THE
unofficial GUIDE®
TO Washington, D.C.

13TH EDITION

D1114394

COME CHECK US OUT!

Supplement your valuable guidebook with tips, news, and deals by visiting our website:

theunofficialguides.com

Also, while there, sign up for The Unofficial Guide newsletter for even more travel tips and special offers.

Join the conversation on social media:

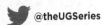 @theUGSeries

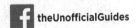 theUnofficialGuides

 theUGSeries

 theUGSeries

#theUGseries

Other *Unofficial Guides*

Beyond Disney: The Unofficial Guide to SeaWorld, Universal Orlando, & the Best of Central Florida

The Disneyland Story: The Unofficial Guide to the Evolution of Walt Disney's Dream

Mini Mickey: The Pocket-Sized Unofficial Guide to Walt Disney World

Universal vs. Disney: The Unofficial Guide to American Theme Parks' Greatest Rivalry

The Unofficial Guide Color Companion to Walt Disney World

The Unofficial Guide to Disney Cruise Line

The Unofficial Guide to Disneyland

The Unofficial Guide to Las Vegas

The Unofficial Guide to Universal Orlando

The Unofficial Guide to Walt Disney World

The Unofficial Guide to Walt Disney World with Kids

THE *unofficial* GUIDE

TO Washington, D.C.

13TH EDITION

EVE ZIBART, RENEE SKLAREW,
AND LEN TESTA

Please note that prices fluctuate in the course of time and that travel information changes under the impact of many factors that influence the travel industry. We therefore suggest that you call ahead or check websites when available for confirmation when making your travel plans. Every effort has been made to ensure the accuracy of information throughout this book, and the contents of this publication are believed to be correct at the time of printing. Nevertheless, the publishers cannot accept responsibility for errors or omissions, for changes in details given in this guide, or for the consequences of any reliance on the information provided by the same. Assessments of attractions and so forth are based upon the authors' own experiences; therefore, descriptions given in this guide necessarily contain an element of subjective opinion, which may not reflect the publisher's opinion or dictate a reader's own experience on another occasion. Readers are invited to write the publisher with ideas, comments, and suggestions for future editions.

The Unofficial Guides
An imprint of AdventureKEEN
2204 First Ave. S., Suite 102
Birmingham, AL 35233
theunofficialguides.com, facebook.com/theunofficialguides, twitter.com/theugseries

Cover design by Scott McGrew
Cover photo © Jon Arnold Images Ltd / Alamy
Text design by Vertigo Design with updates by Annie Long
Index by Ann Cassar

For information on our other products and services or to obtain technical support, please contact us from within the United States at 888-604-4537 or by fax at 205-326-1012.

AdventureKEEN also publishes its books in a variety of electronic formats. Some content that appears in print may not be available in electronic formats.

ISBN: 978-1-62809-048-2; eISBN: 978-1-62809-049-9

Distributed by Publishers Group West
Manufactured in the United States of America

5 4 3 2 1

CONTENTS

LIST *of* MAPS

ABOUT *the* AUTHORS

EVE ZIBART is the author of several *Unofficial Guides,* as well as *The Ethnic Food Lover's Companion.* She spent many (many!) years as a feature writer, nightlife columnist, and restaurant critic for the *Washington Post* and has contributed to numerous magazines, including *Cosmopolitan, US Airways Magazine, Capitol File, Gotham, Philadelphia Style, Ocean Drive,* and others. Her passions are her black cat (she's a Halloween baby) and her vintage sports car (also black).

RENEE SKLAREW was raised in the D.C. area and writes about her hometown for numerous publications, including *The Washington Post, The Washingtonian, Northern Virginia Magazine,* and *VivaTysons Magazine.* She contributed to *Fodor's Washington D.C.* guidebook in 2013 and 2014. She is thrilled to be part of the *Unofficial Guide* team so that she may offer readers her insider's advice about navigating the city from a parent's point of view.

LEN TESTA is the coauthor of *The Unofficial Guide to Walt Disney World, The Unofficial Guide to Disneyland, The Unofficial Guide Color Companion to Walt Disney World,* and *The Unofficial Guide to Disney Cruise Line.* Len leads the team at **TouringPlans.com,** the website and research arm of the *Unofficial Guides.* Len lives in Greensboro, NC.

ACKNOWLEDGMENTS

EVE WOULD LIKE TO THANK the always patient and encouraging Holly "The Queen" Cross; Joe Surkiewicz, who contributed much to the early versions of this book; and Rich Scherr, who personally inspected more than 140 hotels and inns for our accommodations chapter. This book is for Dodger, who has to live with me while I'm working—and when I'm not.

RENEE THANKS HER INTREPID DAUGHTERS, Allison and Danielle, for enthusiastically exploring their hometown's attractions and neighborhoods. Her husband, Eric, is her perfect partner—a passionate traveler, who embraces new foods and cultures by her side whenever possible. The family's shared love of travel brings them ever closer. She also thanks Tim Jackson for his professional guidance and generous spirit, and Kathryn McKay, mentor and fellow travel writer, who opens exciting doors for her, year after year.

LEN THANKS Brian McNichols, who wrote the neighborhood walks and many monument and museum descriptions in our Attractions chapter. Brian don't talk about it, he be about it, and every day he sequel. Len also thanks Laurel Stewart, without whose eye for artistic detail most of the National Gallery reviews would read "Blue. French?" The folks at the Smithsonian, especially Linda St. Thomas and Nick Partridge, were super helpful in getting visitor numbers and facts. Thanks to Fred Hazelton for the crowd predictions; Bernie Edwards at NASA for fact-checking Air and Space, and general awesomeness; Charlotte Blatt at Senator Kirsten Gillibrand's office for tour help; and Joe Biden for Amtrak.

INTRODUCTION

■ WELCOME *to* WASHINGTON

I MOVED TO THE WASHINGTON, D.C., AREA when I was a toddler. As I grew older, I thought everybody's hometown had magical museums that charged nothing to enter, where you could gaze upon massive dinosaur skeletons and walk underneath a whale as long as your house. I thought every kid wandered through art galleries that looked like palaces, where you could see in person paintings by the most famous artists in the world or actually touch a real moon rock.

My parents loved taking my brother and me to the Smithsonian museums, and we were thrilled when guests came to visit. Then we were allowed to climb the legendary steps of "the Lincoln" or ride the paddleboats in the Tidal Basin next to "the Jefferson" (as we called them). I was especially fortunate—when I was in third grade, my father took a job in Switzerland, and we were able to visit eight countries in two years (Switzerland is centrally located!). We toured the magnificent museums of London, Paris, and Rome, and it was there I realized my hometown is an exciting destination, just like the famous European capitals!

I've always been proud of my city and fascinated by the unique people who live here. They're smart. They care about global issues. They love learning. Having moved around the country after graduating from a Midwest college, I never found another place that felt just right. I missed my hometown so much, I cried when I watched newscasters standing in front of The White House. I'm still moved today by so many landmarks—the acres of graves at Arlington Cemetery, the state pillars around the World War II Memorial, and the stark black marble wall of names on the Vietnam Veterans Memorial.

As parents of two daughters, my husband and I believed an early introduction to travel would put them on the path that helped bring the two of us together. When they were still in elementary school, we visited Europe and Asia, making sure to expose them to different cultures and food. It wasn't always easy. Like most American kids, they turned their noses up at falafel and codfish, but luckily we found plenty of pizza and gelato to keep them smiling.

Just like our parents, my husband and I tried to expose our children to history, art, music, theatre, and sports, and we didn't need to travel far. It was all right here in our backyard! There is so much to do in Washington; even after half a century, I haven't visited every attraction or toured every park in the metro area. But I have seen a lot, and there are new sites introduced every year. In 2016 alone, we expect the new streetcar service near Union Station to begin operating, the Old Post Office Pavilion will open as a luxury hotel, and the Smithsonian's collection of 21 world-class museums expands with the opening of the National Museum of African American History and Culture.

Another exciting development is the constant debut of new restaurants, both by renowned chefs and local talents. You won't tire of the food here because we have almost every cuisine—countless Latin American eateries, especially Peruvian and Salvadoran, with Ethiopian and Vietnamese restaurants almost as common as American. There are lots of Middle Eastern and European places, too, but don't miss sampling the seafood from the Chesapeake Bay or D.C.'s famous half smokes. This melting pot is one of the reasons why Washington remains so interesting to visitors across the globe.

Perhaps the increase in tourism is due to the city's presence in popular culture. The mysterious workings of Washington politics are the inspiration for a lot of television shows, books, and movies. The nation's capital seems much more glamorous thanks to shows like *Scandal, Veep, Alpha House, Homeland,* and *House of Cards.* Most people who live here don't know much about the goings-on behind closed doors, but we enjoy the attention. It's fun to identify streets and sights from these shows, though so often they are filmed elsewhere, due to the constraints of post-9/11 security measures.

Many tourists (and residents) are surprised by the city's mercurial weather. Here, conditions fluctuate from epic blizzards that shut down the entire city to record-breaking heat and humidity. Our delightful spring and fall are the optimum seasons to visit. But don't let weather deter your plans. In winter, you'll have the museums to yourself, and in summer, there are plenty of shady trees and cool fountains to break up your trek across the Mall.

The most important things to remember are: Wear comfortable shoes and understand that you can never see everything worth seeing in one visit (not even in two or three visits). Take your time, prioritize, and use this guide to help you plan. Be ready for an unexpected squall or enchanting ethnic festival to deter your progress. It's okay if you don't see all the monuments on this trip; just come back and visit again soon.

—*Renee Sklarew*

ABOUT *this* GUIDE

WHY "UNOFFICIAL"?

MOST "OFFICIAL" GUIDES TO WASHINGTON, D.C., tout the well-known sights, promote local restaurants and accommodations indiscriminately, and don't explain how to find the best value for your vacation. This one is different.

We'll steer you toward the best restaurants, not just the most expensive; we'll dissect the trends so you can tailor your visit to your personal interests; and we'll guide you away from the crowds and lines for a break now and then. We send in a team of evaluators who tour each site, eat in the restaurants, perform critical evaluations of the city's hotels, and visit Washington's hottest nightlife neighborhoods. If a museum is boring, or standing in line for two hours to view a famous attraction is a waste of time, we say so—and, in the process, we hope to make your visit more fun, efficient, and economical. We also keep in mind how family-friendly our recommendations are so visitors can select experiences that best meet their families' needs.

HOW *UNOFFICIAL GUIDES* ARE DIFFERENT

READERS CARE ABOUT THE AUTHORS' OPINIONS. The authors, after all, are supposed to know what they are talking about. This, coupled with the fact that the traveler wants quick answers (as opposed to endless alternatives), dictates that authors should be explicit, prescriptive, and, above all, direct. The authors of the *Unofficial Guides* try to be just that. They spell out alternatives and recommend specific courses of action. They simplify complicated destinations and attractions and allow the traveler to feel in control in the most unfamiliar environments. The objective of the *Unofficial Guide* authors is not to give the most information or all of the information, but to offer the most accessible, useful information.

An *Unofficial Guide* is a critical reference work; it focuses on a travel destination that appears to be especially complex. Our experienced authors and research team are completely independent from the attractions, restaurants, and hotels we describe. *The Unofficial Guide to Washington, D.C.* is designed for individuals and families traveling for the fun of it, especially those visiting D.C. for the first time. The guide is directed at value-conscious, consumer-oriented travelers who seek a cost-effective, comfortable, and convenient travel style.

SPECIAL FEATURES

THE *UNOFFICIAL GUIDE* offers the following special features:

- Friendly introductions to Washington's most interesting neighborhoods
- "Best of" lists, giving our well-qualified opinions on things ranging from burgers to baguettes, four-star hotels to 12-story views

- Listings that are keyed to your interests, so you can pick and choose, plus cross-references to similar attractions
- Advice to sightseers on how to avoid the worst of the crowds, as well as traffic and excessive costs
- Recommendations for lesser-known sights that are away from the attractions at the National Mall but are equally worth a visit
- A neighborhood system and maps to make it easy to find places you want to go to and avoid places you don't
- Advice on avoiding street crime and unnecessary stress
- Hotel descriptions organized by neighborhood, with details that help you narrow down your choices fast, according to your needs
- Focused chapters that include only those hotels, attractions, and restaurants we think are worth considering
- A detailed index to help you find things fast
- Insider advice on crowds, lines, best times of day (or night) to go places, and our secret weapon, Washington's stellar subway system

HOW THIS GUIDE WAS RESEARCHED AND WRITTEN

WHILE A LOT OF GUIDEBOOKS HAVE BEEN WRITTEN about Washington, D.C., very few have been evaluative. Some guides come close to regurgitating the hotels' and tourist offices' own promotional material. In preparing this work, nothing was taken for granted. Each museum, monument, federal building, hotel, restaurant, shop, and attraction was visited by trained observers who conducted detailed evaluations and rated each according to formal criteria.

While our observers may have some particular expertise, they are independent and impartial. Like you, some have visited Washington as tourists or business travelers, while others live in the city. In both cases, they take note of their satisfaction or dissatisfaction.

The primary difference between the average tourist and the trained evaluator is the evaluator's skills in organization, preparation, and observation. The trained evaluator is responsible for much more than simply observing and cataloging. While the average tourist is gazing in awe at stacks of $20 bills at the Bureau of Engraving and Printing, for instance, the professional is rating the tour in terms of the information provided, how quickly the line moves, the location of restrooms, and how well children can see the exhibits. He or she also checks out things like other attractions close by, alternate places to go if the line at a main attraction is too long, and the best local lunch options. Observer teams use detailed checklists to analyze hotel rooms, restaurants, attractions, and recreational activities. Finally, evaluator ratings and observations are integrated with tourist reactions and the opinions of patrons for a comprehensive quality profile of each feature and service.

In compiling this guide, we recognize that a tourist's age, background, and interests will strongly influence his or her taste in Washington's wide array of attractions and will account for a preference for one sight or museum over another. Our sole objective is to provide the reader with sufficient description, critical evaluation, and pertinent data to make knowledgeable decisions according to individual tastes.

LETTERS, COMMENTS, AND QUESTIONS FROM READERS

WE EXPECT TO LEARN FROM OUR MISTAKES, as well as from the input of our readers, and to improve with each new book and edition. Many of those who use the *Unofficial Guides* write to us asking questions, making comments, or sharing their own discoveries and lessons learned in Washington. We appreciate all such input, both positive and critical, and encourage our readers to continue writing. Readers' comments and observations will frequently be incorporated into revised editions of the *Unofficial Guides* and will contribute immeasurably to their improvement.

How to Write the Author

Renee Sklarew
The Unofficial Guide to Washington, D.C.
2204 First Ave. S., Suite 102
Birmingham, AL 35233
unofficialguides@menasharidge.com

When e-mailing us, please tell us where you're from. If you snail-mail us, put your address on both your letter and envelope; the two sometimes get separated. It's also a good idea to include your phone number. Because we're travel writers, we're often out of the office for long periods of time, so forgive us if our response is slow. *Unofficial Guide* e-mail isn't forwarded to us when we're traveling, but we'll respond as soon as possible after we return.

Reader Survey

At the back of the guide, you will find a short questionnaire that you can use to express opinions about your Washington visit. Clip out the questionnaire along the dotted line and mail it to the address above.

The *Unofficial Guide* Website

Visit **theunofficialguides.com** for in-depth information on all *Unofficial Guides* in print.

HOW INFORMATION IS ORGANIZED: BY SUBJECT AND BY LOCATION

TO GIVE YOU FAST ACCESS TO INFORMATION about the *best* of Washington, we've organized material in several formats:

ACCOMMODATIONS Because most people visiting Washington stay in one hotel for the duration of their trip, we have summarized our coverage of hotels with descriptions, charts, maps, ratings, and rankings that allow you to quickly focus your decision-making process. We provide you with a vivid picture of what it's like to stay at a particular hotel—its location, amenities, proximity to attractions and public transportation, price point, and whether they're pet friendly or not (pages 54–73). Plus, the vital information for all accommodations is provided in an extensive chart (pages 93–104).

ATTRACTIONS Attractions—historic buildings, museums, art galleries —draw visitors to Washington, but it's practically impossible to see them all in a single trip. We list them by location and then evaluate each one. These descriptions are the heart of this guidebook and help you determine what to see and when.

RESTAURANTS We provide a lot of detail when it comes to restaurants. Because you will probably eat a dozen or more restaurant meals during your stay, and not even you can predict what you might be in the mood for on Saturday night, we provide detailed profiles of the best restaurants in and around Washington and their quirky hours (many downtown sandwich and coffee shops are open only on weekdays). We also recognize that convenience and budget are important, so we have supplied more Metro-friendly restaurants and dependable local family chains. Restaurants are also listed by location, as well as by cuisine (see pages 255–308).

ENTERTAINMENT AND NIGHTLIFE Visitors may want to try out several different theatres or nightspots during their stay, but again, where you go depends on your particular interests. We describe the best theatres and clubs in Washington, as well as the hottest nightlife neighborhoods (pages 327–332), and list some top destinations for beer-lovers, cocktail loungers, and dancers.

NEIGHBORHOODS Once you've decided where you're going, getting there becomes the issue. To help you do that, we have divided the city into neighborhoods:

- Southwest Waterfront or The Wharf
- Capitol Riverfront and Navy Yard
- Capitol Hill
- H Street Corridor and NoMa
- The National Mall and The White House
- Penn Quarter, Chinatown, and Convention Center
- Foggy Bottom
- Georgetown
- Dupont Circle and Logan Circle
- U Street/Mid City

- Adams Morgan and Columbia Heights
- Upper Northwest: Woodley Park, Cleveland Park, and Tenleytown
- The Maryland Suburbs
- The Virginia Suburbs

All hotel charts, as well as profiles of restaurants and attractions, include the neighborhood. If you are staying at the Hotel Palomar, for example, and are interested in Japanese restaurants within walking distance, scanning the restaurant profiles for restaurants in Dupont Circle or Adams Morgan will provide you with the best choices.

WASHINGTON, D.C.:
Portrait of a City

GEORGE WASHINGTON MAY HAVE BEEN, famously, "first in the hearts of his countrymen," but no such claim could have been made for the city that bears his name. In fact, strange as it may sound today, Washington, D.C., has spent most of its history suffering from a serious inferiority complex.

It wasn't the first or second or even fifth city to serve as the capital. Philadelphia was first and foremost: The Continental Congress briefly adjourned to Baltimore when the British threatened, but they quickly returned, only to retreat again to York, Pennsylvania, with an overnight session in Lancaster. The representatives returned to Philadelphia in 1778, but an uprising five years later (not by British but by their own troops, who were still awaiting their promised pay) sent them first to Princeton, New Jersey; then to Annapolis, Maryland; then to Trenton, New Jersey; then to New York; and—inevitably—back to Philadelphia. (There's a good reason why the city's main boulevard is named Pennsylvania Avenue.)

Washington has never been given much respect, or at least not until relatively recently. The British were particularly hard on their former colony: In 1809, not long before the British Army undertook a severely incendiary approach to renovating the city, the British minister Francis Jackson called it "scantily and rudely cultivated." In 1842, Charles Dickens ironically called it "the City of Magnificent Intentions," filled with "spacious avenues that begin in nothing and lead nowhere; streets, mile-long, that only want houses, roads, and inhabitants; public buildings that need but a public to be complete." Anthony Trollope, who visited America several times in the 1860s, called it as "miserable" a town as could be imagined.

Americans themselves weren't much more impressed with their capital. In 1811, Washington Irving, then dabbling in politics as a lobbyist,

called it a "forlorn . . . desert City," especially when the "casual population"—meaning Congress—had adjourned and removed themselves
for the comforts of home. In July 1814, only about six weeks before
the Battle of Bladensburg and the burning of Washington, Secretary
of War John Armstrong insisted the British wouldn't attack Washington because it wasn't strategically worth it. Even 150 years later, John
F. Kennedy famously described it as a "city of Northern charm and
Southern efficiency."

But in the 21st century, Washington looks every bit the monumental
city the founders envisioned. It may have played a limited role in the
Revolutionary War, but it has rebounded from the fires of 1814, the
too-close-for-comfort battles of the Civil War, riots that nearly erased
whole downtown neighborhoods, crime waves, and so-called urban
renewal stronger and far more beautiful than ever. Although the 9/11
attacks on the Pentagon and New York City may have altered the landscape, physically and mentally, resulting in physical barriers and security queues, officials have found ways to make them more ornamental
and even "natural," replacing jersey barriers with trees and retaining
walls. In fact, the 9/11 tragedy inspired some quite moving monuments
as well. And while you are here, you will likely see even more museums,
memorials, art spaces, and green spaces under construction.

After all, there were those who called the new capital "the American Rome," and while Washington certainly wasn't built in a day, the
wait has been worthwhile.

WASHINGTON BEFORE WASHINGTON

THE HISTORY OF WASHINGTON is the tale of two rivers, the mighty
400-mile Potomac and the much more modest but fortuitously placed
9-mile-long Anacostia. Rock Creek, which is a tributary of the Potomac,
is almost 33 miles long. The same confluence of the Anacostia and
Potomac that would later attract the city's founders to the site also drew
the attention of indigenous peoples. There is archaeological evidence that
Native Americans moved into the region as long as 10,000 years ago,
perhaps longer, and tides of immigration overlapped for millennia.

The Piscataway, the largest Native American nation in the region
and Algonquian speakers, had been permanently established here since
at least 1300, long before Captain John Smith of Pocahontas fame
put them on the map, so to speak. At the time of the English explorations, the Powhaton tribal alliance is estimated to have included
15,000 people. (That, of course, was before the years of warfare and
European-borne epidemics of smallpox and measles.) "Potomac" is
thought to mean something along the lines of "place where people
trade." Oddly, Anacostia, derived from the name the Nacotchtank
tribe gave it, may have a similar meaning: "the trading place." Perhaps
Congress should try reading a little local history.

CHESAPEAKE BAY OYSTERS are a famous delicacy, and once again, as they were in earlier eras, the namesake of many prominent Washington restaurants. They have been a mainstay of the local diet for perhaps 5,000 years. So revered was *Crassostrea virginica* that one possible translation of the Algonquian "Chesapeake" is "Great Shellfish Bay." When the earliest settlers arrived, oysters were not only abundant, they were more like lobsters than the single slurpers of today; early settlers described them as "13 inches long" and "four times as large" as those in England. They became so famous that when the harvest got back up to full speed after the Civil War, Maryland took in 5 million bushels and Virginia another 2 million. Oystering actually sparked what might be called a "pearl rush"—a hectic boom that drew fortune-seekers, bootleggers, and brothel owners—though it was the meat rather than any occasional nacreous gallstone that was valued. The various cliques of oystermen became so competitive that a series of skirmishes (some quite violent), nicknamed the Oyster Wars, lasted into the mid-20th century. Oystering also led to another cottage industry in the Delmarva Peninsula: the making of mother-of-pearl buttons. At its height, around the turn of the 20th century, pearl buttons represented half of all buttons made in the world.

The first Europeans to explore the Washington region were not British, but Spanish; Admiral Pedro Menendez, who also founded St. Augustine, may have sailed up the Potomac River (which he dubbed the Espiritu Santo, or Holy Spirit, which was remarkably unprescient of him) as far as Occoquan, Virginia. Captain Smith came even closer, to what is now Great Falls, Virginia, in 1608, though it is not clear whether he actually landed. Foragers from the Jamestown colony raided an Indian village in Anacostia in 1622; the first permanent English colony on Kent Island was founded in 1631. A few years later, George Calvert, Lord Baltimore, was granted the tract of Virginia north and east of the river—henceforth to be known as Maryland—as a refuge for British Catholics. By the middle of the 17th century, the entire area had been staked out as great tracts and manor seats.

Thanks to the shipping access afforded by the Potomac River, Washington's two most important early cities, "Old Town" Alexandria and Georgetown, were both founded as ports of call; and both had their roots in the region's first great export, tobacco.

Alexandria is located on part of a 6,000-acre grant given in 1669 by the governor of Virginia, as proxy for King Charles II, to a Captain Robert Howson for his services in transporting 120 new colonists to the state. (A nod here to the First Mothers: The tract previously had belonged to Dame Margaret Brent, Virginia's first woman lawyer and an advisor to the governor.) A month later, Howson sold the land to John Alexander for a pound of tobacco per acre. Alexander took the green(s) and ran with them, seeding a long and profitable mercantile tradition.

By 1732, the Alexanders and partner Hugh West had built a tobacco warehouse on the bluffs above the river. In 1749, with the backing of other wealthy planters, the area merchants successfully petitioned the Virginia colonial assembly to create a town near the shipping point. (Entrepreneurism is a small world: Among the petitioners was Lawrence Washington, son-in-law to Lord Fairfax, whose 17-year-old brother George assisted Hugh West's son John in mapping the site. It was in their blood: The Washington fortune was also based on tobacco.) Lots were auctioned off in 1749, and more were sold off in 1763. Even more enterprisingly, in the 1780s, the city added landfill to the Potomac shoreline so that wharves could be built out to the deeper channel of the river, meaning that ocean-going vessels, including foreign imports, could sail all the way to the port.

Meanwhile, a few miles upstream—the farthest point those ocean-going boats could navigate—another tobacco port had taken hold on the Potomac. By the late 1740s, there was already a string of tobacco warehouses and wharves, a tobacco inspection office, and, of course, taverns along the river in Georgetown. Near as it was, Georgetown was actually part of Maryland, not Virginia; in 1751, the provincial legislature approved the purchase of 60 acres from merchants providentially named George Gordon and George Beall. Local legend has it that Georgetown was winkingly named for these "founders," but considering the prevailing attitude of the times, they no doubt saw it as a worthwhile investment.

HISTORY, AS WELL AS GEOGRAPHY, can often be read on maps. While the memory of the local tribes lingers largely on the map (history is indeed written by the victors), the close ties of pre-Revolutionary colonists to the mother country is evident in the majority of county and state names: Virginia (for Elizabeth, the Virgin Queen); Maryland (for Queen Henrietta Maria, wife of the Catholic King Charles I); Prince George's County (for the Danish consort of Queen Anne); Charles County and Calvert County (both for Lord Baltimore, as, of course, is that city); Fairfax County (Thomas Fairfax, sixth Lord Fairfax of Cameron); and so on. Annapolis went through two Anns, first Anne Arundel, wife of Lord Baltimore, and then the future Queen Ann. Old Town Alexandria—which, as noted earlier, was partly surveyed by none other than George Washington—has a King, Queen, Prince, Duke, Princess, and Royal street. Georgetown, or George Towne, as it was then, is another royalist remnant, named not for the father of our country, as many people assume, but for his then-august Hanoverian majesty King George II. But because Washington adheres in general to the L'Enfant grid (enforced by Congress), it has few resonant street signs.

Alexandria and Georgetown had more in common than timing and mercantile advantage; they became the seed ground for war—wars, in fact—and then, eventually, Washington, D.C.

In 1753, as tensions over trading rights and expansion in the Ohio Valley escalated between the British and French, the Virginia governor sent then-22-year-old militia Major George Washington to "invite" the French construction commander to remove himself. He refused, Washington headed to Williamsburg to report, and then, having been promoted to lieutenant colonel, was instructed to defend a fort the governor had ordered built by any means necessary. Washington led a group of about 50 militia and Mingo troops that ambushed a French and Canadian party of about 30. The commander, Villers de Jumonville, was killed in the action, which came to be known as the Jumonville affair.

Unhappily for Washington, the governor was acting without any instructions from the British government, or indeed without the knowledge of any other Virginia officials. The Jumonville affair and its repercussions became one of the prime instigations of the French and Indian War. Major General Edward Braddock, the colonial commander in chief, used Carlyle House in Alexandria, now a museum, as his headquarters. Braddock would lose his life in the war, bequeathing his battle sash to his aide-de-camp, Washington.

 IT WAS ROBERT E. LEE'S FATHER, Washington's close aide Major General Henry "Light-Horse Harry" Lee, who coined the famous epitaph, "first in war, first in peace, and first in the hearts of his countrymen."

Washington did indeed sleep at Carlyle House, probably many times, as he was related by marriage (and various cousins) to Sarah Fairfax Carlyle, but he also had his own town house on Cameron Street and a private pew at Christ Church. He danced and dined with most of the other founding fathers and mothers at Gadsby's Tavern (still operating as a restaurant today). But he also frequented the popular Suter's Tavern in Georgetown, where much of the planning for the creation of the nation's capital took place. The tavern's exact location is unclear: it was somewhere near 31st and K Streets NW, not far from what is now the Old Stone House Museum, where Suter's son rented a room for many years. The fact that the pre–Revolutionary War structure was never demolished is due in part to the assumption for many years that it had served as Washington's Georgetown headquarters, but that has since been discredited.

There was plenty more warfare in Alexandria's future. Partially as a diversion from their attack on Washington, British forces sailed up the Potomac, bombarded the only fort between the Chesapeake Bay and the city (whose commander blew up his own fort after only two hours of battle and was later dismissed from the service), and politely accepted the surrender of the Alexandria mayor. There was so much loot to be had (including sugar, cotton, wine, and, of course, tobacco), combined with shallow waters, that the British naval forces reportedly grounded their ships and were a little late to the Washington bonfire party. This was very good luck for Georgetown because by then the commodore had decided that proceeding up the Potomac to burn the docks in Georgetown was a waste of time.

But Alexandria's later wartime sufferings would be more significant. Only a block from the Carlyle House is the Stabler-Leadbeater Apothecary, now also a museum, where in 1859 then U.S. Army Lieutenant J.E.B. Stuart handed the orders to Colonel Robert E. Lee, also still in the U.S. Army, to quell John Brown's rebellion in Harper's Ferry, powder keg of the Civil War. In 1861, one day after Virginia voted overwhelmingly to secede from the Union, Lee and Stuart followed Virginia into the Confederate fold. Union forces took possession of Lee's family home and plantation just across the Potomac from Washington—now Arlington National Cemetery—and then quickly marched down to Alexandria. Union forces occupied the city for four years, the longest occupation of the conflict.

Washington would be invaded once more, in 1864, by Confederate troops under the command of General Jubal A. Early; that raid, which culminated in the battle at Fort Stevens in Northwest Washington, marks the only time in American history that a sitting president of the United States was present at a battle. Abraham Lincoln was reportedly so fascinated that he kept standing up to watch, oblivious to the bullets flying around him. (The young captain who finally yelled, "Get down, you damned fool!" to the civilian he did not recognize, has been identified by some historians as future Supreme Court Justice Oliver Wendell Holmes Jr.)

The issue of slavery, and/or segregation, continued to haunt the nation's capital long after Appomattox, and to shape Washington in palpable ways, not all unhappy; these are discussed in more detail below.

THE FIRST CITY OF THE NATION (FINALLY)

WELL BEFORE THE CIVIL WAR, the question of whether the nation's capital should be built in the North or the South was a subject of much debate. In fact, while the Congress was in Trenton, some members made an attempt to lay out a site on the Delaware River. Vice President John Adams, voting as president of the Senate, favored Germantown, Pennsylvania. (To some extent, this indicates just how different in culture the two regions of the country already were.) A compromise was finally struck, so the legend goes, at a private dinner Thomas Jefferson hosted for Alexander Hamilton and Washington's ally Light-Horse Harry Lee.

The specific site was selected by George Washington himself, who lived almost his entire life along his beloved Potomac River. The initial design was a diamond shape, 10 miles by 10 miles, or 100 square miles; many of the mile markers around the perimeter, which were laid by Andrew Ellicott and Benjamin Banneker—a farmer, mathematician, astronomer, inventor, and probably the most famous black man in Colonial America—still stand, though they are badly deteriorated.

(Incidentally, although the map directions of the District—Northwest, Northeast, Southwest, and Southeast—are taken from the Capitol building, the geographical center of the city is nearer the White House, a bit north of the Washington Monument, near 17th Street NW. And the official heart of the District of Columbia, and hence the point from which all those "miles to Washington" are measured, can be found on the Ellipse.)

Within that 10-mile square lay a confederation of smaller towns: Washington City, which ended at Rock Creek Park on the west and Florida Avenue and Benning Road on the north; Georgetown, or the Port of Georgetown; Alexandria County, which included parts of Alexandria (the city) as well as present-day Arlington County; and the unincorporated County of Washington. Florida Avenue was then called Boundary Street, which explains why the transportation exhibit in the Museum of American History shows streetcars with that destination.

 DESPITE THEIR ALREADY FAIRLY LONG HISTORY, neither Georgetown nor Alexandria were formally incorporated until after the Revolutionary War. Alexandria was incorporated in 1779 and Georgetown in 1789—just in time, ironically, for both to find themselves surrendered by their states to create the new nation's capital.

Having argued over the location of the new seat of the national government, the founders couldn't even settle on a name for it. (Many of the major buildings on Capitol Hill, including the U.S. Capitol itself, are on land known for more than a century as New Troy, which wouldn't have seemed to be a hopeful omen, though it was a fleeing Trojan prince who legendarily founded Rome.) The property where the White House sits now once belonged to a man named Francis Pope, who punningly called his 400-acre farm Rome and the bordering stream the Tiber (more on this later).

Designer Pierre L'Enfant called it the Capital City; Thomas Jefferson referred to it as Federal Town. It was officially dubbed Washington City in 1791, but modest George never used that name himself, continuing to refer to it as the Federal City. He did, however, allow the city to use his coat of arms as a basis for its flag and to place him on its seal.

Even the casual tourist can understand how important the Potomac and Anacostia Rivers were to the evolution of the Washington area, but what might not be as immediately apparent beneath the sprawl of modern-day development is how formative a role the underlying topography of Washington played.

The entire region—actually, much of the northeastern United States—basically slopes downhill from north to south. The District's highest point, which is Fort Reno Park, a former Civil War defense near the Maryland border off Wisconsin Avenue, is more than 400 feet above sea level. (Its vantage point was the whole point of its location.)

The areas around the city's southern boundaries of the city, i.e., the rivers, are marshy and soft: "Foggy Bottom" was a phrase long before the State Department was built there.

 WASHINGTON NATIONAL CATHEDRAL is 400 feet tall; add 300 feet for the tower, and you have the tallest spot and likely best view in Washington, some 150 feet higher than the Washington Monument.

Tiber Creek, which ran from the Potomac just east of Georgetown toward Capitol Hill, was quite a sizable estuary. According to L'Enfant's plan, which was intended to fulfill Washington's dream of making the city into (yet another) profitable port, it would be dredged into a canal connecting the city to the river and commercial traffic. In the meantime, it was a prominent recreational feature of the city. People swam, fished, and punted along it. President John Quincy Adams and his son John were canoeing on it in 1825 when their vessel sprang a leak and they were forced to swim for shore. (John Jr. walked back to the White House naked, according to Adams's diary.)

Gradually, however, and especially during the Civil War when there were troops bivouacked there, Tiber Creek became more of an open sewer than a swimming hole. Any serious rainfall turned downtown into a swamp, and the air in the city was famously pestilential: It is almost certain that the typhoid fever that killed 11-year-old Willie Lincoln came from the water around the White House. Although the creek was diverted down into a tunnel beneath Constitution Avenue in the 1870s, the land around and above it remains less than ideal: Building the Ronald Reagan International Trade Building at 14th Street and Constitution Avenue required a huge drainage project that unsettled other buildings nearby. In 2006, the water problem contributed to the flooding of the National Archives and Internal Revenue Buildings, many museums, and the entire Mall itself.

 NEAR WHAT WAS THE MOUTH OF TIBER CREEK, and briefly the Washington City Canal, there remains a lockkeeper's cottage, a stone building on the southwest corner of 17th Street and Constitution Avenue NW, not far from the World War II memorial.

In fact, the land under much of what is now the heart of Washington—the Washington, Jefferson, Lincoln, MLK, and World War II Memorials; East Potomac Park and West Potomac Park; and even the Tidal Basin and its famous cherry trees—was originally mudflats or actual waterways, and the Mall extension was created out of sand and gravel dredged from the Potomac. Repeated attempts to alleviate flooding and clear the river also led to the creation of the various channels around the city and even the expansion of what is now Theodore Roosevelt Island and part of the foundation of the Pentagon.

So despite the undoubted advantages of water access, the best options for major construction, and the preferred neighborhoods for housing, tended to be higher and drier. Capitol Hill, then called Jenkins Hill or Jenkins Heights, is naturally elevated, nearly 100 feet up, giving the federal offices a built-in prominence: L'Enfant described it as "a pedestal waiting for a superstructure."

Many of the residential sections of Georgetown are similarly elevated. Several of the historic mansions in Georgetown are situated so high up that, in the early days, their owners could see straight across to the Mall. Tudor Place, home of Washington's step-granddaughter Mary Custis Peter, is about 100 feet higher than the riverfront. Dumbarton House, where First Lady Dolley Madison paused after fleeing the President's House with the Gilbert Stuart portrait of Washington, is 125 feet up. From their vantage points, both Madison and Peter had unimpeded views of the White House going up in flames. (Although it's usually the White House fire that is remembered, the British also torched the Capitol, Treasury Building, Navy Yard, War Office, and what was then the only bridge across the Potomac between Washington and Alexandria, so it must have been quite visible.)

Even Charles Dickens, who was so clearly disillusioned by the state of official Washington, found Georgetown a pleasant exception: "The heights of this neighborhood, above the Potomac River, are very picturesque; and are free, I should conceive, from some of the insalubrities of Washington. The air, at that elevation, was quite cool and refreshing, when in the city it was burning hot."

It's no wonder that the Lincolns, and several of their successors, delighted in moving their households to the summer residence, now the President Lincoln's Cottage museum. Only 3 miles north, it's about 300 feet higher up and enjoys not only cooler but cleaner breezes.

 LINCOLN'S HABIT OF CANTERING ALONE along 16th Street from the White House north to the cottage was so widely known that, in 1865, a would-be assassin took a shot at him—and left a gaping hole through his stovepipe hat.

The bad news is the climate is warming and sea levels are rising. Before the latest round of restoration, the Jefferson Memorial and its sea wall were sinking as much as 8 inches a year, and scientists predict the entire Washington area will drop that much over the next century. Just as the current generation cannot imagine Washington as it was a century ago, so visitors a hundred years from now may find it quite different.

THE GREAT RACE DEBATE

THOUGH WASHINGTON ITSELF saw no action during either the French and Indian or Revolutionary War, crucial campaigns in both were conceived here. Created (and debated) by the then newly independent 13 colonies, it arguably remains the 14th colony—home to both houses of Congress, but without a vote in either—a fact many observers believe is influenced by the large black (and presumably Democrat-leaning) population. The phrase "taxation without representation" was in wide use on both sides of the Atlantic by the mid-18th century; it is alive today, and with good reason, on the license plates of District of Columbia residents. Washington was laid out as a perfect diamond, but (literally) fragmented by the issue of slavery. It showcases monuments to some who did not want them, including Presidents Franklin Roosevelt and Dwight D. Eisenhower, and sequesters statues of some who helped shape America's history, including Benjamin Banneker and until quite recently Frederick Douglass.

African Americans, freed, slave (by one estimate, as many as 20,000), and indentured, served on both sides of the Revolutionary War, as did Native Americans; yet nearly half of the original writers or signatories to the Declaration of Independence, including Washington, Jefferson, Franklin, Lee, Madison, and Monroe, owned slaves, and not all promises of freedom for martial service were honored. (Apparently, not all men—or women—were created equal.)

In 1800, census figures indicate that 30% of Georgetown's population was slave, with more than 200 free blacks as well. Although they represented half the congregation, African American worshippers at Georgetown's Dumbarton Methodist Episcopal Church were relegated to an airless, crowded balcony; so in 1816 they founded Mount Zion United Methodist Church at 27th and Q Streets NW.

There were slave markets all over the Washington area, a couple within view of the Capitol, as Lincoln noted. In 1830, a census of one of Alexandria's markets listed around 150 slaves, two-thirds under 25 years old and five under 10. Georgetown's slave markets operated until the Civil War; the District's largest slave pen was located a stone's throw from where the National Museum of African Art is now. Even Francis Scott Key, who was a devout Episcopalian and nearly became a priest instead of a lawyer, owned slaves. Slaves unquestionably were involved in the construction of the White House and the Capitol building, staffed the hotels and boardinghouses, drove the cabs, hauled the bathwater, and even attended their owners on the floors of Congress.

The issue was as hot, and hypocritical, in Washington as anywhere in the country, especially as Congress and the U.S. Supreme Court repeatedly debated slave vs. free states and slaves as property. Benjamin Banneker, the surveyor of the city, wrote Jefferson a rather scathing letter on the question of slavery. Most people of color in Washington itself in the early 19th century were free—if they could stay that way. In 1841, violinist Solomon Northup, the inspiration for the film *Twelve Years a Slave,* was kidnapped from a hotel (owned by the same James Gadsby as Washington's favorite tavern) where the Newseum stands today.

In 1846, the residents of Alexandria, who feared that the capital would outlaw slavery and thus strangle the slave trade in that busy port, voted to ask Congress to return the portion of the District across the river to the state of Virginia. It was just short of a third of the 100 square miles; you can clearly see on a map how the original diamond is cut off at the southwestern corner by the Potomac. (It's even more obvious on the graphically pared-down Metro subway maps.)

Even on the day of Lincoln's inauguration, the sheriff of Alexandria auctioned off "all free Negroes who have failed to pay their [head] tax in for the years 1859 and 1860," though what was actually being sold was their labor, if that constituted any real difference. Ironically, perhaps the one upside of the Union's occupation of Alexandria throughout the Civil War was the opportunities it offered escaped slaves to establish businesses, either as laborers of various degrees of expertise or as personal servants. By one estimate, as many as 10,000 African Americans moved into Alexandria in a period of 16 months, between 1862 and 1863, and by 1870 roughly half the city's population was black.

In some ways, Washington was forward-thinking on the issue. Slavery was finally outlawed in the District of Columbia in 1862, a year before Lincoln issued the Emancipation Proclamation, and Emancipation Day, April 16, is observed as a holiday in D.C. Howard University was founded in 1867. Black men, though not women, in the District of Columbia were given the right to vote in 1867, three years before the 15th Amendment enfranchised all men. Until the mid-1870s, black office-holders had substantial influence in D.C.

But the imposition of segregation in federal agencies, and the banning of interracial marriage, under President Woodrow Wilson in 1913 (who had specifically promised to work for equal rights), restarted a long train of tensions, eventually resulting in race riots in 1919. What might be the earliest black sit-in occurred in 1943, during FDR's efforts to desegregate the federal government, in the U Street neighborhood, then part of "Black Broadway" (see "Entertainment and Nightlfe," page 328) and now the bustling Mid City area. The Reverend Martin Luther King Jr. led a March on Washington for Jobs and Freedom in 1963 that culminated in his still-gripping "I Have a Dream" speech at the Lincoln Memorial; his assassination in 1968 sparked a week of street battles and fire fights that, ironically, devastated blocks around 14th and U Streets NW, then one of the central points of African American development in the District, and of H Street NE. Both neighborhoods have only in recent years seen a rebirth.

By 1960, "white flight" and the lure of the new suburbs had upset the old ratios; African Americans represented the majority of Washington residents; a decade later it was more than 70%. (One of the District's nicknames, especially in the 1970s and 1980s, was Chocolate City.) Black District residents remained the majority until 2013.

Finally, in 1967, Congress appointed Walter Washington as mayor, and a few years later, District residents were finally allowed to vote themselves for Washington as mayor. All elected District mayors since have been African American. In 2008, Presidential candidate Barack

Obama won the election with 92% of the District vote; four years later, it was still more than 90%.

However, segregation, subtle or overt, remains visible in Washington today. The overwhelming majority of black residents live in the eastern half of the city, especially on the other side of the Anacostia River, and questions of real estate values, health care, and quality of education continue to bedevil the city.

BEAUTIFICATION AND MODERN-DAY WASHINGTON

AS NOTED ABOVE, Washington was not always a pleasure to visit.

Despite the fact that it was conceived in 1791, and Congress and President John Adams officially moved into their new quarters in 1800, construction of the less symbolic sort was spotty at best. Many of the great houses that are now museums were built in the very early 19th century, by prosperous farmers and developers, and mostly in the then much more desirable towns of Alexandria and Georgetown. Pennsylvania Avenue, envisioned as Washington's grand promenade and running directly between the President's House, as it was originally called, and the Houses of Congress, wasn't paved even rudimentarily until 1832 and went through cobblestones, bricks, and even wood surfaces before getting a taste of asphalt in 1876—not that it helped much. The city's first sewer was built beneath Pennsylvania Avenue, too, in 1829 (which again says something about the quality of life in the neighborhood).

Even what we now know as the Mall, one of the most immediately recognizable stretches in the nation, remained far more mud than marble well into the 20th century. The first Smithsonian building, The Castle, opened in 1855, the neighboring Arts and Industries Building in 1881, the National Museum of Natural History in 1910, and the Freer Gallery in 1923, but it was decades before the other buildings were constructed. (And it should be noted that both the Castle and the Freer were primarily funded by bequests, not the federal government.) The Washington Monument wasn't begun until 1848, and was only half a building until 1884. The Lincoln Memorial opened in 1922, the Jefferson Memorial in 1923.

Even more surprisingly, post–Civil War downtown Washington, including areas near the White House, housed some of the most dangerous and degenerate neighborhoods, including Hell's Bottom, Bloody Hill, and Murder Bay, which was where the fortress-like Federal Triangle stands today. (Chillingly, President Lincoln's cortege likely at least brushed the edges of Murder Bay on his way to Ford's Theatre.) Washington even had its own Whitechapel, and though not frequented by a Ripper, it racked up its share of victims.

Poor architect Pierre L'Enfant, who had discovered his passion for the new nation while serving under both Generals Lafayette and Washington in the Revolutionary War, died penniless and brokenhearted in

1825. His vision for the city was considered too grandiose and was repeatedly amended, though he was finally exonerated in 1901 when the McMillan Commission used his original plan to push for the start of Washington's true construction, including the Mall.

L'Enfant's remains were finally exhumed in 1909 from a farm in Prince George's County, taken to the Capitol rotunda to lie in state, and reburied on a hillside in Arlington Cemetery. His gravestone is engraved with a replica of his original design. Even more fittingly, President John F. Kennedy, who had admired the moving monumental view not long before his assassination, is buried at his widow's request just a few yards away.

Nevertheless, the statue of L'Enfant that was commissioned in the hope it would someday stand in the U.S. Capitol remains, at press time, forbidden to enter the halls of the building he helped put on the map. Instead (somewhat like Banneker), he looks directly west toward the White House and points backward toward the Capitol from the lobby of a very large and uninviting government building in Judiciary Square.

The heroes of modern Washington, D.C., are Lady Bird and President Lyndon Johnson, philanthropist David Rubenstein, and, to a lesser extent, Abe Pollin.

While Jacqueline Kennedy was rightly praised for restoring the White House to engage Americans in their own history, Lady Bird Johnson campaigned for the beatification of Washington's byways, parks, and side streets, urging volunteers (and eventually, the National Park Service) to plant the smallest traffic triangle with flowers, dogwoods, and azaleas. Her programs became a sort of adjunct to her husband's vision of the Great Society and helped turn the city from a dutiful destination for schoolchildren into a true tourist attraction.

Financier David Rubenstein is to Washington as John D. Rockefeller Jr. was to New York. He has almost singlehandedly restored the National Archives, paying for the new visitor center and lending it a copy of the Magna Carta. He has been chairman of the board of the Kennedy Center for the Performing Arts since 2010 (to which he has donated $50 million), kicked in $7.5 million to repair earthquake damage to the Washington Monument, $10 million to reconstruct slave quarters at Jefferson's Monticello, picked up the bill for repairs of the Washington National Cathedral, bought a $2 million copy of the Emancipation Proclamation for the nation, and much more. Even the beloved baby pandas of the National Zoo—you know, those famously adorable "sticks of butter"—owe him a huge debt: $4.5 million that went to fund the panda reproduction program.

Abe Pollin, owner of the NBA's Washington Wizards (then the Bullets), the WNBA Mystics, and the NHL Washington Capitals, was a construction tycoon who built athletic stadiums/concert venues first outside the Beltway and then in the center of town. The construction of the Verizon Center in the mid-1990s is often credited with igniting the redevelopment of the Penn Quarter sector of downtown, now perhaps the most vibrant neighborhood of the city.

STILL MOVING FORWARD

AS WASHINGTONIANS FREQUENTLY POINT OUT, the District of Columbia is still more like a colony of the United States because residents have no voting representative in Congress, only a nonvoting seat, and no senator at all—which is why you will see license plates bearing the ironic slogan "Taxation without Representation." (The District's motto, *Justitia omnibus*, or "Justice for all," might also be considered somewhat sarcastic.) Residents of the District couldn't even vote for president until 1961.

Perhaps it's appropriate, then, that Washington is a more international city than an American one, housing as it does the scores of embassies and consulates, the headquarters of the World Bank and International Monetary Fund, the Organization of American States, and so on. And, of course, repeated waves of immigration have made it, if not the melting pot of America, a sizable and simmering one. In 1900 only 7% of the residents had come from other countries; a century later a fifth were foreign-born. By 2020 it's estimated that half of Washington's population will be immigrant. Before 1960 most of the incoming were European; since then, they have been primarily Hispanic and Asian.

The population peaked at more than 800,000 in 1950, making the city the ninth largest in the country; according to the 2013 census estimates, it's now closer to 650,000 (the entire metropolitan area comprises more than 5,600,000 and is expected to reach 7.4 million by the year 2030). Now the mix is just under 50% African American, about 43% Caucasian, and the rest a variety of Hispanic/Latino, African, and Asian minorities.

Today, early in its third century, Washington is again at a cultural and architectural crossroads, considering its massive new Mall development plan, expanding public transportation, embracing the suburbs, and balancing national dignity with "security" barriers. The astounding revitalization of the Pennsylvania Avenue neighborhood and reuse of historical buildings is a belated testament to the vision of Pierre L'Enfant. Destination DC reports the Washington, D.C., area received more than 20.2 million visitors in 2014, and 18.4 million of them were from the United States, while a record number of international visitors, some 1.9 million, joined them (an increase of 16%). We think you'll agree, it's a great place to visit!

PART ONE

PLANNING YOUR VISIT

◼ **WHEN** *to* **GO**

CROWDS

TO GAUGE D.C.'S CROWD PATTERNS, we collected monthly visitor statistics from more than 20 monuments, museums, and attractions from 2012 through 2015, covering more than **110 million visitors**. We also counted daily visitors at D.C.'s most popular museums during research trips, to compare different days of the week.

Washington, D.C.'s tourist attractions are busiest around the National Cherry Blossom Festival, roughly mid-March through mid-April, and from late June through early August, when most US public schools have their summer vacations. The period from late April through late June is also busy. The best times to visit are October (which also has great weather), January, and February (when the weather is worse).

Washington, D.C., Crowd Calender 2016

National Cherry Blossom Festival
March 20–April 17

Marine Corps Marathon
October 23–25

JAN FEB MAR APR MAY JUN JUL AUG SEP OCT NOV DEC

DAY OF WEEK PATTERNS Attractions, monuments, and museums are generally busiest on Saturday and slowest on Tuesday. Ignoring special events, such as legal holidays, here's how each day of the week stacks up in terms of crowds, with Saturday being the busiest and Tuesday the least busy: Saturday, Friday, Sunday, Thursday, Monday, Wednesday, and Tuesday.

Legal holidays and school breaks often combine to move crowds around within a given month. If you're planning a trip to D.C., check out our chart on the facing page to see how crowded we expect every day in 2016 to be.

On individual days, crowds generally peak at attractions between 11 a.m. and 3 p.m. If a museum or monument opens at 10 a.m, arrive by 9:30 a.m. to beat the crowds. Alternatively, if you're touring during summer and a museum has extended hours, it's possible to do a "highlights" tour of even the largest museum between 3:30 and 7:30 p.m.

If you have no restrictions on your travel time, we suggest you scan the "Calendar of Festivals and Events" at the end of this chapter and see which ones might lure you.

WEATHER

WASHINGTON, D.C.'S WEATHER IS BEST in the spring and fall. The city's fabled cherry blossoms bloom at the end of March or early April—not necessarily coinciding with the Cherry Blossom Festival, unfortunately—while fall brings crisp, cool weather and a spectacular display of foliage, especially in the Shenandoah Valley.

WASHINGTON, D.C., WEATHER AVERAGES				
Month	High	Low	Rainfall (Inches)	Number Rainy Days Per Month
January	48° F	29° F	2.8″	14
February	50° F	32° F	2.6″	14
March	59° F	38° F	3.5″	14
April	66° F	47° F	3.0″	14
May	75° F	58° F	4.0″	20
June	85° F	66° F	3.9″	18
July	88° F	72° F	3.7″	17
August	86° F	71° F	3.0″	16
September	81° F	63° F	3.7″	16
October	69° F	51° F	3.4″	16
November	60° F	44° F	3.2″	16
December	59° F	33° F	3.0″	16

Summers are generally brutally hot and humid. Many Washingtonians follow Congress and foreign diplomats and "recess" out of the

Washington, D.C., Crowd Calender by Day

January	1 2 3 4 5 6 7 8 9 10 11 12 13 14 15 16 17 18 19 20 21 22 23 24 25 26 27 28 29 30 31
February	1 2 3 4 5 6 7 8 9 10 11 12 13 14 15 16 17 18 19 20 21 22 23 24 25 26 27 28 29
March	1 2 3 4 5 6 7 8 9 10 11 12 13 14 15 16 17 18 19 20 21 22 23 24 25 26 27 28 29 30 31
April	1 2 3 4 5 6 7 8 9 10 11 12 13 14 15 16 17 18 19 20 21 22 23 24 25 26 27 28 29 30
May	1 2 3 4 5 6 7 8 9 10 11 12 13 14 15 16 17 18 19 20 21 22 23 24 25 26 27 28 29 30 31
June	1 2 3 4 5 6 7 8 9 10 11 12 13 14 15 16 17 18 19 20 21 22 23 24 25 26 27 28 29 30
July	1 2 3 4 5 6 7 8 9 10 11 12 13 14 15 16 17 18 19 20 21 22 23 24 25 26 27 28 29 30 31
August	1 2 3 4 5 6 7 8 9 10 11 12 13 14 15 16 17 18 19 20 21 22 23 24 25 26 27 28 29 30 31
September	1 2 3 4 5 6 7 8 9 10 11 12 13 14 15 16 17 18 19 20 21 22 23 24 25 26 27 28 29 30
October	1 2 3 4 5 6 7 8 9 10 11 12 13 14 15 16 17 18 19 20 21 22 23 24 25 26 27 28 29 30 31
November	1 2 3 4 5 6 7 8 9 10 11 12 13 14 15 16 17 18 19 20 21 22 23 24 25 26 27 28 29 30
December	1 2 3 4 5 6 7 8 9 10 11 12 13 14 15 16 17 18 19 20 21 22 23 24 25 26 27 28 29 30 31

National Cherry Blossom Festival

National Cherry Blossom Festival

Marine Corps Marathon

More Crowded — Less Crowded

January
1st New Years Day
18th Martin Luther King Jr. Day

February
9th Mardi Gras
15th Presidents Day

March
25th Good Friday
27th Easter

May
5th Cinco de Mayo
8th Mother's Day
30th Memorial Day

June
19th Father's Day

July
4th Independance Day

September
5th Labor Day

October
10th Columbus Day

November
11th Veteran's Day
24th Thanksgiving

December
25th Christmas Day

city in August, but that does mean August has its good side: far less traffic and shorter queues, easy restaurant reservations, extended museum hours, and—precisely because so many federal employees are on vacation—less tedious security. Washington is so much less crowded, in fact, that August is when many of the area's most prominent chefs participate in the summer **Restaurant Week**, offering bargain-priced three-course lunch and dinner menus at about $22 and $36, respectively.

Though D.C.'s weather is erratic in winter, it's one of the best times to avoid crowds. On weekdays especially, the Mall is nearly deserted, and museums, monuments, and normally crowd-intensive hot spots, such as the Capitol, are almost congenial. (There's another, winter version of Restaurant Week offered in January, too.) If you take our advice to stay near a Metro station, the subway will get you around town with minimal exposure to the elements.

GATHERING INFORMATION
Before YOU LEAVE

THERE ARE PLENTY OF DEPENDABLE and frequently updated websites that you might want to browse while planning your visit. The official tourism site is **washington.org**, which lists many family-friendly and free seasonal options, events, some package deals you might compare, and so on. It also offers an official visitor's guide, updated twice a year, with maps and local hotel options that you can download.

Another good site for lists of special events and regularly updated information on tourist attractions is **dc.about.com**. D.C. has its own visitor's site, **thedistrict.com**, which includes hotel and travel information, as well as links to event tickets, and more. You also might want to look into **vrc.dc.gov/vrc**, which specifically covers tours of government sites. Also check out **culturaltourismdc.org**, **visitalexandriava.com**, and **visitmaryland.org/capital**, which include many historical attractions. Lastly, check the deals available on **Groupon.com** and **LivingSocial .com.** They often feature discounted tickets to museums (the ones that charge an entry fee), as well as deals on boat and bus tours, sporting events, and festivals.

Several of the major publications in the area have online editions that you can surf in advance of your visit, including *The Washington Post* (**washingtonpost.com**) and *City Paper,* Washington's free weekly "alternative" newspaper, with lists of arts, theater, clubs, and more (**washingtoncitypaper.com**). The *Washingtonian,* the area's preeminent magazine, is strong on lists (top 10 restaurants, hot shopping boutiques, and so on) and provides a monthly calendar of events, dining information, and feature articles (**washingtonian.com**). Check out

Northern Virginia Magazine (**northernvirginiamag.com)** for dining, events, and features on the Virginia side of the Potomac River.

Once you arrive, you'll discover that there are dozens of concerts, art shows, and special events going on all the time around Washington, and many of them are free. Check *The Washington Post*'s Going Out Guide and the Friday Weekend section. *The Post* also owns a free quick-read newspaper, called *Express,* handed out at Metro stations and many street corners.

Where/Washington lists popular things to do around town; it's usually available in your hotel or at airport racks (**wheretraveler.com**). The *Washington Blade,* the LGBT community's weekly, is available in many restaurants and nightspots, especially around Dupont Circle and Capitol Hill (**washingtonblade.com**).

If you're planning to visit any of the Smithsonian museums, their site, **si.edu/visit** will give you a quick first look at the exhibits and floor plans; museums have individual sites as well.

MAKING ADVANCE RESERVATIONS FOR MONUMENTS, MUSEUMS, AND TOURS

THERE ARE A LIMITED NUMBER OF SPACES AVAILABLE for each day's guided tours of major attractions such as the White House or U.S. Capitol. These are almost always filled days or weeks in advance. In addition, you'll have to ask a member of Congress and submit to a background check before being admitted to certain locations, and that makes last-minute visits impossible. The chart on pages 26–27 shows how far in advance you can (and must) make reservations for popular D.C. destinations.

unofficial **TIP**
To email your Congressperson about tour reservations, visit **senate.gov** or **house.gov.** Have ready the birthdate and social security number of everyone in your group.

Even if reservations aren't mandatory, it's still a good idea to make them if you can. Visitors with reservations get placed at the front of any line, which can save hours of time waiting. Also note that while many tours are free, a small fee of around $1.50 may be assessed for making reservations in advance.

If you don't have time or the inclination for much advance work, there's a sort of one-stop shop for brochures, maps, discount coupons, hotel/ restaurant reservation kiosks, and so on: the Tourist Information Center in the D.C. Chamber of Commerce building at 506 Ninth Street NW, near the corner of Ninth and G Streets NW and the Gallery Place subway stop in the heart of Penn Quarter, and not far from the Mall. It's open weekdays 9 a.m.–5 p.m. (202-347-7201; **dcchamber.org**).

unofficial **TIP**
An alternative to a White House tour is a stop in the new interactive White House Visitor Center located at 1450 Pennsylvania Avenue NW and run by the National Park Service.

Continued on page 28

A Guide to Advance Reservations for Major Attractions

WHAT	WHERE TO GET TICKETS	TOUR TIMES
NATIONAL ARCHIVES	archives.gov/museum	Guided, 9:45; other 10:30 to 30 mins before close
WHITE HOUSE	Must go through member of Congress.	Mon.–Thu., 7:30-11; Fri.–Sat., 7:30-1:30
US HOLOCAUST MUSEUM	ushmm.org	
TREASURY BUILDING	Must go through member of Congress.	Sat., 9, 9:45, 10:30, 11:15
WASHINGTON MONUMENT	nps.gov/wamo	
PENTAGON	pentagontours.osd.mil	Mon.–Fri., 9-3
U.S. CAPITOL	visitthecapitol.gov for tickets. Through Congressman for Gallery Passes.	8:50-3:20
FORD'S THEATER NATIONAL HISTORIC SITE	fords.org	Daily, 9-4
DEPARTMENT OF STATE	diplomaticrooms.state.gov	Mon.–Fri., 9:30, 10:30, 2:45
US NAVAL OBSERVATORY	www.usno.navy.mil/USNO	Select Monday evenings
FREDERICK DOUGLASS NATIONAL HISTORIC SITE	nps.gov/frdo	Daily, 9, 12:15, 1:15, 3, 3:30 (walk-ins only), 4 (Apr.–Oct.)
PRESIDENT LINCOLN'S COTTAGE	lincolncottage.org	Tours Mon.–Sat., 10-3; Sun., 11-3
BUREAU OF ENGRAVING AND PRINTING	Must go through member of Congress for advance tickets.	Mon.–Fri, 8:15-8:45, 4-4:45
AMERICAN RED CROSS	E-mail tours@redcross.org or call ☎ 202-303-4233.	Wed. & Fri., 10 & 2
FOLGER SHAKESPEARE LIBRARY	folger.edu	Saturday at noon
DEPARTMENT OF THE INTERIOR	Call ☎ 202-208-4743	Tue. & Thu. at 2
ARLINGTON NATIONAL CEMETERY	arlingtontours.com	No time or date selection necessary
FBI	Must go through member of Congress.	Mon.–Thu.

ADULT COST	MAXIMUM DAYS AHEAD	MINIMUM DAYS AHEAD	NOTES
$1.50	180	3	
	180	21	Background check is required.
$1.00	180		Passes required Mar-Aug; tickets released for Mar-May on 11/30, June-Aug on 2/28/16.
	180	21	Background check is required.
$1.50	90	30	
	90	14	
	90	1	
$4.25	90	1	Tickets released in chunks, usually 7–8 months in advance.
	90	1	Background check may be required.
	90		Seems to be about twice per month.
$1.50	90		
$16.00	90	0	
	90		Tickets only required Mar-Aug; can be picked up at ticket window for other times.
	90	7	
	60	1	This is for READING ROOM TOURS; regular tours do not require tickets.
	60	7	This is for MURALS TOURS; museum visits do not require tickets.
$12.00	30	1	This is for bus tour. ANC Explorer App for self-guided tours.
	35	21	Background check may be required.

Continued from page 25

HOW TO GET TO WASHINGTON, D.C

PEOPLE PLANNING A TRIP TO OUR NATION'S capital have several options when it comes to getting there: by car, train, bus, or plane. We explore these in detail in Part Three: Getting In and Getting Around, but here are some quick points:

- **DON'T DRIVE.** The Capital Beltway, which surrounds the city in the Maryland and Virginia suburbs, is only slightly less congested than New York and Los Angeles. Normal traffic on I-95 can include bumper-to-bumper traffic for up to 60 miles around D.C. Inside the Beltway, D.C. streets are studded with diagonals, traffic circles, one-way streets, massive construction, and reversible lanes. Street parking near popular tourist sites is severely limited, and garage parking is expensive— around $50 per day in many cases—and often inconvenient. If you do drive, park the car and forget it until you leave.

- **TAKE THE TRAIN.** Union Station is the area's train, subway, and bus hub. It is convenient to dozens of cities served by **Amtrak,** and only minutes from a downtown hotel by subway; the Union Station Metro is right alongside the tracks and covered from the weather. If your hotel isn't near a Metro stop, you can easily hail a cab.

- **OR TAKE A BUS.** If you're looking for a bargain, there are a number of well-equipped, inexpensive, and easily booked bus lines these days: **MegaBus, Greyhound,** and others will deposit you at Union Station.

- **OR FLY.** Washington is well served by the airline industry. **Reagan National** is the closest airport and has a dedicated Metro station; **Dulles International Airport** is about 45-60 minutes outside town, and it will eventually have Metro service. **Baltimore/Washington International Thurgood Marshall Airport,** universally known as BWI, is closer to Baltimore than to D.C., but it is accessible by commuter trains and Amtrak, and taking the train to BWI may save you money. See pages 106–110 for full details.

WHERE *to* GO

THE NEIGHBORHOODS

YOU ALSO SHOULD SPEND A LITTLE TIME THINKING about which Washington attractions you are most interested in touring before you choose where you want to stay. There are obvious advantages to being within easy reach, or at least commute, of major attractions. Here are brief descriptions of the areas most visited by tourists, plus some neighborhoods where you might find less expensive hotels, but from where you can easily commute into downtown Washington. These descriptions will help you begin to pinpoint an itinerary and a home base. Remember, though, because there are no distinct lines between each neighborhood, to check a Web-based or conventional map of Washington to see where each hotel is located in relation to museums and other landmarks mentioned in the descriptions below. Most of the attractions are discussed in more detail in Part Four: Attractions. For descriptions of family-friendly lodging found in the following neighborhoods, see Part Two: Accommodations, pages 54–73. The presence of a nearby Metro stop, whether you actually stay in that neighborhood or not, should factor into your plans.

The Southwest Waterfront or The Wharf

THIS NEIGHBORHOOD ON THE WASHINGTON CHANNEL is anchored by the stunning Arena Stage on one end and the historic Maine Avenue Fish Market on the other. In between is a long concrete boardwalk that leads to restaurants and a marina from which some cruises on the Potomac River depart. Developers are building a new Intercontinental Hotel, luxury movie theaters, a waterfront park, a rum distillery, and a music venue called Wharf Hall. Residents are both apartment dwellers and "live-aboards," people who live full-time on their boat. Another notable feature, East Potomac Park, is the narrow peninsula between the riverfront and Washington Channel with a National Park–run recreation area. The Wharf includes Waterfront Metro on the Green Line and L'Enfant Plaza station with multiple lines.

Capitol Riverfront and Navy Yard

THIS NEIGHBORHOOD, A FEW BLOCKS SOUTH of the Mall and near the point where the Potomac and Anacostia Rivers meet, is experiencing a renaissance thanks to the development of Capitol Riverfront, anchored by family-friendly Yards Park, a trapeze school, and a cluster of popular eateries. A few attractions of interest include Nationals Park, home to the Washington Nationals baseball team, Blue Jacket Brewery, Ball Park Boathouse, and the historic Washington Navy Yard. Navy Yard Metro station is on the Green Line.

Capitol Hill

IN ADDITION TO THE CAPITOL ITSELF, and the sprawling grounds surrounding it, this is the home of the U.S. Botanical Garden, Supreme Court, the Library of Congress, Folger Shakespeare Library, Government Printing Office, and on the very edges, the Congressional Cemetery. Every color subway line has at least a couple of stops in the Hill area. Capitol Hill encompasses a residential neighborhood, too, with some of Washington, D.C.'s first homes, dating back to the 1700s. Colorful Eastern Market and the shops and restaurants of Barracks Row act as the

Continued on page 32

Washington at a Glance

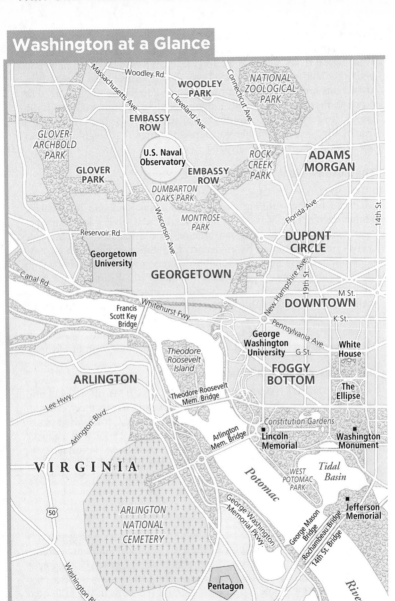

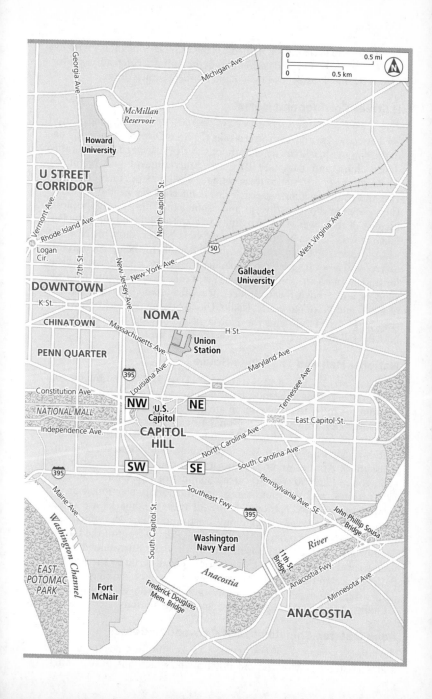

Continued from page 29

neighborhood town center, named for the U.S. Navy members who live in barracks there. On Friday evenings in the summer, catch a free performance by the "President's Own" band on their parade deck.

H Street Corridor and NoMa

THE AREA NORTH AND EAST OF UNION STATION along H Street NE between 11th and 14th Streets (aka the Atlas District) is currently one of the hottest after-hours neighborhoods, with a strip of edgy restaurants, dance clubs, and bars (see Part Six: Entertainment and Nightlife). Although the H Street strip does not have a Metro stop, there is bus service and plans for a new streetcar line connecting the neighborhood to Union Station. Politicos live in and around this hipster neighborhood because of the lower rents, proximity to Capitol Hill, and the Atlas Performing Arts Center. North of H Street NE is NoMa (short for North of Massachusetts Avenue), a neighborhood notable for being comfortably diverse and artsy. It's home to Gallaudet University, a prestigious college for students who are deaf; Union Market, a collection of restaurants, food vendors, and a movie theater under one roof; and also D.C. headquarters of CNN and National Public Radio. Union Station is the closest Metro stop to H Street NE, and the NoMa neighborhood is served by the NoMa-Gallaudet Metro; both are on the Red Line.

National Mall and The White House

THE 1.9 MILES BETWEEN THE CAPITOL STEPS and the Lincoln Memorial encompass the most famous museum strip in Washington and account for more than two dozen attractions, including the Smithsonian's American Art Museum, National Air and Space Museum, National Museum of American History, National Museum of Natural History, National Museum of the American Indian, and, soon, the National Museum of African American History and Culture. But on your first visit, you're likely to want to catch a glimpse of The White House, the U.S. Capitol, and the monuments and memorials positioned in and around the massive National Mall. All these landmarks are spread among expansive parks, including Constitution Gardens, which joins together the war memorials, the Reflecting Pool in front of the Lincoln Memorial, and the Tidal Basin, a body of water surrounded by the famous cherry blossom trees. The National Mall is run by the National Park Service and constantly patrolled by Park police, making it safe to walk around at night. Access the National Mall from the Smithsonian, L'Enfant, Archives, and Federal Triangle Metro stations.

Penn Quarter, Chinatown, and Convention Center

NORTH OF THE NATIONAL MALL, roughly between 14th Street and 3rd Street NW, is the old downtown, which has grown into a vibrant neighborhood with dozens of tourist attractions. Much of the revitalization, like City Center DC, grew around the Verizon Center arena and the Washington Convention Center. In terms of attractions, this area is home to several museums, such as the International Spy Museum, National Building Museum, National Postal Museum, the expanded Ford's Theater museum complex, and Madame Tussauds. The neighborhood also houses Union Station; Koshland Science Center; the Harman Center for the Arts, home to the acclaimed Shakespeare Theatre Company; and the National Law Enforcement Memorial. There are several subway stations here, the busiest being Gallery Place–Chinatown, Metro Center, and Mount Vernon Square (in the Washington Convention Center).

Foggy Bottom

LOCATED WEST OF THE WHITE HOUSE and north of Constitution Gardens on the National Mall, Foggy Bottom got its name from the swampy land on which it was built. The headquarters for the U.S. Department of State and International Monetary Fund, the neighborhood is also home to George Washington University, the National Academy of Sciences, the Octagon Museum, and the new Textile Museum. Other notable sites include Constitution Hall, the Daughters of the American Revolution Museum and Library, The Kennedy Center for the Performing Arts, and, for political junkies, the Watergate Complex. Less well known, but worth noting, is the statue of Albert Einstein and the American art collection in the Department of the Interior. The Foggy Bottom Metro is on the campus of George Washington University.

Georgetown

FAMOUS IN THE 1960S AND 1970S as home to the political establishment/journalism elite (thanks to the charisma of local residents JFK and Jackie), Georgetown is bustling with upscale boutiques, bars, and a variety of restaurants, some with views of the Potomac River. The historic neighborhood of restored town houses is filled with vintage and familiar name-brand shops, and is a good place for antique and trendy furniture shopping (see the "Great Neighborhoods for Window-Shopping" section in Part Seven, pages 340–342). It is home to historical mansions, including Dumbarton Oaks, the Old Stone House museum, and Tudor Place, as well as Georgetown University. Spanning the riverfront, the modern Washington Harbour complex sits beside Georgetown Waterfront Park with dockside restaurants. The water taxi and a few cruise tours operate from there. The Chesapeake & Ohio Canal and towpath begin behind the Four Seasons Hotel and follow the Potomac River upstream for 184 miles to Cumberland, Maryland (see Part Eight: Sports and Recreation). There is no direct subway service, but both Dupont Circle and Foggy Bottom/GWU Metro stations are within walking distance. The Circulator bus runs a regular route from Georgetown to Dupont Circle and Union Station.

Dupont Circle and Logan Circle

DUPONT CIRCLE IS THE CENTER of one of the city's most fashionable neighborhoods, where you'll find elegantly restored town houses, boutiques, restaurants, cafés, bookstores, and art galleries. A stroll down Massachusetts Avenue along Embassy Row leads past embassies and chancelleries, as well as some of Washington's lesser known but exceptional attractions: the Anderson House, the Phillips Collection, and the Woodrow Wilson House. East of Dupont Circle is historic Logan Circle, the only completely residential circle in Washington, where an equestrian statue of General Logan is surrounded by 19th-century Victorian-era brownstones. The neighborhood is the current home of Studio Theatre; Duke Ellington grew up playing music in this park.

U Street/Mid City

SEVERAL BLOCKS NORTH OF LOGAN CIRCLE is U Street Corridor. Although not as well known as Georgetown, the thriving dining and nightlife neighborhood around 14th and U Streets NW, also known as Mid City (accessible from the U Street–African American Civil War Memorial and Museum–Cardozo Metro), is partially a revival of what was known in the early 20th century as the Black Broadway, a moniker bestowed by Pearl Bailey. After decades of decline, it's once again a major music district, home to the restored Lincoln and Howard Theaters, the Black Cat, and the 9:30 Club. There are no hotels in the heart of the neighborhood, but a few are within walking distance. During the daytime, visitors can peruse Mid City's chic boutiques, art galleries, and furniture stores (see Part Seven: Shopping, pages 343–344), as well as sample innovative cuisine at some of Washington's finest restaurants.

Adams Morgan and Columbia Heights

ONE OF WASHINGTON'S OLDEST ETHNIC-CHIC neighborhoods, with a heavy emphasis on Hispanic and African cultures, Adams Morgan doesn't offer much in the way of museums or monuments, but the neighborhood features a collection of globally influenced restaurants, eclectic shops, and casual nightclubs. To visit, take a 10-minute walk over Rock Creek Bridge from the Woodley Park–National Zoo Metro station. Meridian Hill Park, with its acres of terraced gardens and cascading fountains, lies between Adams Morgan and Columbia Heights, an area north of Florida Avenue NW that is under redevelopment and becoming popular with young families. Several large retailers have moved in around the plaza on 14th and Park Road, but it's also known for its taquerias, bakeries, and an expanding bar scene, especially along 14th Street NW near the GALA Hispanic Theatre.

Upper Northwest: Woodley Park, Cleveland Park, and Tenleytown

A MAP QUADRANT RATHER THAN A SINGLE NEIGHBOR-HOOD, referring to everything from Georgetown and Dupont Circle to Friendship Heights, the Upper Northwest is also the most affluent quadrant of the city. It contains mostly residential neighborhoods that have come to be defined by their Metro stations. Tenleytown Metro is in the heart of The American University campus, with its modern Katzen Art Center, and is also the closest stop to the Washington National Cathedral. The National Zoo entrance is halfway between Cleveland Park and Woodley Park Metro stations. Some of the city's most beautiful Victorian homes are in Cleveland Park and Woodley Park, both of which have their own Metro-centered restaurant rows.

Rock Creek Park

THE GREAT SWATH OF ROCK CREEK PARK—more than twice as large as New York's Central Park—is one of the notable recreational assets of the area. Founded 125 years ago, the park is an oasis in the heart of the city that begins at the Potomac River around the Kennedy Center and stretches for 30 miles into suburban Maryland. The Hillwood Museum, with its stunning collection of gardens and French and Russian art, is located off Beach Drive, on the edge of Rock Creek Park, closest to Van Ness–UDC Metro station. Also within its borders are Carter Barron Amphitheatre, site of free summer concerts; the National Zoo; Rock Creek Tennis Center, where the top pro–circuit CitiOpen Tennis Classic is held; a planetarium; a nature center; an equestrian center; a golf course; and numerous playgrounds, picnic areas, hiking trails, and so on. Under the supervision of the National Park Service, Rock Creek has no hotels or restaurants contained in the park, but park rangers offer daily programs for families, including nature hikes and mill demonstrations. For more information, see Part Eight or go to **nps.gov/rocr.**

THE MARYLAND SUBURBS

National Harbor on the Potomac River

NATIONAL HARBOR IS A MODERN WATERFRONT development that spans more than 300 acres and is located on the shores of the Potomac River, across from Old Town Alexandria. The massive Marriott Gaylord Hotel is the anchor that draws both vacationers and conventioneers alike, along with special events such as fireworks shows, concerts, food festivals, and sporting competitions. Another notable addition to the neighborhood is the Capitol Wheel, the 175-foot Eye of London–style observation wheel with panoramic views of Washington, D.C., and Old Town Alexandria. Close to an outlet mall, and, soon, an MGM Casino, the neighborhood is about 6 miles south of Washington, D.C., and offers visitors a resort-like home base. National Harbor runs a free bus shuttle to the King Street Metro station for hotel guests (not offered on federal holidays). A Metro bus (NH1) connects National Harbor to the Branch Avenue Metro station. A water taxi service run by Potomac River Boat Company runs from the Gaylord Hotel and the adjoining National Harbor marina to Old Town Alexandria, where you can pick up a free bus to the King Street Metro station. The trip takes about 25 minutes; check the schedule and prices on **potomacriver boatco.com**. For more information, visit **nationalharbor.com.**

Friendship Heights/Chevy Chase

YOU COULD CALL WISCONSIN AVENUE, which becomes Rockville Pike or Route 355, the Rodeo Drive of Washington—and indeed there was a time when it brought in more retail dollars per square foot than that more-famous Los Angeles address. At the five-way intersection of Wisconsin Avenue, Military Road, and Western Avenue, which marks the division between the District of Columbia and the state of Maryland, is the neighborhood centered on the Friendship Heights Metro. Along with high-rise luxury apartments and expensive homes, this is a major shopping hub, housing not only several malls but also the luxurious Collection at Chevy Chase, a must for couture-fashion and high-end jewelry addicts. See Part Seven: Shopping (pages 344–345) for more on this area.

Bethesda

BETHESDA IS ONE OF THE WEALTHIEST residential communities in the United States. You won't find much in the way of attractions, except for Strathmore Concert Hall and Rock Creek Park, although in the last few decades, Bethesda and North Bethesda neighborhoods have experienced extensive redevelopment, mostly into multiuse retail centers. These neighborhoods may be good for visitors seeking less-expensive yet still urbanlike accommodations. The Bethesda and White Flint Metro stations are a 30-minute ride to the National Mall. The area already draws out-of-towners who have business with the National Institutes of Health and Walter Reed military hospitals. Bethesda is a major dining and shopping area (Apple Store) and has several large hotels and conference centers.

Rockville

CONTINUING UP ROUTE 355 (or the Red Line Metro) from Bethesda, you come to an ambitious town development in Rockville, with a lot of boutiques and excellent ethnic restaurants positioned around county office and judicial buildings. It's a busy area for meetings and corporations, and business lunches and cocktails in the neighborhood are quite popular. (Rockville is actually a broad description that includes Twinbrook, which has its own Metro station.)

THE VIRGINIA SUBURBS

Old Town Alexandria

LIKE GEORGETOWN, Alexandria is a particularly picturesque area, with waterfront parks and homes dating back to Colonial times. Historic sites, such as the Alexandria Black History Museum, the Carlyle House, and Gadsby's Tavern, are part of this dynamic and charming community spanning the Potomac River. The downtown area is popular with locals and tourists alike who enjoy walking, dining, and shopping. The area has a few hotels and a working artist studio/gallery called the Torpedo Factory. The drawback for tourists is that both Metro stops, King Street and Braddock Road, are at the edges of the historic district; however, King Street Metro station provides a free trolley to the waterfront. About 20 minutes south of Old Town is George Washington's Mount Vernon property, a must-see if you have time and transportation.

Tysons Corner and McLean

TYSONS IS A RETAIL MEGACENTER that is being developed into a more walkable community. At the moment, there are numerous luxury hotels in the vicinity and two major shopping malls—Tysons Corner and Tysons Galleria. The new Tysons Metro station, on the Silver Line, makes this a good option for visitors seeking less-expensive but upscale accommodations. Along with dozens of restaurants and brand-name stores, American Girl Place is connected to Tysons Corner Mall. Within a short drive is the entry into Claude Moore Colonial Farm, Great Falls National Park, and Scott's Run Nature Preserve.

Arlington and Rosslyn

ROSSLYN, THE CONCRETE TOWN at the foot of Key Bridge, is a slightly more affordable, convenient option for visitors. Though mostly high-rise, commercial buildings, it's a quick walk to Georgetown, and the area has easy access to waterfront parks and bike trails on the Potomac Heritage Trail. Rosslyn is part of Arlington, home of the magnificent Arlington National Cemetery and the Pentagon. Arlington also encompasses Theodore Roosevelt Island, Pentagon City, and Reagan National Airport. Metro stations that serve this area include Arlington Cemetery, Pentagon City, and Rosslyn on the Blue Line.

Clarendon and Ballston

ALTHOUGH NOT AS NEAR TO D.C. as Rosslyn, these northern Virginia suburbs have been redeveloped around Metro stops as relatively upscale neighborhoods; Clarendon, in particular, is a dining destination and has an Urban Village Market on Saturdays with vendors, and a weekly farmers market on Wednesday afternoons. Ballston is the home of the Kettler Capitals Iceplex, which is open to anyone, and you might get to see the Washington Capitals players practicing. See Part Eight: Sports and Recreation (page 363) for more information.

WHAT *to* PACK

FRANKLY, THE MOST IMPORTANT THING TO CONSIDER when packing is comfortable shoes, and more than one pair of them. This is a culture of concrete and marble, and even if you are using one of the trolleys or shuttles, you're likely to be standing about quite a bit. Wearing walking or running shoes during the day is fine, but don't think you're going to want to pull on those high heels or shiny lace-ups at the end of a long day of sightseeing. Pick your evening shoes (or boots) with reasonable comfort in mind. Two pairs of comfortable shoes are also useful if it happens to rain—you can wear one pair while the other is drying.

Washington is a tourist town, but it's also a high-powered center of world politics. Most restaurants have retreated from having a dress code, but a few upscale spots list jackets for gentlemen as "requested" (as opposed to the "requirement" of earlier times). While it's fine to dine in shorts during the day at less-formal spots, you might feel a social as well as climatic chill if you wear that Hawaiian shirt to a moderately upscale restaurant for dinner. After all, most people will still be in office attire—at least long pants, if not suits. In general, polo shirts are fine in spring and fall; a not-too-bare sundress or reasonably neat pair of khakis will make you look downright respectable.

You should bring a rainproof top in the summer, one nice enough to pass for a jacket; in winter, you can probably get by with a trench coat with a zip-in lining or a walking coat with a sweater. Gloves and hats are important, of course, but when choosing headgear, make sure to bring something that won't blow off. Washington can get both very hot and very cold (sometimes in the same day), but in the spring and fall, a windbreaker-style coat that you could stuff into a bag would be ideal. Many of Washington's museums offer free coat checking, so store those layers and enhance your viewing experience.

Women will find a large scarf or shawl a good interim layer in fall and winter, and it will stand in as a sweater (or throw, or seat cushion) in emergencies. Everyone should carry sun protection, including hats and sunscreen, in their travel bag. And seriously consider dressing in layers to deal with changes in weather.

Take a photo of your passport and other important documents, such as hotel information, as well as prescription medicines in their

unofficial **TIP**
A small flashlight (or flashlight app for your smartphone) may come in handy for reading small or dimly lit museum captions. If you like to read in bed, it might be worth packing one of those mini book lights; hotels are notoriously dim, and your companions may not be on your sleep schedule.

labeled bottles. It's best to store your prescription medicines in carry-on bags, in case your packed bag gets lost.

Pacemakers, metal implants, and surgical pins may set off security machines, so a letter from your doctor describing your condition is a wise precaution.

Though over-the-counter medicines are easy to find at local drugstores, you may want to pack travel-size over-the-counter headache and stomach-upset medications. If you're allergic to bee stings, don't forget the antihistamines. Sunscreen and insect repellent are available in individual packets—a great (non-spill) space saver. Stain-removing packets can be very helpful, too.

Zippered plastic bags keep dry clothes dry and wet clothes separated, keep your underwear together so the luggage inspector doesn't have to sort through them, prevent jewelry from tarnishing and/ or snagging your clothes, and prevent shampoos and lotions from leaking.

You should plan to walk *a lot* (the National Mall is 2 very long miles), so especially in hot weather, pack double sets of thin socks rather than too-thick ones, and carry some precut moleskin bandages: They offer the best possible protection and won't sweat off.

SPECIAL TIPS *for* SPECIAL PEOPLE

TRAVELING WITH CHILDREN (AND PERHAPS GRANDPARENTS)

WASHINGTON IS SO FULL OF INTERNATIONAL ICONS— from the U.S. Capitol to the Washington Monument, the White House to President John F. Kennedy's eternal flame, and the Wright Brothers' biplane to giant pandas—that it's easy to get overambitious about an itinerary.

But there are a few factors to consider if you are planning a family vacation, especially with small children or seniors. While there are attractions that delight toddlers and preschoolers, many are oriented to older kids and adults. Consider adding something into your itinerary at least once per day that will please your kids, such as a rest stop at a friendly garden, a visit to a playground, a show for kids, or a ride on the National Mall carousel.

Although the Smithsonian museums have enhanced their exhibits with many more interactive games, children younger than 8 years old might not be enthralled by seeing the entire National Museum of Natural History or National Air and Space Museum. Children 2 and older will probably enjoy short visits to the art galleries and monuments, but only if you let them out to walk a bit in between (Run Forest,

Run!). You might enjoy taking them to the outdoor sculpture gardens, where they can dangle feet in the fountain or walk among the giant art installations. If your child is fussy, the museums have big restaurants and entertaining museum stores where you can find a snack or treat. Most museums are spacious enough for strollers, but they can get very crowded, and it becomes hard to maneuver the big ones.

If your children are younger and you want to minimize the hassle of commuting to and from downtown, look for lodging near—or with short subway commutes to—the Mall and Penn Quarter.

Children and seniors are more susceptible than adults to overheating, sunburn, and dehydration. Be sure to put sunscreen on children in strollers, even if the stroller has a canopy; their exposed foreheads and feet are particularly vulnerable. Small children don't always tell their parents about a developing blister until it's too late; consider using a lunch or bench break to check their feet. Similarly, excited children may not inform you or even realize that they're thirsty or overheated. Carry plastic water bottles and follow the Chicago rule: Drink early and often.

TIPS FOR INTERNATIONAL TRAVELERS

MOST VISITORS FROM Australia, Chile, Japan, New Zealand, South Korea, Taiwan, the United Kingdom, or western Europe who stay in the United States fewer than 90 days need only a valid, machine-readable passport, not a visa, and a round-trip or return ticket. Canadian citizens need a passport if arriving by air, but most do not need a visa to enter the United States (though if you have any doubts, you can certainly apply for one).

Citizens of other countries must have a passport good for at least six months beyond the projected end of the visit, as well as a tourist visa, available from any US consulate. Contact consular officials for application forms. However, the most current and accurate information can be found by consulting the U.S. Department of State at **state .gov/travel** or US Customs and Border Protection at **cbp.gov/travel /international-visitors.**

Check with the local consulate to see whether travelers from your country are currently required to have any inoculations; there are no set requirements to enter the United States, but if there has been any sort of epidemic in your homeland, there may be temporary restrictions.

International visitors should also remember that the United States does not have a national medical program and that if you require medical treatment you will have to pay for it; you may wish to investigate medical and/or travel insurance. However, throughout the United States, if you have a medical, police, or fire emergency, dial 911, free even on a pay telephone, and an ambulance or police cruiser will be dispatched to help you. (For nonemergency police aid in most areas, dial 311.) You also can contact the **Traveler's Aid Society** International in the Washington area at ☎ 202-546-1127 (**travelersaid.org**). International visitors to Washington who would like a tour conducted in their native language can contact the **Guild of Professional Tour Guides of Washington** at **washingtondctourguides.com.**

If you arrive by air, be prepared to spend as much as two hours entering the country and getting through U.S. Customs. Traveler's checks will be accepted at some hotels if they are in American dollars, although most travelers use credit and debit cards these days. Other currencies can be taken to a bank or foreign exchange and turned into dollars.

Two last reminders: The legal drinking age in the United States is 21, something many European travelers forget. And most of Washington's restaurants and all of its cultural facilities are nonsmoking venues.

TRAVELERS WITH SPECIAL NEEDS

WASHINGTON, D.C., IS ONE OF THE MOST ACCESSIBLE CITIES in the world for those with disabilities. With the equal-opportunity federal government as the major employer in the area, D.C. provides a good job market for disabled persons. As a result, the service sector—bus drivers, waiters, ticket sellers, retail clerks, cab drivers, tour guides, and so on—are well attuned to the needs of people with disabilities. Check **Washington.org** under "Disability Information" for a list of 10 D.C. attractions that are particularly welcoming to people with special needs, and consult **dc.about.com** for an extensive list of accessibility services in the community and at various attractions.

For example, the White House has a special entrance on Pennsylvania Avenue for tourists using wheelchairs (you can also borrow one there), and guides frequently allow visually impaired visitors to touch some of the items described during the tour. The U.S. Capitol offers a variety of special services, including wheelchair loans, interpreters for the hearing impaired, Braille and large-type brochures, and sensory aides; go to **visitthecapitol.gov** and select "Visitors with Disabilities" for information.

The Metro was designed to be accessible from the beginning. As a result, the stations and trains provide optimal services to a wide array of people with special requirements. Elevators provide access to the mezzanine, or ticketing-areas platform, and street level; call the Metro's 24-hour elevator hot line at ☎ 202-962-1825 to check if the elevators at the stations you plan to use are operating. When elevators are out of service (and Metro is constantly struggling with mechanical time-outs and repairs), shuttle buses are provided between the stations that bookend the outage; but depending on your stamina or comfort, you may not wish to go that route.

The edge of the train platform is built with a 14-inch "studded" granite strip that's different in texture from the rest of the station's flooring so that visually impaired passengers can detect the platform edge with a foot or cane. Flashing lights embedded in the granite strip alert hearing-impaired passengers that a train is entering the station. Handicapped-only parking spaces are close to station entrances. While purchasing a fare card is a strictly visual process (unless the station is equipped with new talking vending machines), visually impaired passengers can go to the nearby kiosk for assistance. Priority seating for senior citizens and passengers with disabilities is located next to doors in all cars.

unofficial **TIP**
In many older parts of Washington, D.C., particularly Adams Morgan, Capitol Hill, Dupont Circle, Georgetown, and Old Town Alexandria, restaurants and museums may not be wheelchair accessible; however, some that were not previously accessible may have been renovated by the time you visit—check in advance.

Visitors with disabilities who possess a transit ID from their home city can pick up a courtesy Metro ID or half-fare SmarTrip card that provides substantial fare discounts. The Metro Disability ID Card is good for a month, but appointments are mandatory at Metro Headquarters, 600 Fifth Street NW near the Judiciary Square Metro's F Street exit, from 8 a.m. to 4 p.m. weekdays (until 2: 30 p.m. Tuesdays); call ☎ 202-962-1245 or visit **wmata.com/accessibility** for more information. To request forms for fare discounts, contact the Office of ADA Programs at ☎ 202-962-1558.

The Smithsonian and the National Park Service, agencies that run the lion's share of popular sights in Washington, offer top-notch services to people with disabilities: entrance ramps, barrier-free exhibits, elevator service to all floors, and accessible restrooms and water fountains. Visually impaired visitors can pick up large-print brochures, audio tours, and raised-line drawings of museum artifacts at many Smithsonian museums. For special tours or information about accessibility for visitors with disabilities, contact the individual museum or the Smithsonian Accessibility Office at ☎ 202-633-2921 or e-mail the Accessibility Program at acess@si.edu. More information is available also at **si.edu/accessibility.** For information on the National Zoo's provisions for disabled visitors, go to **nationalzoo .si.edu/visit/accessibility.** For specific information about accessibility on the National Mall, check **nps.gov** to see what is offered in the way of services for people with disabilities at each of the memorials and at Arlington Cemetery.

Old Town Trolleys and Gray Line have on-off Mall and monument and area historic site tours, and they offer handicapped-accessible vehicles with 24- (Old Town) and 48-hour (Gray) advance reservations; visit **trolleytours.com/washington-dc** or **graylinedc.com.**

Unlike the Trolley or Gray Line, the DC Circulator buses don't provide narrated tours, but they do allow customers to get on and off at all the major monuments and several Smithsonian museums for only $1 (good for two hours of riding if you use a SmarTrip card to pay initially). Circulator buses have designated spaces for wheelchairs, and all have motorized ramps for lifting scooters or wheelchairs on and off the bus. These buses do not require riders to make advance reservations, but they do have restricted hours—summer hours are 7 a.m.–8 p.m., and winter hours are 7 a.m.–7 p.m. The DC Circulator charges half price to disabled riders: just 50 cents per trip, and you can pay with your Metro SmarTrip card! With cash, riders must have exact change. For more information, visit **dccirculator.com.**

In spite of all the services available to disabled visitors, it's still a good idea to call ahead to any facility you plan to visit and confirm that services are in place and that the particular exhibit or gallery you wish to see is still available.

A CALENDAR *of* FESTIVALS *and* EVENTS

January

WASHINGTON RESTAURANT WEEK Early to mid-January. More than 150 restaurants offer fixed-price lunch ($22) and dinner ($36) menus; **washington.org.**

February

CHINESE NEW YEAR PARADE February 8, 2016. Marching bands and lion and dragon dancers wind through Chinatown and around the Verizon Center; **chinesenewyearfestival.org.**

ABRAHAM LINCOLN'S BIRTHDAY February 12. A wreath-laying ceremony, music, and dramatic reading of Lincoln speeches inside the Lincoln Memorial; ☎ 202-426-6841; **nps.gov/linc.**

GEORGE WASHINGTON'S BIRTHDAY PARADE Mid-February. The nation's largest, with marching bands, floats, military reenactors, and other units on the streets of Old Town Alexandria; ☎ 703-829-6640; **washingtonbirthday.net.**

March

ST. PATRICK'S DAY PARADE Mid-March. Old Town Alexandria's annual parade of floats, bands, and Irish dancers is booked for the first Saturday of March; **ballyshaners.org.** In D.C. it's the Sunday before March 17 (March 13, 2016) that Irish dancers, bagpipers, and marching bands salute all things Irish along Constitution Avenue NW from Seventh to 17th Streets; ☎ 202-670-0317; **dcstpatsparade.com.**

BLOSSOM KITE FESTIVAL Late March. Competitions in design, performance, and other categories; ☎ 877-442-5666; **nationalcherryblossomfestival.org.**

NATIONAL CHERRY BLOSSOM FESTIVAL March 20–April 17, 2016. The blooming cherry trees surrounding the Tidal Basin are the centerpiece of this two-week festival of concerts, cooking and dance demonstrations, children's activities, restaurant specials, the National Cherry Blossom Parade along Constitution Avenue NW, and the street festival on Pennsylvania Avenue; ☎ 877-442-5666; **nationalcherryblossomfestival.org.**

WHITE HOUSE EASTER EGG ROLL March 28, 2016. Colored-egg collecting and entertainment held the Monday after Easter, rain or shine. Open to children age 12 and younger with supervising adults. Free tickets are distributed through an online lottery system; ☎ 202-456-1414; **whitehouse.gov1.info/easter-egg-roll.**

AFRICAN AMERICAN FAMILY CELEBRATION Late March to mid-April. The free annual Easter Monday jubilee offers an Easter egg hunt, gospel music, storytellers, and food vendors at the National Zoo; ☎ 202-633-4800; **nationalzoo.si.edu/ActivitiesAndEvents/Celebrations/Easter.**

April

THOMAS JEFFERSON'S BIRTHDAY April 13. A military honor guard and a wreath-laying ceremony salute the third president, noon at the Jefferson Memorial; ☎ 202-426-6841; **nps.gov/thje.**

WASHINGTON INTERNATIONAL FILM FESTIVAL Mid- to late April. Scores of new American and foreign films are screened in theaters across town during the annual Filmfest D.C.; ☎ 202-274-5782; **filmfestdc.org.**

SHAKESPEARE'S BIRTHDAY April 19. Annual open house with free cake, children's activities, theater tours, dramatic readings, medieval crafts, and entertainment at the Folger Shakespeare Library; ☎ 202-544-4600; **folger.edu.**

EARTH DAY April 22. The celebration on the Mall, one of the nation's largest, includes music, demonstrations of green technology, celebrity speakers, and vendors; ☎ 202-518-0044; **earthday.net.**

WHITE HOUSE SPRING GARDEN TOURS Late April (weather permitting). Free, timed tickets distributed each day on a first-come basis at Ellipse Visitor Pavilion, 15th and E Streets NW, at 9 a.m.; ☎ 202-456-2200; **whitehouse.gov.**

GEORGETOWN HOUSE TOUR Last Saturday. Tour private homes in Washington's Georgetown district; Go to St. John's Episcopal Church—Georgetown Parish on April 25 at 10 a.m.; tour starts at 11 a.m. and lasts all day; ☎ 202-338-2287; **georgetownhousetour.com.**

May

PASSPORT DC All of May. D.C.'s embassies open their doors to visitors during this month-long annual event. There are festivals, performances, and the opportunity to sample international cuisine at the open houses of participating embassies; ☎ 202-661-7581; **culturaltourismdc.org.**

NATIONAL HARBOR FOOD AND WINE FESTIVAL First weekend. Well-known chefs gather for cooking demonstrations, and a wide variety of food and beverage vendors offer samples of wine and food at this water-front festival; **wineandfoodnh.com.**

NATIONAL CATHEDRAL FLOWER MART May 6 and 7. With lavish exhib-its, floral displays, food vendors, musical performances, and craft sales, this annual fund-raising event for the church gardens is held on the grounds of the National Cathedral; ☎ 202-537-2937; **allhallowsguild.org.**

NATIONAL ZOO ZOOFARI Mid-May. This annual fund-raising gala fea-tures tastings by more than 100 area restaurants, international wines, entertainment, animal demonstrations, and a silent auction at the National Zoo; ☎ 202-633-3045 (tickets); **nationalzoo.si.edu.**

MOUNT VERNON SPRING WINE FESTIVAL AND SUNSET TOUR Mid-May. Taste wines from Virginia vineyards, learn more about George Wash-ington's wine-making efforts, and enjoy live jazz at the first president's estate. Advance purchase is recommended; ☎ 703-780-2000 (informa-tion); **mountvernon.org.**

PREAKNESS STAKES Third Saturday. Running of the second jewel in thoroughbred horse racing's Triple Crown at Pimlico Race Course in Baltimore; ☎ 410-542-9400; **preakness.com.**

NATIONAL MEMORIAL DAY CONCERT Last Sunday. The National Sym-phony Orchestra and guest performers from Broadway, pop, R&B, country music, and more in a free concert on the West Lawn of the U.S. Capitol; ☎ 202-426-6841; **pbs.org/national-memorial-day-concert.**

MEMORIAL DAY CEREMONIES Last Monday. Commemorative events and wreath layings are scheduled at Arlington National Cemetery, the Vietnam Veterans Memorial, World War II Memorial, National Law Enforcement Officers Memorial, Navy Memorial, Air Force Memorial, and the Women in Military Service for America Memorial; ☎ 202-426-6841. Marching bands and veteran units from all over the country parade down Constitution Avenue; ☎ 703-302-1012. And the U.S. Navy Band performs a free concert at the U.S. Navy Memorial; ☎ 202-433-3366; **navyband.navy.mil.**

June

CAPITAL PRIDE FESTIVAL Mid-June. A parade Saturday in the Dupont Circle area and a street festival Sunday along Pennsylvania Avenue with crafts and food vendors winding up a weeklong celebration by the area's LGBT residents; ☎ 202-719-5304; **capitalpride.org.**

DC JAZZ FESTIVAL Late June. More than 100 concerts at nearly 50 venues around town, including the Kennedy Center and the Mall; **dcjazzfest.org.**

GIANT BARBECUE BATTLE June 25-26, 2016. Teams from across the country compete to win prizes for best barbecued pork, chicken, and beef. Entertainment on multiple stages, cooking demonstrations by celebrity chefs, children's activities, and food vendors, along Pennsylvania Avenue between Ninth and 14th Streets NW; ☎ 202-488-6990; **bbqdc.com.**

SMITHSONIAN FOLKLIFE FESTIVAL Late June to early July. Annual two-week festival celebrates the food, music, arts, and culture of a specific nation, region, state, or theme; on the Mall between Seventh and 14th Streets; ☎ 202-633-6440; **festival.si.edu.**

July

FOURTH OF JULY CELEBRATION July 4. Independence Day is commemorated with the National Independence Day Parade along Constitution Avenue NW, the "Capitol Fourth" concert by the National Symphony Orchestra, and guest musical celebrities on the West Lawn of the U.S. Capitol, culminating in fireworks over the Washington Monument grounds; ☎ 202-426-6841; **july4thparade.com.**

USA/ALEXANDRIA BIRTHDAY CELEBRATION Mid-July. The Alexandria Symphony Orchestra celebrates the City of Alexandria's birthday (it's older than D.C.) and America's birthday with a free concert that includes Pyotr Tchaikovsky's "1812 Overture" with cannon fire, followed by fireworks at Oronoco Bay Park on the Potomac; ☎ 703-746-5592; **visitalexandriava.com.**

August

CITIOPEN TENNIS CLASSIC First week. The US Open men's tennis tour (and young women pros) stop at FitzGerald Tennis Center in Rock Creek Park in preparation for New York, complete with top-ranked players; **citiopentennis.com.**

WASHINGTON RESTAURANT WEEK Early to mid-August. More than 150 area restaurants offer fixed-price lunch ($22) and dinner ($36) menus; **washington.org.**

September

LABOR DAY CONCERTS Sunday before Labor Day. National Symphony Orchestra performs a free concert featuring patriotic music on the West Lawn of the US Capitol or at the Kennedy Center (depending on the weather); ☎ 202-467-4600. Monday, the U.S. Navy Band and Sea Chanters perform at the U.S. Navy Memorial; ☎ 202-433-2525; **navy band.navy.mil.**

LIBRARY OF CONGRESS NATIONAL BOOK FESTIVAL First weekend. More than 70 authors of all types gather for readings, signings, and literacy exhibits; formerly held on the Mall but now inside the Washington Convention Center; ☎ 202-707-5000; **loc.gov/bookfest**.

DC BLUES FESTIVAL Early September. Free all-day concert at the Carter Barron Ampitheater in Rock Creek Park off 16th Street. Event includes performances by six bands, with an after-party and petting zoo for kids; **dcblues.org**.

ALEXANDRIA FESTIVAL OF THE ARTS Second weekend. An outdoor festival features sculptures, paintings, photography, fused glass, jewelry, and other works by nearly 200 artists and artisans along King Street in Old Town Alexandria; ☎ 703-746-3301; **visitalexandriava.com**.

BLACK FAMILY REUNION Second weekend. Annual cultural celebration of the African American family, with live entertainment, exhibits, an arts-and-crafts marketplace, and food vendors on the Mall; ☎ 202-737-0120; **ncnw.org/events**.

SHAKESPEARE THEATRE "FREE FOR ALL" Early to mid-September. Free performances at Sidney Harman Hall. Tickets distributed day of show; ☎ 202-547-1122; **shakespearetheatre.org**.

ROSSLYN JAZZ FESTIVAL Early to mid-September. Daylong free outdoor concerts by local and national jazz stars at Gateway Park (near the Rosslyn Metro station); ☎ 703-276-7759; **rosslynva.org**.

SILVER SPRING JAZZ FESTIVAL Mid-September. Daylong free outdoor concerts by local and national jazz stars at the Silver Spring Civic Building, Veterans Plaza (near Silver Spring Metro station); ☎ 240-777-5300; **silverspringdowntown.com**.

ADAMS MORGAN DAY FESTIVAL Second Saturday. Daylong celebration of Washington's most famous multicultural neighborhood with entertainment, children's activities, food vendors, and more; ☎ 502-544-5765; **facebook.com/adamsmorganday**.

H STREET FESTIVAL Late September. Nearly a mile of food vendors, crafts, concerts, performances, kids' activities, plus a beer garden, positioned along H Street NE; **Hstreet.org**.

ALEXANDRIA SEAPORT DAY Date varies. Boat-building demonstrations, model boat–building workshops, exhibits, and boat rides at Waterfront Park in Old Town Alexandria; ☎ 703-549-7078; **alexandria seaport.org**.

October

TASTE OF GEORGETOWN First Saturday. One of D.C.'s best food festivals held at Georgetown Waterfront Park on K Street NW; includes entertainment, food vendors, and a craft beer and wine pavilion; ☎ 202-298-9222; **tasteofgeorgetown.com**.

WHITE HOUSE FALL GARDEN TOURS Mid-October (weather permitting). Free, timed tickets distributed each day on first-come basis at the Ellipse Visitor Pavilion, 15th and E Streets NW, at 7:30 a.m.; ☎ 202-456-1111; **whitehouse.gov.**

BOO AT THE ZOO Last weekend. Halloween trick-or-treating, animal demonstrations, and zookeeper talks at the National Zoo; ☎ 202-633-4800; **nationalzoo.si.edu.**

MARINE CORPS MARATHON Last Sunday. Tens of thousands of runners start at the Iwo Jima Memorial and follow a course along the Mall and back to the Memorial; ☎ 800-786-8762 or 800-RUN-USMC; **marine marathon.com.**

November

CANDLELIGHT TOUR OF KALORAMA HOUSES AND EMBASSIES First weekend. Begin this self-guided walking tour at the Woodrow Wilson House and visit embassies, ambassadors' residences, and other sites; advance purchase only; ☎ 202-792-5807; **woodrowwilsonhouse.org.**

VETERANS DAY CEREMONIES November 11. Commemorations and wreath-laying ceremonies at Arlington National Cemetery, the Navy Memorial, the Air Force Memorial, National Marine Corps Museum, the World War II Memorial, the Vietnam Veterans Memorial, the Vietnam Women's Memorial, and the Women in Military Service for America Memorial; ☎ 202-426-6841; **va.gov/opa/vetsday.**

WASHINGTON CRAFT SHOW Early to mid-November. Nearly 200 artists from across the country display their glasswork, furniture, textiles, and other creations at the DC Armory. **americanfinecraftshowwashington.com**

GAYLORD NATIONAL RESORT'S ICE! Mid-November–early January. Families love touring the huge ice sculptures housed in a tent at National Harbor; ☎ 301-965-4000; **nationalharbor.com/events.**

MOUNT VERNON BY CANDLELIGHT Thanksgiving weekend through early December. Tour the first president's estate by candlelight, along with music, holiday cooking, and fireside caroling; ☎ 703-780-2000 or **tickets@mountvernon.org; mountvernon.org.**

D.C. METROPOLITAN COOKING & ENTERTAINING SHOW Late November. Celebrity chefs, demonstrations, book signings, specialty food vendors, and more at the Washington Convention Center; ☎ 866-840-8822 for tickets or email **tickets@img.com; metrocookingdc.com.**

December

KENNEDY CENTER HOLIDAY FESTIVAL All of November and December. The Kennedy Center celebrates the holidays with free performances (including popular "Messiah" sing-alongs) and ticketed concerts; ☎ 202-467-4600; **kennedy-center.org.**

THE WASHINGTON BALLET'S NUTCRACKER All month. This classic holiday ballet has elaborate costumes and features the city's premier dance company at the Warner Theatre; ☎ 202-363-3606; **washingtonballet.org**.

NATIONAL MENORAH LIGHTING Event coincides with the Hanukkah holiday. Families are invited to attend the free annual ceremony of the lighting of the National Menorah on the grounds of the White House; **nationalmenorah.org**.

PATHWAY OF PEACE Mid-December. The lighting of the National Christmas Tree on the Ellipse, usually by the president and first lady, kicks off a month of free holiday activities, including nightly choral performances and a display of lighted trees representing the states and territories; free passes issued in early November; ☎ 202-208-1631 or 202-619-7222; **thenationaltree.org** or **nps.gov/whho/planyourvisit /national-christmas-tree.htm**.

PEARL HARBOR DAY December 7. A ceremony commemorates the 1941 attack on Pearl Harbor at the Navy Memorial; ☎ 202-380-0710; **navymemorial.org**. Friends of World War II Memorial hosts "Remembering Pearl Harbor" on the National Mall; ☎ 202-426-6841; **wwii memorialfriends.org**.

HISTORIC ALEXANDRIA CANDLELIGHT TOURS Mid-December. Sites include the Lee-Fendall House, Gadsby's Tavern Museum, and the Carlyle House in Old Town Alexandria, with music, colonial dancing, seasonal decorations, and light refreshments; ☎ 703-746-4554; **alexandriava.gov**.

NEW YEAR'S EVE December 31. Family-oriented, alcohol-free "First Night" festivals with concerts, children's entertainers, and other activities are in Alexandria ☎ 703-746-3299; **firstnightalexandria.org** and Annapolis, among others.

PART TWO

ACCOMMODATIONS

DECIDING WHERE *to* STAY

BECAUSE THE BEST WAY TO GET AROUND Washington is on the Metro, and because most of the major attractions are also Metro-accessible, we highly recommend a hotel within walking distance of a Metro station. **Penn Quarter,** which is within a stroll of perhaps two dozen major attractions and many popular restaurants, is served by a handful of stations, giving you plenty of options to come in from farther out: **Crystal City,** for example, has its own Metro station in between Washington National Airport and D.C. itself—cutting commute time in both directions—and is home to a bevy of name-brand hotels and a restaurant strip; despite its urban façade, the neighborhood is flanked by the Mount Vernon trail, a biking and hiking trail that parallels the Potomac River. Be sure to check out our discussion of Washington's neighborhoods, "Where to Go," in Part One (pages 28–38) to help you choose a home base for your visit.

THE MOST ICONIC HOTELS IN WASHINGTON

IF YOU HAVE READ our history section on pages 7–20, you will have realized that while Washington itself has great history, it has been through repeated cycles of depression and redevelopment, especially in what are now some of the most popular tourist areas. So, it has fewer hotels whose legends reach back to earlier eras than do capitals of Europe.

There are a few notable names, however, starting with the **Willard Hotel,** which faces Pennsylvania Avenue a block east of the White House. (Actually, the hotel's roots go back to six 1816 town houses, but it underwent an extensive rehab after a 1922 fire that rousted then-Vice President Calvin Coolidge and several senators.) After two decades of neglect and a multimillion-dollar renovation by InterContinental, it's back to its 1901 Beaux-Arts glory. Its history is impressive, and you can see memorabilia from various guests who've stayed there, such as President Lincoln's hotel bill. Julia Ward Howe wrote the lyrics to "The Battle Hymn of the Republic" while staying there; the newly elected Lincoln lived there while awaiting inauguration; Dr. Martin Luther King Jr. wrote the "I Have a Dream" speech there as well. Its Round Robin Bar claims to be the spot where powerful Kentucky Senator Henry Clay introduced the bourbon (as opposed to brandy) mint julep. The hotel also claims that the term "lobbyist" came from the fact that influence peddlers lurked in its lobby hoping to buttonhole its presidential and diplomatic patrons. Nevertheless, the hotel's list of former guests, from Charles Dickens to Harry Houdini to Gypsy Rose Lee and a positive passel of presidents, is too long to reproduce.

Location, location, location . . . but that's not the only reason the Obama family spent the fortnight before his inauguration at the famed **Hay-Adams Hotel.** Although the building does not truly incorporate the side-by-side mansions of Lincoln private secretary John Hay and author Henry Adams, the grandson and great-grandson of presidents, it was built on that White House–friendly site and retains much of the look and elegance of that mid-19th-century era. (Clover Adams, who famously committed suicide here by drinking photographic cyanide solution, is said to haunt its halls.) Its view across Lafayette Park toward the Executive Mansion is breathtaking (very rarely, during the odd protest scuffle involving tear gas, that might be literally true). Its cocktail lounge, Off the Record, is a favorite among power drinkers and cocktail anecdote collectors alike. The panoramic view of the White House and National Mall from the top floor is unforgettable.

And speaking of location: What is now the **W Hotel** was known for almost a century as the Hotel Washington, and its rooftop POV bar, with views of the White House, Washington and Lincoln Memorials, etc., has long been a classic draw, though it's a little more expensive and trendy than in the old glamorous lazy summer evenings, when its one-name celebrity patrons included Marilyn and Elvis (who met secretly with President Nixon here). Still Italianate on the outside, it is ultramod on the inside, with brilliant jewel tones, animal prints, and a concierge service that promises "whatever you want, whenever . . . as long as it's legal." That includes the club sandwich (available through room service), which made the Travel Channel's Adam Richman swoon.

The **Mayflower,** about four blocks from the White House, has long been nicknamed the "Grande Dame of Washington," famous for the amount of gold and gilt, unsurpassed in the nation except by the Library of Congress (much of it visible in the block-long lobby promenade), and the fact that it has hosted a presidential inaugural ball every four years since Calvin Coolidge's day. (It's the city's longest continually operating hotel, since 1925.) FDR rehearsed his "fear itself" speech here; Truman, who kept a room at the hotel after leaving

1600 Pennsylvania Avenue, called it "the second best address in Washington." Its Town and Country Lounge hosted FBI director J. Edgar Hoover (chicken soup and cottage cheese) and his companion Clyde Tolson at lunch for two decades; the renovated room is now called the Edgar Bar and Kitchen in his, um, honor. It's also a magnet for scandal lovers: Clinton "aide" Monica Lewinsky and Kennedy's mob-related mistress Judith Exner both stayed there; it was also the site of then–New York Governor Eliot Spitzer's partying with a very expensive escort in 2008, which cost him his job.

The much smaller and recently refreshed **Morrison Clark Inn** began its life as two private homes, built in 1864, and served for many years as the Soldier's, Sailor's, Marine's, and Airmen's Club, a prominent First Ladies' charity. It's not a typical hotel—it barely has what passes for a lobby—but more like a romantic B&B with a restaurant, most alluring for those who love the original touches, such as the Shanghai tile roof, Carrara marble fireplaces, antique furniture, and more.

The Beaux-Arts **Jefferson Hotel** was completely renovated in 2009—uncovering a stunning lobby skylight in the process—and now salutes its namesake wine-loving president with Monticello-inspired architectural elements, such as a parquet floor and toile draperies, signed documents and artifacts, a hand-painted silk mural in the Plume restaurant of his own vineyard there, and a glass ceiling that could inspire the first woman president. Quill, the elegant lounge, has an outdoor terrace and an alcove with a library full of signed books (by famous guests who've stayed there). But it also has technological innovations that inventor Jefferson would have loved: free international phone service, as well as Wi-Fi and daily newspaper downloads, plus 24-hour butler service.

Presidential candidate Donald Trump and his children are turning the gorgeously gothic **Old Post Office Pavilion** into a luxury hotel and spa; it is scheduled to open in 2016.

B&BS

unofficial **TIP**
If you expect to stay for an extended period, check the B&B websites; some list furnished apartments that are homier than hotel suites and in more residential areas.

B&BS CAN BE PLEASANT OPTIONS and feel more homey than hotels. They offer more of a "neighborhood" experience—ideally with a subway stop, which generally means dining and services nearby—and with a built-in source of information in the hosts. However, there are a few questions you should ask before making a reservation at a B&B.

- What are the payment options? Do they accept credit cards, cash, and/or personal checks?
- Are young children (or pets) allowed?
- Do all the rooms have private baths or showers?

- What sort of "breakfast" is included?
- Is there a refrigerator and/or microwave in the room?
- Is the entire establishment nonsmoking?
- Does it have free Wi-Fi and laundry service?
- If applicable, are the facilities wheelchair-accessible?
- What is the cancellation policy? Because B&Bs typically operate on a tighter budget than big hotels, the policy may be more stringent.

Among websites with information on Washington-area B&Bs are **abba.com,** the site of the American Bed and Breakfast Association; **bedandbreakfastdc.com;** and **iloveinns.com. SelectRegistry.com** maintains a rigorous evaluation of the quality, ambience, and hospitality offered at B&Bs and Inns. Both **Embassy Circle Guest House** and **Swann House** have achieved this designation. However, there are many options in various neighborhoods worth considering if they meet your needs.

Airbnb

Airbnb (**airbnb.com**) offers an alternative to hotel accommodations. The company describes itself as a "community marketplace," where individuals can offer space in their homes to visitors. These spaces are especially attractive for the budget traveler or families. Rentals can be as small as one guest room to as large as an entire home. Airbnb listings have become popular in the Washington, D.C., area, and there are a variety of accommodations in both downtown neighborhoods and the surrounding suburbs. You will likely find a place that charges substantially less than any D.C. hotel room would cost and, in some cases, find more than one room, which is especially nice for families. It might seem a little intimidating to stay overnight in a stranger's house, but Airbnb is growing in popularity, and the community of reviewers keeps a potential customer informed if they encounter less than stellar accommodations. Len, one of the authors, used Airbnb exclusively for his D.C. research and wouldn't see Washington any other way. Prices range from $60 to $120 per night. Travelers can pay by PayPal or credit card, with a booking fee of 6–12% added on.

VACATION RENTALS

VACATION-RENTAL COMPANIES have millions of live vacation listings and appeal to those seeking a rental house or apartment. Three of the most popular and reputable rental companies are **FlipKey, VRBO,** and **Home Away**—all list vacation rentals in the Washington, D.C., area. Typically, vacation rentals are more spacious than a single hotel room and are often located in residential neighborhoods. Some provide free parking and free laundry facilities.

Guests may search listings in Washington, D.C., by using "tools" that designate price, dates, location, number of bedrooms, neighborhood, child-friendly accommodations, and so on. The owner of the rental property determines cost. Travelers may also search for vacation rentals using **TripAdvisor.com/vacation rentals.** We recommend you read the reviews of the property under consideration on the vacation rental website.

As noted, payment methods vary, but one way to protect yourself against possible fraud is to have a conversation with the owner before you submit any money. During this conversation, ask important questions, such as: Where do I pick up a key? Is the rental near public transportation, and if so, which ones? Where do I park? Most rentals require a down payment to hold your reservation and an additional deposit upfront for damages. This deposit should be refunded within 30 days, unless actual damage occurs. One way to avoid losing your damage deposit is to look around the space when you first arrive and report any problems you encounter directly to the owner.

THE BEST HOTELS FOR FAMILIES BY NEIGHBORHOOD

WHAT MAKES A SUPER FAMILY HOTEL? Roomy accommodations, in-room fridge, great pool (or access to one), complimentary breakfast, child-care options, and programs for kids are a few of the things the Unofficial Guide hotel team researched in selecting the top hotels for families from among hundreds of properties in the Washington, D.C., area. Some of our picks are expensive, others are more reasonable, and some are a bargain. Regardless of price, be assured that these hotels understand a family's needs.

The Southwest Waterfront or The Wharf

Mandarin Oriental Washington, D.C.

1330 Maryland Ave. SW, Washington, D.C.; 202-554-8588; **mandarinoriental.com**

Rate per night $250–$550. **Pool** Yes. **Fridge in room** No. **Pet-friendly** No. **Maximum occupants per room** 4. **Nearby dining** Potbelly Sandwich Shop, Amsterdam Falafel Shop, Five Guys, Maine Avenue Fish Market, Jenny's Asian Fusion, Captain White's Seafood City.

THIS ELEGANT, BUSY HOTEL IS IN THE HEART OF D.C. If you're willing to splurge to stay at D.C.'s most posh hotel, with panoramic views of the Potomac River and a quick walk to the National Mall, then this is your hotel, *if* you can get a reservation. The place is almost always full, due to its location, first-class service, and popularity with business travelers. Yet, it's still worth investigating, especially if you're traveling during a quieter time (unfortunately, that's not during school breaks). Guest rooms are the epitome of luxury and sophistication, with marble tubs, sumptuous linens, and balconies. It's just steps away from Washington's historic Maine Avenue Fish Market, and The Wharf, a multiuse development on the waterfront that should be up and running around late 2016. The hotel is also known for its luxurious Asian-style spa and beautiful Empress Lounge, so you can still experience the Mandarin, even if you're not staying there.

OTHER FAMILY-FRIENDLY HOTELS IN SOUTHWEST RIVERFRONT AND THE WHARF: Intercontinental is scheduled for early 2017. L'Enfant Plaza Hotel is undergoing renovation until 2017.

Capitol Riverfront and Navy Yard
Courtyard Washington Capitol Hill/Navy Yard
140 L St. SE, Washington, D.C.; 202-479-0027; **marriott.com**

Rate per night $180–$300. **Pool** Yes. **Fridge in room** No. **Pet-friendly** No. **Maximum occupants per room** 4. **Nearby dining** Five Guys, Starbucks, Gordon Biersch Brewing, Red Hook Oyster Bar, Subway.

JUST A FEW BLOCKS FROM NATIONALS PARK STADIUM, this sparkling new Courtyard is growing in popularity, as the neighborhood continues to revitalize. The hotel has a heated indoor pool, whirlpool, and fitness center. When weather permits, guests can walk to Washington Canal Park or the nearby Anacostia Riverwalk Trail, which stretches for several miles and has water features and places to play for kids. The Navy Yard Metro station is one block away, which makes getting to the National Mall easy and quick. The modern lobby reflects the recent renovation of the comfortable, clean rooms; configurations vary, but double rooms have two queen beds, while others include sofa sleepers and separate living areas. Some rooms even have a view of the Washington Monument.

Capitol Hill
Capitol Hill Hotel
200 C St. SW, Washington, D.C.; 202-543-6000; **capitolhillhotel-dc.com**

Rate per night $135–$200. **Pool** No. **Fridge in room** Yes. **Pet-friendly** Yes. **Maximum occupants per room** 4. **Nearby dining** Hank's Oyster Bar, Good Stuff Eatery, We the Pizza, Eastern Market.

SUITE LIFE NEAR KEY ATTRACTIONS. This family-friendly hotel is an ideal location for exploring Washington's must-see landmarks, such as the U.S. Capitol Visitor Center, Library of Congress, Supreme Court, historic Eastern Market, National Gallery of Art, and the U.S. Botanic Garden. Located near a combination of residential and federal buildings, all the guest rooms are like small apartments—doubles have two queen beds, and all have kitchenettes and roomy closets. Ask about the Family Getaway Package, which comes with four daily Metro passes (which can be a hassle to buy on your own) and free rollaway beds. Breakfast and Wi-Fi are complimentary, and the hotel hosts a weekday wine reception. This neighborhood has a plethora of restaurants and bars within walking distance, as well as Eastern Market. Capitol Hill Hotel is just one block from Capitol South Metro station, with a friendly staff eager to help plan your day or provide answers to questions.

Holiday Inn Washington-Capitol

550 C St. SW, Washington, D.C.; 202-479-4000; **ihg.com**

Rate per night $110–$180. **Pool** Yes. **Fridge in room** Yes. **Pet-friendly** No. **Maximum occupants per room** 4. **Nearby dining** Mitsitam Native Foods Café in the American Indian Museum, McDonald's, Starbucks, Cosmo Café, Pizza Autentica, Mezza Café.

BEST PLACE TO EXPLORE THE NATIONAL MALL. This hulking behemoth of a hotel overlooks the Smithsonian section of the National Mall. The hotel has a lovely rooftop pool and relaxing courtyard—perfect for families who would like to rest and refuel after a long day of sightseeing but who plan to tour the monuments later that night. You're literally one block from the Smithsonian Air and Space Museum, the Museum of the American Indian, and the Hirshhorn Gallery of Art. Small children love the nearby carousel, and older kids will enjoy renting a bike from Capital Bikeshare to tool around the safe paths of the National Mall. Only two blocks from the L'Enfant Plaza Metro and a little farther to Smithsonian Metro, the hotel also has a McDonald's and CVS right outside the door. Ask for an even number room that faces the courtyard because the street noise can be quite loud. The breakfast buffet is complimentary but is often very crowded if you don't get there early; other options include the in-house Starbucks or the Shuttle Express Deli. The hotel gift shop sells tickets to various tour buses, and full-size washing machines are available to guests. Although the decor is dated, the king rooms have sleeper sofas and feel very spacious. All rooms have a fridge, microwave, coffeemaker, and standard Wi-Fi access.

Residence Inn Washington, D.C. Capitol

333 E St. SW, Washington, D.C.; 202-484-8280; **marriott.com**

Rate per night $180–$600. **Pool** Yes. **Fridge in room** Yes. **Pet-friendly** Yes, deposit required. **Maximum occupants per room** 6. **Nearby dining** Mitsitam Native Foods Café in the American Indian Museum, McDonald's, Good Stuff Eatery, Starbucks, We the Pizza, Tortilla Cafe.

MAKE YOURSELF AT HOME. As in all Residence Inn hotels, this location offers a selection of suites with kitchens and sofa sleepers. What makes this Residence Inn so great is the location—only two blocks to Federal Center Metro station, an 8-minute walk to the National Mall, a 15-minute walk to the U.S. Capitol, and a 10-minute cab ride to Union Station. Although there are a few restaurants nearby, the hotel offers a full complimentary breakfast and small happy hour. It also has clean, spacious rooms with two televisions—nice for families fighting over the TV at night. Other amenities include an indoor saltwater pool, a whirlpool, a fitness center with bright skylights, and lounge chairs on an outdoor deck adjacent to the pool. The hotel was renovated in 2010, so it looks updated and fresh. One cool fact about this hotel: Four different tribes of American Indians own it, and you'll see touches, such as bed covers and the lobby wall, that give a nod to the Smithsonian American Indian Museum nearby.

H Street Corridor and NoMa

Hyatt Place U.S. Capitol

33 New York Ave. NE, Washington, D.C.; 202-289-5599;
washingtondcuscapitol.place.hyatt.com

Rate per night $130–$180. **Pool** Yes. **Fridge in room** Yes. **Pet-friendly** No. **Maximum occupants per room** 6. **Nearby dining** McDonald's, Potbelly Sandwich, Tynan Coffee & Tea, Todd Gray's Watershed, Mint Indian Cuisine, Soi 38.

HIGH-QUALITY HOTEL NEAR THE METRO BUT OFF THE BEATEN PATH. This sparkly-new, two-year-old hotel is located in the NoMa neighborhood. Well-appointed, spacious guest rooms have comfy sleeper sofas, plush bedding, and granite countertops. With free Wi-Fi, an urban sundeck and outdoor pool, a 24/7 café, and free hot breakfast, you get a lot for your money, despite being outside the traditional tourist areas. But with a two-block walk to the NoMa/Gallaudet Metro, or a quick cab ride, you can be at the U.S. Capitol and National Mall in no time. Guests love the Coffee to Cocktails Bar in the lobby and the views of the Capitol dome from the upper rooms. This is a transitional residential neighborhood, with an occasional panhandler and the usual street noise, and it does not yet have many restaurants or shops within walking distance; however, if you're looking for a comfortable hotel, and don't mind a short commute to do your sightseeing, this hotel could be a good choice.

The National Mall and The White House

Hamilton Crowne Plaza Hotel

1001 14th St. NW, Washington, D.C.; 202-682-3801; **ihg.com**

Rate per night: $112–$300. **Pool** No. **Fridge in room** Yes. **Pet-friendly** Yes, on 3rd floor. **Maximum occupants per room** 5. **Nearby dining** Toro Toro, &Pizza, Pret a Manger, The Hamilton, Cosi, Woodward Table.

HISTORIC HOTEL AT AFFORDABLE PRICES. What makes The Hamilton so special is the beauty of this historic building and the exemplary service provided by the staff. It's also centrally located—McPherson Square is one block away, the White House is three blocks away, and the National Mall is less than a mile away. The hotel looks out on Franklin Square Park, and the higher floors have gorgeous nighttime views of the city. Guest rooms vary in size but are all beautifully furnished with smallish bathrooms. Besides the full-service Starbucks in the lobby, the hotel has an elegant restaurant called 14K that serves breakfast, lunch, dinner, and a popular weekend brunch. Room rates are reasonable, but guests are charged for extras like Wi-Fi and breakfast (consider joining the IHG rewards club for discounts).

Hilton Garden Inn Washington, D.C. Downtown

815 14th St. NW, Washington, D.C.; 202-783-7800;
hiltongardeninn3.hilton.com

Rate per night $149–$250. **Pool** Yes. **Fridge in room** Yes. **Pet-friendly** No. **Maximum**

number of occupants per room 4. **Nearby dining** The Hamilton, Starbucks, Cosi.

IDEAL LOCATION FOR SIGHTSEEING. It's hard to beat the quality and price of this Trip Advisor Hall of Fame winner. The hotel maintains the highest level of quality through an exceptional staff, convenient location, and spacious rooms with microwaves, refrigerators, and free Wi-Fi. Feeling more like a boutique hotel than your typical chain, this Hilton is decorated in cheerful prints and features ergonomic chairs for deskwork. In addition to complimentary coffee/tea in the morning and cookies in the afternoon, you can order room service or a cooked-to-order breakfast (for a charge). Other amenities include an indoor pool, in-room fitness supplies, 24-hour pantry/gift shop, guest laundry room, kid's menu, and baby gear. Close to McPherson Square Metro station, the Trolley stop, and Franklin Square Park, guests claim it's a great base for exploring the city's attractions. Valet parking is $41 per night, but ask about Parking Panda; it's less expensive and only a few blocks away. To avoid street noise, ask for a room on a higher floor.

JW Marriott Washington, D.C.

1331 Pennsylvania Ave. NW, Washington, D.C.; 202-393-2000; **marriott.com**

Rate per night $225–$720. **Pool** Yes. **Fridge in room** Yes. **Pet-friendly** No. **Maximum occupants per room** 5. **Nearby dining** Avenue Grill, Starbucks, Brasserie Beck, Bombay Club, Old Ebbitt Grill, The Hamilton.

LUXURY AND COMFORT IN THE HEART OF D.C.'S MAJOR ATTRACTIONS. Renovated in 2015, this large, sophisticated hotel has an excellent location on Pennsylvania Avenue, near some of D.C.'s most popular attractions. The hotel is one block from Metro Center subway station, a 10-minute walk to the National Mall, and has easy access to museums, monuments, the White House, the National Theatre, shopping, and dining. The hotel is a good choice for families because plenty of the guest rooms are large enough to sleep four people, and the junior suites make a great home base for spreading out and exploring the city (rollaway beds are not allowed). Furnished with luxury linens, many of the rooms have city views of the Old Post Office Pavilion and the Washington Monument. Families love the convenience of the indoor swimming pool, whirlpool, well-equipped fitness center, and two on-site restaurants. Babysitting services can be arranged. Steps away from the hotel are two food courts—inside the Ronald Reagan Building and in the Shops at National Place. Check out packages that offer free parking, complimentary breakfast, and last-minute deep discounting available on weekends.

Sofitel Washington, D.C. Lafayette Square

806 15th St. NW, Washington, D.C.; 202-730-8800; **sofitel.com**

Rate per night $200–$500. **Pool** No. **Fridge in room** No. **Pet-friendly** No. **Maximum occupants per room** 5. **Nearby dining** Lincoln Restaurant, Joe's Seafood, Woodward Takeout Food, Devon & Blakely.

PRESIDENTIAL LUXURY WITH EUROPEAN STYLE Just two blocks from the most famous address in the United States, this Sofitel allows you to be a neighbor of the president. Located in historic Lafayette Park, the hotel is within walking distance of almost every major attraction in downtown Washington. The hotel's staff is extraordinarily helpful, and the newly renovated guest rooms are the peak of sophistication and comfort. Sofitel is known for their SoBeds, with signature feather-top linens, and spa-style bathrooms. The restaurant, ICI Urban Bistro, specializes in modern French cuisine, and Le Bar is a fine place to sip French wine, drink the complimentary coffee, or watch the Secret Service agents pass by from the outdoor terrace. The gym is small but has state-of-the-art equipment. The hotel is working to reduce waste with helpful signs and recycling containers. Ask for one of the corner rooms; they feel like a private apartment. Also, inquire about the Petit Prince program, which includes free accommodations and breakfast for up to three kids under 12 years old who share their parents' room. Each family traveling with kids is welcomed with a cookie platter and milk.

Penn Quarter, Chinatown, and Convention Center
Comfort Inn Downtown D.C./Convention Center
1201 13th St. NW, Washington, D.C.; 202-682-5300; **dcdowntownhotel.com**

Rate per night $150–$280. **Pool** No. **Fridge in room** Yes. **Pet-friendly** No. **Maximum occupants per room** 4. **Nearby dining** El Rinconcito, the Pig, Rogue 24, Estadio, Tortino.

AFFORDABLE PRICE AND FRIENDLY SERVICE. This cheery chain hotel is closer to Thomas Circle than Penn Quarter—about a 20-minute walk to the National Mall and closer to several other attractions, including the National Geographic Museum, Ford's Theatre, International Spy Museum, Smithsonian Art Museum, and City Center. Amenities include free breakfast, free Wi-Fi, free coffee and tea, and, in the afternoon, complimentary cookies and popcorn. There's no pool, but the fitness center has machines with their own TVs. Although this is a chain, it feels more like a historic boutique hotel, with a cozy lobby and a breakfast room that gets very crowded. Ask for a room on a higher floor, as the lower ones report some street noise. The hotel caters to business travelers and people attending events at the convention center, so it's quieter on the weekends. Parking is off site, but they have valet service and will drive your car up and back to the garage for you.

Courtyard Washington Convention Center
900 F St. NW, Washington, D.C.; 202-638-4600; **marriott.com**

Rate per night $150–$250. **Pool** Yes. **Fridge in room** Yes. **Pet-friendly** Yes. **Maximum occupants per room** 4. **Nearby dining** Daikaya, Shake Shack, Hill Street BBQ, Oyamel, Zengo, Proof, Starbucks.

HOME IN THE HEART OF THE CITY. This family-friendly hotel in Penn Quarter not only puts you right into the action, but it also shelters visitors in comfortable accommodations at a reasonable price. The hotel was once a bank, with thick, solid walls, so you won't hear the lively street noise (check out the old bank vault door in the lobby). The rooms aren't large—double rooms have full-size beds—but will fit a rollaway bed or crib. They also have spacious suites, a small pool, a hot tub, a fitness center, free Wi-Fi, and complimentary water bottles and snacks in the lobby every day. The hotel is just steps from the Gallery Place/Chinatown Metro, Smithsonian Art Museum, International Spy Museum, and Ford's Theatre and is surrounded by dozens of restaurants and shops. You can catch a sightseeing bus or walk to the National Mall in about five minutes. Some guests complain about the sink being outside the bathroom and the lack of bathtubs, but the hotel is clean, and the staff is eager to accommodate your specific needs. Be sure to make specific requests *when* you book your reservation. This is a great place to stay if you plan to see a concert or sports event at Verizon Center.

Embassy Suites Washington, D.C. Convention Center

900 10th St. NW, Washington, D.C.; 202-739-2001; **embassysuites3.hilton.com**

Rate per night $220–$260. **Pool** Yes. **Fridge in room** Yes. **Pet-friendly** Yes. **Maximum occupants per room** 6. **Nearby dining** DBGB, City Tap House, Casa Luca, Acadiana, Cuba Libre.

TONS OF SPACE AND LOTS OF FREEBIES. This Embassy Suites hotel serves families well, with their sleeper sofas, free buffet breakfast, and evening snacks. You'll get a microwave, mini-fridge, and two LCD TVs in each room. Guests enjoy the free drinks during the evening reception, their indoor pool, Jacuzzi, and the 24-hour business and fitness centers you can use at your convenience. This hotel would make a good home base to go sightseeing, although the neighborhood is not especially attractive. It's about seven blocks to the National Mall and the Smithsonian museums, and on the way you'll pass St. Patrick's Church, Madame Tussauds wax museum, E Street Cinema, and City Center, with its high-end stores, a farmers market, and many great restaurants. It's a short walk to Macy's, a modern department store, and only three blocks to Metro Center station, where many subway lines meet. Recently renovated, the rooms are quite spacious. There's free Wi-Fi for Hilton members, self-service laundry facilities, and the Circulator bus stop is close by.

Fairfield Inn & Suites Washington, D.C./Downtown

500 H St. NW, Washington, D.C.; 202-289-5959; **marriott.com**

Rate per night $140–$250. **Pool** No. **Fridge in room** No. **Pet-friendly** No. **Maximum occupants per room** 6. **Nearby dining** Ping Pong Dim Sum, La Tasca, Zaytinya, Carmine's, Tony Cheung's Seafood Restaurant, Asian Spice, Zengo.

VIBRANT CHINATOWN IS CLOSE TO ALL THE ACTION. Right in the middle of Washington's Chinatown, this Fairfield has signs in Chinese, and many of the surrounding restaurants are either Chinese or have their names spelled out in Chinese letters. Although there is no pool, the fitness center is spacious and well equipped. The hotel serves a generous breakfast buffet every morning, and they also offer free Wi-Fi. Room styles vary—doubles have two queens, and the studio suites have mini-fridges, coffeemakers, and a privacy wall separating the sitting area and the bed. The hotel scores high in cleanliness, location, and value. You're a block or two from the Newseum, Spy Museum, Ford's Theatre, and Madame Tussauds. The Verizon Center is across the street, and there are too many restaurants to count. Guests rave about the proximity to Gallery Place–Chinatown Metro (across the street) and the short walk to the National Mall. The Irish Pub in the building offers room service when you're worn out from your busy day of exploring.

Foggy Bottom
Hotel Lombardy

2019 Pennsylvania Ave. NW, Washington, D.C. (faces I St. NW); 202-793-7281; **hotellombardy.com**

Rate per night $160–$250. **Pool** Yes (off site). **Fridge in room** Some. **Pet-friendly** No. **Maximum occupants per room** 3. **Nearby dining** Primi Piati, Baja Fresh, Elephant & Castle, Kaz Sushi Bistro, Founding Farmers, Prime Rib, District Commons.

HISTORIC HOTEL WITH A PRIME LOCATION. Enter the Hotel Lombardy and you'll experience some old-fashioned hospitality. The hotel has a bright green awning and a friendly doorman welcoming visitors; in fact, the whole staff strives to look after you well. They will gladly set up tours, sell bus passes and tickets to attractions, and more. The lobby is Old World European, with Oriental rugs, a wooden front desk with a little bell, and an antique letterbox. The hotel lounge is the epitome of cozy. Although it's designated as a Historic Hotel of America, the guest room furnishings have been renovated and are mostly contemporary (except for the little floral vanity). Some rooms have city views and small kitchens with a fridge. Despite its address on Pennsylvania Avenue, the hotel faces I Street NW. It's a short walk to both the Foggy Bottom and Farragut West Metro stations and a six-block walk to the National Mall and the White House. You have use of the fitness center and complimentary passes to the pool at the Washington Plaza Hotel in Thomas Circle.

Melrose Georgetown Hotel Washington, D.C.

2430 Pennsylvania Ave. NW, Washington, D.C.; 202-955-6400; **melrosehoteldc.com**

Rate per night $161–$240. **Pool** No. **Fridge in room** Yes. **Pet-friendly** Yes (dogs). **Maximum occupants per room** 4. **Nearby dining** Marcel's, Sweetgreen, CIRCA, District Commons, One Fish Two Fish, Aroma, Founding Farmers, Sea Catch.

A MIX OF HISTORIC BEAUTY AND MODERN COMFORT. Located on the border of Foggy Bottom and Georgetown, this independent boutique hotel is known for its attractive, luxurious rooms and friendly, courteous staff. Although it's about a 20-minute walk to the National Mall, it's only three blocks to Foggy Bottom Metro and a short walk to the Georgetown Waterfront, restaurants, and shopping. You'll find yourself surrounded by George Washington University students, which is why there are so many take-out and fast-casual restaurants nearby. There's also Trader Joe's and Whole Foods within walking distance, where you can stock up on drinks and snacks. There are no coffeemakers in the room, but coffee is served complimentary in the lobby each morning, and they offer to-go cups. Thanks to the thick walls in this historic building, you will rarely be bothered by street noise. The elegant Art Deco–style lobby has a wood-burning fireplace, and there's a gym and free Wi-Fi throughout the hotel. Jardenea, the hotel restaurant, serves breakfast, lunch, and dinner and has an appealing lounge that attracts even the locals. Guest rooms are smartly done, with artwork featuring George Washington and the Constitution. Traveling with kids? Ask about their Munchkin package.

Residence Inn Foggy Bottom

801 New Hampshire Ave. NW, Washington, D.C.; 202-785-2000; **marriott.com**

Rate per night $150–$280. **Pool** Yes, rooftop. **Fridge in room** Yes. **Pet-friendly** Yes. **Maximum occupants per room** 6. **Nearby dining** District Commons, Burger Tap & Shake, Rasika West, Bangkok Joes, Devon Bakery.

CLOSE TO COLLEGES AND KENNEDY CENTER. This neighborhood gets its high energy from the George Washington University college students, and it's busy at all hours of the day and night, making it safe to walk to many destinations, including the Potomac River waterfront and Foggy Bottom Metro. Thanks to the students, there are lots of inexpensive restaurants around here, too, and many stay open late at night. You can walk over to the grocery store in the Watergate building to stock up that full kitchen, and go for a swim in the beautiful rooftop pool. The hotel has the usual suite-style rooms—one-bedroom suites with choice of King or two queens, both with sleeper sofas. It's only one block to Foggy Bottom Metro or Rock Creek Park. Georgetown, the National Mall, and the White House are all within a mile of the hotel.

State Plaza Hotel

2117 E St. NW, Washington, D.C.; 202-861-8200; **stateplaza.com**

Rate per night $100–$150. **Pool** No. **Fridge in room** Yes. **Pet-friendly** No. **Maximum occupants per room** 4. **Nearby dining** Chipotle, Johnny Rockets, Dunkin Donuts, Potbelly Sandwich Shop, Starbucks, Tonic, Whole Foods.

POSSIBLY THE BEST VALUE IN TOWN. Half of the State Plaza Hotel is sparkling and new, and the other half is in the process of renovation, so request a room in the F Street Tower. The hotel's Garden Café serves three meals a day, and after your workout in the fitness center, check out the daily happy hour from 4 to 7 p.m. Suites come in a variety of configurations, including two queens, one king, and one queen bed; all have fully equipped kitchens, with microwave ovens available by request. Some rooms have additional sleeper sofas in separate sitting rooms, which is nice for families who want to spread out. This hotel lobby isn't very welcoming, but the location puts you adjacent to George Washington University, with its many fast-casual restaurants. State Plaza is three blocks from the Foggy Bottom Metro station and just a half mile from the National Mall (closest to the Lincoln Memorial and Vietnam Veterans Memorial). Patrons of this undiscovered gem are often state department employees or George Washington University families.

Georgetown
Avenue Suites Georgetown

2500 Pennsylvania Ave. NW, Washington, D.C.; 202-333-8060;
avenuesuites.com

Rate per night $200–$310; some weekends require a 2-night minimum. **Pool** No.
Fridge in room Yes. **Pet-friendly** Yes, $25 per pet. **Maximum occupants per room** 4.
Nearby dining Charm's Thai, Flavors of India, Marcel's, La Perla.

FULL KITCHENS, SPACIOUS ROOMS, AND FRIENDLY STAFF. Avenue
Suites Georgetown is an independent hotel with a reputation for enthusiastic
service and large guest rooms that resemble apartments, some up to 600
square feet. The property is located midway between Georgetown and Foggy
Bottom; it's four blocks to Foggy Bottom Metro station and within walking distance to popular attractions, such as the White House and the National Mall.
Some rooms have beautiful views of the city, and the neighborhood has a
youthful vibe thanks to its proximity to George Washington University and
Georgetown University. The hotel is also steps from many dining options in different price points. Because the neighborhood is mostly residential, it's busy
and safe at night, with more locals on the streets than tourists. Guest rooms
come in multiple configurations—some have two queen beds and a sleeper
sofa; some have private terraces; but every room has a full kitchen. Trader Joe's
grocery store is across the street, so it's easy to stock breakfast foods, pack a
picnic lunch for a day of sightseeing, and eat in for dinner to save a little money.
Guests are welcome to grill or dine on the outdoor patio. In addition to a small
gym, the hotel offers Saturday morning yoga on the terrace. The Avenue's A
BAR Kitchen has a fireplace lit in the lobby lounge with full food service.

Best Western Georgetown Hotel & Suites

1121 New Hampshire Ave. NW, Washington, D.C.; 866-872-1640;
georgetowndchotel.com

Rate per night $150–$180. **Pool** No. **Fridge in room** Yes. **Pet-friendly** No. **Maximum
occupants per room** 4. **Nearby dining** Baja Fresh, Johnny Rockets, Subway.

GOOD LOCATION AND ROOM TO SPREAD OUT. Although the Best Western is not an upscale hotel, the rooms are spacious—with kitchenettes—and
can comfortably accommodate a family of four. Another plus for families is
that the hotel doesn't charge for children under 17. The parking fee is somewhat less than competitors, at $28 per night, although the garage is across the
street at the Ritz-Carlton. The hotel offers use of a full-service Bally's Gym off-
site, free Wi-Fi, a laundry and dry-cleaning service (great if you're staying for
a while), free continental breakfast, and a coffeemaker in the room. It's just a
short walk to both Foggy Bottom and Dupont Circle Metro stations, and
there's also a Circulator bus that stops nearby. Large student groups often
book this hotel, so it gets very busy. Even at its busiest, the staff remains polite
and helpful. They are eager to point guests to attractions and restaurants.

Although there is no hotel restaurant, this very safe neighborhood features many restaurants and two grocery stores within walking distance.

Fairmont Washington, D.C. Georgetown

2401 M St. NW, Washington, D.C.; 202-429-2400;
thefairmont.com/Washington

Rate per night $150–$350. **Pool** Yes. **Fridge in room** Only in suites. **Pet-friendly** Yes. **Maximum occupants per room** 4. **Nearby dining** Tea Cellar, District Commons, Café Deluxe, Rasika West End.

FAMILY WELLNESS RETREAT. Although not in the beating heart of Georgetown (M Street and Wisconsin Avenue, NW), the Fairmont Hotel is a short walk from the historic neighborhood's shops and restaurants. The Fairmont is actually located in the West End, near a few hotels and 1 mile from the Dupont Circle and Foggy Bottom Metro stations. What makes Fairmont so family-friendly are the extras: free lemonade and board games in the lobby, beautiful garden courtyard, safe residential neighborhood, free bicycles, and gracious service. The rooms have luxurious furnishings and marble bathrooms; some have sleeper sofas or balconies overlooking a courtyard fountain. The hotel has streamlined check-in by providing roving guest-service representatives armed with iPads to facilitate the process. The hotel's Balance Gym Fitness Center and Spa boasts a sauna, whirlpool, steam room, large indoor saltwater pool, and classes in yoga, spin, cross-fit, Pilates, barre, and zumba. Fairmont's Juniper Restaurant has menus that cater to a variety of food preferences, including gluten-free, vegan, and paleo diets. Children age 5 and under eat free, and kids ages 6–11 eat for half price. Two blocks away are running and biking trails in Rock Creek Park. Check out family packages, such as the Smithsonian Experience and Family Adventures.

Park Hyatt Hotel Washington

1201 24th St. NW, Washington, D.C.; 202-789-1234;
parkwashington.hyatt.com

Rate per night $250–$650. **Pool** Yes. **Fridge in room** Only in suites. **Pet-friendly** No. **Maximum occupants per room** 4. **Nearby dining** Rasika West, Marcel's, RIS, Café Deluxe, Burger Tap & Shake, Whole Foods, District Commons, Bobby's Burger Palace, Unum.

SOPHISTICATED COMFORT IN A FASHIONABLE NEIGHBORHOOD. If you love being pampered, consider staying at the Park Hyatt. The hotel is known for exceptional service and outstanding restaurants, including a posh tea buffet on weekends and all-day farm-to-table dining in the acclaimed Blue Duck Tavern. With modern decor, local artwork, and an expansive American book collection, you'll find this hotel a welcoming retreat. Some rooms have spa-inspired bathrooms with separate soaking tubs and rain-style showers, and all are oversize, with plush furnishings and high-tech touches, including free Wi-Fi. Don't miss the Spa Room, indoor saltwater pool and whirlpool, and state-of-the-art fitness center. Borrow a free bike for four hours from the hotel's bicycle valet, along with helmets, locks, water bottles, and trail maps.

Located about 1 mile from Foggy Bottom and Farragut North Metro stations, you'll find an abundance of upscale and family-friendly restaurants in this very safe neighborhood.

Dupont Circle and Logan Circle

Embassy Suites Washington, D.C. Georgetown

1250 22nd St. NW, Washington, D.C.; 202-857-3388;
embassysuites3.hilton.com

Rate per night $160– $220. **Pool** Yes. **Fridge in room** Yes. **Pet-friendly** No. **Maximum occupants per room** 6. **Nearby dining** Meiwah, Bread & Chocolate, Café Deluxe, Rasika West, West End Bisto.

BRIGHT, SUNNY LOBBY AND CENTRAL LOCATION. Embassy Suites is known and loved by traveling families, and this location is no exception. From the cheery lobby to the expansive suites, it's hard to beat this chain hotel situated between Georgetown, Foggy Bottom, and Dupont Circle. One criticism is thin walls and noise, although that is probably because of the open lobby atrium. Nevertheless, travel with earplugs, and don't shy away from this all-suite hotel with the complimentary buffet breakfast every morning and happy-hour snacks and cocktails every night. Adjacent to many international embassies, this hotel is just four blocks away from the Dupont Circle and Foggy Bottom Metro stations and a Circulator bus stop. This charming residential neighborhood is just steps from Rock Creek Park, with its walking and biking trails. Guest rooms are dated in their decor, but all have a coffeemaker, microwave, safe, sink, ironing board, dining table, sofa sleeper, two TVs, and a desk. The indoor pool and fitness center, along with the bountiful koi swimming around the lobby fountain, make this a favorite for families with younger children. Breakfast is usually extremely busy, so try to get there early.

Hotel Madera, A Kimpton Hotel

1310 New Hampshire Ave. NW, Washington, D.C.; 202-296-7600;
hotelmadera.com

Rate per night $119–$420. **Pool** No. **Fridge in room** Some. **Pet-friendly** Yes. **Maximum occupants per room** 6. **Nearby dining** Pizza Paradisio, Raku, Nora, Hank's Oyster Bar, Urbana, Starbucks, Shophouse.

CHECK OUT THE BUNK BEDS AND DELIGHTFUL RESTAURANT. A fresh renovation and the whimsical restaurant put Hotel Madera on our radar. Kimpton Hotels make an effort to welcome kids with a guppy for their guest room, hula hoops, mini bathrobes, free bikes, cribs, and more. Madera also happens to be in a quiet residential neighborhood that is only two blocks from the Dupont Circle Metro and dozens of restaurants, shops, and museums. This small boutique hotel was originally an apartment building. The lobby is miniscule, but some guest rooms have city views, some have balconies, others have kitchenettes, and some even have massage chairs. The double queen room with bunk beds is ideal (if you can reserve one) for a large family, although many of the rooms are spacious. Feel free to bring your pet, no matter how big or small; they are welcome but must be caged when housekeeping enters the room. The Firefly restaurant is popular for its farm-to-table cuisine and opens its floor-to-ceiling windows in good weather. There's also free coffee in the mornings and a wine hour at 6 p.m.

Hotel Palomar, A Kimpton Hotel

2121 P St. NW, Washington, D.C.; 202-448-1800; **hotelpalomar-dc.com**

Rate per night $130–$270. **Pool** Yes. **Fridge in room** No. **Pet-friendly** Yes. **Maximum occupants per room** 4. **Nearby dining** Obelisk, Equinox, Al Tiramisu, Pesce.

TREAT YOURSELF TO FUN. Hotel Palomar will constantly surprise you with the whimsy hidden behind the guest room door. Inside you'll find zebra print bathrobes, leopard print throws, square sinks, and velvet sofas. It's just so much fun to stay here that you won't want to leave. Inside the lobby, you'll see quirky original art, as well as friendly guest-service people who welcome you with good cheer and a glass of wine (wine hour is every evening 5–6 p.m.). The lobby opens to the courtyard, with a sparkling blue outdoor pool nestled between the walls of the hotel, affording lots of privacy. Across the street are several restaurants serving take-out and fast food, and it's only a short walk to dozens of sit-down restaurants too. Besides the close proximity to Dupont Circle Metro, there's also the Circulator bus stop nearby that will whisk you away to Georgetown or Union Station. Palomar guests have the use of free Wi-Fi, complimentary morning coffee and tea, an on-site fitness center, and a yoga mat in every room. Urbana, the hotel restaurant, serves outstanding pizzas, cocktails, and healthful entrees. Palomar even provides the use of free bikes (upon availability). Be forewarned if you're uncomfortable or allergic to animals: You may ride the elevators with someone's furry friend (no size restrictions), as Kimpton Hotels are known for being pet-friendly.

Hotel Rouge, A Kimpton Hotel

1315 16th St. NW, Washington, D.C.; 202-232-8000; **rougehotel.com**

Rate per night $120–$240. **Pool** YMCA facilities. **Fridge in room** Some. **Pet-friendly** Yes. **Maximum occupants per room** 6. **Nearby dining** Nage, Shake Shack, Iron Gate, Suki Asia, Peet's Coffee & Tea.

GET READY FOR SOME BUNK BEDS! At first glance, this might not seem like a family-friendly hotel. The decor is obviously, well, red. There are also white marble statues of bare-chested women on the street outside. The lobby is tiny, but upstairs the hotel has guest rooms with some very intriguing bunk beds hidden in small alcoves. The bunk beds come with an Xbox 360 game console and allow kids to feel they have their own space, while the adults stretch out on their king-size bed. Other suite-style rooms are very spacious with small kitchenettes and sleeper sofas. Kimpton hotels have cute treats, such as a free guppy delivered to your room while you're there, and kids under age 17 stay free. The hotel's breakfast is average, but there's a nightly wine hour for guests. Ask about the hula hoops to use in the room, or a yoga mat if you need to stretch. Though it's not close to the National Mall, Hotel Rouge is only a 10-minute walk to the Dupont Circle Metro, and the neighborhood has dozens of first-class and fast-casual restaurants within four blocks, as well as a Whole Foods grocery store. The hotel is near the National Geographic Museum and five blocks from the White House. If you're looking for something unlike the typical chain, Hotel Rouge may be for you.

U Street/Mid City

Homewood Suites by Hilton Washington

1475 Massachusetts Ave. NW, Washington, D.C.; 202-265-8000; **homewoodsuites3.hilton.com**

Rate per night $180–$270. **Pool** No. **Fridge in room** Yes. **Pet-friendly** No. **Maximum occupants per room** 6. **Nearby dining** Estadio, The Pig, ChurchKey, Le Diplomate, Birch & Barley, Ghibellina.

FAMILY-FRIENDLY HOME BASE WITH A CENTRAL LOCATION. This attractive, spacious suite hotel is located between Dupont Circle, Farragut North, McPherson Square, and U Street Metro stations. Although not in the heart of the U Street Corridor's amazing array of great restaurants and irresistible boutiques, you will enjoy a pleasant stroll past some of Washington's most beautiful homes to get there. Guests rave about the friendly staff and the two-room configuration in this hotel—sleeping and living rooms separated by a wall and door. Rooms have a bedroom ceiling fan, fully equipped kitchen, two TVs, and a sofa sleeper, making them an excellent place to spread out and prepare meals. A hot breakfast is complimentary, as is the evening social (weeknights only). There's a fitness and business center, laundry facilities, and a gift shop. It's about 10 blocks to the National Mall and 8 to the White House, but close to many restaurants, shops, and exercise studios in the U Street Corridor.

Washington Plaza

10 Thomas Circle NW, Washington, D.C.; 202-842-1300; **washingtonplazahotel.com**

Rate per night $150–$200. **Pool** Yes. **Fridge in room** Yes. **Pet-friendly** Service animals only. **Maximum occupants per room** 5. **Nearby dining** City Tap Room, DBGB, Dolcezza, The Pig, ChurchKey, B Too, Thaitanic, Lalibela.

IT'S ALL ABOUT THAT POOL. A big draw to this retro-style hotel is the large outdoor pool with views of the city. Architect Morris Lapidus, who designed the Fontainebleau in Miami, intended the Washington Plaza to feel like a resort in the heart of Washington, D.C. The hotel is about five blocks from Mid City's restaurants, bars, and nightclub strip and reasonably close to other attractions, such as the convention center, National Geographic Museum, the White House, and Verizon Center. Guest rooms are decorated in bright contrasting colors, and some lower-level rooms have balconies with city views. The 15 junior suites include a sitting area and two full bathrooms. The hotel's restaurant, Ten Thomas, serves three meals a day, and in warm weather, guests can choose to be served by the pool. In cold weather, the lounge has a cozy fireplace. There's no fitness center, but the hotel can direct guests to a yoga and Pilates studio nearby. The Washington Plaza is four blocks from McPherson Square and Mount Vernon Square–Convention Center Metro stations.

Adams Morgan and Columbia Heights

Adam's Inn

1746 Lanier Place NW, Washington, D.C.; 202-745-3600; adamsinn.com

Rate per night $79–$179. **Pool** No. **Fridge in room** No. **Pet-friendly** Yes. **Maximum occupants per room** 4. **Nearby dining** Meridian Pint, Room 11, Los Hermanos, Sticky Fingers Sweets & Eats, Radius Pizza.

FEEL LIKE A LOCAL IN THE HEART OF ADAMS MORGAN. This budget-friendly, hostel-style inn has been operating for 30 years and consists of 27 rooms in three connected townhomes. The rooms share a living area where guests can watch television, and the innkeepers serve a continental breakfast, as well as tea, coffee, and snacks throughout the day. Guests have an open kitchen available to them, with a microwave, fridge, toaster, and icemaker. One feature worth noting is the Certified Wildlife Habitat in the Inn's garden area. Choose from rooms with one, two, or three beds, some with shared bathrooms; there is no charge for children under age 8. When booking, note whether stairs are an issue. Although limited parking spaces are available and require advanced reservations, the hotel is close to public bus stops and a 10-minute walk to both the Woodley Park and Columbia Heights Metro stations. Best of all, it's a 15-minute stroll to the south/eastern entrance to the National Zoo.

Courtyard Washington, D.C./Dupont Circle

1900 Connecticut Ave. NW, Washington, D.C.; 202-332-9300; **marriott.com**

Rate per night $180–$250. **Pool** Yes. **Fridge in room** Yes. **Pet-friendly** No. **Maximum occupants per room** 4. **Nearby dining** Mintwood Place, Lia's, City Lights of China, Buca di Beppo.

NEAR NATIONAL ZOO IN UPSCALE NEIGHBORHOOD. Although this hotel isn't technically in either Adams Morgan or Columbia Heights, it is one of the closest to both neighborhoods and has much to offer the traveling family. About a 10-minute walk to Dupont Circle Metro station, this Courtyard is located in a busy neighborhood, with restaurants and shops nearby, and has an attractive outdoor pool. The walk on Columbia Road to the heart of Adams Morgan passes by lovely historic townhomes and Kalorama Park. Once you're in the ethnically diverse and energetic neighborhoods, you may happen upon a farmers market or street vendors. Guest rooms and bathrooms are small but modern and attractive; they have double (not queen) beds and a coffeemaker and mini-fridge. Some rooms feature views of the Washington Monument and the colorful buildings around the hotel. The hotel has a fitness center and complimentary Wi-Fi, but it does not allow rollaway beds. The Bistro serves breakfast and dinner only, but in nice weather, the hotel patio has umbrella tables—perfect for eating takeout. The National Zoo is 1 mile from the hotel.

Upper Northwest: Woodley Park, Cleveland Park, and Tenleytown

Omni Shoreham Washington, D.C.

2500 Calvert St. NW, Washington, D.C.; 202-234-0700; **omnihotels.com**

Rate per night $150–$375. **Pool** Yes. **Fridge in room** No. **Pet-friendly** No. **Maximum occupants per room** 4. **Nearby dining** Open City Diner, Chipotle, Lebanese Taverna, Hot n Juicy Crawfish, New Heights, Starbucks.

HISTORIC HOTEL WITH BEAUTIFUL POOL, NEAR NATIONAL ZOO. The Omni is a Grande Dame; it sits regally above bucolic Rock Creek Park and spreads its literal wings a full block on Calvert Street. The lobby is elegant and enormous, with lots of space to relax and people-watch after a busy day of sightseeing. The rooms have a classic look; suites have luxurious living areas, and many rooms have balconies, with views of the hotel gardens. If you're traveling with kids, ask about special treats, such as milk and cookies delivered to your room on the first night. The garden area has a resort-style pool that makes children screech with excitement. Parents can sit at the outdoor bar and watch them splash around. There's also a fire pit, well-equipped gym, and coffee and gift shop in the lobby area, so you don't need to go far to jump-start your morning. However, there are some things to consider: prices for breakfast items are sky high, the elevators are cramped, and the bathrooms are unimpressive. Also, this hotel hosts a lot of convention crowds and gets very busy. On the up side, Woodley Park Metro is across the street, the National Zoo is a 10-minute walk downhill, and several restaurants and a CVS are within a block of the hotel. You can easily explore Adams Morgan from this location, and although it's not possible to walk to the National Mall from here, it's only three subway stops away.

MARYLAND SUBURBS

National Harbor

Residence Inn National Harbor

192 Waterfront St., National Harbor; 301-749-4755; **marriott.com**

Rate per night $180–270. **Pool** No. **Fridge in room** Yes. **Pet-friendly** Yes. **Maximum occupants per room** 6. **Nearby dining** Rosa Mexicana, Grace's Mandarin, Cadillac Ranch, Public House Restaurant.

HOME AWAY FROM HOME AT ENTERTAINING NATIONAL HARBOR. National Harbor is a sprawling complex of hotels, shops, restaurants, a marina, and other recreational activities. Although it's about 20 minutes from downtown Washington, staying here has its perks. This hotel has views of the riverfront and is adjacent to the lavish Gaylord Resort Hotel, a sandy beachfront, a carousel, boat rentals, and the Capital Wheel, a huge Ferris wheel offering a birds-eye view of the region. The large suites have a bedroom and separate living area, which allows guests to relax and spread out. The hotel provides a free breakfast and has a small fitness center. There are multiple options to get into Washington from here. Besides driving, National Harbor has a courtesy shuttle to the King Street Metro station in Alexandria (across the river). It runs every hour from 6:30 a.m. to 8:30 p.m. Another option, more fun but less convenient, is taking the water taxi from National Harbor to the Alexandria City Marina; the water taxi runs approximately 11 a.m.–11 p.m. during the summer.

Friendship Heights/Chevy Chase

Embassy Suites by Hilton Chevy Chase

4300 Military Rd. NW, Washington, D.C.; 202-362-9300; **embassysuites3.hilton.com**

Rate per night $200–$350. **Pool** Yes. **Fridge in room** Yes. **Pet-friendly** Yes. **Maximum occupants per room** 6. **Nearby dining** Indique Heights, Maggiano's, Cheesecake Factory, Chadwick's, P.F. Chang's, Range.

GREAT SHOPPING DESTINATION, WITH A METRO STOP IN THE BUILDING. Although Friendship Heights is not near any monuments, this location has a lot to love. This prime real estate boasts Washington's most upscale department stores and exclusive boutique shopping. The hotel is located in the Chevy Chase Pavilion mall, with the Friendship Heights Metro directly below the building. Many restaurants surround the hotel, too, although a hot buffet breakfast and an evening happy hour are included in your rate. The atrium in the hotel center opens up to mall shops and restaurants below. All guest rooms have full kitchens and separate living areas. Whole Foods grocery store is within walking distance. An indoor pool, bright bar area, and large fitness center all add value to this hotel stay. Sign up with Hilton to request complimentary Wi-Fi and (sometimes) free parking.

Bethesda

Bethesda Court Hotel

7740 Wisconsin Ave., Bethesda; 301-685-5493; **bethesdacourtwashdc.com**

Rate per night $100–$120. **Pool** No. **Fridge in room** Yes. **Pet-friendly** No. **Maximum occupants per room** 4. **Nearby dining** Woodmont Grill, Black's Bar and Kitchen, Tastee Diner, Original Pancake House, Kabob Bazaar.

BEST-KEPT SECRET IN BETHESDA. This little motor lodge has spruced itself up and increased amenities and services so much that it competes against Hyatt, Hilton, and Marriott very successfully. Just a block from the Bethesda Metro, the motel offers free breakfast, water bottles, and Wi-Fi. It also has an exercise room and laundry services, and it puts you in a convenient and safe neighborhood filled with restaurants and shops. Because it's so small (74 rooms), the staff makes an effort to meet and provide personal service to all their guests. For example, the hotel shuttle will take guests up to 2 miles away, including a local pool in the summer. They have a small courtyard garden, where you can relax after a busy day of touring. Walk or take the free Bethesda Trolley to movie theaters, boutiques, performance venues, diners, and first-class restaurants. Ask for an upper floor. Bethesda Court is a nice option for people who like taking the Metro and want the benefits of a city without the high cost.

Rockville
Cambria Hotel and Suites Rockville

1 Helen Heneghan Way, Rockville; 301-294-2200; **cambriasuitesrockville.com**

Rate per night $90–$130. **Pool** Yes. **Fridge in room** Yes. **Pet-friendly** Yes. **Maximum occupants per room** 4. **Nearby dining** Five Guys Burgers, La Canela, Sushi Damo, Peter Chang, World of Beer, Bar Louie.

SUBURBAN TOWN CENTER WITH CHARM AND METRO ACCESS. This brand-new hotel is located in Rockville Town Center, anchored by the huge modern library and art gallery. Around the town center are dozens of shops, restaurants, a movie theater, an Amtrak stop, and a Metro stop. You can take the Red Line subway from Rockville into Washington in about 45 minutes, then return to this very comfortable hotel room with queen-size beds, a microwave, a sofa sleeper, and room to spread out comfortably. The indoor pool is a big hit with kids, and in winter, the hotel is near an outdoor ice-skating rink. There's also a barista coffee bar and well-equipped gym. Visitors may safely walk around at night to pick up groceries or go out for dinner. Guests complain about the parking fee ($15 per day) despite the location being outside of the city. Unfortunately, you'll be charged to park just about everywhere in the Washington area.

VIRGINIA SUBURBS
Old Town Alexandria
Residence Inn Alexandria Old Town/Duke Street

1456 Duke St., Alexandria; 703-548-5474; **marriott.com**

Rate per night $120–$190. **Pool** Yes. **Fridge in room** Yes. **Pet-friendly** Yes. **Maximum occupants per room** 6. **Nearby dining** Whole Foods, Brabo, Laporta's, Hard Times Cafe, Table Talk Restaurant.

OLD TOWN CHARM AND CONVENIENT TO METRO. Save a little money and still find yourself in one of Washington's most delightful neighborhoods, Old Town Alexandria. Founded around the time of the American Revolution, Old Town boasts dozens of historic landmarks and charming cobblestone streets that will make any history buff swoon. Families love that they can walk or take the Old Town Trolley from this hotel to visit shops, restaurants, and the waterfront parks, and it's also easy to get to D.C.'s best tourist sites, by taking the King Street Metro (Yellow Line) three blocks away. The Residence Inn's suite-style rooms have kitchenettes, a separate living area, sleeper sofas, and come with free hot breakfast There's also a small pool, fitness center, and free Wi-Fi. On weekday evenings, the hotel hosts a happy hour with complimentary food and beverages. This location is also convenient to visit Arlington Cemetery, Mount Vernon, and the 9/11 Memorial at the Pentagon. The upper floors have pretty views, but because the rooms are currently undergoing refreshing, ask for a room away from the construction.

Tysons Corner and McLean

Hilton McLean Tysons Corner

7920 Jones Branch Dr., McLean; 703-847-5000; **hilton.com**

Rate per night $90–$200. **Pool** Yes. **Fridge in room** No. **Pet-friendly** No. **Maximum occupants per room** 4. **Nearby dining** California Pizza Kitchen, Coastal Flats, Nostos, Founding Farmers, Maggiano's, Shamshiry.

CONVENIENT TO AMERICAN GIRL STORE AND LEGENDARY SHOP-PING MALLS. This Hilton happens to be near Hilton International, the corporate offices of the hotel company, and as a result has state-of-the-art gizmos sprinkled throughout. The lobby is especially impressive, with its soaring light installations, illuminated tables, enormous wall monitors, birch wood accents, and multiple fireplaces. Directly off the lobby is Harth, both an 18-hour bar serving wood-fired flatbreads and a farm-to-table restaurant with an outdoor patio and fire pit. Other cool features they've pioneered are beehives on the rooftop and an organic garden; this "farm to table" literally operates in the building. Accommodations are comfortable, even luxurious; ask for a corner room. Although the hotel has a fitness center and indoor pool, they also offer yoga supplies and in-room yoga content on the TV. They even have a "cardio room," or a guest room equipped with a motion trainer (like an elliptical machine), weights, and resistance bands. The bathrooms are pretty luxe, too, with large marble showers. As the hotel is surrounded by an office park, you'll need to use the shuttle to get to Tysons Corner Metro and the Tysons Malls.

Hyatt Regency Tysons Corner Center

7901 Tysons One Place, Tysons; 703-893-1234;
tysonscornercenter.regency.hyatt.com

Rate per night $180–$300. **Pool** Yes. **Fridge in room** No. **Pet-friendly** Yes, small dogs. **Maximum occupants per room** 4. **Nearby dining** Shake Shack, Coastal Flats, Capital Grille, Silver Diner, Brix and Ale, Nostos, American Girl Bistro.

NEAR METRO STOP, SHOPPING, AND FREE PARKING. This is the newest hotel in suburban Virginia, and it is literally connected to Tysons Corner (a mega mall) by an open-air plaza with restaurants, a playground, outdoor games such as Ping-Pong and chess, and outdoor seating around fire pits. The rooms boast floor-to-ceiling windows, as well as separate seating areas, night-light foot sensors (these are awesome!), spa showers, and luxurious linens. Every room has a coffeemaker, but staying on the club floor entitles guests to a continental breakfast, snacks, appetizers, and dessert daily. You don't need to go far to find restaurants, however—there are dozens inside Tysons Corner Mall, plus a huge movie theater. The hotel provides free Wi-Fi, as well as premium service for faster streaming. There's an attractive indoor pool, and the "Stay-Fit" gym is open 24 hours. Barrel & Bushel, the hotel's restaurant, features sit-down meals, room service, and takeout. In partnership with the Tysons' American Girl Store, Hyatt has a package that includes a doll bed souvenir and free breakfast for kids under 10 years old. There's a walkway to the new Tysons Metro station for a 30-minute ride into Washington.

Arlington and Rosslyn

Holiday Inn Rosslyn Key Bridge

1900 North Fort Meyer Dr., Arlington; 703-807-2000; **ihg.com**

Rate per night $150–$250. **Pool** Yes. **Fridge in room** No. **Pet-friendly** No. **Maximum occupants per room** 5. **Nearby dining** Panera Bread, Ruby Tuesday, Heavy Seas Alehouse, Tom Yum District, Pie Sisters.

SPECTACULAR VIEWS, ACROSS THE RIVER FROM GEORGETOWN. Staying in Arlington is a good bet for those who want to save money. Just about every hotel on the Virginia side of the Potomac River will cost you 20% less than comparable hotels in Washington. Holiday Inn Rosslyn Key Bridge happens to sit directly across the Francis Scott Key Bridge from Georgetown. Take the pedestrian walkway, and voila, you're there. The hotel rooms facing the river have panoramic views of Georgetown, the Kennedy Center, and Washington Harbour. You can also hop onto the adjacent George Washington Parkway to drive or bike down to Arlington National Cemetery, Old Town Alexandria, and farther south to Mount Vernon. The Rosslyn Metro station is one block from this hotel, so you can make your way to the heart of D.C. in no time. Guest rooms are average but comfortable. The biggest draws are the free parking (probably because of the tight garage), convenience to D.C., and friendly service. The hotel has a restaurant on the 17th floor that serves a lackluster buffet breakfast, but there are several good restaurants nearby.

Renaissance Arlington Capital View Hotel

2800 South Potomac Ave., Arlington; 703-413-1300; **marriott.com**

Rate per night $103–$200. **Pool** Yes. **Fridge in room** No. **Pet-friendly** No. **Maximum occupants per room** 4. **Nearby dining** Cinnabar, O'Malley's Pub, Kohinoor Dhaba.

Residence Inn Arlington Capital View

2850 South Potomac Ave., Arlington; 703-415-1300; **marriott.com**

Rate per night $250–$500. **Pool** Yes. **Fridge in room** Yes. **Pet-friendly** Yes (ask about sanitation fee). **Maximum occupants per room** 6. **Nearby dining** Crystal City has Jaleo, Farrah Olivia, Buffalo Wild Wings, Good Stuff Eatery, Cosi, Ruth's Chris, Perfect Pita.

TWO HOTELS IN ONE. This modern, chic hotel is a combination of Renaissance's upscale style and Residence Inn's utilitarian suites. Located in the same building, they share amenities, such as a swimming pool, fitness center, and a shuttle to Reagan National airport (and Metro station). Less than 5 miles from both Old Town and downtown D.C., this location offers flexibility and costs less than most hotels in Washington. Despite the close proximity to Reagan National airport, guests say it's well insulated from the airplane traffic. The hotel offers regular shuttle service to nearby restaurants and the Crystal City metro. Guests can easily walk to food trucks, a supermarket, and Pentagon City shopping mall. The Residence Inn offers complimentary breakfast, but not for those staying on the Renaissance side.

GETTING *a* GOOD DEAL *on a* ROOM

HOTEL PRICING IN WASHINGTON IS DRIVEN not only by tourism but also by business, government, and convention trade, which translates to high rack rates (a hotel's published room rate). Even in the suburbs, where you might expect lower rates to be the trade-off for commuting into town, there are few bargains because, no matter how far you are from the Capitol, you are apt to be close to some agency, airport, university, or research complex. The Bethesda Marriott near Grosvenor/Strathmore, for example, is 30–40 minutes away from the Mall but stays full because it's close to the National Institutes of Health.

*un**official* **TIP**
Always use your friendliest voice when asking for favors, and don't call between 10 a.m. and 3 p.m., typical check-out and check-in times; the staff may be too busy to coddle you.

One key factor in getting a better deal is having flexibility on your travel dates. If you're traveling during your kids' school vacation schedule, that, of course, limits your flexibility. But while you're on the phone to the hotel, ask what days may have lower rates.

Another trick that may help you secure a better deal is to check the Internet to see what aggregate sites such as **Trivago.com, Kayak.com,** and **TripAdvisor.com** offer (more about that in the next section). Then, even if you are considering a chain hotel rather than an independent establishment, call the specific Washington location, not the toll-free number, which is likely to be located in some other city. While the central operator may not even be aware of local specials, the in-town reservations desk may be able to offer a few incentives, such as free breakfast or Wi-Fi. He or she will have computer access to your account if you are a member of the chain's rewards club and is likely to want to make you welcome. Ask about specials or added benefits.

*un**official* **TIP**
In addition to the quoted room rates, the District of Columbia imposes a 14.5% hotel tax (including sales tax); hotels in the suburbs, once town and state taxes are figured in, can be almost as high, so add that into your budget.

If you are staying for several days, ask whether you might stay for any additional nights at a reduced rate or even free. Find out whether the clientele is mostly business travelers or families with children (whichever suits you better). And if you're talking to the on-site staff, you can get more specific information about quiet rooms, good views, access to a swimming pool, and the nearest Metro stop.

Find out how old the hotel is, how recently the rooms—and the bathrooms—have been renovated, and whether photos on the hotel's website are up-to-date. Be sure to ask if there is any ongoing construction, either inside the hotel itself or nearby. Just because the work isn't being done on your floor, it may start before you want to get up in the morning, and if you're sensitive to dust or paint smells, which tend to work their way around through the elevators and ductwork, you may have trouble.

If you are driving to Washington, find out if, and for how much, the hotel provides parking; valet and overnight fees can be substantial. Ask about alternative parking garages near the hotel to see if the garage offers discounts to hotel guests.

If your visit to Washington coincides with a major convention or trade show, hotel rooms are likely to be scarcer and more expensive than if you can avoid the big-business traffic. If you have flexibility with travel dates, you might avoid the conventions and trade shows; check the calendar at **dcconvention.com.**

Look into weekend rates and corporate rates. Many hotels that cater to business travelers, who tend to come in during the week and go home on Friday, offer weekend discounts that may be 15–40% lower. Others offer corporate rates of 5–20% off-rack, and you may not have to work for a large company to qualify: just ask. Some hotels will guarantee you the discounted rate when you make your reservation; others may make the rate conditional on your providing a fax on your company's letterhead requesting the rate, or a company credit card or business card on check-in. Membership in AARP or AAA may qualify you for discounts as well.

THE INTERNET ADVANTAGE

ALTHOUGH THE PERSONAL TOUCH IS THE BEST IDEA once you get to the point of making your reservation, it's worth understanding how the Internet affects hotel rates.

Months in advance, hotels establish rates for each day of the coming year, taking into consideration weekend versus weekday demand; holidays, major conventions, trade shows, and sporting events; and the effect of weather on occupancy. If demand is greater than forecast, the rate may rise; if demand is less than expected, the hotel will begin "nudging," incrementally decreasing the rate for the days in question until bookings rebound to the desired level. This sort of rate manipulation isn't new, but, at Internet speed, a hotel can adjust website rates almost hourly. Consequently, major Internet travel sellers, such as Travelocity, Hotels.com, and Expedia, among others, can advertise special deals and rates almost instantaneously. Lower rates and deals are also communicated by e-mail to preferred travel agents, and sometimes directly to consumers via e-mail, print advertisements, or direct-mail promotions.

The easiest way to scout room deals is on **kayak.com,** which scans not only Internet sellers but also national hotel chain websites and some individual hotel websites. You can organize your search by price, location, star rating, brand, and amenities; plus, you can see detailed descriptions of each property, photos, customer reviews, and maps. Kayak provides a direct link to the lowest-price sellers. Other websites to scour include **groupon.com, costco.com, oyster.com,** and **jetsetter.com.**

Also consider **priceline.com,** where you can bid for a room—not at a specific hotel, but within a neighborhood and quality level. If your bid is accepted, you will be assigned to a hotel and your credit card charged (transactions are nonrefundable). Notification of acceptance usually takes less than an hour. Here again, it would be worthwhile to check the convention schedule; a busy time means you can't lowball your offer. Reduce your bid for off-season periods.

Reservation services are live versions of Kayak or Priceline, so to speak, wholesalers and consolidators who deal directly with the public. When you call, you can ask for a rate quote for a particular hotel, or ask for the best available deal in the area where you prefer to stay. You can give them a maximum budget too; chances are, the service will find you something, even if it means shaving a dollar or two off its profit.

If you are coming into town for a convention or trade show, and the sponsoring agency has negotiated a special rate with area hotels for a "block" of rooms, you can use some of these same techniques to figure out whether it really is a good deal. (After all, a lot of travelers simply take for granted the block rate is a bargain, but you are part of a captive audience.) Check the rate offered on the Internet sites; if you think you can do better, book it on the Internet, call one of the (preferably local) reservation services, or try your luck with the hotel directly. Or avoid the crowd altogether; look through our guide for something that suits you better. The earlier you book, the broader your options. Just remember, stay near the Metro.

RESERVATION SERVICES		
Capitol Reservations	☎ 800-847-4832;	hotelsdc.com
Hotels Discounts	☎ 866-675-3584;	hotelsdiscounts.com
Hotels.com	☎ 800-246-8357;	hotels.com
Quikbook	☎ 800-789-9887;	quikbook.com
Washington, D.C., Accommodations	☎ 800-554-2220;	wdcahotels.com

TRAVEL AGENTS AND/OR VACATION PACKAGES

FIRST, FIND OUT WHETHER YOUR TRAVEL AGENT has actually been to Washington because an agent who doesn't know the territory may turn to a tour operator or wholesaler and then pass that package along to you. That allows the travel agent to set up your whole trip with a single phone call and still collect an 8–10% commission, but it may not be the best bargain for you.

Here's why: Package vacations seem like win-win deals for buyers and sellers. The buyer makes one phone call to set up the whole trip: transportation, lodging, meals, tours, attraction tickets, perhaps even golf or spa services. Similarly, by settling everything in a single conversation, the seller avoids multiple sales calls, confirmations, and billing. In addition, some packagers benefit by buying airfares and hotel rooms in bulk at significant savings, bargains theoretically passed along to the buyer.

In practice, however, the seller may be the only one who benefits. Wholesalers typically work with specific airlines or chains rather than looking for deals. Many packages are padded with extras that cost the bundler next to nothing but grossly inflate the retail price, like a "loaded" new automobile. Many of the extras in the package sound enticing but won't get used (most people overestimate how much can be crammed into a single day) or may not be as advertised (we've all had a "hot" hotel breakfast that wasn't).

So you should present your agent with some information up front. Choose a neighborhood, and maybe a second choice, you prefer; if possible, specify a hotel. (Check our ratings in the table on pages 81–87 and our Hotel Information Chart on pages 93–104, use the Internet sites at left, and also see the local website listings in the "Gathering Information" section of Part One.) If you see a good package advertised online or in a travel publication, follow up by calling the hotels or package operator for more information—but don't make the reservation yourself. Even if it seems that you're doing all the work yourself, you should still let the agent do the actual booking. He or she might still get a commission (free to you) and is more likely to know whether the deal is too good to be true. And you should always give your agent a chance to match or better the package once you have a baseline to go by. One word of caution, however: If you make a reservation through anything other than the hotel itself, you must then make any changes or complaints to that service. The hotel will no longer consider you their customer; rather, they expect your proxy to speak and act on your behalf. This can be frustrating if you can't reach the wholesaler or website.

If you are considering booking a package yourself, choose one that includes at least some features you are sure to use; you'll pay for them all, anyway. Spend an hour surfing and estimate what the major components of your trip—airfare, lodging, transportation, museum tickets—would actually cost. If the package costs less, or is even close, go for the convenience factor and book the package. Remember local factors: If offered a choice of rental car or transportation to and from the airport, for example, free transportation would be more useful in Washington than a car. And if at all possible, be flexible about travel time; some specials *do* live up to the hype, but you may have to move fast.

Don't forget that if you have a premium credit card, you probably have a "concierge" too. These are basically unpaid travel agents (at least, not paid by you), and because the cards tend to be accepted almost everywhere these days, these agents can often scout a variety of hotels and packages, find out whether your rewards or points can be transferred to a hotel or airline, and more. They also keep track of short-term fare deals, which can save you a bundle. Again, just try to have an idea of what going rates are.

ACCOMMODATIONS:
Rated and Ranked

WHAT TO LOOK FOR IN A ROOM

EXCEPT FOR THE IMMEDIATELY VISIBLE ISSUES—cleanliness, upkeep, decor—most travelers don't really know what goes into a comfortable hotel room. There is, of course, a discernible standard of quality and luxury that differentiates Motel 6 from Marriott and a Residence Inn from a Ritz; but few hotel guests recognize that comfort is also a matter of engineering and design.

The Unofficial Guide family spends a lot of time in hotels, and we've made quite a study of the factors that make a room a haven. So when our researchers inspect a hotel room, here are a few of the elements they weigh.

SIZE While smaller rooms may be cozy and well designed, a large and comfortably furnished room is preferable for a stay of more than about three days. Air quality matters, too, by which we mean not only central air and heat (with a controllable thermostat in the room) but also freedom from smoke, mold, and odor.

SAFETY AND SECURITY Most hotels these days have already shifted to coded or magnetic-strip entry cards instead of traditional locks that are vulnerable to criminals with skeleton keys or picks; but we prefer doors with dead bolts, peepholes, and chain latches as well. If windows and balcony doors are not sealed, they should have locks and railings. Bathtubs should have nonskid strips; electrical outlets in bathrooms should be away from water sources. Rooms should be equipped with sprinkler systems and blinking fire alerts for hearing-impaired guests. (Note that most safety equipment is standard in better hotels and motels, as newer construction has been subject to regulation for years now, but older structures and, in some states, inns and B&Bs with a minimum number of rooms may be exempt.)

NOISE AND DARKNESS CONTROL Noise can be an issue. Newer hotels are designed so that plumbing (and televisions) are at a distance from the bed, but a lot of rooms still have thin walls and doors that don't close tight, so that bills and even newspapers can be slipped under the door. (That's when a little hallway from the door comes in handy.) If you're a light sleeper, ask the front desk clerk when you check in to keep you away from the elevator—*and* the service elevator—and away from a busy street by asking for a higher floor, if possible. Avoid a room that's directly over a banquet room because events, such as weddings, often last into the night and may keep you awake.

It's essential to have a dark, quiet room where you can sleep without the morning sun or night-light neon interfering. Curtains should be thick and lined, closing completely in the center and extending outside the window frames; inner sheers for daytime are a bonus.

LIGHTING Inadequate lighting is a common problem in American hotel rooms, especially over work areas and beds; table lamps on bedside tables are usually not sufficient for reading. Overhead or general lights should have switches near the door and ideally duplicate switches near the bed or in the bedside console—a set-up common in other parts of the world but only recently working its way into the United States. Some hotels have movement lighting on the floor to prevent nighttime falls.

BATHROOM Shower and bath amenities are increasingly brand name, but there are fewer items in the baskets these days; if you need a razor or shower cap, you may have to call housekeeping. Beware glass shelves, which are generally unsteady, and sometimes dangerous, as well as small; it's better to have one sink and good counter space than two sinks with a little trim. The nap and size of towels is one of those things that just may depend on the price of the room. Some hotels no longer have bathtubs, so if that's important to you, say to bathe your kids, inquire about that in advance.

BEDDING The average quality of beds in hotels is improving, if only because of competition and advertising (eight kinds of pillows, hypoallergenic bedding, and so on). Many beds feel more luxurious than your own. If you're worried about bedbugs, ask whether, and when, the room has been treated. Also, check **Oyster.com** and the public database of user-submitted bedbug reports—**BedBugRegistry.com**—to find out if there are reports of infestations at the hotel you're considering. Remember, these reports are not vetted, but if you're worried, check under the bedding for tiny bloodstains, and store your suitcase in the bathroom.

EXTRAS Small refrigerators are increasingly common, but be aware that newer-generation minibars automatically charge you for a drink even if you just move the can to put in your leftovers. And a room without a coffeemaker is definitely like a day without sunshine.

Finally, check out the cost of the Internet connections (many hotels are providing free Wi-Fi now) and, if you have kids, the gaming system. What's the single most important guideline? Find out what amenities the hotel promises (like an operational swimming pool), and make sure you get what you pay for.

THE HIT PARADE

WE HAVE ASSEMBLED A LIST OF WHAT WE CONSIDER the best hotels in town, using two different criteria. To indicate relative quality—tastefulness, upkeep, cleanliness, and size—we have graded hotels by stars (see the table on the next page). Star ratings apply to *room quality only* and reflect the property's standard accommodations. For most hotels and motels, "standard accommodation" is a room with either one king bed or two queen beds; in an all-suite property, the standard may be a one- or two-room suite. Though many hotels offer luxury rooms and special suites in addition to their standard accommodations, these are not rated in this guide. Star ratings are for rooms only, without regard to a property's facilities or amenities.

Within the broad categories of the star rankings, we also use a numerical rating system of 0–100 to differentiate properties in the same star category. Rooms at the Mandarin Oriental, River Inn, and Hotel Palomar, for instance, are all rated as ★★★★ (four stars); but in the supplemental numerical ratings, the Mandarin Oriental and River Inn are rated 88 and 87, respectively, while the Hotel Palomar is rated 84. This means that within the four-star category, the Mandarin and the River Inn are comparable, and that both have slightly nicer rooms than the Hotel Palomar.

The cost estimates are based on the hotel's published rack rates for standard rooms. Each "$" represents about $50. This list does not factor in location, services, recreation, or amenities. In some instances, a suite is the same price or less than a regular hotel room.

Also remember, please, these ratings are based on samplings, not comprehensive room tours. Even with the best of intentions, we cannot inspect every room in every hotel, especially as we conduct our inspections anonymously and without the knowledge of the management. We check out several rooms selected at random and base our ratings and rankings on those rooms. Occasionally (we hope very rarely), the rooms we inspect are not representative of the entire hotel, and you might be assigned a room that is inferior or scheduled for renovation.

The key to avoiding disappointment is to snoop around in advance. Check out the hotel website before you book, remembering the photos might be of the best rooms, not all rooms. When you or your travel agent call, ask when the rooms were last renovated. If you arrive and are assigned a room that does not live up to expectations, request to be moved. (But be polite; it works better.)

★★★★★	Superior Rooms Tasteful and luxurious by any standard
★★★★	Extremely Nice Rooms What you would expect at a Hyatt Regency or Marriott
★★★	Nice Rooms Holiday Inn or comparable quality
★★	Adequate Rooms Clean, comfortable, and functional without frills (like a Motel 6)
★	Super-Budget

How the Hotels Compare in Washington, D.C.

HOTEL	STAR RATING	ROOM RATING	COST ($=$50)	LOCATION
Jefferson Hotel	★★★★½	92	$x8	Downtown
Hay-Adams Hotel	★★★★½	91	$x7+	Downtown
Park Hyatt	★★★★½	91	$x7+	Georgetown
St. Regis	★★★★½	91	$x9+	Downtown
Four Seasons Hotel	★★★★½	90	$x11+	Georgetown
Ritz-Carlton Georgetown	★★★★½	90	$x11+	Georgetown
Mandarin Oriental	★★★★	88	$x8+	National Mall
Sofitel Lafayette	★★★★	88	$X7-	Downtown
Willard InterContinental	★★★★	88	$X7-	Downtown
Avenue Suites Georgetown	★★★★	87	$$$$$+	Georgetown
Capella Washington, D.C., Georgetown	★★★★	87	$x11+	Georgetown
Madison Hotel	★★★★	87	$x6+	Downtown
River Inn	★★★★	87	$$$$$+	Foggy Bottom
Hotel Rouge	★★★★	86	$$$$-	Dupont Circle/ Adams-Morgan
Ritz-Carlton Washington, D.C.	★★★★	86	$x10-	Dupont Circle/ Adams-Morgan
Residence Inn Dupont Circle	★★★★	86	$$$$-	Dupont Circle/ Adams-Morgan
Westin Washington, D.C. City Center	★★★★	86	$x8-	Downtown
Cambria Suites Washington, D.C. /Convention Center	★★★★	85	$$$$$	Downtown
Capitol Hill Hotel	★★★★	85	$x6-	Capitol Hill
Fairmont Washington, D.C.	★★★★	85	$x6-	Georgetown
The Graham Georgetown	★★★★	85	$$$$$+	Georgetown
Hotel Madera	★★★★	85	$$$$-	Dupont Circle/ Adams-Morgan
Hyatt Place DC/Downtown /K Street	★★★★	85	$$$$+	Downtown

Continued on page 85

Washington, D.C., Accommodations

See "Dupont Circle Accommodations" Map

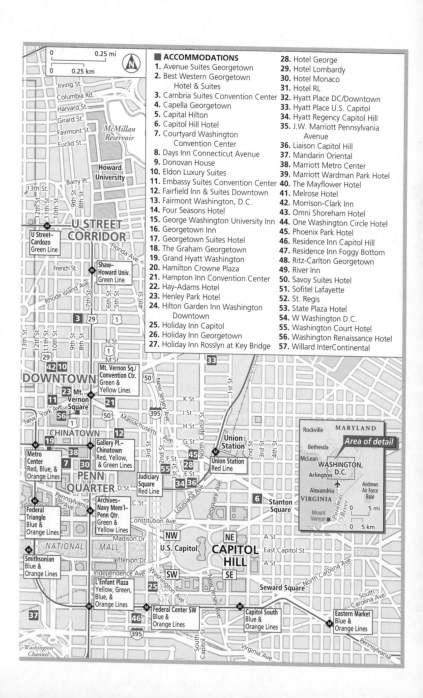

■ **ACCOMMODATIONS**

1. Avenue Suites Georgetown
2. Best Western Georgetown Hotel & Suites
3. Cambria Suites Convention Center
4. Capella Georgetown
5. Capital Hilton
6. Capitol Hill Hotel
7. Courtyard Washington Convention Center
8. Days Inn Connecticut Avenue
9. Donovan House
10. Eldon Luxury Suites
11. Embassy Suites Convention Center
12. Fairfield Inn & Suites Downtown
13. Fairmont Washington, D.C.
14. Four Seasons Hotel
15. George Washington University Inn
16. Georgetown Inn
17. Georgetown Suites Hotel
18. The Graham Georgetown
19. Grand Hyatt Washington
20. Hamilton Crowne Plaza
21. Hampton Inn Convention Center
22. Hay-Adams Hotel
23. Henley Park Hotel
24. Hilton Garden Inn Washington Downtown
25. Holiday Inn Capitol
26. Holiday Inn Georgetown
27. Holiday Inn Rosslyn at Key Bridge
28. Hotel George
29. Hotel Lombardy
30. Hotel Monaco
31. Hotel RL
32. Hyatt Place DC/Downtown
33. Hyatt Place U.S. Capitol
34. Hyatt Regency Capitol Hill
35. J.W. Marriott Pennsylvania Avenue
36. Liaison Capitol Hill
37. Mandarin Oriental
38. Marriott Metro Center
39. Marriott Wardman Park Hotel
40. The Mayflower Hotel
41. Melrose Hotel
42. Morrison-Clark Inn
43. Omni Shoreham Hotel
44. One Washington Circle Hotel
45. Phoenix Park Hotel
46. Residence Inn Capitol Hill
47. Residence Inn Foggy Bottom
48. Ritz-Carlton Georgetown
49. River Inn
50. Savoy Suites Hotel
51. Sofitel Lafayette
52. St. Regis
53. State Plaza Hotel
54. W Washington D.C.
55. Washington Court Hotel
56. Washington Renaissance Hotel
57. Willard InterContinental

Dupont Circle Accommodations

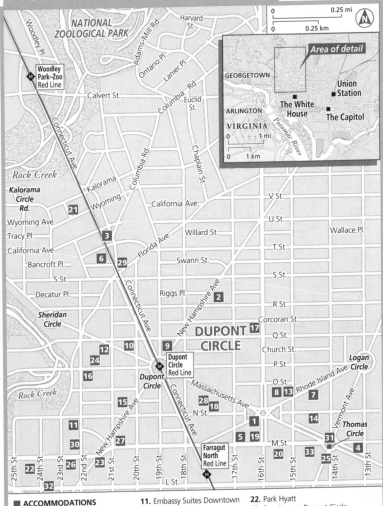

■ ACCOMMODATIONS

1. Beacon Hotel
2. The Carlyle
3. Churchill Hotel
4. Comfort Inn Downtown DC/Convention
5. Courtyard Embassy Row
6. Courtyard Washington Northwest
7. The District Hotel
8. Doubletree Washington, D.C.
9. Dupont Circle Hotel
10. Embassy Row Hotel
11. Embassy Suites Downtown
12. Fairfax Embassy Row
13. Holiday Inn Central
14. Homewood Suites Washington, D.C.
15. Hotel Madera
16. Hotel Palomar Washington
17. Hotel Rouge
18. Hotel Topaz
19. Jefferson Hotel
20. Madison Hotel
21. The Normandy Hotel
22. Park Hyatt
23. Renaissance Dupont Circle
24. Residence Inn Dupont Circle
25. Residence Inn Washington, D.C.
26. Ritz-Carlton Washington, D.C.
27. St. Gregory Luxury Hotel & Suites
28. Tabard Inn
29. Washington Hilton
30. Washington Marriott Hotel
31. Washington Plaza Hotel
32. Westin Georgetown
33. Westin Washington, D.C.

Continued from page 81

How the Hotels Compare in Washington, D.C.

HOTEL	STAR RATING	ROOM RATING	COST ($=$50)	LOCATION
Residence Inn Capitol Hill	★★★★	85	$$$$–	Capitol Hill
Residence Inn National Harbor	★★★★	85	$x7–	Maryland Suburbs
St. Gregory Luxury Hotel & Suites	★★★★	85	$$$–	Dupont Circle/Adams-Morgan
Embassy Suites Convention Center	★★★★	84	$x8–	Downtown
Georgetown Inn	★★★★	84	$x7–	Georgetown
Hamilton Crowne Plaza	★★★★	84	$x6	Downtown
Hotel Monaco	★★★★	84	$x7+	Downtown
Hotel Palomar Washington	★★★★	84	$x6+	Dupont Circle/Adams-Morgan
Melrose Hotel	★★★★	84	$$$$$–	Georgetown
One Washington Circle Hotel	★★★★	84	$$$$–	Foggy Bottom
Tabard Inn	★★★★	84	$$$$$+	Dupont Circle
Westin Georgetown	★★★★	84	$x6–	Georgetown
Capital Hilton	★★★★	83	$x8+	Downtown
Churchill Hotel	★★★★	83	$$$$$–	Dupont Circle/Adams-Morgan
Courtyard Washington Convention Center	★★★★	83	$x10–	Downtown
Doubletree Washington, D.C.	★★★★	83	$x6	Upper Northwest
The Dupont Circle Hotel	★★★★	83	$x7+	Dupont Circle/Adams-Morgan
Eldon Luxury Suites	★★★★	83	$$$$+	Downtown
The Embassy Row Hotel	★★★★	83	$x6+	Dupont Circle/Adams-Morgan
The George Washington University Inn	★★★★	83	$$$$–	Foggy Bottom
Georgetown Suites Hotel	★★★★	83	$$$$–	Georgetown
Grand Hyatt Washington	★★★★	83	$x6+	Downtown
Hotel George	★★★★	83	$x6+	Downtown
Hotel Lombardy	★★★★	83	$$$$–	Foggy Bottom
Hotel Topaz	★★★★	83	$$$$+	Dupont Circle/Adams-Morgan
The Mayflower Hotel	★★★★	83	$$$$+	Downtown
The Normandy Hotel	★★★★	83	$$$$$–	Dupont Circle/Adams-Morgan
Omni Shoreham Hotel	★★★★	83	$$$$–	Upper Northwest
Renaissance Dupont Circle	★★★★	83	$$$$	Dupont Circle/Adams-Morgan
Residence Inn Washington DC /Foggy Bottom	★★★★	83	$$$$–	Foggy Bottom

How the Hotels Compare in Washington, D.C.

HOTEL	STAR RATING	ROOM RATING	COST ($=$50)	LOCATION
Residence Inn Washington, D.C.	★★★★	83	$$$$$	Downtown
Savoy Suites Hotel	★★★★	83	$$$$$+	Upper Northwest
W Washington D.C.	★★★★	83	$x7+	Downtown
Washington Court Hotel	★★★★	83	$$$$$-	Downtown
Washington Renaissance Hotel	★★★★	83	$x6	Downtown
AC Hotel Washington, DC at National Harbor	★★★½	82	$x6-	Maryland Suburbs
The Donovan	★★★½	82	$x7+	Downtown
The Fairfax at Embassy Row	★★★½	82	$x10	Dupont Circle/ Adams-Morgan
Gaylord National	★★★½	82	$x7+	Maryland Suburbs
Hampton Inn Washington, DC-Convention Center	★★★½	82	$x8+	Downtown
Homewood Suites Washington, DC	★★★½	82	$x8-	Dupont Circle/ Adams-Morgan
Hotel RL	★★★½	82	$$$$+	Downtown
Hyatt Place U.S.Capitol	★★★½	82	$$$$$+	Downtown
Hyatt Regency Capitol Hill	★★★½	82	$x6-	Downtown
J.W. Marriott Pennsylvania Avenue	★★★½	82	$$$$+	Downtown
Liaison Capitol Hill	★★★½	82	$x8-	Downtown
Morrison-Clark Inn	★★★½	82	$$$$-	Downtown
State Plaza Hotel	★★★½	82	$$$$-	Foggy Bottom
Washington Hilton	★★★½	82	$$$$$+	Dupont Circle/ Adams-Morgan
Westin Washington National Harbor	★★★½	82	$$$$$+	Maryland Suburbs
Courtyard Embassy Row	★★★½	81	$$$+	Dupont Circle/ Adams-Morgan
Courtyard Washington Capitol Hill /Navy Yard	★★★½	81	$$$$+	Capitol Hill
Courtyard Washington Northwest	★★★½	81	$$$$$	Dupont Circle/ Adams-Morgan
Marriott Wardman Park Hotel	★★★½	81	$$$$	Upper Northwest
Washington Marriott Georgetown	★★★½	81	$$$$$-	Dupont Circle/ Adams-Morgan
Washington Plaza Hotel	★★★½	81	$$$$+	Downtown
Beacon Hotel	★★★½	80	$x6-	Dupont Circle/ Adams-Morgan
Best Western Georgetown Hotel & Suites	★★★½	80	$$$$-	Dupont Circle/ Adams-Morgan
Fairfield Inn & Suites Washington, DC / Downtown	★★★½	80	$x8-	Downtown
Hampton Inn & Suites National Harbor	★★★½	80	$x8	Maryland Suburbs
Hilton Garden Inn Washington Downtown	★★★½	80	$x7-	Downtown

How the Hotels Compare in Washington, D.C.

HOTEL	STAR RATING	ROOM RATING	COST ($=$50)	LOCATION
Washington Marriott Metro Center	★★★½	80	$$$$$	Downtown
Embassy Suites Downtown	★★★½	79	$x7–	Dupont Circle/ Adams-Morgan
The Carlyle	★★★½	78	$$$$$+	Dupont Circle/ Adams-Morgan
Comfort Inn Downtown DC /Convention	★★★½	78	$x7–	Downtown
The Henley Park Hotel	★★★½	78	$$$$+	Downtown
Holiday Inn Capitol	★★★½	78	$$$$–	Capitol Hill
Phoenix Park Hotel	★★★½	78	$$$$	Capitol Hill
Holiday Inn Central/White House	★★★½	77	$$$$–	Upper Northwest
Days Inn Connecticut Ave	★★★½	75	$$$–	Upper Northwest
The District Hotel	★★½	60	$$+	Dupont Circle/ Adams-Morgan

THE BEST DEALS IN WASHINGTON

TAKING BOTH QUALITY AND PRICE of rooms into account, and using a mathematical formula to factor in the fractions, so to speak, we have also assembled a list of the best 30 values in Washington—that is, the biggest bang for your buck. As before, the rankings do not reflect the hotel's location or the availability of restaurants, facilities, or amenities.

We use the hotels' rack rates when calculating value; if you are planning your trip in advance, this guide will help. However, because most hotels offer special rates and incentives at various times, you should look back at the techniques on getting a good deal (pages 74–78).

Remember, these are relative ratings, not recommendations. A reader once complained that he had booked one of our top-value rooms and had been very disappointed—but the quality rating for that property was only ★★½. A ★★½ room at $90 may have the same *value* rating as a ★★★★ room at $200, but that does not mean the rooms will be of comparable quality. Good deal or not, a ★★½ room is still a ★★½ room.

The Top 30 Best Deals in Washington

	HOTEL	STAR RATING	ROOM RATING	COST ($=$50)	LOCATION
1.	St. Gregory Luxury Hotel & Suites	★★★★	85	$$$–	Dupont Circle/ Adams-Morgan
2.	Hotel Madera	★★★★	85	$$$$–	Dupont Circle/ Adams-Morgan
3.	Residence Inn Capitol Hill	★★★★	85	$$$$–	Capitol Hill
4.	Days Inn Connecticut Ave	★★★½	75	$$$	Upper Northwest

The Top 30 Best Deals in Washington

HOTEL	STAR RATING	ROOM RATING	COST ($=$50)	LOCATION
5. The George Washington University Inn	★★★★	83	$$$$–	Foggy Bottom
6. Hotel Lombardy	★★★★	83	$$$$–	Foggy Bottom
7. Omni Shoreham Hotel	★★★★	83	$$$$–	Upper Northwest
8. Hotel Rouge	★★★★	86	$$$$	Dupont Circle/ Adams-Morgan
9. Residence Inn Dupont Circle	★★★★	86	$$$$	Dupont Circle/ Adams-Morgan
10. One Washington Circle Hotel	★★★★	84	$$$$	Foggy Bottom
11. Georgetown Suites Hotel	★★★★	83	$$$$–	Georgetown
12. Renaissance Dupont Circle	★★★★	83	$$$$	Dupont Circle/ Adams-Morgan
13. Hyatt Place DC /Downtown/K Street	★★★★	85	$$$$+	Downtown
14. Courtyard Embassy Row	★★★½	81	$$$+	Dupont Circle/ Adams-Morgan
15. Best Western Georgetown Hotel & Suites	★★★½	80	$$$$–	Dupont Circle/ Adams-Morgan
16. Morrison-Clark Inn	★★★½	82	$$$$–	Downtown
17. Hotel Topaz	★★★★	83	$$$$+	Dupont Circle/ Adams-Morgan
18. The Mayflower Hotel	★★★★	83	$$$$+	Downtown
19. State Plaza Hotel	★★★½	82	$$$$–	Foggy Bottom
20. Holiday Inn Capitol	★★★½	78	$$$$–	Capitol Hill
21. The Normandy Hotel	★★★★	83	$$$$$–	Dupont Circle/ Adams-Morgan
22. Residence Inn Washington DC/Foggy Bottom	★★★★	83	$$$$$–	Foggy Bottom
23. Churchill Hotel	★★★★	83	$$$$$–	Dupont Circle/ Adams-Morgan
24. Marriott Wardman Park Hotel	★★★½	81	$$$$	Upper Northwest
25. Hotel RL	★★★½	82	$$$$	Downtown
26. Holiday Inn Central/ White House	★★★½	77	$$$$–	Upper Northwest
27. Melrose Hotel	★★★★	84	$$$$$–	Georgetown
28. Washington Court Hotel	★★★★	83	$$$$$–	Downtown
29. Phoenix Park Hotel	★★★½	78	$$$$	Capitol Hill
30. Cambria Suites Washington, D.C./Convention Center	★★★★	85	$$$$$	Downtown

WHEN ONLY THE BEST WILL DO

Note: The following lists are in alphabetical order and not by rank.

Best Family-Friendly Boutique Hotels

- **Adams Inn**   Adams Morgan
- **Avenue Suites**   Georgetown

- **The Churchill Embassy Row**   Dupont Circle
- **Fairmont Hotel**   Georgetown
- **Hotel Lombardy**   Foggy Bottom
- **Hotel Melrose**   Foggy Bottom
- **Hotel Madera**   Dupont Circle
- **Hotel Rouge**   Dupont Circle
- **Hotel Sofitel Washington DC**   Downtown
- **Liaison Capitol Hill Hotel**
- **Monaco Hotel**   Alexandria
- **Palomar Hotel**   Dupont Circle
- **State Plaza Hotel**   Foggy Bottom
- **Washington Plaza Hotel**   Downtown

Best Family-Friendly Chain Hotels
- **Best Western Georgetown Suites**
- **Cambria Hotel and Suites**   Rockville, Maryland
- **Comfort Inn Convention Center**
- **Courtyard by Marriott Convention Center**   Penn Quarter
- **Courtyard by Marriott Embassy Row**   Dupont Circle
- **Embassy Suites Hotels**   Dupont Circle, Friendship Heights, Georgetown, Convention Center
- **Gaylord Hotel in National Harbor**
- **Hamilton Crowne Plaza**   Downtown
- **Hilton Garden Inn near McPherson Square**
- **Holiday Inn Capitol Hill**
- **Holiday Inn Downtown**
- **Holiday Inn Rosslyn**   Arlington, Virginia
- **Homewood Suites**   Dupont Circle
- **Hyatt Regency Capitol Hill**
- **Residence Inn Foggy Bottom and DC Capitol**
- **Residence Inn National Harbor**
- **Residence Inn Washington DC in Federal Center SW Metro**

Best Swimming Pools (Indoor and/or Outdoor)
- **Cambria Suites-Convention Center**   Penn Quarter
- **The Capella**   Georgetown
- **Courtyard by Marriott**   Dupont Circle
- **Courtyard by Marriott Convention Center**   Penn Quarter
- **Courtyard by Marriott Foggy Bottom**
- **Courtyard by Marriott Washington D.C.**   Capitol Hill
- **The Donovan**   Dupont Circle
- **Embassy Row Hotel**   Dupont Circle

- **Embassy Suites Chevy Chase Pavilion**   Northwest D.C.
- **Embassy Suites Washington Convention Center**   Penn Quarter
- **Fairmont Washington DC**   Georgetown
- **Four Seasons Washington DC**   Georgetown
- **Grand Hyatt Washington**   Penn Quarter
- **Hampton Inn Washington DC**   White House
- **Hilton Garden Inn**   Bethesda
- **Hilton Garden Inn Washington DC/US Capitol**   Capitol Hill
- **Hotel Palomar**   Dupont Circle
- **Holiday Inn Capitol Hill**   National Mall
- **Holiday Inn Washington DC-Central/White House**   Downtown
- **Holiday Inn Washington Georgetown**
- **Hyatt Regency**   Capitol Hill
- **J.W. Marriott**   Downtown
- **Liaison Capitol Hill**
- **Mandarin Oriental**   Capitol Hill
- **Marriott Wardman Park**   Woodley Park
- **Omni Shoreham**   Woodley Park
- **One Washington Circle Hotel**   Foggy Bottom
- **Park Hyatt Washington**   Georgetown
- **Residence Inn Foggy Bottom**
- **Residence Inn Washington DC/Capitol**   Capitol Hill
- **Ritz-Carlton Pentagon City**
- **Washington Hilton**   Dupont Circle
- **Washington Marriott at Metro Center**   Penn Quarter
- **Washington Plaza**   Thomas Circle
- **Westin Georgetown**

Best Hotel Restaurants

- **Art & Soul in Liaison Capitol Hill**
- **Bistro Bis in the Hotel George**
- **Blue Duck Tavern at the Park Hyatt Washington**
- **Bourbon Steak in the Four Seasons**
- **Brabo in the Lorien Hotel and Spa**
- **Corduroy in Four Points Sheraton Hotel**
- **Decanter at the St. Regis**
- **Edgar at the Mayflower Hotel**
- **Grill Room at Capella Washington DC**
- **ICI Urban Bistro at Sofitel Washington DC Lafayette Square**
- **J&G Steakhouse in the W Washington D.C.**

- Nage at the Courtyard Embassy Row Dupont Circle
- Plume at the Jefferson Hotel
- Poste Moderne Brasserie at the Hotel Monaco
- Rural Society at the Madison Hotel
- Seasons at the Four Seasons
- Tabard at the Tabard Inn
- Westend Bistro at the Ritz-Carlton D.C.
- Zentan at The Donovan

Best Family-Friendly Hotel Restaurants

- 21st Amendment in Holiday Inn Capitol
- America Eats at Ritz Carlton Tysons Corner
- Amuse at Le Meridien Hotel Arlington
- Anthem at Marriott Marquis Washington DC
- Coffee Bean & Tea Leaf in Washington Hilton
- Fire & Sage at Marriott Metro Center
- Firefly in Hotel Madera
- Gordon Biersch Brewing Company in Courtyard Convention Center
- Harth in Hilton McLean Tysons Corner
- High Velocity at Marriott Marquis Washington DC
- Jardenea in Hotel Melrose
- Mansion on O Street
- President's Sports Bar at Renaissance Marriott Hotel
- Skydome Restaurant and Bar in Doubletree Crystal City
- Tom Yum District in Courtyard Arlington Rossyln
- Urbana at Hotel Palomar
- Vantage Point in Holiday Inn Rossyln

Best for High Tea

- **Henley Park Hotel**   Any day with advance reservations
- **Jefferson Hotel**   Saturday and Sunday
- **Mandarin Oriental**   Friday—Sunday
- **Mansion on O Street**   Advance reservations for groups only
- **Mayflower Hotel**   Saturday and Sunday
- **Park Hyatt Washington**   Saturday and Sunday
- **Ritz-Carlton Pentagon City**   Saturday and Sunday
- **Ritz-Carlton Tysons Corner**   Friday—Sunday
- **St. Regis Hotel**   Any day with advance reservations
- **Willard InterContinental**   Friday—Sunday only

Best Hotel Bars

- Amuse at Le Meridien Arlington
- Bar Dupont at Dupont Circle Hotel
- Bar at Urbana at Hotel Palomar
- Cure Bar and Grill in Grand Hyatt
- Empress Lounge at Mandarin Oriental (garden)
- Fairfax Lounge at Embassy Row Hotel
- Firefly (adjoining Hotel Madera)
- Le Bar at Hotel Sofitel
- The Living Room and POV at W Washington
- Loggia Lounge at the Fairmont Hotel
- The Lounge at Bourbon Steak, Four Seasons Hotel
- Off the Record at the Hay-Adams Hotel
- Poste at Hotel Monaco
- Quill at the Jefferson Hotel
- Round Robin Bar at the Willard InterContinental
- Rural Society at the Madison
- Rye Bar at the Capella
- Sky Bar at the Beacon Hotel
- Tabard Inn Bar & Lounge
- Trademark Drink & Eat at the Westin Alexandria

Best Views

- Beacon Hotel   Sky Bar, rooftop
- The Capella   Rooftop bar and pool for guests only
- The Donovan   Rooftop pool
- DoubleTree by Hilton Crystal City   Skydome
- Embassy Row Hotel   Rooftop terrace and pool
- Gaylord National Resort & Convention Center   National Harbor
- The Graham Georgetown   Observatory Lounge, rooftop
- Hay-Adams
- Holiday Inn Rosslyn Key Bridge
- Hyatt Regency Capitol Hill
- Hyatt Arlington Key Bridge
- Liaison Capitol Hill DC   Rooftop pool and lounge
- Key Bridge Marriott
- Lorien Hotel   Presidential Suites
- Mandarin Oriental   Empress Lounge
- W Washington   POV Lounge, rooftop

Hotel Information Chart

AC Hotel National Harbor ★★★½
156 Waterfront Street
National Harbor, MD 20745
☎ 301-749-2299
FAX 301-749-2298
TOLL-FREE ☎ 877-GO-ALOFT
marriott.com

ROOM QUALITY	82
COST ($=$50)	$$$$$$
LOCATION	Maryland Suburbs
NO. OF ROOMS	190
PARKING	Self $16
ROOM SERVICE	—
BREAKFAST	
ON-SITE DINING	•
POOL	—
EXERCISE FACILITIES	•

Avenue Suites Georgetown ★★★★
2500 Pennsylvania Avenue
Washington, DC 20037
☎ 202-333-8060
FAX 202-338-3818
TOLL-FREE ☎ 888-874-0100
avenuesuites.com

ROOM QUALITY	87
COST ($=$50)	$$$$$+
LOCATION	Georgetown
NO. OF ROOMS	263
PARKING	Self $32, valet $42
ROOM SERVICE	•
BREAKFAST	Continental
ON-SITE DINING	•
POOL	•
EXERCISE FACILITIES	•

Beacon Hotel ★★★½
1615 Rhode Island Avenue, NW
Washington, DC 20036
☎ 202-296-2100
FAX 202-331-0227
TOLL-FREE ☎ 800-821-4367
beaconhotelwdc.com

ROOM QUALITY	80
COST ($=$50)	$$$$$-
LOCATION	Dupont Circle/ Adams Morgan
NO. OF ROOMS	197
PARKING	Valet $41
ROOM SERVICE	•
BREAKFAST	—
ON-SITE DINING	•
POOL	Access
EXERCISE FACILITIES	•

Best Western Georgetown Hotel & Suites ★★★½
1121 New Hampshire Avenue, NW
Washington, DC 20037
☎ 202-457-0565
FAX 202-331-9421
TOLL-FREE ☎ 800-263-7212
bestwesternwashingtondc.com

ROOM QUALITY	80
COST ($=$50)	$$$$-
LOCATION	Dupont Circle/ Adams Morgan
NO. OF ROOMS	76
PARKING	Self $27 (off site)
ROOM SERVICE	—
BREAKFAST	Continental
ON-SITE DINING	—
POOL	—
EXERCISE FACILITIES	—

Bethesda Court Hotel ★★★½
7740 Wisconsin Ave.
Bethesda, MD 20814
☎ 301-656-2100
bethesdacourtwashdc.com

ROOM QUALITY	82
COST ($=$50)	$$$$
LOCATION	Maryland Suburbs
NO. OF ROOMS	74
PARKING	Self $15
ROOM SERVICE	—
BREAKFAST	Continental
ON-SITE DINING	—
POOL	—
EXERCISE FACILITIES	•

Cambria Hotel and Suites Rockville ★★★★
1 Helen Heneghan Way
Rockville, MD 20850
☎ 301-294-2200
FAX 301-294-2201
cambriasuitesrockville.com

ROOM QUALITY	84
COST ($=$50)	$$
LOCATION	Maryland Suburbs
NO. OF ROOMS	N/A
PARKING	Self $15
ROOM SERVICE	—
BREAKFAST	•
ON-SITE DINING	•
POOL	•
EXERCISE FACILITIES	•

Cambria Suites Convention Center ★★★★
899 O St. NW
Washington, DC 20001
☎ 202-299-1188
cambriadc.com

ROOM QUALITY	85
COST ($=$50)	$$$$$
LOCATION	Downtown
NO. OF ROOMS	N/A
PARKING	Valet $38
ROOM SERVICE	
BREAKFAST	•
ON-SITE DINING	•
POOL	•
EXERCISE FACILITIES	•

Capella Washington, D.C. Georgetown ★★★★
1050 31st St. NW
Washington, DC 20007
☎ 202-617-2400
FAX 202-617-2499
TOLL-FREE ☎ 855-922-7355
capellahotels.com

ROOM QUALITY	87
COST ($=$50)	$x11+
LOCATION	Georgetown
NO. OF ROOMS	49
PARKING	Valet $53
ROOM SERVICE	•
BREAKFAST	—
ON-SITE DINING	•
POOL	•
EXERCISE FACILITIES	•

Capital Hilton ★★★★
1001 16th Street, NW
Washington, DC 20036
☎ 202-393-1000
FAX 202-639-5784
TOLL-FREE ☎ 800-HILTONS
thecapitalhilton.com

ROOM QUALITY	83
COST ($=$50)	$$$$$$$$$+
LOCATION	Downtown
NO. OF ROOMS	544
PARKING	Valet $56
ROOM SERVICE	•
BREAKFAST	—
ON-SITE DINING	•
POOL	—
EXERCISE FACILITIES	•

Hotel Information Chart *(continued)*

Capitol Hill Hotel ★★★★
200 C Street, SE
Washington, DC 20005
☎202-543-6000
FAX 202-543-6105
capitolhillhotel-dc.com

ROOM QUALITY	85
COST ($=$50)	$$$$$$−
LOCATION	Capitol Hill
NO. OF ROOMS	153
PARKING	Valet $50
ROOM SERVICE	—
BREAKFAST	Buffet
ON-SITE DINING	—
POOL	—
EXERCISE FACILITIES	•

The Carlyle ★★★½
1731 New Hampshire Avenue, NW
Washington, DC 20009
☎ 202-234-3200
FAX 202-387-0085
TOLL-FREE ☎ 800-964-5377
carlylehoteldc.com

ROOM QUALITY	78
COST ($=$50)	$$$$$+
LOCATION	Dupont Circle/ Adams Morgan
NO. OF ROOMS	170
PARKING	Self $15, valet $42
ROOM SERVICE	—
BREAKFAST	—
ON-SITE DINING	•
POOL	—
EXERCISE FACILITIES	Free access

Churchill Hotel ★★★★
1914 Connecticut Avenue, NW
Washington, DC 20009
☎ 202-797-2000
FAX 202-462-0944
TOLL-FREE ☎ 800-424-2464
thechurchillhotel.com

ROOM QUALITY	83
COST ($=$50)	$$$$$−
LOCATION	Dupont Circle/ Adams Morgan
NO. OF ROOMS	144
PARKING	Valet $46
ROOM SERVICE	•
BREAKFAST	—
ON-SITE DINING	•
POOL	—
EXERCISE FACILITIES	•

Courtyard Washington Convention Center ★★★★
900 F Street
Washington, DC 20004
☎ 202-638-4600
FAX 202-638-4601
TOLL-FREE ☎ 800-393-3063
marriott.com

ROOM QUALITY	83
COST ($=$50)	$x10−
LOCATION	Downtown
NO. OF ROOMS	188
PARKING	Valet $59
ROOM SERVICE	•
BREAKFAST	—
ON-SITE DINING	•
POOL	•
EXERCISE FACILITIES	•

Courtyard Washington Northwest ★★★½
1900 Connecticut Avenue, NW
Washington, DC 20009
☎ 202-332-9300
FAX 202-328-7039
TOLL-FREE ☎ 800-321-2211
marriott.com

ROOM QUALITY	81
COST ($=$50)	$$$$$
LOCATION	Dupont Circle/ Adams Morgan
NO. OF ROOMS	147
PARKING	Valet $39
ROOM SERVICE	•
BREAKFAST	—
ON-SITE DINING	•
POOL	•
EXERCISE FACILITIES	•

Days Inn Connecticut Ave ★★★
4400 Connecticut Avenue, NW
Washington, DC 20008
☎ 202-244-5600
FAX 202-244-6794
TOLL-FREE ☎ 800-952-3060
daysinn.com

ROOM QUALITY	75
COST ($=$50)	$$$−
LOCATION	Upper Northwest
NO. OF ROOMS	155
PARKING	Self $20 garage
ROOM SERVICE	•
BREAKFAST	—
ON-SITE DINING	•
POOL	—
EXERCISE FACILITIES	—

The Dupont Circle Hotel ★★★★
1500 New Hampshire Avenue, NW
Washington, DC 20036
☎ 202-483-6000
FAX 202-328-3265
TOLL-FREE ☎ 800-423-6953
doylecollection.com

ROOM QUALITY	83
COST ($=$50)	$$$$$$$+
LOCATION	Dupont Circle/ Adams Morgan
NO. OF ROOMS	327
PARKING	Valet $38
ROOM SERVICE	•
BREAKFAST	—
ON-SITE DINING	•
POOL	—
EXERCISE FACILITIES	•

Eldon Luxury Suites ★★★★½
933 L Street, NW
Washington, DC 20001
☎ 202-540-5000
FAX 202-290-1460
TOLL-FREE ☎ 877-463-5336
eldonsuites.com

ROOM QUALITY	90
COST ($=$50)	$$$$+
LOCATION	Downtown
NO. OF ROOMS	50
PARKING	Valet $25
ROOM SERVICE	—
BREAKFAST	Continental
ON-SITE DINING	—
POOL	—
EXERCISE FACILITIES	•

The Embassy Row Hotel ★★★½
2015 Massachusetts Avenue, NW
Washington, DC 20036
☎ 202-265-1600
FAX 202-328-7526
TOLL-FREE ☎ 800-336-2900
embassyrowhotel.com

ROOM QUALITY	82
COST ($=$50)	$$$$$$+
LOCATION	Dupont Circle/ Adams Morgan
NO. OF ROOMS	231
PARKING	Valet $35
ROOM SERVICE	•
BREAKFAST	—
ON-SITE DINING	•
POOL	•
EXERCISE FACILITIES	•

Comfort Inn Downtown DC/Convention ★★★½
1201 13th Street, NW
Washington, DC 20005
☎ 202-682-5300
FAX 202-408-0830
TOLL-FREE ☎ 800-787-6589
comfortinn.com

ROOM QUALITY	78
COST ($=$50)	$$$$$$$-
LOCATION	Downtown
NO. OF ROOMS	100
PARKING	Valet $30
ROOM SERVICE	—
BREAKFAST	Continental
ON-SITE DINING	—
POOL	—
EXERCISE FACILITIES	•

Courtyard Embassy Row ★★★½
1600 Rhode Island Avenue, NW
Washington, DC 20036
☎ 202-293-8000
FAX 202-293-0085
TOLL-FREE ☎ 800-321-2211
courtyardembassyrow.com

ROOM QUALITY	81
COST ($=$50)	$$$+
LOCATION	Dupont Circle/Adams Morgan
NO. OF ROOMS	156
PARKING	Valet $44
ROOM SERVICE	•
BREAKFAST	—
ON-SITE DINING	•
POOL	•
EXERCISE FACILITIES	•

Courtyard Washington Capitol Hill/Navy Yard ★★★½
140 L Street SE
Washington, DC 20003
☎ 202-479-0027
TOLL-FREE ☎ 800-321-2211
marriott.com

ROOM QUALITY	81
COST ($=$50)	$$$$+
LOCATION	Capitol Hill
NO. OF ROOMS	192
PARKING	Self $30
ROOM SERVICE	•
BREAKFAST	•
ON-SITE DINING	•
POOL	•
EXERCISE FACILITIES	•

The District Hotel ★★★
1440 Rhode Island Avenue, NW
Washington, DC 20005
☎ 202-232-7800
FAX 202-265-3725
TOLL-FREE ☎ 800-350-5759
districthotel.com

ROOM QUALITY	60
COST ($=$50)	$$+
LOCATION	Dupont Circle/Adams Morgan
NO. OF ROOMS	63
PARKING	Valet $30
ROOM SERVICE	—
BREAKFAST	Continental
ON-SITE DINING	—
POOL	—
EXERCISE FACILITIES	—

The Donovan ★★★½
1155 14th Street, NW
Washington, DC 20005
☎ 202-737-1200
FAX 202-521-1410
TOLL-FREE ☎ 800-383-6900
donovanhoteldc.com

ROOM QUALITY	82
COST ($=$50)	$$$$$$$+
LOCATION	Downtown
NO. OF ROOMS	193
PARKING	Valet $48
ROOM SERVICE	•
BREAKFAST	Continental
ON-SITE DINING	•
POOL	•
EXERCISE FACILITIES	•

Doubletree Washington, D.C. ★★★★
1515 Rhode Island Avenue, NW
Washington, DC 20036
☎ 202-232-7000
FAX 202-521-7103
TOLL-FREE ☎ 800-222-TREE
doubletree.com

ROOM QUALITY	83
COST ($=$50)	$$$$$$
LOCATION	Upper Northwest
NO. OF ROOMS	219
PARKING	Valet $41
ROOM SERVICE	•
BREAKFAST	—
ON-SITE DINING	•
POOL	—
EXERCISE FACILITIES	•

Embassy Suites Chevy Chase ★★★★
4300 Military Road, NW
Washington, DC 20015
☎ 202-362-9300
FAX 202-686-3405
TOLL-FREE ☎ 800-EMBASSY
embassysuites.hilton.com

ROOM QUALITY	86
COST ($=$50)	$$$$
LOCATION	Upper Northwest
NO. OF ROOMS	198
PARKING	Self $26
ROOM SERVICE	—
BREAKFAST	Cooked to order
ON-SITE DINING	•
POOL	•
EXERCISE FACILITIES	•

Embassy Suites Convention Center ★★★★
900 10th St, NW
Washington, DC 20001
☎ 202-739-2001
FAX 202-739-2099
TOLL-FREE ☎ 800-EMBASSY
embassysuites.hilton.com

ROOM QUALITY	84
COST ($=$50)	$x8
LOCATION	Downtown
NO. OF ROOMS	271
PARKING	Valet $41
ROOM SERVICE	•
BREAKFAST	Buffet
ON-SITE DINING	•
POOL	•
EXERCISE FACILITIES	•

Embassy Suites Downtown ★★★½
1250 22nd Street, NW
Washington, DC 20037
☎ 202-857-3388
FAX 202-293-3173
TOLL-FREE ☎ 800-EMBASSY
embassysuites.hilton.com

ROOM QUALITY	79
COST ($=$50)	$$$$$$$-
LOCATION	Dupont Circle/Adams Morgan
NO. OF ROOMS	318
PARKING	Valet $42
ROOM SERVICE	•
BREAKFAST	Cooked to order
ON-SITE DINING	•
POOL	•
EXERCISE FACILITIES	•

Hotel Information Chart *(continued)*

The Fairfax at Embassy Row
★★★½
2100 Massachusetts Avenue, NW
Washington, DC 20008
☎ 202-293-2100
FAX 202-293-0641
TOLL-FREE ☎ 888-627-8439
fairfaxwashingtondc.com

ROOM QUALITY	82
COST ($=$50)	$x10
LOCATION	Dupont Circle/ Adams Morgan
NO. OF ROOMS	259
PARKING	Valet $45
ROOM SERVICE	•
BREAKFAST	—
ON-SITE DINING	•
POOL	—
EXERCISE FACILITIES	•

Fairfield Inn & Suites Washington, D.C. Downtown
★★★½
500 H Street, NW
Washington, DC 20001
☎ 202-289-5959
FAX 202-682-9152
TOLL-FREE ☎ 800-228-7697
marriott.com

ROOM QUALITY	80
COST ($=$50)	$x8-
LOCATION	Downtown
NO. OF ROOMS	305
PARKING	Valet $39
ROOM SERVICE	•
BREAKFAST	Continental
ON-SITE DINING	•
POOL	—
EXERCISE FACILITIES	•

Fairmont Washington, D.C.
★★★★
2401 M Street, NW
Washington, DC 20037
☎ 202-429-2400
FAX 202-457-5010
TOLL-FREE ☎ 800-257-7544
fairmont.com/washington

ROOM QUALITY	85
COST ($=$50)	$$$$$$
LOCATION	Georgetown
NO. OF ROOMS	415
PARKING	Valet $48
ROOM SERVICE	•
BREAKFAST	—
ON-SITE DINING	•
POOL	•
EXERCISE FACILITIES	Fee $18

Georgetown Inn ★★★★
1310 Wisconsin Avenue, NW
Washington, DC 20007
☎ 202-333-8900
FAX 202-333-8308
TOLL-FREE ☎ 888-587-2388
georgetowninn.com

ROOM QUALITY	84
COST ($=$50)	$$$$$$$-
LOCATION	Georgetown
NO. OF ROOMS	96
PARKING	Valet $35
ROOM SERVICE	•
BREAKFAST	—
ON-SITE DINING	•
POOL	—
EXERCISE FACILITIES	•

Georgetown Suites Hotel
★★★★
1111 30th Street, NW
Washington, DC
☎ 202-298-7800
FAX 202-333-5792
TOLL-FREE ☎ 800-348-7203
georgetownsuites.com

ROOM QUALITY	83
COST ($=$50)	$$$$-
LOCATION	Georgetown
NO. OF ROOMS	220
PARKING	Self $35
ROOM SERVICE	—
BREAKFAST	Continental
ON-SITE DINING	—
POOL	—
EXERCISE FACILITIES	•

The Graham Georgetown
★★★★
1075 Thomas Jefferson Street, NW
Washington, DC 20007
☎ 202-337-0900
FAX 202-333-6526
TOLL-FREE ☎ 855-341-1292
thegrahamgeorgetown.com

ROOM QUALITY	85
COST ($=$50)	$$$$$+
LOCATION	Georgetown
NO. OF ROOMS	47
PARKING	Valet $48
ROOM SERVICE	•
BREAKFAST	Continental
ON-SITE DINING	•
POOL	—
EXERCISE FACILITIES	•

Hampton Inn Washington, DC Convention Center ★★★½
901 6th Street, NW
Washington, DC 20001
☎ 202-842-2500
FAX 202-842-4100
TOLL-FREE ☎ 800-HAMPTON
hamptoninn3.hilton.com

ROOM QUALITY	82
COST ($=$50)	$x8+
LOCATION	Downtown
NO. OF ROOMS	321
PARKING	Valet $42
ROOM SERVICE	•
BREAKFAST	Buffet
ON-SITE DINING	•
POOL	—
EXERCISE FACILITIES	•

Hay-Adams Hotel ★★★★½
800 16th St. NW
Washington, DC 20006
☎ 202-638-6600
FAX 202-638-2716
TOLL-FREE ☎ 800-853-6807
hayadams.com

ROOM QUALITY	91
COST ($=$50)	$$$$$$$+
LOCATION	Downtown
NO. OF ROOMS	145
PARKING	Valet $49
ROOM SERVICE	•
BREAKFAST	—
ON-SITE DINING	•
POOL	—
EXERCISE FACILITIES	—

The Henley Park Hotel
★★★½
926 Massachusetts Avenue NW
Washington, DC 20001
☎ 202-638-5200
FAX 202-638-6740
TOLL-FREE ☎ 800-222-8474
henleypark.com

ROOM QUALITY	78
COST ($=$50)	$$$$+
LOCATION	Downtown
NO. OF ROOMS	96
PARKING	Valet $38
ROOM SERVICE	•
BREAKFAST	—
ON-SITE DINING	•
POOL	—
EXERCISE FACILITIES	•

Four Seasons Hotel ★★★★½

2800 Pennsylvania Avenue, NW
Washington, DC 20007
☎ 202-342-0444
FAX 202-944-2076
TOLL-FREE ☎ 800-819-5053
fourseasons.com

ROOM QUALITY	90
COST ($=$50)	$x11+
LOCATION	Georgetown
NO. OF ROOMS	211
PARKING	Valet $52
ROOM SERVICE	•
BREAKFAST	—
ON-SITE DINING	•
POOL	•
EXERCISE FACILITIES	•

Gaylord National ★★★½

201 Waterfront Street
National Harbor, MD 20745
☎ 301-965-4000
FAX 301-965-4100
TOLL-FREE ☎ 800-429-5673
gaylordhotels.com

ROOM QUALITY	82
COST ($=$50)	$$$$$$$+
LOCATION	Maryland Suburbs
NO. OF ROOMS	2,000
PARKING	Self $26, valet $39
ROOM SERVICE	•
BREAKFAST	—
ON-SITE DINING	•
POOL	•
EXERCISE FACILITIES	•

The George Washington University Inn ★★★★

824 New Hampshire Avenue, NW
Washington, DC 20037
☎202-337-6620
FAX 202-298-7499
TOLL-FREE ☎ 800-426-4455
gwuinn.com

ROOM QUALITY	83
COST ($=$50)	$$$$-
LOCATION	Foggy Bottom
NO. OF ROOMS	202
PARKING	Valet $41
ROOM SERVICE	•
BREAKFAST	—
ON-SITE DINING	•
POOL	—
EXERCISE FACILITIES	•

Grand Hyatt Washington ★★★★

1000 H Street, NW
Washington, DC 20001
☎ 202-582-1234
FAX 202-637-4781
TOLL-FREE ☎ 800-233-1234
grandwashington.hyatt.com

ROOM QUALITY	83
COST ($=$50)	$$$$$$+
LOCATION	Downtown
NO. OF ROOMS	888
PARKING	Self $40, valet $52
ROOM SERVICE	•
BREAKFAST	—
ON-SITE DINING	•
POOL	•
EXERCISE FACILITIES	•

Hamilton Crowne Plaza ★★★½

1001 14th Street NW
Washington, DC 20005
☎ 202-682-0111
FAX 202-682-9525
TOLL-FREE ☎ 800-980-6429
hamiltonhoteldc.com

ROOM QUALITY	84
COST ($=$50)	$$$$$$+
LOCATION	Downtown
NO. OF ROOMS	318
PARKING	Valet $45
ROOM SERVICE	•
BREAKFAST	—
ON-SITE DINING	•
POOL	—
EXERCISE FACILITIES	•

Hampton Inn & Suites National Harbor ★★★½

250 Waterfront Street
National Harbor, MD 20745
☎ 301-567-3531
FAX 301-766-0105
TOLL-FREE ☎ 888-370-0981
hamptoninn.com

ROOM QUALITY	80
COST ($=$50)	$x8
LOCATION	Maryland Suburbs
NO. OF ROOMS	150
PARKING	Self $16
ROOM SERVICE	—
BREAKFAST	Buffet
ON-SITE DINING	—
POOL	•
EXERCISE FACILITIES	•

Hilton Garden Inn Washington Downtown ★★★½

815 14th Street, NW
Washington, DC 20005
☎ 202-783-7800
FAX 202-783-7801
TOLL-FREE ☎ 800-HILTONS
hiltongardeninn.com

ROOM QUALITY	80
COST ($=$50)	$$$$$$$-
LOCATION	Downtown
NO. OF ROOMS	300
PARKING	Valet $41
ROOM SERVICE	•
BREAKFAST	—
ON-SITE DINING	•
POOL	•
EXERCISE FACILITIES	•

Hilton McLean Tysons Corner ★★★★

7920 Jones Branch Drive
Falls Church, VA 22102
☎ 703-847-5000
FAX 703-761-5100
TOLL-FREE ☎ 800-HILTONS
hilton.com

ROOM QUALITY	85
COST ($=$50)	$$$$-
LOCATION	Virginia Suburbs
NO. OF ROOMS	458
PARKING	Free lot
ROOM SERVICE	•
BREAKFAST	—
ON-SITE DINING	•
POOL	•
EXERCISE FACILITIES	•

Holiday Inn Capitol ★★★½

550 C Street, SW
Washington, DC 20024
☎ 202-479-4000
FAX 202-479-4353
TOLL-FREE ☎ 800-972-3159
ichotelsgroup.com

ROOM QUALITY	78
COST ($=$50)	$$$$-
LOCATION	Capitol Hill
NO. OF ROOMS	532
PARKING	Self $40
ROOM SERVICE	—
BREAKFAST	—
ON-SITE DINING	•
POOL	•
EXERCISE FACILITIES	•

Hotel Information Chart (continued)

Holiday Inn Central ★★★½
1501 Rhode Island Avenue, NW
Washington, DC 20005
☎ 202-483-2000
FAX 202-797-1078
TOLL-FREE ☎ 877-834-3613
inndc.com

ROOM QUALITY	77
COST ($=$50)	$$$$-
LOCATION	Upper Northwest
NO. OF ROOMS	212
PARKING	Self $32
ROOM SERVICE	•
BREAKFAST	—
ON-SITE DINING	•
POOL	•
EXERCISE FACILITIES	•

Holiday Inn Rosslyn at Key Bridge ★★★
1900 N. Fort Myer Drive
Arlington, VA 22209
☎ 703-807-2000
FAX 703-522-8864
TOLL-FREE ☎ 888-465-4329
ichotelsgroup.com

ROOM QUALITY	74
COST ($=$50)	$$$-
LOCATION	Virginia Suburbs
NO. OF ROOMS	307
PARKING	Free lot
ROOM SERVICE	•
BREAKFAST	—
ON-SITE DINING	•
POOL	•
EXERCISE FACILITIES	•

Homewood Suites Washington, DC ★★★½
1475 Massachusetts Avenue, NW
Washington, DC 20005
☎202-265-8000
FAX 202-265-5810
TOLL-FREE ☎ 888-370-0983
homewoodsuites.com

ROOM QUALITY	82
COST ($=$50)	$x8-
LOCATION	Dupont Circle/ Adams Morgan
NO. OF ROOMS	125
PARKING	Self $45 (off-site)
ROOM SERVICE	—
BREAKFAST	Buffet
ON-SITE DINING	—
POOL	—
EXERCISE FACILITIES	•

Hotel Monaco ★★★★
700 F Street, NW
Washington, DC 20004
☎ 202-628-7177
FAX 202-628-7277
TOLL-FREE ☎ 800-649-1202
monaco-dc.com

ROOM QUALITY	84
COST ($=$50)	$$$$$$$+
LOCATION	Downtown
NO. OF ROOMS	184
PARKING	Valet $50
ROOM SERVICE	•
BREAKFAST	—
ON-SITE DINING	•
POOL	—
EXERCISE FACILITIES	•

Hotel Palomar Washington ★★★★
2121 P Street, NW
Washington, DC 20037
☎ 202-293-3100
FAX 202-857-0134
TOLL-FREE ☎ 800-333-3333
hotelpalomar-dc.com

ROOM QUALITY	84
COST ($=$50)	$$$$$$$+
LOCATION	Dupont Circle/ Adams Morgan
NO. OF ROOMS	325
PARKING	Valet $45
ROOM SERVICE	•
BREAKFAST	—
ON-SITE DINING	•
POOL	•
EXERCISE FACILITIES	•

Hotel RL ★★★½
1823 L Street, NW
Washington, DC 20036
☎ 202-223-4320
FAX 202-293-4977
TOLL-FREE ☎ 800-424-2970
redlion.com

ROOM QUALITY	82
COST ($=$50)	$$$$
LOCATION	Downtown
NO. OF ROOMS	99
PARKING	Self $35
ROOM SERVICE	—
BREAKFAST	—
ON-SITE DINING	—
POOL	—
EXERCISE FACILITIES	—

Hyatt Place U.S. Capitol ★★★½
33 New York Avenue NE
Washington, DC 20002
☎ 202-289-5599
TOLL-FREE ☎ 800-233-1234
washingtondcuscapitol.place.hyatt.com

ROOM QUALITY	82
COST ($=$50)	$$$$$+
LOCATION	Downtown
NO. OF ROOMS	N/A
PARKING	Valet $35
ROOM SERVICE	•
BREAKFAST	—
ON-SITE DINING	•
POOL	—
EXERCISE FACILITIES	•

Hyatt Regency Capitol Hill ★★★½
400 New Jersey Avenue, NW
Washington, DC 20001
☎ 202-737-1234
FAX 202-737-5773
TOLL-FREE ☎ 800-233-1234
washingtonregency.hyatt.com

ROOM QUALITY	82
COST ($=$50)	$$$$$$-
LOCATION	Downtown
NO. OF ROOMS	834
PARKING	Valet $58
ROOM SERVICE	•
BREAKFAST	—
ON-SITE DINING	•
POOL	•
EXERCISE FACILITIES	•

Hyatt Regency Tysons Corner Center ★★★★
7901 Tysons One Place
Tysons, VA 22102
☎ 703-893-1234
TOLL-FREE ☎ 800-233-1234
tysonscornercenter.regency.hyatt.com

ROOM QUALITY	84
COST ($=$50)	$$$$+
LOCATION	Virginia Suburbs
NO. OF ROOMS	300
PARKING	Self $14, valet $25, free on weekends
ROOM SERVICE	•
BREAKFAST	—
ON-SITE DINING	•
POOL	•
EXERCISE FACILITIES	•

Hotel George ★★★★
15 E Street, NW
Washington, DC 20001
☎ 202-347-4200
FAX 202-346-4213
TOLL-FREE ☎ 800-576-8331
hotelgeorge.com

ROOM QUALITY	83
COST ($=$50)	$$$$$$+
LOCATION	Downtown
NO. OF ROOMS	139
PARKING	Valet $46
ROOM SERVICE	•
BREAKFAST	—
ON-SITE DINING	—
POOL	—
EXERCISE FACILITIES	•

Hotel Lombardy ★★★½
2019 Pennsylvania Avenue, NW
Washington, DC 20006
☎ 202-828-2600
FAX 202-872-0503
TOLL-FREE ☎ 800-424-5486
hotellombardy.com

ROOM QUALITY	83
COST ($=$50)	$$$$-
LOCATION	Foggy Bottom
NO. OF ROOMS	140
PARKING	Valet $35
ROOM SERVICE	•
BREAKFAST	—
ON-SITE DINING	•
POOL	•
EXERCISE FACILITIES	•

Hotel Madera ★★★★
1310 New Hampshire Avenue, NW
Washington, DC 20036
☎ 202-448-1800
FAX 202-448-1801
TOLL-FREE ☎ 800-430-1202
hotelmadera.com

ROOM QUALITY	85
COST ($=$50)	$$$$-
LOCATION	Dupont Circle/ Adams Morgan
NO. OF ROOMS	82
PARKING	Valet $46
ROOM SERVICE	•
BREAKFAST	—
ON-SITE DINING	—
POOL	—
EXERCISE FACILITIES	—

Hotel Rouge ★★★★
1315 16th Street, NW
Washington, DC 20036
☎ 202-232-8000
FAX 202-667-9827
TOLL-FREE ☎ 800-738-1202
rougehotel.com

ROOM QUALITY	86
COST ($=$50)	$$$$-
LOCATION	Dupont Circle/ Adams Morgan
NO. OF ROOMS	137
PARKING	Valet $45
ROOM SERVICE	•
BREAKFAST	—
ON-SITE DINING	•
POOL	—
EXERCISE FACILITIES	•

Hotel Topaz ★★★★
1733 N Street, NW
Washington, DC 20036
☎ 202-393-3000
FAX 202-785-9581
TOLL-FREE ☎ 800-775-1202
topazhotel.com

ROOM QUALITY	83
COST ($=$50)	$$$$+
LOCATION	Dupont Circle/ Adams Morgan
NO. OF ROOMS	99
PARKING	Valet $45
ROOM SERVICE	•
BREAKFAST	Buffet
ON-SITE DINING	•
POOL	—
EXERCISE FACILITIES	•

Hyatt Place DC/ Downtown ★★★★
1522 K Street, NW
Washington, DC 20005
☎ 202-830-1900
TOLL-FREE ☎ 800-233-1234
dcdowntown.place.hyatt.com

ROOM QUALITY	85
COST ($=$50)	$$$$+
LOCATION	Downtown
NO. OF ROOMS	N/A
PARKING	Valet $42
ROOM SERVICE	•
BREAKFAST	—
ON-SITE DINING	•
POOL	—
EXERCISE FACILITIES	•

J.W. Marriott Pennsylvania Avenue ★★★½
1331 Pennsylvania Avenue, NW
Washington, DC 20004
☎ 202-393-2000
FAX 202-626-6991
TOLL-FREE ☎ 800-228-9290
jwmarriottdc.com

ROOM QUALITY	82
COST ($=$50)	$$$$+
LOCATION	Downtown
NO. OF ROOMS	772
PARKING	Valet $56
ROOM SERVICE	—
BREAKFAST	—
ON-SITE DINING	•
POOL	•
EXERCISE FACILITIES	•

Jefferson Hotel ★★★★½
1200 16th Street, NW
Washington, DC 20036
☎ 202-347-2200
FAX 202-331-7982
TOLL-FREE ☎ 866-270-8102
jeffersondc.com

ROOM QUALITY	92
COST ($=$50)	$x8
LOCATION	Downtown
NO. OF ROOMS	100
PARKING	Valet $50
ROOM SERVICE	•
BREAKFAST	—
ON-SITE DINING	•
POOL	•
EXERCISE FACILITIES	•

Liaison Capitol Hill ★★★★
415 New Jersey Avenue, NW
Washington, DC 20001
☎ 202-638-1616
FAX 202-347-1813
TOLL-FREE ☎ 800-638-1116
jdvhotels.com

ROOM QUALITY	82
COST ($=$50)	$x8-
LOCATION	Downtown
NO. OF ROOMS	343
PARKING	Valet $48
ROOM SERVICE	•
BREAKFAST	—
ON-SITE DINING	•
POOL	•
EXERCISE FACILITIES	•

Hotel Information Chart (continued)

Madison Hotel ★★★★
1177 15th Street, NW
Washington, DC 20005
☎ 202-862-1600
FAX 202-785-1255
TOLL-FREE ☎ 800-424-8578
loewshotels.com

ROOM QUALITY	87
COST ($=$50)	$$$$$$+
LOCATION	Downtown
NO. OF ROOMS	353
PARKING	Valet $59
ROOM SERVICE	•
BREAKFAST	—
ON-SITE DINING	—
POOL	—
EXERCISE FACILITIES	•

Mandarin Oriental ★★★★½
1330 Maryland Avenue, SW
Washington, DC 20024
☎ 202-554-8588
FAX 202-787-6161
TOLL-FREE ☎ 888-888 1778
mandarinoriental.com

ROOM QUALITY	88
COST ($=$50)	$x8+
LOCATION	National Mall
NO. OF ROOMS	400
PARKING	Valet $49
ROOM SERVICE	•
BREAKFAST	—
ON-SITE DINING	•
POOL	•
EXERCISE FACILITIES	•

Marriott Metro Center ★★★½
775 12th Street, NW
Washington, DC 20005
☎ 202-737-2200
FAX 202-347-5886
TOLL-FREE ☎ 800-228-9290
metrocentermarriott.com

ROOM QUALITY	80
COST ($=$50)	$$$$$-
LOCATION	Downtown
NO. OF ROOMS	456
PARKING	Valet $56
ROOM SERVICE	•
BREAKFAST	—
ON-SITE DINING	•
POOL	•
EXERCISE FACILITIES	•

Morrison-Clark Inn ★★★½
1015 L Street, NW
Washington, DC 20001
☎ 202-898-1200
FAX 202-289-8576
TOLL-FREE ☎ 800-332-7898
morrisonclark.com

ROOM QUALITY	82
COST ($=$50)	$$$$-
LOCATION	Downtown
NO. OF ROOMS	54
PARKING	Valet $39
ROOM SERVICE	•
BREAKFAST	Continental
ON-SITE DINING	•
POOL	—
EXERCISE FACILITIES	•

The Normandy Hotel ★★★½
2118 Wyoming Avenue, NW
Washington, DC 20008
☎ 202-483-1350
FAX 202-387-8241
TOLL-FREE ☎ 866-534-6835
thenormandydc.com

ROOM QUALITY	83
COST ($=$50)	$$$$$-
LOCATION	Dupont Circle/ Adams Morgan
NO. OF ROOMS	75
PARKING	Self $34
ROOM SERVICE	—
BREAKFAST	—
ON-SITE DINING	—
POOL	—
EXERCISE FACILITIES	—

Omni Shoreham Hotel ★★★★
2500 Calvert Street, NW
Washington, DC 20008
☎ 202-234-0700
FAX 202-265-7972
TOLL-FREE ☎ 888-444-6664
omnihotels.com

ROOM QUALITY	83
COST ($=$50)	$$$$-
LOCATION	Upper Northwest
NO. OF ROOMS	834
PARKING	Valet $42
ROOM SERVICE	•
BREAKFAST	—
ON-SITE DINING	•
POOL	•
EXERCISE FACILITIES	Fee $10 per day, $18 stay

Renaissance Arlington Capital View Hotel ★★★★
2800 South Potomac Ave.
Arlington, VA 22202
☎ 703-413-1300
FAX 703-413-3648
TOLL-FREE ☎ 888-803-1298
marriott.com

ROOM QUALITY	83
COST ($=$50)	$$$$$$-
LOCATION	Virginia Suburbs
NO. OF ROOMS	300
PARKING	Valet $32
ROOM SERVICE	•
BREAKFAST	—
ON-SITE DINING	•
POOL	•
EXERCISE FACILITIES	•

Renaissance Dupont Circle ★★★★
1143 New Hampshire Avenue, NW
Washington, DC 20037
☎ 202-775-0800
FAX 202-331-9491
TOLL-FREE ☎ 888-803-1298
marriott.com

ROOM QUALITY	83
COST ($=$50)	$$$$
LOCATION	Dupont Circle/ Adams Morgan
NO. OF ROOMS	355
PARKING	Valet $49
ROOM SERVICE	—
BREAKFAST	—
ON-SITE DINING	•
POOL	—
EXERCISE FACILITIES	•

Residence Inn Alexandria Old Town ★★★★
1456 Duke St.
Alexandria, VA 22314
☎ 703-548-5474
FAX 703-684-6818
TOLL-FREE ☎ 888-236-2427
marriott.com

ROOM QUALITY	86
COST ($=$50)	$$$-
LOCATION	Virginia Suburbs
NO. OF ROOMS	240
PARKING	Self $22
ROOM SERVICE	•
BREAKFAST	Buffet
ON-SITE DINING	—
POOL	•
EXERCISE FACILITIES	•

Marriott Wardman Park Hotel ★★★½
2660 Woodley Road, NW
Washington, DC 20008
☎ 202-328-2000
FAX 202-234-0015
TOLL-FREE ☎ 800-228-9290
marriott.com

ROOM QUALITY	81
COST ($=$50)	$$$$
LOCATION	Upper Northwest
NO. OF ROOMS	1,316
PARKING	Self $41, valet $46
ROOM SERVICE	•
BREAKFAST	—
ON-SITE DINING	•
POOL	•
EXERCISE FACILITIES	•

The Mayflower Hotel ★★★½
1127 Connecticut Avenue, NW
Washington, DC 20036
☎ 202-347-3000
FAX 202-776-9182
TOLL-FREE ☎ 800-228-7697
marriott.com

ROOM QUALITY	83
COST ($=$50)	$$$$+
LOCATION	Downtown
NO. OF ROOMS	657
PARKING	Valet $48
ROOM SERVICE	•
BREAKFAST	—
ON-SITE DINING	•
POOL	—
EXERCISE FACILITIES	•

Melrose Hotel ★★★★
2430 Pennsylvania Avenue, NW
Washington, DC 20037
☎ 202-955-6400
FAX 202-775-8489
TOLL-FREE ☎ 800-635-7673
melrosehoteldc.com

ROOM QUALITY	84
COST ($=$50)	$$$$$-
LOCATION	Georgetown
NO. OF ROOMS	240
PARKING	Valet $48
ROOM SERVICE	•
BREAKFAST	—
ON-SITE DINING	•
POOL	—
EXERCISE FACILITIES	•

One Washington Circle Hotel ★★★★
One Washington Circle, NW
Washington, DC 20037
☎ 202-872-1680
FAX 202-887-4989
TOLL-FREE ☎ 800-424-9671
thecirclehotel.com

ROOM QUALITY	84
COST ($=$50)	$$$$-
LOCATION	Foggy Bottom
NO. OF ROOMS	151
PARKING	Valet $40
ROOM SERVICE	•
BREAKFAST	—
ON-SITE DINING	•
POOL	•
EXERCISE FACILITIES	•

Park Hyatt ★★★★½
24th Street at M Street, NW
Washington, DC 20037
☎ 202-789-1234
FAX 202-419-6795
TOLL-FREE ☎ 800-233-1234
parkwashington.hyatt.com

ROOM QUALITY	91
COST ($=$50)	$$$$$$$+
LOCATION	Georgetown
NO. OF ROOMS	223
PARKING	Valet $51
ROOM SERVICE	•
BREAKFAST	—
ON-SITE DINING	•
POOL	•
EXERCISE FACILITIES	•

Phoenix Park Hotel ★★★½
520 N. Capitol Street, NW
Washington, DC 20001
☎ 202-638-6900
FAX 202-393-3236
TOLL-FREE ☎ 800-824-5419
phoenixparkhotel.com

ROOM QUALITY	78
COST ($=$50)	$$$$
LOCATION	Capitol Hill
NO. OF ROOMS	149
PARKING	Valet $48
ROOM SERVICE	•
BREAKFAST	—
ON-SITE DINING	•
POOL	—
EXERCISE FACILITIES	•

Residence Inn Arlington Capital View ★★★★
2850 South Potomac Ave.
Arlington, VA 22202
☎ 703-415-1300
FAX 703-413-3649
TOLL-FREE ☎ 888-236-2427
marriott.com

ROOM QUALITY	86
COST ($=$50)	$$$-
LOCATION	Virginia Suburbs
NO. OF ROOMS	325
PARKING	Valet $32
ROOM SERVICE	•
BREAKFAST	Buffet
ON-SITE DINING	—
POOL	•
EXERCISE FACILITIES	•

Residence Inn Capitol Hill ★★★★
333 E Street, SW
Washington, DC 20024
☎ 202-484-8280
FAX 202-484-7340
TOLL-FREE ☎ 800-393-3063
marriott.com

ROOM QUALITY	85
COST ($=$50)	$$$$-
LOCATION	Capitol Hill
NO. OF ROOMS	233
PARKING	Valet $45
ROOM SERVICE	•
BREAKFAST	Buffet
ON-SITE DINING	•
POOL	•
EXERCISE FACILITIES	•

Residence Inn Dupont Circle ★★★★
2120 P Street, NW
Washington, DC 20037
☎ 202-466-6800
FAX 202-466-9630
TOLL-FREE ☎ 800-331-3131
marriott.com

ROOM QUALITY	86
COST ($=$50)	$$$$
LOCATION	Dupont Circle/ Adams Morgan
NO. OF ROOMS	107
PARKING	Self $35
ROOM SERVICE	•
BREAKFAST	Buffet
ON-SITE DINING	•
POOL	—
EXERCISE FACILITIES	•

Hotel Information Chart *(continued)*

Residence Inn National Harbor ★★★★
192 Waterfront St.
National Harbor, MD 20745
☎ 301-749-4755
FAX 301-749-4756
TOLL-FREE ☎ 800-321-2211
marriott.com

ROOM QUALITY	85
COST ($=$50)	$$$$$$$-
LOCATION	Maryland Suburbs
NO. OF ROOMS	162
PARKING	Self $16
ROOM SERVICE	—
BREAKFAST	Buffet
ON-SITE DINING	—
POOL	—
EXERCISE FACILITIES	•

Residence Inn Washington, D.C. ★★★★
1199 Vermont Avenue, NW
Washington, DC 20005
☎ 202-898-1100
FAX 202-898-1110
TOLL-FREE ☎ 800-392-8990
marriott.com

ROOM QUALITY	83
COST ($=$50)	$$$$$
LOCATION	Downtown
NO. OF ROOMS	202
PARKING	Valet $39
ROOM SERVICE	—
BREAKFAST	Buffet
ON-SITE DINING	—
POOL	—
EXERCISE FACILITIES	•

Residence Inn Washington, D.C./Foggy Bottom ★★★½
801 New Hampshire Avenue, NW
Washington, DC 20037
☎ 202-785-2000
FAX 202-785-9485
TOLL-FREE ☎ 800-331-3131
marriott.com

ROOM QUALITY	83
COST ($=$50)	$$$$$-
LOCATION	Foggy Bottom
NO. OF ROOMS	103
PARKING	Valet $47
ROOM SERVICE	—
BREAKFAST	Buffet
ON-SITE DINING	—
POOL	•
EXERCISE FACILITIES	•

Savoy Suites Hotel ★★★½
2505 Wisconsin Avenue, NW
Washington, DC 20007
☎ 202-337-9700
FAX 202-337-3644
TOLL-FREE ☎ 800-944-5377
savoysuites.com

ROOM QUALITY	83
COST ($=$50)	$$$$$+
LOCATION	Upper Northwest
NO. OF ROOMS	150
PARKING	Free garage
ROOM SERVICE	•
BREAKFAST	—
ON-SITE DINING	•
POOL	—
EXERCISE FACILITIES	Access

Sofitel Lafayette ★★★★
806 15th Street, NW
Washington, DC 20005
☎ 202-730-8800
FAX 202-730-8500
TOLL-FREE ☎ 800-763-4835
sofitel.com

ROOM QUALITY	88
COST ($=$50)	$$$$$$$-
LOCATION	Downtown
NO. OF ROOMS	237
PARKING	Valet $49
ROOM SERVICE	•
BREAKFAST	—
ON-SITE DINING	•
POOL	—
EXERCISE FACILITIES	•

St. Gregory Luxury Hotel & Suites ★★★★
2033 M Street NW
Washington, DC 20036
☎ 202-530-3600
FAX 202-466-6770
TOLL-FREE ☎ 800-829-5034
stgregoryhotelwdc.com

ROOM QUALITY	85
COST ($=$50)	$$$-
LOCATION	Dupont Circle/ Adams Morgan
NO. OF ROOMS	154
PARKING	Valet $42
ROOM SERVICE	•
BREAKFAST	—
ON-SITE DINING	•
POOL	—
EXERCISE FACILITIES	•

W Washington D.C. ★★★★
515 15th Street, NW
Washington, DC 20004
☎ 202-661-2400
FAX 202-661-2405
TOLL-FREE ☎ 800-424-9540
wwashingtondc.com

ROOM QUALITY	83
COST ($=$50)	$$$$$$$+
LOCATION	Downtown
NO. OF ROOMS	317
PARKING	Valet $50
ROOM SERVICE	•
BREAKFAST	—
ON-SITE DINING	•
POOL	—
EXERCISE FACILITIES	•

Washington Court Hotel ★★★★
525 New Jersey Avenue, NW
Washington, DC 20001
☎ 202-628-2100
FAX 202-879-7918
TOLL-FREE ☎ 800-321-3010
washingtoncourthotel.com

ROOM QUALITY	83
COST ($=$50)	$$$$$-
LOCATION	Downtown
NO. OF ROOMS	267
PARKING	Valet $46
ROOM SERVICE	•
BREAKFAST	—
ON-SITE DINING	•
POOL	•
EXERCISE FACILITIES	•

Washington Hilton ★★★½
1919 Connecticut Avenue, NW
Washington, DC 20009
☎ 202-483-3000
FAX 202-232-0438
TOLL-FREE ☎ 800-HILTONS
hilton.com

ROOM QUALITY	82
COST ($=$50)	$$$$$+
LOCATION	Dupont Circle/ Adams Morgan
NO. OF ROOMS	1,119
PARKING	Self $41, valet $49
ROOM SERVICE	•
BREAKFAST	—
ON-SITE DINING	•
POOL	•
EXERCISE FACILITIES	•

Ritz-Carlton Georgetown
★★★★½
3100 South Street, NW
Washington, DC 20007
☎ 202-912-4100
FAX 202-912-4199
TOLL-FREE ☎ 800-241-3333
ritzcarlton.com

ROOM QUALITY	90
COST ($=$50)	$x11+
LOCATION	Georgetown
NO. OF ROOMS	86
PARKING	Valet $52
ROOM SERVICE	•
BREAKFAST	–
ON-SITE DINING	•
POOL	–
EXERCISE FACILITIES	•

Ritz-Carlton Washington, D.C. ★★★★
1150 22nd Street, NW
Washington, DC 20037
☎ 202-835-0500
FAX 202-835-1588
TOLL-FREE ☎ 800-241-3333
ritzcarlton.com

ROOM QUALITY	86
COST ($=$50)	$x10–
LOCATION	Dupont Circle/ Adams Morgan
NO. OF ROOMS	300
PARKING	Valet $51
ROOM SERVICE	•
BREAKFAST	–
ON-SITE DINING	•
POOL	•
EXERCISE FACILITIES	Access $15

River Inn ★★★★
924 25th Street, NW
Washington, DC 20037
☎ 202-337-7600
FAX 202-337-6520
TOLL-FREE ☎ 888-874-0100
theriverinn.com

ROOM QUALITY	87
COST ($=$50)	$$$$$+
LOCATION	Foggy Bottom
NO. OF ROOMS	125
PARKING	Valet $34
ROOM SERVICE	•
BREAKFAST	–
ON-SITE DINING	•
POOL	–
EXERCISE FACILITIES	•

St. Regis ★★★★½
923 16th Street & K Street, NW
Washington, DC 20006
☎ 202-638-2626
FAX 202-683-4231
TOLL-FREE ☎ 800-562-5661
starwoodhotels.com

ROOM QUALITY	91
COST ($=$50)	$x9+
LOCATION	Downtown
NO. OF ROOMS	175
PARKING	Valet $52
ROOM SERVICE	•
BREAKFAST	–
ON-SITE DINING	•
POOL	–
EXERCISE FACILITIES	•

State Plaza Hotel ★★★½
2117 E Street, NW
Washington, DC 20037
☎ 202-861-8200
FAX 202-659-8601
TOLL-FREE ☎ 800-424-2859
stateplaza.com

ROOM QUALITY	82
COST ($=$50)	$$$$–
LOCATION	Foggy Bottom
NO. OF ROOMS	230
PARKING	Valet $45
ROOM SERVICE	•
BREAKFAST	–
ON-SITE DINING	•
POOL	–
EXERCISE FACILITIES	•

Tabard Inn ★★★★
1739 N Street, NW
Washington, DC 20036
☎ 202-785-1277
FAX 202-785-6173
tabardinn.com

ROOM QUALITY	84
COST ($=$50)	$$$$$+
LOCATION	Dupont Circle
NO. OF ROOMS	40
PARKING	Valet $25
ROOM SERVICE	•
BREAKFAST	–
ON-SITE DINING	•
POOL	–
EXERCISE FACILITIES	Access

Washington Marriott Georgetown ★★★½
1221 22nd St. and M Street, NW
Washington, DC 20037
☎ 202-842-1300
FAX 202-872-1424
TOLL-FREE ☎ 800-393-3053
marriottwashington.com

ROOM QUALITY	81
COST ($=$50)	$$$$$–
LOCATION	Georgetown
NO. OF ROOMS	470
PARKING	Self $45, valet $49
ROOM SERVICE	–
BREAKFAST	–
ON-SITE DINING	•
POOL	–
EXERCISE FACILITIES	•

Washington Plaza Hotel ★★★½
10 Thomas Circle, NW
Washington, DC 20005
☎ 202-842-1300
FAX 202-371-9602
TOLL-FREE ☎ 800-424-1140
washingtonplazahotel.com

ROOM QUALITY	81
COST ($=$50)	$$$$+
LOCATION	Downtown
NO. OF ROOMS	340
PARKING	Self $30
ROOM SERVICE	•
BREAKFAST	–
ON-SITE DINING	•
POOL	•
EXERCISE FACILITIES	•

Washington Renaissance Hotel ★★★½
999 Ninth Street, NW
Washington, DC 20001
☎ 202-898-9000
FAX 202-289-0947
TOLL-FREE ☎ 888-236-2427
marriott.com

ROOM QUALITY	83
COST ($=$50)	$$$$$–
LOCATION	Downtown
NO. OF ROOMS	807
PARKING	Self $35, valet $45
ROOM SERVICE	•
BREAKFAST	–
ON-SITE DINING	•
POOL	–
EXERCISE FACILITIES	•

Hotel Information Chart *(continued)*

Westin Georgetown ★★★★
2350 M Street, NW
Washington, DC 20037
☎ 202-429-0100
FAX 202-429-9759
TOLL-FREE ☎ 888-937-8461
westin.com

ROOM QUALITY	84
COST ($=$50)	$$$$$$–
LOCATION	Georgetown
NO. OF ROOMS	263
PARKING	Self $32, valet $42
ROOM SERVICE	•
BREAKFAST	—
ON-SITE DINING	•
POOL	•
EXERCISE FACILITIES	•

Westin Washington National Harbor ★★★★
171 Waterfront St.
National Harbor, MD 20745
☎ 301-567-3999
FAX 301-567-4001
TOLL-FREE ☎ 888-627-7176
starwoodhotels.com

ROOM QUALITY	82
COST ($=$50)	$$$$$+
LOCATION	Maryland Suburbs
NO. OF ROOMS	195
PARKING	Free lot
ROOM SERVICE	•
BREAKFAST	—
ON-SITE DINING	•
POOL	•
EXERCISE FACILITIES	•

Westin Washington, D.C. City Center ★★★★
1400 M Street, NW
Washington, DC 20005
☎ 202-429-1700
FAX 202-785-0786
TOLL-FREE ☎ 800-627-9035
starwoodhotels.com

ROOM QUALITY	86
COST ($=$50)	$x8–
LOCATION	Downtown
NO. OF ROOMS	406
PARKING	Valet $43
ROOM SERVICE	•
BREAKFAST	—
ON-SITE DINING	•
POOL	—
EXERCISE FACILITIES	•

Willard InterContinental ★★★★
1401 Pennsylvania Avenue, NW
Washington, DC 20004
☎ 202-628-9100
FAX 202-637-7326
TOLL-FREE ☎ 800-487-2537
intercontinental.com

ROOM QUALITY	88
COST ($=$50)	$$$$$$$–
LOCATION	Downtown
NO. OF ROOMS	332
PARKING	Valet $42
ROOM SERVICE	•
BREAKFAST	—
ON-SITE DINING	•
POOL	—
EXERCISE FACILITIES	•

PART THREE

ARRIVING *and* GETTING AROUND

▌ COMING *into the* CITY

WE REALIZE THERE ARE MANY FACTORS (cost, number of people traveling together, distance, time, etc.) involved in choosing a mode of transportation, and there are plenty of options when it comes to Washington, each with pros and cons. Here are the basics.

ARRIVING BY CAR

IF YOU DRIVE, you will most likely arrive on one of three interstate highways, I-95 from the north or the south, I-66 from the west, or I-70/270 from the northwest; US 50 from the east; or the Baltimore-Washington Parkway, which parallels I-95 between Baltimore and Washington.

All of these routes connect with Washington's Capital Beltway, I-495, which is where it gets confusing. The Capital Beltway is a 64-mile loop that travels through the Maryland and Virginia suburbs, with Washington, D.C., centered in the middle. At the perimeter and inside the Capital Beltway, six major bridges cross over the Potomac River: two from Maryland into Virginia, and these bridges experience nearly constant bottlenecking, and four from Virginia into Washington, D.C. (and that's how the term "inside the Beltway" was born). The Beltway has a few different names in different parts of town. It's called both I-95 and I-495 because I-95 doesn't cut directly through Washington; instead, it's rerouted along the southern and eastern half of the Beltway. The signage along George Washington Memorial Parkway is so complicated that even locals find themselves headed either to see Lincoln or Jefferson instead of into Virginia, but one rule to remember is to hug the Potomac River shoreline to stay on this scenic road that passes by Reagan National Airport and ends in Old Town Alexandria.

unofficial TIP
You'll hear constant references to the "Inner Loop"
and "Outer Loop" in directions (and traffic reports).
These refer to the twin circles of the Beltway.
Because Americans drive
on the right, the Inner Loop
runs clockwise and the
Outer Loop counterclock-
wise. Those of you from the
UK, grit your teeth.

Much of the highway construction in recent years is designed to make life easier for commuters, but it can make driving even more stressful for outsiders. There are HOV, or high-occupancy, lanes on many area highways, but their hours of restriction vary, as do the number of passengers required to use the lanes; some even reverse from morning to night. Express lanes have opened in the middle of the Beltway around the massive Springfield Interchange, where the Beltway meets I-95 and much of the battling signage begins, and run around the southwest quadrant of 495 to around Tysons, where you can enter the express lanes going south. There are a limited number of exits, and using the express lanes requires an E-ZPass, so we suggest you don't do that. The express road to Dulles Airport parallels the Dulles Toll Road from the Beltway, but it has no exits, so don't try to cheat. There is also a toll road in Maryland, between I-270 and I-95, officially Maryland Route 200 but locally known as the ICC for Intercounty Connector; it has four intermediate exits and also requires an E-ZPass. (Former residents somewhat familiar with the Beltway can look into these additions at **495expresslanes .com** or **mdta.maryland.gov**.)

If at all possible, avoid rush-hour traffic, especially between 6:30 and 9:30 a.m. and about 2:30 to 7 p.m. When locals talk about "gridlock," they are not only referring to politics, but to traffic jams. In particular, try to avoid what is called the "Friday getaway" between Memorial Day and Labor Day. And remember, a majority of commuters have to cross some bridge or other to get into the city; one fenderbender and the highway becomes a parking lot.

ARRIVING BY PLANE

RONALD REAGAN WASHINGTON NATIONAL AIRPORT Of the area's three airports, Reagan National is by far the most convenient, located a few miles south of D.C. on the Virginia side of the Potomac River, and the favored airport of Congress members headed home to their districts. But its proximity to the capital (with its restricted airspace for security reasons) and so many residential neighborhoods has resulted in limits on overnight flights and those outside a 1,250-mile perimeter (because larger jets are louder).

unofficial TIP
All three Washington
regional airports have designated animal relief areas
for those traveling with
pets and USO lounges for
members of the armed ser-
vices and their families
(and service animals). All
three also participate in the
TSA's PreCheck program.

Reagan National is expanding and has added new airlines every year, including Southwest and JetBlue. There's a very convenient

Washington, D.C., and Vicinity

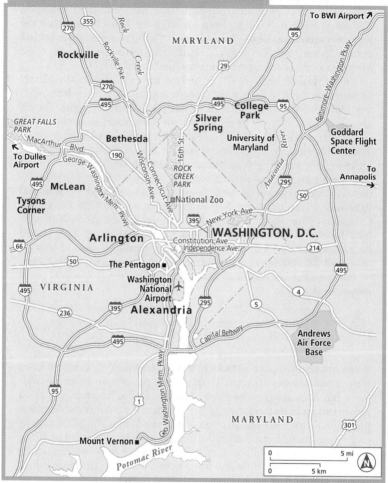

Delta Shuttle to New York La Guardia several times a day. This airport has an original vintage-looking building and two stunning new terminals built to pay tribute to Thomas Jefferson's home, Monticello.

Reagan National offers several options for getting into the city or suburbs. The airport's own Metro station is the most obvious: Both the Blue and Yellow Lines stop here, offering connections to other lines at several crosspoints in the system. Two pedestrian bridges connect the Metro to terminals B and C, although if you have extra baggage or are transferring terminals, you can take a free shuttle. On weekend and holiday mornings, Metrobus numbers 13F and 13G shuttle between downtown, circling around Crystal City, the Pentagon, Arlington Cemetery, Federal Triangle, Penn Quarter, the Smithsonian, and the airport (**wmata.com/bus /timetables**). Two ground-transportation centers located on the baggage claim level provide information on Metro, taxi service, SuperShuttle vans, and rental cars.

Union Station, home of D.C.'s Amtrak trains, is also on the Metro, although on the Red Line, which means you'd have to transfer at Gallery Place or Metro Center to get to Reagan National Airport. There's also an Amtrak stop in Alexandria by the King Street station.

Cab fares are about $22 to downtown or $25 to Union Station. You could certainly rent a car, but you'll have to negotiate some of the busiest traffic just to get out of the immediate area.

SuperShuttle shared-service vans leave every 15 (or fewer) minutes to any destination in the D.C. area. Fares start at $14 (additional members of the party are $10 each) for travel into the District of Columbia. Three SuperShuttle ticket counters are located at National; look for the WASHINGTON FLYER/SUPERSHUTTLE signs posted throughout the airport. For more information, exact fares, and reservations, call ☎ 800-BLUE VAN (258-3826) or go to **supershuttle.com.**

For detailed information about Reagan National Airport, go to **mwaa.com/reagan.**

 THE SMITHSONIAN NATIONAL AIR AND SPACE MUSEUM'S Steven F. Udvar-Hazy annex, 2½ miles from Dulles Airport, houses a Concorde, the space shuttle *Enterprise,* and the *Enola Gay,* among other aviation and aerospace legends.

WASHINGTON DULLES INTERNATIONAL AIRPORT Located 26 miles west of downtown in the sprawling Virginia suburbs, in a soaring landmark building designed by Eero Saarinen, Dulles International is 45 minutes to an hour from the city by car. There is no direct public transportation downtown yet; an extension of the Metro, the Silver Line, is under construction but is not scheduled to open until the end of 2016.

Dulles is primarily known as an international hub—more than 20 international airlines fly here—but a dozen domestic airlines are here as well: United Airlines has a major hub at Dulles.

The building has five terminals, two of which have been renovated. Dulles has Aerotrains, underground passenger trains, between three terminals, though there are still some elevated van-like "Mobile Lounges" in use to Terminal D. For complete information on the airport and services, go to **mwaa.com/dulles.**

Until the Silver Line is complete, Dulles remains the least convenient of the three airports serving Washington, despite the existence of the airport-only Dulles Access Road, which connects with the Capital Beltway and I-66. In fact, Bloomberg recently ranked it the third most frustrating airport in the country, in great part for its location and long security lines. Cab fare is about $76–$86 to downtown Washington.

Washington Flyer coach service to the Wiehle-Reston Metro station leaves about every 30 minutes, seven days a week ($5 one-way); it takes 15–20 minutes, depending on traffic. For more information, call ☎ 888-927-4359 or visit **washfly.com.** SuperShuttle shared-ride vans will take you anywhere in the D.C. metropolitan area; there's usually about a 30-minute wait and fares start at about $29 to the downtown area (additional members of the party are $10 each). Another bus service called Go Buses offers transportation to and from all three D.C.-area airports; visit **theairportshuttle.com** for details on prices and options.

 THIS TAKES SOME TIME BUT WILL SAVE YOU MONEY. Metrobus offers transportation from Dulles Airport to three Virginia stops. Metrobus has service from the L'Enfant Plaza Metro station with stops at the Rosslyn Metro, Herndon–Monroe Park, and the Tysons-Westpark Transit Station, which might be handy for those staying in the Virginia suburbs. The 5A bus leaves L'Enfant Plaza every 25–45 minutes weekdays and on the hour between 6:30 a.m. and 11:40 p.m. on weekends; the trip takes close to an hour and costs $7 each way, but you must have exact change if you don't have a SmarTrip Card from Metro ($4 for seniors and those with disabilities). Be mindful that the bus may be crowded during peak hours. For more information visit **wmata.com/bus/timetables.** For information on SmarTrip service, see the section on "Taking the Metro" on pages 115–123.

If you happen to be staying or working near Dulles Town Center, there is also bus service from there to the airport, with five stops in between. The Dulles 2 Dulles Connector leaves from the town center every 45–60 minutes between 7 a.m. and 6:30 p.m. weekdays. The trip takes about 45 minutes and costs only $1. (This shuttle also stops at the Udvar-Hazy museum.) For more information call ☎ 877-777-2708 or go to **vatransit.org.**

BALTIMORE/WASHINGTON INTERNATIONAL THURGOOD MARSHALL AIRPORT There's a reason "Baltimore" comes first in the name; it's located only 10 miles south of Baltimore's Inner Harbor but about 35 miles—a 50-minute drive in the best of traffic conditions—from downtown D.C.

Although it is a true international port, BWI handles primarily domestic air traffic. It's a Southwest Airlines hub, which accounts for more than half the traffic. Its popularity as a lower-cost, high-efficiency airport has kept business booming; 638 passenger flights per day and more than 22 million passengers came through BWI in 2014. **Aviation.com** has named it one of the Top 10 easiest airports to get to, in great part because, despite its out-of-the-way location, it has public transportation links to Washington via both Amtrak and the Metro. (In contrast to Dulles's bad rating in the *Travel + Leisure* survey, BWI ranked sixth best, with high rankings for on-time flights and swift TSA screening.)

Cab fare from BWI to downtown starts at about $90 without tip. Metrobus B30 offers express service to the Greenbelt Metro station on the Green and Yellow Lines, leaving every 40 minutes seven days per week from about 6 a.m.–10 p.m. weekdays and 9 a.m.–10 p.m. weekends; the fare is $6 ($3 for seniors and disabled passengers), and the transfer onto the subway system is free. Greenbelt is also a stop for the MARC Camden Line (described below), which terminates at Union Station. For information, call ☎ 202-637-7000.

Amtrak has a designated station at BWI, and the free shuttle ride from the airport over to the station takes only a few minutes. The shuttle runs every 12 minutes from 5 a.m. to 1 a.m. and every 25 minutes from 1 a.m. to 5 a.m. (**bwiairport.com/en/travel/ground-transportation**). Depending on the time of day, day of week, and the particular train, one-way tickets to Union Station range from $13 to $39, but there is also an Amtrak stop at New Carrollton, which is a subway stop and might be closer to some Maryland destinations, such as College Park, home of the University of Maryland. Travel time from BWI to Union Station is about 30 minutes, and 15 minutes to New Carrollton; for information call ☎ 800-USA-RAIL (872-7245) or go to **amtrak.com**. MARC trains, which use the same stations as Amtrak, are inexpensive ($4 from Greenbelt to Union Station), but it's primarily a commuter service that is only available on weekdays and infrequently at that; for schedule information call ☎ 866-743-3682 or go to **mta.maryland.gov/marc-train**.

For more information on Baltimore/Washington International Airport, go to **bwiairport.com**.

ARRIVING BY TRAIN

UNION STATION, LOCATED NEAR CAPITOL HILL, is the major Amtrak terminal in Washington. Once inside the newly restored train station (which also houses restaurants, a food court, and plenty of shopping, in case you missed a meal or your best suit), you can jump on the Metro, located on the lower level. To reach cabs, limousines, buses, and open-air tour trolleys, walk through Union Station's magnificent Main Hall to the main entrance.

Amtrak also has a station adjacent to the King Street Metro Station in Alexandria, which might be more convenient for those Virginia-bound. For information and schedules for Amtrak, the national passenger train service, call ☎ 800-872-7245 (TTY 800-523-6590) or visit **amtrak.com**.

In addition to Amtrak, Washington's Union Station is served by the Maryland commuter system (MARC) and Virginia Railway

Express (VRE), which might be useful for those staying with family or friends farther out or who wish to make a day trip to some of the regional attractions.

MARC operates three lines: the Penn Line, connecting to Baltimore's Pennsylvania Station (the Amtrak terminal) with stops at the New Carrollton Amtrak/Metro station and BWI airport; the Camden Line, which ends in downtown Baltimore near the Inner Harbor and the Baltimore Orioles' and Ravens' stadiums; and the Brunswick Line, going northwest through the Montgomery County suburbs along the Potomac River into western Maryland with a stop at Harper's Ferry and an extension to Frederick, Maryland. Note, however, that MARC operates Monday through Friday only. For schedules and more information, go to **mta.maryland.gov/marc-train** or call ☎ 800-325-RAIL (TTY 410-539-3497).

VRE operates two commuter lines, one south to Fredericksburg and the other west to Manassas. Most service is inbound in the mornings and outbound in the afternoons, but some trains serve day-trippers as well. VRE also operates weekdays only; ☎ 703-684-1001 (TTY 703-684-0551) or 800-RIDE VRE (743-3873) or visit **vre.org**.

ARRIVING BY BUS

GREYHOUND MAY BE THE VETERAN on the block and have the most memorable slogan, but it's not up (yet) to the standards of some of the hipper modern bus lines, the routes aren't always direct, and it's not even always a bargain. If you happen to be traveling from New York, Philadelphia, or along the Northeast Corridor, you might also check into some of the new luxury bus lines, which offer free Wi-Fi, bottled water, and/or video screens. Tickets start as low as $1, and though that's obviously a very limited promotional rate, most tickets range from $20 to $50; departure and arrival points vary.

unofficial **TIP**
A convenient way to compare bus fares between Washington, D.C., Baltimore, New York, and Philadelphia is to visit **godcgo.com**, which monitors several bus lines, including Vamoose and Megabus.

As noted in Part 1: Planning Your Visit, the Greyhound bus terminal is near Union Station, which gives you fairly easy access to the subway or taxis, but if you have much more than a carry-on, it's something of a schlep. Coach lines along the corridor have various arrival points, all of them at or very near major Metro subway stops. The **BestBus** (**bestbus.com**) stops at Dupont Circle; **Washington Deluxe Bus** (**washny.com**), which makes a 20-minute pit stop and runs family-friendly movies, will drop you off near the Pentagon City, Dupont Circle, or Union Station Metro stops (the route depends on the time you leave New York); **Vamoose Bus** (**vamoosebus.com**) stops in Bethesda, Lorton, and Arlington. The gimmick at **BoltBus** (**boltbus.com**), which arrives at the Union Station subway station, is that the earlier you make reservations, the cheaper the seats—starting at $1—and if you buy eight trips, the ninth is free, though on average a fare between New York and D.C. is around $30. **Megabus** has many more destinations than cities in the Northeast corridor, some as far flung as Atlanta. Megabus terminates at Union Station, and fares can also dip to the bargain bin if you book several weeks ahead (**megabus.com**).

GETTING *Around*
WASHINGTON

THE LAY OF THE LAND

IN WASHINGTON, GEOGRAPHY ISN'T SO MUCH DESTINY as destination. The District of Columbia is a city of nearly 658,000 people, but metropolitan Washington (formally the National Capital Region), which includes Arlington County, the town of Alexandria, Prince William, Fairfax, and Loudoun Counties in Virginia, and the Maryland counties of Montgomery, Prince George's, and parts of Howard and Frederick, totals nearly 5.8 million residents. Rockville, a few miles north of the D.C. line, is Maryland's second-largest city, after Baltimore. Loudoun County, west of Fairfax County, is the fastest-growing and, according to some surveys, wealthiest county in the nation.

Although it isn't technically accurate, residents generally use "Washington" or "the DMV" (District, Maryland, and Virginia) to refer to the entire metropolitan region, and "D.C." or "the District" to indicate the central city.

Washington's most important geographical features, the Potomac River and, to a slightly lesser degree, the Anacostia River, can be challenges to both tourists and suburban commuters. The few bridges that cross the river are rush-hour bottlenecks; in town, there are a number of particular driving challenges—alternating one-way streets, streets that are two-way most of the time but one-way at certain hours, and, of course, the two blocks of Pennsylvania Avenue immediately in front of the White House, tourist central, that are closed to vehicles— that just add to the confusion. Not to mention constant construction obstructions and detours, accidents, official motorcades. . . .

On the other hand, while it's routinely exhausting to drive around Washington, the street layout—i.e., what tourists need to know on the ground—is more logical than it might seem. Washington's city planner, Pierre L'Enfant, was ahead of his time.

Many of Washington's streets, especially downtown, are arranged in a grid, with numbered streets running north–south and lettered streets going east–west. The Capitol is the grid's center (although if you look at the map, you'll see that the White House is much closer to the geographical heart), with North Capitol, South Capitol, and East Capitol Streets looking like spokes of a wheel protruding out in those directions. What would be West Capitol Street, in effect, is the green swath of the Mall.

What takes getting used to are the avenues—Wisconsin, Massachusetts, New York, New Hampshire, etc.—which are named after states and which cut across the grid diagonally; they tend to lead into traffic circles or park squares that, though picturesque on a map, are the nemesis of many drivers.

To make it worse, those diagonal state place names will disappear for the length of the square: Vermont Avenue temporarily vanishes at either end of McPherson Square; Connecticut Avenue runs toward, and away from, Farragut Square, and so on.

Our advice is to look at the map long enough to understand that underlying pattern—and to count the alphabet on your fingers once in a while. If you are trying to find an address on a lettered street, such as the National Building Museum, at 401 F Street NW, that's fairly obvious: it's on F Street between Fourth and Fifth Streets NW, so the International Spy Museum at 800 F Street NW is quite simply at the corner of Eighth and F Streets in the NW quadrant. (Those NWs are important because there can be multiple examples of the same address; there is, for instance, an Eighth and F Streets SE.)

On the other hand, if you are looking for an address on a numbered street, your digits will come in handy, especially after the 900s. Ford's Theatre at 511 Tenth Street NW is on Tenth between E and F Streets, E being the fifth street. However, there is no J Street NW.

Although longstanding legend has it that it was because Pierre L'Enfant so disliked U.S. Supreme Court Chief Justice John Jay that he refused to acknowledge even the homonym, it was actually because in those days the letters "I" and "J" were written so much alike that it would have caused confusion.

This situation remains impossible to understand even after living here nearly five decades, so don't expect to learn it on your first or even fifth visit. Fortunately, there are many signs that help point you to important attractions and sites, as well as lots of folks on the street who will gladly point you in the right direction. And, *of course,* you can use GPS to navigate (we natives do it all the time).

IT'S NOT JUST THE DRIVING, IT'S THE PARKING

IF WE HAVEN'T ALREADY MADE IT CLEAR why you don't want to drive around Washington, we'll point out the other problem: you'll have to park somewhere.

Though there are more than 17,000 street meters in D.C. alone, many only allow for 2 hours of parking (at up to $2 an hour), and police are quick to issue tickets for expired meters. Street meters and lots may now require you to pay via credit card or have a cell phone–debit charge account; worse, various neighborhoods use different companies for that, so you must be sure where you want to go. Some neighborhoods have "blocks" of parking slots to be paid for at a single machine; others have individual meters. Also, note that a lot of legal spaces turn illegal during rush hour; especially beware of this in Georgetown.

The lingering hope is to find a space after 5:30 p.m., when many *used* to become free. However, increasingly, meters in high-demand areas run until 7 p.m. or, in the "premium demand" zones of Bethesda, Arlington, Penn Quarter, Adams Morgan, Mid City, and Georgetown, until 10 p.m. Plus, if you are in a restricted zone rather than a garage, it is illegal to "add on" more money after your parking expires. Be sure to check the times on parking signs; they may be at the end of the block. Parking tickets will shock you—they usually start at $40.

Note: Unlike many jurisdictions, the District of Columbia enforces meter fares on Saturdays. And if your car is in a traffic lane at rush hour, no matter how much you put in that box, you'll be towed, so don't even think about it. Thousands of vehicles are towed each year for rush-hour violations alone.

Parking garages charge anywhere from $12 to $25 a day or $10 an hour, and many of those are moving toward automated or smartphone payment as well. Valet parking for dinner at a hot spot can easily cost you $20. In some residential neighborhoods, such as Georgetown and Adams Morgan, parking is restricted to 2 hours, unless you have a residential parking permit on your windshield.

Every jurisdiction assesses fair fares differently. For instance, in Arlington, there are color-coded short- and long-term meters—allowing everything from only a half hour up to 10—which cost $1.25 up to 4 hours and $1 an hour, respectively. At least you can use either cash or credit by paying at the Parkmobile stations. Check **transportation.arlingtonva.us/parking** for more information on garages, meters, and fees.

Parking restrictions in most regions are only lifted on Federal holidays or Sundays. You can use your smartphone to pay for all meters in the District of Columbia if you sign up with **parkmobile.com**. Download the app for meters in Bethesda, Wheaton, and Silver Spring in Montgomery County at **mobile-now.com**. Our best advice: Once you have chosen your accommodations, ask the hotel staff or the parking attendant what method of parking is nearest. But before you leave your car anywhere, read the signs.

ALTERNATIVE WHEELS

IF YOU FOLLOW OUR ADVICE TO AVOID DRIVING to Washington but really want to take a day trip or go outside the mass transit circuit, you can rent your wheels without the rent-a-car counter. If you are already a member of the Zipcar auto-sharing nation (which allows you to rent by the hour as well as by the day), there are dozens of pickup locations; go to **zipcar.com** for details.

unofficial **TIP**
If you prefer that someone else provide the pedal power, check the tourist hot spots around the Mall and nightlife neighborhoods for a pedicab; to schedule a pickup or even a tour, contact DC Pedicab (☎ 202-345-8065, **dcpedi cab.com**) or National Pedicabs (☎ 202-269-9090, **nationalpedicabs.com**).

There is also a popular bike-sharing network called Capital Bikeshare, with more than 350 stations around the metropolitan area, especially near subway stations. You can join for a month online, but you can also get a one-day ($8) or three-day ($17) membership right at the kiosk. Once you're a member, you get the first 30 minutes of each trip free, with various hourly rates thereafter; go to **capitalbikeshare.com** for usage fees. For information on suggested commuter routes, maps, and expanded bike lanes in Washington go to **ddot.dc.gov/bike** or **bikewashington .org**. However, be aware that as yet only a few dedicated bike lanes have been put in place downtown, and even locals find them tricky.

The Metro transit system is also bike-friendly. There are free bicycle racks at most Metro parking lots (available on a first-come basis), but you can actually take your bike—classic two-wheelers only, no tandems, etc.—on the subway at non–rush hours during the week (rush hours are 7–10 a.m. and 4–7 p.m.) and all day on weekends and *most* holidays. (Super-crowded days, such as the Fourth of July, are a no-go.) Use the first and last cars only. Children under 16 with bikes must be accompanied by a person above the age of 18. For more information go to **wmata.com/getting_around/bike_ride**.

TAKING THE METRO:
Just Do It

LEAVE THE DRIVING TO METRO

EVEN IF YOU DO HAVE A CAR, adopt the park-and-ride method. The Metrorail system—nearly always called the Metro, though that refers to the Metrobus system as well—connects the outer suburbs to the city with 117 miles of track and 91 stations throughout the Washington area, with more stations under construction. It's the second-busiest system in the country after New York City's, transporting about 700,000 passengers every day, and it's fully accessible. Each of the six color-coded lines—Red, Blue, Green, Yellow, Silver, and Orange—run from the outlying counties through downtown D.C. The Silver line, Metrorail's most recent addition, runs west from the District (piggybacking on some Orange Line stations) to Tysons Corner, with future stations planned in Reston and eventually Dulles Airport.

It's a relatively clean, generally safe, and efficient system that saves visitors time, money, and energy. The trains are fairly quiet, with a mix of seats and straphangers, and heating and air-conditioning that is relatively reliable. The stations are clean, if somewhat stark, with signature arching concrete panel ceilings; because in many stations the electrified tracks run along the wall and the platform is in the middle, this helps protect the walls from graffiti. The wide-open design also explains why Metro is less susceptible to the sort of pickpocketing and petty crime often associated with subways: there are few places for thieves to hide, especially with the extensive closed-circuit TV and car-to-operator intercoms. Metro also has its own police/security force.

Trains operate Monday–Thursday, 5 a.m.–midnight; Friday, 5 a.m.–3 a.m.; Saturday, 7 a.m.–3 a.m.; and Sunday, 7 a.m.–midnight. (Holiday schedules vary; check the schedule at **wmata.com**.) During peak hours (weekdays 5 a.m.–9:30 a.m. and 3 p.m.–7 p.m.), trains run every 4–6 minutes; off-peak hours, the wait averages 12 minutes and can go to 30 minutes late at night and on weekends. Fortunately, the stations now have signs indicating when the next train is expected. Check the brown poles for a list of stops that a train/line makes to make sure you're on the right one. Currently, the system is undergoing expanded track work and repairs, so be prepared to adjust your plans around possible station and rail closures.

Many, though unfortunately not all, street signs in Washington indicate the direction and number of blocks to the nearest Metro station. Station entrances are identified by brown columns with an "M" on all four sides, and the newer ones are marked with a combination of colored stripes in red, yellow, orange, green, silver, or blue that indicate the line or lines serving that station. (The pylon at the entrance nearest the elevator will have a wheelchair symbol on it.)

Because most stations, especially in D.C., are underground, passengers usually have to descend to the mezzanine to ride, buy passes, or add money. Stations have stairs, escalators, and elevators; the escalators in particular have been dogged in recent years with mechanical troubles, and the system is undergoing a vast maintenance and improvement program, but breakdowns are not infrequent. If an elevator is out at a particular station, wheelchair users can ride to the next station, and shuttle service will be available.

 FOR TRIVIA FREAKS, Washington's Metro system might be a tourist attraction in its own right: The Wheaton station boasts the Western

Hemisphere's longest single-span escalators, 230-foot-long behe-
moths that take 2¾ minutes to ride. The Forest Glen station, nearly
200 feet underground, doesn't even have escalators, only elevators.

First-time visitors should get an official Metro Visitor's Kit, which
includes a pocket-size Metro map, sites of interest near Metrorail
stations, and hours and fare information. You can download the kit,
along with Metrobus routes for the District, Virginia, and Maryland,
at **wmata.com/getting_around/visitor_info/visitorkit.cfm**. The Metro
Pocket Guide and map is available for downloading in English and
five additional languages; several others can be read in translation on
the website. If you prefer to have it snail-mailed, call ☎ 888-METRO-
INFO (638-7646) or 202-962-2773, but you need to allow about
three weeks for delivery. However, there is a service kiosk just inside
every station entrance, and the attendants will be happy to help you
sort out your directions. Or ask a local; many will volunteer assistance
if you look bewildered.

You can also purchase Metro SmarTrip cards in advance at **wmata
.com/fares/purchase/store**; they are available in denominations of
$10 and $30. Other online options include one-day passes for $14.50
and a couple of seven-day plans (inner-city for $36 and longer-range
trips for $59.25). There is even an all-access monthly option for $237
for a 28-day pass. (For more information on SmarTrip cards, including how to purchase them, see pages 119–120.)

There are several rules you must follow. Most international visitors
(and New Yorkers) are used to being able to eat and drink on their
subway systems, but consumption of any sort is illegal in Metro stations, buses, and trains. You may carry water or coffee in a mug or a
burger in a bag, but keep it closed. Smoking is also illegal. You must
use earphones for music and/or video devices. Also, observe the signs
for seating reserved for seniors and disabled riders. If you see a parent
with a child or a pregnant woman, please offer your seat.

Warning: Do not shove your arm between subway car doors as
they are closing. These do not respond like elevator doors and *will
not reopen* because of the obstruction. Make sure you don't let a
purse strap or briefcase get caught, either, because you're likely to see
it dragged away.

And though it is not a true rule, there is something that will make
you an object of the fury of hundreds of disgruntled fellow travelers:
standing on the left side of the escalators. Washingtonians are divided
into those who stand on the escalators—*on the right*—and those who
walk up on the left. If you block the left half of the moving stairs, you
are asking for a nasty remark at the very least.

Lastly, although Metro in general is very safe, it is a major people-
mover, which means you may have to endure loud or rambunctious
teenagers, sports fans, theater- or concert-goers, etc. There are isolated

incidents of violence at downtown stations, and although these are rare, you should never be taken by surprise. Don't flash cash, or that iPhone around without having a firm grip. Keep your purse tucked under your arm and zippered. If you feel concerned for your safety, move closer to other passengers, or get out of the train and take the next one.

PARKING AT THE METRO

THERE ARE A FEW THINGS TO KNOW before you drive to the Metro station. First, only 42 stations have parking lots, and most of those are outside the Beltway. (All have bike and motorcycle parking as well.)

None of the 91 stations accept cash at the parking lot exit; you must have a SmarTrip card or credit card to get your car out of the lot on weekdays. Occasionally, the gate will go up, but it's best to assume you're going to pay. (A major exception is Grosvenor/Strathmore; whenever there is a concert or event at Strathmore Hall or concert center, the bars go up for 30 minutes after a show.) Parking fees vary slightly, depending on the station, but are generally $4.50–$6 a day, except on Saturdays, Sundays, and federal holidays, when you can get out of jail (so to speak) for free.

Most Metro lots and garages have close-in areas of parking spaces marked "Reserved." These require a monthly permit but are only reserved until 10 a.m., after which you may grab an empty space. Don't try to slip in too early; Metro police keep an eye out for that, and you'll likely have competition from locals.

There are a limited number of metered spaces that you may be able to grab that allow you to pay in coin (follow the "Short-Term Parking" signs), but these are usually limited to 2 hours and cost $1 per hour. In a few cases, such as Grosvenor, Rockville and Twinbrook, there are meters on the streets and in lots just outside the main parking lot as well; though these have longer allowable hours, they are still $1 for 60 minutes. Even trickier, these meters accept only quarters and $1 coins.

Very few stations allow multiday or longer-term parking (up to 10 days): Franconia–Springfield, Greenbelt, Huntington, and Wiehle–Reston East are all likely farther out than most tourists will be staying, but you could park there and take the Metro into town with your luggage.

PREPARING, AND SQUARING, THE FARE

METRO EMPLOYS A FARE SYSTEM BASED ON DISTANCE, unlike New York, for example, where all trips cost the same regardless of how many stops you pass. One-way fare is a minimum of $2.15 and a maximum of $5.90 at rush hour, and a minimum of $1.75 and a maximum of $3.60 at non–rush hour times. You are required to buy a SmarTrip card for an initial cost of $10, even if you only use it once.

The SmarTrip card costs $2 upfront but entitles you to $8 worth of travel. You can recharge the SmarTrip card at every Metro station. Everyone over the age of 4 must have a fare pass; up to two toddlers per paying adult ride free.

Peak fares are in effect 5 a.m.–9:30 a.m. and 3 p.m.–7 p.m. weekdays and from midnight to closing on weekends. Fares between specific stations are listed at the bottom of the color-coded system maps throughout the station, along with the estimated time of travel.

Metro stations have vending machines for SmarTrip cards, but you can also purchase SmarTrip cards (though not the seniors' version) at Washington-area CVS pharmacies and many Safeway and Giant grocery stores. SmarTrip cards are the size of a credit card and have an electronic chip rather than a strip; the screens read out the balance as you go in and come out.

Though the vending machines can seem rather imposing in their long, square-shouldered ranks, buying a pass is actually fairly obvious: you stick in cash or a credit card, and out comes the SmarTrip card that you will use to get in and out of the subway. (We find it useful to consult our children, who are born to operate technology and seem to understand the directions much faster than adults often do.)

Notice that we said in *and* out. If you are used to a subway system that has a one-price fare for all trips, you may be in the habit of stashing the ticket in your pocket or even disposing of it once you're on board. Here you must hold onto it; otherwise, you may ride forever 'neath the streets and never return. (Not really, of course, but it will be a pain.)

To buy a fare pass from the vending machine, you start with the large orange circle marked, not surprisingly, "1." Next to that are buttons that point to lighted choices on a screen (pretty much like an ATM); if you're using cash, the machine allows you to adjust the actual value—i.e., after your initial purchase of the $10 SmarTrip card, to add value, you may insert change or dollar bills into the machine, and then choose the amount you want on your card. But be forewarned that all change is distributed back to you in coins not dollar bills.

Like all machines that accept paper money, these occasionally turn snarky, spitting back bills they don't like, so use new, stiffer greenbacks whenever you can or try smoothing wrinkled bills before inserting them. You can save yourself both time and aggravation by inserting or charging $10 or $20 at a time, which means you're buying a ticket good for several trips at least.

SmarTrip Cards

For the past several years, Washington-area transit authorities have been working toward a unified system for paying fares. SmarTrip is already a mainstay of the subway system; can be used to exit any Metro station parking lot; and can be used on any Metrobus and nearly every regional bus and shuttle system (including the DC Circulator, described on pages 123–124). The card itself costs $2 in the beginning, but it can be reused indefinitely, which could be a great convenience to business travelers who return frequently or those who have family members in the Washington area. If you register the card when you buy it—and if you buy it online or by mail, it is automatically registered—you can replace a lost card for $2, and all the money that was still on it will be restored. You can also register your card by going to **smartrip.wmata.com.**

All Metrobuses are equipped with SmarTrip readers that work the same way—touch and go—except that you only touch it once and the fare is automatically counted. If you have used the card at a Metrorail station or other Metrobus within the past 2 hours, the SmarTrip box automatically registers your fare as a transfer, and the second trip is free. And anytime you use the SmarTrip card on Metrobus or another related shuttle, you save 20 cents over the cash price.

How to Buy a Metro SmarTrip Card

- Metro farecards are like debit cards; they can be recharged and reloaded.
- You may buy a SmarTrip card with a credit card or cash at the Blue "Dispense" machines in the station.
- Your initial purchase costs $10 upfront, and $2 go toward the purchase of the card, while $8 goes toward your future travel within the Metro system (you can also start with $30 with $28 left to travel on).
- SmarTrip cards can be used to pay at Metro parking lots and on all regional buses. They enable discounted bus transfers too (VRE, Circulator, Dash, RideOn, Fairfax Connector, TheBus, Light Rail, Art, etc.).
- To use your SmarTrip card, touch the entrance emblem at the gate, and touch your exit at the departing gate.
- One card per person only; you can't pass a card back to another passenger.
- All passengers need a SmarTrip card, except for children under 5 years old who may ride free with a paying adult.
- Any balance left over can be reimbursed by sending in your SmarTrip card to WMATA (less the $2 fee for the card).

For more information about SmarTrip, visit **wmata.com/fares /smartrip.**

NEGOTIATING THE STATION

NOW THAT YOU HAVE YOUR SmarTrip card in hand, you can pass the gate into the Metro station proper. Walk up to one of the waist-high gates with the green "Enter" light and white arrow (red-light turnstiles marked "Do Not Enter" do not work both ways) and press your card against the magnetic reader on the right side of the gate (clearly marked with an image of the card).

Once you're inside the gate, there will be escalators with the name of the end station indicating which platform your train will be on. Most stations have a single, middle platform, though some have dual platforms framing the tracks. You can confirm that you're on the correct side of the platform by reading the list of stations printed on the pylons located there. (The Wheaton and Forest Glen stations are the anomalies, so far underground that they have individual tunnels for the north- and southbound trains, so you have less chance of getting on the wrong train.) The route and the appropriate stations are marked with the route color; if there are two routes that use that station but diverge farther on, make sure the station you want to get off at is marked with the correct color, or both.

If you do find that you are headed in the wrong direction, simply reverse course by walking across the platform, if it is in the middle, or go up the escalator over and down; just don't go through the turnstile. The computer doesn't know if you're direction-challenged or not.

Some lines have shorter internal routes at rush hour, so that the busiest stations get more service. If you are staying in Bethesda, for example, you can take a Red Line train marked either Grosvenor–Strathmore or Shady Grove because both are beyond Bethesda. If you're going to Rockville, however, you may have to disembark at Grosvenor–Strathmore and wait for a Shady Grove–bound train. Also, some stations are served by more than one line—both the Blue and Yellow Lines will bring you from Reagan National Airport into town; and the Orange and Blue Lines, Silver and Orange Lines, and Yellow and Green Lines run together for several stops. Check the map or ask the agent.

Above the platform are electronic signs on either track side that tell you how long the wait will be for the next several trains—the estimations are pretty accurate—and how far each particular train is going (Grosvenor vs. Shady Grove, Glenmont vs. Silver Spring, etc.) "Approaching" means the train has left the previous station and is within about a minute of arriving; "arriving" means just that. Trains

*un*official **TIP**
You can use the internal routes to your advantage. For instance, if you get on an inbound train at Rockville that is SRO, get off at Grosvenor–Strathmore and wait for a train that originates there; you'll have plenty of seats to choose from. Headed back in bad weather? Get off at Medical Center, which is underground, and await the next train minus the cold and damp.

*un*official **TIP**
As a train approaches a station, lights embedded in the floor along the granite edge of the platform begin flashing. As the train comes out of the tunnel, look for a sign over the front windshield that states the train's line (Blue, Red, Green, Orange, or Yellow) and sometimes the destination. The terminus, but not the color, is also shown on the side of the train.

go in one direction only (like cars, on the right side forward), so you can tell which way your train is coming.

All trains have live operators who announce the next station over a PA system and give information for transferring to other lines, but you can't always hear them over the din and the static. The newer cars have electronic signs at the front and rear that list the next station. Also, those large station signs on the walls over the tracks are visible through the car windows, so if you check the map and see which stop is just before the one where you want to get off, you'll have a couple of minutes to gather your belongings (or kids) and make your way toward the doors.

Directions are always given as if you are facing forward, even though some seats face the side or the back. So if the conductor says, "Doors opening on the right," he or she means the right if you are facing forward. If you can't hear what the conductor is saying, watch the crowd shifting to one side or the other.

*un**official* **TIP**
Transfers between route lines are free but usually require going up or down a level. A straight-ahead arrow means go forward, but an upward arrow at an angle means look for an escalator.

When you get off the train, in most stations, you will have a choice of turning left or right to an escalator, and the signs are not always terribly instructive. At the Smithsonian station, for example, the choices are "The Mall" (which is almost certainly the one you want) and "Independence Avenue," which means you tunnel beneath the street and come up over on the side with federal buildings. That's not too hard to figure out. At Dupont Circle, on the other hand, one says "Q Street"—which brings you out north of the circle—and the other says "Dupont Circle," which lets you up south of it. So if you aren't sure of the exit in advance, it might be a good idea to ask the kiosk attendant at the first station so you don't have to go through the turnstile before discovering you're taking the long way around. But if worse comes to worst, you'll be only a few blocks away from your intended destination.

Remember, you'll have to use your SmarTrip card to exit. Touch the SmarTrip card to the image on the inside of the gate. The lighted sign on the turnstile will flash to indicate how much the fare cost and how much money is left on your card. You will just walk through and out. If you don't have enough money on your SmarTrip card, the gate will not open and you'll need to go to the Exitfare machines inside the station (they look pretty much like a farecard vending machine). Press the SmarTrip to the reader light, and the digital readout will tell you how much more money you need to exit the station. You'll be able to add on as much as you like, but note: Exitfare machines only accept cash. To add value with a credit card, you'll have to go back to the main farecard machines. If you don't have enough money, consult the train station operator. He or she will grudgingly accompany you through the turnstile to the machines and make you re-touch your card to pay with a credit card.

Before you enter Washington's Metro Station, you may find it useful to download Metro's Trip Planner, an app that helps you determine where you want to go and how much it will cost. It announces upcoming departures at various stations, informs you of elevator or escalator outages, indicates when the next bus is coming, and describes any disruptions that are ongoing. By 2017, Metro plans to make it possible to pay with your smartphone and eliminate SmarTrip cards altogether.

METROBUS AND OTHER BUS SYSTEMS

WASHINGTON'S EXTENSIVE BUS SYSTEM, known as **Metrobus,** serves Georgetown, downtown, and the suburbs, but with 400 routes and more than 1,500 buses, Metrobus is complicated. However, it can be a good option if you're trying to reach places that don't have a Metro station. You should consult your hotel concierge about buses to places like Georgetown, the National Cathedral, and H Street Corridor and have him or her write drown your route for you.

Similarly, while most of Washington's suburbs have good subsidiary bus or shuttle systems that connect to the subway and the District, they're probably too complicated, unless you are staying with friends who can show you the nearest stop.

However, the **DC Circulator** is the most useful bus for tourists, especially those staying downtown or doing sustained sightseeing. These comfortable, convenient buses arrive at their stops every 10 minutes, so you won't need a timetable (except during extremely busy times such as the Cherry Blossom Festival, when downtown traffic is legendary). To board the bus, look for the station signs posted on the sidewalk. Confirm that this bus is going in the direction you want to go. You're allowed to bring strollers on the buses if there's enough room, but you must fold it up when a person using a wheelchair needs to board, as they have priority. The cost of a single trip is $1 in cash, either dollars or coins, but exact change is required. Seniors and riders with disabilities pay 50 cents, or ride free if transferring; children age 4 and under ride free. Circulator buses also accept SmarTrip cards. Another option is to purchase an unlimited-trip pass before you board: a one-day pass costs $3, a three-day pass is $7, and a weekly pass is $11. Visit **commuterdirect.com** to purchase a ticket in advance.

The machines take change or credit cards but no paper bills. There are ticket machines all along the way (and also at the Gallery Place,

unofficial **TIP**
Circulator stop signs are also marked with a fish-shaped red-and-gold logo, while Metrobus stop markers are red, white, and blue. They are often, but not always, at the same intersections. Streetcars on the DC Trolley system resemble the Circulator buses.

Waterfront, and Mount Vernon Square–Convention Center Metro stations). For route maps and more information, go to **dccirculator.com.**

Look for a map published after 2015 to see the latest shuttle routes. In mid-2015 Circulator added a National Mall route (red) that loops around, connecting passengers to key tourist attractions. It originates at Union Station and then stops at the National Gallery of Art, National Museum of American History, Washington Monument, Holocaust Memorial Museum, Thomas Jefferson Memorial, Martin Luther King Jr. Memorial, and the Lincoln Memorial. It continues to the Vietnam Memorial, the World War II Memorial, Smithsonian Visitor Center, National Air and Space Museum, the U.S. Capitol, and then returns to Union Station. You can get on and off at any of these stops and ride for the two hours for free after your initial payment if you use a SmarTrip card.

The DC Circulator's yellow route connects Union Station to Georgetown by way of the Washington Convention Center and K Street NW; the section between downtown (17th and K Streets NW) and Georgetown runs until midnight weekdays and 2 a.m. Fridays and Saturdays. The blue route travels between Dupont Circle and Rosslyn via Georgetown, primarily along M Street NW; and the green route connects McPherson Square (i.e., the Farragut North Metro station) with Woodley Park and Adams Morgan via the trendy 14th Street area and has late-night service (until 3:30 a.m. Fridays and Saturdays and midnight the rest of the week). The purple route, which connects Union Station to the Navy Yard by way of Capitol Hill, stays open late when the Nationals play a home game.

These bright-red Circulator buses, with silver and yellow stripes on the side, are a bargain, and visitors can sign up for Live Twitter Alerts that announce route changes or service disruption on @DCCirculator.

TAXIS *and*
CAR SERVICES

MAJOR WASHINGTON TAXI COMPANIES	
Action Taxi ☎ 301-840-1000	**Red Top** (Arlington and Alexandria) ☎ 703-522-3333
Barwood (Montgomery County) ☎ 301-984-1900	**Washington Flyer** ☎ 202-572-taxi
Diamond Cab ☎ 202-387-2221	**Yellow Cab** (general) ☎ 202-544-1212

For information on cab fares, visit taxifarefinder.com.

WASHINGTON TAXIS ARE PLENTIFUL and relatively cheap; there are more than 150 companies registered with the District of Columbia Taxicab Commission. Many companies also have wheelchair-accessible vans, but you should reserve those a day in advance (and get a confirmation number).

In the District of Columbia, meter fares start at $3.25 for the first few blocks (1/8 mile), then a little over $2 per mile; additional passengers are $1 (up to $3) and baggage in the trunk is 50 cents per piece.

You'll never mistake Pennsylvania Avenue for Park Avenue: Despite the rainbow of names among various cab companies, even yellow, D.C. cabs are now required to have a uniform paint scheme—a rich red, matching the Circulator buses, with a gray swoosh across the side and the company name in black. But you'll still spot Barwood blue, Orange orange, etc. in the suburbs.

Various surcharges may be imposed for a driver waiting ($25 per hour), being sent away without use, when gasoline prices go up, etc. Within the District of Columbia, the maximum fare is $19 absent emergency add-ons (25% in snow emergencies); children under age 6 ride free. The suburban taxi companies have their own rates; if you expect to use them, it is probably a good idea to call or go online to see what they are. D.C. cabs are required to have charge-card machines installed; most suburban cabs have them as well, but it wouldn't hurt to specify if you're calling for a reservation.

Cabbies can pick up other fares as long as the original passenger isn't taken more than five blocks out of the way of the original destination. That's good news if you're the second or third rider and it's raining; it's not so hot if you're the original passenger and are trying to catch a train.

Washington is currently saturated with **Uber** cabs and car services. Download the **Uber.com** app on your phone to set up an account, which includes submitting your credit card number. There are three levels of service. Low-cost **UberX** service involves rides in everyday cars driven by individuals. **UberTaxi** service charges more but involves a professional driver and larger vehicle. You can select a Black Car, with its private driver in a high-end sedan, guaranteed to arrive within minutes of your request. When you're traveling with a group up to six people, consider ordering the UberSUV. If you're looking for a stylish ride, there's also **UberLux,** with a fleet of luxury vehicles with prices to match.

Using Uber involves providing your location for pick up and your destination upon your request. At that time, you will see a range of pricing you can expect to pay for that ride. You can include the tip on your payment, with options of 15–20%. During periods of intense demand, rates may fluctuate, and if tolls or fees are required by the city government, these are passed onto the passenger.

THINGS *the* NATIVES
Already KNOW

WHERE THERE'S SMOKE, THERE'S FINES

IF YOU HAVEN'T ALREADY REALIZED IT, WASHINGTON—the District of Columbia in particular—is predominantly public territory. And since the federal government and the surrounding jurisdictions (even tobacco-proud Virginia) have finally conceded that indoor tobacco smoke is as hard on the human body as it is on art, archival materials, and even infrastructure, smoking is prohibited in all public facilities, including, but not limited to: federal offices; the Smithsonian museums (and all other museums as well) and major memorials; Metrorail and Metrobus, as well as most smaller transit services; performing arts venues and cinemas, the Verizon Center, and other indoor arenas; airports and train terminals; stores and shopping malls; restaurants; and hotel lobbies (and most hotel restrooms). Most open-air facilities—football and baseball stadiums, for instance—have restricted, designated smoking areas. Consequently, if you are a habitual smoker, you'll need to factor that in to your itineraries, or at least calculate where and when you can light up.

In February 2015, the District of Columbia, approved their citizens', age 21 and older, right to possess small amounts (2 ounces or less) of marijuana. Residents are also allowed to grow up to six plants in their home and transfer, not sell, up to 1 ounce of marijuana to another person 21 or older. They may also possess drug paraphernalia such as bongs and rolling papers; however, it's still a crime to sell marijuana and to smoke it anywhere other than inside the home. This means the people you may see smoking pot on the street are not allowed to do so and are committing a crime. You may see an occasional daredevil walking with a joint, but it's not recommended. Marijuana use is not legal in Maryland or Virginia, but possession of 10 grams or less in Maryland will incur only a small fine, and possession of 10–50 grams is a misdemeanor. In contrast, Virginia's laws are much tougher, and anyone in possession of less than half an ounce is eligible for a misdemeanor charge involving up to 30 days in jail and a $500 fine. Above half an ounce, and in Virginia, you could be charged with distribution, which is a felony. Hookah smoking, especially with the large number of restaurants serving Middle Eastern cuisine, is available in many D.C. and Virginia restaurants.

TIPPING

IS THE TIP YOU NORMALLY LEAVE AT HOME appropriate in Washington? Probably, but bear in mind that while a tip is a reward for good service, Washington waiters in particular tend to be a bit spoiled, so be sure you're making a point if you tip lightly. Also, consider your hotel's schedule: If your room is serviced twice a day, it would be nice to leave a tip for both the day and night staff—and it might earn you extra attention. Following are some general guidelines, but in truth, we recommend the high end, especially if you are hanging out at one of the area's retro–cocktail–renaissance bars. Many of these mixologists have become celebrities in their own right, so if you want to command their attention, expect to flash the bigger bucks.

- **Porters, redcaps, and bellmen** At least $1–$2 per bag and $5 for a lot of baggage

- **Cab drivers** 15–20% of the fare; add an extra dollar if the cabbie does a lot of luggage handling

- **Valet parking** $1–$2   • **Waiters** 20% of the pretax bill

- **Bartenders** 10–15% of the pretax bill   • **Chambermaids** $2–$3 per day

- **Checkroom attendants in restaurants or theaters** $1 per garment

- **Shoeshine guys** $2 for shoes, $3–$4 for boots

TELEPHONES

THE WASHINGTON AREA IS SERVED BY SEVERAL AREA CODES: ☎ 202 inside the District; ☎ 301 and ☎ 240 for the Maryland suburbs; ☎ 703 and ☎ 571 for the closer Northern Virginia suburbs across the Potomac River; ☎ 540 for the outer Virginia suburbs; and ☎ 410 and ☎ 443 for Baltimore, Annapolis, and the ocean resorts. The Delaware ocean resorts use the ☎ 302 area code. All calls require the full 10-digit number; depending on your phone or calling plan, you may or may not have to dial 1 first. Most pay phone calls are 50¢—if you can still find one to call from.

RESTROOMS

THE UNOFFICIAL GUIDE FAMILY IS LEGENDARILY ON GUARD for travelers with small bladders and those who've been recently potty-trained. When we enter a marble edifice, we're not just scrutinizing the layout, the flow of the crowd, and the aesthetics: we're checking for the nearest public restrooms.

So how does Washington rate in the restroom department? Really well. That's because of the huge number of museums, monuments, federal office buildings, restaurants, bars, department stores, and hotels that cover the city, nearly all of which have clean and conveniently located restrooms.

Leading any list of great restroom locations should be the National Air and Space Museum on the Mall. For women who claim there's no justice in the world when it comes to toilet parity, consider this: there are three times as many women's restrooms as there are men's restrooms. "And the men don't seem to notice," says a female Smithsonian employee who works at the information desk.

Other facilities of note on the Mall include those at the National Gallery of Art, the Arthur M. Sackler Gallery, the Hirshhorn Museum and Sculpture Garden, and the National Museum of African Art. At the Arts and Industries Building, facilities are located far away from the front entrance (which means they aren't as frequently, um, frequented). The restrooms in The Castle are easier to find and also usually not very crowded—perhaps because tourists tend to go there earlier in the day.

Nearly all the monuments have restrooms equipped for wheelchair users, including the Martin Luther King Jr., Lincoln, and Jefferson Memorials (the last two are downstairs by the museum stores) and the Washington Monument (in the ticket lodge). The restrooms at the National World War II Memorial on the Mall and the FDR Memorial are acceptable. The U.S. Capitol Visitor Center has more than two dozen restrooms, and there are more at the Ellipse Visitor Pavilion, Sylvan Theater, Botanic Garden, and White House Visitor Center. There is a stand-alone facility in Constitution Gardens. During events, port-a-potties are set up temporarily in various locations. Ask a national park ranger for specific directions while on the National Mall.

Downtown hotels, restaurants, department stores, coffee shops, and bars are good bets. You won't find restrooms in Metro stations, although a few stations are located in complexes that do provide restrooms, including Union Station, Metro Center, Farragut North, Friendship Heights, and L'Enfant Plaza; ask the attendant which exit to take.

THE HOMELESS

YOU MAY BE TAKEN ABACK BY THE NUMBER of homeless persons in Washington. Street corners and medians are filled with women and men, asking for money. All along town, you will see people sleeping in blankets and sleeping bags, their possessions piled up next to them. Occasionally, drivers are approached at stoplights by people carrying cardboard signs reading "Homeless—Will Work for Food." Many Metro exits are populated by people begging for money. Although, there are more than 4,000 people living in D.C. homeless shelters, the number of homeless people continues to climb, partially due to the high cost of living in the Metro area.

Many are lifelong D.C. residents who are poor, according to homeless advocacy groups. A disproportionate number are minorities and people with disabilities, mental or physical. And despite any stereotypes, studies show that the homeless have lower conviction rates for violent crimes than the population at large. Whatever you decide, you should be polite; look the person in the eye and say calmly that you can't help right now. We believe that most of these people are what they claim to be: homeless. If you want to give, carry a few dollar bills in outside pockets so that it's not necessary to open a purse or wallet to donate. Just be alert. All the people you encounter on the street are strangers. They are most likely harmless, but they might be unstable.

Following are some recommendations for staying safe from the Metropolitan Police Department: Don't engage in lengthy conversations with a stranger, stay in well-lit areas, keep valuables close, don't walk alone at night, don't wear headphones while walking, and avoid carrying large sums of cash.

CRIME IN WASHINGTON

TWENTY-FIVE YEARS AGO, Washington was slammed as the "Murder Capital of the United States"—even then a slight exaggeration. Since then, however, many of the neighborhoods that were associated with violence have been redeveloped and gentrified; and networks of surveillance cameras have been mounted in high-crime areas. Violent crime and property crime rates in D.C. have dropped by nearly half since 1995, and local law enforcement officials call Washington very safe for tourists.

In fact, there are so many law enforcement layers, public and private, that the District might well be the most closely patrolled 68 square miles in the United States. In addition to the Metropolitan Police Department, there are the U.S. Park Police, which patrols all the monuments and parks, including the Mall; the U.S. Capitol Police, which has jurisdiction over not only the Capitol itself but the 20-square-block area around it; the Secret Service, which patrols the area around the White House, including the Treasury Building, as well as the Vice-President's residence and foreign embassies and diplomats; the Marshals Service, which ensures the safe conduct of the federal judiciary, jurors, and any judicial proceedings; and the D.C. Protective Services, which guards all city buildings and agencies. The Metro transit system has its own police force. Many federal agencies—the FBI, the ICE, the TSA, and the now-famous NCIS, among others—have their own armed officers. On top of that, many museums hire their own police and security guards—the Smithsonian has its own federally trained police force patrolling inside the buildings and around the grounds—as do most embassies, corporations, and international associations. (Which is why you should get in the habit of traveling light and security gate–friendly.) And in case you somehow missed the tragic shooting at Navy Yard, the area's SWAT and special units have mutual aid agreements.

Aside from all the officers on the ground (and horseback, bicycles, motorcycles, Segways, etc.), a network of security cameras has been added around the Mall by the Park Police, and the Metropolitan Police has installed a similar network in high-traffic areas, such as Georgetown, the U.S. Capitol, Union Station, and around the White House. And none of that even takes into account the ever-upgraded high-tech security measures that have become standard since 9/11.

Over the last decade, a new force of uniformed employees, armed only with clipboards, walkie talkies, and perhaps litter sticks, has been making downtown D.C. both safer and cleaner: downtown SAM (Safety, Hospitality and Maintenance) Teams, easily recognized by their bright red, white, and blue attire. Maintenance staff work a fairly common business day, but the safety/hospitality staffers are around until 10 p.m. Monday–Saturday and 7 p.m. on Sundays. Visitors are encouraged to ask for directions, get a restaurant recommendation, or obtain directions to a landmark. If you are alone, one will escort you to the nearest subway, bus, etc.

Note: It is legal to carry concealed handguns in Virginia, even in bars, though some restaurants and malls, including Potomac Mills, have opted to refuse them. In theory, those bar patrons who are packing aren't supposed to be putting it away, but that's hard to enforce. Neither Maryland nor the District recognizes out-of-state gun licenses or permits; the District does not issue any unless the person has received the required amount of firearms training.

Regardless of the level of security, random violence and street crime are facts of life in any large city—or subway system. You just need to be reasonably cautious and consider preventive measures that will keep you out of harm's way, as well as an escape plan just in case. Don't make yourself attractive as a target—or, put another way, make potential assailants see you as a bad risk. Good general strategies include:

- **Don't play solitaire.** You're always less appealing as a target if you're with other people.

- **Be alert, and always have at least one of your arms and hands free.** Thieves gravitate toward people who are staring at a smartphone (or map, marking you as preoccupied *and* unfamiliar with the territory) or encumbered by luggage or packages. Billfolds are harder to snatch from a front trouser or breast coat pocket; purses should be hung across the chest or under the coat. Keep a thumb through your camera strap. Both men and women can assemble a fake wallet, with about $20 in cash and some expired credit cards—the fake ones you get in the mail that read "your name here" are also good for this—while keeping the real money hidden in a pocket or money belt. And move quickly. Police will tell you that a would-be thief has the least amount of control in the first few moments, so short-circuit the crime scenario as quickly as possible. If someone demands your money, take out your billfold (preferably the fake one) and hurl it in one direction while you run shouting for help in the other. Under no circumstance allow yourself to be taken to another location—a "secondary crime scene" in police jargon—without a battle. This move, police warn, provides the assailant more privacy and consequently more control. However, in a worst-case scenario, you may have to submit in hopes of finding a way of escaping en route; keep your cool as much as possible. That said, Washington is not known for pickpocketing.

- **Know where you're going in advance,** and if you get lost, ask a shopkeeper, theater manager, bartender—what *aren't* bartenders good for?—Metro station attendant, or one of those various patrol officers. Be aware of all the public and federal facilities around you. If you think you're in trouble, head for any federal office building for help. They are all patrolled by armed guards who can offer assistance, and even though many (such as embassy guards) are forbidden to leave their posts in case the "emergency" is a ruse, you'll be safe in their presence.

- **Carry as little cash as possible.** If you need to use an ATM, either choose one that is inside a bank lobby or station a friend or family member behind you to make sure nobody reads your PIN. If you are making a transaction requiring you to tell the last four numbers of your Social Security number, punch it in rather than speak it out loud. And stay away from any ATM that looks temporary (at a festival) or exposed or in any way odd; sophisticated scammers have figured out how to put false fronts and magnetic strip readers on less closely guarded machines.

- **Guard your personal information.** If you are an international visitor and need to use your passport for identification or cash-exchange purposes, you should make a photocopy and keep the original in the hotel safe or at least your room safe. If you bring your laptop or notebook computer—and this is equally applicable to smartphones or the like—don't have any bank account or charge-card password information on it. And as an extra precaution, double-check that you haven't checked "remember me" after entering your computer user name and password, either. And *do not* Tweet or post Facebook entries about your vacation while on vacation; not only are you advertising that you are not at home (or in your hotel room), you are likely providing a criminal information that might allow him to pretend he knows you, and gain more information.

- **While it's fairly easy to hail a cab on the street,** late at night it's best to hail one along the busier commercial routes or approach the doorman of a hotel with a dollar or so and ask him to summon one for you. Otherwise, call a reliable cab company (see some examples on page 124) or hail Uber, and stay inside while they dispatch a cab to your door. When your cab arrives, check the driver's certificate, which must, by law, be posted on the dashboard, and make note of the name and cab number. Absolutely never accept an offer for a cab or limo made by a stranger in the terminal or baggage claim area; stick to the official queue. Don't be tricked by people standing at the airport arrival area who offer to give you a ride in a limo and then insist on being paid in cash. Stand in the designated cab area only.

- **The best self-defense device for the average person,** aside from some basic physical training and mental clarity, is Mace spray, which is legal in most states, nonlethal, and easy to use. (However, in D.C., you must register it with the police.) A loud whistle or alarm is another good keychain charm.

- **Scam I am.** Every tourist city has its particular scams, and Washington is no exception. One involves charging for a map or brochure, an especially popular dodge around the top of the Smithsonian Metro. Don't fall for it; the brochures are free in Smithsonian museums. And then there are always those asking for money for train fare or the like: Use your common sense. If they look like they need money, make your own choice. Also, beware of people outside sports and entertainment venues who want to give you a "free hat," as they will promptly request a donation "for the children." Just say "no thank you" and continue on your way.

PART FOUR

ATTRACTIONS

NO CITY IN THE UNITED STATES features as many top-tier museums, monuments, and cultural exhibits as Washington, D.C. If you're a family on vacation, it's possible to fill a week with world-class art and priceless historical objects without spending a dime on admission. Even better, you can get to virtually all of it via relatively reliable, inexpensive public transportation and short walks.

This chapter covers D.C.'s major attractions, with comprehensive reviews and step-by-step touring plans. These will help ensure you'll see all of the city's highlights without long waits in line.

The level of detail in each review depends on two criteria: the popularity of the attraction and how well it explains what you're looking at. We used each attraction's official visitor statistics or estimates to gauge popularity. For example, more than 7 million people visit the **Smithsonian National Air and Space Museum** (pages 147–162) each year, approximately 20 times the annual attendance of the **National Postal Museum** (page 223). Everything else being equal, Air and Space gets approximately that much more coverage.

The other influence of a review's length is how much background material the attraction gives you related to the exhibits you're viewing. For example, the **National Gallery of Art** (pages 165–174) is one of the best (and most popular) art museums in the United States, but its explanation of the works on display is often limited to a few dozen words per room. In those cases, our reviews provide background material on the artists, subject matter, and school or movement, so you know how they all fit together in context.

Some very popular museums set the standard for high-quality exhibit narrative. The **US Holocaust Memorial Museum** (pages 196–199) and the **Smithsonian National Museum of American History** (pages 174–177) include elaborate supporting material covering the origins, timeline of events, and historical consequences of their subjects, often combining photographs, video, and interactive touch-screen displays.

In those instances, there's not a lot for us to add—we couldn't write better background material or summaries than what the museum provides, so our reviews are shorter.

To help you sort through Washington, D.C.'s attractions, we've rated each on a scale from 0 to 5 stars, with 5 as the highest rating. We've also used a hierarchy of categories to help you gauge an attraction's magnitude, as follows.

HEADLINERS The best museums, monuments, and presentations in Washington, D.C., with world-famous exhibits and don't-miss displays, usually done on a massive scale. The **Smithsonian National Museum of Natural History** is an example.

MAJOR ATTRACTIONS Examples include smaller museums with extensive collections in one or two subject areas. The **Smithsonian's Freer and Sackler** galleries of Asian art are examples.

MINOR ATTRACTIONS Monuments, exhibits, and attractions dedicated to a specific group, event, person, or relatively narrow interest. The **U.S. Navy Memorial**, in a plaza between commercial buildings on Pennsylvania Avenue, is an example.

DIVERSIONS Small theater presentations or walk-through attractions, often not unique to Washington, D.C. **Madame Tussauds** museum of wax figures is an example.

Finally, we've grouped our attraction reviews together by neighborhood. This makes it easier for you to plan your days and minimizes the amount of backtracking and transportation needed.

 The **MALL**

ONE OF THE MOST INCREDIBLE THINGS about the L'Enfant plan for Washington is how closely the layout of today's city resembles it. One example is the National Mall, which was set out as a "Grand Avenue" for Washington—the most important thoroughfare in the city. Over time the city shifted much of that role to Pennsylvania Avenue, but the National Mall remains the most grand—and most visited—area of Washington, D.C.

Important Note: The National Mall is undergoing a major turf restoration project where much of the grass is absent and large sections are under visible construction. The project is expected to last until spring 2016.

The National Mall is largely pedestrian only, so be prepared to walk. There are several streets that pass through and surround the area, but parking is almost nonexistent, so driving is not recommended. The area is framed by Metro stations, although Smithsonian (Blue, Orange, Silver) is the only one on the border of the Mall. For visiting the eastern end of the National Mall—the section between the Capitol and the

Washington Monument—the Federal Triangle station (Blue, Orange, Silver), Archives–Navy Memorial (Green, Yellow), and L'Enfant Plaza (Blue, Orange, Silver, Green, Yellow) are all within a few blocks of the Mall. If you are starting your tour as we do, on the Mall's western side, the closest stations are Foggy Bottom or Farragut West (both Blue, Orange, Silver), even though they are about 0.75 mile away.

We start our exploration of the National Mall at the **National Academy of Sciences** at 2101 Constitution Avenue, near the intersection with 22nd Street. Established in 1863 by Congress and President Lincoln, the Academy of Sciences provides unbiased opinions on scientific matters. The impressive headquarters building houses an eclectic interior that immaculately integrates several architectural styles. It can be visited weekdays from 8 a.m. to 5 p.m.

In the front garden of the National Academy of Sciences building sits the **Albert Einstein Memorial.** A 12-foot-high bronze representation of Einstein is seated on marble steps browsing a pad with three of his most important scientific contributions: the photoelectric effect, the theory of general relativity, and the equivalence of energy and matter.

From the Academy of Sciences, you can either walk east along Constitution Avenue and turn into the Mall near 19th Street or walk south to the **Vietnam Veterans Memorial** (pages 199–200) and meander east along the Mall's paths. Either way you will soon come upon a pond surrounded by greenery and pathways. This is **Constitution Gardens,** a serene spot in a bustling city. On the north side of the pond, take the walkway onto the tiny Signer's Island, where you will find a tribute to the 56 signers of the Declaration of Independence, along with some lovely views.

Take time now to walk across the National Mall and enjoy its splendid vistas that are unlike any other American city. Head south toward the **World War II Memorial** (page 201) and the **Washington Monument** (pages 200–201). From there, you truly get a look at the grandeur that was envisioned so long ago. As you cross 14th Street along Jefferson Avenue, you will come upon the only federal office building on the Mall, the Jamie L. Whitten building housing the **U.S. Department of Agriculture.** The two L-shaped wings were built between 1904 and 1908, with the central block added in 1930.

Wandering toward the **Smithsonian Castle** (page 195), you will pass by the small, copper-domed kiosk at 1100 Jefferson Drive SW that is the entrance to the **S. Dillon Ripley Center.** Within this underground center is the **Discovery Theater,** a child-friendly performance space. Shows are sporadic, so check **discoverytheater.org** if you are interested in attending a performance.

In between the Ripley Center entrance and the Smithsonian Castle is a brick pathway that will lead you into one of the most splendid gardens in Washington: the **Enid A. Haupt Garden.** This 4-acre formal garden contains a few different sections, each carefully manicured and featuring fountains, seating areas, and thousands of flowers. The garden makes a wonderful photo op, framed by the grand Smithsonian Castle to the north, the **Freer and Sackler Galleries** (see below) to the west, and the **National Museum of African Art** and the **Arts and Industries Building** to the east.

Directly across the National Mall, in between the **Smithsonian National Museum of Natural History** (pages 179–190) and the **National Gallery of Art** (pages 165–174) is the **National Gallery of Art Ice Rink.** Most of the year it is a simple park with a wide, shallow, circular fountain at its center. In the coldest months, however, it becomes a very popular ice rink, something you no doubt deduced from its name.

We end our tour of the National Mall by leaving it and crossing Constitution Avenue. Across the street from the National Gallery of Art—and across Pennsylvania Avenue from the **Newseum** (pages 190–191)—is the **Andrew W. Mellon Memorial Fountain.** This round fountain is made up of three concentric bronze bowls with a water spout in its center and the signs of the zodiac on its outer ring.

Freer and Sackler Galleries *(a Smithsonian museum)*
★★★

Note: The Freer Gallery will be closed for maintenance from January 2016 through summer 2017. The Sackler entrance address is given below.

URL asia.si.edu. Address 1050 Independence Ave. SW, Washington, D.C., 20013. **What it is** Museums of Asian art. **Scope and scale** Minor attraction. **When to go** Anytime. **Hours** Daily, 10 a.m.–5:30 p.m.; closed December 25. **Closest Metro** Smithsonian (Orange, Blue, Silver); L'Enfant Plaza (Yellow, Green); Red should transfer at Metro Center. **Admission** Free. **Authors' Comments** With the Freer closed through mid-2017, it's possible to tour the Sackler exhibits in about an hour. **Not to Be Missed** Sculptures of South Asia and the Himalayas; *Peacock Room REMIX* by Darren Waterston; and *Monkeys Grasping for the Moon* by Xu Bing.

DESCRIPTION AND COMMENTS Like the Hirshhorn Museum, the Freer and Sackler Galleries are based on the donated art collections of individuals: Charles Lang Freer and Arthur M. Sackler. Freer was a 19th-century railroad car manufacturer who collected both Oriental art and works by 19th-century American artist James McNeill Whistler. Sackler was a 20th-century physician and entrepreneur. He donated his collection of 1,000 pieces of Oriental art and objects to the Smithsonian in 1982, with additional funding to help construct the museum. The collections' similar focus means that the two museums, connected by a short underground tunnel, are effectively combined for both visitors and research.

One of the first exhibits you'll see at the Sackler is **Feast Your Eyes: A Taste for Luxury in Ancient Iran**—a collection of highly decorated gold, silver, and stone objects from Iran and surrounding areas between 400 BC and 700 AD. These are cups, plates, jewelry, and other everyday objects, done in precious metals and ornately rendered.

The National Mall

● **ATTRACTIONS**

1. Ford's Theatre
2. Freer and Sackler Galleries
3. Hirshhorn Museum and Sculpture Garden
4. International Spy Museum
5. Thomas Jefferson Memorial
6. Martin Luther King, Jr. Memorial
7. Korean War Veterans Memorial
8. Abraham Lincoln Memorial
9. National Air and Space Museum
10. National Archives
11. National Building Museum
12. National Gallery of Art: East Building
13. National Gallery of Art: West Building
14. National Museum of African American History and Culture
15. National Museum of American History
16. National Museum of the American Indian
17. National Museum of Natural History
18. Newseum
19. Franklin Delano Roosevelt Memorial
20. Smithsonian American Art Museum and National Portrait Gallery
21. Smithsonian Castle and Information Center
22. U.S. Botanic Garden
23. US Holocaust Memorial Museum
24. Vietnam Veterans Memorial
25. Washington Monument
26. World War II Memorial

That exhibit ends in a large room that houses *Peacock Room* **REMIX:** **Darren Waterston's Filthy Lucre.** This Sackler exhibit is a companion piece to the Freer's Peacock Room, which is closed through mid-2017. With that unavailable, here's some background in order to make sense of this display: The American artist James McNeill Whistler spent much of his working life in London. While there, he was commissioned by Thomas Jeckyll to finish decorating a dining room he had started for Englishman Frederick Richards Leyland.

Depending on whose view you take, Whistler either went a little overboard on the artistic flourishes, or he created one of the greatest examples of interior design ever seen. Leyland thought the former and refused to pay Whistler, who was driven to bankruptcy shortly after, with Leyland as his main creditor. Whistler so hated Leyland that he painted a caricature of Leyland as a peacock in *The Gold Scab: Eruption in Frilthy Lucre.* Freer bought the room from Leyland's heirs and had it transported in its entirety to the United States. It will be on display when the Freer reopens in 2017.

Waterston's REMIX work takes its name from that Whistler caricature. The room is reimagined in the middle of its decay, with faded paint, broken ceramics, and damaged walls. What's also great about this display is that you get to see Waterston's art samples, color, and texture studies for his version, showing how much time, effort, and thought goes into a display of this size and complexity.

Beyond the REMIX room is the hall of **Sculpture of South Asia and the Himalayas.** This area contains intricately carved religious statues of the area's major and minor gods, and there are a couple of exceptional parts. First, the sculptures aren't surrounded by glass or plastic, so you can get in close and see all of the detail work. Second, the explanations provided by the staff are excellent, giving you both the background on how these societies viewed this specific deity, and the symbolism in the specific work you're viewing.

Besides these permanent exhibits, the museums introduce several new topics per year. Upcoming exhibitions include:

Chinamania Starting with Dutch imports in the 17th century, Europe was fascinated with Chinese blue-and-white porcelains, which were highly prized for their craftsmanship. Prices skyrocketed, and these pieces are still collected today. (In fact, Delft pottery became famous in large part because it could do a reasonable copy of Chinese pottery.) This exhibit covers the Chinese porcelain craze from its inception to now.

Turquoise Mountain: Artists Transforming Afghanistan Including ceramics, jewelry, woodworking, and other arts from this area. Through December 2016.

TOURING TIPS The Freer Gallery will be closed through mid-2017 for maintenance and refurbishment. The Sackler exhibits are smaller and can be toured in less than an hour. That makes it a good choice for an in-between stop if you're visiting the nearby Air and Space or Holocaust museums or the Washington Monument.

Hirshhorn Museum and Sculpture Garden
(a Smithsonian museum) ★★★½

URL hirshhorn.si.edu. Address 700 Independence Ave. SW, Washington, D.C. 20560. **What it is** Museum of contemporary art, including painting, sculpture, mixed media, film, and more. **Scope and scale** Major attraction. **When to go** Anytime. **Hours** Daily, 10 a.m.–5:30 p.m.; closed December 25. **Closest Metro** L'Enfant Plaza (Yellow, Green, Orange, Blue, Silver); Red should transfer at Metro Center. **Admission** Free. **Authors' comments** Excellent sculpture garden and enough interesting pieces inside to make a visit worthwhile. **Not to Be Missed** (Third Level) *Family Group* by Reg Butler; *Torso of a Young Man* by Constantin Brancusi; *At the Hub of Things* by Anish Kapoor; *Nude with Leg Up* by Lucien Freud; and *Point of Tranquility* by Morris Louis. (Second Level) Special exhibits. (Lower Level) *"monument" for V. Tatlin* and *untitled (to Helga and Carlo, with respect and affection)* by Dan Flavin; *Belief + Doubt* by Barbara Kruger. (Garden) Rodin and Henry Moore sculptures and *Are Years What? (for Marianne Moore)* by Mark di Suvero.

DESCRIPTION AND COMMENTS This museum is named for Joseph H. Hirshhorn, who amassed a reported $100-million fortune in Canada's uranium mines during the 1950s. With that bankroll, Hirshhorn expanded an art collection that began in his teens, eventually acquiring more than 12,000 works. Those were willed to the Smithsonian upon his death in 1981, along with an endowment to fund the museum that now includes his name (funding is also provided by the US taxpayers and the Smithsonian). Joe's wife, Olga, continued to donate both to this museum and the Corcoran, which recently merged with the National Gallery (see pages 165–174). The museum's current, futuristic building opened in 1974.

The Hirshhorn collection focuses on 19th- and 20th-century modern and contemporary art. Since most of the collection comes from Joe and Olga Hirshhorn, it obviously reflects Joe's and Olga's taste and bankroll. While we are neither art critics nor artists, the Hirshhorns' taste and judgment were very good. If you have even a passing interest in contemporary art, you'll recognize some familiar names in this collection: Brancusi, Calder, Johns, Koons, Moore, (Yoko) Ono, and Rothko.

In addition to paintings and sculpture, the Hirshhorn hosts many rotating special exhibits on the second and third levels. These frequently use video and other multimedia, and they change every few months.

The rest of this section contains brief summaries of the Hirshhorn's better works, starting with the third floor and working down to the sculpture garden outside. We think it's best to start your tour on the third floor and work your way down to the lower level. Because the exhibits can move and change, we've listed the artists alphabetically by last name for easy reference.

THIRD FLOOR

Note: If you take the escalator to the third floor, look to the ceiling for **Spencer Finch's** *Cloud (H2O)* from 2006. Finch's works are known for their attempts to convey transient light and color, so the Hirshhorn staff ingeniously placed this above the escalator. Notice how the wide plane of light is compressed into a smaller space as you approach the third-floor landing. Also walk around the landing to see how the shape and intensity of the light shift with you.

Here's what should be on display:

- **Janine Antoni** *Lick and Lather* **(1994)** Two busts of the same human head and shoulders, one made of chocolate and one of soap. The artist sculpted part of the chocolate head by biting, licking, and gnawing at it, and the soap one by bathing with it. (We humbly suggest the next one be called "Two Doves.")

- **Mary Bauermeister** *In Memory of Your Feelings, or Hommage à Jasper Johns* **(1964)** Bauermeister used "found objects"—a case of glass lenses here—in her work. Why? The use of premade objects, assembled by the artist according to her mood, was supposed to challenge the conventional idea of "what art *is*."

- **Alighiero e Boetti** *Untitled* **(1994)** Boetti's best-known works are a set of intricate, embroidered geographic maps, from the early 1970s to the early 1990s, made by artists in Afghanistan and Pakistan. This watercolor on paper isn't a map, but it is a good representation of his style, and it's probably not a coincidence that it looks like a rug that might have been woven in that region.

- **Louise Bourgeois** *The Blind Leading the Blind* **(1949)** Bourgeois is better known for her sculptures of giant spiders (there's one across the street at the National Gallery's Sculpture Garden), but this is an interesting piece with an only slightly less disturbing background story. As Bourgeois recounts it, one day when she was a child, she was playing under her family's kitchen table while her parents were preparing lunch. That apparently brought up a host of questions in her young mind, such as "What are they doing?" "What is their purpose?" and "How do I relate to them?"—thoughts for which we'd prescribe medication if expressed today.

- **Constantin Brancusi** *Torso of a Young Man* **(1924)** Brancusi is one of the most significant artists in the Modernism movement, and this is an excellent piece done during his peak creative period. *Torso of a Young Man* emphasizes the geometric shape of the torso and thighs while eliminating secondary characteristics you'd see in representational sculpture, such as bone, muscle, and skin. That reduction clarifies the shape so that it's both new and recognizable.

- **Reg Butler** *Family Group* **(1948)** Approach this work from a couple different angles and heights to see the "family" and you'll be rewarded with a clever, abstract view. A second work by Butler—*Musee Imaginaire*—is also on display on this floor.

- **Alexander Calder** *Mobile* **(1958)** By law, every contemporary art gallery must include at least one Calder mobile. If you're a fan, there are several more over at the National Gallery of Art. Calder's *Two Discs* sculpture has a prominent spot in the Hirshhorn plaza too.

- **Nick Cave** *Soundsuit* **(2009)** Nick Cave is famous for these intricate, colorful dance costumes, made of everything from plant fibers to human hair. They're often displayed in museums, but they're also used in theater productions and possibly as Nicki Manaj loungewear. We're not sure. PBS has a short video of them in motion at **youtube.com/watch?v=BpNcmh3rxko.**

- **Christo** *Store Front* **(1964)** Christo was famous for huge, temporary, outdoor art installations; he once wrapped 11 small islands off the coast of Miami in 6.5 million square feet of pink fabric for two weeks. Compared to that, *Store Front* is small and subdued. It's been described as either a commentary on mass merchandising, or a tribute to the architecture of urban retailers and the cities around them.

- **Joseph Cornell** *Untitled (Aviary with Yellow Birds)* **(1948)** Cornell was one of the founders of *assemblage,* arranging existing or "found" objects into visual commentary or as a reminder of a specific place or time. In this case, Cornell has put these birds and the tree they fly to into a box, sort of like a zoo puts nature on display.

- **Robert Delaunay** *Untitled* **(1937)** Delaunay, a painter, was one of the founders of Orphism, an art technique that emphasized bright colors and abstract shapes and linked Cubism to the Abstract movement. This is a bronze sculpture that still shows an emphasis on abstract shape.

- **Lucien Freud** *Nude with Leg Up (Leigh Bowery)* **(1992)** If you've toured the National Gallery of Art, you probably think of portraiture in terms of formal clothes and poses, done in a style that compliments the subject. Freud's approach was the exact opposite. His portraits were designed to be uncomfortable to look at and often used a limited color palette of yellows and browns. (He also really liked painting nudes, so maybe the subjects dictated the colors).

- **Alfred Jensen** *The Sun Rises Twice (Per I, Per II, Per III, Per IV)* **(1973)** This is typical of Jensen's work—a set of calendars, astrological charts, and other artifacts used to measure time, executed in excruciating detail. It's the kind of thing that ends up in a museum or shown on the wall at the beginning of a *CSI* episode.

- **Jasper Johns** *Untitled* **(1954)** Still living as we went to press, Johns is one of the most recognized and influential artists of the past 50 years (even appearing in an episode of *The Simpsons* as himself). He's known for using popular images such as the US map and flag. This isn't one of his more popular works and doesn't seem to display the characteristics for which he's known.

- **Anish Kapoor** *At the Hub of Things* **(1987)** Kapoor was trying to capture the characteristics of "void" when he did this, and we think he succeeded. The piece, roughly the shape of an egg, is done in a deep Prussian blue that seems to absorb light. It's mesmerizing.

- **Ellsworth Kelly** *White Relief over Dark Blue* **(2002)** This is one of Kelly's later works, done in his late 70s, but exhibits many hallmarks of the style he developed over the last 50 years. Kelly was known for crisp lines between colors and the emphasis on basic shapes and colors. The typical Kelly painting would not look out of place as an icon on your iPhone or as the logo for some new Internet company. That is, even though he produced these for years, they're arguably more in style and modern now than at any time before.

- **Sol LeWitt** *13/11* **(1985)** LeWitt was one of the founders of Minimalism, an art movement that, as its name implies, sought to remove from each work any extraneous shapes, colors, or characteristics. This pyramid sculpture is a good example of his output.

- **Morris Louis** *Point of Tranquility* **(1960)** Morris "painted" this piece by pouring a small amount of each paint color into the middle of the canvas; then he tilted the canvas so that the paint ran to the edge. The result resembles a flower, which led to Louis naming this series of works *Floral*. Louis would go on to do similar works, including *Delta Theta,* during the same period.

- **Agnes Martin** *Garden* **(1964)** and *Play* **(1966)** These are two good examples of Martin's minimalist work, which typically feature straight, lightly drawn, colored pencil lines on largely monochromatic backgrounds.

- **Joan Mitchell** *Cercando un Ago* **(1959)** One of a series of similarly named and executed works from Mitchell's early career, this is an example of Abstract Expressionism, the same style as Jackson Pollock and Barnett Newman. Like works from those artists, the point of *Cercando un Ago* isn't to tell a story or replicate a scene—it's to convey emotion.

● **Robert Rauschenberg** *Dam* **(1959)** Part of Rauschenberg's "Combines" work from 1954 to 1962, this supposedly contains "coded messages" to the (then underground) gay community of New York. As far as we've been able to research, though, no one has yet put forth a definitive meaning to any of these words or symbols—the work's meaning seems to have died with Rauschenberg.

We suppose this could be interpreted two ways: First, that the act of displaying the painting is now an art performance itself, celebrating not needing to display "coded messages" to an underground gay community; or second, an open question as to whether there's a difference between undecipherable code—that is, a message that has permanently lost its meaning—and random gibberish.

● **George Rickey** *Marsh Plant* **(1962)** Rickey is known for his kinetic sculptures, and his works display a simple, slender balance. Amazingly, a few of his pieces are still within the budget of a middle-income collector.

● **Mark Rothko** *Blue, Orange, Red* **(1961)** One of the most famous American artists of the last half of the 20th century, Rothko was a pioneer in the Abstract Expressionist movement. Like those on display at the National Gallery (see pages 171-172), this work comes from late in Rothko's "multiform" series—by 1961, he's famous enough in the United States to be invited to meet the Kennedy family in Washington.

● **David Smith** *Agricola I* **(1952)** It's a series of farm tools welded together to look (roughly) like a farmer, then painted red. The most popular interpretation is that the modern farmer depends so much on his tools that it's hard to tell where one ends and the other begins.

● **Hiroshi Sugimoto** *Akron Civic, Ohio* **(1980)** Sugimoto visited cinemas across the United States to do a series of these images. In each, he exposed a single film slide for the duration of a full-length film playing in the theater. This one is from Akron, Ohio.

● **Paul Thek** *Warrior's Leg* **(1967)** It's a copy of a Roman soldier's leg, amputated just below the knee. But the main thing to know was that it was unveiled during the Vietnam War. In that respect, it's similar to Bourdelle's *Great Warrior of Montauban* in commenting on the true cost of conflict.

● **Andy Warhol** *Marilyn Monroe's Lips* **(1962)** Ostensibly this piece—a mechanical reproduction of Monroe's lips 168 times, arranged in a rectangle and writ large—is an observation that overcommercialization damages anything special that we hold dear.

SECOND FLOOR

The second floor is used primarily for short-term special exhibitions. They're worth a visit. New for 2016 is *Suspended Animation,* works by six artists who "use digitally generated images as a tool to question conceptions of reality." These are supposed to be immersive exhibits, which should be fun. We're looking forward to seeing it.

FIRST FLOOR

The first floor is primarily the entrance, security checkpoint, and a set of escalators for getting to the other levels.

- **Jeff Koons** *Kiepenkeri* **(1987)** Koons is a commercial but talented artist. His *Balloon Dog (Magenta),* in the Palazzo Grassi in Venice, manages to convey the hyper-eager personalities of puppies, modeled as a building-size balloon sculpture. But we're not sure about this piece—a copy of another work in Germany, with Koons using stainless steel instead of bronze. It's not as playful or fun as his other work, and it's not clear what stainless steel adds.

LOWER LEVEL

If it's still around, you won't be able to miss **Barbara Kruger's** *Belief + Doubt* because it's plastered all over the walls and floors of the lower level.

- **Dan Flavin** *"monument" for V. Tatlin* **(1967)** and *untitled (to Helga and Carlo, with respect and affection)* **(1974)** These are two installations using fluorescent lights as sculpture. It's a creative idea because, like bronze or steel, these lights both illuminate and cast literal shadows. The hum of the light fixtures adds another element to the installation. Taken together, the light, darkness, and sound make you want to stare at the bulbs, even though you know it's terrible for your eyes.

- **Muguel Angel Rios** *A Morir ('til Death)* **(2003)** Another video, this is one of a game of tops that serves as a commentary about competition and possessing land.

PLAZA

A plaza surrounds the Hirshhorn, and the space is used for some eye-catching work.

- **Tony Cragg** *Subcommittee* **(1991)** It's a collection of giant rubber stamps whose handles resemble human heads. Combine that with the piece's title, and it's kind of funny.

- **Roy Lichtenstein** *Brushstroke* **(1996)** Better known for his pop-art paintings, this is Lichtenstein's attempt to capture in three-dimensional sculpture the essence of the artist's brushstroke motion.

- **Yoko Ono** *Wish Tree for Washington DC* **(2007)** It's safe to say that Ono would be more highly regarded now as an artist if she had never been married to John Lennon. In the years before she met The Beatles, Ono was active in the New York art scene, with her own shows and critical success. This piece, *Wish Tree for Washington DC,* invites viewers to write down their hopes and dreams on small pieces of paper, and then tie them to the tree.

- **James Sanborn** *Antipodes* **(1997)** *Antipodes* is a two-part sculpture and coded message, written in Cyrillic and English. It's similar to Sanborn's more famous work, *Kryptos,* installed at the Central Intelligence Agency headquarters in Virginia. All of the Cyrillic side of this sculpture has been decoded (as have three sides of Kryptos)—it's a couple of Soviet-era documents on how to recruit sources, and some text on dissident Andrei Sakharov. The remaining unsolved sides are the sources of obsession for a remarkably large number of people.

- **Kenneth Snelson** *Needle Tower* **(1968)** Snelson's work is interesting because it uses tension in steel cables to assemble large towers of steel and aluminum pipes. Without tension on the steel cables, the pieces would fall apart. The use of cables allows Snelson to create very tall, delicate works, and to play with perspective near the top of the pieces. This is a good example of his work.

GARDEN

- **Jean (Hans) Arp** *Evocation of a Form: Human, Lunar, Spectral* **(1950)** Arp was already well respected within the art world by the time he made this and would, in a few years, start winning awards for his works. The curves in this torso are a good example of Arp's style, and this particular piece is a good representation of Arp's sculptures.
- **Emile-Antoine Bourdelle** *The Great Warrior of Montauban* **(1900)** Bourdelle was an influential sculptor whose pupils included Giacometti and Matisse. This bronze work, commemorating the townsmen's effort in the Franco-Prussian War, was controversial when it was unveiled. The town thought it was getting a conventional "marching soldiers and parade horses" statue, not a nude in a literal battle of life and death. Many considered the work inappropriate. It took the support of Augustus Rodin (see facing page) to bring around the town. They eventually considered it a faithful representation of war's reality.
- **Anthony Caro** *Monsoon Drift* **(1975)** Caro was an assistant to sculptor Henry Moore (see below), and then switched to Modernism in the 1950s. *Monsoon Drift* is typical of Caro's work, with an emphasis on geometric planes and textures. Also notice that you're allowed to walk right up to this piece. That's by design— Caro's intent was that it be observed up close, not from a distance.
- **Willem de Koonig** *Clamdigger* **(1972)** De Koonig became famous as a painter and took up sculpture later in life. This possible self-portrait was done when he was 68 and is his first large-scale work in bronze. The rough texture and exaggerated features remind us more of Giacometti than, say, Rodin.
- **Mark di Suvero** *Are Years What? (for Marianne Moore)* **(1967)** Di Suvero is widely recognized as one of the first to use a construction crane as an artist's tool. This is considered one of his best works. We have no idea what it means, but it's colorful, proportioned well, and looks good.
- **Barry Flanagan** *The Drummer* **(1990)** It's an 8-foot-tall bronze rabbit with a drum—that you'll be seeing in your dreams for weeks.
- **Alberto Giacometti** *Monumental Head* **(1960)** Giacometti studied sculpture under Antoine Bourdelle (see above) in Paris and was one of the leading sculptors of the 20th century. He's best known for his tall, almost impossibly thin human figures, with rough surfaces and exaggerated features: Imagine this head on a statue about 30 feet tall.
- **Dan Graham** *For Gordon Bunshaft* **(2006)** Graham is known for these outdoor architecture installations that feature unusual mirrors, glass, steel, wood, and stone. In this piece, you can simultaneously see through the glass and see yourself in the mirror. Have one of your group go around to the other side to get the full effect.
- **Henry Moore (Many works)** **(1952–1970)** One of the best-known sculptors of the 20th century, Moore specialized in the kinds of large bronzes you see here. The sculptures all come from Moore's post–World War II style, which featured reclining figures, sometimes of families, whose bodies are often pushed to the limits of abstraction.
- **Susan Philipsz** *Sunset Song* **(2003)** No modern art garden would be complete without a sound installation! In this case, it's Philipsz's *Sunset Song,* which plays at a low, slow way as background music while you're in the garden.

- **Auguste Rodin** *The Burghers of Calais* **(1889),** *Crouching Woman* **(1882),** *Walking Man* **(1900),** and *Monument to Balzac* **(1898)** (See page 171 for an overview of Rodin's career.) Along with *The Age of Bronze* (see page 171), these sculptures are some of Rodin's most important works. Like *The Age of Bronze, The Burghers of Calais* was controversial when it was unveiled. It tells the story of how six city leaders offered to sacrifice themselves to save Calais from the English army, but the sculpture doesn't portray any of them as heroic, noble, or larger than life. Instead, each of the half-dozen appears resigned to their fate. Adding to the unexpected design, the sculpture is installed near ground level, not on a pedestal like traditional public works. The Hirshhorn owns one of only 12 copies of this sculpture.

  Rodin's *Monument to Balzac* has an interesting history. It was commissioned as a tribute by Balzac's friends at the *Société des Gens de Lettres* in Paris after Balzac's death. It did not go well for Rodin. The *Société* was expecting a two-year turnaround for the finished sculpture, but Rodin took seven years to complete just the plaster prototype. And even then, Rodin decided to sculpt Balzac's personality, not his physical appearance, so the subject was hard to identify.

TOURING TIPS The Hirshhorn is rarely crowded enough for lines to form. That makes the museum an excellent stop either before or after a visit to a larger museum such as Air and Space.

Korean War Veterans Memorial   ★★★★

URL nps.gov/kowa. **Address** 10 Daniel French Dr. SW, Washington, D.C. 20245. **Phone** ☎ 202-426-6841 (National Mall & Memorial Parks). **What it is** Beautifully designed monument to those who served in the Korean War. **Scope and scale** Minor attraction. **When to go** Anytime, but it is particularly striking at night. **Hours** Open 24 hours. **Closest Metro** Foggy Bottom or Smithsonian (Orange, Blue, Silver; for Green, Yellow, transfer at L'Enfant Plaza; for Red, transfer at Metro Center). **Admission** Free.

DESCRIPTION AND COMMENTS The Korean War Veterans Memorial is frequently overshadowed by the Vietnam Veterans Memorial nearby. Although perhaps not as emotionally resonant as the Vietnam Memorial, we think the Korean War Memorial is more visually striking. Designed as a small circle intersected by a large triangle, it combines a quiet, contemplative space with powerful, dynamic sculpture.

Dominating the memorial are 19 stainless-steel statues representing various United States armed-forces servicemen. The figures are posed mid-action, patrolling the Korean terrain in full combat gear. On a quiet evening, the alert, mindful statues can cause even the calmest visitor to check over their shoulder for an invisible enemy. One side of the triangle containing these figures is made up of a glossy, black granite wall engraved with photo-realistic images of people, places, and items from the Korean War.

The circular portion of the Korean War Veterans Memorial perfectly offsets the animated triangular area with a reflecting pool surrounded by tree-covered benches. The Pool of Remembrance is a lovely spot to sit and contemplate the reminder spelled out on the section of granite wall that juts into the pool: Freedom Is Not Free.

Abraham Lincoln Memorial   ★★★★★

URL **nps.gov/linc**. **Address** 2 Lincoln Memorial Circle NW, Washington, D.C. 20037.
Phone ☎ 202-426-6841 (National Mall & Memorial Parks). **What it is** A Greek-like
temple dedicated to America's 16th president. **Scope and scale** Headliner. **When to
go** Anytime, although the memorial is most beautiful at twilight. **Hours** Open 24
hours. Park rangers typically available from 9 a.m. until 10 p.m. Closed December
25. **Closest Metro** Foggy Bottom (Orange, Blue, Silver; for Green, Yellow, transfer at
L'Enfant Plaza; for Red, transfer at Metro Center). **Admission** Free.

DESCRIPTION AND COMMENTS When thinking of the memorials and monuments
of Washington, D.C., "classic Greek temple" may not be what immediately
comes to mind. However, the Lincoln Memorial and its towering Doric columns are so ingrained in American culture that it hardly seems out of place.
Anchoring the west end of the National Mall, the Lincoln Memorial is one of
the most beautiful, powerful, and inspiring monuments in the United States.
It attracts more than 5 million visitors per year.

At 99 feet tall, 190 feet wide, and 119 feet deep, it's impossible to overlook
from the Mall. The shallow reflecting pool stretching more than 2,000 feet in
front further enhances your approach. When standing in front of the Lincoln
Memorial, the pool reflects the Washington Monument towering nearby.

Walking toward the Lincoln Memorial, the first noticeable features are the
36 fluted Doric columns that surround the exterior, representing each state in
the Union at the time of President Lincoln's death. These 36 states are inscribed
on the frieze—the area above the colonnade—along with the other 12 states
that joined the Union prior to the memorial's 1922 dedication.

Climbing the 87 steps from the reflecting pool invokes almost as much history as the monument itself. It was on these very steps that Dr. Martin Luther
King Jr. made his famous "I Have a Dream" speech in 1963. (An inscription
where MLK stood memorializes the speech. It's on the landing 18 steps below
the memorial.) These steps have since been the location for innumerable ral-
lies, protests, speeches, and movie settings.

Cresting the stairs brings you face to face with Abraham Lincoln . . . well,
face to knees is more accurate, since President Lincoln in this form is 19 feet tall
(he would be 28 feet tall if he stood). This remarkable, 175-ton President Lincoln sits upon a marble chair in a state of deep contemplation. Although carved
from 28 separate blocks, the figure appears as one and is brought to life with
a probing stare across the reflecting pool. The president looks weary, as if it is
the end of a long period of hard decisions. Even his hands betray his troubled
thoughts—one pawing at the arm of the chair while the other balls into a fist.

On the wall of either side chamber is a different speech—the Gettysburg
Address to the south and the president's second inaugural speech to the
north—topped by stunning murals. These particular speeches were selected to
emphasize President Lincoln's greatest achievements. The Gettysburg Address,
along with being his most well-known speech, spoke of not just ending the Civil
War, but also resuming the path set forth by those who created the United
States of America four score and seven years prior. Likewise, in the president's
second inaugural address, given a mere 36 days before the end of the Civil War,
Lincoln implored the still-broken nation to rejoin and accept each other ". . .

with malice towards none; charity for all." These two speeches helped to stitch a wounded America and illuminate a path toward healing.

The Lincoln Memorial is an exceptionally popular tourist attraction, but it is something everyone must see and reflect upon. If the soaring Washington Monument is the icon of D.C., the Lincoln Memorial is its soul, radiating inspiration through staggering architectural achievement and memories of what great leaders are capable of.

National Air and Space Museum *(a Smithsonian museum)*
★★★★½

URL **airandspace.si.edu**. **Address** Independence Ave. at 6th St. SW, Washington, D.C. 20560. **Phone** ☎ 202-633-2214. **What it is** World-class collection of historic airplanes, spacecraft, and flight memorabilia. **Scope and scale** Headliner. **When to go** As soon as it opens, or after 3 p.m. **Hours** Daily, 10 a.m.–5:30 p.m.; 10 a.m.–7:30 p.m. summer and peak times. Closed December 25. **Closest Metro** L'Enfant Plaza (Green, Yellow, Orange, Blue, Silver; for Red, transfer to Green, Yellow, Orange, or Blue at Gallery Place or Metro Center). **Admission** Free. **Not to Be Missed** (First Floor) *Hughes H-1* (Gallery 105); *Douglas DC-3* (Gallery 102); Boeing Milestones of Flight Hall (Gallery 100); and How Things Fly (for kids; Gallery 109) (Second Floor) *Wright Flyer* (Gallery 209); *Skylab* (Space Race, entrance on second floor); and *Supermarine Spitfire, North American P-51 Mustang* (Gallery 207).

DESCRIPTION AND COMMENTS Air and Space holds the world's greatest collection of flying machines. Its galleries contain more of the aviation world's "firsts"—first airplane, first to land on the moon—than anywhere else. What Air and Space does well is tell the story of the pilots and engineers whose inventions, bravery, and risk-taking took humans from their first flight of 120 feet in 1903, to the first moon landing and back in 1969.

A quick tour of Air and Space can be done in two and a half or three hours, assuming you're willing to skip some galleries and give others a brief walkthrough. A comprehensive tour, including lunch and an IMAX movie, takes five to seven hours, depending on how much time you spend reading the details in each gallery. (Many galleries have 10- to 20-minute movies—we think none of them are mandatory for enjoying or understanding the exhibits.)

Start your visit at the Independence Avenue entrance. During summer and holidays, plan to arrive 20-30 minutes prior to opening; arrive 45 minutes in advance around July 4th and Thanksgiving.

EARLY FLIGHT (Gallery 107)
The Early Flight exhibit is a good place to start a comprehensive tour. The room is designed to look like an early 20th-century airplane festival, promoting "the latest" in aeronautical developments. Near the entrance is a set of displays summarizing man's fascination with flight, from bird-watching to da Vinci's 15th-century helicopter sketches to the first flying gliders and full-scale, powered airplane prototypes. You'll also find photos, models, and posters recounting the first European flight attempts, wall-size displays featuring the Wright Brothers' and Glenn Curtiss's aircraft innovations, and, toward the opposite end of the room, various early designs for gas-powered engines.

National Air and Space Museum First Floor

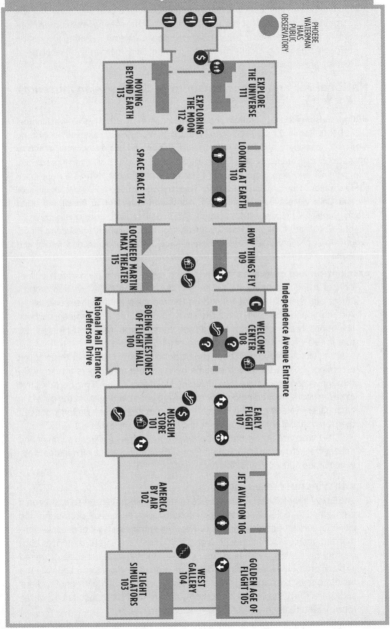

National Air and Space Museum Second Floor

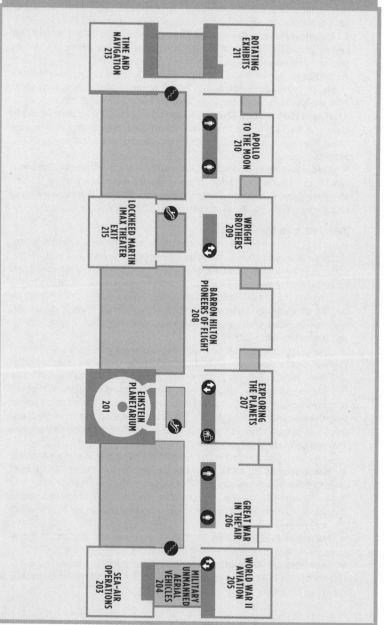

TIME AND NAVIGATION
213

ROTATING EXHIBITS
211

APOLLO TO THE MOON
210

LOCKHEED MARTIN IMAX THEATER EXIT
215

WRIGHT BROTHERS
209

BARRON HILTON PIONEERS OF FLIGHT
208

EINSTEIN PLANETARIUM
201

EXPLORING THE PLANETS
207

GREAT WAR IN THE AIR
206

SEA-AIR OPERATIONS
203

MILITARY UNMANNED AERIAL VEHICLES
204

WORLD WAR II AVIATION
205

The full-size planes on display here show how various builders approached the challenge of maneuvering an airplane once it was in flight. If you have children, point out the differences in where the engine and vertical and horizontal control surfaces are located on each plane. Aircraft on display include:

- **Lilienthal Hang Glider of 1894** Otto Lilienthal, a German, built and flew several unpowered gliders in the 1890s, about a decade before the Wright Brothers' first powered flights.
- **Blériot XI** Made in France, another of these single-wing airplanes was the first to cross the English Channel, in 1909. The one on display here was built in 1914 and flown extensively in South America and the United States.
- **Wright 1909 Military Flyer** This wasn't the world's first airplane—that's in Gallery 209 upstairs—but this model was the first military aircraft ever purchased by the United States, and the one displayed here was flown by Orville Wright.
- **Curtiss D-III Headless Pusher** Curtiss was the first to use discrete ailerons—small flaps on the far, back edges of the wings that move up and down—to turn the plane. Ailerons proved a better solution than what the Wrights were using and are found on virtually all modern planes.

THE JET AGE (Gallery 106)

Marking a huge leap forward into the modern era, both in time and technology, is The Jet Age, next door. In the years leading up to World War II, airplane designers were grappling with the physical limits of how fast and large an airplane could be when powered by traditional piston engines similar in design to the ones seen at the end of the Early Flight gallery. (An engine's pistons have to be larger and move faster for a plane's propeller to spin faster. At very high speeds, the back-and-forth stress on the pistons will shatter the metal they're made of, and the engine will fail.)

The gas turbine engine, invented independently by Dr. Hans von Ohain, a German, and Sir Frank Whittle, a Brit, introduced a completely new method of aircraft propulsion. Like the piston engine, the gas turbine uses the controlled detonation of liquid fuel for propulsion. However, the detonations in a jet engine spin a circular turbine, turning around a central shaft, to produce power. Because the turbine spins in a circle instead of moving up and down like a piston, jet engines don't have the same mechanical stress as piston engines, and they can be made larger and more powerful.

Three early jet-powered military aircraft are on display in The Jet Age:

- **Messerschmitt ME 262A** *Schwalbe* Development of the ME 262 started prior to World War II, and it became the first jet fighter used in combat, in June 1944. At this point in the war, fortunately for Allied pilots, Germany had neither the time nor the industrial capacity to mass-produce enough Me 262s to affect the outcome.
- **McDonnell FH-1 Phantom I** This model was the first production jet fighter to be based from a US Navy aircraft carrier, in 1947.
- **Lockheed XP-80 Shooting Star** This original prototype jet served as the test bed for the F-80 jet fighter, the first operational combat fighter for the U.S. Air Force, from 1944 to 1949.

TOURING TIPS Along the main walkway in this gallery is a collection of gas turbine engines, including the first models produced by von Ohain and Whittle, as well as more advanced versions. Other exhibits include various jet aircraft cockpit displays, showing how vastly more information was conveyed to pilots as the planes they were flying became more complicated. While they're moderately interesting, we think a cursory glance at these is sufficient.

THE GOLDEN AGE OF FLIGHT (Gallery 105)

The Golden Age of Flight room covers the public's expanding fascination with civilian aviation between 1919 and 1939, roughly the time between the World Wars.

The basic principles for powering and controlling an airplane in flight were well known by the end of World War I. With these mastered, airplane manufacturers and pilots began to push the limits of how fast, far, and high their planes could go. Crowds flocked to the new air shows and air races springing up across the United States and Europe; many people were inspired to become amateur pilots themselves. This gallery's displays include trophies, photos, and results from these races, as well as the newspaper and magazine coverage their pilots garnered.

Five aircraft are displayed in Golden Age of Flight:

- **Hughes H-1** Long before he was the reclusive billionaire with the crazy fingernails, Howard Hughes was an aviation legend. Wanting to break the world speed record, Hughes commissioned the design of this plane in 1934. It was built with the most modern aircraft design methods of the time, including wind-tunnel testing, a retractable landing gear and flush rivets for less drag, and two sets of purpose-built wings.

- **Curtiss Robin J-1 Deluxe** In 1935, this airplane used air-to-air refueling to set a world's record for longest sustained flight: 27 days, 5 hours, and 34 minutes from takeoff to landing.

- **Beechcraft Model 17 Staggerwing** By the early 1930s, people were using airplanes for private transportation instead of trains, ships, or cars. And while most early planes were sparsely furnished, focusing more on basic, safe flying than luxury, Beechcraft outfitted its Model 17s with leather interiors, essentially making it the Depression-era equivalent of today's private jet.

TOURING TIPS The gallery's film, *Jimmy Doolittle Remembers,* is one of the better in the museum but not needed on any partial-day tour.

THE WEST END (Gallery 104)

The **West End** of the first floor holds rotating exhibits on a variety of topics. Past presentations include *Hawaii by Air,* recounting the history and dangers of Pacific flight to Hawaii, from its early days to modern, reliable, commercial jet service. The current exhibit, *Art of the Airport Tower,* on display through November 2016, uses photography to illustrate the architectural beauty of airports and airport towers around the world.

AMERICA BY AIR (Gallery 102)

Covering roughly the same 1919-to-1939 time period as The Golden Age of Flight, this gallery focuses on the development of aircraft for America's commercial air service. Spurred on by the US government, the early 1930s saw the rapid development of larger, faster commercial airplanes for passenger service, plus supporting infrastructure such as airports and air-traffic control.

Don't miss the walk-through section of the **American Airlines DC-7,** showing what the inside of a pre–WWII airliner looked like (we're pretty sure airplane bathroom design hasn't changed in 70 years), and the huge **Airbus A320 simulator** performing takeoffs and landings.

Important aircraft on display show the rapid transition from airmail to passenger service; several of the planes made the plane hanging next to them obsolete. Aircraft include:

- **Pitcairn PA-5 Mailwing** Built in 1927, the PA-5 on display here shows the state of most commercial aviation in the United States at that time: The pilot flew in an open cockpit exposed to the weather; there was no room for passengers, but there was capacity for up to 500 pounds of mail. The PA-5 flew at a top speed of around 130 miles per hour.

- **Northrop 4A Alpha** The Alpha is notable because its 1929 design introduced two features now found on virtually all commercial aircraft: *wing fillets,* the smooth, aerodynamic transition area where the wing meets the fuselage; and *stressed-skin construction,* which keeps the airplane's wings and body rigid without heavy internal bracing.

- **Ford 5-AT Tri-Motor** In addition to automobiles, the Ford Motor Company tried its hand at making commercial airplanes between 1924 and 1936. Their most notable achievement was the Tri-Motor, made between 1927 and 1933. When it was introduced, the Tri-Motor was the largest passenger plane in the world, able to carry two pilots, a stewardess, and up to 10 passengers more than 500 miles. The Tri-Motor's airframe was made entirely of metal, while most planes still used wood and canvas, and the plane could be flown with just one of its three engines running. Those three engines produced a whopping 120 decibels of noise, however, *inside the plane.* For comparison, that's 10 decibels louder than sitting in the front row of a Van Halen concert.

- The **Boeing 247-D** This is the plane that ended production of the Ford Tri-Motor. The 247-D could fly 50% faster and 50% farther than the Ford Tri-Motor while carrying the same number of crew and passengers, and on two engines instead of three. Besides speed and range, other 247-D advances included the use of retractable landing gear, plus cabin soundproofing and air-conditioning for passengers.

The airlines' demand for the 247-D was so great that Boeing was unable to fulfill their orders when production started in 1933. That shortage led to the development of the last plane displayed in this gallery, the Douglas DC-3. The DC-3, in turn, quickly ended the production of the 247-D.

- **Douglas DC-3** Trans World Airlines was one of the companies that couldn't get the 247-D. In mid-1933, TWA asked the Douglas Aircraft Company to design an alternative that became the DC-3.

The DC-3 was larger, faster, and more refined than the 247-D, and it proved to be a far more versatile airframe. It could be configured to hold 21 seated passengers, or, for overnight service, 14 passengers in "sleeper" compartments.

More than 600 DC-3 planes were built for the US military through the end of World War II (plus an additional 5,400 built by Russia and Japan). Thousands of used planes entered the post-war commercial market. With spare parts readily available, hundreds are still flying today, including a few commercial airlines.

TOURING TIPS In addition to these planes, the "What Makes an Airliner 'Modern'" and Pan Am Clipper displays are worth a longer look.

THE BOEING MILESTONES OF FLIGHT HALL

The Air and Space Museum's centerpiece display is a priceless collection of some of the world's most important flying machines. Most of these aircrafts' names, their pilots' names, and their achievements will be instantly recognizable.

- **Ryan NYP** *Spirit of St. Louis* Charles Lindbergh was the first solo pilot to fly an airplane, this *Spirit of St. Louis,* nonstop across the Atlantic Ocean, in 1927. While the public regarded Lindbergh's flight as a demonstration of how reliable airplanes had become, at the time the fatality rate was still roughly 50% for pilots attempting long-distance flight records over oceans.

- **Bell X-1** *Glamorous Glennis* Chuck Yeager was the first pilot to break the sound barrier, in this Bell X-1 in 1947. To fly faster than the speed of sound, the X-1 used liquid-fuel rocket motors instead of a piston or jet engine. The X-1 never took off from the ground; it was dropped from a military bomber before igniting its engines. Thus, the X-1 is essentially a missile with wings. Still, it showed that controlled flight could be achieved above the speed of sound.

- **Mercury MA-6** *Friendship 7* John Glenn Jr. was the first American to orbit the Earth, in this Mercury spacecraft on February 20, 1962. The Soviet Union had placed the *Sputnik* satellite into orbit in late 1957, catching the United States off guard and prompting the start of the Cold War's space race. John Glenn's orbital flight in the *Friendship 7* demonstrated that the United States was back in the game.

- **Apollo 11 Command Module** *Columbia* The *Columbia* is the most important man-made object in the history of the world. Launched on July 16, 1969, the Apollo 11 mission was the first to land men on the moon. Neil Armstrong and Buzz Aldrin reached the lunar surface on July 20, and, with pilot Michael Collins, returned safely to Earth in this *Columbia* command module on July 24, 1969.

Why is the *Columbia* the most important object ever made? It represents the point at which humans definitively controlled Earth's materials and mastered the universe's fundamental physical laws. And, not coincidentally, the only nation that has shown the collective will and capability to build one of these things has its basic ideas of freedom and governance displayed for you to read in a couple of documents a few blocks away.

Besides these, the Milestones of Flight Hall includes many other aircraft of notable achievement, from Mars landers to Cold War missiles.

SPACE RACE (Gallery 114)

The Space Race gallery is an open, multistory exhibit area, similar to the Boeing Milestones of Flight Hall, but dedicated to rockets, missiles, test vehicles, and spacecraft developed primarily by the United States and Soviet Union during the Cold War.

Start your tour of this huge area at the front middle of the room, with the display of military missiles. Then turn right and begin a counterclockwise tour of the room beginning at Race to the Moon. Save your walk through Skylab for when you're on the second floor.

Almost the entire right side of this gallery is dedicated to artifacts, models, and memorabilia from the 1960s race to the moon, which ended when the United States landed first, in July 1969.

On display above the middle of the room is an American **M2 Lifting Body** aircraft. The M2s are airplanes without wings—the shape of the body produces the lift needed to fly—and these research vehicles helped the development of the space shuttle. Here's a cool fact for anyone old enough to remember: This Smithsonian's plane, the M2-F3, is the one you see crashing in the *Six Million Dollar Man* TV-show title sequence. The plane was rebuilt and flew again before being donated to the Smithsonian. See **tinyurl.com/NASM-M2F2** for the video.

LUNAR EXPLORATION VEHICLES (Gallery 112)

At the far end of the first floor, in front of the food court, are the Lunar Exploration Vehicles. Here you'll find the **Apollo Lunar Module LM-2,** the second of 12 built for the Apollo moon missions. While this one never flew in space, it shows how relatively small and delicate these spacecraft needed to be, while safely carrying astronauts a quarter-million miles. Also on display are the Apollo 11 spacesuits worn by the Apollo 11 crew.

MOVING BEYOND EARTH (Gallery 113)

This gallery includes relatively modern space artifacts, including spacesuits, large-scale models of the space shuttle, parts of the **Hubble Space Telescope,** and a life-size replica of the **space shuttle crew compartment.** Interactive displays show the Earth, moon, and Mars. While the walk-in space shuttle–crew area is interesting, much of the material here is covered elsewhere in the museum.

EXPLORE THE UNIVERSE (Gallery 111)

This room covers the history of man's observations about the heavens and how they helped us refine our understanding of the universe.

The first third of the exhibit illustrates the development of the telescope, from the early glass and mirror models of **Galileo's 17th-century "optic tube"** and 18th-century British astronomer **William Herschel's 20-foot telescope** to modern satellite observatories currently flying in space.

The technical details of telescope construction get dry quickly, but two things make this gallery worth a visit. First, there's **excellent photography** displayed in the exhibits, showcasing the increasing ability of successive generations of telescopes to see farther and clearer. Second, there's a good, simple explanation of what **Edwin Hubble** did to get his name on the Hubble Space Telescope: discover that the universe is expanding, and expanding faster and faster.

LOOKING AT EARTH (Gallery 110)

This gallery contains a short overview of the technologies used to look at our own planet. Fans of classic airplanes will want to stop in to see the **de Havilland DH-4,** a World War I–era biplane used for military reconnaissance, and the Cold War's **Lockheed U-2** spy plane, whose legacy includes high-altitude spying missions over the Soviet Union and a fairly successful Irish rock band. Besides these, there are several Earth-facing weather-satellite models on display. These aren't the most glamorous topics in the museum, and much of it is covered elsewhere.

HOW THINGS FLY (Gallery 109)

One of the best and most kid-friendly galleries at Air and Space is How Things Fly, sponsored by Boeing. As its name suggests, the gallery is filled with small, hands-on displays, most about the size of a phone booth, that demonstrate the physical principles of airplane and rocket flight: thrust, drag, lift, and weight. Young museum volunteers circulate around the room to explain the displays, answer questions, and reinforce what the displays have to do with flight.

For example, one display has part of an airplane wing submerged in a clear, plastic pipe full of colored water. Push a button to start the display and a pump moves water over the wing, showing how the water on top of the wing has a lower pressure than the water below. The display explains why this happens (the **Bernoulli Principle**) and how the same effect is what creates lift in an airplane wing, allowing it to fly. Other nearby kiosks show the same effect with different toys, ranging from baseballs hung with string to inflated beach balls spinning untethered above an industrial air blower.

Other hands-on displays show **why wings are round** at the front and pointy in the back; how airplane flaps work; how fast different objects fall in air and in a vacuum (explaining drag); and high-speed flight-wing design. For that, several consecutive hands-on displays explain what **"the speed of sound"** means, how to visualize it (using a large coiled spring), and why it's important for anyone designing a fast plane or rocket.

The section on thrust describes how piston, jet, and rocket engines work. There's a great hands-on display that shows kids how, at high altitudes with thin air, airplane propellers stop working while rocket engines keep going. It's an excellent explanation of **why you can't fly a propeller plane to the moon.**

The museum holds short, instructor-led talks throughout the day on a small stage set up inside this gallery. Most of the talks have a hands-on activity, such as **how to build a great paper airplane,** and kids are given plenty of opportunities to ask questions. If you've got the time and your kids have the interest, it's definitely worthwhile (we got some fantastic paper airplane designs).

The last part of How Things Fly includes a chance to sit in a real Cessna 150 cockpit, a sit-down-and-spin lesson on gyroscopes (it's surprising and loads of fun), and a quick lesson on the material sciences that bring us strong, lightweight airplanes and spacecraft.

TIME AND NAVIGATION (Gallery 213)

The name of this room doesn't sound all that fun, but this is a remarkably interesting set of exhibits, and it's definitely worth a visit. If you used a GPS or Sat-Nav system to get to D.C., this gallery explains part of how it did that.

The exhibits start by explaining why knowing the precise time is critical to knowing where you are in the world. This affected navigation throughout history, from Christopher Columbus's time, through the 20th century.

After World War II, the United States and Soviet Union both needed more precise clocks for their global militaries, which grew to include fast, precise missiles and submarines that couldn't see the stars in the sky. The gallery's display on how the US military merged various timekeeping satellite systems into the **Global Positioning System (GPS),** and how it works, is an excellent conclusion to the theme of time and navigation.

APOLLO TO THE MOON (Gallery 210)

This gallery contains artifacts from the Apollo space program, which started in 1961 and ran through the mid-1970s. The gallery is arranged in chronological order, so **start your tour from the entryway closest to the food court** for the displays to make sense.

The bulk of the gallery contains various artifacts from the Apollo missions, from paper manuals describing how to operate the computers to cameras to a **Command Module instrument panel.** There's an interesting display on why the Apollo spacecraft used fuel cells (similar to those in some zero-emissions cars today) instead of batteries.

THE WRIGHT BROTHERS & THE INVENTION OF THE AERIAL AGE (Gallery 209)

The world's first airplane, the **1903 Wright Flyer,** gets its own gallery here on the second floor. Before you see the plane, however, you're introduced to its inventors, Orville and Wilbur Wright, via short biographical scenes. The gallery does a good job of pointing out how the brothers' bicycle shop helped them build the airplane. The gallery also explains well the Wrights' original ideas about propellers and their **extensive research program** (they wrote to the Smithsonian for information!), including the use of wind-tunnel testing, for their first flights.

TOURING TIPS Because of its popularity, the gallery's two walkways are set up as an entrance and an exit. Enter from the side closest to the middle of the gallery, and exit on the far side, closest to the food court. On very busy days, waits can exceed 30 minutes to enter the room, so see this gallery first thing in the morning, or wait until the hour before the museum closes.

BARRON HILTON'S PIONEERS OF FLIGHT (Gallery 208)

A huge display of aircraft in the middle of the second floor, Pioneers of Flight's theme and timeline overlaps considerably with the Golden Age of Flight downstairs, in that it showcases aircraft and pilots that flew farther, faster, and higher than those before them. However, this gallery also notes the achievements of women and African American pilots, pioneers in their own right, in the early days of flight.

Aircraft on display in this gallery include:

● **Douglas World Cruiser** *Chicago* The U.S. Army sent four of these Douglas World Cruisers on an around-the-world flight attempt in 1924: the *Boston,* the *Chicago,* the *New Orleans,* and the *Seattle.* The *Seattle* crashed soon into the trip, in Alaska, and the *New Orleans* went down in the North Atlantic (all of the pilots survived). The *Boston* and *Chicago,* however, made it all the way back, becoming the first airplanes to fly around the world.

● **Curtiss R3C-2 Racer** James Doolittle flew this seaplane to a new world speed record of 245.7 miles per hour in 1927. Doolittle was an accomplished pilot who set several air-speed records. He was also a top-notch engineer, earning a Ph.D from M.I.T. in aeronautical engineering along the way. Doolittle's most famous achievement is surely "Doolittle's Raid"—the high-risk 1942 bombing mission over Tokyo that was the first Allied attack on the Japanese mainland.

- **Lockheed 5B Vega** One of Amelia Earhart's own airplanes, this was also the first aircraft design produced by Lockheed. Earhart used this plane, which she called the "Little Red Wagon" on two record-setting flights, across the Atlantic and the United States, in the early 1930s.

Displays on air races, flying, and rocketry in popular culture (including *Plane Crazy,* a Mickey Mouse cartoon, because you can't escape Disney) line two of the walls of this enormous room.

EXPLORING THE PLANETS (Gallery 207)

These displays cover man's discovery and exploration of the planets in our solar system (and beyond), starting from the invention of the telescope.

Each planet (and Pluto) gets a dedicated section in this gallery, with detailed photos, video, and other data. Along with information on each planet is displayed the spacecraft sent to view or explore it. Among the highlights, there are replicas of **Curiosity, Sojourner, Spirit,** and **Opportunity** (Mars), **Voyager** (Jupiter, Saturn, Uranus, and Neptune), and **New Horizons** (Pluto and beyond).

TOURING TIPS At the risk of losing our Neil deGrasse Tyson Fan Club badges, this gallery is expendable if you're short on time.

LEGEND, MEMORY, AND THE GREAT WAR IN THE AIR (Gallery 206)

The exhibits in this gallery cover the aircraft and aerial tactics deployed in Europe during World War I. Like other galleries, the displays here are arranged chronologically. If you're facing the gallery, enter on the left side (closest to Gallery 207, Exploring the Planets).

While the airplane had little impact on the outcome of the war, the gallery does a good job of describing how the combatants' press and governments benefited from celebrating their aviators and airplanes. Pilots such as **Manfred von Richthofen (the "Red Baron")** became household names, and their fame was used to sell a variety of commercial products, including frozen pizza.

The strength of this gallery is in the full-size aircraft on display, which we've listed below. One notable aircraft displayed as a scale model is the **Zeppelin-Staaken R.IV Bomber.** Its wingspan of more than 138 feet—bigger than a Boeing 747-200—enabled it to carry a 2,200-pound bomb, but it is too large to be displayed here.

Aircraft on display include:

- **Albatros D.Va** The Albatros line of aircraft was Germany's best fighter design in the middle of World War I. In fact, although he's usually associated with a red Fokker triplane, Manfred von Richthofen scored most of his combat victories in an Albatros similar to this one.
- **Royal Aircraft Factory F.E. 8** The presence of the F.E. 8 in this gallery is to show how quickly aircraft design progressed during the war. In the case of the F.E. 8, it was obsolete by the time it made it to the front.
- **SPAD XIII** *Smith IV* The SPAD XIII, designed in early 1917, was based on the design of the earlier SPAD VII. Heavier and bigger than earlier versions, and equipped with two machine guns, the XIII was faster and better armed than most planes of the time. At least five fighter-pilot aces flew in a SPAD XIII, among them American Eddie Rickenbacker.

- **Fokker D.VII** By 1917, Allied airplanes were regularly defeating Germany's fighters. In response, the Germans held a competition to produce improved designs for both fighters and bombers. The Fokker D.VII model shown here was the fighter chosen; it went into production in 1918. The D.VII was substantially better than earlier German fighters. When the war ended, the armistice agreement included specific language that transferred all of the D.VII aircraft to the Allies.

TOURING TIPS Lots of aircraft engines are on display throughout the museum, many of them, frankly, less interesting than the planes near them. The ones in this room, however, are integral to the stories of their planes. Be sure to read about them.

WORLD WAR II AVIATION (Gallery 205)

World War II produced some of the most well-known airplanes in history. In fact, it produced so many famous and significant aircraft that it'd be close to impossible for the Smithsonian to display all of them in this museum. For that reason, Gallery 205 is dedicated to **land-based fighter aircraft** from the European and Pacific theaters. (See below for where to find more aircraft from this era.)

Five aircraft are on display here: Britain's **Spitfire;** America's **P-51D;** Germany's **Bf 109;** Japan's **Zero;** and Italy's **Folgore.** Generations of children, including at least one of this book's authors, grew up building balsa models of these planes, and they'll be familiar to almost everyone with an interest in aviation.

- **Supermarine Spitfire Mk. VIIc** The Spitfire was the best fighter aircraft produced by England during World War II. It was designed by Supermarine's R.J. Mitchell. Prior to World War II, Mitchell had designed the *S.6B,* a racing aircraft that won the Schneider Trophy (shown in Gallery 105) in 1931 and broke the world speed record.

Mitchell started designing the Spitfire in 1934. Like the S.6B, the Spitfire has elliptical wings, which lower drag and improve speed. Through a series of design upgrades before and during the war, the Spitfire got a powerful Rolls Royce engine (the Merlin, shown at the entrance to this gallery) and eight machine guns in its wings.

The combination of speed, agility, and armament helped lead the Spitfire to its finest hour—defeating the attacking German Luftwaffe in the decisive **Battle of Britain** in the summer of 1940.

- **North American P-51D Mustang** Arguably the United States's best fighter aircraft during World War II, the Mustang was fast, maneuverable, well armed, and had a 1,600-mile range. That range would change the course of the war.

Prior to the P-51, the Allies had no fighter aircraft with the range to accompany bomber groups on missions over Germany. Early attempts at flying "self-defending" bombers over Germany proved disastrous, and the Allies were forced to switch to nighttime bombing, which wasn't as effective, or simply accept the losses.

Things changed dramatically when the P-51s started flying with the 8th Air Force in the spring of 1944. The P-51 broke the German air defenses in a matter of months, allowing daytime bombing missions over all of Germany. The head of the German Luftwaffe, Herman Goering, was reported to have said, "When I saw Mustangs over Berlin, I knew the jig was up."

- **Messerschmitt Bf 109** The Bf 109 was Germany's best fighter aircraft of World War II. Designed in the mid-1930s, the BF 109 had already been used in combat in Spain in the late 1930s. That gave the 109s engineers and pilots valuable experience, even before England joined the war.
- **Mitsubishi A6M Reisen "Zero"** This was Japan's best fighter of World War II. It was designed in 1937 to be deployed from navy carriers, and so it had to be lightweight and fast. As a result, the Zero could out-turn and out-climb most American planes. It also had a tremendous range—1,600 miles, about that of a P-51D—and could stay in a dogfight for a very long time. Those characteristics offered a huge advantage over early American naval aircraft at the start of the war, and they forced the Allies to develop new tactics and planes. Still, like the P-51 Mustang, the Zero shot down around 11 airplanes for every one lost.

TOURING TIPS If you want to see more World War II aircraft, two American carrier-based planes sit across the hall in the Sea-Air Operations gallery: the Grumman F4F Wildcat and the Douglas SBD Dauntless. For even more fighters and bombers, including the F4U Corsair, P-40 Warhawk, Focke-Wulf Fw 190, B-29, and more, head to the Smithsonian's **Udvar-Hazy Center** in Chantilly, Virginia, about 30 to 40 minutes outside D.C.

SEA-AIR OPERATIONS (Gallery 203)

This entire gallery is dedicated to naval aviation and is a fitting end to your tour of the exhibits. The highlights here are a replica aircraft-carrier hangar deck and an air-traffic control center, on different floors within the gallery. Huge video screens, actual audio, and real carrier artifacts surround you as you watch footage of jets catapulting off the deck and returning for landings.

Naval aircraft on display in Sea-Air Operations include:

- **Boeing F4B-4** This was one of the US Navy's primary carrier-based fighters in the early and mid-1930s. A biplane, its top speed was around 186 miles per hour and it could carry just under 500 pounds of bombs.
- **Grumman F4F-4 Wildcat** The Wildcat became part of the US Navy's aircraft fleet in 1940, and, like the F4F-3, it was the best carrier-based fighter the United States had in the Pacific until the F6F Hellcat (on display at the Udvar-Hazy Center in Chantilly).
- **Douglas SBD-6 Dauntless** If it's possible for an airplane to change the course of naval history, then the SBD-6 Dauntless did just that.

After Jimmy Doolittle's bombing of Tokyo in April 1942, Japan sent its naval forces farther out into the Pacific, to capture islands and prevent the Allies from establishing air bases for more raids. In particular, Japan sent 21 major ships toward Midway, which was around 2,200 miles from Tokyo and an important refueling point for ships and planes heading out from Hawaii.

What Japan didn't realize was that the United States had just cracked the secret communication code used by Japan's navy, allowing the Allies to know how many ships Japan was sending, where, when, and of what kind. To keep the element of surprise, the United States positioned its aircraft carriers just outside the range of Japanese radar, on the other side of the island.

At Midway, Japan's four aircraft carriers had launched a first wave of bombers against the island's airstrip and fighters to escort them. While those bombers were refueling on the carrier decks (and the fighters waited their turn to refuel), four squadrons of Navy SBDs attacked from different directions. It was incredibly fortunate timing.

The SBDs' bombs ignited massive firestorms on the Japanese carriers—three of them sank in less than 10 minutes. All told, Japan lost four carriers, a heavy cruiser, 248 airplanes, and more than 3,000 men. In contrast, the United States lost one carrier, about 150 planes, and 307 men. It was a huge victory for the Americans, and Japan's navy never recovered.

● **Douglas A-4C Skyhawk** Bucking the trend of each aircraft generation to be larger, heavier, and more complex than the previous one, the Skyhawk was specifically designed to be small, lightweight, and simple. Because of the plane's lightness and speed, it found roles as part of the Navy Fighter Weapons School (you know it as "TOPGUN") and in the Navy's Blue Angels aerobatic team.

IMAX MOVIES, EINSTEIN PLANETARIUM, AND FLIGHT SIMULATORS

The museum's **IMAX movie theater** shows high-definition, large-format movies throughout the day. Naturally, most of the films are related to airplanes or spaceflight; the rest almost always have something to do with American history. Tickets for popular midday shows can sell out, so get your tickets early in the day if you know you want to see a particular film at a specific time. Tickets cost around $9 per person.

In addition to IMAX movies, the **Einstein Planetarium** shows movies on its curved planetarium ceiling. Among the best current offerings is *Dark Universe*, hosted by Neil deGrasse Tyson. It's an exploration of dark matter and dark energy, which make up the vast majority of the stuff in the universe, yet can't be detected or analyzed directly. It's also playing at the Museum of Natural History in New York. Tickets cost around $9 per person.

Finally, the Smithsonian has dedicated an entire gallery room to large **flight simulators** that you can try out for yourself. These are fairly advanced for what they are—way more than an arcade game. With just a little prompting, you can spin one 360 degrees around in a loop. Tickets are $8 per person for a two-person simulator, or you can fly alone for $16. Empty your pockets first.

TOURING TIPS Each of the museum's galleries is dedicated to a specific era of flight, but the galleries are not arranged chronologically. That makes it hard to trace the development of flight technology. The alternative is to walk across the museum to maintain the right historical timeline. Our touring plan avoids skipping around the museum in favor of less walking.

DINING The museum's food court contains a McDonald's, a Boston Market, and a Donato's Pizza. The food court gets very busy at lunchtime. On weekends and during summer, expect waits of 10–40 minutes to order and get your food. According to the staff we spoke with, waits can approach 90 minutes on July 4 and Thanksgiving weekend. If the line for food looks substantially longer than the line to get into the museum, consider going to the cafeteria at the Museum of the American Indian around the corner. There'll be a much shorter wait and better food.

TOURING PLAN

1. Arrive at the Independence Avenue entrance about 20 minutes prior to opening. On summer holidays and weekends, arrive 30 minutes prior to opening. Bring water.

2. If you have kids, tour How Things Fly (Gallery 109) as soon as the museum opens. These hands-on exhibits will be entertaining for all children, and older kids might pick up on a couple of science tips. Also check the daily entertainment schedule for any hands-on labs, such as building paper airplanes.

3. Begin a clockwise tour of the first floor's exhibits with Early Flight (107). Note how each airplane on display uses completely different methods to stay in control during flight.

4. Continue to The Jet Age (Gallery 106), and tour the jet exhibits. See the Messerschmitt Me 262A *Schwalbe.*

5. Tour The Golden Age of Flight (Gallery 105). See the Hughes H-1 and the Curtiss Robin J-1 Deluxe.

6. Briefly tour the rotating exhibits in Gallery 104.

7. There is a lot to see in See America By Air (Gallery 102). Don't miss the walk-through of the American Airlines DC-7, the Ford 5-AT Tri-Motor, and the Douglas DC-3. Also check out the Airbus flight simulator.

8. See everything in the Boeing Milestones of Flight Hall (Gallery 100), including the Apollo 11 Command Module, the *Spirit of St. Louis,* and the Bell X-1.

If you want to see an IMAX movie, get tickets now.

9. Tour Space Race (Gallery 114). The exhibits are arranged chronologically, so enter it from the side farthest from the Milestones of Flight Hall. Save the Skylab tour until you're on the second floor.

10. Briefly tour the Space Shuttle mock-up in Moving Beyond Earth (Gallery 113).

11. Check out the Apollo Lunar Module LM-2 in Lunar Exploration Vehicles (Gallery 112).

12. If you have time, check out the Big Bang exhibits in Explore the Universe (Gallery 111) and the history of satellites and spy planes in Looking at Earth (Gallery 110).

13. Eat lunch. If the line to get food is more than 45 minutes, consider leaving the museum for the cafeteria at the National Museum of the American Indian, around the corner. The food is better, with far fewer crowds.

14. Pick up your tour on the second floor with Time and Navigation (Gallery 213).

15. Tour Apollo to the Moon (Gallery 210) if you didn't get enough at Space Race on the first floor.

16. the world's first airplane in The Wright Brothers & the Invention of the Aerial Age (Gallery 209).

17. Tour the Barron Hilton Pioneers of Flight (Gallery 208). See the Douglas World Cruiser Chicago and Amelia Earhart's Lockheed 5B Vega.

18. If you have the time and interest (in planetary exploration), see the exhibits in Exploring the Planets (Gallery 207). Otherwise, continue to the next step.

19. See Legend, Memory, and the Great War in the Air (Gallery 206), including the Albatros D.Va and the Fokker D.VII.

20. See the famous WWII fighter aircraft in World War II Aviation (Gallery 205).

21. Check out the carrier flight-deck simulators in Sea-Air Operations (Gallery 204).

22. See an IMAX movie or visit any missed exhibits.

National Archives ★★★

URL archives.gov. Address Constitution Ave. NW between 7th and 9th Streets, Washington, D.C. 20565. **Phone** ☎ 202-357-5000. **What it is** Home of the U.S. Declaration of Independence, Constitution, and other important American documents. **Scope and scale** Major attraction. **When to go** Anytime; last admission is 30 minutes prior to closing. **Hours** Daily, 10 a.m.–5:30 p.m. Closed 4th Thursday of November, December 25. **Closest Metro** Federal Triangle (Blue, Orange, Silver); Archives (Yellow and Green); Gallery Place/Chinatown (Red). **Admission** Free. **Authors' comments** Make reservations if visiting during summer or holidays; see **TOURING TIPS** for details. Photography is prohibited throughout the Archives. **Not to Be Missed** (Record of Rights gallery, ground level) 1297 Magna Carta; (Rotunda for the Charters of Freedom, upper level) U.S. Declaration of Independence, U.S. Constitution, and Bill of Rights.

DESCRIPTION AND COMMENTS The National Archives is the United States's warehouse for official, historic, and important public records. Besides the U.S. Declaration of Independence and Constitution, it holds more than 10 billion pages of documents; 12 million maps, charts, and architectural drawings; 25 million photos; and 700,000 sound and video recordings. The Archives also holds millions of records on US military service and family genealogy.

The Archives's presentations are spread over two floors: The **ground level** contains an orientation area, the *Record of Rights* exhibition, and the Archives's store. The **upper level** contains the *Charters of Freedom Rotunda,* holding the Declaration and Constitution, plus other exhibits pulled from the Archives collection and shown on the same floor. There's also a **lower-level** basement for the Archives's small café.

GROUND LEVEL

The *Record of Rights,* in the David M. Rubenstein gallery, is a permanent exhibit on the evolution of US citizens' rights over time. It begins with a look at the English **Magna Carta** from 1297. Magna Carta was originally written in 1215 by rebellious wealthy English landowners fed up with King John's often-capricious treatment and above-the-law behavior. The original document was essentially a peace treaty between the two sides, spelling out a specific list of rights and responsibilities each side would agree to live by.

Magna Carta is just the start of *Record of Rights.* When it was ratified in 1788, the U.S. Constitution contained no explicit guarantees for equality; freedom of speech, religion, or assembly; the right to bear arms; or any of the protections now known as the Bill of Rights, which was ratified in 1791. Specifically, the Constitution's guaranteed rights were generally understood to apply only to white men: Women couldn't vote; slavery would be legal for almost 75 more years, and racial discrimination exists to this day.

National Archives

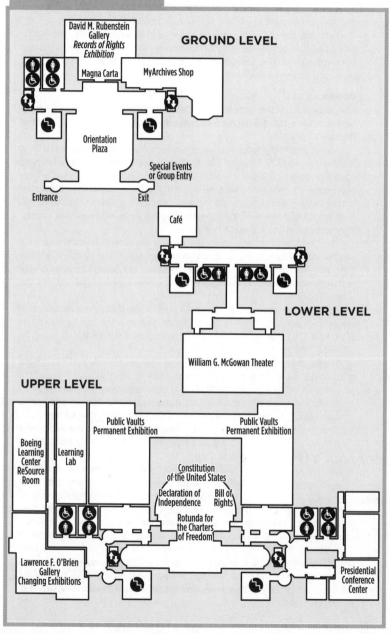

GROUND LEVEL

David M. Rubenstein Gallery
Records of Rights Exhibition

Magna Carta

MyArchives Shop

Orientation Plaza

Special Events or Group Entry

Entrance   Exit

Café

LOWER LEVEL

William G. McGowan Theater

UPPER LEVEL

Public Vaults Permanent Exhibition

Public Vaults Permanent Exhibition

Boeing Learning Center ReSource Room

Learning Lab

Constitution of the United States

Declaration of Independence

Bill of Rights

Rotunda for the Charters of Freedom

Lawrence F. O'Brien Gallery Changing Exhibitions

Presidential Conference Center

However, as *Record of Rights says,* the long-term trend for civil rights is inclusion and expansion. What this exhibit does well is show the timeline of people and events that have contributed to this expansion, from the adoption of the 14th Amendment to the Voting Rights Act of 1965 and beyond.

That said, the civil rights material covered in *Record of Rights* also is covered in exhibits at the Library of Congress, the National Museum of American History, the Newseum, and other locations around Washington, D.C. If time is short, you only need to choose one of these.

UPPER LEVEL

The centerpiece of the Archives is the **Charters of Freedom Rotunda,** containing the original **U.S. Declaration of Independence, Constitution,** and **Bill of Rights.**

Admittance to the rotunda is done in groups of around 30 people at a time, roughly every 5 to 10 minutes. The documents are encased in protective glass cases lining about half the rotunda's circumference, starting with the Declaration on the left and ending with the Bill of Rights on the right. Once you're admitted to the rotunda, you're told to walk directly to whatever document you wish to view first. However, most people instinctively head left and form a long, slow processional to visit each text in turn.

The Declaration on display is the original document, written on animal parchment by Thomas Jefferson's own hand, and signed first by John Hancock. Though it is on display, the Declaration is entirely unreadable because of age and wear. However, excellent copies of the document are available just past the rotunda's exit.

The Constitution on display at the Archives is also the original document. It was written across five sheets of parchment, four of which can be viewed by the public. (The fifth page of the Constitution deals only with how it would be ratified by the states; it is shown rarely.)

The Bill of Rights on display is the original *1789 Joint Resolution of Congress,* proposing 12 additions to the newly adopted Constitution. Articles 3 through 12 were ratified in 1791 and became the first 10 amendments—the Bill of Rights.

Besides these documents, the **East Rotunda Gallery** displays one or two notable objects from the Archives's vaults. Displays change about every two months. Past exhibits have included **the original Coca-Cola bottle and patent** and **Japan's** *Instruments of Surrender* **from World War II.**

unofficial **TIP**
You can search the National Archives's documents at **archives.gov/research.**

Also in the upper level is the **Lawrence F. O'Brien Gallery,** used for rotating, in-depth presentations on a single subject from American history. The most recent is *Spirited Republic: Alcohol in American History,* covering our country's long and often contentious relationship with beer and spirits.

TOURING TIPS Make an advance reservation to avoid a long, outdoors wait to enter the Archives if you're visiting during spring break, summer, or a holiday. Reserved visits are available from 10:30 a.m. to 90 minutes before closing, daily. Admission to the Archives is free, but there's a $1.50 per-person fee for reservations. Visit **archives.gov/museum/visit/reserved-visits.html** to get started.

US military personnel in uniform or with valid military ID can enter through the Special Events entrance on the corner of Constitution Avenue and 7th Street.

The museum advises against bringing backpacks, large bags, or metal jewelry into the building. Also keep your camera at home—photography is prohibited throughout the building.

National Gallery of Art and Sculpture Garden ★★★★½

URL nga.gov. **Address** Constitution Ave. NW between 4th and 7th Streets, Washington, D.C. 20565. **Phone** ☎ 202-737-4215. **What it is** One of America's best art museums; collection of European and American works with special emphasis on 17th- to 19th-century Dutch and Flemish paintings, Impressionists, and modern art and sculpture. **Scope and scale** Headliner. **When to go** Anytime. **Hours** Monday–Saturday, 10 a.m.–5 p.m.; Sunday, 11 a.m.–6 p.m. Closed January 1 and December 25. Hours vary for the sculpture garden, but 10 a.m.–6 or 7 p.m. is common. **Closest Metro** Smithsonian (Blue, Orange, Silver); Archives 7th Street Exit (Yellow and Green); Judiciary Square 4th Street Exit (Red). **Admission** Free. **Authors' comments** Excellent small café on ground floor. **Not to Be Missed** (First Floor) *Ginevra de' Benci* by Leonardo da Vinci (Gallery 6); Works by Raphael (Gallery 20); Works by Rembrandt (Gallery 48); *Girl Holding a Balance* by Vermeer (Gallery 50A); *Ellen Peabody Endicott* by John Singer Sargent and *Symphony in White, No. 1* by James McNeill Whistler (Gallery 69); and Impressionist works by Monet, Renoir, Pissarro, van Gogh, Gauguin, Degas, Seurat, Cézanne, and Picasso (Galleries 80–90; tour in reverse). (Ground Floor) *The Thinker* and *The Age of Bronze* by Augustus Rodin (Gallery 2); Equestrian models in beeswax by Edgar Degas (Gallery 4); *Number 1, 1950 (Lavender Mist)* by Jackson Pollock (Gallery 39); *No. 1* and an untitled work by Mark Rothko (Gallery 39); and female heads in various early 20th-century sculpture styles (Gallery 41). (Sculpture Garden) *Typewriter Eraser, Scale X* by Claes Oldenburg and Coosje van Bruggen; *Aurora* by Mark di Suvero; *Cheval Rouge (Red Horse)* by Alexander Calder; *House I* by Roy Lichtenstein; *Graft* by Roxy Paine; *An Entrance to the Paris Métropolitain* by Hector Guimard.

DESCRIPTION AND COMMENTS The National Gallery of Art (NGA) is one of the world's best collections of art. Within the United States, only New York's Metropolitan Museum compares in terms of scope, scale, and quality. The NGA's collection is so large that it spans two buildings and an outdoor park. The **West Building** focuses on European and American painting and small sculpture, from 13th-century religious canvasses to mid-20th-century Picassos and Rothkos. The **East Building** (currently closed for renovation; reopens 2016) contains modern art from around 1900 to the present. The **Sculpture Garden** contains even more modern art, on a larger scale and outdoors.

The NGA recently acquired the **Corcoran Gallery** collection of more than 17,000 works from Europe and America. About a third of these will be integrated into the NGA's displays by the end of 2016. In the meantime, below you'll find comprehensive tours of the West Building and Sculpture Garden.

THE WEST BUILDING: MAIN FLOOR

Start your tour on the main floor of the West Building. The main floor is divided into four quadrants, with the rotunda separating east and west, and the long hallways of the gallery dividing north and south. Galleries are numbered,

National Gallery of Art

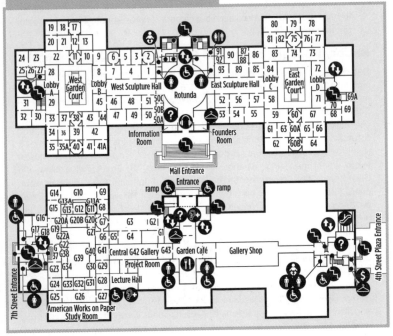

starting with 1 immediately left and back of the rotunda, and proceeding counterclockwise. The last gallery, 93, is just off the rotunda to the right rear.

- **Galleries 1 through 29** cover European art from the 13th century to around 1650. The vast majority of these works are devoted to themes from early Christianity, and they are important and beautiful. That said, there are only so many paintings of Saint Jerome that you need to see, especially if you've got children. Here's what you need to know and view in these galleries to save time and interest.

unofficial **TIP**
To keep small children interested in the art, have them find the oldest paintings that contain a dog or cat.

Start with the d'Arezzo painting *Madonna and Child Enthroned with Four Saints* in Gallery 1. Thirteenth-century paintings were concerned almost exclusively with religious subjects and the morality lessons they conveyed, without regard for background, realism, or perspective. *Madonna and Child* is a good example: a front-facing, two-dimensional image of Mary and Jesus; the basic outline of a simple throne on which they're seated; and small, full-body representations of four saints in what would be the background scene. The infant Jesus has the features of a tiny adult, not a child, and there's little evidence of a maternal bond with Mary. (That would also change over time.) Notice also that most of the art in this room was painted on wood panels, not canvas.

Next, pop in to Gallery 4 and take a look at *The Annunciation* by Fra Carnevale from around 1445, about 150 years after the d'Arezzo. It's still a religious painting, but there's a background scene with a tree, blue sky, and clouds. In addition, the lines of the garden squares and those of the building facades all converge to a single point in the distance, giving the viewer the impression of depth and perspective.

Gallery 6 has the only painting by Leonardo da Vinci in the United States, a portrait of *Ginevra de' Benci* from around 1474. Here, the background contains a juniper bush, which da Vinci chose because of its association with faithfulness. Da Vinci also painted the back of this panel, decorating it with juniper, a palm branch, and a laurel wreath. An inscription reads (in Latin) "Beauty adorns virtue."

If you're a fan of Renaissance art, check out the NGA's **Raphael** collection in Gallery 20. *Saint George and the Dragon,* the *Alba Madonna,* and the *Niccolini-Cowper Madonna* are here, plus a portrait of *Bindo Altoviti.* Raphael was a contemporary of both Michelangelo and da Vinci, and the three are considered the masters of the Italian Renaissance period (roughly 1490 to 1530).

Of his many skills, Raphael was known for his realistic paintings of people, and the *Bindo Altoviti* is a good example. Notice how well defined Altoviti's hair is, and how the light hits it. Compare the *Altoviti* to the adjacent *Portrait of a Young Woman* by Girolamo di Benvenuto from 1505, to see how much more lifelike were Raphael's works than his contemporaries.

unofficial **TIP**
Such is the largess of the NGA that they've got a Rembrandt—*Portrait of a Man in a Tall Hat*—in the West Stair Lobby. Just like at our house.

There's more Italian Renaissance in Gallery 23, with **Titian** portraits and allegorical works (his *The Feast of the Gods,* with Bellini, is in Gallery 12), and **Tintoretto** and **Veronese** in Gallery 24.

If you have small children, make your way over to Gallery 29 and a quick lesson on perspective. Position your children at the far left of *The Lute Player* by **Orazio Gentileschi,** and have them focus on the neck of the violin on the table (it's facing toward them). Next, have the kids move slowly to the right side of the painting, while keeping their eye on the violin. They should see the violin's neck "follow" them as they move. That's perspective in action.

The National Gallery's collection of **Dutch, Flemish, and Netherlandish** art is one of its strengths, and the displays begin around Gallery 39, which shows Netherlandish sculpture and painting beginning around 1400. The galleries are arranged roughly chronologically, so you can see the evolution of subject matter, detail, and perspective of these artists as with those of the Italian Renaissance.

Our tour of the highlights includes Gallery 42, which features early 17th-century Flemish portraits by **Anthony Van Dyck** and **Peter Paul Reubens.** (Van Dyck served an apprenticeship in Reubens's studio.) Although he wasn't British, Van Dyck was part of the royal court of King Charles I, and he did many portraits of royalty and nobility during this time.

unofficial **TIP**
More Van Dyck and Reubens portraits can be found in Gallery 43. Reubens's allegorical paintings are in Gallery 45.

The one Peter Paul Reubens work in Gallery 42 is an early one, *Marchesa Brigida Spinola Doria,* from 1606, but it's amazing in its detail and technique. Notice Reubens's ability to capture light shimmering in the fabric of the marchesa's silver gown and the detail in the gown's lace collar.

Next, head to Gallery 48 for 17th-century works by **Rembrandt** and his students. Considered the best of the Dutch painters, and among Europe's finest, Rembrandt van Rijn was known for his unembellished portraits (including many self-portraits—see his 1659 *Self-Portrait* here) and narrative scenes from the Bible and mythology.

Like his peers, Rembrandt used light and darkness to govern the mood of a painting. In Gallery 48, notice how his portrait subjects' noses are used as the dividing line between lighter and darker areas of the canvas. Even in the landscape *The Mill* here, the "nose" of the windmill is the demarcation between sunlight on the right and storm clouds on the left.

Works from the last 15 years of Rembrandt's life are in **Gallery 51,** plus those of his workshop. These are both portraits and biblical scenes, and they tend to use darker colors than his earlier paintings.

No trip through the Dutch artistic scene would be complete without a visit to **Vermeer,** in Gallery 50A. Vermeer is known for capturing incredible details in his work and for his very realistic depictions of the interplay of light and dark. A couple of the Vermeers in this room are fantastic. *Woman Holding a Balance* shows a young woman standing at a table, holding a small scale. The sun streams into the room from a window above and to the left, and the light falls unevenly on the textured gray wall behind her, as well as the blue robe she's wearing. The sunlight also falls on the pearls and gold she's weighing, while in the background is a painting of The Last Supper.

Galleries 51 through 59 include works from Europe and England from Vermeer's time (circa 1630) through the 18th century, organized by region and artist rather than by year. Spanish art, including works by **Goya,** are in Gallery 52; French artists are in galleries 53 through 56. British landscapes, including those by **J.M.W. Turner** and **John Constable,** are in Gallery 57; portraits are in Gallery 58.

Gallery 59 is a transition from British portrait artists to American, around the time of the American Revolution. Two early portraits by Rhode Islander **Gilbert Stuart** are here: *The Skater (Portrait of William Grant)* and *Sir Joshua Reynolds.* *The Skater* launched Stuart's career as a portrait artist. He went on to paint more than 1,000 subjects, including US Presidents Washington through John Quincy Adams. An unfinished Stuart work of Washington is the basis for George's image on the back of the US $1 bill; you can view the painting at the National Portrait Gallery nearby.

If you're a fan of American landscapes, and the **Hudson River School** style in particular, you'll want to see Gallery 60's four-panel installation *The Voyage of Life* by **Thomas Cole,** the school's founder. In this series, Cole expressed human life as a solitary boat trip down a river. More Hudson River School artists, including Cole, **A.B. Durand,** and **Albert Bierstadt,** are in Gallery 64, as well as in Lobby C off the East Garden Court.

If you've got the time, stop off in Gallery 69 to see two wildly different approaches to portrait paintings

unofficial **TIP**

If you follow the Hudson River School artists, the Smithsonian Museum of American Art has a slightly better collection than NGA, including many works by Albert Bierstadt.

by Americans **James McNeill Whistler** and **John Singer Sargent.** Sargent was considered the best portrait painter of his era, and these four examples are a good representation of his skill. Then contrast Sargent's style with that of Whistler, in which one color usually dominates the canvas. The upper two-thirds of *Symphony in White No. 1: The White Girl,* for example, are essentially different shades of white surrounding the girl's face.

IMPRESSIONISM

Main floor rooms 80 and above are dedicated to Impressionism. Up to this point, we've been touring the galleries in numerical order, starting with Gallery 1. If you want to follow Impressionism's development from the early 19th century on, though, start with Gallery 93 and work your way down to 80.

In Gallery 93, start with **Jean-Baptiste-Camille Corot's** 1838 landscape *A View near Volterra.* Painted 25 years before the birth of the Impressionist school, it's a fairly traditional landscape. But notice the fallen tree, vegetation, and path in the foreground. Rocks are shown as little more than taupe ovals, made with short brush strokes; the white moss on the tree is represented by white down strokes with a stiff brush; and the nearby shrubs are loosely arranged dabs of green. If John Singer Sargent had painted this, you'd be able to identify the species of each plant by its leaf edges, and the horse would be wearing a burgundy robe with lace bridle.

Moving to Gallery 92, you can see in the landscapes of **Eugène Boudin** a continued shift away from detailed representation and toward capturing the colors and shapes seen at a particular moment in time. In *Jetty and Wharf at Trouville,* pay attention to how Boudin paints the clothing and faces of the people in the lower right, especially the mother, father, girl in a white-and-blue dress, and their dog.

Galleries 90 and 89 hold works by Paris-based artists around the beginning of the Impressionist movement, roughly 1864 to 1867. Gallery 90 has mostly portraits (and one still life) from **Paul Cezanne, Edgar Degas, Edouard Manet,** Monet, and Renoir. Because they're portraits, it's easy to compare how these artists represented their subjects' faces. Renoir's 1864 *Mademoiselle Sicot,* for example, is a fairly conventional approach; you can even make out the detail in her earrings.

But compare the Renoir to Monet's *Bazille and Camille (Study for "Déjeuner sur l'Herbe")* adjacent, then Manet's *The Tragic Actor* after that. Manet specifically avoids trying to blend the pinks and yellows of the man's skin in with the brown and gray brush strokes under his eyes and the shaded side of his face. He's going out of his way to contrast the color of skin and shadow. (An even larger contrast is Paul Cézanne's *Antony Valabrègue* nearby.)

Monet's faces for *Bazille and Camille* are even less defined—you can kind of make out a couple of ears, a mouth, and Bazille's beard—but those aren't the focus. Monet wants you to look at the dress, which spans three-quarters of the canvas, and the interplay of light and fabric.

Gallery 89 mostly covers the years 1869 to 1880, and it includes Manet's *The Railway;* Renoir's *Pont Neuf, Paris;* **Camille Pissarro's** *Place du Carrousel, Paris;* Bazille's *Edmond Maître;* and **Mary Cassat's** *The Loge.* Cassat was an American living in Paris and was part of the Impressionists' circle. Her work here exhibits all of the characteristics of that style—notice how Cassat chose the audience as her subject, not the performers.

There's more Pissaro in Gallery 88, which covers 1880 to 1891, but the real draw here is **Georges Seurat,** father of *pointillism.* Remember that one trait of Impressionism is the use of short brush strokes and bold, unblended colors. Seurat took this to the extreme by using thousands of tiny dots of color to create entire paintings. Stand as close as the security guards will allow you to get to Seurat's *Seascape at Port-en-Bessin, Normandy* and you'll see nothing but those tiny dots. Step back 3 feet and the dots form an ocean, sky, coastline, and mountains.

Gallery 87 is devoted entirely to **Claude Monet** landscapes from the period 1894 to 1908. The National Gallery has an interesting arrangement here, showing how Monet painted the same subject in different ways depending on the time of day.

Gallery 86 focuses on portraiture and scenes from the lives of everyday Parisians, mostly through works by **Mary Cassatt** from 1878 to 1905.

More **Monet landscapes** are in Gallery 85, including *The Japanese Footbridge.* In 1893, Monet bought some land with a pond next to his house in Giverny, France, and diverted a small stream to run through the property. This work is one of 12 he painted from the exact same spot in his yard that year.

A dozen paintings from **Paul Cézanne** are in Gallery 84, covering the years 1873 to 1906, most from 1890 on. What's interesting here is how Cézanne's style changes from Impressionism to focusing on the geometric shapes of his subjects. That shift would influence Pablo Picasso, among others, in the early part of the 20th century.

The two early works, *House of Père Lacroix* from 1873 and *Landscape near Paris* from 1876, are in the Impressionist style, with bright colors and an emphasis on light and color, and lots of quick brush strokes.

You can see Cézanne's style change, however, by 1883's *Houses in Provence: The Riaux Valley near L'Estaque.* Look at how Cézanne painted the hills and grasses in the foreground, using aggressive, short, diagonal strokes, all in the same direction. Also notice how Cézanne played with depth, perspective, and shape in the houses. Two other paintings, 1888's *Harlequin* and *Boy in a Red Waistcoat,* show Cézanne manipulating color and geometry.

More well-known artists are in Gallery 83, including **Edgar Degas, Paul Gauguin,** and **Vincent van Gogh.** To paraphrase Augustus Saint-Gaudens (Gallery 66), insanity is to art as garlic is to salad. And in that case, it's a good thing that Vincent van Gogh wasn't a chef because he exhibited signs of mental illness for most of his short, prolific life. Although van Gogh was Dutch, he lived in Paris from 1886 to 1888 and counted Pissarro, Gauguin, and Toulouse-Lautrec among his close friends.

Both van Gogh and Degas were fans of Gauguin's style, which most notably departed from Impressionism by painting natural objects in artificial colors. His travels to the South Pacific, including Tahiti, came at a time when Europe was fascinated with that part of the world. Gauguin's works from this time on display here include *Fatata te Miti (By the Sea), Parau na te Varua ino (Words of the Devil), The Bathers,* and *Te Pape Nave Nave (Delectable Waters).* Take a good look at how Gauguin paints the human bodies in *Te Pape Nave Nave* and see if you can spot similarities in Picasso's *Two Youths* next door.

Our tour of Impressionism ends in Gallery 80, which features works by Picasso, **Henri de Toulouse-Lautrec,** and **Amedeo Modigliani.** The works in this gallery show the transition of Paris-based artists from Impressionism to new styles, as the late 19th century gave way to the early 20th.

Three Picasso works are also in Gallery 80. One is *Le Gourmet,* from 1901, the beginning of Picasso's "blue period" (roughly 1901 to 1904) in which blue is the primary color for most of his work. And notice the way Picasso purposely painted the table out of perspective in this scene. Over the last 700 years, starting from Gallery 1, we've seen artists not use perspective, then experiment with it, try to copy it faithfully, and, here with Picasso, throw the convention away.

WEST BUILDING: GROUND FLOOR

Start in **Gallery 2,** which is given over to sculptures by **Auguste Rodin,** a French sculptor most active in the early 20th century. At the entrance to the room is *The Thinker,* probably the most known of Rodin's works. Although it's shown here by itself, *The Thinker* was designed to be only one part of a huge entrance mural for Paris's Museum of Decorative Arts, depicting scenes from Dante's *Inferno.* The mural was never completed. Several of Rodin's designs for individual figures still survive, however, including *The Kiss (Le Baiser)* here.

Rodin's reputation today is as one of the 20th century's most important sculptors. And while he was fortunate to have heard this in his lifetime, his earliest work was criticized and controversial. The piece in question is *The Age of Bronze,* at the far end of Gallery 2, 1875–1876. It's a life-size male nude, first done in plaster (in Gallery 3), then in bronze. When it was exhibited in 1877, it scandalized Paris because of its contemporary aesthetic; at the time, nude models were generally seen only in works of mythological or historical scenes.

Also in Gallery 2 are three **Edgar Degas** studies for *Little Dancer Aged Fourteen,* and the work itself, in the center of the room. Like *The Age of Bronze,* the use of a contemporary subject (and a working-class girl at that) was novel for Parisians of the time. The other interesting thing about these works is that they're made of colored beeswax designed to look like bronze. Beeswax was cheaper and easier to work with, allowing Degas to achieve the same look as bronze, but faster.

Gallery 4 also has three **Monet** paintings (*The Seine at Giverny* from 1897, *Jerusalem Artichoke Flowers* from 1880, and *Morning Haze* from 1888) and two **Renoirs** (*Girl with a Basket of Oranges* and *Girl with a Basket of Fish,* from 1889.

Next, make your way to Gallery 39, featuring mid-20th-century American artists **Alexander Calder, Jasper Johns, Jackson Pollock,** and **Mark Rothko.**

Pollock and Rothko were part of the Abstract Expressionist movement in post–World War II New York. Because we can't hope to understand it (and think the definition as much a Rorschach test as the art itself), we won't attempt to describe the movement other than to say it rejected most of the last couple thousand years of artistic convention and progress. There are no recognizable people, places, or things to be found here. This said, Pollock's *Number 1, 1950 (Lavender Mist)* is undeniably art, pretty, and makes us feel good. (The artistic among you are screaming, "That's the whole point!" right now. We can tell.)

We're also fans of Rothko's "multiform" work, two examples of which are here: an untitled work from 1955 and *No. 1* from 1961. The untitled work is characteristic of the late stage of Rothko's career, utilizing vertical blocks of contrasting color (here red, black, and white). Also, these paintings are huge—50 square feet or more—on purpose. Rothko pointed out that with small paintings, the viewer is acutely aware of being an outside observer to the scene. In contrast, Rothko wanted his viewers to feel like they were inside the art, often suggesting they get within a couple of feet to better experience it.

If you're ever in a museum and see bits of sheet metal in primary colors all hanging together from the ceiling, chances are it's an **Alexander Calder** mobile. There's one here.

Head to Gallery 41 next. Yes, there are a couple of **Picassos** hanging here (*Pedro Mañach* and the collage *Guitar*), a **Mondrian** (*Tableau No. IV; Lozenge Composition with Red, Gray, Blue, Yellow, and Black*), and a nice portrait by **Henri Matisse** (*La Coiffure*), but the theme you want to recognize here is that most of the room is given to works that represent the human head in different styles. There's the Matisse painting, then Ernst Ludwig Kirchner's *Two Nudes* and *Nude Figure,* both from 1907. Those are examples of Expressionism, in which the artists tried to convey feeling and emotion instead of a faithful representation of reality.

There's also **Joan Miró's** somewhat less abstract *Head of a Catalan Peasant* painting from 1924. But the sculptures make up the best part of the theme, showcasing the same idea in different styles from the early 20th century:

- Matisse's *Figure decorative* from 1908 is perhaps in the style of **Fauvism,** which (like Impressionism) valued form over strictly realistic representation;
- Picasso's *Head of a Woman (Fernande)* from 1909 is a kind of 3-D **cubism;**
- Modigliani's *Head of a Woman,* 1910–11, is in the **Modernist** style;
- Kirchner's *Head of a Woman* from 1913 is an **Expressionist** take.

What is Matisse's *Pot of Geraniums* doing in this room? We're not sure, but the French are an inscrutable people, their artists more so. Just go with it.

End your tour of the West Building with a walk through Gallery 42, showing **Masterpieces of American Furniture** from the Kaufman Collection, covering the years 1700 to 1830. These years cover the William and Mary; Queen Anne; Chippendale; Federal; and Empire styles. If your group includes anyone who's done some woodworking, the pieces and craftsmen represented here will be familiar to them. Don't miss the Philadelphia high chest, the Newport block-and-case desk, or the Willard tall-case clock.

SCULPTURE GARDEN

The National Gallery's Sculpture Garden sits just west of the Gallery's main building, and just east of the Smithsonian Museum of Natural History. It contains almost two dozen large modern and contemporary works, situated around a central fountain that doubles as an ice rink (from mid-November through mid-March).

While most works are indeed sculpture, art forms from mosaics to industrial design are also represented, covering the years from 1902 to the present. Going clockwise from the corner of Constitution Avenue and 9th Avenue, here are the highlights:

- **Marc Chagall,** *Orphée* **(1969)** This mammoth 170-square-foot mural or glass tile loosely depicts the legend of the Greek artist Orpheus, who was said to entrance all living things with his music. Look closely and you may see references to Chagall's emigration to the United States in the early 1940s.

- **Claes Oldenburg and Coosje van Bruggen,** *Typewriter Eraser, Scale X* **(1998)** It's a giant, colorful, circular eraser, almost 20 feet tall. Sure, if you're an art critic, it's easy to point out that making small everyday objects big is a straightforward way around not having any other ideas. On the other hand, the tilt of the rubber wheel and spread of the eraser's blue "fingers" suggests a lightness of movement that belies its 5-ton weight. We love it. Other examples are in Seattle and Las Vegas.

- **Louise Bourgeois,** *Spider* **(1996)** In our review of Ms. Bourgeois' work at the Hirshhorn (see page 140), we mention that she's also known for a series of bronze sculptures depicting giant spiders. Here's one of them, and it's exactly as terrifying as you imagine. It's got to be extra scary after dark, but ahhh, we're busy that night. Let us know if you happen to walk by it.

- **Tony Smith,** *Wandering Rocks* **(1967)** A series of squat, three-dimensional shapes that represent rocks, this is one of five such installations around the world. The interesting thing about the installations is that Smith apparently never said how the pieces are supposed to be arranged relative to each other, instead leaving the decision up to the curators. That makes the "wandering" part of the title appropriate.

- **Mark di Suvero,** *Aurora* **(1992)** di Suvero has another large outdoor sculpture over at the Hirshhorn—*Are Years What? (for Marianne Moore)* (see page 144)—done 25 years earlier than *Aurora,* and it's nice to be able to compare both of these within a short walk. *Aurora's* steel beams and curves are bound to a dense central mass, and all of the steel has been left unpainted to rust. In contrast, *Are Years What* is light, open, and bright red. They both work, but in different ways, and that's a good example of how an artist can use material and void together.

- **David Smith,** *Cubi XI* **(1963)** When the singularity occurs and our robotic overlords have taken over, mankind's last collective thought might be, "These robot bodies look familiar." So if you see *Cubi XI,* you can at least go out knowing where you've seen them before. Smith has a second sculpture here—*Cubi XXVI*—although it's more evocative of di Suvero's *Are Years What* over at the Hirshhorn than Smith's *Cubi XI.*

- **Alexander Calder,** *Cheval Rouge (Red Horse)* **(1974)** Calder is better known for his mobiles, but this sculpture, an abstract representation of a horse (or horses), is great, capturing the flowing curves of an equine body, plus the rounded projection of a horse's chest and neck.

- **Roy Lichtenstein,** *House I* **(1998)** *House I* is a mesmerizing case study on the use of perspective. It's a set of flat, two-dimensional panels, painted to look like a three-dimensional home. You'll find yourself walking past it at different angles just to see how the effects are done. Kids love it.

- **Roxy Paine,** *Graft* **(2008)** *Graft* is a concrete and stainless steel, life-size tree that's positively captivating in the right light. The work's title is a play on the word's definitions, which include splicing part of one tree on to another, so that they both grow together, and corruption, which we've heard happened once in Washington, D.C.

- **Hector Guimard,** *An Entrance to the Paris Métropolitain* **(1902)** Guimard designed the entrances for Paris's then-new subway system in 1900, and to say that the style caught on is an understatement. Done in the Art Nouveau style, more than 80 of them still exist today (and they're protected national treasures). The few that have been removed due to wear have been snapped up and restored by collectors and museums as iconic examples of France's Belle Epoque aesthetic.

TOURING TIPS Besides the permanent collection, the NGA dedicates substantial space to ongoing temporary exhibits, and these are worth at least a walk-through. As we went to press, these exhibits included photography, metal-work prints, and a retrospective of French artist Gustave Caillebotte.

When the East Building reopens in 2016, it will take at least one and a half days to see everything at the NGA. For now, you can tour the West Building in one long day (with lunch), and walk through the Sculpture Garden on your way to and from other attractions along the National Mall.

The NGA's small cafeteria serves excellent food at reasonable prices, with friendly service. And the area around the fountain is a popular place for locals to have lunch when the weather is nice.

National Museum of African American History and Culture *(a Smithsonian museum)*

URL nmaahc.si.edu. **Address** 14th St. and Constitution Ave., Washington, D.C. **What it is** New museum dedicated to African American history and culture. **Scope and scale** Headliner. **When to go** Anytime after its 2016 grand opening. **Closest Metro** Federal Triangle (Blue, Orange, Silver; for Red transfer at Metro Center; for Green, Yellow transfer at Gallery Place). **Admission** Free.

DESCRIPTION AND COMMENTS Scheduled to open to the public in late 2016, the National Museum of African American History and Culture will be located on the National Mall at Constitution Avenue and 14th Street. The museum is being built of glass and bronzed metal, giving it a glowing sheen that will undoubtedly stand out from its neoclassic neighbors. A small welcome center sits on that corner during construction, although staffing is based on volunteers, so its operating times are inconsistent. An exhibit titled Through the African American Lens is currently being housed in the National Museum of American History (see facing page) until it is moved into the new building.

National Museum of American History *(a Smithsonian museum)* ★★★★½

URL americanhistory.si.edu. **Address** 1400 Constitution Ave. NW, Washington, D.C., 20001. **Phone** ☎ 202-633-1000. **What it is** Museum of the United States' historic events, artifacts, and popular culture memorabilia. **Scope and scale** Headliner. **When to go** Anytime. **Hours** Daily, 10 a.m.–5:30 p.m.; often until 7:30 p.m. summer and holidays. Closed December 25. **Closest Metro** Smithsonian or Federal Triangle (Blue, Orange, Silver). **Admission** Free. **Not to Be Missed** Price of Freedom (Floor 3 East); Star-Spangled Banner (Floor 2 East); Food Exhibition (Floor 1 East); Transportation and Technology exhibits (Floor 1 East); Innovations, Creativity and Enterprise exhibits (Floor 1 West).

DESCRIPTION AND COMMENTS What makes the Smithsonian National Museum of American History excellent is its staff's ability to make engaging displays out of almost any part of the country's past, from huge, in-depth examinations of US military conflicts to *The Muppets*. There's something here to entertain every member of your family, and they may learn something along the way.

The west side of Floor 2 is undergoing refurbishment through the end of 2016, the west side of Floor 3 until 2017. That makes it easier to tour the entire museum in a long morning or afternoon, including lunch.

Start your tour on Floor 3 East, with the *Price of Freedom,* a walk-through educational exhibit on the causes, campaigns, and outcomes of every American conflict since the Revolutionary War. Each war is given its own section, and the entire collection takes up almost a third of Floor 3. Within each war, photos, video, and soldiers' memorabilia describe what the fighting was like, along with personal and newspaper accounts of the war effort. Even relatively minor skir-mishes, such as the Spanish-American War, get wall-sized treatments within the exhibit; the Civil and World Wars are multiple hallway-length presentations. A great many of the items on display are shown at child-friendly heights, too, mak-ing it easier for kids to engage. The one downside to all this detail is that you can be overwhelmed with facts by the time you reach Iraq and Afghanistan. Pace yourself by not overdoing it in the first big section (on the Revolutionary War).

Also on Floor 3 are the *Gunboat Philadelphia,* a partially restored ship sunk during battle in the Revolutionary War; *First Ladies,* which shows the gowns and china patterns of America's presidential spouses; and *American Presidency,* describing the daily responsibilities and lives of America's presidents, through photos, video, and personal objects. Each of these is worth a quick walk-through; they're not nearly as long or in-depth as *Price of Freedom.*

Next, make your way to Floor 2 Center and the *Star-Spangled Banner* ex-hibit. The US national anthem was written by Francis Scott Key after a long nighttime battle outside Baltimore, Maryland, during the War of 1812. During the fight, the British Navy attacked Maryland's Fort McHenry while Key, an American, was stuck on the HMS *Tonnant,* trying to negotiate the release of American prisoners. Because it was night, Key couldn't determine how well his fellow Americans were doing in the fight. Given the power of the British navy at the time, things didn't look good for the Yanks.

The flag you see here is the same one Key saw at morning above Fort McHenry 200 years ago, signifying that the US defenses had held. This marked the penultimate major battle in the war, which ended a few weeks later. In the days and years after the battle, the flag was flown in all kinds of weather, and parts were snipped off as souvenirs. Today it sits in a dimly lit, climate-controlled environment to help preserve its color and fabric.

In Floor 2 East is *American Stories,* a collection of the museum's memora-bilia on different subjects (and often pop culture). You're likely to see anything from Dorothy's ruby slippers from *The Wizard of Oz,* to Kermit the Frog, to a piece of Plymouth Rock. The objects usually don't have anything to do with each other, and there's often enough variety for everyone in the family to find something interesting.

Also worth seeing on Floor 2 East is the preview of the **National Museum of African American History and Culture Gallery** (see the previous page for

National Museum of American History

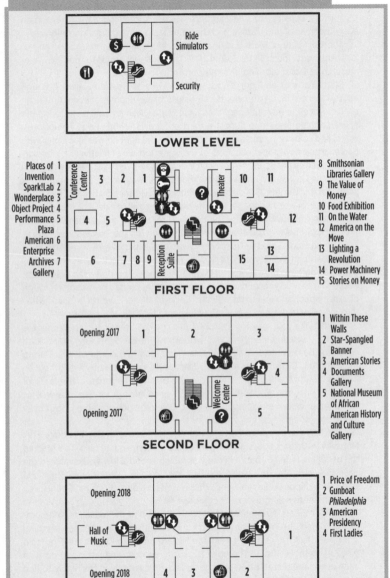

LOWER LEVEL

Ride Simulators
Security

Places of 1
Invention
Spark!Lab 2
Wonderplace 3
Object Project 4
Performance 5
Plaza
American 6
Enterprise
Archives 7
Gallery

Conference Center

3 2 1

Theater

4 5

6 7 8 9

Reception Suite

10 11

12

13
14
15

8 Smithsonian
Libraries Gallery
9 The Value of
Money
10 Food Exhibition
11 On the Water
12 America on the
Move
13 Lighting a
Revolution
14 Power Machinery
15 Stories on Money

FIRST FLOOR

Opening 2017 1

2

3

4

Welcome Center

Opening 2017

5

SECOND FLOOR

1 Within These
Walls
2 Star-Spangled
Banner
3 American Stories
4 Documents
Gallery
5 National Museum
of African
American History
and Culture
Gallery

Opening 2018

Hall of
Music

Opening 2018

4 3 2

1

THIRD FLOOR

1 Price of Freedom
2 Gunboat
Philadelphia
3 American
Presidency
4 First Ladies

details on the new museum, which opens in 2016). Here you'll find a collection of personal memorabilia from African Americans, spanning the earliest days of the nation through today. While some of it is from well-known African American celebrities, much of it is clothing, household items, and personal effects from everyday Americans. It's interesting because it shows both assimilation and the preservation of unique cultural signifiers. Also, don't miss the Woolworth's lunch counter from Greensboro, North Carolina, where four legends from North Carolina A&T State University (Len's alma mater) staged a sit-in in 1961 to protest segregation. #AggiePride.

After this, make your way to Floor 1. Start on the east side, with the *Food Exhibitions*. It begins with a look at TV chef Julia Child's kitchen. From there you'll see displays on everything from how prepackaged meals have changed American family dinners to the impact that microwaves, migrant labor, and California wines have had on what Americans eat.

The next series of exhibits are roughly related: *On the Water* and *America on the Move* are transportation-related displays, covering shipping, railroads, cars, and trucks, from the 1700s through the late 20th century. You'll see full-size vehicles (including trains!), huge dioramas, and some excellent narrative to link it all together. It's one of the best parts of the museum.

Beyond these are *Lighting a Revolution*, which explains how Edison's lightbulb helped the Industrial Revolution, and *Stories on Money*, which covers the history of coins and money, with a focus on American currency and its role in society.

The latest big display to open at the museum is its **Innovation Wing** on Floor 1 West, which traces the history of capitalism in the United States through a series of objects and case studies. If your group contains kids, you can point out (for example) how much of the early US economy was dominated by farming, agricultural products, and slavery. The Industrial Revolution changed that, and with it, the relationship between capital and labor. Give the museum credit for not shying away from that topic: one of the graphs on display shows how labor's share of productivity gains has flattened out over the past few decades, one reason why middle-class wages have stagnated.

Finally, the hallways and common areas of the museum typically display collections of less well-known Americana, from lightbulb collections to unusual machines sent to the US Patent Office. You could spend a few enjoyable, air-conditioned hours just browsing these too.

TOURING TIPS The museum's size makes it easy to tour even on busy days. On holidays and at other peak times, you'll find it easier to arrive 30 minutes before opening, or after 3 p.m.

The museum's cafeteria has an excellent selection of food, prepared well, at somewhat high prices (but remember admission is free). Service is excellent.

National Museum of the American Indian
(a Smithsonian museum) ★★★½

URL nmai.si.edu. Address 4th St. and Independence Ave. SW, Washington, D.C. 20560. **Phone ☎** 202-633-1000. **What it is** Museum dedicated to the cultures and history of indigenous North and South Americans. **Scope and scale** Major attraction. **When to go** Anytime, but weekdays are less crowded. **Closest Metro** L'Enfant Plaza.

(Green, Yellow, Orange, Blue, Silver). **Admission** Free. **Hours** Daily, 10 a.m.–5:30 p.m. Closed December 25. **Not to Be Missed** Our Universes: Traditional Knowledge Shapes Our World; *Nation to Nation: Treaties between the United States and American Indian Nations;* and The Great Inka Road: Engineering an Empire.

DESCRIPTION AND COMMENTS The National Museum of the American Indian is dedicated to preserving the history, culture, and arts of the Western Hemisphere's indigenous peoples. To that end, the museum is housed in one of the most attractive buildings on the National Mall—a curved, limestone four-story building designed to look like a natural rock formation.

We suggest starting your tour on the fourth floor, with the film *Who We Are,* in the Lelawi Theater. This 13-minute film introduces modern native communities and is a good introduction to the style of the rest of the museum.

Next, see the *Our Universes* exhibition, also on the fourth floor. This is a large set of eight walk-through rooms, each focusing on one tribe's religious and cultural views. The tribes span the Americas, from the Quechua in Peru, to the Kha'p'o of New Mexico, to the Yup'ik of Alaska. Within each room, handmade artifacts illustrate each group's daily lives and religious beliefs.

Also on the fourth floor is *Nation to Nation:* **Treaties between the United States and American Indian Nations.** Since the United States was formed, its government has negotiated more than 350 treaties with the independent nations of indigenous Americans. Eight of those treaties are highlighted here, showing not only the end result (spoiler alert: the United States broke all of them), but how each side approached the negotiations with respect to ownership, representation, language, and the very concept of a treaty.

One of the great things about the museum is that its definition of "American Indian" includes South America. In fact, there's an excellent, large exhibit on the third floor, titled **The Great Inka Road: Engineering an Empire,** that explores the Inka empire and its contemporaries. In a massive feat of early engineering, the Inkas built a 24,000-mile system of roads across mountains and jungles, linking together their civilization with others from Ecuador to Argentina to Chile.

Besides relating the history of the road, this 8,500-square-foot exhibit also shows objects from everyday South American life, including clothing, tools, and jewelry. The highlights of this exhibit are the photographs, though, which show how difficult it must have been to put roads across these lands. Amazingly, many of these roads are still in use today as the primary transportation network for many people.

*un*official **TIP**
See an amazing woven bridge built along the Inka Road at **youtu.be/dqI-D6JQ1Bc.**

On your way out, check the performance schedule for the Rasmuson Theater on the first floor. Short programs of native music and dance that are entertaining and informative are often performed throughout the day.

TOURING TIPS The museum's Mitsitam Café serves tasty, interesting food based on Native recipes from North and South America—from buffalo burgers to smoked rhubarb turkey with house-made mustard. Check the latest menu at **mitsitamcafe.com/content/menus.asp.** The café's proximity to the Air and Space Museum (the café is one block east) means that it's easy to head here for lunch, rather than stand in line for Air and Space's fast food.

National Museum of Natural History
(a Smithsonian museum) ★★★★

URL The museum's informative, kid-friendly website is **mnh.si.edu**. **Address** 1000 Constitution Ave. NW, Washington, D.C. 20004. **Phone** ☎ 202-633-1000. **What it is** World-class exhibits of dinosaurs, animals, humans, plants, and geology, and the forces that shape them. **Scope and scale** Headliner. **When to go** Anytime. **Hours** Daily, 10 a.m.–5:30 p.m.; summer hours until 7:30 p.m. Closed December 25. **Closest Metro** Federal Triangle or Smithsonian (Blue, Orange, Silver); Archives 7th St. Exit (Yellow and Green); Judiciary Square 4th St. Exit (Red). **Admission** Free. **Authors' comments** Excellent coverage of evolution, including how it works and how scientists verify that it is true. Note that the National Fossil Hall, which makes up about 20% of the museum's first floor, is closed for renovation through 2018. **Not to Be Missed** (First Floor) Henry the Elephant (rotunda); African dioramas on evolution (Mammal Hall); Hall of Human Origins; right whale model (Ocean Hall); and coral reef (Ocean Hall). (Second Floor) Triceratops skeleton (Bones); T Rex skeleton (Bones); How the moon was formed (Geology, Gems, and Minerals); mine displays (Geology, Gems & Minerals); crystal color and shape displays (Geology, Gems, and Minerals); and The Hope Diamond (Geology, Gems, and Minerals). (Ground Floor) Easter Island Stone Figure (Constitution Ave. exit) and T-Rex skull (Constitution Ave. exit).

*un*official **TIP**
Try the museum's virtual tour at **mnh.si.edu/vtp/1-desktop.**

DESCRIPTION AND COMMENTS

FIRST FLOOR

The museum's two-story rotunda is the approximate center of the building, and it's a good place to reunite if your group is separated. On the first floor of the rotunda is an African elephant named Henry. He's posted in a state of alert, using his senses to investigate what's going on around him. The idea, of course, is that you should also be ready to explore what's around you in the museum.

The rest of this section is a detailed exhibit-by-exhibit tour of both museum floors. A complete tour of the museum can easily take an entire day or more. Instructions in the tour below tell you the parts you can skip if you've got half a day or less.

Mammals Tour the first floor in a clockwise direction, beginning with the Mammals hall. It's an impressive place to start because you're immediately surrounded by lots of big animals. To your left is a two-story display with a life-size moose, white rhino, panda bear, and a score of other creatures; to your right is a similar case with walruses, chimpanzees, horned sheep, and more. Hanging from the ceiling above you is a life-size manatee mother and child, as if they were swimming above you in a stream.

The museum's strength is its ability to explain clearly the scientific basis for the things you're seeing. In the case of mammals, large panels near the hall entrance explain the characteristics that distinguish mammals from other creatures. Specifically, mammals have:

- hair;
- mothers that nurse their young with milk;
- special small ear bones that amplify sound;
- warm-blooded, self-regulating body temperatures;

National Museum of Natural History

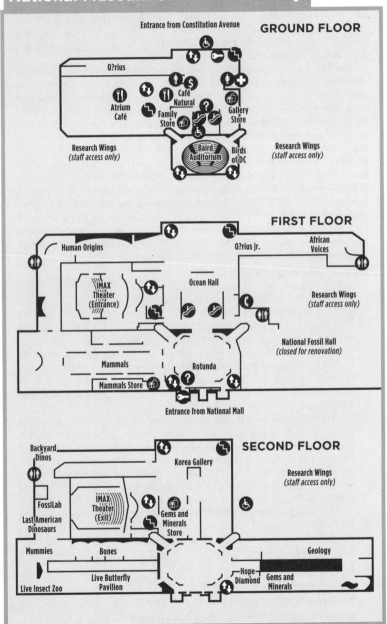

GROUND FLOOR

Entrance from Constitution Avenue

Q?rius

Atrium Café

Café Natural

Family Store

Gallery Store

Research Wings *(staff access only)*

Baird Auditorium

Birds of DC

Research Wings *(staff access only)*

FIRST FLOOR

Human Origins

IMAX Theater (Entrance)

Ocean Hall

Q?rius jr.

African Voices

Research Wings *(staff access only)*

National Fossil Hall *(closed for renovation)*

Mammals

Rotunda

Mammals Store

Entrance from National Mall

SECOND FLOOR

Backyard Dinos

Korea Gallery

Research Wings *(staff access only)*

FossiLab

IMAX Theater (Exit)

Gems and Minerals Store

Last American Dinosaurs

Mummies

Bones

Geology

Live Insect Zoo

Live Butterfly Pavilion

Hope Diamond

Gems and Minerals

- and brains with a neocortex, used to process complex information such as spatial reasoning, social interactions, and speech.

The Mammals hall focuses on the first four characteristics. You'll see more about brain development in the Hall of Human Origins later on this floor.

The story of mammals would be impossible to tell without referencing **evolution,** so the museum introduces here the six elements of the evolutionary process: **environmental change, natural selection, adaptation, innovation, diversification,** and **extinction.** As you view the exhibits in this hall, you'll see signs on display explaining the relevant part of the evolutionary process.

For example, in the **Africa** scenes a few feet away, you'll see how, as the continent's landscape changed from tree-filled rainforest to savannah, giraffe necks got longer in order to reach the leaves on the remaining, higher trees.

*un**official* TIP

Regarding evolutionary diversification, the museum notes that there are more than 4,000 species of rodent, but fewer than 20 species of aardvark.

Just beyond the Africa section is a hallway. To the left are mammals from Australia and South America; to the right is North America. We'll cover these shortly. In front of you, though, is a tall display showing the family tree of *morganucodon oehleri,* the **common ancestor of all mammals,** from around 210 million years ago. A small bronze cast of *m. oehleri* is nearby; it's the thing that looks like a shiny mouse. The museum has named it Morgie and decided it's a she.

Beyond the Morgie display is the **Evolution Theater,** showing a six-minute movie about evolution. The film focuses primarily on the interaction of environmental change and natural selection, with a couple of cameos by Morgie. Limited seating is provided. The movie isn't mandatory for understanding evolution or any part of the museum and can be skipped.

To the left of the Evolution Theater are displays with mammals from Australia and South America.

Australia is the only place on Earth where you'll find koalas and kangaroos, and this section of the museum highlights how those species have adapted to their environment.

The other interesting display in this area is on the monotremes, which include the **platypus** and **echidna,** and are found only in Australia and New Guinea. The echidna looks like the tiny result of a wild night between a porcupine and an anteater—they're adorable, and there should be a cartoon character based on one.

*un**official* TIP

If you're touring the museum for half a day or less, skip Australia and South America and head to your right, through the North America mammals and to the Human Origins hall.

Next on the tour is **South America,** just down the side hall from Australia. More mammals live in South America than anywhere else on Earth. These exhibits focus on the animals that live in the rainforest canopy and how they get their food.

When finished with South America, head across the hall to the exhibit on **North America's mammals.** North America's climate and landscape vary tremendously, from rainforests to tundra, and from very warm to very cold. The mammals shown here demonstrate the ability to adapt to these different conditions. The museum separates the cold-weather mammals from the rest of the displays, to focus on those animals' ability to stay warm and find food through the winters.

The remainder of North America's exhibits covers the prairies and forests. Because the prairies are, like Africa's savannas, wide-open expanses of land in which animals can't hide from predators, you'll see animals here have developed characteristics similar to those in Africa. In particular, the **bison** and **pronghorn antelope** have long legs to help them run fast. They also tend to live in herds for safety.

THE HALL OF HUMAN ORIGINS

The museum's Hall of Human Origins shows how humans have evolved over the past six million years in three major areas: the separation into a distinct branch of the apes, the adaptation to a changing Earth's climate, and the changes needed to survive as humans spread to all corners of the globe.

The museum begins the story by noting that humans are primates and part of the "great apes" family that includes orangutans, gorillas, bonobos, and chimpanzees. We share a common ancestor with chimpanzees, one that lived between six and eight million years ago. Two of the major things that set human ancestors apart from other ancient apes are the ability to walk upright on a regular basis, plus small canine teeth in both males and females. Walking upright makes it easier to get around a wide variety of landscapes, and smaller teeth may have been the result of eating more meat and fewer plants, since plants required bigger teeth to tear and chew.

The first display you'll see when entering the hall is that of **four fossil skulls** from human ancestors, the earliest of which dates to around six to seven million

unofficial **TIP**
Learn more about the origins of the human species at **HumanOrigins.si.edu**.

years old. Along with each skull is a short explanation of how ape-like and human-like the species was. The oldest fossil, known as *sahelanthropus tchadensis,* was found in Chad in 2001. What's interesting about this fossil is that it shows the place where the spinal cord meets the brain shifting to underneath the skull from the back of the skull. That's an indication that the animal could walk upright on a regular basis. Coupled with small canine teeth, it's enough for many scientists to accept *s. tchandensis* as the earliest entry on our branch of the family tree.

The next major display, titled **One Species, Living Worldwide,** is a collection of human (*homo sapiens*) skulls from around the world, dating from **4,700** to **200,000** years old. These skulls show how these populations spread from Africa to Europe, Asia, and beyond.

What were humans like before 200,000 years ago? The next section discusses that, in a display titled **Two Species, One Survivor,** comparing Neanderthals to modern humans.

Neanderthals (*homo neanderthalensis*) are the closest extinct relative to modern humans, sharing a common ancestor from around half a million years ago. Both species evolved to live in a wide variety of climates, used tools and fire, and lived in shelters. Sometime between 40,000 and 28,000 years ago, however, when both humans and Neanderthals were living in Europe, a combination of climate change, competition, and other forces drove the Neanderthals to extinction.

The wall opposite the Neanderthals contains **Imagination Takes Wing** and **A World of Symbols,** a look at the art, language, music, and decorative arts created by early humans between 30,000 and 60,000 years ago.

A museum display such as Human Origins runs the risk of *fossil fatigue,* where all the skulls start to look the same, and important but tiny distinctions are often overlooked or skipped. To get around that, Human Origins has built a **series of replica heads,** with hair, eyes, and skin, of the major human ancestors, including *homo heidelbergensis, homo erectus,* and Neanderthals. Each head is in a glass case, set to the average height of that species. We'd love to see these sold in the gift shop.

Beyond the replica heads is another interactive kiosk, titled **What Would You Look Like as an Early Human?** A small digital camera takes your photo and slowly morphs your face so that it has the features of one of eight species. Kids love it, and although there are several kiosks available, there's usually a short wait of a few minutes to get in front of a camera.

The last model in Human Origins is that of an *australopithecus afarensi,* commonly known as **Lucy.** Found in Ethiopia, these 3.2-million-year-old bone fragments continue the story of ape-to-human transition started at the beginning of the hall. Among Lucy's human-like traits are angled knees and a short, broad pelvis, both indications that Lucy spent a great deal of time walking upright. But, as we said with Morgie the mammal, evolution is a slow process, and Lucy still retains some ape-like traits, including long arms and fingers, and flexible feet. All of these characteristics indicate that Lucy spent a lot of time in trees too.

OCEAN HALL

The Hall of Human Origins ends at the back of Ocean Hall, a major exhibition space dedicated to marine animals. Because of the way the exhibits are organized, it's better to start your tour at the front of the hall, near the archway to the rotunda. Work your way to the back of Ocean Hall from there, and then turn right into African Voices.

Ocean Hall is a rectangle divided into three parts along its length. The middle part is the main hall, containing most of the large animal specimens and displays showing where they live. The smaller left side contains marine fossils dating back billions of years, illustrating how life evolved in the seas. The right side is broken into small, separate rooms with multimedia presentations about various ocean topics, such as how the oceans affect Earth's climate.

We'll cover the main floor of Ocean Hall first. The front of the hall, just off the rotunda, contains presentations on the ocean's **biodiversity.** Three large glass cases contain dozens of ocean animals, photos, and informative posters; in one case, a 20-foot tall, pink-and-white jellyfish extends out from its case, its head near the ceiling and tentacles flowing back inside the glass.

The goal of these biodiversity displays is to illustrate the questions scientists ask themselves when trying to organize and make sense of all these animals:

- Who is it related to?
- Where does it live?
- How big (or small) is it?

Each display case has a section devoted to each question. In one of the *Who is it related to?* examples, there's a nice set of around three-dozen **cone snail** shells. One of the *Where does it live?* sections holds the giant jellyfish and uses it to explain why where an ocean animal lives greatly affects its body shape. Finally, the *How big (or small) is it?* sections are a bit unclear to us. There's a section on how big sharks can get, for example, and one that compares the size of underwater kelp forests to tiny phytoplankton invisible to the human eye, but neither of them really explains how size factors into a classification scheme.

The center of Ocean Hall is dedicated to a 43-foot-long **North Atlantic Right Whale** named *Phoenix*. Researchers have studied Phoenix from her birth in 1987 (she's still alive as of this writing), and the displays in this part of the gallery show her growing up, her migration patterns, diet, and more. There's also quite a bit on the whaling industry, from how it got started supplying whale oil for homes and industry, to the destructive impact on global whale populations.

The back of Ocean Hall is dedicated to the open ocean. Separating this section from the rest of the hall is a long, thin display case holding a **giant squid,** 36 feet long and weighing more than 300 pounds.

Beyond the giant squid, the hall is organized into three areas, depicting life in different ocean zones. In the shallow **Surface Zone,** sunlight is abundant and makes photosynthesis possible. That means plankton can live, and they provide food for a wide variety of other animals.

The next-deepest layer is the **Twilight Zone,** where there's much less sunlight and food. Animals that live here have developed huge eyes to see better in the dark, as well as larger mouths (compared to their body size) for eating anything they can catch. Also, many animals found at these depths have developed some kind of bioluminescence.

The bottom of the sea is known as the **Deep Ocean** and is described by the museum as essentially a river of mud. There's very little food here, and there is enormous pressure due to the volume of water above. This means that most bottom-dwelling animals are either stationary or slow-moving, with large mouths and watery bodies that float easily.

When you're at the back of Ocean Hall, look right for a small room titled **The Polar Oceans.** This pathway goes through another series of ocean exhibits that lead you back toward the rotunda for the last part of the Ocean Hall tour.

The Polar Oceans documents how fish, animals, and people have evolved to live with ice, constant cold, and darkness six months out of the year. How do animals survive in these temperatures? Many mammals, like **polar bears** and **penguins,** have developed a layer of blubber fat that acts as insulation from the cold, especially when they're in the water.

The **Shores and Shallows** section of the hall contains some of the gallery's best models. One shows a huge model of a Chesapeake Bay estuary, with real water, plants, and blue crabs. Another shows **beach erosion** in action, in a clear, plastic-walled model filled with sand and water.

The third display in this section is a **coral reef packed with colorful fish and plants.** It's a mesmerizing collection of **yellow angelfish, pajama cardinalfish, bicolor blenny, shrimp, anemone,** and more, modeled after reefs found in the Indo-Pacific Ocean. Kids love it, and there's often a group of people standing wide-eyed in front of it. The thing to notice is how many different species share this relatively tiny space. They've evolved behaviors to share the space—for example, being active at different times of the day, or staying within a relatively confined area of the reef.

If you're touring the museum for half a day or less, take a break for lunch, and then begin your tour of the second floor with our coverage below. If you've got more time, however, continue walking the rest of Ocean Hall.

The last two small parts of this side of Ocean Hall are **Global Ocean Systems,** showing how the oceans interact with Earth's atmosphere and soil, and **Ocean Today,** with the latest news on marine research.

Once you're back at the front of Ocean Hall near the rotunda, bear left to the **Journey Through Time** area. The first display, on **the evolution of predator fish,** is based on the idea that you may not be having enough nightmares. We say that because all of these fish look terrifying: 25-foot-long **placoderms** with spear-like jaws; **helicoprionid sharks,** whose mouths are described as "a buzz saw with fins"; **mosasaurids,** 50-foot-long, air-breathing, marine lizards; **ammonites,** creatures the size of a grown man with the looks of a giant, angry snail with tentacles; and, of course, the **giant great white shark.**

Next up is a section titled **The Explosion of Early Life,** starting with 3.5-billion-year-old microbes, which gave off oxygen as part of their photosynthetic respiration cycle. These microbes were apparently the main form of life on the planet for a couple of billion years, up until around 600 million years ago, when many more diverse forms of life, including multicelled algae and hard-shelled animals started to appear.

One of the hard-shelled organisms that flourished around this time was the **trilobite.** We're being charitable when we describe these fossils as giant ocean cockroaches, and they are indeed distant relatives of both insects and lobsters. Fortunately, a mass extinction wiped them out. The last set of displays in Ocean Hall explains how this happened.

There have been five mass extinctions in the Earth's history, and scientists are debating whether we're in the sixth right now. Extinction events can be caused by many things. In the case of the trilobites, evidence suggests that a volcanic eruption did them in—along with 95% of everything else alive—in the **Permian-Triassic extinction** of 250 million years ago. Causes of extinction also can come from space, as in the huge meteor that slammed into Mexico 65 million years ago, wiping out the dinosaurs and marking the end of the **Cretaceous** period.

Your tour of Ocean Hall is finished after the displays on mass-extinction events. If you're doing a comprehensive tour of the museum, continue to the back of Ocean Hall, turn right, and walk through the **Mud Masons of Mali** photography exhibit and **African Voices.** If you're touring the museum for half a day or less, head to the second floor's exhibits now.

AFRICAN VOICES

African Voices is an ongoing special exhibit of Africa's peoples, cultures, and economies, and their influence around the world. The exhibit is divided into themed sections on either side of the gallery, described below. If time is short, however, the gallery's center walkway, called **Walk Through Time,** summarizes much of the content.

African Voices is the last part of our tour of Natural History's first floor. We suggest taking a break for food and restrooms now, before beginning the tour of the second floor.

SECOND FLOOR

Exhibits on the museum's second floor tend to be more kid-friendly and (with a few exceptions) require less familiarity with their background science to enjoy. Like the first floor, we'll tour the second in roughly a clockwise direction starting with **Butterflies + Plants,** just off the rotunda. We'll end up back at the rotunda after seeing **Geology, Gems, and Minerals.**

● **Butterflies + Plants** This gallery explains how evolution creates diversity, using butterflies and flowers as an example. More than 170 million years ago, there were neither flowers nor butterflies. The fossil record shows, however, that five moth species existed, flying at night and feeding on plant pollen and leaves. Flowers first appear in the fossil record around 102 million years ago, bringing nectar as a new food source. Moths seem to have evolved a short, tube-like tongue to eat the nectar, and the moths' flying from flower to flower helped to pollinate these new plants.

A giant meteor caused a mass extinction at the end of the Cretaceous period around 65 million years ago, taking with it the dinosaurs and most other forms of life. It took millions of years for the Earth to be repopulated, and with the old species wiped out, new forms of life sprang up. Some of the plants that evolved during this time were deep-throated flowers, whose pollen and nectar were hard to reach. Several moth species evolved even longer tongues to reach this food, however, and around 48 million years ago, we see **the first daytime moths—butterflies.**

Also in this hall is a **Live Butterfly Pavilion,** a remarkably large, plastic dome holding thousands of actual butterflies and the plants that support them. There's a separate charge (around $7 per person) to enter the pavilion, and there's often a short wait because of its limited capacity. Once inside, however, there are additional displays on the co-evolution of butterflies, moths, and plants.

Beyond the butterflies is the **Live Insect Zoo,** ingeniously sponsored by Orkin Pest Control. The main draws here are the various insect terraria, with land- and water-based bugs. Most of these glass cases are arranged a foot or two off the ground, at the correct height for small children to peer into without being held by an adult.

The middle section of the zoo explains the evolutionary traits that allow insects to populate every nook, cranny, and crack on Earth: **high reproductive rates, short lives,** and **specialization.** That allows billions of tiny gene crossovers and mutations to happen every day, ensuring that different biological forms get tested.

*un*official **TIP**
If you want your kids to ever sleep at night, walk quickly past the next part of the tour, which includes huge bugs from 300 million years ago, such as giant cockroaches, scorpions, spiders, and more.

Farther down the gallery is a large interactive display showing how **insects live in and around our houses.** It features kid-size computer screens and chairs, allowing kids to explore several species found in most homes.

After the insects is a relatively small area with **Egyptian mummies,** artifacts, and the religious beliefs behind them. To prepare a deceased family member for the afterlife, they were often buried with the things they'd "need," such as cooking utensils, tools, and other everyday objects. Also buried with the dead were offerings to the gods in the form of **animal mummies,** such as cats, crocodiles, and birds—even a highly prized **Apis bull.**

● **Last American Dinosaurs** One of the largest and best exhibits on the second floor is a collection of dinosaur fossils from the Hell Creek Formation in the United States's upper Midwest and Rocky Mountains. Here you'll find a **30-foot, three-horned Triceratops skeleton** and a **40-foot Tyrannosaurus Rex.** The great thing about these dinosaurs is that they stand at ground level, are easy for kids to see, and have no plastic or glass case around them. You can't touch them, but you'll be close enough to appreciate the size of these animals.

The most important part of the Dinosaurs gallery is the explanation of how these animals went extinct. In 1980, the father-and-son team of Luis Alvarez (a physicist) and Walter Alvarez (a geologist) published a paper observing that rock formations around the world all include a thin layer of clay containing ash, shocked quartz crystals, tiny diamonds, and unusual quantities of minerals such as **iridium, typically found on asteroids.** The theory presented by the Alvarezes was that a huge asteroid crashed into Earth 66 million years ago, sending up dust and debris around the globe, blocking sunlight, and then killing most plants and their consumers up the food chain.

It was a controversial idea not initially accepted by most geologists, who pointed out that an asteroid big enough to do that kind of damage would have left an enormous impact crater, which the Alvarez team had not found. However, two geologists using radar to look for oil deposits in Mexico later realized that such a crater did exist, in the ocean off the coast of the Yucatán peninsula. That crater, more than 110 miles wide and 12 feet deep, has been dated to exactly the same age as the worldwide clay ring with the iridium deposits. While some scientists today believe that volcanoes and climate change helped kill off the dinosaurs, the "impact hypothesis" is the generally accepted cause of the dinosaur's extinction.

At the end of the Last American Dinosaurs section is a small hallway with an exhibit titled **Backyard Dinosaurs.** It features a map showing where in the United States you'd find rocks of the right age to contain dinosaur fossils.

Also along this back hallway are rooms dedicated to special exhibits. Each of these is a large space, capable of hosting substantial displays on multiple topics. **Special Exhibit Gallery 3** was being renovated as we went to press; its most recent theme was *Beyond Bollywood,* a look at the lives of Indian immigrants in the United States. Adjacent to that is **Special Exhibit Gallery 2,** which most recently hosted a large-format photography exhibit titled *Wilderness Forever – Celebrating the Wilderness Act's 50th Anniversary,* with more than 60 nature photos of landscapes, wildlife, people in nature, and inspirational moments.

Between these is the **Korea Gallery,** a small room off the hallway that focuses on Korean culture and language. It's a relatively quick walk-through, with interesting explanations on the evolution of the Korean writing system, the history of Korea's kingdoms, and Korean clothing, paintings, and ceramics.

In Special Exhibit Gallery 1 is another photography exhibit, **Into Africa.** It's an ongoing exhibit, also using large-format photos. These were taken by *National Geographic* photographer Frans Lanting during his trips to Africa over the past 15 years.

The **Bones** gallery, off the rotunda to your right, shows how animals that do the same thing—such as climb, fly, or swim—have evolved similar skeletal features, even when the species aren't that closely related. For example, sloths and apes have curved feet and hands for climbing trees. The interesting thing about these displays is that they're almost all complete skeletons, not individual bones or bone fragments. **Children will find it easier to identify the animals** related to each skeleton, and it'll be easier to see the similarities.

A subset of the displays in Bones is called **Skeletons in Motion,** which shows the evolution of joints, muscles, and bone shapes for birds that fly, swim under water, and run (with specific coverage of aquatic, semiaquatic, and terrestrial birds). There's also a set of displays showing the **evolution of skeletons, limbs, and motion,** and jaws and teeth for eating. We consider these among the best in the Bones gallery.

When you've reached the Mummies exhibit at the end of Bones, turn around and walk back through Bones and to the other side of the rotunda, to Geology, Gems, and Minerals. We'll start our tour of this U-shaped gallery on the left and end back at the rotunda.

GEOLOGY, GEMS, AND MINERALS GALLERY

The first part of the hall is **The Solar System through Time,** showing the evolution of Earth's eight-planet solar system over the past 4.6 billion years. A three-minute video here explains how the sun formed first, and then its gravity attracted the space dust and rocks that formed the other planets. Beyond this is **a massive collection of meteorites** collected from around the world, explaining where these come from in the universe, what they're made of, and how you can tell whether a rock is a meteorite. (Spoiler alert: A good clue is if the rock has high concentrations of elements like iridium, generally rare on Earth.) Another section of Geology deals with **how Earth's moon was formed.**

After the solar system is **an informative section on plate tectonics**—definitely enough for some chit-chat during your next cocktail party.

In 1912, a German named **Alfred Wegener** came up with the idea of *plate tectonics,* saying that all of the continents were once joined together into a single continent some 300 million years ago and had broken apart and drifted into their current positions. Wegener couldn't explain how the plates moved, though, and his theory was not widely accepted. It took until the mid-1960s, when exploration of the deep ocean showed sea-floor spreading, to confirm these theories.

unofficial **TIP**
Regardless of whether you take the short or long tour through Geology, Gems, and Minerals, don't miss the **Hope Diamond,** in its own room at the end of the hall to the right.

Today, plate tectonics, continental drift, and a molten-core Earth are the accepted explanations for natural phenomena such as earthquakes, volcanoes, mountain ranges, and more. The gallery covers each of these in detail, showing how the Earth's huge plates come together and split apart.

Past the display on plate tectonics, volcanoes, and earthquakes is the **Rocks Gallery,** with a variety of short displays on the many features of rocks (we're not making this up).

One of the best sections of this hall is the **Mine Gallery,** built to resemble the inside of several important mines from around the United States. The

Franklin-Sterling Hill mine in New Jersey, for example, contains more than 330 mineral species, many of which **glow in the dark.** The museum dims the lights in this part of the mine to show how these minerals fluoresce, and **kids love it.**

Almost all of the remainder of this gallery is dedicated to exhibits on **gems and minerals.** Be forewarned that there are thousands of rocks on display here, and it would take a day or more to examine the details of each one. We've outlined the hall's major subjects below, such as "diversity" and "how gems grow," and we think **the sections on crystal color and shape are not to be missed.** If time is short, the middle of this hall forms a "Fast Track" summary of the displays on either side.

One of the most kid-friendly areas in Geology, Gems, and Minerals is on **color;** its centerpiece is a huge display of minerals arranged to form all the colors of the rainbow. Minerals get their color in two ways. The **base color** of a pure mineral is always the same, regardless of where it's found, because it's based on the wavelengths of light that are absorbed by the molecular structure of the mineral. For example, rubies are red because red light isn't absorbed by the aluminum and oxygen atoms that make up all rubies.

The color of a mineral is also affected by **impurities** that are mixed in with its elements. The museum demonstrates how mixing a tiny amount of copper in with other minerals produces a green tint because copper doesn't absorb green light.

The final major section of gem characteristics covers **the shape of gems and minerals.** The museum shows off dozens of different shapes for the same basic calcite crystals, showing how the impurities and forming process change its structure. A highlight here is **a huge purple quartz you can touch.**

The last part of Geology, Gems, and Minerals is a **jewelry exhibit,** with earrings owned by Marie Antoinette and other royalty. The highlight is the famous **Hope Diamond,** found in India in the 1600s and owned over the centuries by French and British aristocrats, before being donated to the museum in 1958 by jeweler Harry Winston.

IMAX MOVIES AND DINING   The museum's food court–style restaurant is on the first floor, featuring sandwiches, roasted meats and vegetables, pizza, pasta, and hamburgers. There's ample seating, but the area where you order and pick up your food is tiny and chaotic. If you've got small children, it'll be easier for one adult to find seats for everyone and keep the kids with them, while other adults order and deliver all the food.

Besides the exhibits, the museum offers a rotating series of nature-based **IMAX movies.** These are usually 20–30 minutes in length, many in 3-D. They're generally well done but not mandatory for understanding or enjoying the museum.

TOURING PLAN

1. Enter the Natural History Museum via the ground-floor entrance on Constitution Avenue. Head to the **rotunda** on the first floor and view **Henry the Elephant.**

2. Begin a clockwise tour of the first floor with **Mammal Hall.** See the African and North American animal exhibits. Skip Australia and South America on half-day tours.

3. Continue to the **Hall of Human Origins,** including the fossil skulls, *Burying the Dead,* and *Surviving the Dry Times* interactive displays.

4. Tour the center of **Ocean Hall.** On full-day tours, also view the displays on the left and right walls.

5. Full-day tours should see **African Voices,** behind Ocean Hall.

6. Take a break for lunch on the ground floor.

7. On the second floor, begin a clockwise tour with the **butterfly exhibit** and **Live Insect Zoo.**

8. Full-day tours should see **Mummies.**

9. Tour **Last American Dinosaurs** and Backyard Dinos.

10. Full-day tours should see **Special Exhibitions 3, 2, and 1,** plus the **Korea Gallery.**

11. Tour **Geology, Gems, and Minerals,** starting from the back and working toward the rotunda.

12. Browse any missed exhibits, see an IMAX movie, or shop the museum store for souvenirs.

Newseum   ★★★

URL newseum.org. Address 555 Pennsylvania Ave. NW, Washington, D.C. 20001. **What it is** Museum dedicated to journalism, reporting, and the role of the press in society. **Scope and scale** Major attraction. **When to go** Anytime. **Hours** Daily, 9 a.m.–5 p.m.; closed 4th Thursday of November, December 25, and January 1. **Closest Metro** Archives (Yellow, Green); Judiciary Square (Red); Blue, Orange, Silver should transfer to Red at Metro Center. **Admission** $23 for adults 19–64, $19 for seniors 65+, $14 for children 7–18 (free for children under 7). Military, AAA, and college discounts are available with proper ID. **Authors' comments** News junkies (like us) and history buffs will love it. If you're not one of those, it's probably too expensive for a few hours of touring. **Not to Be Missed** Reporting Vietnam (Level 6; through September 12, 2016); Today's Front Pages (Level 6); News History Gallery (Level 5); Big Screen Theater (Level 3); and Pulitzer Prize Photographs Gallery (Level 1).

DESCRIPTION AND COMMENTS Reviewing the Newseum is essentially a review of modern news reporting: A core slice of it is excellent and reminds you that the Fourth Estate is vital to a functional democracy. The rest of it you've probably seen for free on the web.

The Newseum's **Today's Front Pages** exhibit, on Level 6, is an example. In its one long hallway hangs today's full-color front page from 80 newspapers, including one from every US state and selected editions from around the world. Thirty years ago, this would have been an amazing display available only to large corporations with multimillion-dollar data and communications systems. Even today, it's still impressive to look at. But we all know that those pages are less current than the newspapers' own websites, which we get on our phones at zero cost.

That said, there are several excellent exhibits in the Newseum, many of which should provoke a discussion on the current state of news reporting, what its goals should be, and how news organizations should be paid for their work.

One of the best exhibits is **Reporting Vietnam,** also on Level 6. The media's coverage of the war in Vietnam, especially the in-country television reporting, had a major influence on how Americans viewed the war. Television news wasn't widespread for World War II or the Korean War, and negative stories about those conflicts were frequently censored or suppressed by either the US government or the news organizations doing the reporting.

Vietnam was different. It was covered by television crews delivering same-day footage of front-line battles, often sending images of wounded or dead soldiers and civilians directly to American living rooms during dinner. Those images evoked a more powerful antiwar sentiment than any text description could hope to attain.

*un*official **TIP**
The bathrooms' tile walls have real, badly written newspaper headlines printed on them, such as "Panel Urges Cloning Ethics Board" and "Woman Found Dead in Trunk Kept to Herself, Neighbors Say."

Another good exhibit is **News History Gallery,** on Level 5. This is a collection of more than 300 important newspaper front pages from the middle of the 15th century to today, covering events as they happened, from the American Revolution to the bombing of Pearl Harbor, the Kennedy assassinations, moon landings, and 9/11.

Another impressive hall is the **Big Screen Theater,** also on Level 5. This houses a series of huge video displays, each tuned to a different news source from around the world. On days with major stories, it's interesting to see how each news organization covers those events. On slow news days, which happened when we visited, it becomes obvious that 24-hour news channels have to produce 24 hours of content, whether it's all newsworthy or not. Regardless, you could easily spend half an hour here just catching up.

Another attraction worth seeing, on Level 3, is the **9/11 Gallery,** a collection of newspapers, videos, and artifacts from the terrorist attacks in New York and Washington, D.C., on September 11, 2001.

Finally, stop by the **Pulitzer Prize Photographs Gallery** on Level 1 before you leave. As with the famous newspapers, you'll probably recognize many of these iconic photos. What makes a visit worthwhile is the background stories about how each photo was taken.

TOURING TIPS The Newseum's suggested itinerary starts with the Concourse, one floor below the museum's entrance on Level 1. From there you'll take an elevator to Level 6 and work your way back down to the exit on Level 1. It's a good touring strategy, and the one we recommend.

Smithsonian American Art Museum and National Portrait Gallery ★★★½

URL americanart.si.edu and **npg.si.edu**. **Address** 8th and F Sts. NW, Washington, D.C. 20004. **Phone ☎** 202-633-7970. **What it is** Museums of American art and portraits of famous Americans. **Scope and scale** Major attraction. **When to go** Anytime. **Hours** Daily, 11:30 a.m.–7 p.m.; closed December 25. **Closest Metro** Gallery Place/Chinatown (Red); Metro Center (Blue, Orange, Silver); Archives (Green, Yellow). **Admission** Free. **Authors' comments** Good Hudson River School collection; interesting modern art. **Not to Be Missed** *America's Presidents* collection (Portrait

Gallery, Floor 2); Hudson River School art by Durand, Bierstadt, Colman, and Church (American Art, Floor 2); modern art collection (American Art, Floor 3).

DESCRIPTION AND COMMENTS These two museums occupy opposite halves of the same building, allowing you to tour both in one visit. All told, it takes anywhere from 2 to 8 hours to tour both, depending on your level of interest.

We suggest starting your tour on the Portrait Gallery's first floor, with the *American Origins* exhibit. This series of portraits is arranged by date, starting with pre–Revolutionary War settlers and American Indians, including Pocahontas. Three of the collection's 17 rooms are dedicated to the Civil War–era photography of Matthew Brady, and these are among the best in the museum.

Next, make your way to the second floor and the *America's Presidents* collection, the centerpiece of the Portrait Gallery. One of the first you'll see is Gilbert Stuart's painting of George Washington, known as *The Athenaeum Portrait,* from 1796. It's the basis for the image of Washington found on the US $1 bill. And while most of these portraits are the kind of formal numbers you'd expect, check out Chuck Close's unique take on Bill Clinton's head while you're there.

Beyond America's Presidents is *The Struggle for Justice,* dedicated to Americans who have fought for civil rights equality throughout the years. Subjects include Frederick Douglas, Betty Friedan, Cesar Chavez, Leonard Crow Dog, and more.

The second floor also hosts a revolving set of special exhibits on portraiture. On our most recent visit in late 2015, it was Elaine de Koonig's abstract and figurative portraits, including several of John F. Kennedy.

The Portrait Gallery's third floor has portraits on *20th Century Americans,* covering the 1950s to the 1990s. Beyond that, the *Bravo!* exhibition features portraits of entertainers from John Phillip Sousa to John Wayne; the *Champions* set is drawn from the sports world, with everyone from Arthur Ashe to Casey Stengel.

Once you're done with the third floor of the Portrait Gallery, make your way back to the first floor to start a tour of the American Art Museum. The first-floor exhibits include *Experience America* and *Folk and Self-taught Art.* Of the two, the *Experience America* section is more interesting. This includes art commissioned by the Works Progress Administration during the Depression, giving funding to everyday and lesser-known artists around the country. The pieces span every genre (and probably a few new ones) and show how many talented artists probably live in every neighborhood in the country.

The second floor of American Art is arranged chronologically, with rooms dedicated to Early America, Western Art, the Civil War, Impressionism (with several by Mary Cassat), the Gilded Age, and Modernism (including Georgia O'Keeffe). Of these, the Western Art collection of Hudson River School art is the best. It starts with **Asher Durand's** *Dover Plains, Dutchess County, New York,* then moves to **Frederick Church's** *Aurora Borealis* and *Cotopaxi* and **Thomas Cole's** *The Subsiding of the Waters of the Deluge,* before finishing with **Albert Bierstadt's** *Gates of Yosemite; Cathedral Rocks, Yosemite Valley;* and the magnum opus *Among the Sierra Nevada, California.* There's also a set of **Frederick Remington** bronze, *The Bronco Buster.*

Smithsonian American Art Museum and National Portrait Gallery

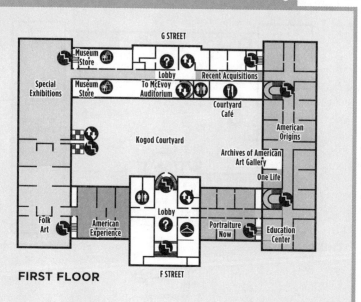

FIRST FLOOR

G STREET

Museum Store

Special Exhibitions

Museum Store

Lobby

Recent Acquisitions

To McEvoy Auditorium

Courtyard Café

American Origins

Kogod Courtyard

Archives of American Art Gallery

One Life

Lobby

Folk Art

American Experience

Portraiture Now

Education Center

F STREET

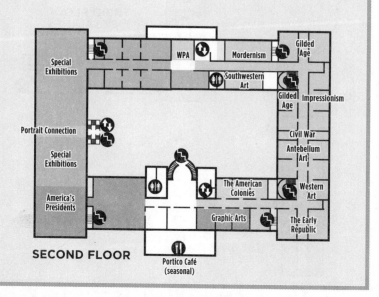

SECOND FLOOR

Special Exhibitions

WPA

Mordernism

Gilded Age

Southwestern Art

Gilded Age

Impressionism

Portrait Connection

Special Exhibitions

Civil War

Antebellum Art

America's Presidents

The American Colonies

Western Art

Graphic Arts

The Early Republic

Portico Café (seasonal)

Smithsonian American Art Museum and National Portrait Gallery

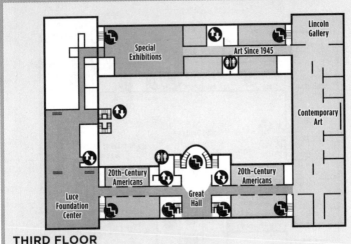

THIRD FLOOR

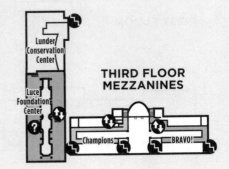

THIRD FLOOR MEZZANINES

FOURTH FLOOR

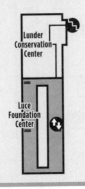

The third floor of American Art is dedicated to post-1940 (i.e., Modern) art. It's a huge, open space, allowing for works of size to be displayed, including large-format video and image-based works. Our favorite is **Nam June Paik's** *Electronic Superhighway: Continental U.S., Alaska, Hawaii.* It's a collection of small televisions, arranged in the shape of the United States, each showing film snippets from American cinema. The nearby *Megatron Matrix,* also by Paik, is a 215-monitor display of disparate video and audio clips, also mesmerizing.

TOURING TIPS Both museums are served by a small cafeteria located across an enclosed, tranquil courtyard.

Smithsonian Castle and Information Center ★★½

URL si.edu/Museums/smithsonian-institution-building. **Address** 1000 Jefferson Dr. SW, Washington, D.C. 20560. **Phone ☎** 202-633-1000. **What it is** Primary visitor information center in a beautiful castle-like building. **Scope and scale** Diversion. **When to go** Anytime. **Hours** Daily, 8:30 a.m.–5:30 p.m.; closed December 25. **Closest Metro** Smithsonian (Orange, Blue, Silver; for Green, Yellow, transfer at L'Enfant Plaza; for Red, transfer at Metro Center). **Admission** Free.

DESCRIPTION AND COMMENTS The story of the grand, red-sandstone Smithsonian Institution Building starts with the story of James Smithson, founding patron of the Smithsonian Institute. Smithson was an English chemist and mineralogist who came from wealthy parents and had no children of his own. A clause in Smithson's will gifted all of his wealth to the government of the United States, a country that he never visited, to found "an establishment for the increase and diffusion of knowledge among men" that was to be called the Smithsonian Institute.

The first building was completed for the Smithsonian Institute in 1855 and is lovingly referred to as "the Castle," although it is officially called the Smithsonian Institution Building. The Castle contains the primary visitor information center as well as all Institution administrative offices. The interior is just as beautiful as the exterior, with the vaulted ceilings more closely resembling a church nave than an administration building. It also houses a few exhibits about the Castle itself and the Smithsonian, as well as the remains of James Smithson himself, which were moved to the Castle in 1904.

U.S. Botanic Garden ★★★

URL usbg.gov. **Address** 100 Maryland Ave. SW, Washington, D.C. 20024. **Phone ☎** 202-225-8333. **What it is** Park, garden, and greenhouse. **Scope and scale** Minor attraction. **When to go** Anytime. **Hours** Conservatory and gardens, daily, 10 a.m.–5 p.m. (including holidays), with extended summer hours possible; park hours are dawn to dusk. **Closest Metro** A three-block walk from Federal Center SW (Orange, Blue, Silver); Yellow, Green, and Red can transfer at Metro Center. **Admission** Free. **Authors' comments** Colorful, fragrant, informative look at flowers and plants. A nice, living break from stone buildings and monuments. **Not to Be Missed** Conservatory; National Garden.

DESCRIPTION AND COMMENTS The U.S. Botanic Garden (USBG) was originally created in 1850 to hold plants from American expeditions around the country and world. Its **Conservatory** fulfills that duty in a 300-foot-long Victorian glass-and-steel structure with a four-story central dome.

Inside the dome, the USBG has replicated a jungle rainforest environment, with live, towering trees, vines, and plants. Stairs and an elevator allow you to reach the top, where you can see how different layers of the jungle ecosystem come together to support life. It's a wonderful, lush place to visit, especially in winter, when the colorful flowers and plants contrast with the cold outdoors.

The Conservatory's mission also includes raising and propagating **rare and endangered plants.** Many of these, such as the yellow coneflower and holywood, are found in the United States, but most come from around the world.

Outside the Conservatory is the **National Garden,** highlighting plants and gardens of the Mid-Atlantic region. It includes an organic Rose Garden with dozens of different varieties and colors; a Butterfly Garden, showing plants such as milkweed, which attracts and nurtures butterflies and other pollinating insects; and a water garden.

TOURING TIPS Free tours are offered by the Botanic Garden, though the schedule isn't fixed. Check with the Visitor Information desk when you arrive.

The indoor Conservatory can be toured at any time of the year, but the outdoors National Garden is best toured in the spring and fall, when more plants are blooming.

The USBG has only a limited amount of on-site parking, all dedicated to handicap-accessible access. Metered parking is available within a few blocks.

US Holocaust Memorial Museum ★★★★

URL ushmm.org Address 100 Raoul Wallenberg Place SW, Washington, D.C. 20024-2126. **What it is** National memorial and guide to the World War II Holocaust, with educational exhibits on other past and current genocide campaigns. **Scope and scale** Major attraction. **When to go** Anytime. Free timed passes required for admission to the permanent collection March–August; see Touring Tips for details. **Hours** Daily, 10 a.m.–5 p.m., but elevators to the permanent collection close at 4:10. **Closest Metro** Smithsonian (Orange, Blue, Silver); Yellow and Green can transfer at L'Enfant Plaza; Red can transfer at Metro Center. **Admission** Free. **Authors' comments** Some of the best historical narratives we've seen. A comprehensive tour takes 2–3 hours. **Not to Be Missed** Permanent Exhibition and *Some Were Neighbors: Collaboration & Complicity in the Holocaust.*

DESCRIPTION AND COMMENTS The US Holocaust Memorial Museum documents and preserves the memories of Germany's genocidal campaign against Jews and others during the 1930s and 1940s. The museum also chronicles modern-day genocide events throughout the world.

The museum's displays are deeply personal and present some of the best historical narratives we've ever seen. Using a combination of photos, film, audio, and actual artifacts, the exhibits chronicle how Hitler rose to power in 1930s Germany and began a systematic campaign of oppression against Jews and other minorities. And while the Holocaust was unspeakably brutal, one of the most disturbing (and effective) things the museum shows is how, step by step, the German people were convinced to go along with Hitler's plans. If you've ever thought, "That couldn't happen today," this museum will change your mind.

US Holocaust Memorial Museum

CONCOURSE

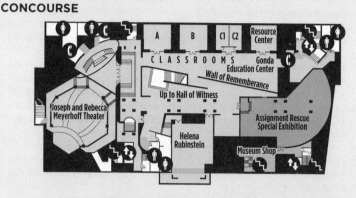

FIRST FLOOR

SECOND FLOOR

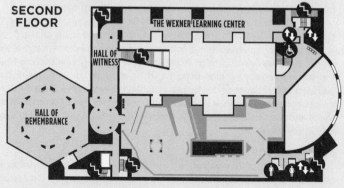

FIRST FLOOR AND PERMANENT EXHIBITS

The centerpiece of the museum is its Permanent Exhibition, spread across three floors. Elevators take you to the top floor, *Nazi Assault – 1933 to 1939,* showing how the Nazis came to power in Germany, in large part by blaming Jews for Germany's post–World War I problems. Once in power, the Nazis continued the persecution, using more powerful government tools, including terrorism. Along with this timeline, newspaper headlines from the rest of Europe and the United States show how these events were portrayed in other countries.

The middle floor of the Permanent Exhibition is *The "Final Solution" – 1940 to 1945,* showing Germany's policies and treatment of Jews and persecuted minorities throughout Europe during World War II. Among its many moving displays is a scale model of the Auschwitz concentration camp, which Germany built using the most modern ideas of efficiency, industrialization, and mass production—essentially a factory of death built by German engineers.

The last floor of the Permanent Exhibition is *Last Chapter,* covering the defeat of Germany in 1945, liberation of the Jews from the concentration camps, the quest for some measure of justice from those responsible, and the eventual establishment of Israel.

Back on the first floor, *Remember the Children: Daniel's Story* is an age-appropriate overview of the Holocaust's buildup and events in Germany as told from the perspective of a young German Jewish boy named Daniel.

GROUND FLOOR

The ground floor contains three exhibits. The first is *A Dangerous Lie: The Protocols of the Elders of Zion,* a series of wall-size screens on the history of the *Protocols* book. It originally appeared in Russia in 1905 and purported to describe meetings of Jewish leaders planning to rule the world by influencing the economies, media, and culture of major nations. It was soon exposed as pure fiction, based on a 19th-century satirical work about the French government (that never mentioned Jews). Still, the "exposé" spread around the world. Hitler was apparently influenced by it, and the Nazi Party published almost two-dozen editions before World War II. It's still available today.

The second exhibit on the ground floor is the **Children's Tile Wall,** with thousands of ceramic tiles mounted along one of the floor's long walls. Each tile was decorated by a child, depicting his or her thoughts about the Holocaust.

One of the best exhibits in the Holocaust Museum is *Some Were Neighbors: Collaboration & Complicity in the Holocaust,* the last exhibit on the ground floor. It uses personal narratives from a small group of Jews to explain how the Nazis got everyday Germans to go along with their plans of oppression and extermination. Perhaps the most unsettling thing about this presentation is that you come away convinced that there was nothing inherently evil about the German population prior to the Holocaust; they weren't all that different from us today, and the same techniques could allow it to happen again, the same way, almost anywhere.

SECOND FLOOR

The six-sided **Hall of Remembrance** is a large, indoor, open memorial space for quiet reflection and prayer. Outside the Hall is a memorial to selected **Jewish**

resistance fighters during World War II, from France to the Balkans to inside Auschwitz, with flags, photos, and their stories on display.

Also on the second floor is *From Memory to Action,* in the Wexner Center. *From Memory to Action* covers modern genocide campaigns in Rwanda, Bosnia-Herzegovina, Darfur, and Cambodia. The second half of *From Memory to Action* documents Cambodia's quest for justice against those responsible in the Khmer Rouge government and features displays from Syrian refugees. Beyond is the **Holocaust Survivors and Victims Resource Center,** and past that are stairs from which you can access the first and ground floors.

TOURING TIPS Admission to the museum is free, but timed-entry tickets are required to access the Permanent Exhibition March through August, when the museum is most crowded. Reserve these online up to five months in advance at **tinyurl.com/USNHMMtickets,** where you can also choose your entry time to the exhibits. You can also get these passes in person on the day of your visit, but you may not be able to choose the time of your entry to the exhibits.

The museum recommends that children be age 11 and above to view the Permanent Exhibition, some of which contains graphic displays of suffering and death. If you have younger children, a Family Guide to appropriate exhibits is available online at **tinyurl.com/USHMM-FamilyGuide.**

TOURING PLAN

1. Obtain timed-entry tickets for the museum's Permanent Exhibition up to five months in advance at **tinyurl.com/USNHMMtickets.** If possible, request an entry time to the exhibition about an hour after your planned arrival time, to allow you to view the rest of the museum.

2. Arrive at the museum about an hour before your entry time. Head to the second floor and view the **Hall of Remembrance.**

3. Tour *From Memory to Action,* also on the second floor.

4. See the anti-Semitism exhibit *A Dangerous Lie* on the ground floor, then tour the Children's Tile Wall.

5. Tour *Some Were Neighbors* in the Rubinstein Auditorium, also on the ground floor.

6. Return to the first floor and walk through *Remember the Children* if you have children.

7. When it's time to enter the Permanent Exhibition, take the elevators from the first floor and begin your tour.

8. Revisit any missed exhibits before leaving the museum.

Vietnam Veterans Memorial ★★★★½

URL **nps.gov/vive**. Address 5 Henry Bacon Dr. NW, Washington, D.C. Phone ☎ 202-426-6841 (National Mall & Memorial Parks). **What it is** Simple, striking, stirring, and somber memorial to those lost in the Vietnam War. **Scope and scale** Major Attraction. **When to go** During Daylight. **Hours** Open 24 hours. Park Rangers typically available during daytime and evening. Memorial is better seen in daylight. **Closest Metro** Foggy Bottom (Orange, Blue, Silver; for Green, Yellow, transfer at L'Enfant Plaza; for Red, transfer at Metro Center). **Admission** Free.

DESCRIPTION AND COMMENTS Most of the monuments and memorials in Washington are of larger-than-life individuals or symbolic of a vast group of people. Not so at the Vietnam Veterans Memorial, which lists the name of every American who made the ultimate sacrifice during the Vietnam War: more than 58,000 of them. The deeply personal nature of seeing each name carved into the angular, black granite wall means that what's often reflected in its glossy surface are subdued faces.

The wall is sunk into the ground just north of the Lincoln Memorial's Reflecting Pool and is one of the most moving installations in the capital. There are nearby directories for visitors looking for specific names and pencils and paper that can be used for rubbings of the wall.

The Vietnam Veterans Memorial is not just the wall, however, but two statues that add corporeal form to the spirit of all those who served. *The Three Servicemen* stand to the southwest of the wall, looking toward the names of those they fought alongside. The *Women's Memorial*—directly south of the wall—depicts some of the many responsibilities of the serving women.

TOURING TIPS To show proper reverence to the fallen and those paying their respects, loud conversations, interviews, chewing gum, and music are discouraged. In addition, camera tripods are not allowed on the sidewalks near the wall, and absolutely no walking on the ground at the top of the wall is permitted.

Washington Monument ★★★

URL **nps.gov/wamo**. Address 2 15th St. NW Washington, D.C. 20245. **Phone** ☎ 202-426-6841 (National Mall & Memorial Parks). **What it is** A 555-foot-tall marble obelisk honoring the first President of the United States of America. **Scope and scale** Major attraction. **When to go** First thing in the morning, unless you have a prepurchased ticket. **Hours** 9 a.m.–10 p.m. from Memorial Day through Labor Day, 9 a.m.–5 p.m. otherwise. Closed July 4 and December 25. **Closest Metro** Smithsonian (Orange, Blue, Silver; for Green, Yellow, transfer at L'Enfant Plaza; for Red, transfer at Metro Center). **Admission** Free, although there is a $1.50 service charge per ticket for prepurchasing.

DESCRIPTION AND COMMENTS The towering Washington Monument dominates the skyline of Washington, D.C. The 555-foot-tall marble obelisk is the most pronounced object in the city and serves as a wonderful orientation point for touring the National Mall. It also serves as a magnificent viewing platform, allowing half a million visitors per year access to its apex.

Upon making it inside—after considerable security—you are whisked by elevator to the 500-foot level to see 360-degree views of downtown D.C. On the ride, the elevator operator points out many of the memorial stones, which were donated by various states, cities, countries, and organizations. The 500-foot observation level and the level just below it are also home to historical photos and information about President George Washington, as well as the fascinating construction process of the monument built in his honor.

An engineering marvel, the monument's marble blocks are held together almost solely by gravity, with the visible mortar acting basically as weatherproofing. The Washington Monument has withstood blizzards, hurricanes, and millions upon millions of visitors for more than 130 years. It stands as a beacon for tourists, patriots, and engineers, piercing the Washington, D.C., sky as a reminder of what can be accomplished.

TOURING TIPS Tickets are necessary to visit the top of the Washington Monument, although they are free of charge. Tickets can be obtained on the day of your visit at the Monument Lodge on 15th Street, adjacent to the Monument, but we recommend buying them online ahead of your visit. On the Washington Monument's website, tickets can be purchased several months in advance, although an exact date and time is necessary, as is paying the $1.50 per-ticket service fee. Helpfully, the ticketing website lets you see the number of available tickets for every hour of every day so you can see how necessary they are. If you choose to line up for same-day tickets, be warned that they will be very scarce in the summer months, when lines start forming as early as 7 a.m., with the ticket office opening at 8:30 a.m.

World War II Memorial   ★★★½

URL nps.gov/wwii. **Address** 1750 Independence Ave. SW, Washington, D.C. 20245. **Phone** ☎ 202-426-6841 (National Mall & Memorial Parks). **What it is** Memorial to the American involvement in World War II. **Scope and scale** Major attraction. **When to go** Anytime. **Hours** Open 24 hours. Park Rangers typically available from 9 a.m. until 10 p.m. Closed December 25. **Closest Metro** Smithsonian (Orange, Blue, Silver; for Green, Yellow, transfer at L'Enfant Plaza; for Red, transfer at Metro Center). **Admission** Free.

DESCRIPTION AND COMMENTS World War II was a pivotal period for many countries. For the United States, it represented a time—some would say the last time—when the entire country was united in a singular cause. The World War II Memorial represents this unity by lining an oval-shaped base with 56 pillars representing the US states and territories that defended the country: the 48 states (at the time), along with the territories of Alaska and Hawaii, the District of Columbia, the Commonwealth of the Philippines, Puerto Rico, Guam, American Samoa, and the U.S. Virgin Islands.

These pillars form the ends of the memorial's oval, with 43-foot arches acting as midpoints for the curves. Each side represents a different WWII campaign, with the north being "Atlantic" and the south "Pacific." In the center of the memorial is a 246-foot-wide, shallow, fountain-laden pool. The walls of the memorial are inscribed with scenes depicting each stage of a soldier in the war, from troops being issued uniforms right through a handshake agreement of peace. The Freedom Wall is found on the western side, complete with 4,048 gold stars: one for every 100 Americans who died during the war.

A more playful detail is the two obscure "Kilroy was here" messages found behind the service gates on either side. This is a nod to the popular graffiti doodle at the time, which was co-opted by World War II troops and found scribbled in many European locations. It became a kind of secret rallying cry for the people in war-torn areas.

The TIDAL BASIN

WASHINGTON, D.C.'S TIDAL BASIN was designed to function exactly as its name implies, by controlling the flow of water from the tidal section of the adjacent Potomac River. What it has become is a serene vista surrounded by elegant monuments and beautiful flowering cherry trees. The Tidal Basin is a highly visited area just south of the Lincoln Memorial (pages 146–147) and Korean War Veterans Memorial (page 145). The closest Metro station is Smithsonian (Blue, Orange, Silver), although it is about a half mile from the station to the water, and the basin itself is about 2 miles around.

In between the Smithsonian Metro station and the Tidal Basin are some interesting sights, one of the most fascinating being the **Bureau of Engraving and Printing** at 14th and C Streets Southwest. Tours are available and, while learning how money is made may not sound compelling, it is a wonderful visit. Tours in the off season—September through February—do not require tickets and are available Monday through Friday between 9 and 10:45 a.m., and again between 12:30 and 2 p.m. From March through August, tickets are necessary for tours, which are available between 9 and 10:45 a.m., 12:30 and 3:45 p.m., and 5 and 6 p.m. To obtain tickets, head to the ticket booth on Raoul Wallenburg Place (formerly 15th Street Southwest), which opens at 8 a.m. and closes when the tickets are gone. Another alternative is to request tickets through your congressional office, although those tours are only offered April through August between either 8 and 8:45 a.m. or 4 and 4:45 p.m. All tours are free of charge.

Walk north toward Independence Avenue and turn left, and you'll be at the edge of the Tidal Basin, which introduces you to the stunning views across the water toward the Jefferson Memorial (see facing page). As you approach the west side of the basin, at 1900 Independence Avenue, you come upon the location of the **District of Columbia War Memorial:** an open, stand-alone, Doric rotunda designed as both a memorial and a bandstand, with every concert being a tribute to the fallen. A 2010 restoration also added more attractive pathways and lighting, enhancing the entire setting of the beautiful memorial.

Continuing around the edge of the Tidal Basin—which itself is a lovely path—you will come upon the Martin Luther King, Jr. Memorial (page 204) followed by the Franklin Delano Roosevelt Memorial (page 204), both large, sweeping monuments with equally sweeping views.

We would be remiss if we discussed the Tidal Basin without mentioning the famous flowering cherry trees and the yearly festival centering on them. The cherry trees were planted near the Tidal Basin in 1912 as a gift of friendship from the people of Japan. The flowering trees are heavily admired in Japan, equated with the evanescence of life. These were the second set of trees sent from Japan because the first set were found to be infested and were burned to avoid potential damage to native plant life. During World War II, the trees were referred to as the "Oriental" cherry trees to try and stall any retaliation against them in protest against the Japanese involvement in the war. The shell game seems to have been successful because only four trees were damaged.

The first **Cherry Blossom Festival** was held in 1935 and is now a yearly event. The festival itself runs from late March into mid-April—specifically March 20 through April 17, 2016—although the actual blooming of the trees does not always cooperate. In 2013 through 2015, the blossoms didn't reach full bloom until the second week of April, although, in contrast, they hit that mark on March 20 in 2012. There is no way to be sure of exactly when full bloom will be, but as the festival is approaching, start checking **nps.gov/cherry** for the estimated dates. Even if your visit doesn't coincide with "full bloom," any level of flowering is lovely and gives the impression that you're walking through a magical forest. For visitor information, check **national cherryblossomfestival.org.**

Thomas Jefferson Memorial ★★★★★

URL nps.gov/thje. Address 13 E Basin Dr. SW, Washington, D.C. 20242. **Phone** ☎ 202-426-6841 (National Mall & Memorial Parks). **What it is** Beautiful monument to the third President of the United States in a charming setting. **Scope and scale** Headliner. **When to go** Anytime. **Hours** Open 24 hours. Park Rangers typically available from 9:30 a.m. until 11:30 pm. **Closest Metro** Smithsonian (Orange, Blue, Silver; for Green, Yellow, transfer at L'Enfant Plaza; for Red, transfer at Metro Center). **Admission**: Free.

DESCRIPTION AND COMMENTS Many visitors overlook the attractive, stately Thomas Jefferson Memorial—it receives less than half the attendance of the Lincoln Memorial. Although adjacent to the National Mall, just across the Tidal Basin, its separation deters many tourists. Despite the distance, the outstanding design and relatively tranquil setting are worth the trip.

The Jefferson Memorial is an open-air, circular, domed, 165-foot-wide structure supported by a total of 54 columns. It is augmented at its main entrance by a 102-foot-wide triangular portico. While both neoclassical and charming, the design is also very similar to the Rotunda at the University of Virginia—a building designed by Thomas Jefferson himself. There may be no better method of tribute than allowing President Jefferson to indirectly design his own monument.

The interior naturally features a statue of the president, in this case a 19-foot-tall bronze sculpture of Thomas Jefferson standing casually with a confident smile. The quality and detail are beautiful, as are the Thomas Jefferson quotes that adorn just about every surface.

Equally as stunning as the monument is its setting: on the shores of the Tidal Basin. The exact spot was chosen because it is in a direct line with the White House, thus completing the "four-point" plan of the National Mall—Lincoln Memorial to Capitol, White House to Jefferson Memorial, with the Washington Monument as the fulcrum. From the steps of the Jefferson Memorial, a wonderful vista appears of the basin, the Martin Luther King, Jr. Memorial, the White House (through some trees), and the Washington Monument.

TOURING TIPS The blooming of the cherry blossom trees that surround the Tidal Basin gives the entire area a gorgeous pink glow, although those blossoms bring the crowds with them. If you are visiting during the Cherry Blossom Festival (late March to mid-April), go earlier in the day.

Martin Luther King, Jr. Memorial   ★★★★

URL nps.gov/mlkm. **Address** 1850 West Basin Dr. SW, Washington, D.C. 20245. **Phone** ☎ 202-426-6841 (National Mall & Memorial Parks). **What it is** Inspirational monument to a civil rights icon. **Scope and scale** Minor attraction. **When to go** Anytime. **Hours** Open 24 hours. Park Rangers typically available from 9 a.m. until 10 p.m. Closed December 25. **Closest Metro** Smithsonian (Orange, Blue, Silver; for Green, Yellow, transfer at L'Enfant Plaza; for Red, transfer at Metro Center). **Admission** Free.

DESCRIPTION AND COMMENTS "With this faith, we will be able to hew out of the mountain of despair a stone of hope."

These words were spoken during Dr. Martin Luther King Jr.'s seminal "I Have A Dream" speech and form the basis for the memorial built in Dr. King's honor. Located along the northeast bank of the Tidal Basin, the Martin Luther King, Jr. Memorial sits adjacent to the Franklin Delano Roosevelt Memorial and across the water from the Jefferson Memorial.

The memorial itself is that metaphorical stone of hope—a monolith featuring a 30-foot-tall carving of Dr. King—hewn out of the figurative mountain of despair behind it. The granite statue, along with the two semicircular sections of wall surrounding it, features 16 inspirational Martin Luther King Jr. quotes and fantastic views of the basin. Dr. King's words remind visitors of the light he shone onto the civil rights movement—specifically as a result of his most well-known speech, given within view of this memorial.

Franklin Delano Roosevelt Memorial   ★★★½

URL nps.gov/frde. **Address** 400 West Basin Dr. SW, Washington, D.C. 20242. **Phone** ☎ 202-426-6841 (National Mall & Memorial Parks). **What it is** Sprawling memorial for the 32nd President of the United States of America. **Scope and scale** Minor Attraction. **When to go** Anytime. **Hours** Open 24 hours. Park Rangers typically available from 9:30 a.m. until 11:30 p.m.; interpretive programs every hour from 10 a.m. until 11 p.m. Closed December 25. **Closest Metro** Smithsonian (Orange, Blue, Silver; for Green, Yellow, transfer at L'Enfant Plaza; for Red, transfer at Metro Center). **Admission** Free.

DESCRIPTION AND COMMENTS At 7.5 acres, the Franklin Delano Roosevelt (FDR) Memorial utilizes a space large enough to befit America's longest-serving president. FDR was elected to the highest office in the United States four times (prior to the implementation of term limits) and served for 12 years, ending with his death in 1945. Located on the Tidal Basin—between the Martin Luther King, Jr. Memorial and the Jefferson Memorial—the FDR Memorial honors him with elegance and dignity by featuring four areas, each highlighting a different aspect of his presidency. In every area, water is used to represent the turmoil of the times, from the straight, downward crash of the Great Depression to the chaos of World War II to the stillness that followed his passing.

unofficial **TIP**
The FDR Memorial is the only one to honor a first lady or presidential pet.

TOURING TIPS It's easiest to see the FDR Memorial and MLK Memorial (see previous page) when going between the Jefferson and Lincoln Memorials.

PENNSYLVANIA AVENUE

PENNSYLVANIA AVENUE RUNS FROM MARYLAND into Georgetown, but when people speak of it, they likely mean the stretch from the Capitol to the White House. The original city plan called for a magnificent throughway linking these two titans of United States government, and Pennsylvania Avenue became that link.

Sections of Pennsylvania Avenue are easily accessed by the Metro system. On the eastern end—closer to the Capitol—are the Archives–Navy Memorial (Green, Yellow), Gallery Place (Red, Green, Yellow), and Judiciary Square (Red) stations; on the western end—closer to the White House—are the Federal Triangle (Blue, Orange, Silver) and Metro Center (Red, Blue, Orange, Silver) stations.

We start our tour on the eastern end, at the northeast corner of Pennsylvania Avenue and 7th Street Northwest, where the simple Grand Army of the Republic Memorial stands. Dedicated in 1909, it is a monument to the once-popular organization of Civil War soldiers.

Across Pennsylvania Avenue, you can't help but notice the neoclassic facade of the National Archives (pages 162–165), but there is another interesting tribute directly adjacent to the Hancock statue. The **United States Navy Memorial** honors all who have served in the Navy, Marine Corps, Coast Guard, and Merchant Marine. The memorial plaza features a statue—The Lone Sailor—fountains, naval flags, and 26 bronze reliefs. Make sure you look down while you're there because underfoot is the Granite Sea, an inlaid map of the world's oceans.

Continuing on Pennsylvania Avenue, the **J. Edgar Hoover F.B.I. Headquarters Building**—between 9th and 10th Streets—stands out from its surroundings, but not necessarily in a good way. When designed in the 1960s, the stylistic preferences of the time won out over the classic architecture of much of Washington, resulting in a poured concrete exterior. In addition, the differing height restrictions of Pennsylvania Avenue and E Street (behind the building) mean that it looks like the F.B.I. Building is wearing another, smaller building on top of it.

Farther along Pennsylvania Avenue, past the Internal Revenue Service headquarters, is the **Old Post Office,** located at the corner of 12th Street. Built between 1892 and 1899, the former headquarters for the U.S. Post Office is the third tallest building in Washington—behind the Washington Monument and the Basilica of the National Shrine of the Immaculate Conception.

At 1300 Pennsylvania Avenue is the **Ronald Reagan Building and International Trade Center,** which, at 3.1 million square feet, is the largest structure in Washington (by square footage). It includes a large food

The White House Area

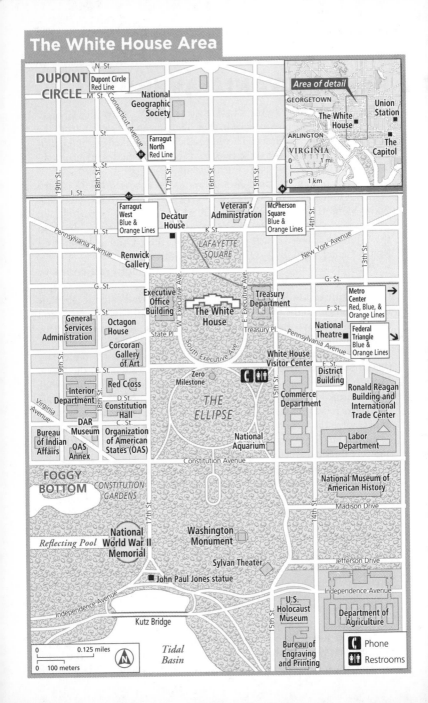

DUPONT CIRCLE

N. St.

Dupont Circle
Red Line

M. St.

Connecticut Avenue

National Geographic Society

L. St.

Farragut North Red Line

K. St.

19th St.
18th St.
17th St.
16th St.
15th St.

I. St.

Area of detail

GEORGETOWN

Union Station

The White House

ARLINGTON

VIRGINIA

The Capitol

0   1 mi
0   1 km

Farragut West Blue & Orange Lines

Decatur House

Veteran's Administration

McPherson Square Blue & Orange Lines

14th St.

Pennsylvania Avenue

H. St.

K St.

LAFAYETTE SQUARE

New York Avenue

13th St.

Renwick Gallery

G. St.

W. Executive Ave.

E. Executive Ave.

Executive Office Building

The White House

Treasury Department

F. St.

Metro Center Red, Blue, & Orange Lines

General Services Administration

Octagon House

State Pl.

Treasury Pl.

Pennsylvania Avenue

National Theatre

Federal Triangle Blue & Orange Lines

Corcoran Gallery of Art

South Executive Ave.

White House Visitor Center

E. St.

District Building

Virginia Avenue

19th St.

E. St.

Interior Department

Red Cross

D St.

Constitution Hall

18th St.

C. St.

Zero Milestone

THE ELLIPSE

Commerce Department

Ronald Reagan Building and International Trade Center

Bureau of Indian Affairs

DAR Museum

OAS Annex

Organization of American States (OAS)

National Aquarium

Labor Department

Constitution Avenue

FOGGY BOTTOM

CONSTITUTION GARDENS

National Museum of American History

Madison Drive

Reflecting Pool

17th St.

National World War II Memorial

Washington Monument

14th St.

Jefferson Drive

Sylvan Theater

■ John Paul Jones statue

Independence Avenue

Independence Avenue

15th St.

Department of Agriculture

Kutz Bridge

U.S. Holocaust Museum

0   0.125 miles
0   100 meters

Tidal Basin

Bureau of Engraving and Printing

📞 Phone
🚻 Restrooms

court that is a good lunch stop while touring. The food court is open weekdays from 7 a.m. to 7 p.m., Saturday from 11 a.m. to 6 p.m., and Sunday from noon to 5 p.m. (March 1 through August 31 only).

Crossing to the north side of Pennsylvania Avenue, you come upon **Freedom Plaza,** named in honor of Martin Luther King Jr., who developed his "I Have a Dream" speech nearby. North, across the street from Freedom Plaza, is the site of the historic **National Theater,** which first opened its doors on December 7, 1835. Over the years, the National Theater has been the site of many Presidential Inaugural Balls, and it was the theater where President Lincoln first saw a young actor named John Wilkes Booth.

As you continue west along Pennsylvania Avenue, you will see the 1908 John A. Wilson building that houses the District of Columbia government on the corner of 14th Street between 14th and 15th Streets.

Directly west across 14th Street from Freedom Plaza is the charming **Pershing Park,** which contains a square fountain that is used for ice skating in the winter months. The park is named for John J. Pershing, the American commander in Europe during World War I.

On the northwest corner of the intersection with 14th Street is the historic **Willard Hotel**—officially now the InterContinental The Willard Washington D.C. The Willard brothers began running an inn on this corner in 1847. It expanded several times and eventually became the elegant building it is today. The Willard has hosted P.T. Barnum, Buffalo Bill, Charles Dickens, and 10 different US presidents, and Mark Twain wrote two books at the hotel in the early 20th century.

As you continue on the last bit of Pennsylvania Avenue before you get to the White House (see below), you pass right in front of the Greek revival–style **U.S. Department of the Treasury** building fronted by a statue of Alexander Hamilton, the first Secretary of the Treasury. The Treasury Building is open for tours, but advance reservations are required and must be made through your Congressional office. Tours are typically available Saturday mornings at 9 a.m., 9:45 a.m., 10:30 a.m., and 11:15 a.m. The Treasury Department does not produce currency; for those tours, visit the Bureau of Engraving and Printing (page 202).

White House ★★★★

URL **whitehouse.gov**. **Address** 1600 Pennsylvania Ave. NW, Washington, D.C. **Phone** ☎ 202-456-7041. **What it is** The home of the current President of the United States. **Scope and scale** Headliner. **When to go** Whenever you can get reservations. **Hours** Tours are available Monday–Thursday 7:30 a.m.–11:30 a.m. and Friday and Saturday 7:30 a.m.–1:30 p.m. **Closest Metro** Federal Triangle (Blue, Orange, Silver) or Metro Center (Red, Blue, Orange, Silver; for Green, Yellow, transfer at Gallery Place). **Admission** Free.

DESCRIPTION AND COMMENTS One of the perks of being President of the United States is that you get to live in the White House. Of course, a downside is that

White House

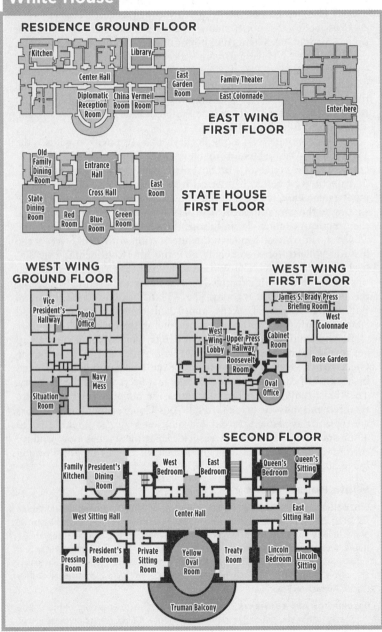

RESIDENCE GROUND FLOOR

Kitchen
Library
Center Hall
East Garden Room
Family Theater
Diplomatic Reception Room
China Room
Vermeil Room
East Colonnade
Enter here

EAST WING FIRST FLOOR

Old Family Dining Room
Entrance Hall
East Room
State Dining Room
Cross Hall
Red Room
Blue Room
Green Room

STATE HOUSE FIRST FLOOR

WEST WING GROUND FLOOR

Vice President's Hallway
Photo Office
Navy Mess
Situation Room

WEST WING FIRST FLOOR

James S. Brady Press Briefing Room
West Colonnade
West Wing Lobby
Upper Press Hallway
Cabinet Room
Roosevelt Room
Rose Garden
Oval Office

SECOND FLOOR

Family Kitchen
President's Dining Room
West Bedroom
East Bedroom
Queen's Bedroom
Queen's Sitting
West Sitting Hall
Center Hall
East Sitting Hall
Dressing Room
President's Bedroom
Private Sitting Room
Yellow Oval Room
Treaty Room
Lincoln Bedroom
Lincoln Sitting
Truman Balcony

there are tours traipsing through your house and an innumerable number of sightseers taking photos on your front sidewalk.

The White House has a long history, with its cornerstone having been laid on October 13, 1792. Located in the figurative—and just about the literal—center of Washington, the iconic mansion faces the Washington Monument in the center of the National Mall. The structure is made from sandstone with a lime-based whitewash covering that eventually led to its name. It was in the year 1800 when the first executive inhabitants moved in—President John Adams and First Lady Abigail Adams.

Expansion began rather quickly after President Jefferson moved in, only a few months after the Adams family moved out. Jefferson added single-story wings for storage and greatly improved the landscaping. All was for naught, however, as in 1814 the British burned the White House into little more than a shell during the War of 1812. James Hoban, the original architect, was enlisted to rebuild the President's House. He completed the project in less than three years, despite the original taking eight years.

Adding onto or redecorating the White House became a right of passage for many presidents. Features that became necessities, such as running water and electricity, were naturally added, but porticos, libraries, gardens, and Tiffany glass also were all introduced to the mansion over time. The most drastic changes came in 1902 when President Theodore Roosevelt—in addition to officially establishing the name "White House"—oversaw a complete renovation that expanded the wings into offices and extra living spaces that are still there today.

In the early 1950s, the foundation and structural supports were updated to catch up to the massive strain the additions were placing on them. Since their completion in 1952, there have been no major architectural or design changes, although each president and first lady still likes a little redecoration now and again.

TOURING TIPS Tours are available for the White House, although they are self-guided tours. It is akin to walking through a museum—there are no guides, merely guards in each room who are willing to answer questions (and to make sure you don't do something you're not supposed to). As you might expect, most of the White House is off limits, with only a selection of public rooms open to touring. That said, it is an interesting experience and one that everyone should attempt to have.

Getting a tour of the White House, however, is the single most difficult reservation to obtain in Washington. Tickets have to be requested from your member of Congress (or embassy for non-US residents), and whether or not you are selected is based largely on the number of tickets that congressional office has and their responsiveness. You are allowed to make a request for tickets six months in advance, and all requests must be made at least three weeks ahead of your visit. While we can sadly not guarantee a White House tour, here are the steps that give you the best chance.

1. As soon as you know the dates of your visit (and it is within 180 days), locate your congressman. For your representative, go to **house.gov** and enter your zip code at the top; for your senator, go to **senate.gov** and select your state from the dropdown box at the top.

2. From your congressman's website, find the menu for Tours and Tickets (it might be under a "Services" subheading), and fill out all information.

3. This is where it gets tricky: You may get an e-mail or phone call from your congressman's office within a few days, you may get one in a few months, or you may never hear from them at all. If you do not hear from them at all, about five or six weeks before your visit, try contacting them directly to ask about your request status. It may not help, but it won't hurt either.

4. Hopefully at some point you will receive an official request from your congressman for more detailed information on those visiting and the specific dates you are available for a tour. Once that information is sent in, the tour can be scheduled by the White House. Tours are available from 7:30 a.m. to 11:30 a.m. Monday through Thursday, and 7:30 a.m. to 1:30 p.m. Friday and Saturday. The specific time and date within your availability range cannot be selected nor can it be changed, so consider that when choosing your available dates.

5. If all goes well, you will be confirmed on a White House tour approximately two to three weeks prior to your visit. The last step is to call ☎ 202-456-7041 on the morning of the scheduled tour. Unfortunately, the high security level of the building means that tours are canceled for many things. Make sure yours is still on before you head to 1600 Pennsylvania Avenue.

If you do participate in a tour, limit what you bring with you. Cameras with detachable lenses, video cameras, tablets (such as iPads), tripods, monopods, and selfie sticks are all banned, although cell phones and compact cameras are allowed for still photography only. Video recording, live streaming, talking on the phone, and texting while inside the White House are not allowed. No bags, strollers, or food are permitted, and there are no storage facilities, meaning that you either have to abandon your tour or throw out the offending object. If you're in doubt about whether something will be allowed, don't bring it. Another important note is that there are no restrooms available for public use in the White House—despite having 35 of them. So make sure you use the ones in the Ellipse Visitor Pavilion just south of the White House before you go in.

■ CAPITOL HILL

CAPITOL HILL—STRETCHING AROUND and several blocks to the east of the U.S. Capitol—is one of the District's largest residential neighborhoods. Although there are few hotels in Capitol Hill, there are numerous places of interest and many sights that showcase the city's charm and history.

Ebenezer United Methodist Church, which was founded by African American parishioners in 1827 (the current structure was completed in 1897), sits on the corner of D Street and 4th Street SE. (A model of the original sits along 4th Street). This church once housed the city's first publicly financed school for black children. A few blocks away at 225 7th Street SE is the huge **Eastern Market,** which has been the place where locals buy produce, baked goods, meats, and cheeses since

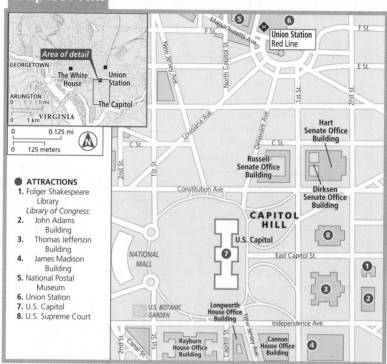

Capitol Hill

Area of detail

GEORGETOWN
The White House
Union Station

ARLINGTON
0   1 mi
0   1 km

The Capitol

VIRGINIA

0   0.125 mi
0   125 meters

● **ATTRACTIONS**
1. Folger Shakespeare Library
   Library of Congress:
2. John Adams Building
3. Thomas Jefferson Building
4. James Madison Building
5. National Postal Museum
6. Union Station
7. U.S. Capitol
8. U.S. Supreme Court

Union Station Red Line

Hart Senate Office Building
Russell Senate Office Building
Dirksen Senate Office Building
CAPITOL HILL
U.S. Capitol
NATIONAL MALL
East Capitol St.
U.S. BOTANIC GARDEN
Longworth House Office Building
Independence Ave.
Rayburn House Office Building
Cannon House Office Building
Constitution Ave.

1871. The indoor South Hall Market is open Tuesday through Sunday, with weekends bringing the outdoor, year-round farmers market and arts and crafts market.

Heading toward the U.S. Capitol building (pages 214–216), right near both the Library of Congress (pages 212–214) and the Supreme Court (page 217), are the Folger Shakespeare Library (201 East Capitol Street) and the Sewall-Belmont House and Museum (144 Constitution Avenue Northeast). **The Folger Library** houses the world's largest collection of Shakespeare's works, but the building itself is much of the draw. The Shakespeare-related reliefs and quotes carved into its white marble exterior are matched in grandeur only by its Tudor-style great hall. The Folger Library is open from 10 a.m. to 5 p.m. Monday through Saturday, and noon to 5 p.m. on Sunday, with free tours offered at 11 a.m. (Monday–Saturday only), 1 p.m. (daily), and 3 p.m. (Monday–Friday only).

While not as grand, the **Sewell-Belmont House** holds more history in its simpler bricks. It has been the seat of the National Women's

Party since 1929 and contains exhibits about suffrage and the campaign for the Equal Rights Amendment. It is only accessible by tour, which is $8 and given on Fridays and Saturdays at 11 a.m., 1 p.m., and 3 p.m., and can be scheduled at **sewallbelmont.org.**

To the southwest of the Capitol, across Independence Avenue from the United States Botanic Garden Conservatory (pages 195–196), is the lovely and often overlooked **Bartholdi Park.** This 2-acre park is meant as a demonstration garden—to show visitors what they can do at home—and has at its center a 30-foot-tall 1876 fountain designed by Frederic Auguste Bartholdi, the creator of the Statue of Liberty. Speaking of colossal statuary, moving north (directly in front of the Capitol's west front) is one of the hardest-to-miss tributes in Capitol Hill: the Ulysses S. Grant Memorial.

The **Ulysses S. Grant Memorial** marks the eastern edge of the National Mall, with the Civil War's Union Commander (and later, President of the United States) poetically staring at the likeness of the president who helped end that very war: Abraham Lincoln, who is 2 miles away. The entire marble structure is 252 feet wide and is punctuated by the 17-foot-tall equestrian statue of President Grant astride his horse Cincinnati, which rests on a 22-foot-tall marble pedestal.

Continuing to the north side of the Capitol brings you to the **Robert A. Taft Memorial and Carillon,** which lies in a park just north of Constitution Avenue, between 1st Street Northwest and New Jersey Avenue Northwest. This memorial consists of a bronze statue of the former senator (and son of President William H. Taft) and a 100-foot bell tower. One block farther north sits the **Japanese American Memorial to Patriotism During World War II,** which honors Japanese Americans who triumphed over adversity to serve their fellow Americans.

Capitol Hill does not contain many Metro stations. It is bordered by both the Eastern Market and Capitol South stations (Blue, Orange, Silver) to the south, and the Union Station stop (Red) to the north, but you will likely have to do a little walking to fully enjoy this area.

Library of Congress ★★★

URL loc.gov. **Address** 10 1st St. SE, Washington, D.C. 20540. **Phone** ☎ 202-707-5000. **What it is** Library for the U.S. Congress, but open to the public. **Scope and scale** Major attraction. **When to go** Anytime. **Hours** Monday–Saturday, 8:30 a.m.–5 p.m. Last entrance at 4:30 p.m. Closed 4th Thursday of November, December 25, and January 1. **Closest Metro** Capitol South (Orange, Blue, Silver); Yellow, Green, and Red can transfer at Metro Center. **Admission** Free. **Authors' comments** Beautiful building and decorations, good exhibits. **Not to Be Missed** The Great Hall; Main Reading Room; special exhibits.

DESCRIPTION AND COMMENTS The Library of Congress is the world's largest library collection, holding more than 23 million books and 135 million other documents. Although it is literally the library for the U.S. Congress's research

Library of Congress

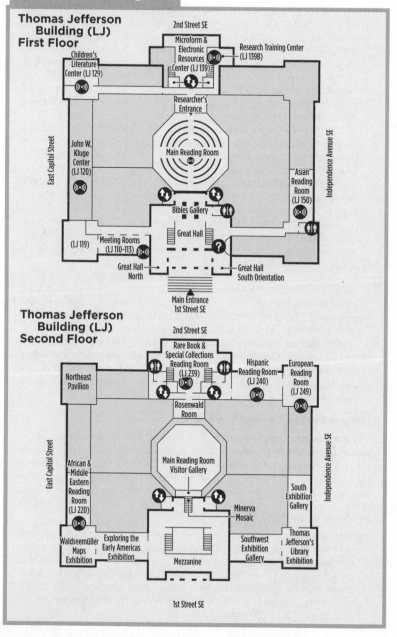

Thomas Jefferson Building (LJ) First Floor

2nd Street SE

Children's Literature Center (LJ 129)

Microform & Electronic Resources Center (LJ 139)

Research Training Center (LJ 139B)

Researcher's Entrance

John W. Kluge Center (LJ 120)

Main Reading Room

East Capitol Street

Independence Avenue SE

Asian Reading Room (LJ 150)

Bibles Gallery

Great Hall

(LJ 119)

Meeting Rooms (LJ 110-113)

Great Hall North

Great Hall South Orientation

Main Entrance 1st Street SE

Thomas Jefferson Building (LJ) Second Floor

2nd Street SE

Rare Book & Special Collections Reading Room (LJ 239)

Hispanic Reading Room (LJ 240)

European Reading Room (LJ 249)

Northeast Pavilion

Rosenwald Room

Main Reading Room Visitor Gallery

East Capitol Street

Independence Avenue SE

African & Middle Eastern Reading Room (LJ 220)

Minerva Mosaic

South Exhibition Gallery

Waldseemüller Maps Exhibition

Exploring the Early Americas Exhibition

Mezzanine

Southwest Exhibition Gallery

Thomas Jefferson's Library Exhibition

1st Street SE

needs, anyone can use the library's materials while inside the building, with proper ID.

Most people opt to tour the library rather than read in it, and for good reason: It's a beautiful building. Completed in the Beaux-Arts style (as are New York's Public Library and Grand Central Terminal) in 1897, the **Great Hall** inside the building features soaring ceilings and dozens of murals by some of America's great artists. These murals cover a range of topics, and each usually gets several scenes across a wall or ceiling. Topics include everything from the evolution of the written word, to good and bad government, to how to live a nice life. Along with these are statues, carvings, and other decorations, celebrating science, reason, printing, and more.

The main floor of the Great Hall contains two priceless Bibles on display: a *Gutenberg Bible* and the *Giant Bible of Mainz,* both from 15th-century Germany during the Renaissance that led (eventually) to the ideas of government on which the United States is based.

The **Main Reading Room,** on the second floor, is topped with a 160-foot rotunda, also elaborately decorated. Even if you're not planning to read, you can tour the room from the second floor.

Besides the architecture, the library hosts a series of permanent and rotating exhibits. Permanent exhibits include displays of entertainer Bob Hope's personal memorabilia (including his legendary file of jokes) and one dedicated to composer George Gershwin.

The rotating exhibits are thoughtfully done and very good. Since you're in a library, these displays focus on important documents. Past themes have included maps, political cartoons, The U.S. Civil Rights Act of 1964, and chamber music.

TOURING TIPS The library's architecture is a big draw, so expect waits of 20 to 30 minutes to get through security and into the Great Hall.

Free, guided, one-hour tours are available on the half-hour from 10:30 a.m. to 3:30 p.m. weekdays, and at 2:30 p.m. on weekends. Reservations aren't available. On most non-busy days, plan on arriving around 20 minutes before the tour to get a space; on busy days, arrive 45 minutes to an hour ahead, put your name in, and grab a snack while you wait.

United States Capitol ★★★★

URL visitthecapitol.gov. Address East Capitol St. NE & 1st St. SE, Washington, D.C. **Phone** ☎ 202-226-8000. **What it is** The seat of Congress in a majestic building. **Scope and scale** Headliner. **When to go** Anytime with a scheduled tour, early in the morning to simply browse the visitor center. **Hours** Tours are available Monday–Saturday, 8:50 a.m.–3:20 p.m. **Closest Metro** Union Station (Red) or Capitol South (Blue, Orange, Silver). Transfer from Green, Yellow at either Gallery Place or L'Enfant Plaza. **Admission** Free.

DESCRIPTION AND COMMENTS In the original plan for Washington, D.C., the focal point was a grand, wide strip of land anchored at one end by the presidential residence and at the other by the building meant to house the Congress. Remarkably, that is exactly how it was built, and the United States Capitol still anchors the east end of the National Mall. Rising 288 feet above Capitol Hill, the grand, domed, neoclassical Capitol Building has been beckoning visitors for more than 200 years.

U.S. Capitol

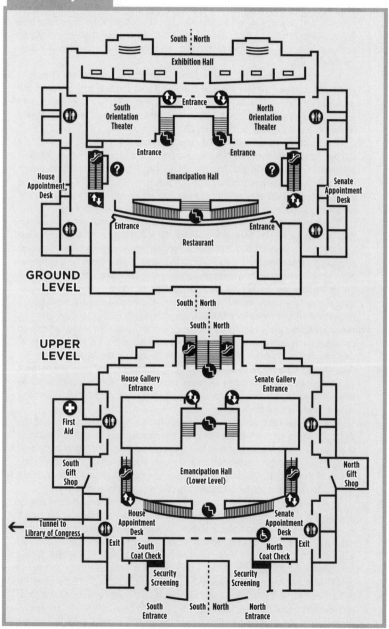

GROUND LEVEL

- South | North
- Exhibition Hall
- South Orientation Theater
- Entrance
- North Orientation Theater
- Entrance
- Entrance
- House Appointment Desk
- Emancipation Hall
- Senate Appointment Desk
- Entrance
- Entrance
- Restaurant
- South | North

UPPER LEVEL

- South | North
- House Gallery Entrance
- Senate Gallery Entrance
- First Aid
- South Gift Shop
- Emancipation Hall (Lower Level)
- North Gift Shop
- Tunnel to Library of Congress
- Exit
- House Appointment Desk
- Senate Appointment Desk
- Exit
- South Coat Check
- North Coat Check
- Security Screening
- Security Screening
- South Entrance
- South | North
- North Entrance

The cornerstone of the Capitol was set in place by George Washington himself on September 18, 1783, following a parade leading to the construction site. The spectacle demonstrated how important the Capitol was to be, both symbolically and practically—especially when compared with the ceremony-free laying of the White House's cornerstone the previous year. The United States Congress officially met in the first section completed—the north wing—in November of 1800.

It only took 50 years for the needs of the Capitol to outgrow the structure, which led to major expansions in the building that symbolically matched the expansion of America. Today's U.S. Capitol Building is 751 feet from end to end and 350 feet at its widest point. Within is where you will find the 435 members of the House of Representatives and 100 senators.

The most recent addition to the Capitol complex is the U.S. Capitol Visitor Center, located belowground on the east side of the building. The Visitor Center contains exhibits on the Capitol, gift shops, and a restaurant that serves from 8:30 a.m. to 4 p.m. Monday through Saturday. The Visitor Center can be toured without a ticket or advance reservation, although it is the staging point for tours, so it becomes quite busy during the middle of the day.

The massive dome of the U.S. Capitol is undergoing a multiyear restoration that is expected to be completed before the inauguration of America's 45th president on January 20, 2017. The current refurbishment includes restoring and weatherproofing the exterior, and the next phase will focus on the interior and the space between the inner and outer shells. That means that for the time being, visitors will be seeing scaffolding outside and a "safety donut" suspended from the dome inside. While not aesthetically pleasing, the work is necessary and should make for a fittingly grand reveal in 2017.

TOURING TIPS Tours of the U.S. Capitol Building are available Monday through Saturday, with tour times ranging from 8:50 a.m. to 3:20 p.m. While same-day passes are available near the information desk in the Visitor Center, we recommend reserving passes in advance at **visitthecapitol.gov,** where tours can be booked approximately 90 days prior to your visit. It is also possible to get tours via your congressional office, and some congressmen even offer smaller tours led by staffers.

The tour will take you through some of the many impressive areas of the Capitol. The centerpiece is the Rotunda, the circular room beneath the dome that rises 180 feet and culminates in a fresco titled *The Apotheosis of George Washington.* You also will see National Statuary Hall, which was the original location of the House of Representatives but now contains many statues. There are 100 total statues in the Capitol's collection—two from each state.

If you wish to tour the Senate and House galleries, they are open whenever Congress is in session, but they are not included on the regular tour. To obtain passes to the galleries, you must get them through your congressman. For international visitors, you must inquire about the availability of passes at the marked appointment desks on the upper level of the Visitor Center. Those with passes are admitted to the galleries Monday through Friday between 9 a.m. and 4 p.m.

Be advised that liquids, food, and bags larger than 18 x 14 x 8.5 inches are not allowed in the Capitol Building. The galleries are even more restrictive: Non-medical electronic devices, cameras, strollers, and bags of any size are not allowed, but there is storage available near the entrance to the galleries.

U.S. Supreme Court ★★

URL supremecourt.gov. **Address** 1 1st St. NE, Washington, D.C. 20543. **Phone** ☎ 202-479-3000. **What it is** The highest court within the United States judicial branch of government. **Scope and scale** Diversion. **When to go** Anytime. **Hours** Monday–Friday, 9 a.m.–4:30 p.m.; closed weekends and federal holidays. **Closest Metro** Capitol South (Orange, Blue, Silver), Union Station (Red); Yellow and Green can transfer at Metro Center. **Admission** Free. **Authors' comments** A quick, interesting, air-conditioned stop on the way to another attraction.

DESCRIPTION AND COMMENTS There are two reasons to visit the Supreme Court: to hear an important case argued or verdict announced and to tour the building.

Of the two, touring the building is vastly easier and requires less coordination. There are no guided tours and only a handful of exhibits, all on the ground floor. The best of these exhibits is dedicated to the history and architecture of the Supreme Court building. Besides that, another highlights the career of Sandra Day O'Connor, the first female Supreme Court Justice, and a third covers the history of legal education in the United States. There's also a 24-minute film on the history of the Court, covering its roots in the U.S. Constitution and important cases over the years.

It's also possible to hear one of those important cases being held live in front of the court. Sessions start on the first Monday in October and usually run through late April. The Supreme Court's website lists its calendar for hearing cases for the current session, so you'll typically know around 30 days in advance the date on which a case will be argued.

> *unofficial* **TIP**
> Lines to hear important cases will begin to form the night before the Supreme Court hears oral arguments.

On the day the case is heard, two lines will form outside of the building, both on a first-come, first-serve basis. One line is for people who want to hear the entire case's oral arguments; the other is a line of people who'll get admitted to the court's gallery for three minutes each, to hear snippets of the case.

TOURING TIPS The Supreme Court has no on-site parking and very limited public parking nearby. Your best bet is to park at Union Station, but if you're doing that, you're probably better off just taking the Metro.

As with the White House and Congress, access to the Supreme Court is controlled tightly, with lots of security. Leave behind any nonessential items, and allow 20 minutes to get through the scans.

CHINATOWN, PENN QUARTER, *and* JUDICIARY SQUARE

FOR GENERAL PURPOSES, Penn Quarter and Judiciary Square each are bordered by Pennsylvania Avenue Northwest to the south and Massachusetts Avenue and New York Avenue to the north, with Chinatown making up a few square blocks at the north end of this polygon. Where exactly these three neighborhoods begin and end is debated, but it is reasonable to say that Judiciary Square expands from I-395 on its eastern border to 6th Street, while Penn Quarter makes up the rest of the territory over to somewhere around 13th Street.

Now that the cartography is out of the way, we can discuss the multitude of things to do in these areas. In addition to several sights well worth seeing, the Penn Quarter/Chinatown section of the city was the focus of much attention in the 1990s and 2000s and now boasts many shopping, dining, and nightlife options. What makes these options extra attractive is that the Penn Quarter area is well serviced by the Metro. The Gallery Place-Chinatown station (Red, Green, Yellow) and the Metro Center station (Blue, Orange, Red, Silver) mean that you can easily reach anywhere in this neighborhood with no more than a few blocks walk.

We are starting our tour, however, in the Judiciary Square neighborhood, which itself is serviced by the Judiciary Square Metro station (Red). Whichever way you look coming off of the Metro, you are likely to see a courthouse of some kind (it isn't called Judiciary Square for nothing). In fact, much of the neighborhood is utilized by government buildings, with the U.S. Tax Court, D.C. Superior Court, Metro Police, D.C. Court of Appeals, U.S. Court of Appeals for the Armed Forces, and the U.S. Government Accountability Office (among others) all residing in the Judiciary Square neighborhood.

The **District of Columbia Court of Appeals**—on Indiana Ave between 4th and 5th Streets—was designed in 1820 to serve as both the courthouse and city hall to Washington, D.C. The southwest corner of the complex (at 4th and Indiana) features the **Darlington Memorial Fountain,** complete with a gilded bronze statue of a nude "Maiden and Fawn" dedicated to Joseph J. Darlington, the former leader of the Washington Bar Association. There was controversy at the time of its design (1922) because the symbolic connection with Darlington and a forest nymph were not immediately apparent. Honestly, we still don't get it.

From the Court of Appeals, crossing E Street to the north walks you right into the **National Law Enforcement Officers Memorial.** Two long, curving, tree-lined marble walls frame a tranquil reflection pool in this memorial to the more than 20,000 American officers who have been killed in the line of duty.

Directly to the west, across 5th Street, is the **Marian Koshland Science Museum.** Open 10 a.m. to 6 p.m. daily (closed Tuesdays), this museum features interactive exhibits designed to spur teens and adults into conversation and action regarding today's most important scientific issues. The cost for an adult ticket is $7.

For a glimpse into D.C.'s cultural history, walk east along F Street past the beautiful structure housing the National Building Museum (pages 221–223) until you come to 3rd Street. Here you will find the **Holy Rosary Church,** the last vestige of one of the few Italian communities in D.C.

For even more historical culture, head over to Washington's **China-town,** the center of which is found on H Street Northwest between 6th and 7th Streets. The **Friendship Archway,** a traditional Chinese gate that rises to a height 60 feet above H Street and contains more than 270 depictions of dragons, is located on that street. Also along H Street is where you will find several decently authentic Chinese restaurants.

Just around the corner from the Friendship Archway (at 7th and F Streets) sits the **Verizon Center,** a 20,000-seat sports and concert venue. Although the arena constantly hosts other events, it is primarily used as the home for the NBA's Washington Wizards, NHL's Washington Capitals, WNBA's Washington Mystics, and Georgetown University's Men's College Basketball team. Bars and restaurants surround the Verizon Center.

Walking down G Street toward 9th, you pass the classic facade of the American Art Museum and National Portrait Gallery (pages 191–195), and just a block south (on 8th and F) is the International Spy Museum (pages 220–221), but we're heading to **Martin Luther King, Jr. Memorial Library** at the intersection of G and 9th Streets. The glass-and-metal building serves as the central branch of the D.C. Public Library and contains a substantial Washingtonia collection on the city's history, and the Black Studies Center, which focuses on African American culture.

At the corner of F Street Northwest and 10th Street, half a block north of Ford's Theatre (see below), is **Madame Tussauds,** the famous exhibitor of lifelike wax figures. The Washington, D.C., branch naturally focuses on local figures—including all 44 US Presidents—as well as civil rights leaders and the usual assortment of personalities from Hollywood, sports, and media. The price ranges from $16.29 to $23.27, depending on the type of ticket and if it's purchased in advance, but the figures and the interesting sets (news desks, offices, living rooms) make for fun photos.

Over on the western edge of Penn Quarter—where H Street, 13th Street, and New York Avenue Northwest all meet—sits the **National Museum of Women in the Arts.** This is the only major museum in the world dedicated exclusively to recognizing the achievements of women artists. The collection includes 4,500 objects and an 18,500-volume library and research center. Admission is $10 for adults, and the museum is open from 10 a.m. to 5 p.m. (12 to 5 p.m. Sundays).

Ford's Theatre ★★½

URL fordstheatre.org. Address 511 Tenth St. NW, Washington, D.C. 20004. Phone ☎ 202-347-4833. What it is Both a working theater and a museum with displays about the assassination of President Lincoln. Scope and scale Minor attraction. When to go Anytime. Hours Entry is available 9 a.m.–4:30 p.m.; box office opens at 8:30 a.m. for same-day tickets; closed December 25. Closest Metro Metro Center (Red, Orange, Blue, Silver; for Green, Yellow, transfer at Gallery Place). Admission Free, although a timed-access ticket is required.

DESCRIPTION AND COMMENTS Ford's Theatre was opened in 1861 as a venue hosting stage productions. It is best known for the infamous shooting of President Abraham Lincoln. On the evening of April 14, 1865, the President was at Ford's Theatre to view a performance of the comedy *Our American Cousin* when John Wilkes Booth—an actor who often worked the theater's stage—shot Lincoln in the head. Lincoln was taken to the Peterson House directly across the street, where he died the following day.

Following that tragic event, Ford's Theatre was closed for more than 100 years. It didn't reopen until it was deemed a national historic site in 1968. Since then, it has acted as both a working theater and a museum dedicated to President Lincoln's final days, his murderer, and the conspiracy surrounding the assassination.

Exhibits display the clothes Abraham Lincoln wore to the show that night, the play's program, the murder weapon, and John Wilkes Booth's diary, among other artifacts. The museum also examines the conspiracy surrounding the assassination, including Booth's gang of Confederate sympathizers, their initial kidnapping plot, and the synchronized murders that were supposed to coincide with the president's (including the non-fatal stabbing of Secretary of State William Seward and the not-attempted assassination of Vice President Andrew Johnson).

Admission to Ford's Theatre includes entry to the **Peterson House** and the **Center for Education and Leadership,** both across 10th Street from the theater. The Peterson House is more commonly referred to as "The House Where Lincoln Died" (it's true). Inside are displays about the president's final hours and the ultimately unsuccessful fight to save his life. Next door to the Peterson House, the Center for Education and Leadership explores the aftermath of the assassination, the hunt for John Wilkes Booth, and the lasting impacts of Lincoln's presidency.

If you're in the mood to see a play, Ford's Theatre also regularly puts on performances that are open to the public. Tickets range from about $27 to about $108 (including Ticketmaster fees) depending on the performance.

TOURING TIPS Visiting Ford's Theatre is free, but a ticket is required. The easiest way to get a ticket is via the theater's website (through Ticketmaster). Tickets go on sale anywhere from one to four months in advance. Advance tickets are generally available a few days ahead on all but the busiest times. A small number of tickets are distributed at the theater box office for same-day visits, but these tickets are first-come, first-served and not guaranteed to be available.

International Spy Museum ★★★

URL spymuseum.org. Address 800 F St. NW, Washington, D.C. 20004. **Phone** ☎ 202-393-7798. **What it is** Museum on spies, spy tools, and espionage. **Scope and scale** Diversion. **When to go** Anytime. **Hours** Usually 10 a.m.–6 p.m., but check website for earlier openings. Closed 4th Thursday of November, December 25. **Closest Metro** Gallery Place/Chinatown (Yellow, Green, Red); Blue, Orange, Silver can transfer at Metro Center or L'Enfant Plaza. **Admission** Adults (ages 12–64) $22; children (ages 7–11) $15; children 6 and under are free; seniors, military, law enforcement $16. **Authors' comments** Impressive.

DESCRIPTION AND COMMENTS The International Spy Museum (ISM) is a tribute to spies, spy technology, and secrets. Opened in 2002 in a town full of high-quality, free museums and monuments, the Spy Museum's engaging, fun exhibits have allowed the for-profit museum to succeed while charging $22 for admission. If you're at all interested in this kind of thing, it's time (and money) well spent.

The ISM's permanent exhibits cover six areas: Starting in **Covers and Legends,** you get an alternate identity (complete with documentation) and an introduction to spying as a career. Next comes **School for Spies,** where you get to see all of the cool gadgets, tools, and tech that spies use to gather secrets, evade detection, and stay one step ahead of their targets. In **The Secret History of History,** you'll learn the stories of spies throughout history, how they worked, and whom they helped. **From Ballroom to Battlefield** covers how spies and espionage worked during the US Civil War.

One of our favorite exhibits is **Spies Among Us,** which features codes and code-breaking stories from World War II.

If you want to sleep at night (instead of hoarding generators and batteries), skip **The 21st Century** exhibition, which shows how modern life would be disrupted if a cyberattack were launched against the US electricity grid.

unofficial **TIP**

Unofficial Tip (in code!):

Gur VFZ'f nqivfbel obneq vapyhqrf sbezre urnqf bs gur PVN, SOV, XTO, ZV5, naq fgnss sebz gur AFN.

Besides the permanent exhibits, the ISM has a rotating set of special exhibits. The most recent is *Exquisitely Evil: 50 Years of Bond Villains,* featuring the villains from the James Bond movie franchise, their weapons of destruction, plans, and movie props. The best part of the exhibit is when real-life spies tell stories of how their missions sometimes got as exciting as a Bond movie.

The ISM also hosts a one-hour, interactive spy game called **Operation Spy** (ages 12 and up). Your team's assignment is to track down a bomb device and the person who stole it, in a foreign town called Khandar. You'll need to make contact with a local agent (without drawing attention), break out of a room, decrypt a secret transmission, and more. It's fast paced but fairly straightforward, even for small children. If you've got the time, it's fun.

Operation Spy costs $15 without museum admission, or $29 including museum admission. Buy tickets in advance on the website, and arrive 20 minutes in advance for orientation.

TOURING TIPS The gift shop's most popular item is a black T-shirt that reads, "Deny everything." (We bought one to wear around the office.)

National Building Museum ★★★

URL nbm.org. Address 401 F St. NW, Washington, D.C. 20001. **Phone** ☎ 202-272-2448. **What it is** Exhibits on different styles of interior and exterior architecture, the evolution of building design, and how buildings influence our lives. **Scope and scale** Minor attraction. **When to go** Anytime. **Closest Metro** Gallery Place/Chinatown (Red, Yellow, Green); Blue, Orange, and Silver lines can transfer to Red at Metro Center. **Admission** $8 for adults; $5 for children, students, and seniors. Special exhibits require extra admission, typically around another $8 per person. **Hours** Monday–Saturday, 10 a.m.–5 p.m.; Sunday, 11 a.m.–5 p.m. Closed 4th Thursday of November and December 25. **Authors' Comments** The rotating exhibits are hit or miss, but there are usually one or two that make a visit worthwhile. **Not to Be Missed** House and Home (second floor).

DESCRIPTION AND COMMENTS The National Building Museum is dedicated to examining the influence of architecture and buildings in our lives. Its exhibits cover a wide range of ideas, from the evolution of American home design and building materials to rethinking the boundaries of public and private spaces.

The museum typically has around six exhibits open, spread over two floors. Past exhibits have covered how local culture and climate affect building design; architecture for surviving natural disasters; and an indoor "beach" made from a million white, translucent, plastic balls (it was amazing—we have photos). At least a couple of exhibits will have large video installations or films, and these are nice breaks if you've been walking around D.C. all day.

The **House and Home** exhibit on the second floor is one of the museum's best, showing the evolution of the American home in concept, design, building materials and techniques, decoration, and use. Each area gets its own dedicated space. The "design" segment includes 14 detailed, scale models of iconic homes, from Fallingwater to Monticello. To illustrate building materials and techniques, full-scale model rooms are built along one long wall of the exhibit, starting with post-and-girt, through adobe bricks, to steel, glass, and concrete. The best part about this display is that you're encouraged to touch the materials and walk inside the models.

Also in House and Home are two multimedia presentations: *Welcome Home,* showing different designs for 21st-century residential architecture, including one-room apartments and spaceship-like college dormitories; and *From Home to Community,* examining the role of individual houses in six American neighborhoods.

Three special exhibits are running in 2016. The first, **New American Garden,** takes a look at the low-water, low-maintenance landscaping movement started by the Washington, D.C., architecture firm of Oehme, van Sweden & Associates. These landscapes, created with ornamental grasses and perennials instead of manicured lawns, started a "sustainable landscape" trend that continues today. The exhibit shows several residential and commercial installations, from concept design to implementation to how the landscapes have fared over the past 20 years.

The second special exhibit for 2016, **Small Stories,** showcases 12 different dollhouses, some more than 300 years old. The "twist" on this display is that it will have an ongoing narrative about the "residents" that "live" in the dollhouses. You'll think it's inspired, weird, or both.

The third exhibit for 2016, **St. Elizabeth's—The Architecture of an Asylum,** explores the changing theories of mental-illness treatment from the 19th to the 21st centuries, using the example of the Government Hospital for the Insane, as St. Elizabeth's was originally known. The building was later converted to a federal office building (So the residents could work from home? – Len) and then to a mixed-use urban development.

The museum typically has two ongoing, hands-on play areas for kids: **Building Zone,** for children ages 2 to 6, includes giant foam blocks to build with, picture books about architecture, construction-themed toys, and an eco-friendly play house; and **Play Work Build,** for older children and adults, features smaller building blocks, virtual design tools, and more. These areas tend to be some-what crowded, and it'll take some patience and time to complete a design.

TOURING TIPS Because the museum charges admission, it's not usually as crowded as some of the free sites. It is popular with parents and small children, however, especially on weekends.

National Postal Museum *(a Smithsonian museum)*   ★★★

URL postalmuseum.si.edu. **Address** 2 Massachusetts Ave. NE, Washington, D.C. 20002. **Phone** ☎ 202-633-5555 **What it is** Exhibits on America's postal history—much more interesting than it sounds. **Scope and scale** Minor attraction. **When to go** Anytime. **Hours** Daily, 10 a.m.–5:30 pm. Closed December 25. **Closest Metro** Union Station (Red; for Orange, Silver, Blue, transfer at Metro Center; for Yellow, Green, transfer at Gallery Place). **Admission** Free.

DESCRIPTION AND COMMENTS Located in the building that served as the Washington city post office from 1914 through 1986, the Smithsonian National Postal Museum is surprisingly delightful. Examining the history of postal service and philately (stamp study and collection) in America doesn't sound particularly interesting, but it is presented in a fascinating way in a stately, gorgeous building.

Walking in, the first thing you see is the 90-foot-high atrium ceiling and the three vintage airmail planes suspended from it. From there you'll learn the history of mail delivery—from the stagecoach to the train to the truck.

TOURING TIPS The galleries are well designed and logically presented but involve a fair amount of reading to absorb the full scope of the subject. While simply entering the museum and browsing is certainly worthwhile (after all, it's free), this may not be the best stop for children. Unless they're budding philatelists, of course.

Union Station   ★★★

URL unionstationdc.com. **Address** 50 Massachusetts Ave. NE, Washington, D.C. 20002. **Phone** ☎ 202-289-1908. **What it is** Major transportation hub, with food and shopping. **Scope and scale** Diversion. **When to go** Anytime. **Hours** The station is open 24 hours; restaurants are usually open 6 a.m.–9 p.m. weekdays, 9 a.m.–9 p.m. Saturday, and 7 a.m.–6 p.m. Sunday. Stores usually open 10 a.m.–9 p.m. Monday–Saturday, 12–6 p.m. Sunday. **Closest Metro** Union Station (Red); Orange, Blue, and Silver can transfer to Red at Metro Center; Yellow, Green can transfer at Gallery Place/Chinatown. **Admission** Free. **Authors' comments** Impressive architecture; nice place for a quick lunch if you're nearby.

DESCRIPTION AND COMMENTS Union Station is the central hub for Amtrak, Acela, and Maryland, Virginia, and West Virginia train lines, the Washington Metro's Red Line Metro trains, plus bus service by Greyhound, Megabus, Bolt-Bus, and more. If you're taking a train, bus, or Metro to Washington, it'll probably stop here.

Built between 1903 and 1907, Union Station is one of the busiest train depots in the United States, serving more than 40 million passengers per year. As the main hub for the nation's capital, the station's architecture is suitably grand, done in a classical style with soaring archways, long halls, and lots of columns.

It's also got a decent variety of food and retail opportunities, especially for breakfast and lunch.

TOURING TIPS The Union Station parking garage holds almost 2,200 spaces and charges $9 for the first hour for unvalidated tickets ($3 for validated), up to a maximum of $24 per day. See **unionstationdc.com/parking** for rates.

◧ LOGAN CIRCLE

LOGAN CIRCLE IS PRIMARILY A RESIDENTIAL NEIGHBORHOOD north of the White House and east of Dupont Circle. Much like Dupont Circle, Logan Circle is centered around its namesake traffic circle, one of the circles laid out in L'Enfant's original city plan. The Logan Circle neighborhood contains few sights but is rich in history and is a wonderful spot to mingle with real Washingtonians living their lives. The area has no Metro stops within its borders, but there are several that surround the relatively small neighborhood. McPherson Square Metro station (Orange, Blue, Silver) is to the south, Mt. Vernon Square (Green, Yellow) is to the east, and Shaw-Howard U (Green, Yellow) is to the northeast.

Let's start our look at Logan Circle by visiting another circle: Thomas Circle at the intersection of Massachusetts Avenue, Vermont Avenue, M Street, and 14th Street Northwest.

Thomas Circle is named for the Civil War General George Thomas, whose statue graces its center. In the 1860s, Logan Circle featured a horse-drawn railway that led the middle- and upper-class residents downtown farther north into Logan Circle. Today it is a simple, small, urban, green space. Standing in Thomas Circle, however, you can't help but notice the two towering steeples jutting into the skyline to the north.

The most noticeable from Thomas Circle is the neoclassical **National City Christian Church** at 5 Thomas Circle Northwest. The building was designed by the same architectural firm as the Thomas Jefferson Memorial and National Archives, which seems obvious once you know. President Lyndon Johnson worshiped here, and this was the site of his state funeral in 1973. Turning slightly to the right brings the **Luther Place Memorial Church** into full view. Completed in 1873, the gothic revival church features a bronze statue of Martin Luther that was dedicated in 1884.

Farther north at 1318 Vermont Avenue is the former home of **Mary McLeod Bethune** and the current site of the **Memorial Museum** in her honor. Mary McLeod Bethune was a civil rights leader and educator who founded the National Council of Negro Women in 1935. The house is open seven days a week from 9 a.m. to 5 p.m., with the last guided tour at 4 p.m.

Walking a short block north brings us finally to the neighborhood's center, Logan Circle. This large traffic circle is the only one in the city that is fully surrounded by residences, giving it a very homey feel. It is not uncommon to see neighbors enjoying the grass in the middle of the circle around the 25-foot-tall **statue of John A. Logan,** who was a Civil War commander, congressman, and resident of 4 Logan Circle.

Some of the houses around Logan Circle are quite impressive, such as Nos. 1 and 2 on the southwest side, which is a Second Empire–style double house built around 1880. Moving clockwise you will see numbers 4 through 14, which are representative of the cohesive, yet wildly different, styles of the time. The variant rooflines, mixed materials, and irregular level of detail make for a charming scene.

U STREET CORRIDOR

THE NEIGHBORHOOD JUST NORTH OF LOGAN CIRCLE is known as the U Street Corridor because it centers around that very street. More specifically, when locals refer to "U Street," they generally mean the area between 9th and 15th Streets, including U Street and the two or three blocks to the north and south. The U Street area is served by the U Street–African American Civil War Memorial–Cardozo Metro station (Green, Yellow).

The city of Washington, D.C., is a diverse one, and there is perhaps no area of the city more important to that diversity than U Street. It seems that almost every building is steeped in the history of African Americans in the District. The story of U Street starts, as most do in this section of the city, just after the Civil War, when demand for more housing increased. The increasingly diverse and, at the time, segregated nature of the city made U Street, a neighborhood that was unofficially divided from the predominantly white areas to its south and west, popular with black citizens.

A side effect of this division was that U Street became a place where African Americans could excel at a time when they were being repressed elsewhere. For instance, the **Prince Hall Masonic Temple** at 1000 U Street (completed in 1930—the ground floor is a CVS) and the **True Reformer Building** at 1200 U Street (1903) were both designed and financed by African Americans.

The U Street Corridor is also known for music, specifically jazz. **Club Caverns**—later called Crystal Caverns, now Bohemian Caverns—is at 2001 11th Street (at the intersection with U) and still features jazz often. The **Howard Theater,** a few blocks away at 620 T Street, was closed for many years, but it recently has been reopened as a music venue once again. Both of these clubs were home to the best jazz musicians of the time, including Louis Armstrong, Nat King Cole, Miles Davis, Duke Ellington (who was from the U Street area), Ella Fitzgerald, and Billie Holiday.

Any discussion of U Street seems remiss without mentioning **Ben's Chili Bowl** at 1213 U Street. Sure it's a great place to get a chili dog and a shake, but it's more important for what it is than what it serves. Ben's was opened in 1958 and has been a staple of U Street through the music boom, the riots following the assassination of Dr. Martin Luther King Jr., the degradation of the neighborhood in the 1970s and 1980s, and the recent redevelopment. If you stop by, you may even see one of the many celebrities who have eaten at Ben's.

Added more recently to the U Street Corridor is the **African American Civil War Memorial and Museum,** found at 1925 Vermont Avenue. This museum was opened in 1999 to honor the United States Colored Troops by telling their stories through photos, documents, and presentations. These soldiers who fought for freedom during the Civil War are also the focus of a memorial in the street in front of the museum. The museum is free to the public and open Tuesday through Friday from 10 a.m. to 6:30 p.m., Saturday from 10 a.m. to 4 p.m., and Sunday from noon to 4 p.m.

◼ DUPONT CIRCLE/KALORAMA

THE NEIGHBORING AREAS OF DUPONT CIRCLE and Kalorama are both official Historic Districts. They are located in northwest Washington, D.C., approximately 1.5 miles north of the Lincoln Memorial end of the National Mall. Like many city neighborhoods, the boundaries are not agreed upon, but the center of Dupont Circle is very easy to find—it is the large traffic circle of the same name. Kalorama is the neighborhood just to the northwest, with the dividing line being Florida Avenue. The easiest access point is via the Dupont Circle Metro station (Red), located at the traffic circle.

The **Dupont Circle** traffic circle was begun in 1871 (then called Pacific Circle) and named for Rear Admiral Samuel Francis Du Pont, whose statue once graced its central park (it was moved by his family in 1921—the same family that started the DuPont corporation and was profiled in the Academy Award–nominated film *Foxcatcher*). The circle now surrounds a double-tiered marble fountain.

At one time, stately mansions lined Dupont Circle, the last of which is the **Patterson Mansion,** found at 15 Dupont Circle (at its intersection with P Street). This Italianate house was built in 1901 and served as temporary quarters for President Calvin Coolidge in 1927 while the White House was being renovated.

Moving west along R Street, and passing about a half block north of the Phillips Collection (pages 228–230) on 21st Street, you will start noticing more large houses, some of which have flags. These are some of the many foreign embassies that blanket these neighborhoods. Turning right onto 22nd Street and crossing Decatur Place brings you to something you don't expect to find in the middle of a street . . . stairs. Called the **Spanish Steps,** this wide, lavish, Italianate staircase was built in 1911 to allow pedestrians access to a street that was simply too steep for a carriage.

Cresting the top of the steps brings you to S Street, which is lined with gorgeous residences, a few embassies (namely Lao at 2222 and Myanmar at 2300), and the quaint Mitchell Park. At 2340 S Street, you will come upon the **Woodrow Wilson House,** President Wilson's post-presidential residence. Adult tickets are $10 from 10 a.m. to 4 p.m. Tuesday through Sunday. Visitors can see the mansion much the way it was when President Wilson retired to it in 1921.

Continuing out to Massachusetts Avenue brings you right into the heart of **Embassy Row,** the section of Massachusetts Avenue stretching from Dupont Circle all the way up to the Naval Observatory. This segment of Massachusetts Avenue and the surrounding streets is where most of the foreign embassies to the United States are located.

For one day each year, usually in early May, many embassies open their doors to visitors. Quite a few even have demonstrations of cultural dress, dances, food, fashion, and so on. Truthfully, there are two different days: one for European Union countries, and one for all others. For more information, check the Passport DC section of **cultural tourismdc.org.**

Walking southeast down Massachusetts Avenue, at 2118, is where you will find **the Society of the Cincinnati**—the nation's oldest patriotic organization. Founded in 1783 by soldiers who served in the American Revolution, the society aimed to spread appreciation in American independence. The current society utilizes its location in the **Anderson House** to display its broad collection of historical documents, newsreels, artifacts, and art. The exhibits can be viewed for free between 10 a.m. and 4 p.m. Tuesday through Saturday, and between noon and 4 p.m. Sunday.

Farther down Massachusetts Avenue—along the 1500 block of 20th Street—the **Dupont Circle FRESHFARM Market** operates every Sunday, offering fresh foods, flowers, and herbal products. At this point you are almost back to Dupont Circle, but if you continue south on 20th Street until you come to its intersection with New Hampshire Avenue, you will see the fortress-like **Heurich House,** also referred to as the Brewmasters Castle. This house was built to be the residence of Christian Heurich, a German immigrant who made his fortune brewing beer (the brewery closed in 1956).

A few blocks away at 1725 Rhode Island Avenue Northwest—near the intersection of M Street and Connecticut Avenue—is the deceptively plain **Cathedral of St. Matthew the Apostle.** What is deceptive is that this 1890s church only seems plain on the outside. Meanwhile, the recently restored interior is mesmerizing with decorative mosaics, polished marble, and murals painted from the floor to the top of its dome—200 feet off the floor. Self-guided tours of the church are allowed at any time except when mass is taking place.

Farther south—and probably not quite in the Dupont Circle neighborhood anymore—is the **National Geographic Museum** at 1145 17th

Street Northwest. Sitting right on the corner of 17th Street and M Street, this museum features many frequently changing exhibits that are interactive and feature the photographic work of *National Geographic*. The displays are usually in-depth looks at specific places (such as Jerusalem 3D, running through March 31, 2016) or nature exhibits (Pristine Seas runs through March 27, 2016). The cost is $15 for adults, and the museum is open from 10 a.m. to 6 p.m. daily. If you are visiting, the Farragut North Metro station (Red line) is much closer than Dupont Circle.

The Phillips Collection ★★★★

URL phillipscollection.org. Address 1600 21st St., Washington, D.C. 20009. **Phone** ☎ 202-387-2151. **What it is** Private art collection turned museum of Impressionist and modern masters. **Scope and scale** Major attraction. **When to go** Anytime. **Hours** Sunday, 12–7 p.m.; Tuesday, Wednesday, Friday, and Saturday, 10 a.m.–5 p.m.; Thursday, 10 a.m.–8:30 p.m. **Closest Metro** Dupont Circle (Red; for Blue, Orange, Silver, transfer at Metro Center; for Green, Yellow, transfer at Gallery Place). **Admission** Collection is by donation only Tuesday through Friday. Saturday and Sunday, adults $10, students and seniors $8, under 18 free. **Not to Be Missed** Works described below.

DESCRIPTION AND COMMENTS Duncan Phillips began displaying his collected art in his family's Dupont Circle home in 1921, even while the family still resided there. The original 1897 Georgian Revival house still makes up the part of the museum on the corner of 21st and Q Streets, although the Phillips family moved out in 1930 to accommodate the ever-growing gallery. In 1960 Duncan Phillips added what is now known as the Goh Annex—named after a Japanese businessman who funded its renovation—directly adjacent to the house. The third and final building that makes up the Phillips Collection is a former apartment building, the Sant Building, which was added in 2006 as part of a major expansion that also added 30,000 subterranean feet.

Housed within the collection are works by such modern masters as Cézanne, Degas, O'Keefe, Renoir, Rothko, and van Gogh. The museum continues to add contemporary artists. Special exhibits are also frequent, although there is a $2 increase on the weekend admission while exhibits are running. That same $12 adult fee is charged to view any visiting exhibit on weekdays as well, although seeing only the permanent collection still remains an option for non-weekend visitors.

If you find yourself overwhelmed by the size and scope of the major museums, the Phillips Collection might be perfect for you. Likewise, if you are a lover of Impressionist and modern art, the Phillips Collection might be perfect for you too.

Here's what we consider not to be missed:

● **Paul Cézanne,** *Mont Sainte-Victoire* Cézanne painted the landscape featured in this piece more than 30 times. This version is one of his earlier works, which still features curving lines and a sense of realism. In his later years, Cézanne began to depict everything—including Mont Sainte-Victoire and the surrounding French countryside—in terms of their base geometric shape, bridging the gap between Impressionism and Cubism. Some of what was to come from Cézanne can be seen in this painting, specifically in the farmland and its blocky buildings.

- **Wolfgang Laib—The Laib Wax Room** On the second floor of the Phillips House is where you will find one of the most strangely pleasant art installations in the Phillips Collection. The room is as it sounds: lined with beeswax. The small 6-x-7-foot room contains about 440 pounds of wax molded by the German artist and lit by a single bare light bulb. The experience is meant to be meditative, but we are boorish and find it a bit comical. As we stood in the Laib Wax Room contemplating life, we also began contemplating whether beeswax tasted like anything. We can neither confirm nor deny that it does or does not.

- **Georgia O'Keeffe,** *My Shanty, Lake George* Georgia O'Keeffe is one of America's most important artists—credited with helping popularize modern art in this country. She is best known for her magnified paintings of small objects, and The Phillips Collection features some of those (*Pattern of Leaves* is particularly excellent). *My Shanty, Lake George* showcases another wonderful aspect of O'Keeffe's painting, however—her ability to use her precision painting to great effect in a landscape. The hard, straight edges of the shanty are perfectly contrasted by the hazy flowers, wispy trees, and curving mountains, giving the painting a sharp focus despite its dreamlike surrounding.

- **Pierre-Auguste Renoir,** *Luncheon of the Boating Party* The most well-known and popular piece in The Phillips Collection, *Luncheon of the Boating Party* is a work that encapsulates everything that is loved about Renoir. He painted happy things—beautiful women, flowers, pets, party scenes—and this painting contains all of those things. Renoir was a true Impressionist, painting without outlines and clipping the edges of the scene, conveying motion and implying that the party continued off canvas. He also refused to use black in his painting—he said it is not a color—instead using dark blue for shadows.

Despite the casual, energetic look of his style, Renoir spent many hours perfecting each of his paintings, including this one. That does not show, however, because the life and liveliness of the scene jumps off the canvas. Much like a real party, you can even tell which people are flirting and which have had a little too much wine. This is a masterpiece by a master; expect to spend a little extra time looking it over.

The Repentant St. Peter—**versions by El Greco and Francisco Goya** The Phillips Collection boasts not one, but two paintings titled *The Repentant St. Peter,* both done by master painters. The far older version is by Domenikos Theotocopoulos—simply known as El Greco for obvious reasons—painted in the early 17th century. El Greco was a Renaissance artist known for elongated figures and harsh light, and his portrait of St. Peter is no different. The thin apostle looks pleadingly skyward toward a bright light, while seemingly on the verge of tears. Like most of El Greco's works, *The Repentant St. Peter* is full of emotion, yet distant due to the strong use of color and Byzantine style.

Contrasting the El Greco with the Francisco Goya version is striking. Goya is an artist without a category, known mostly for painting rebellious, unforgiving images depicting the corrupt side of humanity. He painted this rare religious subject sometime around 1824, and his St. Peter is portly and strikingly solitary. Unlike El Greco's, this St. Peter is bathed in soft light, and while he still pleads with the heavens, there is depth in his face—a face that is rugged and worn—suggesting complex emotions.

- **Mark Rothko—The Rothko Room** On the second floor of the Sant Building sits the Rothko Room, space dedicated solely to Mark Rothko and his large color-field paintings. Rothko used hidden paint strokes to make blocks of color—the edges blurred into their background—to evoke emotion. The paintings allow the viewer to attach their own feelings to the art—joy, anger, fear, sadness, disgust, or maybe a feeling of confusion over why color blocks are considered art (not our feeling, but a common one nonetheless). Sadly, Rothko's color palette often reflected his own mood, and it became blacks and browns shortly before he took his own life in 1970.

- **Vincent van Gogh,** *Entrance to the Public Gardens in Arles* Painted in 1888, the thick, haphazard brush strokes seen so often in van Gogh's works are evident here, especially in the sky. While no doubt a tranquil scene, the dynamic style of the surrounded walkway and shadowy visitors hint at the feelings within van Gogh's troubled mind. This is not one of van Gogh's best works, but the mastery of place, emotion, and dynamism shows just how talented the Dutchman was.

FOGGY BOTTOM

ALTHOUGH THE NAME FOGGY BOTTOM sounds a tad risqué, the popular neighborhood is logically named. The topography of the area was perfectly shaped to hold the fog that used to roll in from the Potomac. This and the preponderance of smoke-spewing factories in this blue-collar neighborhood are thought to have led to the colorful name.

Foggy Bottom is tucked just west of the White House (pages 207–210) and just north of the National Mall; it is bordered to the north by Pennsylvania Avenue and to the west by the Potomac River. The Foggy Bottom Metro station (Orange, Blue, Silver) is the easiest entry point into the neighborhood, so start your tour of the area at its northern border one block north of the station—the lovely **Washington Circle.**

Walking along K Street and left onto 25th Street takes you right into the center of the working-class past of Foggy Bottom. Halfway down 25th Street you will see alleys on either side: Snows Court to the east and Queen Anne's Lane leading to the delightfully named **Hughes Mews** to the west. In Pierre L'Enfant's original city plan, each block of housing contained open space in its center. The industries of the area—the gas works and brewery, in particular—drew many immigrants looking for work. The flood of Irish and German workers, later expanded by freed slaves, meant that Foggy Bottom needed more houses. Alleyways such as these became strings of simple, inexpensive row houses, many of which still exist in one form or another. Our recommendation is to take a stroll into Hughes Mews, where the row houses still look simple but are definitely no longer inexpensive.

Continuing down 25th Street and curving toward Virginia Avenue brings you face to face with one of the most infamous names in Washington: Watergate. Specifically, the **Watergate Complex** is the name of a group of five buildings containing apartments, offices, and a hotel. The curvilinear design of the buildings is refreshing, yet a bit shocking after seeing so many square, stone structures. The building you will likely be most interested in is the office building at 2600 Virginia Avenue. This office is where, in 1972, the Democratic National Committee headquarters was broken into. The ensuing investigation pointed to members of President Richard Nixon's own administration, which ultimately led to the president's resignation in 1974. The name "Watergate" has been synonymous with scandal ever since.

While we're still talking history, now is a good time to mosey onto the campus of George Washington University. The university itself has been in this location since 1912, but we're looking for something a little older and more obscure. On the southeast corner of H Street and 24th Street Northwest lies the **American Meridian.** A strip of gray stone in the sidewalk shows the line where the United States marked the convergence of the eastern and western hemisphere from 1848 to 1884 (before the Prime Meridian in Greenwich, England was accepted worldwide). This line also was used to calculate the straight borders of several western states, as a nearby plaque spells out.

Also found on the George Washington University campus—at 701 21st Street, at the intersection of G Street—is the **George Washington University Museum and the Textile Museum.** The bulky name is a result of the 2011 combination of multiple museums under one roof. The University Museum displays items related not just to the history of George Washington University, but also to the history of Washington itself. Its Washingtonia collection contains rare maps, books, and other documents concerning the city's history. The joint museum is open Monday and Wednesday through Friday from 11:30 a.m. to 6 p.m., Saturday from 10 a.m. to 5 p.m., and Sunday from 1 to 5 p.m.; an $8 donation is suggested.

A few blocks due south down 21st Street, you can't miss the massive **U.S. Department of State** building, which takes up all the area between 21st and 23rd Streets and C and D Streets. The Harry S. Truman building is the central hub for all American foreign relations and diplomatic missions. Contained inside are the luxurious **Diplomatic Reception Rooms**—rooms where dignitaries meet, converse, and occasionally sign treaties. Tours are available of the Reception Rooms, but they must be made in advance (up to 90 days) at **diplomaticrooms .state.gov.** Tours are available Monday through Friday at 9:30 a.m., 10:30 a.m., and 2:45 p.m.

Moving farther east on C Street (you'll have to make a quick right, then left on Virginia Avenue to stay on C Street), you'll find yet another massive government building, the **U.S. Department of the Interior.** C and E Streets border the huge structure to the north and south, and 18th and 19th Streets border it to the east and west, respectively.

Directly across 18th Street, between C and D Streets, is the **Daughters of the American Revolution** complex, consisting of Constitution Hall and Memorial Continental Hall, which contains a museum and a library. Daughters of the American Revolution (DAR) is a women's organization dedicated to promoting patriotism through non-political volunteerism. All members must prove lineal descent from a Revolutionary patriot.

Constitution Hall is the most well known of the DAR structure's sections. Washington, D.C.'s largest concert hall, it opened in 1929 as the DAR convention site, and every US President since Calvin Coolidge has attended an event here. Constitution Hall is still the go-to for large events in the city.

To the south of Constitution Hall, across C Street, is the small **Art Museum of the Americas** (201 18th Street, near Virginia Avenue), with the related **Organization of American States** behind it (200 17th Street). The Organization of American States is committed to regional solidarity and cooperation among the 35 independent states of the Americas. Tours of the impressive marble building are technically available but are apparently discouraged, because the price is, frankly, outrageous at $100 for a half hour. By comparison, the one-and-a-half-hour group tour for $200 (up to 20 people) is a bargain. The Art Museum of the Americas specializes in Latin American and Caribbean art and is showcased in a beautiful 1912 Spanish Colonial building. The Art Museum of the Americas is open from 10 a.m. to 5 p.m. every day except Monday, with free tours.

Walking up 17th Street, you are on the eastern border of Foggy Bottom with the Ellipse—and soon the White House—on your right. After you cross D Street, you may want to stop to admire the headquarters of the **American National Red Cross** at 430 17th Street. The building was constructed between 1915 and 1917, and not only does it mimic the neoclassic style of the White House, it also houses art and artifacts that have been collected by the Red Cross since its inception in 1881. Free guided tours are offered that include their central exhibit—three stained-glass Tiffany windows. Tours are Wednesday and Friday at 10 a.m. and 2 p.m.; for reservations, e-mail tours@red cross.org or call ☎ 202-303-4233.

Another small yet intriguing museum—**the Octagon Museum**—is found at the intersection of 18th Street and New York Avenue Northwest. Open for relatively short amounts of time (Thursday through Saturday from 1 to 4 p.m.), the free museum examines design and architecture. The building is part of the display, as is its long history. Built in 1801, the residence known as the Octagon (although it's really more of a hexagon, but who's counting?) was the home of a wealthy Virginia family. It was such a magnificent house that President Madison lived in it for six months after the British burned the White House in 1814.

As you make your way toward the White House by going east on New York Avenue, you will be facing one of the most staggering buildings in what is a city of staggering buildings. The **Eisenhower Executive Office Building** is officially at 1650 Pennsylvania Avenue Northwest, but in reality it's where New York Avenue and 17th Street meet. This colossus was built between 1871 and 1888 to house the Departments of State, War, and the Navy, and is one of the finest examples of French Second Empire architecture (mostly baroque, but with mansard roofs). The building is now the location of most of the White House staff, including a secondary office for the vice president.

We will end our tour of Foggy Bottom by leaving it ever so slightly. Just north of the White House on Pennsylvania Avenue between 15th and 17th Streets sits Lafayette Square, a charming park dotted by inspiring statues. It was originally planned as part of the White House complex until, in 1804, President Jefferson separated it from the White House grounds by allowing Pennsylvania Avenue to continue through it. In 1824 the name was changed from "President's Park" to honor General Lafayette, the French officer who fought for the United States in the American Revolutionary War.

John F. Kennedy Center for the Performing Arts ★★★

URL **kennedy-center.org**. **Address** 2700 F St. NW, Washington, D.C. 20566. **What it is** Highbrow performing-arts center with free public shows daily. **Scope and scale** Diversion. **When to go** Anytime. **Hours** Showtimes vary; free daily shows at 6 p.m. **Closest Metro** Foggy Bottom (Orange, Blue, Silver); Red can transfer at Metro Center; Yellow and Green can transfer to Red at Gallery Place/Chinatown, then to Orange, Blue, Silver at Metro Center. **Admission** Free to walk around; tickets for events are additional. **Authors' comments** The modern buildings form a de facto public plaza perfect for lunch, an after-dinner walk, or people watching.

DESCRIPTION AND COMMENTS The Kennedy Center is the home for the National Symphony Orchestra, the Suzanne Farrell Ballet, and the Washington National Opera. It's also the place to find local and traveling theater presentations, and jazz, classical, and chamber music.

The Kennedy Center's **Millennium Stage** offers free performances daily, usually at 6 p.m. Most of these are musicians, ranging from Washington National Opera preview performances to ska.

Free, **guided tours** of the Kennedy Center are available daily, from 10 a.m. to 5 p.m. weekdays and 10 a.m. to 1 p.m. weekends. These 40-minute walks cover the three big performance halls, five theaters, and the Hall of States and Hall of Nations, holding gifts given to the Kennedy Center by various countries and territories around the world. Each tour ends with a trip to the rooftop terrace, which affords some of the best views of D.C. While you probably can get a same-day tour without a reservation, you can reserve a tour spot for free on the center's website if you know you'll be there on a specific day.

If you're looking for a bite to eat, the **KC Café,** inside the center, serves sandwiches, salads, and other light fare from 11:30 a.m. to 8 p.m. daily. A pricier option for dinner is the **Roof Terrace Restaurant,** open from 5 to 8 p.m. daily (plus a Sunday brunch from 11 a.m. to 2 p.m.).

TOURING TIPS A free round-trip shuttle is offered between the Kennedy Center and Foggy Bottom Metro; look for signs on the left as you exit the Metro escalator. The shuttle runs every 15 minutes, 9:45 a.m.–midnight Monday–Friday, 10 a.m.–midnight Saturday, noon–midnight Sunday, and 4 p.m.–midnight on federal holidays.

The Kennedy Center parking garage is open daily from 6 a.m. to midnight. Parking for events is $23. There's a vehicle height limit of 6 feet for most cars, with a limited number of spaces for trucks and SUVs up to 7 feet.

GEORGETOWN

GEORGETOWN PREDATES THE CREATION of the District of Columbia. It was officially authorized as a town in the colony of Maryland in 1751, and it was named George Town, after King George II. With its location on the Potomac River, Georgetown was originally settled as a port that specialized in shipping tobacco to Europe and the West Indies. Congress officially incorporated Georgetown into Washington City in 1871; unlike most Washington neighborhoods, Georgetown has well-defined borders. It stretches from the Potomac River in the south up to Dumbarton Oaks Park, and from Foundry Branch Valley Park in the east to Rock Creek and Potomac Parkway in the west.

There are many historical locations to go along with the trendy shopping on M Street and Wisconsin Avenue, and the sky-high housing prices of this chic neighborhood. Past residents of Georgetown include Alexander Graham Bell, Thomas Jefferson, John F. Kennedy, and Elizabeth Taylor. If you want to visit Georgetown, however, you'll have to do it without the Metro because there are no stations in the neighborhood. The closest Metro stations are Foggy Bottom (Orange, Blue, Silver) and Dupont Circle (Red), but they are each 0.5 mile from Georgetown's eastern edge and almost 2 miles from Georgetown University on its west side.

Speaking of **Georgetown University,** it is an institution of higher learning that is synonymous with the neighborhood it is named after. With its campus sitting on a rise in western Georgetown overlooking downtown D.C. and the Potomac River, The Hilltop—as early students referred to it—can be seen from many surrounding areas.

If you would like to take a full tour of Georgetown University, the school supplies an eight-page pdf file on their website, although it is a little difficult to find. Go to **uadmissions.georgetown.edu/visiting** and scroll to "More Information" at the bottom where there is a link to "Self-Guided Tour."

On the eastern end of **Georgetown Waterfront Park** is the **Washington Harbour,** a retail and dining space housed in a postmodern complex built on the edge of the Potomac.

One block north of the Washington Harbour, on Thomas Jefferson Street, you will cross a small canal. This simple waterway holds a great deal of history for Georgetown. The **Chesapeake and Ohio (C&O) Canal** was begun in Little Falls, Maryland on July 4, 1828, and upon its completion in 1850 ran 184.5 miles along the Potomac River. Today, the C&O Canal is almost completely intact for its entire length and remains an impressive engineering feat.

As you emerge onto 31st Street, glance at the large, brick **Canal Square building** at 1054. This simple building holds some of the history of our nation's computing power. Developed to more quickly process census data, a punch-card tabulating machine that used electric current to sense holes in punched cards and keep a running total was created by Herman Hollerith. Hollerith built that technology into the Tabulating Machine Company in 1896 and organized it at this Canal Square building. The Tabulating Machine Company, through several mergers and buyouts, eventually became a building block in the company we came to know as IBM.

Turning right onto M Street, past stores like Brooks Brothers and Barneys New York, you will come upon a seemingly out-of-place simple stone house at 3051 M Street—this is the **Old Stone House.** While the name may not be original, the Old Stone House is; it is the oldest structure in Washington, D.C., still on its original foundation. Dating from 1765, the house is a wonderful example of Revolutionary War–era construction, and its attached garden is a lovely English-style space. The house and park are open daily from 11 a.m. to 6 p.m.

Heading back to 31st Street and turning right, you will see the dignified Georgetown Post Office and former customhouse at 1215 31st Street. This building, completed in 1858, was constructed when Georgetown was utilized as a port of entry to the country. It was established with the custom house on its second floor and a post office on its first. The post office remains in operation today.

Continuing about 0.5 mile north on 31st Street brings you to the grand **Tudor Place** at 1644 31st Street. The large house was built in 1816 and remains today as it was when it was lived in, and the 5.5-acre garden still contains many trees and shrubs cultivated by the original owners. While it is still unknown why the owners referred to their neoclassical mansion as "Tudor Place," the name stuck. Tudor Place is open from February through December, Tuesday through Saturday from 10 a.m. to 4 p.m. and Sunday from noon to 4 p.m. A guided tour is available and is $10 for adults, although a self-guided, garden-only tour is available (with map) for $3. Admission is half price in February.

Farther north, across R Street at 1703 32nd Street sits the **Dumbarton Oaks museum and gardens.** The house was built in 1801, but after being purchased by Mildred and Robert Woods Bliss in 1920, it was expanded to house their art collection. The attached gardens contain a beautiful swimming pool (no swimming), a strictly manicured pebble garden, a rose garden, and the ellipse, a peaceful oval surrounded by boxwoods, with a fountain at its center. The museum is free of charge and open Tuesday through Sunday from 11:30 a.m. to 5:30 p.m. The gardens cost $10 for adults and are open Tuesday through Sunday from 2 to 6 p.m., mid-March through October, closing at 5 p.m. the remainder of the year.

Returning to R Street and heading east to the intersection of 30th Street will find you standing in front of the impressive brick gatehouse of Oak Hill Cemetery, the historic 22-acre resting place of many Civil War–era government officials.

From the gatehouse of the cemetery continue down 30th Street, taking a left on Q Street toward Dumbarton House at 2715 Q Street. These few blocks are wonderful examples of Georgetown's elegant, historic, and pricey townhouses and tree-lined streets. Arriving at the walled-in Dumbarton House, you are greeted by an exceptional example of Federal period architecture. Completed somewhere around the year 1800, Dumbarton house has been restored, along with its impressive period furniture and decorative arts collections. The house is open Tuesday through Sunday from 11 a.m. to 3 p.m., with the last entry at 2:45 p.m. Guided tours are available if scheduled in advance—call ☎ 202-337-2288 to schedule. Admission is $5 for adults.

NORTHWEST WASHINGTON, D.C.

NORTHWEST IS THE LARGEST OF WASHINGTON, D.C.'S quadrants and likewise contains the most tourist sights, such as the National Zoo (page 239) and the National Cathedral (page 238). Northwest is also the location of most of the neighborhoods covered in this guide, from Judiciary Square to Georgetown to Dupont Circle.

Despite being the largest sector, Northwest is only lightly covered by the Metro system. The Blue, Orange, and Silver lines run through the southern area near the National Mall, while the Yellow and Green lines brush along the eastern edge, through the Logan Circle and U Street neighborhoods. Much of the heavy Metro lifting in Northwest, however, is done by the Red line, which angles through the middle of the area. What that means is that large swaths of Northwest are not easily accessed by the Metro, so having a car will help greatly when visiting the following sights.

At 2401 Foxhall Road Northwest is the beautiful **Kreeger Museum,** a former private home that sits on 5 acres of gardens punctuated by sculptures and surrounded by woods. The Kreeger museum focuses on 19th- and 20th-century art, with works by Monet, Picasso, and Renoir. The museum is open Friday and Saturday from 10 a.m. to 4 p.m. and Tuesday through Thursday for tours only at 10:30 a.m. and 1:30 pm. Reservations are required for the Tuesday through Thursday tours and can be made at **kreegermuseum.org.** The Sculpture Garden is open Tuesday through Saturday from 10 a.m. to 4 p.m. Museum admission is $10 for adults, but the Sculpture Garden is free of charge.

Northwest on Massachusetts Avenue from the Dupont Circle and Kalorama neighborhoods are two interesting stops: the **Kahlil Gibron Memorial**—at 3100 Massachusetts Avenue—and the **United States Naval Observatory** at 3450. The Kahlil Gibron Memorial and surrounding garden are dedicated to the Lebanese-American poet. The bench and part likeness, part abstract sculpture are surrounded by flowers and a peaceful fountain. The U.S. Naval Observatory is on a large, circular complex and provides astronomical data and conducts research for both the US government and the general public.

The home of the Vice President of the United States is also on the Naval Observatory grounds, at Number One Observatory Circle. The house was built for the superintendent of the observatory, but it was so nice that it was commandeered by the chief of naval operations, and then the vice president. Tours are available of the Observatory grounds, but they are very limited—offered only on selected Monday evenings. Tours must be scheduled in advance and can be made around 90 days prior to your visit via **www.usno.navy.mil/usno.**

Farther north, **Hillwood Estate, Museum, and Gardens** is located at 4155 Linnean Avenue Northwest. The former home of Marjorie Merriweather Post, a businesswoman, diplomat, and art collector, the house contains a museum displaying thousands of objects collected by Ms. Post and is surrounded by a manicured formal garden. Self-guided tours are available Tuesday through Sunday from 10 a.m. to 5 p.m., as are docent-led tours that begin at 11:30 a.m. and 1:30 p.m. A donation of $18 for adults is suggested and, although it is not necessary, tickets can be purchased online at **hillwoodmuseum.org.**

Finally, we come to one of the best parks in Washington: **Rock Creek Park.** A massive park stretching across a large section of Northwest D.C., Rock Creek Park contains a nature center, planetarium, and miles and miles of beautiful trails. The nature center is open from 9 a.m. to 5 p.m. Wednesday through Sunday. The planetarium features ranger-led programs on Wednesday at 4 p.m. (Young Planetarium), and Saturday and Sunday at 1 p.m. (Seasonal Night Sky) and 4 p.m. (Exploring the Universe). Both buildings are located at 5200 Glover Road Northwest, although the park itself spans several miles.

National Cathedral ★★★★

URL cathedral.org. Address 3101 Wisconsin Ave. NW, Washington, D.C. 20016.
What it is Neo-Gothic church with impressive stained glass and gargoyle carvings.
Scope and scale Minor attraction. **When to go** Anytime. **Hours** Monday–Friday, 10
a.m.–5:30 p.m.; Saturday, 10 a.m.–4:30 p.m.; Sunday, 1–4 p.m. Summer hours until
8:30 p.m. Tuesday and Thursday, mid-June to late August. **Closest Metro** Tenley-
town/American University (Red). **Admission** Free for worship, prayer, and spiritual
visits. Secular tours and visits are $11 for adults, $7 for children ages 5–17, free for
children 4 and under. $6 admission for seniors, students, active military, and veter-
ans. **Authors' comments** One of America's great examples of church architecture.
Not to Be Missed Stained-glass windows; gargoyles and other carvings.

DESCRIPTION AND COMMENTS The National Cathedral is the seat of the diocese
of the Episcopal Church in Washington, D.C. More than that, though, it's one
of the prettiest churches in the United States, and one of the country's largest. Its collection of stained-glass windows and gargoyle carvings (including
one of Darth Vader) and its church organ draw an estimated 400,000 visitors per year.

The inside of the cathedral is formed by long halls of tall, vaulted, Gothic
arches, similar to those of Notre Dame de Paris or Chartres. The National Cathedral, though, is several hundred years younger than those: Construction
started in 1907 and ended in 1990, although carving, detail, and restoration
work continue today.

One of the cathedral's most famous features is its set of **231 stained-glass
windows,** in styles ranging from Gothic to modern. Most of the windows represent religious themes, people, and events, but there are dozens dedicated to
significant people and events in American history, from explorers Lewis and
Clark to industrialist Andrew Carnegie to the Battle of Iwo Jima to the first men
on the moon. That window, officially named the "Sci-
entists and Technicians" window, contains an actual
piece of moon rock and is informally known as "The
Space Window."

Besides the stained glass, the cathedral is also
known for its **gargoyles.** More than 20 of these exist
around the outside of the church, and they're actually
part of the roof's drainage system. Each gargoyle is unique, and many of them
have contemporary themes. The one of Darth Vader, on the Northwest Tower,
is the most famous, but others include "Crooked Politician" (also the Northwest
Tower), "Horse Skeleton" (Southwest Tower), "Artist" (Southwest Tower), "Alli-
gator" (South Nave), and "Bearded Bulldog" (South Transept, East Side). Check
gargoyles.cathedral.org/gargoyle/indexA.php for a complete list and locations before your visit. Because they're up high, it helps to bring a set of binoc-
ulars to spot these carvings.

The cathedral boasts several towers open to small public groups. The **Classic Tower Climb** is a six-story, 333-step climb that takes around 90 minutes. It
takes place in the central tower, which holds the church's bells, and affords
some of the best views of Washington, D.C., plus visits to the stained-glass windows. The **Gargoyle Tower Climb** takes place in and around the cathedral's
two western towers, including a walk outside on the open-air walkway between

unofficial **TIP**
Among those buried at the
National Cathedral are
Helen Keller and President
Woodrow Wilson.

the towers, for better viewing of the gargoyles. The tours have a 48-inch height and five-person minimum requirement, and they are strenuous climbs. Check the cathedral's website for details and reservations.

TOURING TIPS It's a 1.5-mile walk from the Tenleytown Metro stop to the cathedral, mostly downhill (and uphill on the way back). An alternative to walking is to take any 30-series bus (31, 32, 36, or 37) from the west side of Wisconsin Avenue, going south. Get off at Woodley Road (again, about 1.5 miles), and the cathedral will be on your left.

If you're driving, the cathedral has an underground parking garage—look for the signs as you approach. Cost is roughly $6–$7 per hour weekdays ($22 maximum), $7–$10 flat rate on weekends. See the website for specifics.

Guided tours are available 10–11:15 a.m. and 1–3:30 p.m. Monday–Friday; 10–11:15 a.m. and 1–3 p.m. Saturday; and 1–2:30 p.m. Sunday. Tours last 30 minutes, do not require advance reservations, and are included in the admission price.

Smithsonian National Zoological Park   ★★★½

URL nationalzoo.si.edu. Address 3001 Connecticut Ave. NW, Washington, D.C. 20008. **Phone ☎** 202-426-6841 (National Mall & Memorial Parks). **What it is** A large zoo and one of the only places to see pandas in the United States. **Scope and scale** Minor attraction. **When to go** Morning or evening to avoid the heat; anytime during the off season. Pandas are best viewed between 8 a.m. and 2 p.m. **Hours** Grounds: Daily, 6 a.m.–8 p.m. (6 p.m. in winter—generally November through March); exhibit buildings: Daily, 10 a.m.–6 p.m. (4:30 p.m. in winter); shops and concessions: 9 a.m.–5 p.m. (4:30 p.m. in winter). Closed December 25 and shortened hours for special events such as Halloween parties. **Closest Metro** Woodley Park-Zoo or Cleveland Park (Red; for Blue, Orange, Silver, transfer at Metro Center; for Yellow, Green, transfer at Gallery Place/Chinatown). **Admission** Free; parking $22.

DESCRIPTION AND COMMENTS There are many wonderful things about the Smithsonian National Zoological Park—commonly referred to as the National Zoo—but undoubtedly the two best are the price and the pandas. Let's begin with the price, which is zero dollars. That's because the zoo is under the larger Smithsonian umbrella, so there is no admission fee.

Be forewarned that the National Zoo is built entirely on a hill. The basic layout is simple: A main path—the 0.8-mile Olmsted Walk—meanders the length of the zoo, with various exhibits and trails leading off of it. The design is such that you will rarely be far away from Olmsted Walk, but you should continuously check the park's signs to make sure you haven't missed anything. When you get to the bottom of the hill, you turn around and go right back up. With the exception of a side trail that starts at the Kids Farm at the very bottom and winds through the Amazonia exhibit, most of what you pass on the way up is the same as on the way down.

So what will you actually see at the National Zoo? In short: quite a bit. There are about 1,800 animals from 300 different species including apes, elephants, big cats, orangutans, bears, and bison (added in 2014). What really draws the crowds, though, are the pandas. After the famous couple Hsing Hsing and Ling Ling lived at the National

unofficial **TIP**
If you decide to drive, park in Lot D near Kids Farm. You'll go uphill first, leaving the downhill for the second, more tired, half of the tour.

National Zoological Park

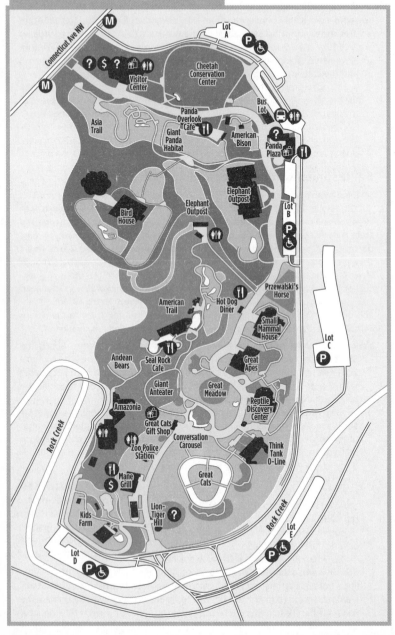

Zoo for 28 years, Washington, D.C., welcomed Mei Xiang and Tian Tian in 2000. Their rental agreement with the Chinese government expires in 2015, but it is assumed that it will be extended. After all, they have had cubs together: Tai Shan in 2005 (who now lives in China) and Bao Bao in 2013, who will remain at the zoo until she turns 4. Most recently, a panda cub named Bei Bei was born on August 22, 2015, and he will make his public debut on January 16, 2016. Only three other American zoos—Atlanta, Memphis, and San Diego—boast resident pandas.

The National Zoo can require a lot of walking, but it allows the opportunity to see many animals that you're not likely to see at other zoos. Receiving their funding entirely through the Smithsonian Institute not only means that admission is free, but also that all additional money spent at the zoo goes directly toward education outreach, research, and conservation efforts.

TOURING TIPS Admission is free, but you'll pay for just about everything else. Even a park map will set you back a few dollars, if you need one—the zoo is well signed and there are frequent in-park maps. An alternative is their mobile app, although that is $1.99, and we've found it sluggish and, unfortunately, not very useful.

Parking is currently $22 and can be reserved in advance via **parkingpanda .com,** something useful since parking fills quickly. The good news is that the zoo is right between two Metro stops, Woodley Park–Zoo and Cleveland Park. The walk is about 0.5 mile from either, although the slope of Connecticut Avenue means that you'll be walking slightly uphill from the Woodley Park station to the zoo but slightly downhill from Cleveland Park. There are also several restaurants near each station, good for a meal before or after the zoo, or to pick up food for an in-zoo picnic, which is allowed (no alcohol).

▌ NORTHEAST WASHINGTON, D.C.

NORTHEAST D.C. ENCOMPASSES THE AREA north of East Capitol Street and east of North Capitol Street. It is made up of many different, smaller neighborhoods as well as a few impressive sights. The Metro snakes throughout Northeast along the Orange, Green, Yellow, and Red lines, but the stops are spread out and not always near where you're trying to go. Luckily the extra space of the less dense Northeast means that parking is usually easier.

At the far north—and technically slightly into Northwest at 140 Rock Creek Church Road Northwest—is the small, charming, and historical **President Lincoln's Cottage.** President Lincoln lived in the house for a little more than a year during the Civil War and visited often to escape the bustle of the White House. Tours of the cottage, including several of Lincoln's possessions, require tickets, and purchasing in advance is advised. Tickets are $15 for adults and can be reserved at **lincolncottage.org** for times between 10 a.m. and 3 p.m. Monday through Saturday and 11 a.m. and 3 p.m. Sunday. The Georgia Avenue Petworth Metro station (Green, Yellow) is the closest to the cottage but is still almost 1 mile away.

Near the easternmost point of Washington, D.C., where the Anacostia River flows into Maryland, parklands surround the river. On the western bank of the river is the **United States National Arboretum,** a 446-acre collection of trees, plants, and flowers being cultivated for scientific and educational purposes (see below).

On the western bank of the Anacostia are the **Kenilworth Aquatic Gardens** at 1550 Anacostia Avenue NE. In 1880 Walter Shaw bought a parcel of land that contained a pond and some wetlands thought to be worthless. He turned them into small but impressive water gardens that, following his death, were saved by Shaw's daughter Helen, who successfully lobbied for the federal government to purchase them. The natural, bird-friendly wetlands and lily-covered ponds are open 8 a.m.–4 p.m. November through March and 9 a.m.–5 p.m. April through October. There is no admission fee. The Aquatic Gardens are part of the larger Kenilworth and Anacostia Parks, a riverside area containing miles of pathways and athletic fields. The Aquatic Gardens are about a half-mile walk from the Deanwood Metro station (Orange).

U.S. National Arboretum ★★★

URL usna.usda.gov. Address 3501 New York Ave. NE, Washington, D.C. 20002-1958. **Phone** ☎ 202-245-2726. **Scope and scale** Diversion. **When to go** Anytime. **Hours** Arboretum: 8 a.m.–5 p.m. daily; closed December 25. National Bonsai Museum: 10 a.m. to 4 p.m. November through February; closed on Federal holidays. **Closest Metro** Take the Blue/Orange line to Stadium Armory station, and then catch the B2 bus at the corner of East Capitol St. and SE 19th St., going toward Mt. Rainier. Get off 14 stops later at the corner of NE Bladensburg Rd. and NE Rand Place, and it's a two-block walk from there. Allow an hour each way. **Admission** Free. **Authors' comments** Surprisingly rich and detailed gardens; very friendly staff. **Not to Be Missed** National Herb Garden and Friendship Garden.

DESCRIPTION AND COMMENTS The 446-acre National Arboretum campus is run by the US Department of Agriculture, about 6 miles northeast of the National Mall. The Arboretum's size and gardens make it one of D.C.'s hidden gems. The USDA staff is exceptionally helpful and able to get answers to gardening questions for every gardening zone in the United States.

Our favorite exhibit here is the **National Herb Garden,** with more than 800 varieties of herbs from around the world, spread over 2 acres of land. It's colorful, aromatic, beautifully landscaped, and organized well. The Herb Garden is organized into 10 dedicated areas, each covering a specific use of herbs in daily life, such as fragrances, dyes, medicines, and beverages. You're invited to touch and smell the herbs during your walk too. The Herb Garden also includes an impressive collection of **roses** in more than 100 varieties.

Also at the Arboretum is **Friendship Garden,** demonstrating how to landscape with decorative perennials, from day lilies to ornamental grasses. A separate area nearby holds the Arboretum's **Perennial Gardens,** showcasing peonies, daffodils, and more when they're in bloom (February through July). If you're visiting in April or May, also catch the azaleas in bloom at the **Azaleas Collection,** covering a set of trail with rolling hills in the southwest side of the properties.

TOURING TIPS Spring (especially April and May) and fall are the best times to visit for moderate temperatures. The plants are most active (and in bloom) from April through October. If you're traveling during summer, get there at 8 a.m. before the heat takes over. Free on-site parking is available.

ARLINGTON, VIRGINIA

ARLINGTON IS THE NORTHERN VIRGINIA COUNTY that was once donated to the United States government in order to form the District of Columbia. Look at a map of the border of Washington, D.C., and it makes more sense: Arlington is the chunk across the Potomac River that keeps America's capital from being a perfect square. Today, Arlington is a bustling suburb of the District with wonderful views across the river and easy access into Washington via Metro—and to everywhere else via **Ronald Reagan International Airport.** It makes a good base of operations for visiting Washington.

There are a few notable sights located within Arlington itself, namely Arlington National Cemetery and the Pentagon (whose address is Washington, D.C., although it is decisively in Arlington). Also found very close to the Pentagon is the **United States Air Force Memorial,** punctuated by its three shiny, metallic, curved spires. The three variant spires, ranging from 201 to 270 feet tall, represent three jets soaring skyward. Rounding out the lovely memorial are four bronze statues making up the Honor Guard, a glass etching of F-16 aircraft, and a wall displaying the names of the Air Force's Medal of Honor recipients.

Also accessible from Arlington—although technically in Washington, D.C.—is **Theodore Roosevelt Island.** This 88.5-acre island sits in the middle of the Potomac River and can be accessed via car from the northbound lanes of the George Washington Memorial Parkway or via footbridge from near the Key Bridge in Arlington. There are numerous pathways throughout the forested island, as well as a memorial to President Theodore Roosevelt that includes a 19-foot-tall likeness. The island is open from 6 a.m. to 10 p.m. every day and is only a 10- to 15-minute walk from the Rosslyn Metro station. There are only about 90 parking spots on the island, so arriving early is recommended if you are not walking.

Arlington National Cemetery   ★★★★

URL **arlingtoncemetery.mil**. **Address** Arlington National Cemetery, Arlington, VA 22211. **What it is** National cemetery and memorials for US military personnel and those who died in service to the country. **Scope and scale** Major attraction. **When to go** Early morning during summer, afternoon during winter. **Hours** October 1–March 31, daily, 8 a.m.–5 p.m.; April 1–September 30, 8 a.m.–7 p.m. **Closest Metro** Arlington Cemetery (Blue). **Admission** Free to walk; guided bus tour is $12 for adults, $9 for seniors, $6 for children ages 4–12 (free for children under 4). Many military discounts are available. **Authors' comments** No food or drink is permitted inside the cemetery. **Not to Be Missed** Tomb of the Unknowns, Iwo Jima Memorial, and John F. Kennedy grave.

DESCRIPTION AND COMMENTS Arlington National Cemetery is the final resting place for more than 400,000 Americans, the vast majority from the country's military branches. In addition, it is home to memorials to civilians whose actions or sacrifice also bring honor to the United States in combat or other service. Its 624 acres of gravestones, tombs, mausoleums, and monuments are a visual reminder of the human cost of America's place in the world.

Arlington Cemetery was created in 1864 by the American government during the US Civil War. By that time, the conflict had produced enough dead to fill the two other nearby cemeteries used for military burials, and the United States was looking for more land. That came in the property belonging to former US General Robert E. Lee, who had betrayed the United States by siding with the Confederate States in the war. The US military seized the Lee family's land and began burials within a few weeks. Lee's family was eventually restored ownership in 1882, and they sold the land back to the government in 1883. Lee's home—**Arlington House**—still stands inside the cemetery and is open for tours.

Arlington Cemetery receives more than 4 million visitors per year. Its most popular monuments, described below, are the graves of the Kennedy family, the Tomb of the Unknowns, and the Iwo Jima Memorial. In addition to these, Arlington's residents include hundreds of well-known figures, from baseball's supposed inventor (and Civil War general) **Abner Doubleday,** to boxer (and U.S. Army sergeant) **Joe Louis.** Stop by the Welcome Center for help in locating a particular gravesite.

The tombs of **President John F. Kennedy,** wife Jacqueline Kennedy Onassis, two of their children, and the president's brothers Robert and Edward, are buried in section 45. Although all US Presidents are eligible for burial at Arlington because of their status as commander-in-chief of the armed forces, Kennedy is one of only two to be located here. The other is **William Howard Taft,** who, after his term as president, went on to become the chief justice of the Supreme Court.

The **Tomb of the Unknowns** is in section 35 in the southern part of the cemetery. It contains the remains of one unidentified US military service member from each of three wars: World Wars I and II, and the Korean War. It had previously also held remains from an unidentified Vietnam casualty who was later identified through DNA testing and reinterred near his family's home. Because of the possibility of DNA testing, no remains of any Vietnam veteran are yet interred in the tomb.

Soldiers from the U.S. Army guard the Tomb of the Unknowns around the clock. Changing of the guard happens every 30 minutes while the park is open in the summer, every hour while open in winter, and every two hours after park closing.

The **U.S. Marine Corps War Memorial,** better known as the **Iwo Jima Memorial,** sits just outside the north end of the cemetery, past section 27 and across Marshall Drive. Its design is based on the famous photograph taken by reporter Joe Rosenthal on February 23, 1945, showing six American men raising the US flag on Mount Suribachi during the Battle of Iwo Jima in World War II. The memorial was opened in 1954 and is dedicated to all US Marines who have died in service.

Arlington National Cemetery

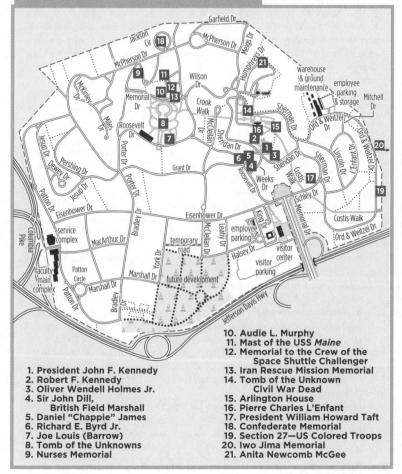

1. President John F. Kennedy
2. Robert F. Kennedy
3. Oliver Wendell Holmes Jr.
4. Sir John Dill,
   British Field Marshall
5. Daniel "Chappie" James
6. Richard E. Byrd Jr.
7. Joe Louis (Barrow)
8. Tomb of the Unknowns
9. Nurses Memorial
10. Audie L. Murphy
11. Mast of the USS *Maine*
12. Memorial to the Crew of the
    Space Shuttle Challenger
13. Iran Rescue Mission Memorial
14. Tomb of the Unknown
    Civil War Dead
15. Arlington House
16. Pierre Charles L'Enfant
17. President William Howard Taft
18. Confederate Memorial
19. Section 27—US Colored Troops
20. Iwo Jima Memorial
21. Anita Newcomb McGee

TOURING TIPS The easiest way to see Arlington's highlights is by taking one of the guided bus tours from the Welcome Center. Tours cost $12 for adults, $9 for seniors, and $6 for children ages 4–12, and are free for children under age 4. Discounts are available for active and retired military personnel and their guests—check the website for details. Buses depart about every 20 minutes starting at 8:30 a.m. The last bus leaves one hour before closing.

The Pentagon ★★½

URL pentagontours.osd.mil. **Address** 1400 Defense Pentagon, Washington, D.C. 20301. **Phone** ☎ 703-697-1776 **What it is** America's largest government office building and headquarters of the Department of Defense. **Scope and scale** Diversion. **When to go** Anytime. **Hours** Entry is available on weekdays from 9 a.m. to 3 p.m.; closed on all federal holidays. **Closest Metro** Pentagon (Blue, Yellow; for Orange, Silver, Green, transfer at L'Enfant Plaza; for Red, transfer at Gallery Place). **Admission** Free, although a timed-access ticket is required.

DESCRIPTION AND COMMENTS Built during the initial rush of World War II, the Pentagon is the headquarters of the United States Department of Defense. As you might assume from the name, the Pentagon is a gigantic, 29-acre, five-sided building. The entire structure was built in just 16 months by a crew of 4,000 working around the clock, with everything completed on January 15, 1943. The finished building contains five concentric rings of five floors (plus two belowground), and there is a 5-acre courtyard at its center. At its maximum, the Pentagon held almost 33,000 workers.

If you are interested in seeing the interior of the Pentagon, one of the world's largest office buildings, tours are available for free, although tickets are required. The tickets can be requested on the Pentagon's website anywhere from 14 to 90 days before your visit. Tickets will not be issued if your visit is less than 14 days from the time of your request. The tour involves facts and history on the four branches of the military, a look at the indoor September 11th memorial, an opportunity to examine a Medal of Honor, as well as other exhibits related to the building and the United States Military.

● **Pentagon Memorial** The Pentagon was struck by American Airlines flight 77 during the attacks of September 11, 2001, exactly 60 years to the day that construction on the building began. The plane penetrated three of the five rings on the building's west side, killing 184 people on the airplane and in the Pentagon. A memorial to those 184 victims is found on the west side of the Pentagon, with elegant benches dedicated to each one. It is an open and serene yet solemn space.

TOURING TIPS For those taking a tour, be aware that there is no parking at the Pentagon. Parking is available at the Pentagon City Mall, a short walk away, but taking the Metro is your best bet. You also are advised to check in for your tour one hour prior to its start for security screening purposes. It probably won't take the full hour, but the security process is very strict and will not be rushed.

SUBURBAN VIRGINIA

Smithsonian Air and Space Museum Udvar-Hazy Center ★★★★

URL airandspace.si.edu/visit/udvar-hazy-center. **Address** 14390 Air and Space Museum Parkway, Chantilly, Virginia 20151. **What it is** Collection of historic airplanes, spacecraft, and memorabilia. **Scope and scale** Major attraction. **When to go**

Anytime. **Hours** Usually daily, 10 a.m. to 5:30 p.m. Summer hours may run until 7:30 p.m. **Closest Metro** None, but public transportation is an option (see Touring Tips). **Admission** Free for the museum, around $15 per car for parking. **Authors' comments** Excellent collection of WWII and modern military aircraft; famous commercial and general aviation planes; Gemini, Mercury, and Apollo spacecraft. **Not to be Missed** Lockheed SR-71 Blackbird; Air France Concorde; B-29 *Enola Gay;* Space Shuttle *Discovery;* and Observation Tower Tour.

DESCRIPTION AND COMMENTS The Udvar-Hazy Center is the second half of the Smithsonian's Air and Space collection. Located next to Dulles International Airport in Chantilly, Virginia, Udvar-Hazy has enough space to hold the planes and spacecraft that don't fit in the downtown museum.

Pick up a museum map as you enter the facility. The **Boeing Aviation Hangar,** straight back from the entrance, holds about two-thirds of the center's exhibits, and all of the aircraft and memorabilia. Most of the Boeing hangar is dedicated to military aircraft, with a particular focus on examples from World War II. The rest holds commercial and general aviation aircraft, including ultralights and helicopters. The **James S. McDonnell Space Hangar,** accessible at the center-back of the Boeing Hangar, is dedicated to space flight, with missiles, spacecraft, and satellites.

The first airplane you'll see in the center is Betty Skelton's **Pitts Special S-1C** *Little Stinker* aerobatic biplane, painted in dramatic red and white, and parked on the entrance walkway to the Boeing Aviation Hangar.

unofficial **TIP**
See the Udvar-Hazy Center's IMAX movie schedule and book tickets online at **tinyurl.com/Udvar-IMAX.**

Beyond the Pitts are two World War II–era fighters marking the entrance ramp and stairs to the hangar's main floor: the **Curtiss P-40E Kittyhawk** and the **Vought F4U-1D Corsair.** The P-40E Kittyhawk was one of the few modern fighter designs available to the Allies at the start of World War II. The F4U-1D Corsair was designed in 1938 as a carrier-based fighter, built around what was the largest engine and propeller ever used on a fighter aircraft. In fact, the prop was so big that the Corsair's wings had to be bent into a gull shape for ground clearance.

Head down the ramp to your right and start a counterclockwise tour of the Boeing Aviation Hangar with Modern Military Aviation. There are more than 100 aircraft on display throughout the floor, and we'll guide you through the highlights of the collection.

At the end of the ramp, turn left and start a counterclockwise tour of the floor with the **Modern Military Aviation** section first. The first plane on display is the prototype of the **Lockheed Martin X-35B Joint Strike Fighter,** the latest and most expensive fighter in the U.S. Air Force inventory. The prototype on display here served as the technology platform, demonstrating the feasibility of (among other things) short takeoffs and vertical landings.

Bear to the left of the X-35B and walk a short way to the display of **Cold War Aviation** airplanes. The museum has done a nice job here of putting the US planes of each era next to their Soviet counterparts. On your right are the two planes that fought for air superiority over Korea: The **North American F-86 Sabre** and the **Mikoyan-Gurevich MiG-15.**

Udvar-Hazy Center Boeing Hangar

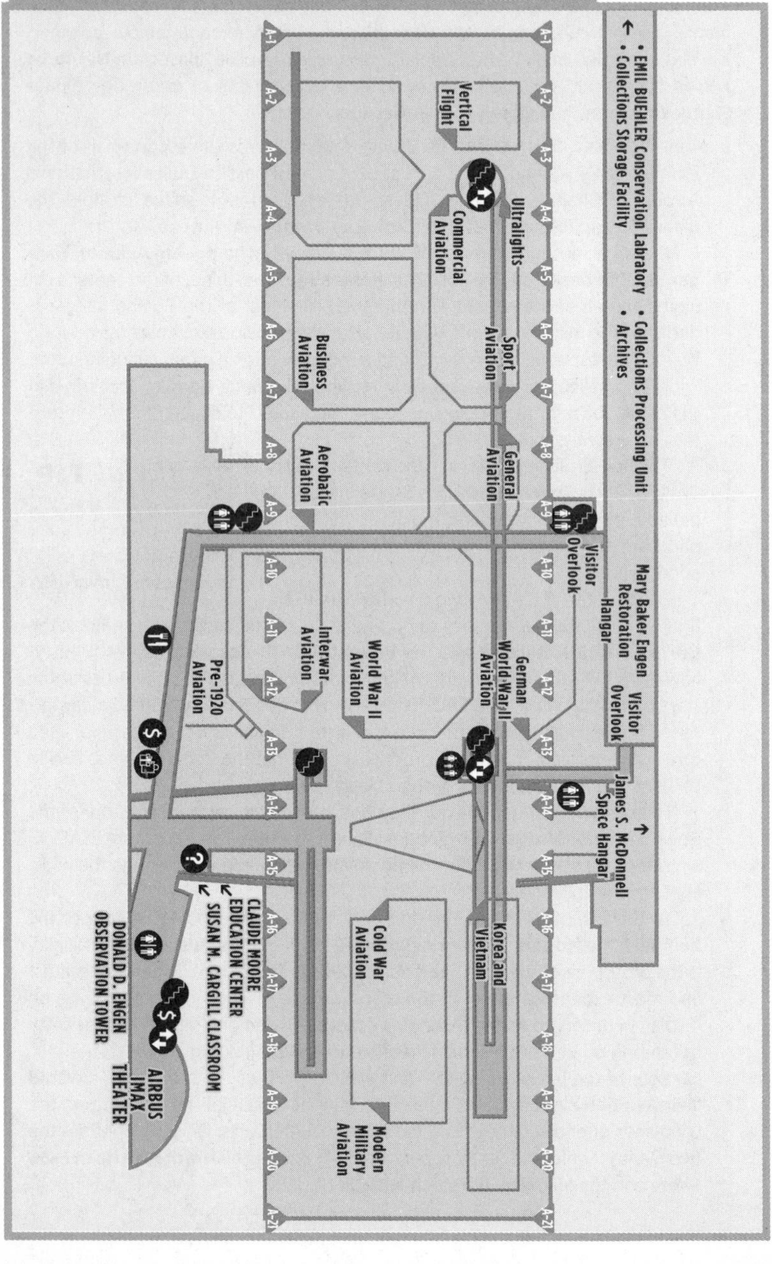

The Soviet Union introduced the MiG-15 into combat over Korea in November of 1950, and it quickly dominated the skies. In fact, the United States stopped flying piston-engine aircraft over Korea because of the MiG-15 and fast-tracked the release of the F-86 Sabre as a result.

The F-86 was one of the first fighters the United States developed as World War II came to an end. Its swept wings are the result of aerodynamic data obtained from German scientists during the war, showing that swept wings handled better than straight wings at speeds greater than 600 miles per hour.

Besides swept wings, the Sabre had six .50-caliber machine guns attached to radar-assisted gun sights. With these gun sights, the F-86 could shoot down an enemy aircraft at distances farther than 1 mile away. As a result, the F-86 had a 10:1 kill ratio versus the MiG-15 in combat.

Across the walkway from these Korean War fighters are their counterparts from the Vietnam War: the Russian **Mikoyan-Gurevich MiG-21** and American **McDonnell F-4 Phantom.**

The F-4 Phantom entered service in the US Navy in 1959, and it was the Navy's first fighter jet able to fly at twice the speed of sound. It was used primarily to defend the Navy's carriers, but it was also a solid attack plane. It could be fitted with a variety of air-to-air and air-to-ground missiles, depending on the need. The plane on display here flew combat missions over Vietnam from 1972–1973; its one confirmed victory came against a MiG-21.

The **Lockheed SR-71 Blackbird** reconnaissance aircraft is the centerpiece of the Cold War Aviation gallery. The Blackbird is the world's fastest jet-engine aircraft. How fast? The Air Force won't say, but various sources list its top speed at around 2,200 miles per hour. That number is, in the words of Tony Scalia, pure applesauce—the plane on display here averaged 2,124 miles per hour *on its flight to the museum* (setting the current transcontinental speed record of 64 minutes), and there are credible claims from SR-71 pilots saying they hit 2,500 miles per hour when evading enemy missiles.

unofficial **TIP**
During its record-breaking flight to the museum, this SR-71 flew from St. Louis to Cincinnati in 8.5 minutes.

Beyond the Cold War Aviation gallery is an area dedicated to World War II aviation. A subsection here includes German aviation, with a **Focke-Wulf Fw 190,** one of Germany's fighter mainstays, and a **Messerschmitt Me 163 Komet,** a rocket-powered fighter prototype that actually included a pilot. It was able to fly at more than 600 miles per hour, far faster than Allied aircraft. Unfortunately, the plane could only store enough fuel for eight or nine minutes of flight, after which it landed unpowered and unable to evade American fighters. That made it impractical as a mass-produced attack aircraft, but it's still an interesting design.

The **Boeing B-29 Superfortress** *Enola Gay* displayed here deserves special mention, as it dropped the world's second atomic bomb, on Hiroshima, Japan, on August 6, 1945. It also flew on the atomic bombing of Nagasaki three days later, performing weather reconnaissance before the bombing.

The left side of the Boeing Aviation Hangar is dedicated to general and commercial aviation. If you're near the *Enola Gay,* turn so that you're facing the Space Hangar, and then turn left at the main walkway near the Junkers Ju 52.

The **Junkers Ju 52** was a 17-passenger commercial plane that debuted in 1932. It was to German aviation what the Ford Tri-Motor or Douglas DC-3 (see page 152) was to American aviation. The Ju 52 could fly from small, primitive fields, making it a favorite of countries around the world trying to build up their air transportation networks cheaply. More than 4,800 Ju 52s were built, and they continued to fly commercially well into the 1960s. A handful of them still fly today.

The **Boeing 367-80 "Dash 80"** shown here is the original prototype for what would be known as the Boeing 707, one of the most successful aircraft designs in history. More than 850 707s were built, in dozens of variations. Millions of Americans got their first jet ride in a Boeing 707.

The prototype on display is notable not only because it's the first 707—it also performed one of the most famous aerobatic maneuvers in the history of flight. Test pilot Tex Johnston barrel-rolled the Dash 80 over Lake Washington during a boat race on August 7, 1955. No one had ever seen a plane this large do a roll, and, for decades after, the feat was considered an urban legend. Home-movie footage surfaced a few years ago, however, taken by a spectator at Lake Washington, confirming the Dash 80's feat. You can see the video here: **youtube.com/watch?v=3IV9PZW1N9U.**

The star of the commercial aviation section is the **Air France Concorde** in the middle of the floor. The Concorde was the world's first commercial, supersonic plane, able to fly from London to New York in less than four hours, at more than twice the speed of sound.

The Concorde on display here was the first delivered to Air France in 1976. It flew almost 18,000 hours before being retired in 2003. It was given to the people of the United States by Air France to commemorate the 200th anniversary of the French Revolution and ratification of the U.S. Constitution.

Next, make your way to the back of the Boeing Hangar and in to the **James S. McDonnell Space Hangar.** The highlight in this area is the Space Shuttle Discovery, the oldest surviving shuttle in the US fleet. It flew 39 missions and spent a year in orbit around the Earth. Among its flights, it carried the Hubble Space Telescope and 77-year-old John Glenn, the oldest person to ever fly in space. Discovery was retired in 2011.

Finally, the center is adjacent to Washington Dulles International Airport, and you can take an elevator ride up to the center's **Observation Tower** for a 360-degree view of Dulles's runways, plus aircraft on approach and at takeoff. Besides the view, the tower holds an exhibit on how the US air-traffic control system works.

TOURING TIPS The Udvar-Hazy Center is larger and less crowded than the main Air and Space Museum downtown. Still, it can take up to 20 minutes to get in during holidays and for special exhibits. Your best bet is to arrive at opening or after 3 p.m.

Capacity for the **Observation Tower Tour** is limited, and tours end at 4:30 p.m. No reservations are available, so try to get in line first thing in the morning or around 12:30 p.m., when other visitors may be taking a lunch break.

It's possible to reach the Udvar-Hazy Center from the main Air and Space Museum downtown using Metro and buses, though the trip takes 90 minutes one way versus 60 minutes by car. To get there, take the Silver line to Wiehle-Reston

East, then take Fairfax Connector Bus 983 to the Center. You'll need $1.75 exact fare per person or a SmarTrip card because drivers don't carry change.

The center's on-site food court is a McDonald's.

SOUTHWEST *and* SOUTHEAST WASHINGTON, D.C.

THE SOUTHERN SECTORS OF WASHINGTON, D.C., do not have as many tourist attractions as the rest of the city but still offer reasons to visit. The dividing line between the north and south areas of the District is East Capitol Street, and the west and east areas are separated by South Capitol Street. While the Southwest and Southeast are serviced by the Green, Blue, Orange, and Silver Metro lines, some of the locations listed below are not within easy walking distance of stations. The good news is that their remoteness means parking is often available for self-drivers.

East Potomac Park is the peninsula that separates the Potomac River from the Washington Channel, and its point—called **Hains Point**—marks the end of the Anacostia River as it flows into the Potomac. This 1.5-mile-long sliver of land is home to the East Potomac Golf Course, a miniature golf course, and a long, cherry tree–lined path with river views. The park is pleasantly quiet and connects via trail to the Tidal Basin, but it is sadly in an underwhelming state with bald spots in the grass and holes in the pathways.

South of the marina—at the intersection of P Street Southwest and the Washington Channel—is the surprising **Women's Titanic Memorial.** We call it surprising for two reasons: For one, most wouldn't expect to find a memorial to the ill-fated ocean liner in Washington, D.C. It is dedicated to the men who died so that women and children could have their spots on the lifeboats and was commissioned by the "Women of America." The second surprising thing? The statue depicts a woman in a pose shockingly similar to that struck at the bow of the ship in the famous 1997 *Titanic* film, despite the statue being erected in 1931.

Moving over to Southeast D.C., 1500 S Capitol Street SE is where you will find **Nationals Park,** the home of Major League Baseball's Washington Nationals. Opened in 2008, the park was built specifically for the Nationals. The Washington Monument and U.S. Capitol dome can be seen from the upper decks on the first-base side. For tickets to a baseball game, check their website at **washington.nationals.mlb.com**— the season traditionally runs from April into October, with the playoffs following that. Start making plans now to attend the 2018 MLB All-Star Game, which has been awarded to Nationals Park.

A few minutes of walking east along a boardwalk on the Anacostia River brings you to the **Navy Yard,** which was established in 1799. A former shipyard and ordinance-manufacturing facility, it is now home to the Chief of Naval Operations, Naval Sea Systems Command, and many other integral Navy functions. Several naval advances, including pre–Civil War nautical cannons and shipboard airplane catapults, were designed and tested here. The **National Museum of the US Navy**—located in a former Naval gun factory—contains displays on the history and important events of the Navy and is open daily from 9 a.m. to 5 p.m.

Farther up the Anacostia River is the large and lesser-known **Congressional Cemetery.** The gatehouse is at 1801 E Street Southeast and is only about three blocks from the Stadium-Armory Metro station (Blue, Orange, Silver). Congressional Cemetery was begun in 1807 and is lined with beautiful brick pathways and 67,000 humble grave markers. Open from dawn to dusk, the 35-acre cemetery is so named because Congress bought several hundred sites in 1830 and built monuments to those who died in office. According to the cemetery's website, one does not have to be a member of Congress to be buried there, but you do have to be dead.

A few blocks northeast of the Stadium-Armory Metro station is **Robert F. Kennedy Memorial Stadium,** commonly called RFK. RFK is the home of Major League Soccer's DC United, although a soccer-specific stadium is being planned near Nationals Park. The American soccer season runs from March through October. For tickets, visit **dcunited.com.**

Across the Anacostia River at 1411 W Street Southeast sits the **Frederick Douglass National Historic Site.** Douglass was an escaped slave who became an impressive speaker against slavery, even inspiring Lincoln to use the Civil War as a chance to improve the country. The hill that the house sits on supplies sweeping views, including the Washington Monument and the Capitol dome in the distance. All tours of the Frederick Douglass house are guided, with a maximum of 10 people; therefore, reservations are encouraged. They can be made at **recreation.gov** or ☎ 877-444-6777 for a $1.50 fee. Tours are at 9 a.m., 12:15 p.m., 1:15 p.m., 3 p.m., 3:30 p.m. (cannot reserve, walk-in only), and 4 p.m. (April through October only). While the Frederick Douglass house is within walking distance of the Anacostia Metro station (Green), the surrounding neighborhood is not one of Washington, D.C.'s best. There is a parking lot available for those driving.

PART FIVE

DINING

The **WASHINGTON CUISINE SCENE**

IN THE LAST 15 YEARS, and even more rapidly over the past 8–10 years, Washington has evolved from an extremely predictable restaurant town, in which dining out was more a matter of convenience or expense account entertaining than pleasure, to one of the top-10 culinary centers in the country—and, like Las Vegas or Los Angeles, it's one of the places the biggest-name chefs want to plant a culinary flag.

The traditional French and Italian (or steak and seafood) restaurants that were the norm in Washington have been replaced by market-fresh, innovative, healthful, and sustainable cooking—as well as, paradoxically, by a raft of throwback American burger bars and blue plate diners. (The **Riggsby** in Dupont Circle even makes sly reference to "old" Washington by describing its menu as "American with a flash of 'Old School Continental.'") Several kitchens, most notably **Minibar** and **Rogue 24,** highlight the imaginative and technically demanding style loosely referred to as molecular gastronomy.

Even more exciting are the number of chefs who are turning back the clock to the true roots of ethnic cuisines, whether the chefs are native to the region or simply admirers. Scores of good restaurants in the Washington area are turning out Afghan, Algerian, Argentine, Balkan, Belgian, Burmese, Ethiopian, Filipino, Honduran, Korean, Laotian, Mediterranean, Northern Thai, Peruvian, Sri Lankan, Turkish, Uzbek, and Yemeni, as well as the more familiar Chinese, French, Indian, Italian, and so on.

And in a surprising but admirable twist, José Andrés, a star of both Spanish and American television and who astonished Washington diners when he created Minibar, has even launched a campaign to educate Americans about their own culinary heritage. In the not-quite-20 years since he moved here, Andrés has introduced a generation (and a half) to Spanish tapas at **Jaleo,** Greek-Turkish meze at **Zaytinya,** authentic Mexican at **Oyamel,** a little-known Peruvian-Chinese ethnic tradition at **China Chilcano,** and the pleasures of veggie-centric dining at **Beefsteak** (named for the tomato, not the steer). His **America Eats Tavern** in The Ritz-Carlton, Tysons Corner grew out of a year-long collaboration with the National Archives inspired by historic cookbooks and menus, such as the "vermicelli 'mac' 'n' cheese prepared like pudding" from a recipe given out in 1802 by pasta-maker Lewis Fresnaye, a refugee from the French Revolution. At brunch, you can have the authentic Hangtown fry—the oyster-bacon-eggs dish prized by lucky gold seekers in 1849. All the food is sourced from American artisans, including the suckling pig jambalaya. Andrés even owns a Spanish food truck called **Pepe**—the traditional diminutive of José.

 AS IS OBVIOUS FROM THE EXPLOSION of what might be called food truck/survivor reality competitions, food trucks of all ethnicities, originality, and pop-up parking are not just a trend—they're a lifestyle, especially at lunch. There are at least three sites claiming to monitor all mobile meal activity around town: **foodtruckfiesta.com** and its various mobile apps, **foodtrucksdc.com,** and **roaminghunger.com/dc,** or check *Washingtonian* magazine's daily blog update at **washingtonian .com/blogs/bestbites/food-trucks/dc-food-truck-locations.**

FIXED PRICE MENUS

A WORD OF WARNING TO VISITORS watching their budgets as well as foodie blogs: A growing number of restaurants now offer *only* prix fixe or tasting menus, an almost imperial edict previously limited to the most famous of culinary figures such as Patrick O'Connell, Eric Ziebold, or José Andrés. Also keep in mind that these fixed prices do not include wine pairings, tax, or tips, and likely require reservations well in advance.

Johnny Monis of the extraordinary haute-Greek **Komi** offers only one fixed price meal starting at $135; his tiny Thai restaurant next door, **Little Serow,** has a single $45 offering. Popular chef R. J. Cooper's **Rogue 24** restaurant near Mount Vernon Square at least offers a choice of tasting menus, priced from $45 for three courses to $125 for the 24-course "journey." The nearby **Seasonal Pantry** is really a sort of supper club, with a table for 12 and a menu of whatever the chef feels like cooking, or charging, which is usually about $150. **G by Mike Isabella** is a sandwich shop by day but a four-course dinner ($40) by night. At **Minibar,** Andrés's team offers only a $250 menu, but three levels of wine pairings. These days, the menu at the **Inn at Little Washington** ranges from $178 to $208, depending not on the number of courses but on the day of the week. And Nobu Yamazaki, owner-chef of **Sushi Taro,** has revamped that long-respected but predictable restaurant into a cutting-edge vision of Japanese classics (if that's not a contradiction), with fresh fish flown in daily from Tokyo's Tsukiji market and four *kaiseki*-style menus, ranging from $80 to $180 before pairings and a few extra options. (Unlike the others, Sushi Taro does an à la carte lunch.) It makes one almost nostalgic for **Obelisk** chef Peter Pastan, who has stuck to his five-course fixed price menu for nearly 30 years and still holds at $75 (though up to $85 on weekends).

BE SURE TO DOUBLE-CHECK a restaurant's reservations policy: Many are stringent—**Seasonal Pantry** allows for no more than 6 of its 12 seats to a single party—or nonexistent, as at **Little Serow, Compass Rose, Rose's Luxury,** and the small but trendy **Etto** pizzeria. **Pearl Dive, Estadio,** and **Toki Underground** offer only very few reservations, and generally before dinner rush (the "senior special" for hipsters).

PRIME DINING NEIGHBORHOODS

ALONG WITH THE AWAKENING of the Washington palate has come a rearrangement of the dining map. While Georgetown remains a busy shopping and nightlife area, it is no longer a dominant restaurant strip (with a few notable exceptions), and the ethnically mixed Adams Morgan neighborhood, though still intriguing, is gentrifying and graying slightly. Upscale redevelopment created around various suburban Metro stations—most notably **Ballston** and **Clarendon** in Virginia, and **Bethesda** and **Rockville** in Maryland—have lured both established and first-time restaurateurs to those mini-cities. Just as an example, the restaurants in and around what has been branded Rockville Town Center offer Indian-French fusion, Japanese, Korean fusion, Lebanese, Peruvian, Russian–Tajik, Southeast Asian fusion, Szechuan, Taiwanese, tapas, and Thai, and there's a classic but pleasingly moderate French bistro, two brewpubs, an Irish pub, a global-fare martini bar, as well as buffalo wings, burgers, frozen yogurt, ice cream, Korean chicken, tortillas . . . well, you get the idea.

While we have included some less-convenient standouts in the restaurant profiles following, for the most part we have stuck to areas that are easily accessible to visitors, especially via public transportation, and preferably around popular attractions where hunger may strike. Our profiles are organized by neighborhood, but if you would like to see a listing of restaurants by cuisine, check out the table on pages 307–308.

Continued on page 259

Washington, D.C., Dining

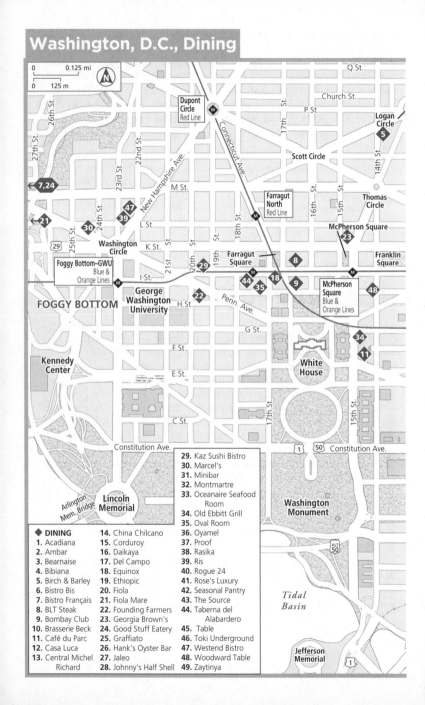

Dupont
Circle
Red Line

Q St.

Church St.

Logan
Circle
5

Scott Circle

Farragut
North
Red Line

Thomas
Circle

McPherson Square
23

7,24

47
39

21

30

Washington
Circle

Franklin
Square

Farragut
Square

8

Foggy Bottom–GWU
Blue &
Orange Lines

George
Washington
University

44
35   18

9

48

McPherson
Square
Blue &
Orange Lines

FOGGY BOTTOM

22

Penn. Ave.

G St.

34

11

Kennedy
Center

F St.

White
House

E St.

C St.

Constitution Ave.

Constitution Ave.

Arlington
Mem. Bridge

Lincoln
Memorial

Washington
Monument

Tidal
Basin

Jefferson
Memorial

29. Kaz Sushi Bistro
30. Marcel's
31. Minibar
32. Montmartre
33. Oceanaire Seafood
    Room
34. Old Ebbitt Grill
35. Oval Room
36. Oyamel
37. Proof
38. Rasika
39. Ris
40. Rogue 24
41. Rose's Luxury
42. Seasonal Pantry
43. The Source
44. Taberna del
    Alabardero
45. Table
46. Toki Underground
47. Westend Bistro
48. Woodward Table
49. Zaytinya

◆ DINING
1. Acadiana
2. Ambar
3. Bearnaise
4. Bibiana
5. Birch & Barley
6. Bistro Bis
7. Bistro Français
8. BLT Steak
9. Bombay Club
10. Brasserie Beck
11. Café du Parc
12. Casa Luca
13. Central Michel
    Richard
14. China Chilcano
15. Corduroy
16. Daikaya
17. Del Campo
18. Equinox
19. Ethiopic
20. Fiola
21. Fiola Mare
22. Founding Farmers
23. Georgia Brown's
24. Good Stuff Eatery
25. Graffiato
26. Hank's Oyster Bar
27. Jaleo
28. Johnny's Half Shell

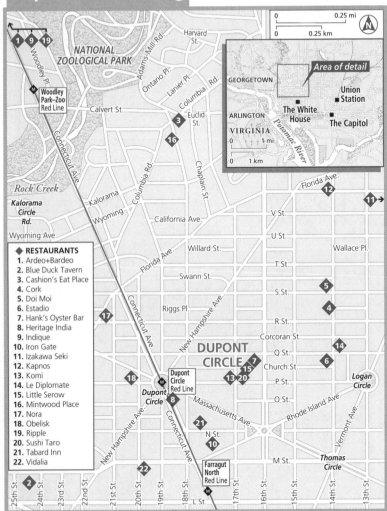

Dupont Circle Dining

0   0.25 mi
0   0.25 km

NATIONAL
ZOOLOGICAL PARK

Harvard St.

Woodley Park–Zoo
Red Line

Adams-Mill Rd.

Ontario Pl.

Lanier Pl.

Columbia Rd.

Calvert St.

Euclid St.

Area of detail

GEORGETOWN

Union Station

ARLINGTON

The White House

The Capitol

VIRGINIA

Potomac River

0   1 mi
0   1 km

Rock Creek

Kalorama Circle Rd.

Kalorama

Wyoming

Columbia Rd.

Chaplain St.

California Ave.

Florida Ave.

V St.

U St.

Wallace Pl.

Wyoming Ave.

Willard St.

T St.

◆ **RESTAURANTS**
1. Ardeo+Bardeo
2. Blue Duck Tavern
3. Cashion's Eat Place
4. Cork
5. Doi Moi
6. Estadio
7. Hank's Oyster Bar
8. Heritage India
9. Indique
10. Iron Gate
11. Izakawa Seki
12. Kapnos
13. Komi
14. Le Diplomate
15. Little Serow
16. Mintwood Place
17. Nora
18. Obelisk
19. Ripple
20. Sushi Taro
21. Tabard Inn
22. Vidalia

Florida Ave.

Swann St.

Riggs Pl.

New Hampshire Ave.

S St.

R St.

Corcoran St.

Q St.

Church St.

P St.

O St.

DUPONT CIRCLE

Dupont Circle Red Line

Dupont Circle

Massachusetts Ave.

Rhode Island Ave.

Logan Circle

Vermont Ave.

N St.

M St.

Thomas Circle

Farragut North Red Line

L St.

Connecticut Ave.

Woodley Pl.

Woodley Pl.

New Hampshire Ave.

25th St.
24th St.
23rd St.
22nd St.
21st St.
20th St.
19th St.
18th St.
17th St.
16th St.
15th St.
14th St.
13th St.

Continued from page 255

Each restaurant profile features a quick heading that allows you to check out the restaurant's star rating, cuisine, and cost.

STAR RATING encompasses the entire dining experience, not only the flavor and quality of the food but also presentation, service, and ambience. It also takes into account the value for the expense—too little for what you paid, or a bargain for the money. Five stars is the highest rating possible and connotes the best of everything. Four-star restaurants are exceptional, and three-star restaurants are well above average. Two-star restaurants are good. One star is used to indicate an average restaurant that demonstrates an unusual capability in some area of specialization—for example, an otherwise unmemorable place that has great barbecued chicken.

COST generally includes an appetizer (or dessert) and entrée with side dish; drinks and tip are excluded. But it is not a hard-and-fast rule because some restaurants serve only a fixed-cost meal.

INEXPENSIVE	$25 or less per person
MODERATE	$26–$40 per person
EXPENSIVE	$41–$60 per person
VERY EXPENSIVE	More than $60 per person

DISABLED ACCESS In the key information, this category will tell you if a restaurant is wheelchair accessible—this means front door, dining room, and restroom access; but be sure to call and double-check before you go, as restaurants remodel or upgrade all the time. If you can manage a few steps or use an unmodified bathroom, it might be worth calling the restaurant for more information about the facilities.

IF YOU LIKE THIS At the end of the profile, we may offer alternative suggestions—restaurants featuring similar fare nearby in case the one profiled is already full, restaurants in another part of town from the same chef or company, and more.

PENN QUARTER AND DOWNTOWN

PENN QUARTER REFERS TO AN AREA from around the Verizon Center from roughly Seventh and G Streets Northwest to about Tenth Street Northwest and south to Pennsylvania Avenue, but its influence is gradually spreading into the old law-and-lobby offices downtown toward K Street Northwest. It surrounds most of the downtown theater venues, so it's usually filled with a mix of new-downtown condo dwellers, tourists, business types, pretheater diners, and post-sports/concert drinkers. It is also just a few blocks south of Mount Vernon Square, making it convenient not only to the majority of museums and tourist attractions but also to the convention center.

*un*official **TIP**
The most reenergized areas in the city for dining, loosely defined, are **Penn Quarter,** the **Mid City/Logan Circle** area, the **Atlas District,** and **Capitol Hill.** But, of course, downtown is still expense account territory.

unofficial TIP

The huge new City Centre has brought in New York stars Daniel Bouloud (DBGB) and David Chang (Momofuku Milk Bar); a (franchise) version of Miami Joe's Stone Crabs; the Bangkok-based Mango Tree; and, to uphold local pride, an Italian market/café from Roberto Donna protégé Amy Brandwein (Centrolina).

Among the best restaurants in Penn Quarter are **China Chilcano, Jaleo** (page 266), **Oyamel** (page 269), **Zaytinya** (page 270), and the *laboratorio* of deconstruction **Minibar** (page 267)—all under the watchful eye of Catalonian superchef José Andrés. And all except Minibar are family-friendly, especially during the day. **The Partisan** is the sandwich/charcuterie/café adjunct to Red Apron butchery, and for those who know offal, it's a must-stop. (And yes, they make burgers.) Other highly regarded options include **701, Acadiana** (page 261), **Bibiana, Bistro d'Oc** (a surprisingly affordable café across from Ford's Theatre), **Central Michel Richard** (page 262), **Corduroy** (page 262), **Cuba Libre, Daikaya Ramen and Izakawa** (page 263) (cheap and quick ramen downstairs, more elaborate upstairs), **Del Campo, Fiola** (page 264), **Graffiato** (page 265), **Oceanaire** (the steak house for seafood lovers), **Poste, Rasika** (page 270), **Rogue 24, Sei** (nightclub-cool sushi), the **Source** at the Newseum, **Seasonal Pantry, Table,** and **Tosca**.

Among the more affordable, family-friendly, and something-for-everyone eateries are the large **Clyde's Gallery Place** (part of a dependable local chain) and its even larger sibling **The Hamilton,** which almost has a different menu for every room; the Tex-Mex **Austin Grill** is also a good local bet and inexpensive. In addition to its Texas-style (via New York) fare, **Hill Country Barbecue** offers a live band to back "rock and twang" karaoke on Wednesdays. Also from New York comes **Carmine's** Italian behemoth: When they say family-style, they mean it, so your hotel room better have a refrigerator.

Teaism, an inexpensive, mostly fusion-flavored café—and also local—is one of the few places in the neighborhood, other than coffeehouses and carryouts, that is open for breakfast, and it is famously sensitive to dietary restrictions.

Chinatown is a ghost of its glory days, but there are still bargains to be had at **Eat First, New Big Wong** (a late-night hangout for area chefs), **Chinatown Express,** and noodle-centric **China Boy. Matchbox** is a labyrinthine pizzeria/trattoria with a fiery decor to match; it may be easier to get into the simpler **Ella's Wood-Fired Pizza.**

unofficial TIP

Planning a touring marathon? Start the day at **Woodward Takeout Food,** or WTF, for biscuits with fried chicken, bacon, cheddar, and honey butter. Everybody else does.

Farther into downtown, moving toward the White House, are the upscale **Bombay Club** (page 261), **Brasserie Beck, Café du Parc, Del Frisco's Double Eagle, Equinox** (page 264), **Founding Farmers, Georgia Brown's** (page 265), **Occidental Grill, Old Ebbitt Grill** (page 268) (also in the Clyde's family), **Oval Room** (page 269), and **Woodward Table** (a lovely Southern remake of a historic building).

Acadiana ★★★ SOUTHERN MODERATE

901 New York Ave. NW; ☎ 202-408-8848; **acadianarestaurant.com**
Downtown

Reservations Recommended. **Metro** Metro Center or Mount Vernon Square. **Wine selection** Very good. **Disabled access** Good. **Open** *Brunch:* Sunday, 11 a.m.–3 p.m. *Lunch:* Monday–Friday, 11:30 a.m.–2:30 p.m. *Dinner:* Monday–Thursday, 5:30–10:30 p.m.; Friday–Saturday, 5:30–11 p.m.; Sunday, 5–9 p.m.

THE PREMISE On the ground floor of this very sleek office building is an elegant surprise: a Creole-nostalgic dining room with lush banquettes, chandeliers, and platters bought in New Orleans. (The restrooms are almost baroque.)

THE PAYOFF Like the architecture, the kitchen updates Louisiana classics such as beer-battered soft-shell crab étouffée; New Orleans–style barbecued shrimp spiked with Worcestershire sauce; grillades and grits; and panfried duck with dirty rice, collard greens, and red pepper jelly glaze. The bar is ideal for quick dining: gumbo, trio of deviled eggs, corn, crab and/or turtle soup, and fried pork boudin balls. The hot biscuits with pepper jelly were addictive before biscuits were trendy. Sunday brunch is topped with bargain (quality) booze and jazz. In good weather, crawfish boils are held on the patio.

Bombay Club ★★★½ MODERN INDIAN EXPENSIVE

815 Connecticut Ave. NW; ☎ 202-659-3727; **bombayclubdc.com**
Downtown

Reservations Recommended. **Metro** Farragut North, McPherson Square, or Farragut West. **Wine selection** Very good. **Disabled access** Good. **Open** *Brunch:* Sunday, 11:30 a.m.–2:30 p.m. *Lunch:* Monday–Friday, 11:30 a.m.–2:30 p.m. *Dinner:* Monday–Thursday, 5:30–10:30 p.m.; Friday–Saturday, 5:30–11 p.m.; Sunday, 5:30–9:30 p.m.

THE PREMISE This luxe-look Raj-retro restaurant was among the first to bust the lowbrow carryout stereotype and show Indian cuisine at its best and spice-brightest. Visually stunning, with gleaming silver, white linen, and lounge chairs that almost seem to be equipped with Pimm's cups, it's a beauty. In nice weather, there is outdoor seating.

THE PAYOFF The menu may look classic (the lamb vindaloo is a local favorite), but the food is anything but predictable: "kebabs" include duck with chilies and nutmeg (second choice: duck in an elegant cashew-and-apricot sauce); samosas are stuffed with shiitakes and fresh corn or butternut squash and peas. If you're a sampler with a fairly good appetite, check out the three *thalis*—one veggie, one seafood, and one omnivore (lamb, chicken, seafood, and veggies). Vegetarians will be astounded and delighted here. The $22 Sunday brunch ($32 with unlimited sparkling wine) is very popular.

IF YOU LIKE THIS Bombay Club's corporate sibling, **Rasika West End,** has launched its own Sunday brunch, a more street food–minded menu, and curries that are the Indian equivalent of an Italian mama's Sunday family dinner.

Central Michel Richard   ★★★½
MODERN AMERICAN   EXPENSIVE

1001 Pennsylvania Ave. NW; ☎ 202-626-0015; **centralmichelrichard.com**
Downtown

Reservations Strongly recommended. **Metro** Federal Triangle, Metro Center, or Archives–Navy Memorial–Penn Quarter. **Wine selection** Very good. **Disabled access** Good. **Open** *Brunch:* Sunday, 11 a.m.–2:30 p.m. *Lunch:* Monday–Friday, 11:30 a.m.– 2:30 p.m. *Dinner:* Monday–Thursday, 5–10 p.m.; Friday–Saturday, 5–10:30 p.m.

THE PREMISE This is currently the sole restaurant from superchef Michel Richard (described as a bistro but priced like a four-star), and it pays tribute to Richard's unique mix of culinary devotion and quirky humor. Visually, Central is something like a Swedish contemporary retro-diner: blond wood with wine-colored accents and industrial chic metals, a long Les Halles–retro white marble bar, see-through wine cellars and meat locker, and fry baskets that resemble Container Store mesh pencil pots.

THE PAYOFF Though its culinary Elvis is only rarely in the house, Central remains one of Washington's best restaurants, annoying as it can occasionally be (loud, and with a pushy I'm-a-regular lunchtime swagger crowd, even when the waiter ignores them). Some of its longest-running items remain favorites: a $30 lobster burger (really more like a lobster-scallop mousse on brioche); short ribs braised for two days in both wine and beer; "faux gras" (chicken pâté); and delicate skate with lentils. And the (seriously) KFC-inspired bucket of lunch-to-go fried chicken (six pieces, six nuggets, and mashed potatoes) is $30. (It does make a pretty astounding picnic.)

Corduroy   ★★★½   MODERN AMERICAN   EXPENSIVE

1122 9th St. NW; ☎ 202-589-0699; **corduroydc.com**   Downtown

Reservations Recommended. **Metro** Mount Vernon Square. **Wine selection** Very good. **Disabled access** Not accessible. **Open** *Dinner:* Monday–Saturday, 5:30–10:30 p.m.

THE PREMISE This renovated town house—not immediately visible because of its small, you-have-to-know signing—has been lightened and brightened with exposed brick, slate floors, blond wood, deep leather chairs, splashy abstract art, Noguchi-meets-Tribeca lighting, and a small bar upstairs. One of the last to demand a little respect from diners, Corduroy keeps a supply of long pants for short-sporting tourists and wrap skirts for women.

THE PAYOFF Tom Power, one of Washington's most under-celebrated chefs, was in the vanguard of the local/seasonal movement, and even his more elaborate dishes have a becoming modesty of presentation. The menu is not extensive because it is so market-driven, but game and seafood are always good bets here and are fresh enough to be crudo, in whatever ethnic language: crab blinis, scallop tartare, lobster carpaccio, or seared tuna sushi. Heftier dishes include guinea hen two ways (roasted and confit) with woodsy maitake mushrooms, and charcoal-grilled pork loin. Check out the $70 "chef's surprise" five-course tasting menu.

IF YOU LIKE THIS Power has opened an almost dizzily (or tipsy) different spot next door called **Baby Wale**—not a typo, but a type of corduroy—with a huge bar and a bar-food menu that sounds so simple (New Jersey hot dogs, ramen, pizza, lobster rolls, and a meatball casserole with lamb, antelope, *and* beef), but the execution puts them in the haute spot. He should have called it Power Play. Best gender-neutral restroom signs ever. Unhappily, neither restaurant is open for lunch.

Daikaya Ramen and Izakawa ★★★½
JAPANESE   INEXPENSIVE/MODERATE

705 6th St. NW; ☎ 202-589-1600; **daikaya.com**   Penn Quarter

Reservations Recommended (upstairs only). **Metro** Gallery Place–Chinatown or Dupont Circle. **Wine selection** Very good. **Disabled access** Good. **Open** *Ramen shop:* Sunday–Wednesday, 11 a.m.–10 p.m.; Thursday–Saturday, 11 a.m.–11 p.m. *Izakawa: Brunch:* Sunday, 11 a.m.–3 p.m. *Lunch:* Monday–Friday, 11:30 a.m.–2 p.m. *Dinner:* Sunday–Wednesday, 5–10 p.m.; Thursday–Saturday, 5–11 p.m.

THE PREMISE This ramen is nothing like the dry dollar-store stuff, and in fact is made for Daikaya in Sapporo (you may see the fresh noodles drying on a rack). An *izakawa* is traditionally a sort of Japanese pub that turns out small plates for drinkers (*sakaya* is a sake bar). Two of Washington's true food stars are partners in this double-decker establishment—Daisuke Utagawa, whose Sushiko was among Washington's first great Japanese restaurants, and Katsuya Fukushima, who was for many years chef at José Andrés's groundbreaking Minibar. The laser-cut steel exterior bears the Japanese kanji for "water," and at night the backlight turns it into a lit lantern, which is what indicates that an *izakawa* is open. The textiles and vintage posters are imported, the "wallpaper" is sheets of manga, and the exposed wood is traditional; the blue-and-yellow chevron-painted bar suggests the ramen carts that are a fast-meal fixture at Japanese train stations.

THE PAYOFF Downstairs is the no-reservations ramen bar, where, if you get a seat by the kitchen counter, you can see the noodles being boiled, the bean sprouts being charred, and the long-simmered broths (chicken, pork, beef, or a vegan version) being prepared. Dumplings are just about the only other option. (Slurping is encouraged.) Upstairs is the *izakawa,* where nibbles include grilled eggplant, grilled or baked oysters, ginger-spiked turkey wings, grilled avocado, miso-braised mackerel (to be eaten bones and all), monkfish liver (*ankimo*) with ratatouille (not so sushi-bar conventional), pork-stuffed rice balls (something like the Japanese version of *arancini*), and skewers of not only the usual suspects but beef tongue and pork with Brussels sprouts. This is one of the wackiest (and best) spots for brunch: Japanese-style fried chicken and waffles with wasabi-spiked sauce, eggs Benedict with *tonkatsu* sauce instead of hollandaise, a croissant with sea urchin and white miso, a gin rickey with green-tea soda, and more.

IF YOU LIKE THIS You may not be able to get both cooking styles in one spot, but **Izakawa Seki** (profiled on page 274) is near the U Street–African American

Civil War Memorial–Cardozo Metro at 11th and V Streets NW. For the ramen, head to **Toki Underground** in the Atlas District (profiled on page 281).

Equinox ★★★ MODERN AMERICAN EXPENSIVE

818 Connecticut Ave. NW; ☎ 202-331-8118; **equinoxrestaurant.com**
Downtown

Reservations Recommended. **Metro** Farragut West or Farragut North. **Wine selection** Very good. **Disabled access** Good. **Open** *Lunch:* Monday–Friday, 11:30 a.m.–2 p.m. *Dinner:* Monday–Thursday, 5:30–10 p.m.; Friday–Saturday, 5:30–10:30; Sunday, 5:30–9 p.m. Friday–Saturday, 5:30–10:30 p.m.

THE PREMISE The unobtrusive decor at Equinox—cerulean drapes and gauzy overhead swags leading the eye to the glass-enclosed "atrium" patio—is a good metaphor for chef-owner Todd Gray's polished and reticent technique. Gray and wife-partner, Ellen Kassoff-Gray, were in the vanguard of the organic, humane, local, and sustainable food movement (although they make a few import exceptions for quality, such as Italian white truffles in season). Before opening Equinox, Gray spent many years as the on-site chef at Roberto Donna's Galileo, then Washington's premiere Italian restaurant, and the fresh pastas prove it, but he has devoted this kitchen to what he calls mid-Atlantic regional, heavy on fresh seafood. Kassoff is vegan, and Equinox not only always has serious vegetarian ("plant-based") entrées, but the Sunday brunch buffet is also entirely vegan.

THE PAYOFF The menu changes frequently, but in general, expect light sauces based on reductions and natural flavors, and contrasting sweet and sour, delicate and pungent, or rich and acid within a single dish. Recent examples include a pale ale–braised squab with chestnut and port–braised cabbage; agnolotti with eggplant and house-made ricotta; and oat-crusted salmon with lobster mushrooms and bok choi. The locally famous truffle mac and cheese and the warm rosemary cheese puffs are not allowed to disappear from the menu.

IF YOU LIKE THIS Gray designed the menus for the Salamander Resort as well as the more "public" **Market Salamander,** in horsey-trendy Middleburg.

Fiola ★★★★★ ITALIAN VERY EXPENSIVE

601 Pennsylvania Ave. NW; ☎ 202-628-2888; **fioladc.com** **Downtown**

Reservations Highly recommended. **Metro** Archives–Navy Memorial–Penn Quarter or Gallery Place–Chinatown. **Wine selection** Very good. **Disabled access** Good. **Open** *Lunch:* Monday–Friday, 11:30 a.m.–2:30 p.m. *Dinner:* Monday–Thursday, 5:30–10:30 p.m.; Friday, 5:30–11:30 p.m.; Saturday, 5–11:30 p.m.

THE PREMISE Though he's worked all over the world, Washington considers Fabio Trabocchi a prodigal chef. This is the same space that once was Bice, Trabocchi's first American kitchen, and few second acts have been more welcome. Fiola is easily the area's best Italian restaurant, and it has a volume level you can actually converse over. The decor is like a Frank Lloyd Wright concoction—part rustic (stacked-stone walls) and part *Mad Men* (white leather banquettes, massive cut-glass chandeliers, a touch of gilding, and what looks like a Murano glass basin in the restroom). The menu equivalent: House-made spaghetti with sea urchin, mussels, and scallops is elegant and intoxicating.

THE PAYOFF Think big and assured: lobster-stuffed ravioli in a gingery sauce (a signature dish going back to the chef's days at Maestro at The Ritz-Carlton, Tysons Corner); carpaccio and tartare ("Italian sushi"); tortellini stuffed with lamb belly and served with sweetbreads and fennel confit; a roast veal rib eye sauced with sweetbreads and osso bucco; prosciutto-wrapped veal chop; pheasant with butternut agnolotti; or fresh pappardelle with suckling pig/veal ragù. Maria's Menu items, named for his wife, are healthy by design, but you can always get a simple grilled fish (or fresh sweet calamari). For a really special occasion, spring for the four- or six-course tasting menus, $105 and $120 before wine pairings.

IF YOU LIKE THIS **Casa Luca** near Mount Vernon Square (named for their son) may be more "rustic," but it's not much more casual, in execution or price—it's the Ferrari of Italian comfort food. And see **Fiola Mare** on page 290.

Georgia Brown's ★★½ SOUTHERN MODERATE

950 15th St. NW; ☎ 202-393-4499; **gbrowns.com** Downtown

Reservations Recommended. **Metro** McPherson Square or Farragut North. **Wine selection** Good. **Disabled access** Good. **Open** *Brunch:* Sunday, 10 a.m.–4 p.m. (last seating at 3:30 p.m.) *Lunch and dinner:* Monday–Thursday, 11:30 a.m.–10 p.m.; Friday–Saturday, 11:30 a.m.–11 p.m.; Sunday, 5:30–10 p.m.

THE PREMISE Low-Country cuisine is uptown again, and this sophisticated take on Southern garden-district graciousness, with vinelike wrought iron overhead, sleek wood curves, and conversation nooks, has stuck to its roots while taking note of the buzz around Charleston and Savannah. Homesick Southerners can indulge in the fried chicken livers and still look uptown, because they're dressed with a mustard-soy emulsion (the cornmeal-crusted catfish fingers come with Washington's local heater, mumbo sauce).

THE PAYOFF This is a mix of "new" Low-Country and church suppers: diver scallops; pepper-crusted tuna; kitchen-sink gumbo with duck confit, chicken, crab, shrimp, okra, and andouille (and a slightly simpler *perlau* for okra-phobes); shrimp and andouille over grits; Southern fried chicken marinated in buttermilk and served with collard greens; and fried or jerk catfish. What keeps this on the list is the Sunday all-you-can-eat brunch with live jazz because, although it's not cheap ($42), the buffet is only the beginning—you get to take a second entrée home for later. Even better might be happy hour (3–7 p.m.), where a list of surprising small plates—not just chicken livers and catfish fingers but also shrimp tacos and meatball sliders—are just $6 with your drink.

IF YOU LIKE THIS **Acadiana** (see page 261) is more strictly New Orleans.

Graffiato ★★★½ ITALIAN/PIZZA INEXPENSIVE

707 6th St. NW; ☎ 202-289-3600; **graffiatodc.com** Penn Quarter

Reservations Recommended. **Metro** Gallery Place–Chinatown or Mount Vernon Square. **Wine selection** Very good. **Disabled access** Good. **Open** Sunday–Thursday, 11:30 a.m.–10 p.m.; Friday–Saturday, 11:30 a.m.–11 p.m. Bar and Pizza Oven open 1 hour later.

THE PREMISE *Top Chef* contestant Mike Isabella has fashioned a love song to the Italian American (real) delis of his childhood. The decor is warehouse-chic (metal lawyer's chairs, exposed brick, laboratory lights), but the real clues to Isabella's passions are the wood-burning oven downstairs (try to snag one of the nearby barstools) and the showcase ham bar on the second floor. Translation: artisan pizza, smoky-roast pasta sauces, and locally cured meats.

THE PAYOFF The oven is more than a pretext for making pizza—though, when you consider such options as the Countryman (fontina, black truffles, and soft-cooked egg), the Bella (cauliflower, mozzarella, mushrooms, and artichoke), or the White House (three cheeses, black pepper honey, and prosciutto), you might not need any explanation. Nevertheless, its presence permeates the menu: the roasted potatoes for the gnocchi with pork, and even the scallops are smoky. Think you've had beet salad? Try the smoked beet/sheep's-milk ricotta/pickled-orange version. Other surprises include roasted chicken thighs with a pepperoni sauce (brunch); an egg, bacon, cheese, and potato breakfast pizza that will ruin you for carryout egg sandwiches; squid ink fettuccine (with clams, calamari, and Italian sausage); and skate with tomato-braised lentils. Chef's tasting menu at dinner is $55; "Jersey shore" happy hour includes duck-fat fingerlings and pan pizza.

IF YOU LIKE THIS Isabella's group now also includes the nearby super-sandwich shop **G by Mike Isabella** and **Kapnos,** profiled on page 274.

Jaleo ★★★½ SPANISH MODERATE

480 7th St. NW; ☎ 202-628-7949; **jaleo.com** Downtown
7271 Woodmont Ave., Bethesda; ☎ 301-913-0003 Maryland suburbs
2250-A Crystal Dr., Crystal City; ☎ 703-413-8181 Virginia suburbs

Reservations Recommended, although walk-ins are given full respect. **Metro** Archives–Navy Memorial–Penn Quarter (Penn Quarter); Bethesda (Bethesda); Crystal City (Crystal City). **Wine selection** Good. **Disabled access** Good. **Open** *Downtown:* Sunday–Monday, 11 a.m.–10 p.m.; Tuesday–Thursday, 11 a.m.–11:30 p.m.; Friday–Saturday, 11:30 a.m.–12:30 a.m. *Bethesda:* Sunday–Thursday, 11 a.m.–10 p.m.; Friday–Saturday, 11 a.m.–midnight. *Crystal City:* Sunday–Thursday, 11 a.m.–10 p.m.; Friday–Saturday, 11 a.m.–11 p.m.

THE PREMISE These fine tapas restaurants from superchef José Andrés are a lot like Andrés himself, simultaneously faithful and irreverent. (The cocktail and wine menus come on an iPad, just for a start.) A renovation replaced the downtown restaurant's signature John Singer Sargent mural of a gypsy tango with a painting of *Footloose*-like dancing feet (and a foosball table); chicken fritters are served in a Cinderella-meets–Michael Jordan glass sneaker; gazpacho is served as a sauce from which tomatoes and bread emerge like the rocks of a Zen garden. (The Crystal City branch, on the other hand, has a much more aristocratic feel, with its gold-stenciled purple wallpaper and Joan Miró–like swirls.) Though the menus are very similar, small distinctions reflect the locations and patrons: Downtown has a pretheater menu; Downtown and Bethesda have a three-course express lunch menu; and Crystal City's Sunday brunch is all-you-can-eat family-style paella.

THE PAYOFF Tapas change frequently, but among recent choices are grilled sausages over white beans, named for the late senator and fan Daniel Patrick Moynihan; oysters gin and tonic; a sort of sea urchin crostini; five types of paellas, including a porcini–veggie version, a squid ink *fideuà,* and a soupy lobster risotto; rabbit confit with apricot puree; grilled quail; sliders of black-foot Ibérico pork; four-cheese grilled sandwiches with honey; "wrinkled" potatoes with red-and-green mojo sauces; and the crispy-thin pan *tomate* that is closer to flatbread than crostini. They may not be called charcuterie and cheese boards, but varieties of fine Ibérico hams, sausages, and cheeses are a strong presence, both as stars and supporting characters. Nevertheless, vegetarians could spend a whole day here. Daily specials and particularly seasonal rarities are extremely good bets.

IF YOU LIKE THIS If you like the idea of duck, achiote-roasted pork, or beef tongue tacos, head to **El Centro DC** or its sibling **El Centro Georgetown.** And although it is a chain restaurant, **Barcelona** in Mid City has an extensive tapas selection.

Minibar ★★★★★   **MODERN AMERICAN VERY EXPENSIVE**

855 E St. NW; ☎ 202-393-0812; **minibarbyjoseandres.com**   Penn Quarter

Reservations Required. **Metro** Gallery Place–Chinatown or Archives–Navy Memorial–Penn Quarter. **Wine selection** Extremely good. **Disabled access** Good. **Open** *Dinner:* Tuesday–Saturday, 2 seatings per night.

THE PREMISE José Andrés indisputably blew minds, and traditionally equipped kitchens, when he opened the first really mini-Minibar in the mid-1990s, and it continues to lead the way in gustatory experimentation, making Andrés the James Beard Award chef of 2011. It may be titanium–credit card expensive—$250 per person before any of the wine-pairing choices ($75, $125, or $200) or well-deserved tips—but more than two dozen courses, incredible technique, and almost flawless flavors make this a 10 in all ways. Though "expanded" to 12 seats (with two seatings nightly), this is still a hot ticket; reserve as early as possible (website only), up to three months in advance. The two "tables," really kitchen-side bars, of six are seated with a 30-minute split to allow for fluid service. Diners have a ringside seat as waves of chefs use liquid nitrogen, sous vide, smoking, searing, and occasionally the cotton candy spinner to transform familiar foods into bubbles, foams, and toys (a meringue rubber duckie with "brains" of foie gras or a similar piggy with bacon ice cream). This is smoke and mirrors of the most delicious kind, but it will not suit the traditionalist or the humorless. Andrés trained at the world-famous El Bulli, the birthplace of deconstructed gastronomy, and he has done mentor Ferran Adrià proud. Amazingly, as elaborate as the menu is, Minibar can accommodate vegetarians and some allergies; when you make your reservations, there is a questionnaire, and the staff will check back with you to get it exactly right.

THE PAYOFF Some of the indulgence is flavor, some is texture, and some is eye candy (tricks); some of these two- and three-bite dishes involve 8–10 steps. Olive oil quivers in a drop like a jelly bean; "carrots" are actually pastry-tube-squeezed concentration of puree; classic tapas are reinvented, with Marcona almonds transformed into an ice and then topped with a foam of blue cheese, or fava beans in a cream of clam. There are also pigs' tail "curry" in a meringue bun; "pizza" on a paper-thin wafer with freeze-dried tomato dust and *burrata*; and "dragon's breath," for which you swallow two shots and breathe out smoke, if not fire.

IF YOU LIKE THIS If you don't have the money or the advance time, you can try to get into **Barmini,** the equally adventurous cocktail-lab side of the restaurant, glittering with vintage barware, which also serves as the dessert room for dinner (reservations are a good idea, though they do accommodate a few walk-ins). The small bites here, though not the same as the dinner menu, will give you a sense of the staff's incredible imagination—sea urchin panino or a bánh mì burger. On the other hand, if you really want to impress somebody, reserve José's Table, a private room for six that costs $3,000. For a similarly extravagant, if slightly less "scientific," menu, check out **Rogue 24** in historic Blagden Alley.

Old Ebbitt Grill   ★★½   AMERICAN   MODERATE

675 15th St. NW; ☎ 202-347-4800; **ebbitt.com**   Downtown

Reservations Recommended. **Metro** Metro Center or McPherson Square. **Wine selection** Good. **Disabled access** Very good (through G Street atrium). **Open** *Brunch:* Saturday–Sunday, 8:30 a.m.–4 p.m. *Breakfast:* Monday–Friday, 7:30–11 a.m. *Lunch:* Monday–Friday, 11 a.m.–5 p.m. *Dinner:* Monday–Friday, 5 p.m.–midnight; Saturday–Sunday, 4 p.m.–midnight.

THE PREMISE The Old Ebbitt Grill is a Washington landmark, sentimentally if not actually: The original opened nearby in 1856, has a list of presidential patrons to equal any in Washington, and has been in this location for more than 30 years. It doesn't get a lot of food-trend buzz, but it doesn't need the business: The mahogany main bar, white-linen-and-wood dining room, and classic oyster bar around back off the atrium are almost constantly humming with lawyers, lobbyists, interns, and tourists. (Don't miss the antique marble staircase or the carved-glass partitions showing the White House, Capitol, and Treasury Buildings.) All four bars—yes, four—have art and decor worth exploring. If you're planning to come around Cherry Blossom Festival, Fourth of July, inauguration, or other busy times, make even your breakfast reservations early. The Old Ebbitt takes its White House neighborhood location seriously, but not too seriously. That is, it gives out pagers to patrons waiting for tables, but the staff democratically seats the ties and T-shirts side by side.

THE PAYOFF The restaurant is part of the local Clyde's group, which guarantees good service and quality. The menu runs an all-American gamut but with interesting updates: chili-braised pork osso bucco, lamb shank, jambalaya, calf's liver, mussels fra diavolo, crab cakes, local seafood, and the Clyde's burger, a local standard. The oyster bar is lovely, and the oyster-centric wine list is first-rate. Even the (very extensive) late-night menu is lively, with Korean pork belly tacos and empanadas alongside seafood, sandwiches, chowders, and even steaks. Annually, during the brief halibut season in Alaska, the Old Ebbitt and its Clyde's cousins have a halibut celebration that is a command performance for seafood lovers.

IF YOU LIKE THIS The half-price raw bar happy hours are another Clyde's tradition, and remarkable: half price every day 3–6 p.m. and after 11 p.m., and that includes the lobster and shrimp as well as shellfish. No doubt that has something to do with the restaurant selling 20,000 oysters a week. Both the **Clyde's of Georgetown** and **Clyde's–Gallery Place** also have extensive late-night options, and Gallery Place has oyster happy hours as well.

Oval Room ★★★½
MODERN AMERICAN MODERATE/EXPENSIVE

800 Connecticut Ave. NW; ☎ 202-463-8700; **ovalroom.com** Downtown

Reservations Recommended. **Metro** Farragut North or McPherson Square. **Wine selection** Very good. **Disabled access** Good. **Open** *Lunch:* Monday–Friday, 11:30 a.m.–2:30 p.m. *Dinner:* Monday–Thursday, 5:30–10 p.m.; Friday–Saturday, 5:30–10:30 p.m.

THE PREMISE For many years, this White House–neighborhood restaurant was famous for a mural featuring its famous patrons: Frank Sinatra, Nancy Reagan, then-Senate wife Elizabeth Taylor, Henry Kissinger, and so on. It no longer needs the self-promotion: Though sleekly redesigned, it's still a hangout for Executive Mansion staffers and people-watchers.

THE PAYOFF This is an accomplished if not revolutionary menu, but it's a steal at lunch, when suits know to go to the bar for the One Dish–One Dessert–One Drink $20 special. In fact, if you are touring and can hang most of your appetite on a late lunch, you will find quite a variety: a corned duck breast Reuben; a cured pork belly Cubano; linguine with root vegetable sauce; pan-seared monkfish; guinea hen; *burrata* with julienned cucumber and artichoke; or a riff on Cobb salad with confit of tuna in the mix.

Oyamel ★★★½ **MEXICAN MODERATE**

401 7th St. NW; ☎ 202-628-1005; **oyamel.com** Downtown

Reservations Accepted. **Metro** Archives–Navy Memorial–Penn Quarter or Gallery Place–Chinatown. **Wine selection** Good. **Disabled access** Good. **Open** *Brunch:* Saturday–Sunday, 11:30–3 p.m. *Dinner:* Sunday–Wednesday, 11:30 a.m.–midnight; Thursday–Saturday, 11:30 a.m.–2 a.m.

THE PREMISE *Oyamel* refers to a kind of tree that is the destination of monarch butterflies that annually migrate to Mexico, hence the fabulous mobile of a butterfly flurry (look for the Day of the Dead butterfly, which is when the monarchs generally arrive in Mexico). While Oyamel accepts reservations, it holds aside plenty of tables for walk-ins. This is particularly popular with kids because everybody likes salsa and chips (free), tangy guacamole made tableside, fries in mole . . . you get the idea.

THE PAYOFF Do not confuse this with Tex-Mex. This is dedicated Mexican street food, which might include hanger steak and eggs with refried beans and salsa verde on a house-made corn tortilla; a fine spicy version of menudo (tripe soup), the classic weekend hangover remedy; local pork spareribs; and so on. And if you think you've had tacos, try those fresh corn tortillas filled with seared house-cured pork belly with chilies and pineapple; confit of suckling pig, cracklings, and tomatillos; braised beef tongue; turkey leg confit blanketed with an almost Middle Eastern pecan, almond, and sesame mole; belly *chicharrónes*; and many more. Vegetarians and vegans have plenty of options here, including seasonal veggie mole; plantain and squash fritters stuffed with black beans; and a sort of Swiss chard, hazelnut, and dried-fruit pilaf. (We're not sure what grasshoppers count as, but sautéed with tequila and guac, they make a pretty amazing taco.) In addition to good wine, beer, and tequila lists, Oyamel serves a mean margarita—several, in fact. The lunch special includes two appetizers and a taco (or one appetizer and a sweet) for $20—in this case, the little bites range from spicy cactus paddles to mahimahi ceviche (one of many) with avocado and olives, several taco options (from wild mushrooms to braised beef tongue), spicy shrimp, and so on.

IF YOU LIKE THIS While each has a different take on small plates, the Mediterranean **Zaytinya** (profiled on page 270), Spanish **Jaleo** (profiled on page 266), and Chinese-Peruvian **China Chilcano** are all within eyeshot.

Rasika ★★★ INDIAN MODERATE/EXPENSIVE

633 D St. NW; ☎ 202-637-1222; **rasikarestaurant.com** Penn Quarter

Reservations Strongly recommended. **Metro** Gallery Place–Chinatown; Archives-Navy Memorial–Penn Quarter; or Judiciary Square. **Wine selection** Good. **Disabled access** Good. **Open** *Lunch:* Monday–Friday, 11:30 a.m.–2:30 p.m. *Dinner:* Monday-Thursday, 5:30–10:30 p.m.; Friday–Saturday, 5–11 p.m.

THE PREMISE Chef Vikram Sunderam has raised the concept of Indian fare to new heights and has made Rasika one of Washington's very best restaurants; in 2015 he won the James Beard Award for best Mid-Atlantic chef. The variety of seating areas—lounge, tables near the exposed kitchen, a communal table, and smaller private areas—and the rich spice colors (cinnabar red, paprika, saffron gold, and twinkling glass) give a nod to this modern Indian's eclectic take on classic ingredients.

THE PAYOFF The menu is divided into *tawa* (griddle) dishes; *sigri* (barbecue), more like sautéing or wok-frying; and entrées, which include the curries, tandoori dishes, stews, and so on (plus breads, savories, and sides). These go beyond the usual offerings to include venison chop, duck, lamb with red chilies or caramelized onions and tomatoes, and Indonesian-hot lobster *peri peri*. Vegetarian options, which can be ordered in half portions as side dishes, are very good, especially the baby eggplant sauté, mushrooms with peas and cashews, okra with dry mango powder, and the cauliflower and green peas with ginger and cumin. Even the chutneys are fresh (in both senses): eggplant ginger, tomato–golden raisin, and the more familiar mango.

IF YOU LIKE THIS Rasika West End near Dupont Circle is very similar but maybe a little less polished (except for the chef's table downstairs) and offers Sunday brunch as a fringe benefit. See also its corporate sibling, the elegant **Bombay Club** in Farragut Square (page 261).

Zaytinya ★★★½ GREEK/MIDDLE EASTERN MODERATE

701 9th St. NW; ☎ 202-638-0800; **zaytinya.com** Downtown

Reservations Available evenings. **Metro** Gallery Place–Chinatown or Metro Center. **Wine selection** Very good. **Disabled access** Good. **Open** Sunday–Monday, 11:30 a.m.–10 p.m.; Tuesday–Thursday, 11:30 a.m.–11 p.m.; Friday–Saturday, 11:30 a.m.–midnight.

THE PREMISE Not Middle Eastern in the usual sense, or in its looks, Zaytinya—which means "olive oil" in Turkish—is specifically Eastern Mediterranean. This is a showpiece: big, high, and airy minimalist room; white and angular with a soaring atrium-style ceiling; cut-through shelving walls stocked with lit candles; a long (and very busy) bar; half-hidden dining nooks and niches; a fireplace; and a mezzanine overlooking the Manhattan-style communal table in the center of the main dining room. It's loud, it's lively, and it's delicious. After all, it's another José Andrés production.

THE PAYOFF First things first: The endless hot-from-the-oven pita, as inflated as a balloon, is to most pita bread as a soufflé is to scrambled eggs. And you don't even have to choose from among the half-dozen dips—you can order a combo. The menu does change frequently, but among indicative dishes are lamb mini-meatballs with cinnamon oil and dried fruit; potato-crusted snails; prawns in smoked tomato sauce; giant favas with tomatoes and red onions; traditional pressed mullet caviar; squid and octopus in a variety of treatments; braised lamb shanks; imported Turkish pastrami; feta- and tomato-stuffed quail; crab cakes with shaved fennel; flaming cheese; fried eggplant; veal cheeks with chanterelle puree; grilled pork and orange-rind sausage; braised rabbit with lentils; and fried mussels with pistachios. For vegetarians and vegans, this is a throwback Garden of Eden, with dozens of options.

IF YOU LIKE THIS Though not close to a Metro station, the bright and lively (and often overlooked) **Café Divan** at the top of Georgetown has an almost equally lengthy list of more traditional Turkish meze and entrées, from lamb and veal *döner* kebab to wood-fired flatbreads. (Take your Armenian godmother's word for it—it's good.)

MID CITY AND LOGAN CIRCLE

IN THE FIRST PART OF THE 20TH CENTURY, Mid City was the "Black Broadway" and the premier African American cultural center, but it was devastated by the fiery riots of 1968 around 14th and U Streets Northwest. So it's only fitting that U Street was among the first to see signs of new life toward the turn of the 21st century.

These days, along the blocks of U Street Northwest between about 10th and 14th Streets, and on the blocks of 14th Street from just above U Street down toward P, you'll find the most literary of Washington cafés: the new-American **Café Saint-Ex,** named for aviator and *The Little Prince* author Antoine de Saint-Exupéry; **Bar Pilar,** named for Ernest Hemingway's boat; the Belgian pub **Marvin,** named for local-boy soul star Marvin Gaye, who lived in Belgium toward the end of his life; **Busboys and Poets,** a combination bookstore, café, bar, and poetry lounge named for black poet Langston Hughes, who was working as a busboy at the Wardman Park Hotel when he began writing (now with several locations); and the New Orleans–flavored **Eatonville,** named for black novelist Zora Neale Hurston's hometown. (Take that, Harlem!)

This area boasts a lot of bargains. It has replaced Adams Morgan as Washington's Little Ethiopia, and there are quite a few restaurants from which to choose, but **Dukem** and **Etete** are the most popular. **Dino's Grotto** is a moderate Italian kitchen that could easily stay under budget, especially if you stick to the admirable antipasti and pastas. And, of course, this area is home to the legendary **Ben's Chili Bowl,** which refused to close after the riots and is still dishing out chili half-smokes (half pork and half beef smoked sausage on a bun topped with mustard, onions, and chili) to stars and presidents alike, and the **Florida Avenue Grill,** which calls itself "the oldest soul-food restaurant in the world"—and at 70-plus, it just might be.

More recently, however, higher-end restaurants and lounges have moved into the area—notably the no-reservation **Compass Rose** (*Rose* for the owner, and *compass* for the number of ethnicities covered in its small-plate menu); **Izakawa Seki** (page 274)**; Kapnos** (page 274)**; Le Diplomate** (page 275)**; Masa 14** (a fusion small-plates collaboration between Richard Sandoval of Zengo and Kaz Okochi of Kaz Sushi Bistro, complete with roof terrace); and **Policy.** On the comfort side, **Etto** is a small (and also no-reservations) pizzeria with benefits—that is, charcuterie and cocktails. The **Fainting Goat** may call itself a neighborhood joint, but it's one where the "liver parfait" is duck, the lasagna is made with lamb neck and rapini, and the beef tartare has bone marrow to boot—and it's pretty cheap.

Just a few blocks south of this cluster, and gradually beginning to merge with it, is Logan Circle, which is technically centered on 13th and P Streets Northwest but which also serves as the shorthand name for the growing P and 14th Street nightlife district. Among the top names there are the affordable **Doi Moi** (page 273) and **Estadio** (page 273)**;** the stylish gastropub **Birch & Barley** (below)**/ChurchKey; Posto,** which offers more than 110 bottles of Italian wine to go with its wood-fired pizza (now that's amore!)**; Pearl Dive Oyster Bar** and its **Black Jack** bar above; and **Logan Tavern,** a casual but often surprisingly deft neighborhood hangout.

Birch & Barley ★★★ MODERN AMERICAN EXPENSIVE

1337 14th St. NW; ☎ 202-567-2576; **birchandbarley.com** Logan Circle

Reservations Recommended. **Metro** Dupont Circle, Mount Vernon Square, or Shaw–Howard University. **Wine selection** Good. **Disabled access** Good. **Open** *Brunch:* Sunday, 11 a.m.–3 p.m. *Dinner:* Tuesday–Thursday, 5:30–10 p.m.; Friday–Saturday, 5:30–11 p.m.; Sunday, 5–8 p.m.

THE PREMISE This brick-and-board neighborhood hangout is one of the city's best gastropubs, with a beer list that tops 550 (and correctly designed glassware to match). The decor points to the mission; in fact, the display of copper draught lines behind the bar is nicknamed the pipe organ, for good reason—it makes strong men sing, if not weep. Birch & Barley is one of those two-for-one establishments: B&B is the more formal dining room and, if you can get the bar, has better service and a more restrained noise level. Church-Key (Get it? A pairing of bottle openers and beer ingredients?) upstairs is a more informal bar, with a younger, clubbier, and louder crowd. The menu is shorter, but the beer list is the same. Even better, if you have time in advance, reserve seats at the kitchen counter.

THE PAYOFF Beer is the breadwinner here, and so are some of the breads, including fresh pretzels and flatbreads, and pasta. But the predictable beer-bar fare—house-made charcuterie, fried chicken and waffles, a brat burger with beer-braised kraut—shouldn't obscure the more surprisingly brew-friendly entrées: pan-seared mackerel with sunchokes and fennel, honey-roasted duck bread with leg confit, a version of Belgian waterzooi with oysters, leek and wolffish, and so on. Sweetbreads with grilled Asian pear and cashew butter? Sign us up. Brunch is what a Sunday day-killer ought to be: fig and prosciutto flatbread, cavatelli with corn pudding and maitakes, or house-brined corned beef hash with duck eggs.

IF YOU LIKE THIS If you're more into wine than beer, check out nearby **Cork,** which offers dozens of wines by the glass and a mix of small plates (not happy hour quick bites but real food) and midsize ones to share.

Doi Moi ★★★ ASIA FUSION INEXPENSIVE

1800 14th St. NW; ☎ 202-733-5131; **doimoidc.com** Logan Circle

Reservations Recommended. **Metro** U Street–African American Civil War Memorial–Cardozo. **Wine selection** Very good. **Disabled access** Good. **Open** *Brunch:* Saturday–Sunday, 11 a.m.–2 p.m.; *Dinner:* Monday–Thursday, 5–10 p.m.; Friday–Saturday, 5–11 p.m.; Sunday, 5–9 p.m.

THE PREMISE This celebration of Southeast Asian street food mixes noodles, skewers (really fresh head-on shrimp), dumplings, curries of a refreshingly broad flavor spectrum, and family-style platters of roast chicken, ribs, or chargrilled whole fish. (The name means "new changes," a Vietnamese term that could be applied both to the kitchen and to the neighborhood.) This is a playful as well as deft kitchen: Noodles sometimes turn into origami. Don't underestimate the spice ratings here.

THE PAYOFF Street food may have inspired it, but the upscale wine and beer lists are American benefits. (The wacky-sweet drink-desserts are true cultural fusions.) Except for the family dishes, however, some plates may seem small. Doi Moi's brunch is anything but typical; the restaurant also has an extremely lengthy vegan/veggie and gluten-free menu, with its own mild-to-spicy range.

Estadio ★★★ SPANISH INEXPENSIVE

1540 14th St. NW; ☎ 202-319-1404; **estadio-dc.com** Mid City

Reservations Available only for parties of 6 or more. **Metro** U Street–African American Civil War Memorial–Cardozo or Dupont Circle. **Wine selection** Very good. **Disabled access** Good. **Open** *Brunch:* Saturday–Sunday, 11 a.m.–2 p.m. *Lunch:* Friday, 11:30 a.m.–2 p.m. *Dinner:* Monday–Thursday, 5–10 p.m.; Friday–Saturday, 5–11 p.m.; Sunday, 5–9 p.m.

THE PREMISE It might seem like just another tapas bar in a neighborhood crammed with small plates, but Logan Circle's Estadio remains a prime choice. The look is post-Moorish occupation, so to speak: patterned tiles, wrought iron, stone, heavy wood, and a touch of steel; food might be plated on wood boards or even slate.

THE PAYOFF The open-faced *montaditos* are not your grandmother's tea sandwiches: foie gras with scrambled eggs or with duck breast, lump crab with jalapeños, and so on; the two-sided kind include pork belly with *shishito* peppers, blood sausage, and grilled vegetables. Grab a toothpick and nosh on chorizo, *manchego* (among a dozen or so cheeses), anchovies, or artichokes; or go big with pork loin, halibut *romesco,* spicy grilled chicken, mussels, and so on. The sherry and Madeira lists are unusually extensive and are mixed into some delectable cocktails.

IF YOU LIKE THIS Estadio's sibling restaurants are the Southeast Asian **Doi Moi** (page 273) and the wine-centric **Proof.** More seriously, pork-aholics should check out **The Pig** down the street, where "nose to tail" is no joke.

Izakawa Seki ★★★½ JAPANESE EXPENSIVE

1117 V St. NW; ☎ 202-588-5841; **sekidc.com**   Mid City

Reservations Accepted for parties of 5–8 only. **Metro** U Street–African American Civil War Memorial-Cardozo or Shaw–Howard University. **Wine selection** Good. **Disabled access** Good. **Open** *Dinner:* Sunday–Monday and Wednesday–Thursday, 5–11 p.m.; Friday–Saturday, 5 p.m.–midnight.

THE PREMISE Remember when the average Japanese restaurant offered something for everyone—teriyaki, sushi, soup, noodles, and fried nibbles? For a while, that was considered American because in Japan, many restaurants specialize in only one of the above, but with the introduction of the *izakawa* style, basically the Japanese version of neighborhood pubs, variety is back in style.

THE PAYOFF It's not only that the sushi is so fresh, but it's also offered in ways that are haute in the old country but still new here: oversize scallops, flown in daily, glazed with soy and miso in the broiler and finished with an egg-creamy sauce, or slow-braised pork belly (and that pork broth is recycled to bathe udon noodles). Grilled yellowtail jaw is a classic, but grilled beef tongue with sharp miso should be. Even heartier are the Korean-flavored short ribs and the skewered grilled pork belly. And if you remember when your non-sushi-savvy buddies would say, "You eat sea urchin???," introduce them to the real sake drinker's test: liver-cured squid or squid in fermented *nattō* sauce.

IF YOU LIKE THIS See **Daikaya** in Penn Quarter (profiled on page 263).

Kapnos ★★★½ GREEK MODERATE

2201 14th St. NW; ☎ 202-234-5000; **kapnosdc.com**   Mid City

Reservations Accepted. **Metro** U Street–African American Civil War Memorial-Cardozo. **Wine selection** Very good. **Disabled access** Good. **Open** *Brunch*: Saturday–Sunday, 11 a.m.–3 p.m. *Dinner:* Monday–Wednesday, 6–10 p.m.; Thursday, 6–10:30 p.m.; Friday–Saturday, 5–11 p.m.; Sunday, 5–10 p.m.

THE PREMISE The name means "smoke" in Greek. The restaurant has *two* hickory-burning spit grills laden with goat, duck, lamb, chicken, even suckling pig (all this within eyeshot of the bar), *and* a bread oven. And the chefs here are Mike Isabella (see Graffiato, page 265) and George Pagonis, who grew up, professionally speaking, spitting lamb as Isabella's sous-chef at Zaytinya (page 270). (He also grew up in his family's long-running Greek diner in Alexandria.)

THE PAYOFF The starter spreads, such as taramosalata (whipped roe smoothed with pureed cauliflower) and *melitzanosalata* (eggplant, roasted peppers, and walnuts) come on hot flatbread from that stone oven. Other small plates include a not-quite-raw lamb tartare, charred Brussels sprouts with white anchovies and kalamatas, and a sort of Greek-soup pasta with cheese, wild mushrooms, and a poached egg. The grilled octopus with *harissa*-spiked yogurt is a signature; the goat is proof against any denial. Larger meze include slices of the lemon- and olive oil–marinated lamb, roasted duck in a phyllo pastry, and a sort of Mediterranean potatoes Anna in phyllo with yogurt and a fried duck egg. If there are enough of you, order the whole dorado with an almost North African preserved lemon–artichoke drapery or a whole lamb shoulder. Kapnos has a nightly special: moussaka on Mondays, rabbit on Tuesdays, duck on Wednesdays, and so on. The chef's-choice tasting menu is $75.

IF YOU LIKE THIS G by Mike Isabella is next door and gets the leftover good stuff for sandwiches. There are similar restaurants, though more casual, in Bethesda (**Kapnos Kouzina**) and Ballston (**Kapnos Taverna**).

Le Diplomate ★★★½ FRENCH MODERATE

1601 14th St. NW; ☎ 202-332-3333; **lediplomatedc.com** Logan Circle

Reservations Recommended. **Metro** Dupont Circle; U Street–African American Civil War Memorial–Cardozo; or Shaw–Howard University. **Wine selection** Good. **Disabled access** Good. **Open** *Brunch:* Saturday–Sunday, 9:30 a.m.–3 p.m. *Midday:* Saturday–Sunday, 3–5 p.m. *Dinner:* Sunday–Tuesday, 5–10 p.m.; Wednesday–Thursday, 5–11 p.m.; Friday–Saturday, 5 p.m.–midnight.

THE PREMISE Stephen Starr, the José Andrés of Philadelphia, owns Italian, German, and even Cuban and Japanese restaurants, and he knows the value of atmosphere. The decor here reportedly topped $6 million, with "authentic" nicotine stains on the ceiling, lipstick-red banquettes, silvered mirrors, a bread bakery display (the bread is a high spot in general), floors that look as if they'd been tangoed on, and conservatory windows on the garden-room roof. Predictably, it became a local foodie rave, but even with a little settling in time, it's a very hot spot. Business diners, be warned: This is as loud as a real French market.

THE PAYOFF Foie gras "parfait" layered with chicken liver or a more rustic boar-and-venison pâté; mushroom tart in fine pastry; steak *frites* (hanger steak here, basted with butter) or mussels and fries; skate; escargots; tartare; beef bourguignon; lamb shank with couscous; and duck confit, with the richness cut by kumquats and kale. In addition to the more-usual shellfish appetizer, such as oysters and lobster halves, look for live scallops and king crab legs, and beef tongue carpaccio. The brunch is almost as lengthy (side of black sausage?). Le Diplomate also offers its version of a blue plate special, only a little fancier: lobster risotto, cassoulet, bouillabaisse, and even prime rib on Saturday.

IF YOU LIKE THIS **Bistro d'Oc,** an underrated, hospitable, and relatively affordable bistro in Penn Quarter, is just across the street from Ford's Theatre (and is great for pre- or postshow dining.) Though not nearly so elaborate, **Bistro Cacao** on Capitol Hill is within eyeshot of Union Station and has outdoor seating; it's a favorite of Hill staffers and a few bosses as well.

CAPITOL HILL

OVER THE DECADES, Capitol Hill has endured waves of restaurant revival and retreat. (There was a time when its most "cosmopolitan" spot was the Thai-Roma restaurant. Seriously.) And, depending on your style of nostalgia, the latest round of gentrification has replaced some of the city's best dive bars and pubs with "retro" or faux diners.

The Hill's most truly venerable restaurant is the long-running political annex **Monocle** ("Senate side" of the Capitol, as the website puts it), whose classic mid-Atlantic steak and seafood menu remains as dignified as its reputation for discretion. Among other popular power stops are **Charlie Palmer Steak,** the spare but elegant **Bistro Bis** (page 278), and the Louisiana lovers' **Johnny's Half Shell** (page 279), sort of the Monocle bar for younger pols and aides. Spike Mendelsohn, who placed fifth on *Top Chef*, has a trio of hot spots in the 300 block of Pennsylvania Avenue Southeast that range from the inexpensive retro burger-and-shake shop **Good Stuff Eatery** (page 278) to **We, the Pizza** next door to his ode to the classic French bistro **Béarnaise** (page 278). The more relaxed bistro **Montmartre** (page 280) also tosses pizza at its next-door hideaway **Seventh Hill.**

When it comes to breakfast, three names rise to the top, starting with the budget-friendly **Bayou Bakery** from New Orleans–born chef David Guas, who starts weekdays with beignets, oatmeal, and biscuit sandwiches, and warms into muffulettas, gumbos, étouffée, deviled eggs, and so on. (Don't miss the "eat dat" nightly dinner special.) **Market Brunch** inside the Eastern Market spins out pancakes, shrimp and grits, and so on, but weekends are packed. And the diner-revival **Ted's Bulletin** takes the old joke about Saturday night vs. Sunday morning— that is, alcohol-laced milk shakes and "burritos of shame"—to a whole new level.

Other popular spots include the Florentine **Acqua al 2** (from a D.C.-bred soccer star who became chef at the original); **Sonoma,** with 45 wines by the glass or even half glass; and the new neo-rustic charcuterie gastropub **Barrel,** with the motto: "Bourbon. With Balls."

One of the more recent dining and nightlife centers of Capitol Hill is known as Barracks Row, a stretch of Eighth Street Southeast between Pennsylvania Avenue and the Washington Navy Yard.

Among its many choices are **Ambar** (page 277) (Serbian and Croatian fare—something like Turkish via Hungary), **Belga Café** (mussels plus classic Belgian), **Café 8** (*pide*, a sort of Turkish pizza), the farm-to-table **Garrison** (from a chef who was planting his own herbs a decade ago), and the no-reservations foodie swoon **Rose's Luxury.** There is also **Cava Mezze,** another branch of Ted's Bulletin; **Matchbox; Medium Rare** (steak *frites*); **Senart's Oyster Bar and Grill** (two fireplaces); plus sushi, Tex-Mex, Cuban, Italian, and Thai—and an equally lengthy list of carryout options.

The area between the Washington Navy Yard and Nats Park is also an up-and-coming area, variously called Capitol Riverfront, The Yards, Yards Park, or Navy Yard because of its proximity to that Metro station. The neighborhood was home to one of Washington's earlier breweries, and appropriately it now houses two brewpubs: the chain **Gordon Biersch** and the home-grown **Bluejacket.** Among its most popular eateries are **Osteria Morini;** a branch of **Bonchon,** a very popular Korean-based fried chicken spot; one of **Nando's Peri-Peri,** an equally spicy Afro-Portuguese chain; one of Danny Meyer's hot **Shake Shacks;** the mostly Italian **Scarlet Oak;** and the Mexican **Agua 301.**

And a huge new development under construction on the southwest end of Capitol Hill, near the old Maine Avenue waterfront (itself a fun place for an informal meal), is scheduled to house not only hotels and several music venues but also a menu of new restaurants, including a Filipino place from Old Town Alexandria mavens Cathal and Meshelle Armstrong.

Ambar ★★★ BALKAN INEXPENSIVE

523 8th St. SE; ☎ 202-813-3039; **ambarrestaurant.com**   Capitol Hill

Reservations Recommended. **Metro** Eastern Market. **Wine selection** Good. **Disabled access** Good. **Open** *Brunch:* Saturday–Sunday, 10 a.m.–3:30 p.m. *Lunch:* Monday–Friday, 11 a.m.–2 p.m. *Dinner:* Sunday–Thursday, 4–10 p.m.; Friday–Saturday, 4–11 p.m.

THE PREMISE This Serbian tapas joint serves dishes ranging from stuffed cabbage to Weiner schnitzel. (The restaurant describes itself as the meeting of southeastern Europe and Southeast D.C.) The room is long and sleek, with wood accents that echo the name: *Ambar* are barnlike corncribs of Serbia.

THE PAYOFF The wide-ranging menu echoes the many countries that meet in middle Europe, including Greece, Turkey, Hungary, Austria, and a touch of France: asparagus topped with a quail egg, kebabs, flatbreads, grilled calamari, hummus, mussels, grilled duck breast, veal stew, veal and vegetable soup, burgers, Parmesan-crusted sirloin, and even Brussels sprouts with bacon. (Dishes may be small, but they are meticulously presented.) The all-you-can-eat $49 dinner option is a round-the-world voyage if you're really hungry.

IF YOU LIKE THIS There are some familial resemblances in the Russian-Uzbek menu at **Rus Uz** (**rus-uzcuisine.com**) in Ballston.

Béarnaise ★★★ FRENCH MODERATE

315 Pennsylvania Ave. NW; ☎ 202-450-4800; **bearnaiserestaurant.com**
Capitol Hill

Reservations Recommended. **Metro** Capitol South. **Wine selection** Brief. **Disabled access** Good. **Open** Tuesday–Friday, 11 a.m.–10 p.m.; Saturday, 10 a.m.–3 p.m. and 5:30–11 p.m.; Sunday, 10 a.m.–3 p.m.

THE PREMISE Chef-owner and former *Top Chef* and *Iron Chef America* contestant Spike Mendelsohn has worked his way through plenty of famous kitchen lines in the "big" dining cites, but he was raised in Montreal, and this family-style and family-run steak-*frites* bistro is an homage to his hometown. It definitely has the bistro look: black-and-white tile, "weathered" silver mirrors, and latticework windows.

THE PAYOFF It's technically "moderate, but with benefits." Order the filet or rib eye, or choose the grass-fed 8-ounce flatiron for $28 and you'll also get all-you-can-eat fries, as well as salad or soup. (There is actually a choice of sauces in addition to the eponymous béarnaise, but if you are a serious béarnaise freak, order the Brussels sprouts.) The other items are classics: escargots, onion soup, smoked trout, steak tartare, pâté, pork chop, mussels (and *frites*), duck confit (and *frites*), and, well, *frites*.

IF YOU LIKE THIS Medium Rare—one location a Metro stop away at Eastern Market, the other at the Cleveland Park Metro—offers (only) a fixed price dinner of bread and pâté, salad, and steak *frites* for $19.75.

Bistro Bis ★★★½ FRENCH EXPENSIVE

15 E St. NW (in the Hotel George); ☎ 202-661-2700; **bistrobis.com**
Capitol Hill

Reservations Recommended. **Metro** Union Station. **Wine selection** Very good. **Disabled access** Good. **Open** *Brunch:* Saturday–Sunday, 11:30 a.m.–2:30 p.m. *Breakfast:* Daily, 7–10 a.m. *Lunch:* Monday–Friday, 11:30 a.m.–2:30 p.m. *Dinner:* Daily, 5:30–10:30 p.m.

THE PREMISE The name sounds like affectionate shorthand for bistro, but it also means "encore"; this was the second restaurant from Sallie and Jeff Buben of the new-Southern favorite Vidalia. It's a long sleek space divided into a series of semidetached blond wood and etched-glass dining "suites," and somehow, it makes you feel that your companions may be billing you by the hour (which, considering the number of pols and pollsters around, they might be).

THE PAYOFF This is semiclassical but freshly toned French fare: quenelles not of pike but of scallops mousse and lobster; foie gras with hazelnuts and apples; bouillabaisse; sweetbreads with trumpet mushrooms and veal tongue; and a rack of lamb that dips across the Mediterranean to North Africa to pick up *merguez*, artichokes, olives, sun-dried tomatoes, and bulgur. Brunch here is not "traditional" but happily more of the same.

Good Stuff Eatery ★★★ AMERICAN DINER INEXPENSIVE

303 Pennsylvania Ave. NW; ☎ 202-543-8222; **goodstuffeatery.com**
Capitol Hill
3291 M St. NW; ☎ 202-337-4663 Georgetown
2110 Crystal Dr., Crystal City; ☎ 703-415-4663 Virginia suburbs

Reservations Recommended. **Metro** Capitol South or Eastern Market (Capitol Hill); Foggy Bottom–GWU (20-minute walk; Georgetown); Crystal City. **Wine selection** Very good. **Disabled access** Good. **Open** *Capitol Hill:* Monday–Saturday, 11 a.m.– 10 p.m. *Georgetown:* Monday–Saturday, 11 a.m.–10 p.m.; Sunday, 11:30 a.m.–9 p.m. *Crystal City:* Monday–Saturday, 11 a.m.–11 p.m.; Sunday, 11:30 a.m.–9 p.m.

THE PREMISE This was the first, and most modest, kitchen from *Top Chef* Spike Mendelsohn and his family; though curiously, having decided to restore to the nation's capital the heartland hamburger, hand-cut fries (from family farm–grown potatoes), and 30 or so milk shakes from fresh-daily custard, he has since spread the love as far as Saudi Arabia.

THE PAYOFF This is a manageable menu, where the burgers come topped with various cheeses, eggs, mushrooms, bacon, tomatoes, and so on. The burgers may be old-fashioned, but that old mustard-and-ketchup condiment bar now offers sriracha, mango, Old Bay, and chipotle mayo. There are a few tributes: the applewood bacon, Roquefort, horseradish, and onion jam version is called the Prez Obama, and the free-range turkey burger with Swiss cheese and herbs on whole wheat honors Michelle. (No doubt the chef has been planning recipes that Trump the competition.) There is also a cheese-stuffed portobello version; an Asian-flavored one with pickled daikon and Thai basil; and bunless versions wrapped in lettuce. And it's really a bargain: Even the double is only $8.50.

IF YOU LIKE THIS The **Ted's Bulletin** group is somewhat similar in concept (burgers and sandwiches of your dreams) but way more over the top (peanut butter, spinach, and herbed cheese spread), with more options (Reubens and Rachels or short ribs and white cheddar on Texas toast) and boozy milk shakes. It's also heftier and somewhat more expensive.

Johnny's Half Shell ★★★ SEAFOOD EXPENSIVE

400 N. Capitol St.; ☎ 202-737-0400; **johnnyshalfshell.net** Capitol Hill

Reservations Accepted. **Metro** Union Station. **Wine selection** Good. **Disabled access** Not accessible. **Open** *Lunch:* Monday–Friday, 11:30 a.m.–2:30 p.m. *Dinner:* Monday–Friday, 5–10 p.m.; Saturday (April–October), 5–9 p.m. May be closed Saturday, November–March; call ahead for hours.

THE PREMISE Ann Cashion has led Washington diners from Spain (Jaleo) to the Deep South (the original Cashion's Eat Place), and these days she and co-owner John Fulchino tip the hat to New Orleans's retro oyster bars (the ones in the business district but with Bourbon Street prices). Cocktails are definitely Bourbon Street in size, and if you wonder why it was dubbed Death in the Afternoon, order one. It's no surprise that its happy hour is a Capitol Hill hot spot.

THE PAYOFF Two words: Trotter tots. Yes, Johnny's makes pork croquettes with bread-and-butter pickles, and it's shorthand for the whole menu. For every richer dish (chicken étouffée, crab imperial), there's a more moderate version: The crispy whole flounder is Thai-inspired with a lime dipping sauce, eggplant, and sesame-rice-wine vinegar sauce. You can go with the fried oyster po'boys (on bread flown in from New Orleans) or grilled squid over wilted arugula or charbroiled oysters; a dark and dirty gumbo; and barbecued shrimp over cheese grits. In good weather, there is outdoor seating and live jazz on Friday and Saturday nights.

Montmartre ★★½ FRENCH MODERATE

327 7th St. SE; ☎ 202-544-1244; **montmartredc.com**   Capitol Hill

Reservations Recommended. **Metro** Eastern Market. **Wine selection** Good. **Disabled access** Fair. **Open** *Brunch:* Saturday–Sunday, 10:30 a.m.–3 p.m. *Lunch:* Tuesday–Friday, 11:30 a.m.–2:30 p.m. *Dinner:* Tuesday–Thursday, 5:30–10 p.m.; Friday–Saturday, 5:30–10:30 p.m.; Sunday, 5:30–9 p.m.

THE PREMISE This is the sort of place that makes *cozy* seem like part of the word *café:* a single sunny-sponged room of about 50 seats with a tiny bar at the back, lively views of the sidewalk to the front and the kitchen to the rear, classic French posters, and elbow-to-elbow tables.

THE PAYOFF The menu sounds familiar but with a few tweaks: beef bourguignon using cheeks; braised rabbit saucing linguine with olives and shiitakes; duck confit salad; caramelized scallops with sweet potato puree and cauliflower; and shrimp with goat cheese risotto. Forget the carrots: The rack of lamb is brightly accompanied by potato gratin, turnips, *piquillo* peppers, cauliflower, and Tuscan kale. Montmartre has joined in on the blue plate–special trend, offering cassoulet, coq au vin, and so on.

IF YOU LIKE THIS See the profile of **Béarnaise** on page 278. The owners of Montmartre have spun off a pizza place, **Seventh Hill Pizza,** out of the side door, so to speak.

ATLAS DISTRICT

WHILE THE H STREET NORTHEAST NEIGHBORHOOD is still more of a music-and-nightlife playground, it has recently blossomed with an increasing number of good and quite varied ethnic options. One of the first on the street was **Granville Moore's,** a Belgian-inflected gastropub whose mussels and *frites* helped launch a local craze (and helped owner-chef Teddy Folkman beat Bobby Flay in a throw down). It also has a brunch hefty enough to erase a nightlife crawl. **Toki Underground** (page 281), an energy-monster ramen dive, is hugely popular, especially with said nightlife types, and is largely responsible for the ramen craze in Washington; these days, its larger and broader-minded (Cambodian to Taiwanese) sibling, **Maketto,** is equally popular, if not quite so inexpensive.

Taylor Gourmet was the creation of two homesick Philly boys, offering hoagies and Italian bites on same-day bread and delis, and it now has several area locations. (See the list of "Best Local Chains" on page 304.) **Liberty Tree** pays homage to New England with the likes of lobster mac and cheese, clam chowder, lobster rolls, and brick-oven pizza, as well as heartier dishes. **Ethiopic** (page 281), at the west end of the stretch at Fourth Street Northwest, is one of the best Ethiopian kitchens in the city; **Sidamo Coffee and Tea** a few doors down offers the traditional Ethiopian coffee service every Sunday at 2 p.m. **Dangerously Delicious Pies** serves up baked-fresh classic sweets, quiches, and deep-dish savory pies stuffed with everything from tofu curry to beer brats to steak and mushrooms. **&Pizza** is a booming local chain.

Sticky Rice features pan-Asian bites and rice or noodle bowls, with options for vegan and gluten-free noodles, but the swank **Hikari Sushi and Sake Bar** has a roof deck, a more extensive menu (mostly Japanese but with a bit of Korean, Thai, and Vietnamese as well), and an even more impressive sake list.

Ethiopic ★★★ ETHIOPIAN INEXPENSIVE

401 H St. NE; ☎ 202-675-2066; **ethiopicrestaurant.com** Atlas District

Reservations Suggested. **Metro** Not Metro accessible. **Wine selection** Good. **Disabled access** Good. **Open** Tuesday–Thursday, 5–10 p.m.; Friday–Sunday, noon–10 p.m.

THE PREMISE There are a lot of similar restaurants in this area, but perhaps none as photo-friendly, thanks in part to a facade face-lift that turned it into an almost Capitol Hill look-alike, with exposed brick, Federal windows, and calligraphy-covered columns. The ingredients are clearly high quality. Some sidewalk seating is available.

THE PAYOFF The menu will be generally familiar to most fans of Ethiopian fare, but this one has attitude—that is, the kind of heat Ethiopians themselves go for. *Doro wat,* the chicken leg/hard-boiled egg dish that is the unofficial national dish, can be had mild or spicy; the *tibs* (boneless leg of lamb) is marinated until tender; and there is also a curried lamb, not just a sauced one, and chickpeas done as a spicy dumpling. The crunchy fried croaker is a cheap ($2!) treat, and there are plenty of veggie/vegan options. The *injera* is authentically teff-based.

Toki Underground ★★½
JAPANESE/CHINESE INEXPENSIVE

1234 H St. NE; ☎ 202-388-3086; **tokiunderground.com** Atlas District

Reservations Not accepted. **Metro** Union Station (15-minute walk). **Wine selection** See "The Payoff" below. **Disabled access** Not accessible. **Open** *Lunch:* Monday–Saturday, 11:30 a.m.–2:30 p.m. *Dinner:* Monday–Wednesday, 5–10 p.m.; Thursday, 5–11 p.m.; Friday–Saturday, 5 p.m.–midnight.

THE PREMISE It might not have been the first place to concentrate on ramen, but it certainly struck the biggest hipster nerve: The "decor" consists of wind-up Taiwanese action figures, Japanese anime, paper lanterns in faux trees, graffiti-like swirls of paint, an antique pinball machine, and skateboards in all directions. Because it's all walk-up traffic (in both senses—it's on the second floor) and only seats about two dozen (on stools), the line starts at 5, and the wait can be substantial. Erratically, it uses the Little Serow model and gives you a time you might be seated and takes your cell phone number.

THE PAYOFF It's a short menu, mostly dumplings (five kinds, fried, panfried, or steamed) and bowls of ramen, along with a few specials (Korean-flavored barbecue) and pumped-up American desserts, such as snickerdoodles with pepper flakes and chocolate-chip cookies with red miso icing. (The chef was born in Taipei but raised in Tokyo and then nearby Woodbridge, Virginia; he teaches the odd Cambodian cooking class.) Except for the vegetarian version, the ramen recipes all start with a 24-hour-simmered porky broth. Toki Underground has a good sake list, interesting Asian beers, and cocktails.

IF YOU LIKE THIS The chef has recently opened a much larger outpost nearby called **Maketto.**

DUPONT CIRCLE AND FOGGY BOTTOM

IN DUPONT CIRCLE, consistently coming in with all stars flying is **Komi** (page 284), Johnny Monis's fixed price Greek feast, but equally striking is his take-no-prisoners Northern Thai **Little Serow** (page 285)—also tasting-menu only. Elsewhere in the neighborhood are **Restaurant Nora,** whose chef Nora Poullion was organic and sustainable before the terms were being bandied about; the revived **Iron Gate** (page 283); the romantic **Tabard Inn** (page 288), with patios and fireplaces; the long-running and still impressive **Obelisk** (page 286); and the special-occasion **Sushi Taro** (page 287). **Pizza Paradiso,** one of the first "gourmet" pizzerias in town, was cofounded by Obelisk chef Peter Pastan; **Annie's Paramount Steak House** (the family type) has been a gay refuge for many years but makes no distinctions.

On the family-friendly side are two sort of ethnic sammie shops: the New York–style **DGS** delicatessen and the Philly-homesick **Bub and Pop's.** Also good for families are **Firefly,** which is technically moderately priced but can be done cheaper, and it's exceedingly child-friendly, and **Hank's Oyster Bar** (page 283), also moderate, but the bar snacks are a bargain. **Ankara** does its happy hour on the patio (when possible), but its *pide* (Turkish pizza), kebabs, and meze are affordable at all hours.

Headed west from Dupont Circle through Midtown toward Georgetown are the **Palm, Ris, WestEnd Bistro, Blue Duck Tavern, Marcel's** (page 286), and **Vidalia,** where bar bites are the bargain way to go South.

South of this area and west of the White House is Foggy Bottom, which is not a major restaurant area in itself, but several museums and monuments in the neighborhood draw visitors there—and because it is executive branch/commission central, this is a hot spot for after-5 specials and bar dining. Top picks include the classic Spanish **Taberna del Alabardero,** which has a small bar with tapas specials and first-class Ibérico ham; **Kaz Sushi Bistro** (page 284); **Del Campo,** a highly rated and very pricey South American chophouse but with bar food you can easily afford; and **Founding Farmers,** featuring such hearty heartland fare that you can make do with small dishes (and a breakfast hefty enough to get you through that waiting line at the Washington Monument). During the day, look to the retro Americana burger-to-pizza **Tonic; District Commons** for flatbreads (and pretzel bread), mussels, soups, and small or big salads; Andrés's eat-your-veggies **Beefsteak;** and **Burger Tap & Shake,** which is just what it sounds like.

Hank's Oyster Bar ★★½
SEAFOOD   INEXPENSIVE/MODERATE

1624 Q St. NW; ☎ 202-462-4265; **hanksdc.com**   Dupont Circle
633 Pennsylvania Ave., SE; ☎ 202-733-1971   Capitol Hill
1026 King St., Old Town Alexandria; ☎ 703-739-4265   Virginia suburbs

Reservations Not accepted. **Metro** Dupont Circle; Eastern Market or Capitol Hill South; King Street (Old Town Alexandria). **Wine selection** Good. **Disabled access** Good. **Open** *Dupont Circle:* Monday–Tuesday, 11:30 a.m.–1 a.m.; Wednesday–Friday, 11:30 a.m.–2 a.m.; Saturday, 11 a.m.–midnight; Sunday, 11 a.m.–11 p.m. *Capitol Hill:* Monday–Wednesday, 11:30 a.m.–11 p.m.; Thursday–Friday, 11:30 a.m.–midnight; Saturday, 11 a.m.–midnight; Sunday, 11 a.m.–11 p.m. *Old Town Alexandria:* Monday–Friday, 11:30 a.m.–midnight; Saturday–Sunday, 11 .am.–midnight.

THE PREMISE Jamie Leeds, once a Manhattan import as an upscale new American chef, has turned to her roots (Hank was her father) with a series of New England–style fish houses (she calls it urban beach food). Though the menus are similar, each has its own twist and decor, but all with a cool pun on fish warehouse chic. At the Capitol Hill branch, she has hooked into the signature cocktail bar-within-a-bar trend (with a nice local beer and wine selection). Like Jeff and Barbara Black, Leeds has partnered with a prime Virginia oyster farm for her own brand, and she uses the empty shells to restore the beds.

THE PAYOFF Even with the influx of carpetbagger lobster rolls, Hank's are deservedly popular. The other staples include crab cakes, fried Ipswich clams, popcorn shrimp, and calamari. Daily specials generally include grilled seafood, lobster or shrimp and grits, and plenty of raw, steamed, or grilled seafood (Leeds recently lost nearly 150 pounds). Leeds's other signature is a "meat and two," a blue plate daily special that ranges from molasses-braised short ribs to oven-roasted or fried chicken to grilled duck breast or chops. Leeds recently opened a second restaurant in Old Town, an old-style Italian spot called **Hank's Pasta Bar,** as well as a playful small-bites/cocktail bar in Petworth called **The Twisted Horn.**

IF YOU LIKE THIS **Johnny's Half Shell** is a little richer (in sauce and price); see page 279.

Iron Gate ★★★½
MODERN AMERICAN/STEAK   MODERATE

1734 N St. NW; ☎ 202-524-5202; **irongaterestaurantdc.com** Dupont Circle

Reservations Recommended. **Metro** Farragut North or Dupont Circle. **Wine selection** Good. **Disabled access** Very good. **Open** *Brunch:* Saturday, 11–2:30 p.m. *Lunch:* Tuesday–Friday, 11:30 a.m.–2:30 p.m. *Dinner:* Monday–Thursday, 5:30–10 p.m.; Friday–Saturday, 5:30–11 p.m.; Sunday, 5:30–9 p.m.

THE PREMISE This has been among the city's most picturesque spots for years—built from an old stable, half hidden down a lantern-lit alley, and with some of the most alluring fireplaces in town. After a period of decline, it has reopened, with a little updating and with rising-star chef Tony Chittum, as a modern eclectic tavern with southern Italian and Greek flavors, including

Sardinian and Sicilian (he's a native of the Eastern Shore, but his wife is Greek). Long a proponent of local sourcing, Chittum is turning regional seafood and game on rotisseries and in a wood-burning grill and oven. The dining room has only fixed price menus—four courses for $60, six for $80, and a chef's choice for $110; the à la carte menu is served in the bar and on the long-beloved patio (now year-round). Neither are huge spaces, so walk-ins at crush hour could be tough.

THE PAYOFF Try "corned" octopus; phyllo pie with Angus beef, feta, and grape leaves (sort of risotto pot pie); dill *gemelli* with braised rabbit and mustard sauce; and local artisan charcuterie. Don't miss the "spit-roasted whole animal" du jour (meant for at least two), which might be poultry or game. The Iron Gate is one of the few restaurants that boasts a few ghosts.

IF YOU LIKE THIS See the profiles of **Kapnos** (page 274) and **Komi** (page 284).

Kaz Sushi Bistro ★★★½
JAPANESE   MODERATE/EXPENSIVE

1915 I St. NW; ☎ 202-530-5500; **kazsushibistro.com**   Foggy Bottom

Reservations Recommended. **Metro** Farragut West or Farragut North. **Wine selection** Fair. **Disabled access** Not accessible. **Open** *Lunch:* Monday–Friday, 11:30 a.m.–2 p.m.; *Dinner:* Monday–Saturday, 5:30–10 p.m.

THE PREMISE Chef-owner Kaz Okochi earned many of his fans while working at Sushiko (page 296), where he originated many of what he calls his original small dishes, both cold and hot. The quality of the more traditional sushi is first-rate, of course, but you can get good sushi in a number of places; instead, order *omakase,* the chef's choice ($80–$120), or a plate-at-a-time tasting menu. Although the dining room is calm and attractive, with a mini-fountain wall in front and abstract *maguro*-colored wallpaper, it's more fun to sit at the smallish sushi bar in the rear.

THE PAYOFF Though he does not advertise his hot dishes as *izakawa* fare, Kaz (who prefers to go by his first name) offers a variety of meat and veggie dishes that go beyond the usual sushi bar fare: sake-poached scallops; lobster salad; glazed and grilled baby octopus; spicy broiled green mussels; foie gras infused with plum wine; Japanese-style duck confit in miso; or torched salmon. When fugu, the famous blowfish, is in season, Kaz (one of the few sushi chefs in Washington certified to handle the potentially lethal fish, although it now comes pre-butchered from Japan) makes traditional multicourse fugu meals (about $150). Kaz also offers *okonomiyaki,* a Japanese comfort food staple, but not that common here.

IF YOU LIKE THIS Kaz is a partner in Mid City's rooftop hot spot **Masa 14** with (mostly) Latin specialist Richard Sandoval, which turns out a whole different range of fusion small plates.

Komi ★★★★   MODERN AMERICAN   VERY EXPENSIVE

1509 17th St. NW; ☎ 202-332-9200; **komirestaurant.com**   Dupont Circle

Reservations Strongly recommended (see "The Premise"). **Metro** Dupont Circle or U Street–African American Civil War Memorial–Cardozo. **Wine selection** Good. **Disabled access** Not accessible. **Open** *Dinner:* Tuesday–Saturday, 5:30–until.

THE PREMISE Johnny Monis, a local boy and still brushing 30, is indisputably one of Washington's best and most consistent chefs; he won the James Beard Award for best Mid-Atlantic chef in 2013. As the website points out, this is a "leisurely" meal: While you're likely to get your first little treat (roasted dates stuffed with mascarpone and dotted with sea salt are now a signature) the moment you're seated, the pace of the overall dinner is relaxed. The menu has a Mediterranean accent—Komi is a small beach town near Monis's Greek grandparents' home—and with only a dozen tables and candlelight decor, this town house really feels almost like a family gathering. (No table holds more than four, so reservations are tight, and they can only be made by telephone starting at noon one month in advance, at most.) In the same family spirit, be prepared to eat at least part of your meal by hand—and we don't mean the homemade lollipops that come with the bill. Komi serves beer and wine only.

THE PAYOFF This is not for control freaks: There is no printed menu, only the multicourse (a dozen or more) chef's-choice dinner for $150. It starts with a variety of meze that sets the leisurely tone, moves generally from seafood to meat, and most often culminates in roasted goat to be hand-rolled into pita with *tzatziki*. But what happens along the way is a fine and eclectic mystery: foie gras *torchon*; pasta with squash, black truffles, and lamb's tongue; rabbit pâté bruschetta; roast suckling pig; a pork chop with artichokes; sea bass; crispy pork belly; prosciutto-wrapped octopus; house-made tagliatelle with sea urchin; blood sausage–stuffed ravioli; salmon belly tartare; braised baby octopus; amberjack in a smoked turbot aspic; pork belly souvlaki with pickled cucumber; or goat liver ragù.

IF YOU LIKE THIS Minibar (profiled on page 267) is the only competition in town for super-foodies.

Little Serow ★★★★½ THAI EXPENSIVE

1511 17th St. NW; no phone; **littleserow.com**   Dupont Circle

Reservations Not accepted. **Metro** Dupont Circle. **Wine selection** Good. **Disabled access** Not accessible. **Open** *Dinner:* Tuesday–Thursday, 5:30–10 p.m.; Friday–Saturday, 5:30–10:30 p.m.

THE PREMISE This quirky restaurant may be a destination for only the most dedicated foodies because there are no reservations—there isn't even a telephone—and it has a market-driven menu that changes weekly, no patron changes allowed. (*Serow* rhymes with "arrow" and refers to a pronghorn goat native to Southeast Asia.) As at Komi (profiled above) next door, chef-owner Johnny Monis offers only a prix fixe menu ($49 for seven courses) of authentically spicy northern Thai food, adjusted weekly, and served family style in a small room with 28 tall barlike stools. The doors open at 5:30, so get in line early (in good weather, perhaps an hour), and if you don't get in the first time, the hostess will sign you up for a table; you'll get a text. If you can't take the heat, stay out of this kitchen (though it seems to be letting up a little); happily, the supply of sticky rice (which is traditionally used as a utensil, though you get spoons and forks here) is unending. The beverage pairings are fascinating—a mix of beers, wines, and vermouths.

THE PAYOFF Typical ingredients include eggplant, snakehead (yup, Frankenfish), mackerel, catfish, shrimp, pork rinds used as scoops for a funky dip of chicken livers, Thai whiskey-marinated pork ribs, and spicy tofu. Flavorings include mint, rice powder, peanuts, chilies, shrimp paste and dried shrimp, dried squid, tamarind paste, Thai whiskey, Kaffir lime, and galangal and ginger. While there are vegetarian dishes, the menu points out that there may be meat, shellfish, and nuts as ingredients that are not listed, so it may not be ideal for all diners.

IF YOU LIKE THIS Though it's no larger, and also serves only chef's-choice menus ($30–$40), **Thai X-ing** in Mid City offers home-style Thai with vegetarian, fish, or even vegan variations if the entire table agrees—and it takes reservations ($10 surcharge for five or more).

Marcel's ★★★★
FRENCH-BELGIAN EXPENSIVE/VERY EXPENSIVE

2401 Pennsylvania Ave. NW; ☎ 202-296-1166; **marcelsdc.com**
  Foggy Bottom

Reservations Highly recommended. **Metro** Foggy Bottom–GWU. **Wine selection** Very good. **Disabled access** Very good. **Open** *Dinner:* Sunday, 5–9:30 p.m.; Monday–Thursday, 5–10 p.m.; Friday–Saturday, 5–11 p.m.

THE PREMISE This cool ultra-lounge-look retreat is a showplace for unapologetically classic French fare with a Belgian accent. The long marble bar is a showpiece, and the partially exposed (and elevated) kitchen is not so intrusive as elsewhere. Chef-owner Robert Wiedmaier gets bigger and more Belgian all the time, turning out confits, root vegetables (including the various endives, of course), artichokes, and flavorful but not heavy sausages. But there is an element of playfulness—matching pan-seared salmon with black-eyed peas and bacon. Wiedmaier now has several restaurants, but this was the first and remains the best. Another draw is the three-course pretheater menu for $70. You can have two courses early, take the restaurant's complimentary limo to the Kennedy Center for a show, and then return in the limo for dessert. Prix fixe menus range from $95 for four courses to $155 for seven, but the entire table does not have to participate. And no worries—all dishes can be ordered à la carte as well.

THE PAYOFF The boudin *blanc* is a signature dish and not to be missed, and so are game dishes in season, such as a sort of venison Wellington with loin and foie gras wrapped in phyllo with black trumpet mushrooms; pheasant and foie gras tortellini with chanterelles; or roulade of rabbit stuffed with sausage over caramelized cabbage. Seafood fans look for the likes of pesto-marinated sardines bruschetta; squid-ink tagliatelle with escargots and crispy sweetbreads; cold-smoked cod with blood orange and paprika croutons; and seared scallops with butternut squash and applewood bacon hash.

IF YOU LIKE THIS In Old Town Alexandria's Lorien Hotel, Wiedmaier's **Brabo** has a menu of similar swagger.

Obelisk ★★★½ ITALIAN VERY EXPENSIVE

2029 P St. NW; ☎ 202-872-1180; **obeliskdc.com** Dupont Circle

Reservations Required. **Metro** Dupont Circle or Farragut North. **Wine selection** Good. **Disabled access** Not accessible. **Open** *Dinner:* Tuesday–Saturday, 6–10 p.m.

THE PREMISE This cozy town house dining room is elegant and good-humored, and it feels like a real home's dining room; the 30 or so customers, staff, and accoutrements—not only the room's floral centerpiece and silver chest but also the displays of grappa and breadsticks—are intimate but relaxed. Chef Peter Pastan long ago—almost 30 years—figured out the cure for overlong, overrich menus: He offers only a five-course fixed price menu ($75, $85 on weekends), with three, perhaps four choices per course. Vegetarians, but not strict vegans, can be accommodated.

THE PAYOFF Among typical dishes are fritto misto; caramel-soft onion and cheese tart; crostini; quail terrine; fresh *burrata* (still one of the best in town); light pastas (squab-stuffed agnolotti with chanterelles or sheep's-milk cheese ricotta with green-tomato sauce); and Tuscan porterhouse or suckling pig carved tableside. Game birds and mixed grills are likely options, and Pastan is happily not in the habit of overcooking, either. After all that comes a fine bit of cheese. Pastan, cofounder of **Pizzeria Paradiso** and **2Amys,** knows the value of a really good bread dough—more than one, in fact, as witnessed first off by the astonishingly light breadsticks.

IF YOU LIKE THIS Though less "insider," **Siroc** in McPherson Square has a somewhat similar style in a slightly larger—and wheelchair-accessible—building.

Sushi Taro ★★★★ JAPANESE VERY EXPENSIVE

1503 17th St. NW; ☎ 202-462-8999; **sushitaro.com**   Dupont Circle

Reservations Strongly recommended. **Metro** Dupont Circle. **Wine selection** Good. **Disabled access** Not accessible. **Open** *Lunch:* Monday–Friday, 11:30 a.m.–2 p.m. *Dinner:* Monday–Saturday, 5:30–10 p.m.

THE PREMISE This lovely second-floor retreat spent decades as a dependable but traditional haven for Japanese businessmen and sushi lovers until owner Nobu Yamazaki (son of the founder and long a stalwart of classic sushi-making) went aggressively upmarket, staking out a series of fixed price *kaiseki* menus ranging up to $180, though the traditional version, which leans on cooked dishes, and the sushi *kaiseki,* which alternates between sushi and cooked dishes, are both $80. What would in most restaurants be the sushi bar here is called the *omakase* counter, meaning that if you sit there, you are also treated to a chef's-choice banquet of a handful of small plates followed by *sashimi* and sushi. You can only make reservations for the counter a month in advance and cancel five days before without a penalty. Note that no-shows will be charged $100.

THE PAYOFF This is not Japanese for the tentative; the quality is too high to be playing with your money. (At these prices, asking $5.50 for fresh wasabi seems like ungilding the lily; on the other hand, on some days if you order a tasting menu, you get a bottle of sake or bargain drinks.) Also, to those accustomed to oversize, Americanized sushi, these correctly bite-size pieces may seem small. Happy hour specials are available at the bar with discount sake, *maki* rolls, and appetizers. There are a few à la carte options at dinner, as well as at lunch (mostly posted on social media), but among specials worth the budget busting might be fugu; grilled fish and fresh bamboo with sake rice; Alaskan king crab; and wild prawns and winter melon with snapping turtle "jelly." It has not gone so far as to ban them, but Sushi Taro is straightforward about having limited space to accommodate small children.

Tabard Inn ★★½ MODERN AMERICAN MODERATE

1739 N St. NW; ☎ 202-331-8528; **tabardinn.com**   Dupont Circle

Reservations Strongly recommended. **Metro** Farragut North or Dupont Circle. **Wine selection** Good. **Disabled access** Not accessible. **Open** *Brunch:* Saturday–Sunday, 10:30 a.m.–2:30 p.m. *Breakfast:* Monday–Friday, 7–10 a.m.; Saturday–Sunday, 7–9 a.m. *Lunch:* Monday–Friday, 11:30 a.m.–2:30 p.m. *Dinner:* Sunday–Wednesday, 5:30–9:30 p.m.; Thursday–Saturday, 5:30–10 p.m.

THE PREMISE This almost theatrically Old English jumble of rooms has a courtyard at its heart (as all good English country inns should), a series of small dining rooms with surprisingly lighthearted decor (a garden-path mural up the stairs, for example), and a wood-lined library with couches and a fireplace, ideal for a winter afternoon, cocktail before dinner, or after-dinner cordial. The outdoor patio (first come, first seated) is a summer favorite; even the private dining room (for no more than 14) is a romantic standby.

THE PAYOFF To be honest, this kitchen is solid and a bit safe—duck breast, crab cake, pork chop, and mixed platter of house-cured charcuterie—but it's really the atmosphere that bumps this onto the list. There are nice vegetarian options here as well: black-bean burger, mushroom risotto, or corn-and-macadamia risotto; butternut ravioli; and so on. Weekend brunch is a local favorite, primarily because of the fresh-fired doughnuts.

IF YOU LIKE THIS The newly revamped **Iron Gate** (profiled on page 283) is another of the few in-town spots with a garden retreat.

GEORGETOWN

THE SPELLBINDING **Fiola Mare** (page 290) in Washington Harbour has river views as impressive as its food. **Sequoia,** which is sort of the other bookend along the harbor development, has similar views and is less expensive, but the food is less interesting. In between is **Farmers Fishers Bakers,** an offshoot of Founding Farmers in Foggy Bottom, which emphasizes seasonal and sustainable surf, turf, tacos, pizza, and a gigantic "farmers market brunch" on weekends.

unofficial **TIP**
Filomena has been every mama's child's Italian refuge for decades, with a home-style kitchen table to prove it; plus it has a window display nobody else can match—real Italian mamas hand-making the pasta every day.

With a canal and footpath view above the river, **Sea Catch** has a cool marble bar and raw bar, as well as outdoor seating in summer and fireplaces in winter. **Chez Billy Sud** is a calmly handsome Southern French bistro, while **Bistro Français** (page 289) has for decades served moderately priced old-style French dishes to other chefs well into the wee hours. The **Pizzeria Paradiso** in Georgetown has a *birreria*—a cellar full of brews. **Leopold's Kafe,** a sweets and savories pastry shop with European café benefits, opens at 8 a.m. daily.

Café Milano's Italian food is a little big on price but even bigger on famous face-watching. Every list of special-event romantic dining spots includes **1789,** a lovely and surprisingly quiet Federal town house with an intimate bar and fireplaces (but no wheelchair access). **Martin's Tavern,** where you can see the booth where then-Senator John F. Kennedy proposed to Jacqueline Bouvier, has been championing comfort food for more than 80 years and offers its substantial brunch every day. The **Clyde's** on M Street is the chain's original location and remains a family favorite. **Unum** (as in "e pluribus") is a small but deft seasonal American dinner spot with a fittingly small and fairly inexpensive menu. **Kintaro** is also small and limited, but from two veteran sushi chefs.

Up the Wisconsin Avenue hill toward Glover Park are the Turkish family fallback **Café Divan;** the classic French **Bistro Lepic** in its pretty two-story town house; **Heritage India,** with its spicy Southern Indian offshoot **Malgudi** downstairs; and a rather guilty but hilarious pleasure, the very old-style **Old Europe,** a moderately priced German restaurant whose spring asparagus festival—a pound at a time—is a local tradition.

Bistro Français ★★½ FRENCH MODERATE

3128 M St. NW; ☎ 202-338-3830; **bistrofrancaisdc.com**   Georgetown

Reservations Suggested. **Metro** Foggy Bottom–GWU. **Wine selection** House. **Disabled access** Good. **Open** Sunday–Thursday, 11 a.m.–3 a.m.; Friday–Saturday, 11 a.m.–4 a.m.

THE PREMISE This old reliable hasn't changed much since the word *bistro* was new to Washington: hanging pots, rotisserie spits, frankly well-used flatware, and clanking trays. Its famous late-night service (until 3 and 4 a.m. on weekends) makes it a recovery sanctuary, and the fact that many local chefs eat here after hours (the smoked salmon is still named for its fan Michel Richard) should be a good clue. In this trend-driven age, BF gets the Rodney Dangerfield treatment from the fashionable crowds, and sometimes feels a little bedraggled in response. But don't let that scare you off; after all, there are plenty of restaurants that *pay* to look worn. And are you eating the decor?

THE PAYOFF The steak and *frites* here is probably the standard against which most others should be measured, and tripes à la mode has become discouragingly hard to find (as, curiously, is squab). Many bistro classics here—especially Dover sole, coq au vin, and its signature spit-roasted chicken—will remind you why they are perennials. Think making steak tartare out of tenderloin is a waste of pallid flavor? Try the flank steak version here instead. But daily specials are often even better: duck confit, roast game birds, or lamb with artichokes.

IF YOU LIKE THIS The similarly nostalgic **La Chaumiere** down M Street isn't open as late, but it does have one romantic advantage: an amazing fireplace.

Fiola Mare ★★★★★
ITALIAN SEAFOOD   VERY EXPENSIVE

3050 K St. NW; ☎ 202-628-0065; **fiolamaredc.com**   Georgetown

Reservations Strongly recommended. **Metro** Foggy Bottom. **Wine selection** Very good. **Disabled access** Very good. **Open** *Brunch:* Saturday–Sunday, 11:30 a.m.–2 p.m. *Lunch:* Tuesday–Friday, 11:30 a.m.–2:30 p.m. *Dinner:* Monday–Thursday, 5–10:30 p.m.; Friday–Saturday, 5–11 p.m.; Sunday, 5–10:30 p.m.

THE PREMISE This is a $5-million blockbuster, both visually and culinarily (the huge walls of glass and nautical-natty stripes make it look like a yacht from some angles and a gigantic fish tank from others). The main bar has fabulous view of the river, but the speakeasy-trend Bar Piccolo is the hot spot. In fact, though it passes as a special occasion spot (and is seriously large), it's busy enough at all times to suggest advance planning.

THE PAYOFF Fabio Trabocchi's father is from the Marches region of Italy, along the coast east of Tuscany, and *Fiola* means something like "faithful one" or "sweetheart." Seafood runs from raw (crudo, tartare, carpaccio, *sashimi*) to seared skate wing to olive oil–poached sea bass with oyster foam and caviar to whole fish carved tableside to mixed grills. And it's not scant fare: If Ariel had ever eaten "Under the Sea"—lobster, branzino, sea urchin, langoustines, scallops, mussels, *plus* foie gras and maitakes—she would never have been able to rise to the surface. Fortunately, there is a Maria Menu with healthier options here as well. A few signature dishes from Fiola have been carried over, such as the lobster ravioli and Wagyu beef (not everyone's a pescatarian), but they are almost concessions to mixed parties.

IF YOU LIKE THIS A few blocks away is **Sea Catch,** a much more limited but also less-expensive canal-side spot with $1 oysters at happy hour and a fairly lengthy bar-bites menu.

WOODLEY PARK, CLEVELAND PARK, AND ADAMS MORGAN

THESE METRO NEIGHBORHOODS bookend the National Zoo, so we have grouped them together. (Cleveland Park is north and uphill from the zoo entrance and, despite the name, a little closer; however, the Woodley Park–National Zoo–Adams Morgan station is down the Connecticut Avenue hill, so if you have small children or company with walking difficulties, start high and end low.)

Cleveland Park was a major restaurant center a few years ago, and while some of its best spots are gone, there are still several of note, including **Ardeo + Bardeo, Indique** (page 291), and **Ripple** (page 292).

At the Woodley Park end are **New Heights,** an eclectic modern American restaurant with a history of allowing local top chefs of all types to exercise their imaginations (and a view down Connecticut Avenue); **Bar Civita,** a new and mostly home-made supper table from the founder of Liberty Tavern; and a branch of **Lebanese Taverna.**

According to the folks who run the subway system, Adams Morgan also belongs in this neighborhood, though it's a few minutes' stroll. Best bets there are **Mintwood Place** (page 292), alongside the beloved **Perry's** (known for its drag brunch and rooftop dining), their neighbor **Cashion's Eat Place** (page 291), and **Roofers Union,** the upscale pub-fare hangout from the chef of Ripple.

As you walk the Calvert Bridge between Woodley Park and Adams Morgan, you will pass a Washington institution very nearly as venerable as Ben's Chili Bowl: **Mama Ayesha's.** This Middle Eastern family spot was opened back in 1960 by a longtime embassy cook and chef and still serves traditional meze, kebabs, and stuffed veggies Mama's way.

Cashion's Eat Place ★★★ NEW SOUTHERN MODERATE

1819 Columbia Rd. NW; ☎ 202-797-1819; **cashionseatplace.com**
Adams Morgan

Reservations Recommended. **Metro** Woodley Park–Zoo/Adams Morgan or Columbia Heights. **Wine selection** Good. **Disabled access** Not accessible. **Open** *Brunch:* Saturday–Sunday, 10:30 a.m.–2:30 p.m. *Dinner:* Sunday and Tuesday, 5:30–10 p.m.; Wednesday–Saturday, 5:30–11 p.m. (Friday–Saturday, after-dark menu, 11 p.m.–1 a.m.)

THE PREMISE This deliberately low-key, upscale café—jazz and R&B over the sound system and a reclining nude over the bar—was one of this multiethnic neighborhood's first destination restaurants and locavore from day one. Its name refers to original chef Ann Cashion, a Mississippi native who helped found Jaleo but went home-style when she opened this Southern showplace that drew plenty of celebrity attention (think the Clintons). Chef-owner John Manolatos has added a touch of the Mediterranean (halibut brandade-stuffed squash blossoms) while using as much regional produce as possible. (Cashion herself is now at Johnny's Half Shell, profiled on page 279.)

THE PAYOFF The entrées are straightforward and robust (breast of game hen and leg confit, or a juicy pork burger), but for my money, it's worth throwing it all on the mini-banquette of appetizers: tagliatelle with lump crab, rabbit liver mousse, or wild mushroom-and-dandelion risotto. There's sidewalk seating in good weather.

IF YOU LIKE THIS Just a few doors away is **Mintwood Place** (profiled on page 292), and the whiskey-centric **Jack Rose Saloon** around the corner on 18th Street deals out even more heartland Southern biscuits, oysters, fried chicken livers, fried chicken skins, and rabbit with marrow-fat beans.

Indique ★★★ INDIAN MODERATE

3512-14 Connecticut Ave. NW; ☎ 202-244-6600; **indique.com** Cleveland Park

Reservations Recommended. **Metro** Cleveland Park. **Wine selection** Good. **Disabled access** Good. **Open** *Lunch:* Friday–Saturday, noon–3 p.m.; Sunday, 11 a.m.–3 p.m. *Dinner:* Monday–Thursday, 5:30–10:30 p.m.; Friday–Saturday, 5:30–11 p.m.; Sunday, 5:30–10:30 p.m.

THE PREMISE Indique is a visually stunning retreat, a whitewashed and jewel-toned room with an interior "courtyard" and a little balcony seating. This street snack–inspired but polished restaurant is brisk and accommodating. Even dining in the bar is relaxing. It also proves to hotheads that there's plenty of flavor without chili—and vice versa.

THE PAYOFF Enjoy anise-flavored crab cakes with coconut flakes; baby eggplant in a sesame, peanut, and cashew cream; okra with mango powder; shrimp and scallop masala; buttery chicken tikka *makhani*; a truly "not-for-the-fainthearted!" chicken with toasted Tellicherry peppercorns; veggie samosas; boneless lamb strips with brown spices; all sorts of fried and stuffed breads and crepes with chutneys; and various regional versions of what might be called Indian trail mix. This is a great place for vegetarians, with a good list of dishes with or without seafood. Here you can get the more familiar dishes, such as tandoori shrimp, lamb kebab, and mustard-kicky calamari, as small plates.

IF YOU LIKE THIS The same group also owns the great bargain **Bombay Bistro** near the Rockville court complex, which is more traditional than the fusion-ish **Spice Xing** nearby.

Mintwood Place ★★★½
FRENCH-AMERICAN EXPENSIVE

1813 Columbia Rd. NW; ☎ 202-234-6732; **mintwoodplace.com** Adams Morgan

Reservations Recommended. **Metro** Woodley Park–Zoo or Columbia Heights. **Wine selection** Good. **Disabled access** Not accessible. **Open** *Brunch:* Saturday–Sunday, 10:30 a.m.–2:30 p.m. *Dinner:* Tuesday–Thursday, 5:30–10 p.m.; Friday–Saturday, 5:30–10:30 p.m.; Sunday, 5:30–9 p.m.

THE PREMISE This stylish understated restaurant, with a mix of bistro furniture, tiled open kitchen, and industrial-rustic decor, has a sense of humor sharp enough to match its ingredients: The striking cocktail snack of crunchy escargot-studded hush puppies, served on a cast-iron grill plate, might be one of the best and brightest inventions in the city—and rescues those under-respected snails from the usual garlic tsunami.

THE PAYOFF The second-best small plate is the suckling pig croquettes on a bed of corn punctuated with mole; third is the chicken liver tartine. (This is a seasonal menu, of course.) The classics are respectful and assured (steak tartare, beef bourguignon, cassoulet, hanger steak and *frites,* Niçoise-style dorado with olives and fennel), but put your faith in the unexpected, such as calf's-heart confit with baby collard greens—also a starter. Italian pork roast is a Sunday-night special, but it's first come, first served.

Ripple ★★★ MODERN AMERICAN MODERATE/EXPENSIVE

3417 Connecticut Ave. NW; ☎ 202-244-7995; **rippledc.com** Cleveland Park

Reservations Recommended. **Metro** Cleveland Park. **Wine selection** Extremely good. **Disabled access** Good. **Open** *Brunch:* Sunday, 11 a.m.–2:30 p.m. *Dinner:* Daily, 5 p.m.–until.

THE PREMISE It may seem as if every new restaurant these days has one of those ad-agency mission statements—"dedication, determination, focus, and finesse";

"nourish the palate"; "food is the focus; wine is the passion"—but Ripple has two: "Eat, drink, gather" and "local, seasonal, sustainable," which pretty much describe this increasingly confident comfort food haven, that and the haute/hot grilled-cheese menu. (C&C, or cheese and charcuterie, is common these days, but Ripple's assortment is particularly fine.) Chef Marjorie Meek-Bradley's résumé—stints under Thomas Keller, José Andrés, and Marcus Samuelsson—is impressive enough to be its own ad campaign. The other hint to the team's philosophy is the communal table, straight out of an Italian farmhouse.

THE PAYOFF Sweetbreads with a punch of plum; cavatelli infused with a touch of cocoa and paired with spicy sausage and chilies, like an Italian take on mole; chicken two ways, roast with sausage; saddle of lamb with moussaka sharpened with grape leaves; and a spicy seafood stew with seared scallops and brandade. As to the grilled-cheese sandwiches (available at happy hour and late-night only), there are a half dozen house creations, but you can make your own from an array of cheeses, breads, spreads, and relishes.

IF YOU LIKE THIS **Ardeo+Bardeo,** just down the block, is a first-class alternative.

MARYLAND SUBURBS

Bethesda and Chevy Chase

COAUTHOR EVE ZIBART refers to Bethesda as having "So many restaurants, so little time." The ethnic options include Yannick Cam's **Bistro Provence** (page 294); a branch of **Jaleo** (page 266) and a less-expensive semi-offshoot, **Guardado's,** from a former Jaleo chef; the Belgian **Mussell Bar;** the often-surprising modern American **Persimmon;** the elegant **Passage to India; 4935 Bar and Kitchen,** which dabbles in Indian, Salvadoran, Italian, and a little French (and if you're careful, not too expensively); **Olazzo,** an affordable throwback to your Italian grandmother's Sunday dinners; and **Penang,** which has a huge menu of Malaysian, Thai, and Chinese dishes that are generally afford-able and mixable.

unofficial **TIP**
The **Bethesda Crab House** is a traditional grab-your-mallet steamer shop; if your family's never been to one, it could be a fun night.

Several of the more serious Japanese res-taurants reside here—**Tako Grill, Yuzu,** and **Matuba,** among others—along with a few broader Asian kitchens such as **Raku. Bangkok Garden** is a quiet restaurant whose repeat Thai clientele speaks to its quality. **Vieux Logis** is the sort of old-fashioned French you can take your in-laws to, and also check out its elaborate murals. **Moby Dick House of Kebob** has been turning out cheap pita rolls, dips, and veggie options for a decade.

Among the newer challengers are **Kapnos Kouzina,** a more casual offshoot of the popular Kapnos downtown; **Villain & Saint,** a Summer of Love–themed hangout (high calorie vs. healthier), but more afford-able than most of its neighbors—and with some live music to boot; **Barrell & Crow,** a modern twist on surf and turf with a weakness for Southern deep-fried; **Urban Heights,** from the Belgian creator of

Mussell Bar, et al, but specializing in small plates from Japan to the Philippines to India; and the margarita-minded and intentionally kitschy **Gringos & Mariachis.**

Among the American entrées are **Black's Bar & Kitchen,** definitely a happy hour contender for oyster lovers; **Café Deluxe,** whose kids' menu is not lengthy but comes with crayons; **Food Wine & Co.** (page 295); **Grapeseed American Bistro & Wine;** and **PassionFish,** which has an unusually large happy hour menu and an equally good kids' list.

*un***official TIP**

The **Bethesda Tastee Diner,** one of three left (along with Silver Spring and Laurel), is an original Jerry Mahoney "dining car," dating from 1953. It's open 24/7, except December 25, and has hosted plenty of politicians and celebrities—even Julia Child.

Chevy Chase, especially the booming Chevy Chase shopping area around the intersection of Wisconsin and Western Avenues Northwest (actually the Montgomery County/D.C. border), has attracted some major restaurants, notably **Meiwah** (Asian fusion), **Range** (page 295), **Sushiko** (page 296), and **Lia's** (Italian).

Bistro Provence ★★★
FRENCH MODERATE/EXPENSIVE

4933 Fairmont Ave., Bethesda; ☎ 301-656-7373; **bistroprovence.org**
   Maryland suburbs

Reservations Recommended. **Metro** Bethesda. **Wine selection** Very good. **Disabled access** Good. **Open** *Lunch:* Wednesday–Sunday, 11:30 a.m.–2:30 p.m. *Dinner:* Daily, 5:30–9:30 p.m.

THE PREMISE It looks as if it were transported whole from some old Manhattan brownstone firehouse, even though it is in fact a new building. (The penguins carved into the overhead arch commemorate the icehouse that once stood on the site.) The decor is true bistro—chandeliers and honey-gold walls or exposed brick—with a stunning stacked-stone courtyard in the back and a (mostly for show) duck press. Warning: This is not a big space, and it can be loud.

THE PAYOFF In the 1980s, Yannick Cam's Le Pavillon was a nouvelle cuisine sensation in a very conventional Continental cream-sauce town. Since then, restless perfectionist Cam has been in and out of a series of Provençal, Brazilian, Catalonian-Spanish, and French–country inn establishments, and although this is nominally a bistro, the food is inherently upscale. Regardless of "ethnicity," when Cam is good, he's very, *very* good. A sampling of his (all-organic) style: roast lobster over tiny lentils or scallops over asparagus risotto; duck confit over sautéed potatoes; a boudin *blanc* of poultry and foie gras; saffron risotto with seafood; and veal chop or hanger steak. The fairly reticent menu doesn't do the meticulous preparation justice. It is pricey, but with such appetizers as wild mushroom–stuffed squid, fricassee of escargots with oyster mushrooms and eggplant, and the lobster, you could get away with a lot of flavor for less.

Food Wine & Co. ★★★
MODERN AMERICAN **MODERATE**

7272 Wisconsin Ave., Bethesda; ☎ 301-652-8008; **foodwineandco.com**
Maryland suburbs

Reservations Recommended. **Metro** Bethesda. **Wine selection** Very good. **Disabled access** Good. **Open** *Lunch:* Monday–Friday, 11:30–2:30 p.m. *Dinner:* Sunday–Monday, 5–9 p.m.; Tuesday–Thursday, 5–10 p.m.; Friday–Saturday, 4–11 p.m.

THE PREMISE This place might be easily underrated, but it's unexpectedly ambitious: a raw bar and mussels (one with pork belly and cider), charcuterie and cheese, flatbreads, charred octopus, bone marrow, and (not your grandmother's) tater tots . . . and that's before you get to the large plates. Decor is dark and clubby, but oddly careful not to telegraph its style; apparently, the high-volume level tells you what you need to know about this "neighborhood bistro." The list of wines by the glass is appreciably long, but FWC has even more craft beers. Happy hour goes all evening after 4 on Tuesday and Thursday.

THE PAYOFF The lamb burger with *harissa*-tomato compote and yogurt and the "vintage" Angus flatiron steak are signature dishes; the brick roast chicken is first-rate. The potato tots with cheese made their way through a tsunami of tweets, and reviews, to be named one of the 40 dishes Washingtonians "had to eat" in 2013. The list of daily specials is quite impressive: seared lamb liver; pan-roasted cod with watermelon relish, lime, and peppercress; and a petite filet with chestnut spaetzle and kale, butternut squash, and apples.

IF YOU LIKE THIS The nearby **Grapeseed** paved the way for a menu like this and is equally accomplished. It also offers half-size wine pairings.

Range ★★½ **MODERN AMERICAN** **EXPENSIVE**

5335 Wisconsin Ave. NW (in Chevy Chase Pavilion); ☎ 202-803-8020;
voltrange.com **Chevy Chase**

Reservations Recommended. **Metro** Friendship Heights. **Wine selection** Very extensive. **Disabled access** Good. **Open** Monday–Friday, 4–10 p.m.; Saturday–Sunday, 11:30 a.m.–10 p.m.

THE PREMISE This 14,000-square-foot complex from local fave and almost *Top Chef* Bryan Voltaggio (who got his start at Charlie Palmer Steak) has its finger in almost every kind of pie—raw bar and crudo, the ubiquitous charcuterie and artisan cheese, bakery, rotisserie, and wood-burning oven pizza—and nearly everything is performed within view. The bread station turns out not just ciabatta and focaccia (and pizza and flatbread) but also biscuits, corn bread, and sourdough; pair them with flights of hams or tastings of lamb. The ovens are hot, and the recipes smokin' (literally), but the decor is cool—lots of marble, glass-fronted coolers, and synchronized LED "art" that recalls the old Michel Richard Citronelle—and the music is typically alternative or indie rock. The equally ambitious cocktail menu includes the spicy Scotch-based Vegan Sacrifice, so-called because the ice cube is made of clarified veal stock.

THE PAYOFF In some ways, Voltaggio may have bitten off more than he could chew, or char; the multi-format restaurant is almost constantly evolving but still adventurous: roasted pork belly with vanilla and fennel; beef cheeks paired with pickled tongue; and such impressive curiosities as pig's face and curried lamb neck. At press time, Voltaggio was working on changing up the menu and adding house-made beer to the menu.

IF YOU LIKE THIS If you are still coddling that cigar habit, Range has a smoking annex, **Civil Cigar Lounge,** with what is almost certainly the fanciest menu any stogie ever met; happily for the other diners, the ventilation system is state-of-the-art.

Sushiko ★★★½ JAPANESE MODERATE

5455 Wisconsin Ave., Chevy Chase; ☎ 301-961-1644; **sushikorestaurants.com**
Maryland suburbs

Reservations Recommended. **Metro** Friendship Heights. **Wine selection** Very good. **Disabled access** Good. **Open** *Lunch:* Daily, noon–3 p.m. *Dinner:* Sunday–Thursday, 5:30–10 p.m.; Friday–Saturday, 5:30-10:30 p.m.

THE PREMISE Thanks to its unusual seasonal dishes, Sushiko attracts a broad, generally knowledgeable, and fairly affluent crowd. (The original location opened in 1976, making it D.C.'s oldest sushi bar.) This has made it possible for the kitchen (and sushi bar) to offer both traditional and improvisational fare based on market availability and traditional seasonal factors.

THE PAYOFF You'll find first-quality sushi and *sashimi,* as well as seasonal small dishes (either traditional or contemporary), involving and often combining fish, both cooked and raw, with seaweeds, wild greens, grains, herbs, caviar, and sometimes unexpected American touches. If you want to see what the chef can do, order one of the special menus: You'll be full but not stuffed. Spring for real wasabi; you'll never go back to the canned stuff. The sake list is not great, but the French wine list may come as a pleasant surprise— creative director Daisuke Utagawa was in the forefront of pairing wines, particularly Bordeaux, with seafood.

National Harbor

While National Harbor primarily served the convention crowd, it has ramped up its seasonal attractions, such as Christmas extravaganzas and food and wine festivals; is not far from an 80-store outlet mall; and will be near an MGM resort and casino (once it's completed). It also has a somewhat smaller version of the London Eye, an outdoor stage, and river-cruise/water-taxi service to Old Town Alexandria. It does have a number of restaurants (the Gaylord Hotel alone has a half dozen, including the **Old Hickory Steakhouse**), ranging from burgers, crab cakes, pizza, and pub fare to the new-Southern **Succotash,** the New York chophouse **Bond 45,** and the Jersey Shore import **McLoone's Pier House.**

Silver Spring

Two of the neighborhood's most promising new spots are curiously opposite in flavor: the loungy, eclectic nose-to-tail **Urban Butcher** and **All Set,** a mostly Nantucket-themed (and priced) seafood restaurant. Among other favorites within walking distance of the Metro are

Olazzo and **Cubano's;** several Ethiopian restaurants, including **Abol, Abyssinia, Bete, Kefa,** and **Lucy** (among others); **Ray's the Classics,** dedicated to the idea of butcher-cut, old-fashioned real steaks; **Mandalay,** one of the few Burmese kitchens in the region; and **Adega Wine Cellars and Cafe,** which also offers fairly light fare and flatbreads, with lots of veggie options.

Additionally, in and around the Fillmore and AFI Silver Theatre, there are a number of family options, some franchise, but many mom-and-pop.

Wheaton

A long time ago, coauthor Eve Zibart wrote a column for *The Washington Post* that began, "In Wheaton, the International House of Pancakes is not a joke." Even then, Wheaton was home to an unusually eclectic group of ethnic restaurants, particularly Thai. Today, though it's not a major tourist hotel spot, it still has a remarkable spread within easy distance of the Metro. Just for a small start, consider **Nava Thai, Ruan Thai,** and **Thai Taste by Kob;** the Korean-Japanese **Woomi Garden;** Vietnamese vs. Japanese–style noodle shops **Mi La Cay, Pho Hiep Hoa,** and **Ren's Ramen;** the Caribbean **Kantuta;** the Salvadoran **Rios;** plus Irish and Scots pubs; and even one of the area's longest-running kosher delis, **Max's.** The dim sum at **Hollywood East Café** is very popular, as is the roast poultry at the Chinese **Paul Kee** and **Full Key** (not a typo; they're not related). Almost all of these are both budget- and family-friendly—and yes, the IHOP is still chugging along.

> *unofficial* **TIP**
> Think you know hot dogs? You can have organic beef, chicken, veggie, Reuben-style, Coney Island–style, Fenway Park–style, Chicago-style, Saigon-style, even Peking duck–style—among others— at **Haute Dogs and Fries.**

VIRGINIA SUBURBS

Old Town Alexandria

Old Town Alexandria may be known to tourists mostly for its historic buildings, but it is also home to several first-rate restaurants, notably **Restaurant Eve** (page 298), as well as **Eammon's** fish-and-chipperies; Southern nostalgic **Majestic;** and **Society Fair,** a sort of not-Italian Eataly that combines a butcher shop, wine bar, bakery, demonstration kitchen, and bistro under one roof—and all from the husband-wife team of Cathal and Meshelle Armstrong. The best French restaurant in town is **Bastille** (page 298), along with its more casual offshoot **Bistrot Royal,** from another husband-wife team, Christophe and Michelle Poteaux.

Belgian fave Robert Wiedmaier of Marcel's, et al, has a high-end spot adjoining the Lorien Hotel called **Brabo** (tasting menus start at $60 a person). **Vermilion** has been a Southern-American staple for many years; **Magnolia's on King** is another haute new-Southern showcase. And **Geranio** has been turning out updated but not trend-driven Italian for repeat diners for even longer.

Old Town has pubs and taverns in abundance. Be sure to check the menus on the sidewalk when possible; many charge tourist-trap prices. Best view probably goes to the chain but savvy **Chart House,** a glass-enclosed family favorite at the end of a pier.

Bastille ★★★ FRENCH EXPENSIVE

606 N. Fayette St., Old Town Alexandria; ☎ 703-519-3776;
bastillerestaurant.com Virginia suburbs

Reservations Recommended. **Metro** Braddock Road. **Wine selection** Very good. **Disabled access** Very good. **Open** *Brunch:* Saturday–Sunday, 11:30 a.m.–2 p.m. *Lunch:* Tuesday—Sunday, 11:30 a.m.–2:30 p.m. *Dinner:* Tuesday-Sunday, 5–10 p.m.

THE PREMISE Chef-owners Christophe Poteaux, a classically trained but not hidebound French chef, and Pennsylvanian dessert chef Michelle Poteaux met (and married) when they were working at the Watergate Hotel. Both are by nature seasonally inspired and locavores; after all, French bistro food was farm-to-table before there was such a term.

THE PAYOFF Everything old is new again, and this is the kind of food that converted Julia Child. Crispy pork belly paired with pork cheeks, paella (Languedoc style), braised lamb shoulder, foie gras with roasted pears, *moules-frites,* fine cheese . . . but if beef tartare, hanger steak, and quail were on every restaurant's midafternoon getaway-bar menu, the world would be a happier place. A local not-so-secret indulgence is Michelle's meat loaf burger. There are a variety of tasting menus, $39–$70.

IF YOU LIKE THIS The original location of Bastille, at 1201 Royal St., is now **Bistro Royal,** a more casual and intimate location that will impress your friends.

Restaurant Eve ★★★★
MODERN AMERICAN VERY EXPENSIVE

110 S. Pitt St., Old Town Alexandria; ☎ 703-706-0450; **restauranteve.com** Virginia suburbs

Reservations Strongly recommended. **Metro** King Street. **Wine selection** Extremely good. **Disabled access** Good. **Open** *Lunch:* Monday–Friday, 11:30 a.m.–2 p.m. *Dinner:* Monday–Saturday, 5:30–10 p.m.

THE PREMISE Chef Cathal (pronounced Ca-*hall*) Armstrong is Irish by nature, French by nurture—he spent his childhood summers in France—and has cooked Latino fusion, French bistro, modern Southern, and Italian. He also keeps a full-time charcuterie chef on duty. But this ambitious kitchen is all-American, locavore, and as organic and sustainable as possible. The building itself is elegant but almost self-effacing; the fireplace bar is a beauty.

THE PAYOFF While the tasting menus (including a family-style Filipino banquet) are still fairly expensive (and worth it), there are more casual options than in Eve's earlier days, especially at lunch. The menu (fixed price in the dining room, à la carte in the bistro) is market-driven, so unusually variable but typical—and intentionally under-described—dishes include veal sweetbreads, poached lobster, loin of rabbit with roasted porcini or braised rabbit en croûte, venison sausage with farro, and squab breast—plus a mystery dish marked "You must be brave to order this dish." This is the flagship not only of Armstrong but also of his wife, Meshelle, who has Filipino roots, and some of their most recent menu explorations are tryouts for a Filipino restaurant that they plan to open along the D.C. waterfront.

IF YOU LIKE THIS Eve, named for Armstrong's daughter, has two siblings—**Eamonn's,** a Dublin-style fish-and-chips shop named for Armstrong's son, and the knock-and-enter retro "speakeasy" **PX** above that. There's also the eclectic comfort food **Majestic** and the butcher/baker/wine bar/exhibition kitchen called **Society Fair** (which serves in part as storage pantry for the house-made charcuterie and breads for Eve and the others).

Ballston

As a neighborhood populated by a number of government agencies, nonprofits, and college students (both full-time and commuting), Ballston is starting to move from mostly casual dining to more upscale spots, including several offshoots of downtown establishments. Even at dinner, Mike Isabella's **Kapnos Taverna** can provide plenty of meze and shellfish at budget-friendly prices. Robert Wiedmaier's **Mussel Bar & Grille** has more than mussels and *frites* (and steak and *frites*), including raw-bar specials, brick-oven pizza, and grilled entrées. **Rus Uz** is one of the few Eastern European (read: Russian-Uzbek) kitchens in the area, offering caviar-filled puffs, more than a baker's dozen piroshki, authentic stroganoff and chicken Kiev, pilaf, and cabbage rolls—and all startlingly inexpensive. **Rustico** is a beer-centric spot that pairs easily with grilled poultry and meat, as well as burgers. **Rocklands Barbecue and Grilling Co.**'s name tells you pretty much what you need to know, but it's a hometown business, not a New York import (ahem). **Grand Cru Wine Bar and Bistro** is also just what it sounds, except that the menu might be a little more polished than you might expect.

Clarendon

A few years ago, Clarendon was one of hottest dining districts in the area, but it has recently fallen prey to one of those low cycles. Nevertheless, it still has several notable eateries, including **Liberty Tavern** (page 300) and its casual sidekick **Lyon Tavern; Ray's the Steaks** (page 300); the surprisingly inventive **Green Pig Bistro;** a branch of the popular **Cava Mezze;** the modern-Indian **Tandoori Nights;** the deservedly popular music hall and deft (and veggie-friendly) café **IOTA;** and the similarly music-minded **Galaxy Hut,** which has made inexpensive comfort food, and in particular grilled cheese (nine basics plus options), into an art form. **Mala Tang** is especially welcome on a chilly night, specializing in Sichuan street food and individual, rather than table-size, hot pots. Most intriguingly, Clarendon is now home to an offshoot of one of the Washington, D.C. area's most revered ethnic restaurants, and a pioneer in the Vietnamese cultural boom of Northern Virginia: **Four Sisters Grill** may not have the 100-plus items of its parent restaurant in Eden Center, but its spread of hand snacks, bánh mì, and rice and noodle dishes are a relaxing bargain.

Liberty Tavern ★★★
MODERN AMERICAN   INEXPENSIVE/MODERATE

3195 Wilson Blvd., Arlington; ☎ 703-465-9360; **thelibertytavern.com**
Virginia suburbs

Reservations Recommended. **Metro** Clarendon. **Wine selection** Good. **Disabled access** Good. **Open** *Brunch:* Saturday–Sunday, 9 a.m.–3 p.m. *Lunch:* Monday–Friday, 11:30 a.m.–2:30 p.m. *Dinner:* Sunday–Thursday, 5–10 p.m.; Friday–Saturday, 5–11 p.m.

THE PREMISE Almost a decade ago, this lovingly restored historical building—exposed brick, a fabulous staircase, and a carved Masonic symbol over the door—became one of the neighborhood's central hangouts when Clarendon was just emerging from an ethnic-food hideaway to a gentrification-food destination, and its quality, and artisanal and sustainable ingredients (including farmhouse cheeses), hasn't diminished. There are two wood-burning ovens, one for pizza and the other for everything else; all the pizzas, even the ones with duck confit or fennel sausage, are $10 after 10 p.m. in the bar.

THE PAYOFF The menu isn't overtly unusual but unusually deft: charred octopus with *bottarga* and preserved lemon; duck confit salad with pears and fennel; crispy duck ribs; an elevated squid ink (*spaccatelli* with sea urchin, shrimp, and chilies); and pork porterhouse with sweet-and-sour eggplant and potato tart. The Monday special is pickled-brined fried chicken with two sides and a biscuit for $15—and the chicken is also on the very extensive all-you-can-eat brunch menu.

IF YOU LIKE THIS Liberty Tavern has an offshoot restaurant, **Lyon Hall,** just down the street; it has a slightly heavier German tone, with more of the pâtés, sausages, schnitzel, and cassoulet. The frankfurter made from short ribs is a local fave.

Ray's the Steaks ★★★½   STEAK   EXPENSIVE
2300 Wilson Blvd., Arlington; ☎ 703-841-7297; **raysthesteaks.com**
Virginia suburbs

Reservations Not accepted. **Metro** Court House. **Wine selection** Very good. **Disabled access** Good. **Open** Daily, 5–10 p.m.

THE PREMISE Michael Landrum, a veteran of Morton's and Capital Grille, established this populist, almost subversive steak house (say it out loud) that keeps up the quality but slices the price. Yes, it's theoretically "expensive," but it verges on moderate because, while other major steak house chains routinely charge $10–$12 a side, Ray's includes the creamed spinach and mashed potatoes in the price of the steak.

THE PAYOFF Signature dishes include steak tartare served like a deviled egg; crab royale; crab bisque with sherry; three-cheese-and-lobster mac; and the cowboy steak, an oversize bone-in rib eye. New York strip and filet mignon are the backbones of the menu, served in a half dozen ways. Though all the steaks are first-rate, the most intriguing, and sometimes the bargain, are the old-fashioned butcher cuts less familiar to diners: *onglet* (well, maybe hanger steak isn't unfamiliar anymore) and, if you are fortunate, an occasional *coulotte,* the eye of the strip.

IF YOU LIKE THIS While Landrum has had to scale back after an ambitious but unfortunately timed expansion, he still has **Ray's to the Third,** a more tavern-like spot not far way at the Metro; **Ray's The Classics** across from the Silver Spring Metro now belongs to a former staffer but retains much of the menu, the good wine list, and the free spinach and potatoes. Both still serve Landrum's once-famous burgers, made from the scraps of those fine steaks; they also take reservations.

Crystal City

Crystal City is a canny place to stay, for many reasons. You are one subway stop from Reagan National Airport (which makes for quick flight arrivals and departures). It has plenty of hotels and a fairly extensive retail-restaurant strip, much of it covered. (And then there's Food Truck Thursdays. . . .) There are plenty of franchise offerings and quick stops, as well as names such as **McCormick and Schmick, Morton's, Ruth's Chris,** and even **Ted's Montana Grill,** but among the better (less-expensive) local bets are **Bar Louie,** a **Good Stuff Eatery** (page 278), a **Jaleo** (page 266), **Neramitra Thai,** and **Athena Pallas.** Crystal City was home to one of the first Ethiopian café clusters outside D.C., and it still has several, including **Demera** and **Harar Mesob.** And the Filipino **Bistro 7101** (which is not an address, but a reference to the number of islands in the archipelago) is fairly new but rousing quite a buzz.

DINING DESTINATIONS: RESTAURANTS WORTH A DRIVE

The Inn at Little Washington ★★★★★
MODERN AMERICAN   VERY EXPENSIVE

Middle and Main Streets, Washington, VA; ☎ 540-675-3800; **theinnatlittlewashington.com**   Virginia suburbs

Reservations Required. **Metro** Not Metro accessible. **Wine selection** Extremely good. **Disabled access** Good. **Open** *Dinner:* Wednesday–Monday, 2 seatings per night.

THE PREMISE For an astonishing 35 years, this culinary legend—it has been profiled in *The New Yorker* and selected by *Travel & Leisure* as the second-finest hotel in the United States and eighth-finest in the world—has been Washington's most popular distant dining destination, even if it isn't in *that* Washington. Chef Patrick O'Connell makes magic in gourmet (and gourmand) circles all over the country. But it is without doubt a special-occasion destination: The prix fixe menu ranges from $178 on weeknights to $208 on Saturday before wine (or the tip, which you should expect to be generous because of the layers of service), although holiday menus may vary. The kitchen tables flank the huge fireplace and seat up to six apiece, though it will set you back more than double, but consider that you are paying for some of the most meticulous and labor-intensive cooking in the country. And although the dinner is purportedly four courses, there are plenty of extras along the way. If you really want a vegetarian gastro-orgasm, this is your chance. Incidentally, this exquisite mansion is worth wandering about, as is the garden, where you will get a glimpse into the bustling kitchen.

THE PAYOFF O'Connell's strength is a sense of balance: Dishes are never overwhelmed or overly fussy, and local produce is emphasized (he was among the first to credit sources), which guarantees freshness and inventiveness. The menu changes continually, and because you will need advance reservations (accepted up to a year in advance), in this case it's really worth it to bring up the website and drool. However, some of the standards include lamb carpaccio with Caesar salad ice cream; a duo of hot and cold foie gras with Sauternes gelée; and pepper-crusted tuna "pretending to be a filet mignon" and capped Rossini-style with foie gras. Everyone remembers his or her first passion here—homemade white-chocolate ice cream with bitter-chocolate sauce or an array of perfect dime-size biscuits with country ham—and for some Washingtonians, driving down to the other Washington becomes an addiction, a compulsion.

IF YOU LIKE THIS Minibar (page 267) and **Komi** (page 284), though different in approach, would be the top in-town foodie destinations. Meantime, O'Connell is generous with his recipes, often posting them on the website or mailing out newsletters.

L'Auberge Chez François/Jacques Brasserie ★★★★
FRENCH MODERATE/VERY EXPENSIVE

332 Springvale Rd., Great Falls, VA; ☎ 703-759-3800;
laubergechezfrancois.com Virginia suburbs

Reservations Required for dinner (see below). **Metro** Not Metro accessible. **Wine selection** Very good. **Disabled access** Very good. **Open** *Lunch:* Tuesday–Saturday, 11:30 a.m.–1:30 p.m.; Sunday, noon–3 p.m. *Dinner:* Tuesday–Friday, 5–9 p.m.; Saturday, 2 seatings (4:30–6:30 p.m. and 8–9:30 p.m.); Sunday, noon–7:30 p.m.

THE PREMISE This has been one of the most beloved and romantic dining sites in the area for 40 years—a real country inn with exposed beams, family photos, and memorabilia saluting the late paterfamilias, Alsatian-born chef François Haeringer (who was a downtown fixture for 20 years before that). François's son Jacques, himself the star of a TV show, has taken over, but blood is thicker than broth, and there is no major shake-up in sight. "Expensive" or not, this is a bargain; entrées run about $70–$80 but are really (large) whole dinners with salads, appetizers, and desserts (get the Grand Marnier soufflé), plus bread and cheese and a bit of sorbet. More recently, Jacques has turned the picture-book patio and garden into a more casual but still classic bistro and bar. Reservations for the brasserie can only be made by telephone; L'Auberge reservations also can be made online. Although the two- to four-weeks' notice rule still applies, competition has increased, along with cancellations: It may be worth it to call in the late afternoon, especially during the week. You can't make reservations for the Christmas-light-festooned terrace, incidentally; just call to make sure it's open (about May–September) and then show up.

THE PAYOFF Here are classics, such as rack of lamb, frogs' legs, chateaubriand (for two), and duck breast with calvados; the true choucroute royal garni, with Alsatian sauerkraut, sausages, smoked pork, duck confit, and foie gras; game in season, such as medallions of venison and roast duck or a "hunter's duo" of venison chop and grilled quail; sweetbreads with wild mushrooms; seafood fricassee with shrimp, scallops, lobster, crab, rockfish, and salmon in Champagne sauce or a relatively lighter poached lobster with jumbo crabmeat; and some trendier riches such as braised Wagyu beef cheeks with wild mushrooms. "Papa Ernest's Grill" includes beef, veal, lamb, and lobster; talk about a moveable feast.

IF YOU LIKE THIS If you don't have a car, see the profile of **Marcel's** in Foggy Bottom on page 286; though it leans to Belgium rather than Alsace, it has a similarly updated classical flair.

The **BEST**

Best Brunches

- **Belga Café**   Barracks Row
- **Birch & Barley**   Mid City
- **Blue Duck Tavern**   Midtown
- **Bombay Club**   Downtown
- **Cashion's Eat Place**   Adams Morgan
- **Doi Moi**   Logan Circle
- **Farmers Fishers Bakers**   Georgetown
- **The Four Seasons Hotel**   Georgetown
- **Georgia Brown's**   Downtown
- **The Hamilton**   Downtown
- **The Irish Inn at Glen Echo**   Glen Echo, MD
- **Jaleo**   Penn Quarter; Bethesda, MD; Crystal City, VA
- **Le Diplomate**   Logan Circle
- **Old Angler's Inn**   Potomac, MD
- **Old Ebbitt Grill**   Downtown
- **Perry's**   Adams Morgan
- **Tabard Inn**   Dupont Circle
- **Ted's Bulletin**   Multiple locations

Best Burgers

- **BGR The Burger Joint**   Multiple locations
- **Bobby's Burger Palace**   Downtown; Montgomery Mall (Bethesda, MD); College Park, MD; Potomac Mills, VA
- **Bourboun Steak**   Georgetown
- **Burger Tap & Shake**   Foggy Bottom, Tenleytown
- **City Burger**   Bethesda, MD
- **Elevation Burger**   Multiple locations
- **Five Guys**   Multiple locations
- **Good Stuff Eatery**   Capitol Hill; Georgetown; Crystal City, VA; Manassas, VA; Burke, VA
- **Ray's the Classics**   Silver Spring, MD
- **Ray's to the Third**   Rosslyn, VA

- **Shake Shack**   Penn Quarter; Dupont Circle' Downtown; Tysons Corner, VA; Union Station
- **Z-Burger**   Multiple locations

Best Hotel Fine Dining

- **Bistro Bis**   Hotel George, Capitol Hill
- **Blue Duck Tavern**   Park Hyatt, Midtown
- **Bourbon Steak**   Four Seasons Hotel, Georgetown
- **Brabo/Brabo Tasting Room**   Lorien Hotel, Old Town Alexandria, VA
- **Café du Parc**   Willard InterContinental, Downtown
- **Firefly**   Hotel Madera, Dupont Circle
- **The Grill Room**   Capella Hotel, Georgetown
- **Nage**   Marriott Courtyard, Dupont Circle
- **Occidental Grill**   Willard InterContinental, Downtown
- **Old Hickory Steakhouse**   Gaylord Hotel, National Harbor
- **Pinea**   W Hotel, Downtown
- **Plume**   Jefferson Hotel, Downtown
- **Poste Moderne Brasserie**   Hotel Monaco, Penn Quarter
- **The Riggsby**   Carlyle Hotel, Dupont Circle
- **Rural Society**   Loews Madison Hotel, Downtown
- **Tabard Inn**   Dupont Circle
- **WestEnd Bistro**   Ritz-Carlton, Midtown
- **Zentan**   Donovan Hotel, Dupont Circle

Best Local Chains

- **Austin Grill**   Penn Quarter; Rockville, MD; Old Town Alexandria, VA; Silver Spring, MD; Springfield, VA
- **Chef Geoff's**   Downtown; Northwest D.C.; Rockville, MD; Tysons Corner, VA; Chevy Chase, MD (as Lia's)
- **Clyde's** *(also as Hamilton's, Tower Oaks Lodge, and Willow Creek Farm)*   Multiple locations
- **Jaleo**   Penn Quarter; Bethesda, MD; Crystal City, VA
- **Lebanese Taverna**   Multiple locations
- **Mamma Lucia**   Multiple locations
- **Tara Thai**   Multiple locations
- **Tastee Diner**   Bethesda, MD; Silver Spring, MD; Laurel, MD
- **Taylor Gourmet**   Multiple locations
- **Ted's Bulletin**   Multiple locations

Best Museum Restaurants

- **National Air and Space Museum Wright Place Food Court** *(best for kids)*
- **National Gallery of Art Sculpture Garden Pavilion Café**

- **National Gallery of Art West Building Cascade Café**
- **National Museum of American History Stars & Stripes Café** *(best for families)*
- **National Museum of the American Indian Mitsitam Café**
- **National Museum of Natural History Fossil Cafe** *(best for kids)*
- **National Museum of Women in the Arts Mezzanine Café**
- **Newseum The Source** *(best gourmet fare)*
- **U.S. Holocaust Memorial Museum Cafe** *(best for vegetarian, kosher)*

Best Pizza

- **&Pizza**   Multiple locations
- **Comet Ping Pong**   Northwest D.C.
- **Ella's Wood-Fired Pizza**   Penn Quarter
- **Etto**   Mid City
- **Ghibellina**   Logan Circle
- **Graffiato**   Penn Quarter
- **Il Canale**   Georgetown
- **Inferno Pizzeria Napoletana**   Darnestown, MD
- **Matchbox**   Penn Quarter; Rockville, MD; Logan Circle; Potomac Mills, VA
- **Pete's New Haven Style Apizza**   Columbia Heights; Tenleytown; Clarendon, VA
- **Pizzeria Paradiso**   Dupont Circle; Georgetown; Old Town Alexandria, VA
- **Potomac Pizza**   Chevy Chase, Rockville, Potomac, Gaithersburg (all MD)
- **Seventh Hill**   Capitol Hill
- **2Amys**   Northwest D.C.
- **We, the Pizza**   Capitol Hill

Best Restaurants Worth a Drive

- **Inn at Little Washington**   Washington, VA
- **Harriman's at Salamander Inn and Resort**   Middleburg, VA
- **L'Auberge Chez François/Jacques' Brasserie**   Great Falls, VA
- **L'Auberge Provencale**   Boyce, VA
- **Restaurant at Patowmack Farm**   Lovettsville, VA

Best Steaks

- **BLT Steak**   Downtown
- **Bobby Van's**   Downtown, Penn Quarter
- **Bourbon Steak**   Georgetown
- **Capital Grille**   Penn Quarter; Chevy Chase, MD; Tysons Corner, VA
- **Charlie Palmer Steak**   Capitol Hill
- **Del Campo**   Penn Quarter
- **Del Frisco's Double Eagle**   Downtown

- **Fleming's Prime Steakhouse & Wine Bar**   Tysons Corner, VA
- **Joe's Seafood, Prime Steak & Stone Crab**   Downtown
- **Mastro's Steakhouse**   Downtown
- **Morton's**   Downtown; Crystal City, VA; Georgetown
- **Palm**   Downtown; Tysons Corner, VA
- **Prime Rib**   Downtown
- **Ray's the Classics**   Silver Spring, MD
- **Ray's the Steaks**   Arlington, VA
- **Rural Society**   Downtown
- **Ruth's Chris Steak House**   Multiple locations
- **STK Washington**   Dupont Circle

Best Sushi Bars

- **Izakawa Seki**   Mid City
- **Kaz Sushi Bistro**   Foggy Bottom
- **Kotobuki**   Northwest D.C.
- **Murasaki**   Tenleytown
- **Nagoya**   Rockville, MD
- **Niwano Hana**   Rockville, MD
- **Sei**   Penn Quarter
- **Sushiko**   Chevy Chase, MD
- **Sushi Taro**   Dupont Circle
- **Tako Grill**   Bethesda, MD
- **Tono Sushi**   Woodley Park
- **Yirasai**   Chevy Chase, MD
- **Yuzu**   Bethesda, MD

Best Sweetshops

- **Astro Doughnuts and Fried Chicken**   Penn Quarter
- **Baked and Wired**   Georgetown
- **Bakeshop**   Clarendon, VA
- **Bayou Bakery**   Capitol Hill; Arlington, VA
- **Dangerously Delicious Pies**   Atlas District
- **District Doughnut**   Barracks Row
- **Dolcezza Gelato**   Multiple locations
- **GBD Fired Chicken and Doughnuts**   Dupont Circle
- **Georgetown Cupcake**   Georgetown; Bethesda, MD
- **Pitango Gilato**   Penn Quarter; Logan Circle; Capitol Hill; Reston, VA
- **Rare Sweets**   Downtown
- **Ray's to the Third**   Rosslyn, VA

Restaurants by Cuisine

CUISINE AND NAME	OVERALL RATING	PRICE
AMERICAN *(see also Modern American and Southern)*		
Good Stuff Eatery	★★★	Inexpensive
Old Ebbitt Grill	★★½	Moderate
BALKAN		
Ambar	★★★	Inexpensive
ETHIOPIAN		
Ethiopic	★★★	Inexpensive
FRENCH		
L'Auberge Chez François/Jacques Brasserie	★★★★	Moderate/V. Expensive
Marcel's	★★★★	Very Expensive
Mintwood Place	★★★½	Expensive
Bistro Bis	★★★½	Expensive
Le Diplomate	★★★½	Moderate
Bistro Provence	★★★	Moderate/Expensive
Bastille	★★★	Expensive
Béarnaise	★★★	Moderate
Montmartre	★★½	Moderate
Bistro Français	★★½	Moderate
GREEK		
Kapnos	★★★½	Moderate
Zaytinya	★★★½	Moderate
INDIAN		
Bombay Club	★★★½	Expensive
Indique	★★★	Moderate
Rasika	★★★	Moderate/Expensive
ITALIAN		
Fiola and Fiola Mare	★★★★★	Very Expensive
Obelisk	★★★½	Very Expensive
Graffiato	★★★½	Inexpensive
JAPANESE		
Sushi Taro	★★★★	Very Expensive
Sushiko	★★★½	Moderate
Daikaya Ramen and Izakawa	★★★½	Inexpensive/Moderate
Izakawa Seki	★★★½	Expensive
Kaz Sushi Bistro	★★★½	Moderate/Expensive
MEXICAN		
Oyamel	★★★½	Moderate

Restaurants by Cuisine *(continued)*

CUISINE AND NAME	OVERALL RATING	PRICE
MIDDLE EASTERN		
Zaytinya	★★★½	Moderate
MODERN AMERICAN		
The Inn at Little Washington	★★★★★	Very Expensive
Komi	★★★★★	Very Expensive
Minibar	★★★★★	Very Expensive
Restaurant Eve	★★★★	Very Expensive
Central Michel Richard	★★★½	Expensive
Corduroy	★★★½	Expensive
Iron Gate	★★★½	Moderate
Oval Room	★★★½	Moderate/Expensive
Ripple	★★★	Moderate/Expensive
Birch & Barley	★★★	Expensive
Equinox	★★★	Expensive
Food Wine & Co.	★★★	Moderate
Liberty Tavern	★★★	Inexpensive/Moderate
Range	★★½	Expensive
Tabard Inn	★★½	Moderate
PAN-ASIAN		
Doi Moi	★★★	Inexpensive
Toki Underground	★★½	Inexpensive
SEAFOOD		
Johnny's Half Shell	★★★	Expensive
Hank's Oyster Bar	★★½	Inexpensive/Moderate
SOUTHERN		
Acadiana	★★★	Moderate
Cashion's Eat Place	★★★	Moderate
Georgia Brown's	★★½	Moderate
SPANISH		
Jaleo	★★★½	Moderate
Estadio	★★★	Inexpensive
STEAK		
Ray's the Steaks	★★★½	Expensive
Iron Gate	★★★½	Moderate
THAI		
Little Serow	★★★★½	Expensive

PART SIX

ENTERTAINMENT *and* NIGHTLIFE

WASHINGTON NIGHTLIFE:
More Than Lit-Up Monuments

WASHINGTON AFTER-HOURS used to be an oxymoron. Public transportation set its clock by the bureaucracy, commuters had too far to go (and come back the next morning) to stay out late, and big expense-account money was lavished on restaurants and buddy bars. Besides, Washingtonians suffered from a persistent cultural inferiority complex that had them running to buy tickets to see touring theatrical companies while not-so-benignly neglecting home-grown troupes.

unofficial **TIP**
Drinking and dining are major elements of nightlife culture these days; check the "best" lists and neighborhood descriptions in Part Five: Dining as well.

Nowadays, though, the joke about Washington nightlife being an oxymoron is just that: a joke. It's not that there's too little nightlife around, it's that there's too much. Washington is a hodgepodge of big-city bustlers, bureaucrats, yuppies, journalists, diplomats, artists, immigrants, CEOs, and college students, and the fact that many of these groups overlap, and others evolve, means you can dabble in a little of everything.

Washington's theatre is underestimated (by tourists, at least) but acknowledged within the theatrical community as excellent—and it's booming, both physically and intellectually. It boasts what might be considered a trio of Shakespeare theatres, including one that evokes the Bard's own London Globe; numerous ethnic theatres (Hispanic, Jewish, Irish); and touring venues hosting the best of Broadway and London. In the past decade, the expansions of Signature Theatre, Studio Theatre, and most impressively, the highly regarded Arena Stage, plus the opening of the Music Center at Strathmore in Bethesda (and just in 2015, its offshoot AMP in Rockville), the Clarice Smith

Performing Arts Center at the University of Maryland, and other multispace performance venues, have established Washington as one of the country's premiere arts centers.

To top it off, the John F. Kennedy Center for the Performing Arts has begun a $100-million, 6,000-square-foot expansion project that will add three outdoor performance and rehearsal pavilions, gardens and outdoor dining, large-scale rehearsal spaces for opera and ballet, and even classrooms for what might be one of its most important legacies: the training of arts management. Also, a pedestrian bridge will enable visitors to access the center from either the Georgetown waterfront or the Lincoln Memorial without having to dodge traffic.

unofficial **TIP**
One of the Kennedy Center's new pavilions will float on the Potomac River (which President Kennedy loved almost as much as President Washington), clad in a translucent glass that the architect says "glows like a Japanese lantern," perhaps a nod to those famous cherry trees.

And nightclubs come in as many flavors as their patrons: dance halls, live-music venues, comedy showcases, salsa bars, specialty bars, sports bars, billiard bars, espresso bars, gay bars, strip bars, singles scenes . . . you could look it up. (And you probably should look it up: We just don't have enough space to tell you everything.)

In the last few years, a kind of nightclub renaissance has revitalized whole neighborhoods, a shift that has been particularly visible in areas that once were nearly deserted after rush hour, or at least after cocktail hour. The H Street NE neighborhood between 12th and 15th Streets, famously hard-hit by riots after the assassination of Reverend Martin Luther King Jr. and left desolate for nearly 30 years thereafter, has become one of the most idiosyncratic and entertaining—almost pop-up—nightlife areas in town, nicknamed the **Atlas District** after its own restored cinema–turned–performing arts center. The U Street/Mid City corridor centered on 14th and U Streets NW has become a lively restaurant and socializing center.

Because **Penn Quarter** (sometimes referred to as Gallery Place) is the hottest dining/drinking neighborhood in the area, and because the Verizon Center sports and concert arena is smack-dab in the middle of it, it's also a late-night celebrity-spotting scene. **Adams Morgan** may be less exuberant than the intentionally showstopping Atlas District, but it still has a major after-dark vibe. **Dupont Circle** remains the heart of Washington's LGBT community and their hangouts. **K Street NW,** long the domain of pinstripers and wannabe hipsters (but only from 9 to 5), is keeping them pinned in place with dance music and expensive bottle service. And even though **Georgetown** isn't much of a live-venue center anymore, it still has a few first-rate draws for night owls. Outside the District lines, **Bethesda** to the north in Montgomery County and **Clarendon** to the south in Arlington are both magnets for music and dining. Even better, almost all these neighborhoods are accessible by, or at least fairly near, subway stations. See more information on all these areas beginning on page 327.

THE BIG-TICKET VENUES

WASHINGTON BOASTS MORE THAN A DOZEN major theatrical venues—not even counting the Kennedy Center's eight (soon to be 11) venues separately—and a wealth of smaller residential and repertory companies, university theaters, and small special-interest venues for itinerant troupes. The "big six" are where national touring companies, classical musicians, and celebrity productions are most apt to show up, offer the most complete handicapped accessibility, and have arguably the most accessible websites.

unofficial **TIP**
If you are considering taking a (free) tour of the Kennedy Center, wait until later in the afternoon; stick around for the (also free) Millennium Stage show and take in the rooftop view.

Downtown Destinations

On any given night at the **Kennedy Center for the Performing Arts,** you might see the resident National Symphony Orchestra in the 2,500-seat **Concert Hall;** a straight drama or classic farce in the 1,200-seat **Eisenhower Theater;** and a Broadway musical, Kabuki spectacular, or big-name ballet company in the 2,300-seat **Opera House** (that is, when the Washington Opera is not in residence). Philip Johnson's steeply canted and gracious **Terrace Theater,** a gift from the nation of Japan, is an intimate venue of fewer than 500 seats, ideally suited for experimental or cult-interest productions, specialty concerts, and showcases. In the even smaller **Theater Lab,** designed to accommodate the avant-garde and cabaret, the semi-improv comedy whodunit *Shear Madness* has been in residence for nearly three decades.

The smallest venue, the **KC Jazz Club** (actually just the Terrace-level gallery, tricked out cabaret-style) is open only on weekends but hosts such first-rate groups as the Roy Hargrove Quintet and the Chick Corea Trio. It also presents cutting-edge discussions on quintessential jazz moments (Roots' pianist Ray Angry conducting a reimagining of Sarah Vaughn and Clifford Brown's 1954 recording), Washington jazz traditions (NPR's now-25-year-old "Jazz Piano Christmas"), and some startling one-chance double-bills such as the Branford Marsalis Quartet with the Terrance Blanchard Quintet or classical star Jeremy Denk and Kennedy Center Artistic Director for Jazz Jason Moran. And the **Family Theater** in the lobby level is one of the most up-to-date venues in the complex—the setting for musicals, folk music, all-ages pops concerts by the National Symphony Orchestra, and even educational (disguised as sci-fi) plays.

Perhaps most remarkable, however, is the Kennedy Center's gift to music lovers: the free **Millennium Stage,** which provides national and top local acts in an indoor venue at 6 p.m. every day of the year, usually in the 630-foot-long Grand Foyer (which, as docents love to point out, could easily cradle the not-quite-555-foot Washington Monument, though it might bust out part of the ceiling), but occasionally in the Theater Lab. The Kennedy Center is at Virginia and New Hampshire Avenues NW, next to the Watergate; the closest subway station is Foggy Bottom, and the center operates a free shuttle from the station. For tickets and information, call ☎ 202-467-4600 or visit **kennedy-center.org.**

The other major downtown venues are in or near Penn Quarter and accessible by several Metro stations.

The critically acclaimed **Shakespeare Theatre Company** (STC) moved first from its beloved but cramped home at the **Folger Shakespeare Library** on Capitol Hill into the 450-seat **Lansburgh Theatre** on Seventh Street NW, which it still operates, and then migrated to the **Sidney Harman Center for the Arts** around the corner on F Street (named for the philanthropist and public servant who donated generously for its construction and who, appropriately, was one of the founders of Harman Kardon audio company). The new building houses jazz, dance, film, and chamber music, as well as theatrical productions; the Lansburgh houses smaller touring shows or quirkier Shakespeare Company productions. Each season, STC produces four classic plays, three by Shakespeare, and regularly corrals major stage and screen stars to headline. It also puts on another of Washington's very best freebies: the annual Shakespeare "Free for All" series in late August and early September. The Harman Center is across from the Verizon Center and the Gallery Place–Chinatown Metro; the Lansburgh Theatre is just a minute closer to the Archives–Navy Memorial–Penn Quarter stops. For information call ☎ 202-547-1122 or 202-638-3863, or visit **shakespearetheatre.org.**

*un*official **TIP**
The Folger Shakespeare Library is home to the lovely period-style Elizabethan Theatre—where Shakespeare and other classic plays are mounted, along with early-music concerts by the Folger Consort—and owns an unrivaled collection of 79 First Folios and other manuscript treasures. The family-friendly celebration of Shakespeare's birthday in April is a local favorite.

ESPECIALLY IN TERMS OF ARTS AND HISTORY, there are three additional background heroes of Washington. **Donald W. Reynolds,** whose philanthropy spanned numerous states and foundations, gave essential donations to create what is now the twinned National Portrait Gallery–Smithsonian American Art Museum; he also made possible the extensive visitor center and exhibit galleries that were added to Mount Vernon in 2006. Developer **Robert H. Smith** donated hugely to the University of Maryland (including the Clarice Smith Performing Arts Center, named for his wife), the auditorium at Mount Vernon, and the restoration of James Madison's Montpelier; he also served as chairman of the board of the National Gallery of Art during an era of expansion from 1993 to 2003. And Smith's partner and brother-in-law **Robert Kogod** was key to the creation of the beloved glass-covered canopy between the Portrait Gallery and American Art Museums, as well as the expansions of Signature Theatre, Arena Stage, Clarice Smith Center, and Shakespeare Theatre, among others.

The National Theatre is a not-for-profit venue, nor is it a federal venue: It got its name from its founders—some of the few early proud Washingtonians—who wanted the nation's capital to have a theatre rivaling those in other big cities. That was in 1835, a quarter-century before John T. Ford turned an abandoned Baptist church into an entertainment venue. The National has been in nearly continual operation ever since ("nearly," because it refused for four years in the late 1940s and early 1950s to integrate). On the night Lincoln was assassinated at Ford's Theatre, he had dropped off his young son Tad at a performance of *Aladdin and the Wonderful Lamp* at the National. The National also hosted the world debut of *West Side Story* in 1957. Though it is now managed by the Shubert Organization, which books its touring Broadway productions there and often uses it for pre-Broadway tryouts, it also offers a nice lineup of free programs— Monday night films, Saturday-morning family shows, and so on. The National is at 13th and Pennsylvania Avenue NW, near the Federal Triangle or Metro Center stations (☎ 202-628-6161; **nationaltheatre.org**).

The Warner Theatre, a 1922 silent-movie house and vaudeville venue, survived a two-year restoration marathon in the early 1990s and is now a rococo delight. It is the home of one of Washington's most beloved traditions, the Washington Ballet's version of *The Nutcracker.* Although it is emphasizing more legitimate theatrical bookings and musicals, and is booked by the national powerhouse Live Nation, it still occasionally harkens back to the days when it was one of the best small-concert venues for popular music (the Rolling Stones played a surprise show here in the late 1970s, and the reclusive Brian Wilson chose the Warner for his *Smile* and final *Pet Sounds* tours) or big-name comedians. The Warner is at 13th and E Streets NW, near Federal Triangle or Metro Center (☎ 202-783-4000; **warnertheatredc.com**). Look for the walk-of-fame autographs on the sidewalk out front.

And **Ford's Theatre,** where the balcony box in which Abraham Lincoln was shot remains draped in black (and spectrally inhabited, according to rumor), has emerged from a $9-million renovation with

unofficial **TIP**
One of the main proponents of a "national theater" was William Wilson Corcoran, he of the Renwick and Corcoran Gallery and numerous other Washington institutions. A successful tycoon at a young age, he contributed not only to area colleges and churches (and Oak Hill Cemetery) but also to the fund to rescue Mount Vernon from foreclosures and for firewood for the poor.

state-of-the-art audiovisual equipment, better restrooms, an expanded theatrical season, and a Lincoln museum in the basement that includes his blood-spattered overcoat and the Derringer that John Wilkes Booth used to shoot him. Its holiday complement to the Warner's *Nutcracker* is its annual production of *A Christmas Carol,* which ranges from very traditional to extremely spooky. Located on 10th Street NW between E and F Streets, Ford's is near several subway stops on various lines (☎ 202-347-4833; **fordstheatre.org**).

It's not of the same size or profile, but the long-itinerant but undiminished **Woolly Mammoth** now has a 265-seat courtyard-style venue near the Lansburgh at Seventh and D Streets NW. Located in the heart of Penn Quarter, it has won more than two-dozen Helen Hayes Awards, many for premiering new works (☎ 202-393-3939; **woollymammoth .net**). And the restored **Historic Sixth and I Street (NW) Synagogue** has begun offering a wide array of music—Clannad, Béla Fleck, Kathy Mattea, Suzanne Vega, and so on—as well as readings and panels (☎ 202-408-3100; **sixthandi.org**).

Midtown Draws

Several of Washington's smaller, special-interest theaters are clustered around the revitalized Mid City/Logan Circle neighborhood, not a long walk from the Dupont Circle Metro. The most important is **Studio Theatre** (14th and P Streets NW; **studiotheatre .org**), which unveiled a three-stage expansion a few years ago. What was the home of **Source Theatre** at 14th and R is now home base to several small troupes, including Washington Improv Theater and the Constellation Theatre Company (**sourcefestival.org**).

*un**official* **TIP**
Dickens's *A Christmas Carol* is a Washington tradition in all sorts of ways: The Keegan Theatre produces *An Irish Carol,* a somewhat more adult version whose central character is not a money lender but a publican.

The **Keegan Theatre,** which specializes in American and Irish plays (though not at all stereotypical—its 2015–2016 season includes *American Idiot* and *Cat on a Hot Tin Roof*), has grown from a basement ensemble to having a permanent home at the 115-seat Church Street Theatre (1743 Church Street NW; **keegan theatre.com**). Among other niche-specific troupes are **Theater J,** a few blocks away at 16th and Q Streets NW (**washingtondcjcc.org /center-for-arts/theater-j**); and the 40-year-old Spanish-language (with subtitles) **GALA Hispanic Theater** in the beautifully restored 270-seat Tivoli Theater at 14th Street NW and Park Road, two blocks north of the Columbia Heights Metro (**galatheatre.org**).

A little farther north in Mid City along the U Street corridor is the revitalized **Lincoln Theatre** (**thelincolndc.com**), across the street from the U Street–African American Civil War Memorial–Cardozo Metro. This 1922 beauty, once the heart of the "Black Broadway" neighborhood, now hosts a range of theatrical productions (including some pre-Broadway tryouts) and concerts; it's also a major venue for the annual Duke Ellington Jazz Festival in June.

 THE COTTON CLUB AND APOLLO THEATER may be more famous, but Washington's "Black Broadway" was in full bloom long before the Harlem Renaissance, and outlasted it by decades. The area around U Street had become an upscale black Victorian neighborhood even before the end of the Civil War, but starting in the early 20th century, a slew of black-owned nightclubs and restaurants drew not only an elegant crowd but also some of the greatest names in entertainment, particularly jazz. This included Louis Armstrong, Pearl Bailey (who is believed to have coined the term "jazz"), Cab Calloway, Duke Ellington (who grew up in the neighborhood and truly fell in love with the piano hanging around the Howard Theatre), Ella Fitzgerald, Billie Holiday, and Sarah Vaughan.

Though not directly accessible by Metro, the multistage **Atlas Performing Arts Center,** a restored Deco movie theater, is an easy free trolley ride away (from Gallery Place–Chinatown or Union Station). The Atlas acts as home base for the Washington Savoyards (a Gilbert & Sullivan troupe), the African Continuum Theatre, the Capital City Symphony, Joy of Motion Dance Theatre, Scena Theatre, and several other community arts groups (14th and H Streets NE; **atlasarts.org**).

On the Waterfront

The biggest excitement in recent Washington theater circles was the late-2010 opening of the soaring and state-of-the-art **Arena Stage,** formally known as the Arena Stage at the Mead Center for the American Theater. Founded 65 years ago as a haven for the preservation and encouragement of American theater, the Arena was already one of the country's most influential theaters before it emerged from the two-and-a-half-year, $135-million reconstruction—renovation is too small a word—as a towering, 200,000-square-foot glass-and-concrete vessel, the largest performing arts center in the region since the Kennedy Center. In fact, Arena, along with Nationals Stadium, has sparked a revitalization not only of the theater scene but also of the entire Southwest sector.

The new Arena, which is more than twice the size of the old, has three venues: the 500-seat Kreeger Theater; the 680-seat Fichandler Stage, which was the original Arena Stage and which has been embedded in the new design; and the completely new, 200-seat Kogod Cradle, which is like a chambered nautilus, with a semicircular entrance ramp on the outside and a slat-sided "basket" of a stage within. Designed by Bing Thom, the complex includes bars and an upscale catered café; glass walls, wood columns, sloping floors, and long steel elbow bars; and a rock garden, lots of overhung walkways, and mysterious vistas.

Arena Stage is only a couple of blocks from the Waterfront-SEU Metro stop. The entire stretch of the waterfront in that area, with

Arena and the Nationals baseball park as the catalysts, is being redeveloped with hotels and apartment buildings, a marina, and more transportation options. Visit **arenastage.org** for more information.

Superb Suburbanites

As dominant as the downtown theatrical scene may seem, the suburbs on all sides of the District have more opportunities than we can list here. Check the "Guide to the Lively Arts" in *The Washington Post* Friday "Weekend" section or the free *City Paper,* for a full listing, but here are some of the most important.

In the past few years, a number of impressive performance venues have been developed in the Maryland suburbs, several accessible by subway. The **Clarice Smith Performing Arts Center,** on the College Park campus of the University of Maryland, offers almost as many venues as the Kennedy Center (and in several cases, even more cutting-edge acoustical and recording technology): the 1,100-seat Dekelboum Concert Hall, with its modern-Gothic arches and choral loft; the 180-seat Dance Theatre; the 650-seat proscenium Kay Theatre; the 300-seat Gildenhorn Recital Hall; the intimate 100-seat Cafritz Foundation Theatre; and the 200-seat "black box"–style Kogod Theatre. Smith Center offerings have ranged from Chinese opera and the Shanghai Traditional Orchestra to Phillip Glass and Laurie Anderson, Liz Lerman Dance Company and Merce Cunningham Dance Company, the Kronos Quartet, and the Abbey Theatre—plus productions featuring the university's dance, music, theater, and voice departments. It also plays host to several national and international competitions every year. The Clarice Smith Center is at University Boulevard and Stadium Drive in College Park; you can take the Green Line Metro to the College Park station and take one of two free shuttles to the Stamp Student Union, or take the campus "Circuit" shuttle directly to the complex (**claricesmithcenter.umd.edu**).

Closer in, and very Metro accessible via an underground pedestrian tunnel, is the **Round House Theatre** on East-West Highway, catty-corner from the Bethesda Metro station (**roundhousetheatre .org**). Round House mounts a mix of family, experimental, classic, and premiere productions. Just a bit farther from the Bethesda Metro, an eight-minute walk at most, is one of the area's most important children's and family theaters, **Imagination Stage,** which began as a school for the performing arts and moved into its two-stage complex, with rehearsal and classroom space, in 2003 (**imaginationstage.org**).

The **Montgomery College** campus in Rockville has a fine acoustic facility. Most of its concerts feature area jazz or classical performances, and they are free. You'll have to take a Ride-On from the Rockville Metro, or stroll maybe 10 minutes (**cms.montgomerycollege.edu**).

And although they require cars (or friends), there are two other prominent venues in Montgomery County. The historic **Olney Theatre,** on Route 108 in Olney, Maryland, started out in 1938 producing high-quality summer stock (over the years, its marquee has listed Tallulah Bankhead, John Carradine, Carol Channing, Hume Cronyn, Jose Ferrer, Lillian Gish, Helen Hayes, Ian McKellan, Gloria Swanson, and Jessica Tandy). Now open year-round, the Olney offers a variety of children's, classic, touring company, and musical productions, as well as free Shakespeare in the summer (**olneytheatre.org**). The increasingly popular **BlackRock Center for the Arts** in Germantown Town Center (**blackrockcenter.org**) also has three venues: a 210-seat main stage, a 130-seat dance theater, and an outdoor performance stage for theatrical productions, festivals, concerts, and outdoor family films. Among recent artists booked there are Alvin Ailey II, the Baltimore Symphony Orchestra Chamber Players, Richie Havens, Janis Ian, and the Marcus Roberts Trio; top local acts the Nighthawks, Mary Ann Redmond, and Seldom Scene; and indie filmmakers and storytellers.

The Virginia suburbs are equally star-studded. The fascinating **Synetic Theater** (**synetictheater.org**), which calls itself "D.C.'s premier physical theater," rethinks fantastic and often supernatural stories—Shakespeare, Edgar Allen Poe, *Don Quixote, King Arthur,* and even *Dracula* and *Frankenstein*—as intensely visual dream works mixing ballet, modern dance, artscapes, multimedia, and mime. Its "Wordless Shakespeare" plays are fascinating—and one reason it occasionally mounts pieces at the Kennedy Center or Lansburgh Theatre downtown. Its home stage is about a block from the Crystal City Metro.

Though not Metro accessible, one of Washington's most successful companies is **Signature Theatre,** whose crystalline two-story center launched the redevelopment of the Shirlington Village of Arlington. Signature has sent several of its theatrical productions to Broadway and frequently brings in national names for locally mounted productions of both established and avant-garde theater and cabaret (**sig-online.org**). Remarkably, every seat at every Signature production's initial run is only $25, one-third the full cost. Signature is also remarkable for devoting whole seasons to the work of a single playwright.

The Center for the Arts at George Mason University in Fairfax is not Metro accessible, but if you have access to a car, it also hosts opera, jazz, popular music, cabaret, symphony performances, "new" circuses a la Cirque du Soleil, and so on (**cfa.gmu.edu**).

CUTTING CURTAIN COSTS

THOUGH MANY OF THESE professional productions can be pricey and often sell out, there are ways to trim the ticket tab for less-popular or longer-running shows. **Ticket Place,**

unofficial **TIP**
The bottom line is, always ask if there's a way to boost your bottom line. What's to lose?

operated by the Cultural Alliance of Greater Washington, sells half-price tickets online (plus a service charge) for some same-day shows and concerts (**ticketplace.org** or **culturecapital.tix.com**). There is a service charge, and all sales are final.

Gold Star (**goldstar.com**) is one of several online/social media sites that sends out notices of discount offers, not only to shows (many of them at major venues) but also to museums, cruises, clubs, and so on.

In addition, several venues, including the Kennedy Center and Arena Stage, offer discounts to special groups, typically students (and sometimes teachers), seniors, patrons with disabilities, military, Metro subway patrons, or those willing to stand or stand by. As noted above, Signature Theatre bears two-thirds of the cost of all seats to its new productions. Call the venue's box office and just say you're from out of town and don't really know all the ins and outs of ticket pricing; operators will do the best they can for you. Or check the website for opportunities.

In the meantime, don't overlook the myriad freebies available, particularly during good weather. In addition to the several mentioned above—the Shakespeare Theatre Company's "Free For All" series, the nightly Millennium Stage performances at the Kennedy Center, the National Theater's Saturday mornings, and so on—several public sites frequently hold concerts of classical, jazz, pop, and folk music, and even some medieval consorts. Among them are the **Washington National Cathedral, National Gallery of Art,** and the **Library of Congress.** For information on these, plus the handful of smaller theaters and itinerant companies, check their websites, or read *The Washington Post* on Friday or online.

*un**official* **TIP**

Here's something longtime residents may not want you to know: The popular National Symphony Orchestra holiday concerts are always packed with patrons, but there are also full dress rehearsals that are a little easier to get into. The Memorial Day and Fourth of July rehearsals are the day before; the Labor Day rehearsal is usually in the afternoon a few hours before the performance.

If you are visiting in midsummer, be sure to investigate the Smithsonian's answer to the Millennium Stage (in terms of gifts to the public): the **Folklife Festival** on the Mall, which for two weeks every year, around the last week of June and the first week of July (culminating around the Fourth of July fireworks display), celebrates a region of the United States and an international culture, complete with all-day live concerts, performances, and food demonstrations.

There are several other warm-weather outdoor music venues downtown, including the **Woodrow Wilson Plaza** at 13th and Pennsylvania Avenue NW and **Freedom Plaza** at 14th and Pennsylvania. The **National Mall** is the site of many festivals during the year in addition to the Folklife Festival, notably on Memorial Day, the Fourth of July, and Labor

Day, when the National Symphony Orchestra and special guest celebrities offer family concerts. Wednesdays are entertainment nights on Georgetown's waterfront (make it a double-header—hit the Kennedy Center's Millennium Stage first and walk over). West Potomac Park has become a site for some of the newer music festivals and fund-raisers.

Washington is also home to another type of free concert: the **armed-services bands.** From about Memorial Day to Labor Day, ensembles from the four branches perform evening concerts, generally starting at 7:30 or 8 p.m., Monday, Tuesday, Wednesday, and Friday before the west front of the Capitol; Tuesday at the Navy Memorial at 7th and Pennsylvania Avenue NW; Wednesday at the Sylvan Theater near the Washington Monument and at Fort Myer in Rosslyn (the most "traditional" in costume but, unhappily, the least accessible); and Friday (a little later, 8:30 p.m.) at the Marine Barracks on Capitol Hill. Sunday matinees at Constitution Hall are the largest, featuring well-known entertainers in patriotic and martial, country, jazz, pop, and some classical music (**usarmyband.com**). You're welcome to bring picnic bags to the outside performances, but as with all National Park Service concerts, including the NSO holiday concerts on the Mall, alcohol is not permitted.

LIVE MUSIC

WASHINGTON IS A DRAW FOR MUSIC LOVERS of all types, from classical to college-radio rock, indie to outrageous, retro to roots, and from hole-in-the-wall to the Washington Mall. Venues range from a few hundred to a few thousand to super-size sports arenas. D.C. has boasting rights to a number of breakout artists and trends over two centuries. John Phillip Sousa and Duke Ellington were both homegrown innovators, and so were Jefferson Airplane guitarist Jorma Koukonen, soul agnostic Marvin Gaye, go-go "godfather" Chuck Brown, the late soulful singer Eva Cassidy (whose version of "Somewhere Over the Rainbow" was featured during the "In Memoriam" segment of the 2015 Emmy Awards), seminal punk Dischord Records, early femme-confessional pianist Tori Amos, and Dave Grohl of Nirvana and Foo Fighters, to name a very few. And while there are obviously commercial interests involved in booking the midsize and larger sites in particular (consider the merger of Ticketmaster and Live Nation), a lot of the credit for the vital live music scene in the area belongs to the stubborn musicians and underground entrepreneurs who have established venues and support networks for themselves and one another.

unofficial **TIP**
If you intend to book tickets for big shows, don't be confused by the name of the website; make sure you are dealing directly with the venue whenever possible, not being shuffled onto a secondhand or resale site that will cost more.

The Larger Venues

As in many big cities, the downtown sports arenas do double duty as mega-rock concert venues, especially the 20,000-plus-seat **Verizon Center** (aka the Phone Booth) downtown, home to the Washington Wizards and Mystics NBA teams, and the Capitals NHL team. As it's an all-season indoor venue, and has more hookups for lights and tech, that's where the off-season and theatrically elaborate tours tend to stop: Lady Gaga, the Police, Paul Simon, James Taylor and Carole King, and those orchestral music/light show spectaculars (Trans-Siberian Orchestra, *Star Wars* in concert, *Dinosaurs*, and so on). Verizon Center has its own entrance from the Gallery Place–Chinatown Metro.

Though only partially covered, the 42,000-seat **Washington Nationals ballpark,** at the Navy Yard Metro, has hosted Billy Joel and Elton John, Dave Matthews, Paul McCartney, and Bruce Springsteen. (Nats Park is also used for live simulcasts of the Washington Opera.) The old **RFK Stadium,** at the Stadium-Armory stop, is still used as an occasional entertainment venue: the Roots, Stone Temple Pilots, and various all-day hip-hop and even Irish music festivals play RFK. The massive Wharf development along the Southwest waterfront, a City Center–like mix of retail, residential, and cultural sites, is scheduled to include a 6,500-seat music venue managed by Seth Hurwitz, owner of the seminal 9:30 Club.

More progressive rock acts, which draw strong college and post-grad audiences, tend to be booked into college sports spaces, such as George Washington University's **Smith Center** or Georgetown's **Gaston Hall.** National acts with midsize audiences—revived rockers (including John Mellencamp and the Allman Brothers), R&B, gospel, soul, and folk—are often booked into the **DAR Constitution Hall** alongside the Ellipse. And the woods-lined, 3,700-seat **Carter-Barron Amphitheatre** in Rock Creek Park hosts occasional (and frequently free) gospel, soul, jazz, ska, and R&B concerts in summer, along with some family film nights.

Outside the city are several of the area's largest venues, which are not so easily accessible but are regular summer commutes for Washingtonians. Perhaps the most sentimentally popular outdoor commercial venue, and the only one with any sort of Metro connection, is the most sophisticated of them: **Wolf Trap Farm Park** off Route 7 in Vienna, Virginia, which offers almost nightly entertainment—pop, country, jazz and R&B, MOR (middle-of-the-road) rock, and even ballet and Broadway musical tours—and picnicking under the stars during the summer at its **Filene Center** amphitheater. (It also operates a full-service restaurant.) During the winter season, Wolf Trap shifts to its small (220 seats) but acoustically great **Barns**—literally two rebuilt vintage barns—which book everything from Wolf Trap's own highly regarded opera company to Joan Armatrading, American pop songbook historian John Eaton, the Flying Karamazov Brothers, Rickie Lee Jones, and Chris Smither, as well as some of the best local acts. On summer nights, the Metro operates a $5 round-trip shuttle service from the West Falls Church station to the Filene Center, but watch your watch: The return shuttle leaves either 20 minutes after the final curtain or at 11 p.m., whichever is earlier, in order to ensure that riders don't miss the Metro.

The gorilla in the Beltway backyard is **Jiffy Lube Live** just off Interstate 66 outside Manassas, Virginia. It's a surprisingly attractive amphitheater with 10,000 covered seats and lawn seating for another 15,000 people (and parking lots and hillsides for tailgates and picnicking). Operated by Live Nation, the largest promoter in the country, it books the full range of big-ticket acts: Mary J. Blige, Iron Maiden, Kiss, Tim McGraw, Pearl Jam, Tom Petty, Rush, Taylor Swift, and Kanye West. And since Live Nation and Ticketmaster are now one, it's all booked through Ticketmaster (☎ 202-397-SEAT; **livenation.com**).

Merriweather Post Pavilion (MPP) in Columbia, Maryland, which also mixes under-cover and lawn seating, has the busiest pop-rock outdoor arena and mixes old-favorite rock and pop tours with younger-draw and cult acts (Béla Fleck, Incubus, Norah Jones, Kid Rock, Lilith Fair, Tom Petty, Phish, Snoop Dogg, Virgin Fest). Keep in mind it is some distance from Washington and can only be reached by car. It's more likely to have some of the multi-act, all-day festivals, and partly for that reason, perhaps, has upgraded its concessions. MPP, booked by locally based IMP Productions, which also owns the prestigious 9:30 club, sells tickets through Ticketfly (☎ 877-4FLYTIX; **ticketfly.com**).

The 10,000-seat **Eagle Bank Arena** (formerly Patriot Center) at George Mason University in Fairfax tends to carry the big-name country concerts, as well as college-draw rock and pop. The adjoining GMU Center for the Arts, described on page 317, is a lovely midsize venue for classical and jazz music and drama.

Midsize Settings

Here we mean the smaller theaters and largest clubs, between, say, 300 and 2,000 seats. One of the most impressive is the **Music Center at Strathmore Hall** in North Bethesda, which, happily for tourists, has a dedicated pedestrian overpass from the Grosvenor-Strathmore Metro station. A beautiful blond-wood space with comfortable chairs and first-rate acoustics, it seats 2,000, and books national classical and pop singers, visiting symphony orchestras, and folk and blues society shows. (The original Strathmore Hall Mansion, a much more intimate affair, hosts tea-time concerts (harp, Japanese koto, violin) on Tuesdays and Wednesdays, as well as summertime concerts and family films on the lawn; it also has art galleries and crafts shows.) For information on programming, visit **strathmore.org.**

Strathmore's new extension, **AMP** (as in "amping up" the options), is about a mile north in the Pike & Rose mixed-residential development near the White Flint Metro, and has seats for 240 plus 350 SRO spaces. Most shows—and the variety is rather eccentric—are Thursday to Saturday. Its main advantage over its parent is freshly prepared (rather than café-style) fare from the ChurchKey group and a much more elaborate cocktail list.

In Silver Spring, a short stroll from the Silver Spring Metro, the 2,000-seat **Fillmore** actually holds 2,000 spaces of SRO, and a handful of "premium" seats. It opened its doors with a sold-out Mary J. Blige concert, and has followed up with classic rock/reruns (Blondie, Cheap Trick, Guns N' Roses, Slayer, Steve Winwood); dance-hall pop (Kelly Rowland); alt-folk (Levon Helm); semi-indie songwriters (Sarah Bareilles and Gavin DeGraw); new-breed country hunks and punks (Chris Young, Kid Rock); tribute bands; and even heavy-metal cult icon Megadeth and comic Andrew Dice Clay. The sound system is vast, showy, and bass-heavy. In terms of decor, the club also seems to want to cover all bases, mixing bordello red drapes, oversize pop art and cartoon graphics, vintage concert posters, chandeliers, and a few lighting effects.

The **Hamilton** downtown is actually a huge, sprawling restaurant with benefits (that is, a nice concert hall on the lower level). It belongs to the local stalwart Clyde's chain, and the upstairs menu includes sushi (a first for the group), plus a full sweep of upscale appetizers and sandwiches, steaks, seafood, and pasta—all available fairly late. The Hamilton Live, as the downstairs music room is called, seats 300, with another 200 standing-room spaces. Bookings range from classic rock to up-and-coming iTunes, jazz, R&B, folk, blues, and country: Bobby Blue Bland, Dr. John, Emmylou Harris, NRBQ, Bucky Pizzarelli, Leon Russell, Spyro Gyra, Booker T., and the Tubes, plus the very occasional bluegrass act or comedian—oh, and Chubby Checker. It has also picked up on the tribute-band craze. You could eat upstairs and then go down for the music, but the Hamilton adheres to the new standard operating procedure: general admission/first come, first seated, and otherwise SRO. It's also all-ages, so depending on which antiquated rock band you're seeing, the line may be even longer. If you're a fan of gospel brunches, this is one of the most expansive Sunday spreads around.

As mentioned before, the 1,800-seat Warner Theater still occasionally books musical acts. George Washington University's **Lisner Auditorium** seats 1,500. Wolf Trap's cold-weather facility, the Barns, holds nearly 400 but occasionally pulls up the main-floor seats for "dance parties."

The **9:30** club, arguably the most important music venue in the region, holds 1,200 ("seats" not being exactly the word) for an amazingly eclectic range of music: alt, country/top 40, hardcore, hip-hop, prog, reggae, semi-punk, and true rock. Consider a scrapbook that includes Blondie, the BoDeans, James Brown, Elvis Costello, the Damned, Bob Dylan, Five for Fighting, Fugazi, Joan Jett, Sergio Mendes, Liz Phair, Radiohead, Smashing Pumpkins, Squeeze, Richard Thompson, Justin Timberlake, Suzanne Vega, and Dwight Yoakam. (Before you go, be sure you know who's playing: The crowd that pays up for Ice-T isn't the same as the one for Marshall Crenshaw, They Might Be Giants, or Anthrax.) It's close to the U Street–African-American Civil War Memorial–Cardozo Metro, but being an old building, it has limited wheelchair access.

unofficial **TIP**
The 9:30 is one of an increasing number of area clubs that believes in seating democracy—that is, general admission SRO—so it's first come, first stand (with very few exceptions); you might find an odd ledge to lean on, and there are a few stools around the mezzanine.

The **Birchmere** in Alexandria, the premiere site for country, bluegrass, new-alt, and ethnic folk acts, holds about 500 (with a smaller roadhouse-style second stage). This is a serious eclectic venue and easily the biggest for new acoustic, alternative, bluegrass, and country acts, such as hometown heroine Mary Chapin Carpenter, Rosanne Cash, Lyle Lovett, Marty Stuart, and Jerry Jeff Walker; Shawn Colvin, Fountains of Wayne, k.d. lang, Patty Loveless, Nick Lowe, Don McLean, Maria Muldaur, and Suzanne Vega; and a few old rockers such as Frank Marino and Mahogany Rush. The bad news—it's not anywhere near the Metro, and although it is a table-service restaurant, all seating is first come, closest in. If you go, go early and expect to stand in line. (But don't worry—it's a bit of a tailgate atmosphere.)

The **Black Cat** in Mid City was another early breakthrough on the music scene and is still a main attraction, booking a mix of hot regional and early-national alternative rock, funky-punk, post-punk, Brit-pop, indie rock, and revivals, from Arcade Fire, Death Cab for Cutie, Kings of Leon, the White Stripes, and Hank Williams III to the Damned, Foo Fighters, Fleshtones, Zombies, et al. The main stage can hold about 1,000 fans; the smaller back room holds only about 150, so that goes to up-and-coming bands and (mostly) DJs. In keeping with the neighborhood playground style, the main-floor bar has pinball and

unofficial **TIP**
Another thing to know about the Washington nightlife scene is that an increasing number of these venues are cash-only, which eliminates some underage freeloading (at best) and greatly increases the bartending speed. Make sure you know the policies at any club before you head out.

pool tables. This is not a swank joint, but it's not scuzzy, either. If you can make it to the box office, you'll save the ticket fee; it's all cash-only with an ATM on site. Get there early for a concert—the check-in system is fairly slow because Black Cat is an all-ages club, so IDs are closely scrutinized and 21-and-over hands have to be stamped for alcohol consumption.

The **State Theatre**, a renovated Art Deco movie house in Falls Church that is a 10-minute walk from the East Falls Church Metro, books rock, blues, reggae, Cajun R&B, jam, alt-country, folk, and indie bands, not to mention cult heroes, been-there-done-that-and-hope-to-again dinosaurs, and one-hit-wonders. Cases in point: Asleep at the Wheel, Hanson, Radiators, Leon Russell, the Smithereens, Toots and the Maytals, Johnny Winter, Wu-Tang Clan, and the odd burlesque show. It also hosts a lot of tribute bands, which can lead to hilarious fan dance duels: Madonna vs. Michael Jackson, for instance. It holds about 215 upstairs but has cocktail tables and standing room on the ground floor.

One of the first attractions to put Clarendon on the map, **IOTA** had the best lineup of acoustic rock, neo-roots, soft psychedelic, progressive, and eclectic melodic rock in town every night of the week for many years. (Its slogan is "Live Music Forever.") Three blocks from the Clarendon Metro, it began as a sort of antiestablishment local musicians' showcase and has hosted any number of stars at the start of their careers (Jack Johnson, Norah Jones, John Mayer, Jason Mraz), as well as indie and alt-rock faves such as Bottle Rockets, John Doe, Drive-by Truckers, Alejandro Escovedo, and so on. However, while you can plan to go in advance, you can't do anything more than that: There are no advance-ticket sales, and admission is first come, first served—which, because it only holds about 160 people, means you'd best be prepared to make friends.

One of the other most interesting music clubs in the area is also in Virginia, and unfortunately it's also not Metro-accessible. **Jammin' Java** is the real deal—locally owned (by three musician brothers), open seven days a week, and as eclectic as 9:30. It books rock, country, folk, blues, punk, even daytime children's entertainers and cult favorites such as Marshall Crenshaw, Enter the Haggis, Daniel Lanois, and former Squeeze front man Glenn Tilbrook. Not long ago, Paul Kelly spent two nights working his way through his songbook alphabetically. The club's drawbacks include seating (there are a few advance-reservation tables; otherwise, it might be folding chairs or standing) and a surprisingly loud volume level (consider that the owners are music producers).

The new kid on the block is **Gypsy Sally's**, a 300-seat-plus venue almost hidden along the Georgetown waterfront that books what its owners describe as "Americana," including alt-country, blues, and bluegrass. The adjoining Vinyl Lounge is a lovely throwback where the decor is Summer of Love, and the music really is on vinyl. Now one of the last live music spots in this once after-dark destination, Gypsy Sally's pays homage to those now-shuttered Georgetown stages such as the Bayou, the Cellar Door, and Desperado's. Google them sometime.

Specialty Clubs

Jazz has a long history in Washington, and the old "Black Broadway" is a very good place to start. Just along U Street, near the U Street–African American Civil War Memorial–Cardozo station and the Lincoln Theatre, are several clubs offering jazz nearly every night, including **Bohemian Caverns,** an old revitalized jazz club at 11th and U Streets NW that also spins occasional funk and go-go dance music; **Twins Jazz Lounge,** at 1344 U Street, which offers live jazz every night; and the **Howard Theatre,** a few blocks away at 620 T Street NW.

The grand old jazz club of Washington, in terms of big-name bookings and length of uninterrupted service, is **Blues Alley** in Georgetown, which has hosted the biggest names in jazz and (more rarely) R&B or soul for 40 years: Jerry Butler, Charlie Byrd, Dizzy Gillespie, Ramsey Lewis, Arturo Sandoval, and every member of the Marsalis family— sometimes together. The menu is more or less New Orleans–style, with entrées named for stars (Sarah Vaughan's filet mignon, Maynard Ferguson's shrimp and peppers pasta). It's an old Georgetown townhouse, so it's not the most luxurious environment—there is little elbow room, and wheelchair access is limited—and since table seating is first come, first served, put in your dinner reservation and show up early. Actually, bar seating is first come, first served as well.

One of the relative newcomers to the scene is the **Bethesda Blues and Jazz** club, another refitted Art Deco cinema, with dinner tables right up to the apron (except when the front area is cleared for dancing), and live entertainment nightly. The management uses "jazz and blues" in the broadest terms: doo-wop, harmonic, horns, jazz orchestra, Latin, lounge, New Orleans beat, piano trios, swing, tango, zydeco, occasionally classic country and bluegrass (Ralph Stanley!), a little funk, and top-flight tributes to big-band, pop, rock, and soul artists. There is even the occasional burlesque troupe. The club also has been supportive of top-tier local bands and has an admirable "listening club" policy, which nudges patrons to remember to lower their voices and ditch the cell phone. It's an easy walk from the Bethesda Metro, and it's wheelchair friendly as well.

Washington's equivalent of the Lincoln Center Jazz Orchestra, the **Smithsonian Jazz Masterworks Orchestra,** calls the National Museum of American History home; the ensemble plays infrequently but has the advantage of access to original transcriptions and even recordings of classic performances.

The Old Naval Hospital on Capitol Hill near the Eastern Market Metro has been renovated as the **Hill Center,** a home for art, cultural nonprofits, and music, especially jazz. The **Carlyle Club** at the edge of Old Town Alexandria is an elegant throwback, a 1930s-style supper club with retro cocktails and, again, a Creole-inflected menu. During warm weather, the outdoor **Gallaudet Pavilion,** near the burgeoning

Union Market along the re-emerging New York Avenue Northeast corridor, hosts jazz and other pop-up concerts.

Other friendly places to hang out and listen to jazz include the **Zoo Bar** on Connecticut Avenue, a couple of blocks south of the Cleveland Park Metro stop just across from the main gate of the National Zoo; and the New Orleans–vibe **Bayou** on Pennsylvania Avenue just east of Georgetown.

For R&B and blues, check out the venerable (and authentically worn) **New Vegas Lounge,** just off the 14th and P Street strip near Logan Circle.

Irish bars, real or otherwise, do a flourishing business in Washington, with the help of a resident community of performers. Among the Metro-accessible pubs with live music at least a couple of times a week—and preferably at least one fireplace—are the **Dubliner** on Capitol Hill and its near semi-sibling rival **Kelly's Irish Times,** and the theatrically "authentic" **Fado Irish Pub** near the old Chinatown–Gallery Place entrance.

The Dubliner across from Union Station is not the oldest Irish bar in town (though it is more than 40 years old), but it has become the clan leader: it's centrally located, politically connected, and has provided the training ground for founders of a half dozen other bars, including Kelly's. It's also one of the few places in Washington to offer live music seven nights a week. Fittingly, the Dubliner also has one of the most colorful histories, filled with romantic intrigue, boom-and-bust bank troubles, and riotous St. Patrick's week parties. The Dubliner is filled with antiques, such as the 1810 hand-carved walnut bar in

unofficial **TIP**

Though Washington, D.C., once claimed to be the bluegrass capital of the country, the bluegrass scene is sadly down to the occasional booking at small or midsize venues.

the back room. The front bar is louder and livelier, often populated by the surviving members of the Dubliner's Irish football and soccer teams. The snug is a discreet heads-together, take-no-names hideaway in the finest tradition, and the parlor is where the tweeds gather. In warm weather, there's patio seating. Be sure to have at least one Guinness on draft: The Dubliner pours an estimated quarter-million pints a year, making it the largest purveyor of Guinness in the country.

Drop by Kelly's Irish Times for a breather and the *Finnegans Wake* crazy-quilt of literary pretense, political conversation, and interns' raves downstairs. Then call a cab. Please.

Ri-Ra in Georgetown has "late-night" Irish bands (that is, 9:30 or later) on weekends. Despite its name, and a sophisticated take on Irish fare, **Flanagan's Harp and Fiddle** in Bethesda has a lineup that includes not just Irish and folk but a wide range of blues, jazz, pop, and rock acts, including Eve's fave Mary Ann Redmond. In Old Town Alexandria, **Murphy's** on King Street has nightly entertainment, and the nearby **Pat Troy's Ireland's Own,** just off King on North Pitt Street, spotlights Alexandria's famed pipe-and-drum corps on the first Thursday of the month.

Washington is full of jokes—and that's the first one. Despite being an unending source of humor for TV talk-show hosts and commentators, the nation's capital itself seems to have a fairly limited tolerance for hearing its own favorite sons or daughters skewered. These days, though several venues have the weekly or monthly stand-up special, the only full-time comedy spot is the **DC Improv** below Dupont Circle near the Farragut North Metro (and tantalizingly close to Lobbyville, K Street NW). The most loyal opposition is offered by the **Capitol Steps,** a group of former and current Hill staffers who roast their own hosts by rewriting familiar songs with punishing, though not too pointed, lyrics. The Steps are a popular tourist attraction and perform every Friday and Saturday at the Ronald Reagan Building and International Trade Center at 13th Street and Pennsylvania Avenue NW (Federal Triangle). But be aware they have lobbyists' fees—$45 a ticket unless there is a forum of at least 10 of you. Not quite so funny.

NIGHTLIFE NEIGHBORHOODS

AS SUGGESTED EARLIER, NIGHTCLUBS AND RESTAURANTS have a tendency to form clusters, which makes cruising or cocktailing relatively easy for visitors. This also means that in general you'll have plenty of company, and if you're not in easy reach of the Metro, you won't have much trouble hailing a cab. However, in some cases, it may also mean that the price is tight: The more celebrity-conscious clubs and VIP-wannabe lounges will definitely put a dent in your platinum card. Just make sure you know which bubbly you're ordering.

In terms of live entertainment, the two brightest strips in Washington are along H Street, in the sometimes rowdy but sweet-tempered Atlas District, and the slightly more sedate U Street/Mid City neighborhood. Not surprisingly, nightlife strips often become dining destinations; many of the areas referred to below appear as "Prime Dining Neighborhoods" in the Dining chapter as well.)

Mid City: "U" R There

The edgy-cum-trendy area around 14th Street and U Street NW, which locals have branded the Mid City neighborhood, has been, for the last several years, evolving from fly-by-fortnight bars to boutiques that suggest more stability (home decor and accessories, import furniture, and so on) and lots of nightclubs and restaurants. It has one of the greatest concentrations of rooftop bars in the area, and it's accessible via the U Street–African American Civil War Memorial–Cardozo Metro, which has entrances at 13th and 10th Streets.

As mentioned above, among the more important musical addresses in Washington are two Mid City attractions, which actually helped launch the neighborhood revival: the **9:30 club** and the **Black Cat.** And U Street is the old Black Broadway, and home to a number of everything-old-is-new-again jazz clubs.

At the corner of 11th and U, next to Bohemian Caverns, is the four-level dance club **LIV,** which is rarely live but spins a mix of old school, reggae, R&B, and 1980s and 1990s dance pop. Across 11th Street you'll hit the cavern club-ish **U Street Music Hall,** a "DJ-owned-and-operated" basement with a 1,200-square-foot, 500-capacity cork dance floor, dueling bars, dark charcoal walls, and two prohibitions: no bottle service and (at least in the blind-your-neighbor sense) no photos.

Other clubs with strong music calendars are the **Velvet Lounge** near Ninth on U, which is drink-spilling tight downstairs (stand-up bar and DJ) and up (prog-metal, dream-state rock, and indie-lounge rockers squeezed into a living room–size space); and **DC9** (around the corner on 9th just below U), a much more upscale and larger space for indie rock and late-night DJs, with a rooftop deck (and less-than-bottle-service prices).

But Mid City also has several nightspots with quite different characters.

At the corner of Eighth and U Streets NW is **Town Danceboutique,** a lighthearted but technically serious two-level, 20,000-square-foot gay club that offers both upscale drag shows and DJs. At the corner of 9th and U, you'll find **Nellie's Sports Bar,** which may not have been the first gay sports bar in the area, but it's the most fun, with Tuesday drag bingo, Wednesday "smartass trivia," and weekend back-slapping football on the flat-panel TVs—and a rooftop bar to boot. (Nellie's version of "beat the clock" means rooftop drink prices go up $1 every hour; you've been warned.) **Black Jack,** the mussels and muffuletta bar above Pearl Dive Oyster Bar, manages to squeeze in two bocce courts, complete with stadium seating.

unofficial **TIP**
The other side of the all-cash nightclubs is "bottle service," which basically means you spend five or six times the wholesale cost for a bottle of booze to have it brought to the table instead of standing in line. Think Grey Goose is worth $325?

The **Saloon** at 12th and U is famous for its rules: no standing, no TVs, no stool hogging—in other words, you're there to enjoy a drink and conversation with your neighbor. Really. And at the far end of the strip past 16th Street is **Chi-Cha Lounge,** which also deserves some founding-father praise; here the shtick is hookah and South American snacks.

Atlas District: Bring Your "H" Game

The Atlas District, a three-block stretch of H Street NE centered around the **Atlas Performing Arts Center,** is without question the quirkiest entertainment district in the Washington area. Bars, dance halls, and restaurants all juggle DJs and games: mini-golf, tabletop shuffleboard, bocce, Skee-Ball, karaoke, dress-up, and even the irregular burlesque.

Some of the more irresistible attractions are clustered between 11th and 15th Streets NE (just to get you going). Starting at the 11th Street end, there's **Little Miss Whiskey's Golden Dollar,** which looks like a bit of fine New Orleans decadence (if Annie Oakley had run the bar), complete with wrought-iron benches, a courtyard fountain, DJs ranging from yacht rock to 1980s alternative—and "Kostume Karaoke" on alternate Wednesdays. In the next block is **Vendetta,** which has two 25-foot bocce courts and a vaguely Italian menu.

Between 13th and 14th is the H Street *Playgroundus maximus,* the **H Street Country Club,** which boasts a two-level, nine-hole adults-only mini-golf course—with miniature D.C. landmarks, including the Lincoln Theatre, a gauntlet of lobbyists, and a graveyard full of zombie presidents among the traps—plus Skee-Ball, shuffleboard, and, logically for H Street, Mexican food. The nearby **Star and Shamrock,** as the name suggests, is sort of a retirement-home joke setup: a combination Jewish deli and Guinness-Harp pub with bingo and trivia nights.

Up from that is the **Rock & Roll Hotel,** a one-time funeral home renovated not as a real overnighter but as a midsize (capacity 400) 18-and-older rock venue with VIP suites, pool tables upstairs, and a huge rooftop deck. This is another gamesters' hangout: To stay in the Friday night spelling bee, you have to down a brew or a shot between rounds, which is one reason the upper reaches are 21-and-up.

And then there's the **Biergarten Haus,** which can make space for 300 mug-huggers and pig-roast pickers in the (obviously) beer garden at long wooden tables amid the odd strolling accordion players and tuba bands. And trivia. The rest of it looks like an Alpine lodge, more or less.

Cross 14th Street and you can play pool, Foosball, or "booze clues" trivia at the pub **Argonaut.** (If you're afraid of dogs, duck Saturday afternoons: It's "mutts happy hour" on the patio.) It's also one of the area's last havens of bluegrass on Thursday nights.

Adams Morgan: The Big Mixer

It's reasonably calm by day—when you can easily see the building-side murals that are one of its hallmarks—but by night, Adams Morgan is a combination carnival midway and meet-market madhouse, and there's no way tourists, or even locals, can hit more than a few of its popular lounges in one visit. (Weekends after midnight, you'd be lucky to find room to move, even down the middle of the street.) And the fact that it's one of the city's older row-house neighborhoods makes it charming to look at, but many of its establishments have accessibility issues. (And some of those that are "officially" accessible have some pretty minimal bathroom facilities.)

Most of the hot spots lie along 18th Street NW between Kalorama and Columbia Roads, and on Columbia Road itself. Just stick your head into a few of them—the trendier, lounge-life nightclubs with white sofas, pastel drinks, and DJs; the truculently retro beer bars and dives; and the live-music and dance venues—and, well, pick your spot.

The grandmother of all Adams Morgan music clubs is **Madam's Organ,** which has three floors plus a rooftop tiki bar and live music (blues, jazz, R&B, bluegrass) every night, and a famously, um, pulchritudinous eponymous mural, in whose honor all redheads pay only half price for Shiner Bock. Amongst all the upscaling, the neighborhood has always supported a few recalcitrant dive bars, the matriarch/patriarch of which is **Millie and Al's** (when the oversized "Attention Shoppers!"–style light bulb comes on and the skeleton dances, the Jell-O shots are only $1). The jazz staples are **Tryst,** which has live music, and **Columbia Station,** back on a nightly schedule.

Long a center of Washington's Central American and South American communities, Adams Morgan also has some of the area's nicer Latin jazz and samba joints, including **Rumba Café, Bossa Bistro,** and **Habana Village.**

Midtown Redux

Downtown's new nightlife began with the turn-of-the-millennium revival of downtown Connecticut Avenue south of Dupont Circle, long a strictly commercial-business area, and one that regularly defeated attempts to push the expense-account-restaurant envelope. The five-pointed-star intersection at Connecticut, M, Jefferson, and 18th Streets NW, just above Farragut North, marks the heart of what emerged in the mid-1990s as one of Washington's first semi-underground-luxe nightlife neighborhoods.

unofficial **TIP**
The invitation list is just about the only way around a hefty cover charge at many clubs these days; if you use Twitter or Facebook, find yourself a friend on the guest list or ask about a password.

The grandfather of the area is the **18th Street Lounge,** a baroquely restored turn-of-the-20th-century mansion with languorous couches, working fireplaces, a rooftop deck, and DJs and live entertainment (reggae, Brazilian jazz, eclectic) nightly. Across Connecticut are the four-and-a-half bars **Midtown** (the private Red Bar is inside the loft level, and it offers one of the few rooftop bars in the neighborhood); the swanky subterranean **Heist;** the nautical-naughty dance hall **Current;** the much more casual football (meaning soccer) sports pub **Lucky Bar;** and the intentionally retro frat-boy beer-bar **Big Hunt,** where you might stumble over some off-the-record pols drinking $3 PBR, if you consider that a deal. At the opposite end of the style spectrum are the still young but celebrity-heavy **Huxley,** where even the "library" is SRO, and **Ozio,** which got on the cigar and martini over-aged boy-bar bandwagon in

DRINKS, ANYONE?

WASHINGTON WAS IN THE FOREFRONT of the cocktail revival, ever since groundbreaking mixologist Todd Thrasher opened his **PX** "speakeasy" in Old Town Alexandria a decade ago, followed by the nearby **TNT.** In recent years, several other bars dedicated to the making of original and authentic cocktails have emerged, notably the aptly named speakeasy-style **Gibson** in the heart of Mid City, and the similarly "secret" **Sheppard** in Dupont Circle; the bar at **Proof** in Penn Quarter; the tiny, and hence reservation-only, **Dram and Grain** in the basement of Jack Rose (see below); **Wisdom and the Eddy Bar** "apothecary" at Hank's on Capitol Hill; and **Policy** in the U Street corridor.

Craft whiskey is fashionable as well, especially in Adams Morgan, where the three-story **Jack Rose Dining Saloon** boasts a running tally of "2,390 bottles of whisk(e)y on the wall," its sibling **Bourbon** offers 125 or so, and **Smoke and Barrel,** a barbecue house, provides similar bourbon (and scotch and rye) benefits. **Black Whiskey** in Logan Circle has dozens of small-batch whiskies, the **Irish Whiskey Public House** downtown boasts more than 50 whiskies (and as many beers), and **Barrel** on Capitol Hill offers close to 100. And the Georgetown outpost of the **Rí Rá** Irish pub chain (a beautiful mash-up of rescued/salvaged Irish pubs, a bank, and even a theater) offers not flights but "duels" of rare whiskies costing up to $180.

Clear liquor fans should not worry: **MXDC** has a tequila menu of more than 100 brands, and you'll find about the same number of vodkas at the **Russia House** or the D.C. branch of New York's **Mari Vanna** at either end of Dupont Circle (which means you'll see a lot of hockey imports hanging out as well).

Washington now has a handful of small craft distilleries producing a variety of whiskies, gin, and vodka, which is only appropriate, as the capital lays (perhaps exaggerated) claim to some classic cocktails: the rickey, first made in the 1880s at Shoomaker's Bar on E Street NW as a morning tonic for lobbyist "Colonel" Joe Rickey (and now the official drink of the District); and the mint julep, which was popularized at the Round Robin Bar around the corner in the Willard Hotel—which, coincidentally, is said to be where the word "lobbyist" originated.

the mid-1990s and is still in the rut. (If you're networking with a stogie-sucking stockbroker, here's your spot.)

A short walk away, the area between McPherson Square and Franklin Square, centered roughly at K Street NW around 14th Street—also previously a canyon of office buildings largely empty at night—has come to life, with landlords now looking to lure in after-hours crowds at the street and even basement level. Most of these clubs are using VIP bottle service to promote a high-class dress code—and also to boost the tabs, all of which are likely to be serious. But be warned: These generally cater to the younger and apparently more hearing-challenged crowds, and both the names and themes waver over the years.

The Park at 14th is a perfect example—a four-story Deco luxe-look lounge and so-called supper club created by some of Washington's most experienced club owners for, let us say, slightly more experienced patrons. (It sells tickets to parties "hosted" by the likes of Ludacris and Diddy.) From the second- and, especially, fourth-floor balconies, VIP drinkers can lord it over the mere mortals below. **Capitale** is less formal but not much less expensive; if you are really on an expense account, the weekends-only **Shadow Room** allows you to touch-screen your cocktail orders, DJ requests, and valet summons from your table—that is, for a four-figure minimum. Around the corner on Vermont Avenue is the boho-bordello **Josephine,** named for Napoleon's beloved, and just as expensive.

Penn Quarter

Because this is mostly a dining mecca, that means primarily cocktail culture, but because the Verizon Center is at the heart of the neighborhood, at least a half dozen of the non–white linen hangouts are sports bars. Of course, if you're not a home-towner, or a hockey fan, there are a few homier options.

In fact, Penn Quarter is picking up on the Atlas District game-night trend. At the bi-level **Iron Horse Tap Room,** the steeds referred to are not locomotives but vintage motorcycles, several of which hang about the place. It's not a biker bar except in name, however; upstairs it's lounge-a-lot territory, and downstairs are Skee-Ball machines, shuffleboard tables, and a plentiful supply of TVs, 20 beers on tap, and as many bourbons. Iron Horse shares ownership with the even more games-away-from-the-game **Rocket Bar** at Seventh and G, which sports a subterranean vibe with 17 flat-panel TVs. As mentioned previously, **Fado** looks Irish antique, if you don't mind the cost. **RFD** is for the beer-o-phile (with 30 taps and 300 bottle choices), and **City Tap House** hauls in craft beers from around the country; **Capitol City** and **District Chophouse** brew their own.

PART SEVEN

SHOPPING

NEW YORKERS USED TO SAY WASHINGTON was a conservative town with no style. News flash—things have certainly changed here. As Washington continues to attract young professionals to the workforce, everyone, from the buttoned-up legal firms to the halls of Congress, has noticed. These youthful, entrepreneurial types have livened up arenas where the suit-and tie crowd once ruled. They demand "casual day" every day, and even the most traditional of workplaces have begun to accept standard attire mixed with edgy accessories. To see what Washington's most fashionable are wearing, check out **thepresidentwears prada.com** or **northernvirginiamag.com.**

Washington also attracts a fair number of visitors for whom museums mean nothing. They come here to shop. These folks enjoy sifting through merchandise at the haute boutiques, eclectic bodegas, and super-stocked shoe stores. They peruse little grocers packed with international spices. They come to lay claim to original art and rare books. In fact, nowadays, many people plan their vacations around the shopping, not the other way around.

As a result of Washington's high median household income, the city has some of the most exclusive shops in the nation. In addition, the increasingly diverse population demands more international offerings from their stores. This means Washington's visitors will find a very wide variety of products and shopping opportunities during their visit.

On weekend afternoons and around the holidays, roads leading to the shopping centers are as congested as commuter routes during rush hour. The stretch of I-95 south of Washington around the **Potomac Mills** factory outlet complex in Dale City—far and away the largest tourist draw in the state of Virginia—is nearly always backed up to a crawl in both directions. **Arundel Mills,** from the same folks who brought you Potomac Mills, bookends the metropolitan area on the north side of the interstate. The **Tanger Outlets** at National Harbor and the **Leesburg Corner Premium Outlets** on Route 7 west of Tysons Corner offer a budget-boggling spread of shopping options.

But shoppers aren't relegated to suburban malls. Oh, no. They can shop to their heart's content at the many mixed-use developments in downtown Washington too. Consider the uber-fashionable **City Center,** just a block from the Convention Center. Visitors make their way to City Center to stop for ice cream, and then peek their heads into Hermès, David Yurman, and Burberry.

The streets of Georgetown are another must-see area for shopping enthusiasts. Dozens of well-known retailers have individual stores on Wisconsin Avenue NW and M Street NW. Some fashion-forward websites, known for their strong online presence, have opened brick and mortar versions where you can try on clothes (Bonobos) or sample the latest technology (Apple and Microsoft).

Maybe you're the shopper craving the pioneer spirit of new designers and vintage finds. If so, there are a number of neighborhoods where the stylistas are more daring. The U Street Corridor has a line of shops that cater to the particular customers who work in the arts or attend Howard, Georgetown, and American Universities. The curated pieces sold here guarantee you won't see yourself coming and going.

Outside of town, Alexandria has always attracted spirited shopkeepers, and even if you don't buy anything, it's fun to window shop here. For an idea of what you may see on the streets of D.C., check out **DistrictofChic.com** (of course, we can't all rock those clothes, but it's fun to get ideas).

There are still plenty of old-school, traditional conservative dressers, but the city's flourishing creative culture can be seen on the street; these urban dwellers embrace trends and add playful accessories, such as designer bags, jewelry, and scarves. Some outfits you'll see in restaurants and on the street may have been inspired by D.C.'s famous television characters—Olivia Pope from *Scandal* and Claire Underwood from *House of Cards*. Tourists, however, should not worry too much about fashion; instead, focus on comfortable shoes and dress for the ever-changing weather.

MALL SHOPPING

SERIOUS BUYERS AND BARGAIN HUNTERS, as opposed to those recreational window shoppers, will have to decide up front whether they are willing to bring, rent, or borrow a car (or something even larger) or stick to using public transportation. Although we have repeatedly recommended against driving in Washington, if one of the big outlet malls is a major part of your itinerary, that would be one reason to override us. (You should still park outside the Beltway, though.) In most cases, there are hotels and motels built nearby for just that reason.

But unless you really plan to load up—and if so, you'll have to budget a lot of time as well as money—there are a few malls within the District of Columbia itself and in the surrounding suburbs that you can reach by public transportation. And in addition to the formal malls, Washington has a growing number of neighborhoods with intriguing boutiques and stores, often the same neighborhoods that have trendy restaurant and entertainment options, so you can really make a day, or night, of it.

SUPERMALLS AND OUTLETS

WASHINGTON MAY HAVE ITS MILLION-DOLLAR HOUSES, expense-account restaurants, and pricey private schools—and if you want to see its answer to Manhattan, see the section on the neighborhood of Chevy Chase on pages 344–345—but it also has a surprising number of discount outlets. For every socialite flashing a Hermès Birkin bag or CEO tugging at his Armani suitcoat, there are savvy shoppers quietly gloating over their discounted Kate Spade dress or their Jack Spade tie. (And these days, the ratio is probably a lot more uneven.) After all, the reason to buy good quality items is that they last a long time, so why not buy leather goods from one season back, when you're going to use them for 10 years? And if you only want something for a year or so, then a quirky boutique or discount store is definitely the way to go.

Forty-five minutes south of Washington off I-95 is **Potomac Mills Mall** in Dale City, Virginia, one of the world's largest outlet malls, with more than 200 shops covering 1.6 million square feet of retail delirium (**simon.com/mall**). Potomac Mills draws more visitors each year than any other Virginia tourist attraction—about 24 million shoppers, maneuvering feverishly into 8,000 parking spaces. It's nearly impossible to hit all of the stores, which include Bloomingdale's, Burlington Coat Factory, Costco, Tommy Bahama, H&M, T.J. Maxx, BCBG Maxazria, Nordstrom Rack, Banana Republic, Under Armour, Bose, Guess, Ann Taylor, H&M, Levi's, Movado, True Religion, Timberland, Nike, Saks Fifth Avenue OFF 5TH, Last Call from Neiman Marcus, Disney Store, and Brooks Brothers. It also has an 18-screen AMC multiplex with a 3-D IMAX screen, a Bobby's Burger Palace from celebrity chef Bobby Flay, a Cheesecake Factory, and a dozen other noshing options. IKEA, which was the mall's original anchor, has moved into a huge space of its own right across the street.

Northeast of Washington, at the intersection of the Baltimore-Washington Parkway and Route 100 near Baltimore-Washington Airport (about 2 miles east of I-95), is Potomac Mills' sibling, behemoth **Arundel Mills** in Hanover, Maryland (**simon.com/mall**). More than a million square feet of name brands echo the Virginia complex, but Arundel Mills trumps them with entertainment options, including a 24-theater multiplex (with XD) that looks like an Egyptian pyramid, a Medieval Times restaurant/theater that looks like an 11th-century castle, and a Bass Pro Shops Outdoor World, with a sort of medieval archery lane, a waterfall, and a rock-climbing wall. And then there's that casino, Maryland Live!, open 24 hours a day with six restaurants, including branches of local raves the Prime Rib and Phillips Seafood (and a Burger Palace); a stage from Annapolis's Ram's Head live music club; and a brewpub. Oh, and a Dave & Buster's Sports Café with billiards, arcade games, and shuffleboard.

To the west of town, perhaps 15–20 minutes past the various Tysons Corner malls (see below) at the intersection of Route 7 and the Route 15 Bypass, is the **Leesburg Corner Premium Outlets** (**premiumoutlets .com**), with many of those same names, plus Michael Kors, Charlotte Russe, Juicy Couture, Kate Spade New York, Nautica, White House Black Market, and True Religion. And instead of IKEA, it offers Restoration Hardware and Williams-Sonoma, plus the Kitchen Collection and Le Creuset.

Most recently, **Tanger Outlets** has opened an 80-store shopping center in the National Harbor development, which is across the Potomac River from the District in Maryland and about 8 miles south of the White House. It features Le Creuset, Adidas, Elle Tahari, Converse, H&M, Tommy Hilfiger, Michael Kors, Brooks Brothers, Calvin Klein, Chico's, Halston Heritage, Oakley Vault, J. Crew, Steve Madden, and Coach.

CITY MALLS

THERE ARE A FEW MALLS WITHIN THE DISTRICT LIMITS. **The Shops at Georgetown Park** (**shopsatgeorgetownpark.com**), which anchors

unofficial **TIP**
Though a little walk from a Metro station, check out the greater M Street shopping scene; see "Great Neighborhoods for Window-shopping," below.

the intersection of M Street and Wisconsin Avenue, is the most extravagant in appearance, featuring a lush Victorian design that fronts for some popular retailers, including DSW, Forever 21, Anthropologie, T.J. Maxx, Home Goods, H&M, J. Crew, and a branch of the famous Dean & Deluca market. It is also home to a large entertainment complex, Pinstripes, which has 14 bowling alleys, six bocce courts, a bistro, and a wine cellar. It still fronts the original Clyde's of Georgetown and J. Paul's retro turn-of-the-20th-century oyster bar/saloon. (In any case, you cannot go hungry in Georgetown; nearly every space that isn't a shop is a restaurant.) There are also several restaurant/bars on the waterfront in Washington Harbor that are particularly attractive in summer (families will like Sequoia and Farmers Fishers Bakers).

A major Washington landmark has been partly reborn as a shopping center: **Union Station,** which in addition to the Amtrak station has its own subway stop. Union Station is a grand Beaux Arts building whose two-story arcade of shops now boasts a number of familiar names, including some that travelers might find particularly useful in the case of mislaid luggage: Ann Taylor, Aerosoles (a great place to find comfortable shoes for sightseeing), Body Shop, L'Occitane, Victoria's Secret, Swatch, Francesca's (reasonably priced, fashion-forward clothes), and Jos. A. Bank (men's classic clothing), along with several purveyors of ties, jewelry, and accessories. There's even an Art of Shaving spa for those whose business trip might have been seriously last minute.

In addition to a large and quite varied food court, Union Station has several sit-down restaurants, including a Bold Bite (gourmet hot dogs), Johnny Rockets (burgers and fries), Thunder Grill for Southwestern and Tex-Mex, and Shake Shack (famous for its milkshakes). Plus, you'll find a couple of elevated-view bars and a multiplex cinema.

There is also a 500,000-square-foot big-box shopping complex at 14th and Irving Streets NW in Columbia Heights, called **DCUSA**, that houses a Target, Bed Bath & Beyond, Staples, Best Buy, Mattress Discounters, Radio Shack, DSW, Petco, and Marshalls. The Columbia Heights Metro and a parking garage are also part of this complex. If you're in town because your teenager is going to college in Washington or just got an internship, this might be a good one-stop spot for you.

unofficial **TIP**
Though both Mazza Gallerie and the Chevy Chase Pavilion shopping malls are (just) within the District boundaries, and with easy Metro access, they are really part of the larger border-crossing shopping district in Chevy Chase; see the description in "Great Neighborhoods," below.

SUBURBAN MALLS

WASHINGTON'S MAJOR SUBURBAN MALLS are probably similar to what you have back home, though perhaps a little bigger, and most of them are easily accessible by subway, including the multimall Tysons Corner area, just west of the Beltway, which is now accessible by Metro, thanks to the opening of the Silver Line and the Tysons Metro station.

Montgomery Mall (westfield.com/montgomery) does not have subway access, but for serious shoppers, it's only a 10-minute cab ride from the Grosvenor/Strathmore Metro station; or on weekdays you can catch a Ride-On bus at the White Flint Metro or Grosvenor/Strathmore. (There is even an Avis Rent-a-Car at the Sears Auto Center if you're *really* shopping.) Westfield Montgomery Mall is anchored by Nordstrom, Sears, and Macy's, and includes Apple, Vera Bradley, J. Crew, J. Jill, Sephora, Under Armour, Bonobos, ECCO, Kiehl's, Lily Pulitzer, bebe, Stuart Weitzman, Madewell, Tesla, Liljenquist & Beckstead jewelers, Forever 21, Zara, and Vineyard Vines. It also has a large food court, a Cheesecake Factory, Blaze Pizza, Naples, yet another Bobby's Burger Palace, and the luxurious ArcLight Cinema.

The formerly dowdy **Wheaton Mall** (westfield.com/wheaton), one block from the Wheaton Metro stop, is now a corporate sibling to Montgomery Mall and offers a very similar line-up of stores: J.C.

Penney, Macy's, As Seen on TV, Old Navy, H&M, Zumiez, Dick's Sporting Goods, and DSW, plus its own Giant grocery store, food court, Costco, Target, and a six-screen multiplex.

One of the area's most elaborate malls is **The Fashion Centre at Pentagon City** (**simon.com/mall**) in Arlington, Virginia—a beautiful conservatory-style building filled with 170 primarily high-end retailers (it belongs to the same folks as Potomac Mills and Arundel Mills): Macy's, Henri Bendel, Hugo Boss, Kate Spade, Nordstrom, Coach, Club Monaco, Tourneau, Swarovski, Apple, Sephora, A|X Armani Exchange, Michael Kors, and Microsoft. The Fashion Centre also leads (through the parking garage) to a second fairly extensive shopping and (mostly) restaurant complex called **Pentagon Row** (for listings, go to **pentagonrow.com**). At the other end, the Fashion Centre connects to the Ritz-Carlton Hotel, where you can have an elegant meal or high tea in the lounge. The Pentagon City Metro stop, on the Blue Line, has a tunnel with direct access to Pentagon City mall.

The **Tysons Corner** neighborhood, just west of the Beltway, is so large, it is a city in its own right, and now, with the opening of Tysons Metro station, developers are trying to make it more pedestrian friendly. Centered on the intersection of Chain Bridge Road/Route 123 and Leesburg Pike/Route 7, between the towns of Vienna and McLean, Tysons is actually a sort of Siamese twin supermall, with the original Tysons Corner Center hosting the slightly more predictable list of stores (**shoptysons.com**) and the Tysons Galleria (**shoptysons galleria.com**) having a few more upscale names. Between the two, Tysons is estimated to serve some 60,000 shoppers daily at nearly 400 shops, including Nordstrom, Lord & Taylor, Prada, Tory Burch, Louis Vuitton, Bloomingdale's, Crate & Barrel, Versace, Max Mara, Gucci, Bottega Veneta, Macy's, Chanel, Cartier, BCBG Max Azria, Coach, Ermenegildo Zegna, Hugo Boss, Burberry, and Bally Shoes. There are dozens of sit-down restaurants of various flavors, especially the big-name steak chains such as Morton's, along the corridor, not to mention the snack shops and food courts. In fact, the "food court" at the Galleria is a hub of sit-downs, including Maggiano's and Lebanese Taverna. And the Galleria adjoins the Ritz-Carlton Hotel, whose restaurants include America Eats, the heritage-theme menu from superchef José Andrés.

There is actually a third shopping section in Tysons Corner, seriously upscale, known as the **Shops at Fairfax Square,** a sort of minimall of super-label shops, including Tiffany & Co, Miele, and an Elizabeth Arden Red Door Spa that you can hit after working out at the Equinox Fitness Center and before chowing down at Chef Geoff's.

FLEA MARKETS

WASHINGTON IS NOT YET A GREAT FLEA MARKET TOWN in the way that New York City is, but the most well-established flea is

Sunday's **Georgetown Flea Market** (in the parking lot of Hardy Middle School on Wisconsin Avenue between 34th and 35th Streets NW). It's manned by more than 50 vendors of vintage jewelry, rugs, sterling, flatware, architectural remnants, and occasionally political memorabilia. *Lonesome Dove* author Larry McMurty, who used to run a second-hand bookstore in the neighborhood, based parts of his novel *Cadillac Jack* on the market (**georgetownfleamarket.com**).

Other regular gathering spots that are subway accessible include the **Bethesda Flea Market** at 7155 Wisconsin Avenue, an easy walk from the Bethesda station (open Wednesday, Friday, Saturday, and Sunday; **farmwomensmarket.com**); **the Sunday Flea Market at Eastern Market** on Seventh Street SE, a two-block, closed-to-vehicles street festival that's just a few steps from the Eastern Market Metro station (**easternmarket.net**); and **Friends in the Marketplace,** which calls itself the Funky Fleamarket, near the NoMa–Gallaudet Metro stop (open Saturdays and Sundays; **facebook.com/groups/funkyfleamarket**).

MUSEUM SHOPS

IF BY SHOPPING YOU MEAN THE SORT OF SOUVENIRS you take home for the family, you can combine your sightseeing with your shopping. Some of Washington's greatest finds are in its museum gift shops. A museum's orientation is a good guide to its shop's merchandise: prints, art-design ties, and art books fill the **National Gallery of Art** shop; model airplanes and other toys of flight are on sale at the **Air and Space Museum,** and so on. The largest Smithsonian shops are at the **Museum of American History,** which sells toys, clothing, musical instruments, and recordings from countries highlighted in the exhibits; although all the museums have some items reflecting the collection. Some of the hippest gifts are currently on view—sort of—at the **International Spy Museum,** which stocks video and CD copies of old spy TV shows and themes, pens disguised as lipsticks, disguises for people, and miniature cameras. The **Newseum** has an exceptional collection of media-related merchandise, and while there aren't many souvenirs at **Madame Tussauds,** you can take selfies with the wax celebrities.

Several museum shops are overlooked by tourists. Among the best are the **National Building Museum** shop, which sells design-related books, jewelry, architecturally inspired greeting cards, and gadgets; the **Arts and Industries** shop, a pretty Victorian setting stocked with Smithsonian reproductions; the **National Museum of the American Indian,** with its turquoise and silver jewelry, Zuni pottery, hand carvings, and rugs; the **National Museum of Women in the Arts,** with Frida Kahlo dolls and Rosie the Riveter bookends; the **National Museum of African Art** shop, a bazaar filled with colorful cloth, Ethiopian crosses, and wooden ceremonial instruments, such as hand drums and tambourines; the **Hirshhorn Museum,** with its selection of gifts for the photography enthusiast; the **Arthur M. Sackler Gallery** shop, with cases full of brass Buddhas, Chinese lacquerware, jade and jasper jewelry, feng shui kits, and porcelain; the **Renwick Gallery,** which stocks unusual art jewelry and handblown glass; the Shakespeare-lovers' treasure trove at **Folger Shakespeare Library** (everyone needs a Shakespeare magnetic poetry kit); and the shop at the **John F. Kennedy Center for the Performing Arts,** stocked with videos, opera glasses, and other gifts for Jackie and John lovers (such as costume jewelry inspired by the late former First Lady).

The **Hillwood Museum** has jewelry and ornaments inspired by Marjorie Merriweather Post's famous collection of Fabergé eggs and Russian porcelains. The expanded shop at **Mount Vernon** offers reproductions of Martha's cookbook, George's key to the Bastille, and period china and silver patterns. The DAR, or **Daughters of the American Revolution Museum** shop, sells Americana-themed memorabilia, such as decorated china, jewelry, clothes, flags, and quilts. The shop at the **National Geographic Museum** offers clothing, jewelry, toys, and accessories from all around the globe. The **Cathedral Store** on the grounds of the National Cathedral features stone gargoyles, prayer books, rose-window silk scarves, statues of religious icons, and rosaries.

A visit in mid-September may mean you'll catch the **Museum Sidewalk Sale** at the Kennedy Center. This all-day event features those same treasures—books, textiles, jewelry, and prints—at significantly lower prices. Another excellent shopping opportunity comes during late November: the annual **Museum Shop Around,** held at the Mansion at Strathmore, where (for a fee of $8) shoppers will find merchandise from all the Smithsonian museums and others under one convenient roof.

GREAT NEIGHBORHOODS
for WINDOW-SHOPPING

WASHINGTON HAS A NUMBER OF NEIGHBORHOODS made for window-shopping—especially in the case of the Chevy Chase–Friendship Heights neighborhood, almost entirely *re*–made for window-shopping.

GEORGETOWN

GEORGETOWN HAS THE CITY'S LARGEST WALK-AND-SHOP DISTRICT. The picturesque streets include a combination of chains, independents, and boutique shops. And thanks to the crowds of teens and 20-somethings that hang out on Georgetown's sidewalks on weekends, many of these keep late hours for impulse shopping (which is, after all, another type of after-hours entertainment).

The central point of Georgetown's consumer compass is the intersection of M Street and Wisconsin Avenue NW, so you can use the Banana Republic or Calvin Klein stores there as locators. Or you could use the gilded dome of the PNC Bank at the same intersection as a marker; it's hard to miss.

Among the boutiques on M Street east of Wisconsin are Alex & Ani, Michael Kors, The Walking Company, Niccolo, Hu's Wear, Kate Spade, Dr. Martens Store, CUSP (which hands out cupcakes and free fortunes to customers), Sterling & Burke (sort of the Brit-style Louis Vuitton but with more for men), Rag & Bone, IKE BEHAR, Diesel, BJ Vines, Brooks Brothers, Dawn Price Baby, Wink, and Sports Zone, along with Anthropologie and BHLDN Anthropologie for Weddings.

This is also the stretch where you can play around with cosmetics and spa products to your heart's content, thanks to the very hot French chain Sephora (where you can try on nearly 100 brands of lipstick and take beauty classes), Bluemercury (which is both a spa and sells custom creams and exotic oils), L'Occitane, and the all-organic London-based LUSH.

*un**official* TIP**
Inside Georgetown Tobacco is a treasure trove of intricate, hand-painted Venetian Carnival masks elaborate enough to make the Phantom of the Opera change his tune, so to speak.

Jewelry junkies should visit Ann Hand, a Washington designer who makes statement pieces with a patriotic flare, and Jewelers' Werk Galerie, a gallery representing more than 50 established art jewelers, selling cutting-edge pieces from around the globe (located in Cady's Alley off M Street NW).

To the west of Wisconsin Avenue on M Street, in addition to the Shops at Georgetown Park, with big-name bargain brands like T.J. Maxx, Forever 21, H&M, and Home Goods, are boutiques such as Steven Alan, the southern-prep Billy Reid, Aldo Shoes, BCBG, Coach, the North Face, Relish (inside Cady's Alley—see below), Intermix, Lululemon, and Lucky Jeans, as well as one Dean & Deluca's specialty foods and housewares.

Wisconsin Avenue north of M Street has also become an open-air parade of boutiques, including UGG Australia (with a huge collection of America's favorite boots), Tory Burch, Jack Spade, Adidas, Ralph Lauren, Zara and its tonier sibling Massimo Dutti, Streets of Georgetown, bebe, Abercrombie & Fitch, Sassanova shoes, Vineyard Vines, the Apple Store (probably the busiest store in the neighborhood), Madewell (a boutique-ish branch of J. Crew), Maxstudio, TUMI Luggage, and as you climb the hill, Appalachian Spring, Tugooh Toys, the Milano Collection, and Comfort Shoes (which may come in handy if the shoes you brought start to hurt).

Everything old is new again, and Georgetown has (once again) become quite the men's fashion warehouse. As if the previously named shops weren't enough, there is Sherman Pinkney, Suitsupply in the Four Seasons Hotel, Camper on M Street (just off Wisconsin at 32nd and O), Bonobos Guideshop in Cady's Alley, and the haute British emporium Jack Wills on Wisconsin just south of M Street. And if you can't afford the flash the first time around, check out Second Time Around on M and Reddz Trading Company on Wisconsin for high-style resales.

Anyone interested in home design and accessories should be sure to make it to the 3300 block of M Street and cruise Cady's Alley, which is actually a hidden semi-mall (parts of it old warehouse buildings) housing high-end stores that may upend your concept of environment. Among stops worth making are the super-chic Italian design stores Contemporaria and Boffi, the two-story Danish-sleek BoConcept, the high-end bathroom supplies at Waterworks, German kitchens of Poggenpohl, the indoor-outdoor chic Janus et Cie, and Design Within Reach, aka DWR. (If you get hungry, the fine Austrian-style Leopold's Kafe & Konditorei is right in the Alley's pedestrian intersection.) And sticking with the theme, a large CB2 store, an offshoot of Crate & Barrel, and West Elm have parked themselves on M Street just west of Cady's Alley. Wisconsin Avenue is home to the luxury furniture design store Restoration Hardware.

ADAMS MORGAN AND MID CITY

HISTORICALLY, ADAMS MORGAN AND U STREET NW—part of what local businesses are now promoting as the Mid City neighborhood—had little connection. Adams Morgan is a multiracial residential area adjoining exclusive Kalorama. It was known as the heart of the Hispanic and, a little later, the Ethiopian immigrant communities. Over the past 15–20 years, Adams Morgan has developed into an eclectic nightlife and dining area, especially along 18th Street NW.

U Street, at the north end of the Shaw neighborhood, was the closest thing Washington had to a Harlem, thanks to its national-circuit jazz and vaudeville venues and the proximity of Howard University. The restored Lincoln Theatre, where such black musical and theatrical luminaries as Duke Ellington and Cab Calloway performed (along with the Howard Theatre a few blocks east in Shaw), is one of the few surviving reminders of a time when U Street NW was known as the "Black Broadway." (Ben's Chili Bowl, the legendary diner in the same block, is nearly as old, having celebrated its 50th anniversary in 2008 with an all-star party.) A victim of the 1960s riots in Washington, Shaw is enjoying a revival, with a wave of young couples investing in renovating the old town houses as restaurants and small businesses.

In recent years, these historically distinct and ethnically heterogeneous areas have become increasingly popular with younger, hip, and international crowds. Two particular developments—art galleries, performance venues, and trendy restaurants along 14th and U

Streets; and the opening of the U Street/African-American Civil War Memorial/Cardozo subway station—have increased popularity and attracted more pedestrian traffic.

Today, Adams Morgan is more of a dining and nightlife area, perhaps with a slightly older audience, while U Street or Mid City, which first attracted attention as a bar and restaurant frontier, has developed into a busy strip of popular stores, including a substantial number of home furnishings shops that cater to all kinds of styles.

Among **Adams Morgan**'s melting pot of restaurants, which range from falafel shops to rooftop bars, are African and Hispanic clothing stores and craft boutiques, racks of Mexican wedding dresses, religious icons, and perhaps a medicinal herb or two. The busiest strip is along 18th Street NW between Florida Avenue and Columbia Road.

The Tibet Shop showcases striking Himalayan jewelry, clothing, furnishings, crafts, and painted altars. Toro Mata is sort of its Peruvian counterpart, a South American showcase of hand-crafted art and home furnishings. Mercedes Bien is a smart and eclectic cache of vintage clothing and accessories. Commonwealth, an upscale and contemporary clothing and shoe store, is pricey but worth investigating. Adams Morgan is also home to used books and record stores; see "Specialty Shopping," pages 349–351.

For architectural remnants—mantels, stained and leaded-glass windows, chandeliers, door handles, and columns—check out the Brass Knob, which has been a fixture on 18th Street for more than 30 years. The four-story Skynear Designs trades in more modern, even luxurious, furniture, including hand-painted pillows, repro armoires, whimsical wrought iron, and acrobatic light fixtures.

Mid City, or the "new-U," is the commercial cluster that runs along U Street NW roughly between 9th and 16th Streets and down 14th Street from U south to P Street and Logan Circle. It's a haven for hipsters from all eras, and the boutiques reflect that.

Among them are Dr. K Vintage, a boutique that lines up rockabilly couture for cowboys and gents alike; Junction, a vintage couture boutique; and Lettie Gooch, an eclectic boutique that separates clothing by occasion. Redeem aims to bring swagger and a little urban grit to luxury casual wear. Even more intriguing, Redeem houses Mutiny, a sort of curated display of craft apothecary and ephemera for the modern J. Peterman guy.

The other, and perhaps even more impressive, field of Mid City art is home furnishings. Room & Board is almost its own big-box store, a four-story showcase for custom interiors from Arts and Crafts to midcentury modern and contemporary, also emphasizing green products. The folk at Foundry apply reimagining into reupholstering; it could be an HGTV set.

unofficial **TIP**
Need a really hip hostess gift? Batch 13 is not a cocktail shaker shop but a specialty liquor store, ideal for delving into locally sourced spirits and mixers.

Designer showcase Lori Graham Home spotlights midcentury and slightly tongue-in-cheek glam in everything from chandeliers to armchairs, plus local artists' works. Mitchel Gold + Bob Williams' oversize seating brings relaxed shopping to a whole new level (dogs welcome). Home Rule has figured out that home and kitchen accessories don't have to be humorless, or even expensive; while Muléh is filled with eco-friendly furnishings for both home and body from Indonesia and the Philippines. And Beige, on Florida Avenue just north of U Street, is more or less just what it sounds like, a haven for those who think "neutral" is a primary color.

Millennium Decorative Arts is one of several retro-kitsch shops in the area, mixing Waring blenders and fondue pots with the real retro stuff, such as Eames chairs and a Saarinen pedestal table. The style at Good Wood, on the other hand, is classic country—it specializes in 19th-century American furniture, including arts and crafts, andirons, and stained glass—but at Sunday-auction prices.

Despite the vintage-sounding name (and some pieces are truly classic), Miss Pixie's Furnishings & Whatnot is a treasure trove of fine and funky vintage furniture and spot-on tchotchkes, whose owner frequently dispenses cookies or perhaps a winter warmer.

CHEVY CHASE

A HYBRID D.C.–MONTGOMERY COUNTY NEIGHBORHOOD— and a commercial gold mine—has emerged around the Friendship Heights Metro station in the last decade. At the intersection of Western and Wisconsin Avenues, which also serves as the boundary between the two jurisdictions (and the multi-exit Friendship Heights Metro station), there are two substantial shopping malls; a third complex anchored by Bloomingdale's and a huge Whole Foods, as well as a full-size Lord & Taylor, a fully renovated Saks Fifth Avenue with a legendary ladies' shoes department, and Brooks Brothers; several trendy new restaurants; a couple of mini shopping strips; and a one-block complex containing some of the most luxe shops in Washington.

On the southwest corner of Wisconsin and Western Avenues is **Mazza Gallerie** (**mazzagallerie.com**), home to Neiman Marcus, Saks Fifth Avenue for Men, Nordstrom Rack, Kron Chocolatier, Ann Taylor, Williams-Sonoma, and a multiplex to park the kids.

Across the street is the **Chevy Chase Pavilion** (**ccpavilion.com**), which has its own Embassy Suites Hotel (so you can shop till you drop for a nap), as well as J. Crew, H&M, CVS, Cheesecake Factory, and World Market. More notably, however, it's home to the multiformat eatery Range from almost Top Chef Bryan Voltaggio; see page 295 in Part Five: Dining for a description. South of Chevy Chase Pavilion, facing Wisconsin Avenue NW, are three popular discount stores: Nordstrom Rack, Marshalls, and DSW Shoes, beside Maggiano's Little Italy restaurant.

A little north of Mazza Gallerie on Wisconsin Avenue between Western and Willard Avenues is the **Shops at Wisconsin Place** (**shopwisconsinplace.com**), which includes Bloomie's, MAC Cosmetics, Anthropologie, BCBG Maxazria, Cole Haan, Talbots, etc., plus a Capital Grille and a wine bar. Facing Bloomingdale's is a spanking bright Saks Fifth Avenue, with all its designer collections; and another block up Wisconsin past Willard Avenue are Chico's, Banana Republic, and Gap. Brooks Brothers is on the next corner.

In the 5400 block of Wisconsin on the east side is a little bit of Manhattan in Maryland—specifically, the corner of Fifth Avenue and 55th Street—where the jewelry royalty cluster of Tiffany & Co., Bulgari, and Cartier are studded amid the complex called **The Collection at Chevy Chase** (**thecollectionatchevychase.com**). (Four other dependable local jewelers are also in the neighborhood, if you want to do some serious comparison shopping: Boone & Son and Adam Keshishian, as well as Pampillonia and Chas Schwartz & Son in Mazza Gallerie.)

Ralph Lauren's two-story boutique—which looks like a European prince's hunting lodge downstairs and a Hollywood starlet's bedroom upstairs—rubs structural shoulders in the Collection at Chevy Chase with Jimmy Choo, Gucci, Louis Vuitton, and Dior. And sharing a parking lot is Saks Jandel, which is not affiliated with the Fifth Avenue brand but carries many Fifth Avenue designer names and houses a Vera Wang Bridal Boutique.

On Wisconsin facing the Collection is Santa Maria Novella, a very high-end boutique for Italian lotions, perfumes, etc. Not surprisingly, there are also several trendy restaurants in this neighborhood (Indique Heights, Lia's, Sushi-Ko, and the more midstream but dependable Clyde's), as well as a number of chain choices.

DUPONT CIRCLE

ALTHOUGH IT IS PROBABLY BEST KNOWN for its restaurants and nightlife, Dupont Circle is also a draw for shoppers looking to enrich the mind—it's full of fine art galleries and bookstores. Most of these are on the north side of the circle: the art galleries are generally clustered along R Street in the two blocks just west of Connecticut Avenue, leading you toward the Phillips Collection (see "Specialty Shopping," below).

One of the first (founded in 1976) combination bookstore/cafés in the country is Kramerbooks & Afterwords, at Connecticut and Q Streets, which stays open 24 hours a day on weekends; just off the circle at 20th and P Streets, you'll find Second Story Books, a terrific source for used books.

Collectors will enjoy a visit to Capital Coin & Stamp Co. or Fantom Comics, and craft enthusiasts may want to check out the city's most popular make-it-yourself jewelry store, Bedazzled.

South of the circle, on Connecticut Avenue NW, between N and K Streets, are several high-end retailers that cater to the law-and-lobby offices in the area, such as Tag Heuer, Brooks Brothers, Betsy Fisher, and Rizik's (a prominent local women's shop). Find a wide selection of irresistible gifts (to give yourself or bring home) at Chocolate Moose and Proper Topper; the latter was formerly a men's haberdashery but now caters to women, babies, and children.

Dupont Circle is home to a fine estate-jewelry shop called Tiny Jewel Box and precious gem specialists, Boone and Sons. If you want to dress for success without financial stress, look into Secondi, a very upscale women's consignment store on Connecticut near R Street. For those who love finding unique pieces for the home, check out Tabletop, or stop in Pansaari for some chai tea and Indian spice mix.

QUICK STOPS

MOST SHOPS ON CAPITOL HILL ARE IN and around **Eastern Market** (see "Flea Markets" on pages 338–339) on 7th Street between Pennsylvania and Independence Avenues SE. There are also a few stores in the blocks around the Library of Congress side of the Capitol. Otherwise, the major shopping center of the hill is **Union Station,** which has dozens of name chains (see pages 336–337).

Also on Capitol Hill, you'll find a handful of independent shops along Pennsylvania Avenue SE, including Metro Mutts, a pet supply store; Boutique on the Hill, a women's clothing store; and Toy Soldier Shop, with displays of castles, books, and collectible toy soldiers from every battle.

Another retail street is 8th Street SE, also known as **Barracks Row** because of the Navy Barracks located there. Although the neighborhood is predominantly restaurants and pubs, there are two bike shops, Capitol Hill and City Bikes; Capitol Hill Sporting Goods; Capital Teas; DCanter, selling wine and hosting regular tasting events; and Hill's Kitchen supply store.

Although the **Penn Quarter** neighborhood is prime dining and museum territory, its shopping tends to be mostly on the supply side: chain clothing stores (H&M, Forever 21, Urban Outfitters, Banana Republic, Ann Taylor, Jos. A. Bank) and a few trendier spots (Zara, Peruvian Connection, Anthropologie, and Mia Gemma Jewelers). You'll generally find them along F and G Streets NW between 9th and 14th. With the establishment of **City Center,** however, many new luxury stores have opened here recently, especially those selling high-end handbags—Louis Vuitton, Paul Stewart, Longchamp, and Burberry. International brands are also well represented: Hermès, Loro Piana (Italian cashmere apparel), Caudalie Boutique and Spa, and an Italian-style gelato boutique called Dolcezza. Sports fans should check out the shops around the Verizon Center: The Jersey Store and The Home Team Store represent both local D.C. teams and competitors' merchandise.

Though **Bethesda** is primarily known as a dining destination, Bethesda Row, a "new town"-style mixed-use development near the Bethesda Metro station, anchors an interesting mini–street mall, with a covered pedestrian shopping area. Among the boutiques in and around the arcade are Ginger, the name-your-denim-brand Luna, Le Creuset, Amethyst, Bluemercury, Aveda, Drybar, the half-new, half-vintage Current, Lou Lou, Lululemon, Secolari olive oil bar and Vino Volo wine bar, Calypso St. Barth, Bonobos, and Sassanova designer shoes. The block is also home to Apple and Bang & Olufsen stores and a Barnes & Noble. Urban Country takes vintage style furniture and goes industrial wink-wink with it. There are also branches of the notorious Georgetown Cupcake (with usually a shorter wait than at the original) and Luke's Lobster (of New York food-truck craze).

In **Old Town Alexandria,** the main intersection for tourists is Washington Street (the George Washington Parkway) and King Street; the more interesting shops are along King Street.

In addition, many other town centers built around Metro stops— **Ballston, Clarendon,** and **Crystal City**—have shopping options. A standout is the **Fashion Center at Pentagon City,** which is directly connected to the Pentagon Metro station. This glitzy indoor mall features upscale anchors, including Nordstrom and Macy's, plus the Ritz-Carlton Hotel. There's also a huge Forever 21 and GAP Kids, as well as an open food court area that attracts a lot of businesspeople at lunchtime. **The Mosaic District** in Fairfax County has a modern line-up of local boutiques, luxury fashion stores, and popular restaurants.

■ SPECIALTY SHOPPING

Antiques

The stretch of Wisconsin Avenue north of M Street in Georgetown, where the clothing boutiques cluster, is also home to several notable antiques dealers, especially between O and Q Streets. Among the best are **Carling Nichols,** which specializes in 18th- and 19th-century Chinese pieces; **John Rosselli & Associates,** a branch of the old-line New York firm; **David Bell; Gore Dean,** the house and garden antiques collection of local Martha Stewart, Deborah Gore Dean; **Darrell Dean** (no relation); **Blair House; Miller & Arney; Oliver Dunn, Moss & Co., Catharine Roberts; Marston Luce; Cherry Antiques;** and the longtime Georgetown secret, **Christ Child Opportunity Shop,** where, on the second floor, you'll find silver and silver plate, china, paintings, and other cherishables on consignment from the best Georgetown homes. **Cotes Jardin,** which deals in 18th- and 19th-century French furniture, is on O Street NW just west of Wisconsin Avenue.

A partitioned town house at 2918 M Street NW features **Michael Getz,** offering a collection of works by such artists and studios as Tiffany, Lalique, Daum, and Icart. Here you can find heavy wrought irons, ivory-handled fish services and magnifying glasses, cream pitchers and perfume bottles, elegant cocktail shakers, candelabras, ornate photo frames, and a breathtaking collection of silver napkin rings. Next door, **Cherub Antiques** also displays art, glass, and silver, but its emphasis is on enamelware, ceramics, and heavier pieces. Shops with antiques, both formal and more offbeat, stretch up Wisconsin toward Q Street.

One of the largest concentrations of antiques shops, about 30 in all, is on **Antique Row** in Kensington, Maryland, about 4 miles from the D.C. line. Most are along Howard Avenue, with smaller shops east of Connecticut Avenue and larger warehouses west of Connecticut. Whatever your era, country, or style, you're likely to find it here.

However, Washington's *very* serious antiques-seekers get out of town—driving an hour or more to the countryside of Maryland, Virginia, West Virginia, or Pennsylvania for the bargains. Frederick, Maryland, about an hour north of Washington, is particularly popular with area antiquers. The biggest single group is at the 130-dealer **Emporium Antiques** on East Patrick Street in Frederick (**emporiumantiques.com**), though walking the Main Street neighborhood and the streets just off it will turn up scores of others.

*un*official **TIP**
While some antiques neighborhoods thrive on weekends, Sundays are a toss-up; do a little web surfing before you hit the road.

Art, Prints, and Photography

Collectors will want to focus on Washington's most concentrated selections of art for sale—traditional, modern, photographic, and ethnic—found around Dupont and Logan Circles. The best shops are centered on the crossroads of Connecticut Avenue and R Street and spread a couple of blocks in each direction—where there are a dozen galleries within two blocks. Several of these galleries are affiliated with the Phillips Collection. Gallery openings are generally on the first Friday of the month, and the galleries stay open until 8 p.m. Some highlights include **Marsha Mateyka,** who represents local art celebs Sam Gillian and Gene Davis, and the nonprofit **Hillyer Art Space,** which promotes many local artists.

In Logan Circle, galleries are located on 14th Street, between P and Q Streets: **Adamson Gallery** (one of Washington's premier print and photography sources), **Curator's Office,** and the high-end folk art specialist **Hemphill Fine Arts,** all of which share an address at 1515 14th Street NW. Nearby are **Gallery Plan B** and the Warhol Foundation–endowed **Transformer.**

Art enthusiasts who find themselves in Georgetown should concentrate their time on Wisconsin Avenue at the intersection of Reservoir

Road. Top galleries there include **Cross Mackenzie, Maurine Littleton,** and **Robert Brown.** These galleries are adjacent to a park and an ice cream store, so that can be your reward for your kids keeping their hands off expensive art.

Penn Quarter, the neighborhood between the National Portrait Gallery and Pennsylvania Avenue, has a few galleries worth noting, including **Flashpoint Gallery,** at 9th and G Streets NW, and **Civilian Art Projects** (which often mounts shows with social or political agendas) on Seventh Street near K Street NW. There are sometimes exhibits at the **Goethe-Institut** on Seventh Street as well.

One of the largest art "warehouses" is the former **Torpedo Factory Art Center** near the waterfront in Old Town Alexandria, where 82 artist studios on three floors feature a range of media—painting, sculpture, jewelry, and more. You can buy their work or simply watch; an estimated 700,000 visitors a year do just that.

Bookstores

Washingtonians love to read, and fortunately that's why many independent bookstores are still in business. These local owners find success through regular readings by famous authors, as well as hosting children's events. One of the busiest is **Kramerbooks & Afterwords Café and Bookstore** in Dupont Circle. What makes this place special is the curated collection of books, especially a wide selection of travel books. It is also a delightful place to grab a cocktail or have a meal, as the bookstore is connected to the café. Shoppers are welcome to read while they eat!

Second Story Books, at 20th and P Streets NW in Dupont Circle, is among the city's oldest purveyors of rare books, and with its Rockville warehouse boasts more than a million editions. The fine **Idle Time Books,** at 2767 18th Street NW in Adams Morgan, also stocks vintage LPs, CDs, and more. Mid City is home to one of the branches of **Big Planet Comics** (1520 U Street NW), a major source for graphic novels and comics. Stop in one of the many **Busboys and Poets** bookstores/cafés to peruse tomes with a liberal bent.

In Georgetown, **Bridge Street Books** (2814 Pennsylvania Avenue NW) has a lovely ambiance and specializes in political writing and social commentary from both sides, as well as literary fiction, philosophy, and poetry. Nearby you'll find **The Lantern** (3241 P Street NW), a used bookstore with proceeds funding college tuition for needy girls.

The **Library of Congress** (**bookstore.gpo.gov**) is another place to pick up books, and don't miss the Smithsonian museum shops, especially the **National Building Museum** and the **National Gallery of Art.** Also in Capitol Hill is the well-established **Capitol Hill Books,** which carries a wide selection of mysteries, obscure biographies, and used books from all genres.

Politics & Prose, intellectual Washington's favorite hangout, specializes in psychology, politics, and the works of local authors—and hosts many of their book-signing parties. They have an excellent kids' section and an expert staff who love to recommend books to satisfy every curiosity (5015 Connecticut Avenue NW; **politics-prose.com)**

Recently, a Washingtonian used Kickstarter to open another independent bookstore, **Upshur Street Books** (827 Upshur Street NW). Located near the Georgia Avenue Petworth Metro station, the store has the support of D.C.'s most famous literati—George Pelicanos and Alice McDermott—and the owners host regular reading events for children.

Although it's not widely advertised, **the Shops at Mount Vernon** (**mountvernon.org**) have the largest bookstore in the country dedicated to George Washington.

Like their parents, Washington kids also have a passion for reading. The younger set is well served by a handful of independent bookstores that have survived through their deep connection to their community. **Fairy Godmother** (319 7th Street SE), near Eastern Market in Capitol Hill, has both toys and books packed into a cramped space, but your kids will love the whimsical selection of fiction and nonfiction literature.

The Children's Playseum, on Bethesda Avenue in downtown Bethesda, not only sells books and toys, but it's also a perfect place to bring your preschool-age kids to reward them for good behavior after touring D.C. With a few themed rooms, kids are free to interact and play, pretend, paint, try on costumes, and buy gently used books (starting at $1–$8). On that same block is Bethesda's massive **Barnes & Noble** (4801 Bethesda Avenue), with the lower of its three levels dedicated to kids books, and **Tugooh Toys** (4823 Bethesda Avenue) for educational books and toys (a second location is at 1355 Wisconsin Avenue in Chevy Chase). Also in Chevy Chase, you'll find **Barston's Child's Play** (5536 Connecticut Avenue NW) stuffed full of games, toys, and books for all ages.

In the Virginia suburbs, check out **Kinder Haus Toys** (170 N. Filmore) in Arlington. Nicknamed "Wonderland" by fans, it's packed with books, European toys, and designer kids clothing. **Hooray for Books** (1555 King Street) is in the main shopping area of Old Town Alexandria; they host daily story time readings and book signings.

Food and Farmers Markets

If you enjoy shopping for gourmet food, regional specialties, and unusual treats, you can't beat Washington's food and farmers markets. Year-round, stop in Capitol Hill's indoor **Eastern Market** (7th and North Carolina Streets SE) to sample international cuisine, find local produce, and peruse a variety of handmade arts and crafts. During the week, Eastern Market has a busy deli, fresh-baked goods, and local cheeses (it's known for having the best pancakes too). On weekends, the attached open-air venue features handmade crafts and antiques.

Union Market (1309 5th Street NE) opened three years ago in a renovated building built in 1800s, and it has become a catalyst in the development of this once-blighted neighborhood. Today, Union Market, near the NoMA–Gallaudet University Metro station, hosts a concentration of modern food purveyors under one roof, selling everything from oysters to gelato to empanadas. You can dine in or take food home.

In the heart of Georgetown, Manhattan's **Dean & Deluca Market** (3276 M Street NW) features regional specialties such as Maryland crab cakes, pantry items from around the world, and elegant gourmet gift boxes. Near the Dupont Circle Metro, **Glen's Garden Market** (2001 S Street NW, facing 20th Street) is filled with prepared foods, beer and wine, local products, cheeses, and produce. The market regularly hosts wine and beer tastings on its outdoor patio.

In fair weather, don't be surprised to walk through Washington right into a fresh-air farmers market. The vendors set up in different locations in the city on different days. To find out where they'll be when you visit, check the website: **freshfarmmarkets.org.**

Political Memorabilia

You can easily find GOP or Demo-leaning T-shirts and buttons in most quickie souvenir shops, but serious collectors might want to check out **Political Americana** at 1331 Pennsylvania Avenue NW (near the JW Marriott) or **Capitol Coin and Stamp** in Farragut Square at 1001 Connecticut Avenue, which carries a broad selection of campaign items, posters, and ephemera.

Records and CDs

Adams Morgan and Mid City are home to a number of good independent record and music stores catering to vinyl vets, as well as cutting-edge, indie, and world music. Among them are **Crooked Beat Records** (2318 18th Street NW); **Smash Records** (2314 18th Street NW), which complements its punk and rock 'n' roll collections with vintage clothing; **Red Onion Records and Books** (18th and T Streets NW); and **Hill & Dale Records** (1054 31st Street NW). See also the listings for Second Story and Idle Time Books, above.

Vintage Clothing

The Greater Washington area is a Mecca for vintage shoppers. In D.C., head to Mid City and Georgetown for the most options; see descriptions in "Great Neighborhoods" above. Some standouts include **Meeps Vintage** (18th Street NW); **Junction** (U Street NW); **Mercedes Bien Vintage** (18th Street NW); **Fia's Fabulous Finds** (806 Upshur, Petworth, D.C.); **Analog** (716 Monroe Street NE, Brookland); **Bartered Threads** (12th

Street NE, Brookland); **Frugalista** (Mount Pleasant Street NW, Adams Morgan); **Crossroads Trading Co.** (14th Street NW, Mid City); **Dr. K's Vintage** (U Street NW, Mid City; **Legendary Beast** (U Street NW, Mid City); **Joint Custody** (U Street NW, Mid City); and **Junction Vintage** (U Street NW, Mid City).

In Maryland, try **Lipstick Lounge** (212 Main Street, Gaithersburg); **Chic to Chic** (Luanne Drive, Gaithersburg); **Mustard Seed** (Wisconsin Avenue, Bethesda); **Polly Sue's Vintage** (Laurel Avenue, Takoma Park); and **Reddz** (on M Street in Georgetown and Woodmont Avenue in Bethesda).

In Virginia, vintage enthusiasts recommend **New to You** (W. Broad Street, Falls Church); **Chic Envy** (Fairfax Corner, Fairfax); **Amalgamated Classic Clothing and Dry Goods** (Mount Vernon Avenue, Alexandria); **Mint Condition** (Saint Asaph Street, Alexandria); **Diva Consignment** (South Pitt Street, Alexandria); and **Elinor Coleman Vintage** (South Columbus Street, Alexandria).

Washington Souvenirs

When the legions of buses arrive in Washington, they are often dropped off at **Souvenir City** (1001 K Street NW), a store full of D.C.-themed keepsakes such as shot glasses, mini-monuments, and postcards. Another popular tourist stop is the **Washington Welcome Center** (1001 E Street NW) near Ford's Theatre and the Old Town Trolley tour stop. This conveniently located facility sells tickets to various tours but also carries replicas of the White House, license plates, key chains, magnets, stuffed animals, and even Presidential toilet brushes. Right next door is **Honest Abe's Souvenir** (506 10th Street NW), a shop with President Lincoln–emblazoned merchandise. Another option is to check out the merchandise sold by street vendors; they sell D.C. T-shirts, sweatshirts, caps, and bags. Adjacent to the Treasury Department on 15th Street, you'll find **White House Gifts** (1440 New York Avenue NW). This whimsical collection includes talking Hillary Clinton dolls, patriotic memorabilia, Air Force One miniatures, and even has the "Oval Office" movie set where you may take your own photos.

The National Zoo probably sells the most kid-friendly souvenirs, especially panda-mania gifts, stuffed animals, and toys. One lesser-known but very entertaining souvenir to take home is a Capitol Steps CD. This local theatre troupe performs satirical musical numbers that skewer politicians and current events, and you can buy a recording from the show. Performances take place every Friday and Saturday night at 7:30 p.m. at the **Ronald Reagan Building and International Trade Center** (☎ 703-683-8330).

Of course, the museum shops are the best source of high-quality souvenirs. All the **Smithsonian** and private museums sell merchandise in their gift shops. Each museum has themed items; for example, at

National Archives you'll find books on genealogy. At the **National Postal Museum,** collectors go gaga over the multitude of stamps from every era. One favorite stop is **The Newseum,** where you'll laugh over the entertaining political gags, shirts, and posters—all celebrating national and international news coverage of both historical and current events.

We especially love the collection housed in the beautiful **White House Visitor Center** (1450 Pennsylvania Avenue NW) run by the White House Historical Association. Besides the clever interactive exhibits, you'll find ornaments, umbrellas, and pins, all with the presidential seal. For kids they sell playing cards, toys, models, and educational books that will help them remember their trip to the nation's capital.

Watches

Washington's answer to Tourneau is **Alan Furman & Co.,** which offers up to 50% off on Rolex, Patek Philippe, and Cartier (near White Flint Metro, 12250 Rockville Pike, second level; **alanfurman.com**). **Benson's Jewelers** has an exclusive line of Swiss-made watches and Quartzline watches worth a look (near Metro Center, 1331 F Street NW). **Fink's Jewelers** in Dulles Town Center has a serious selection of Longine, Tag Heuer, Yurman, and more (near Reston Metro, 21100 Dulles Town Center, Sterling, VA). **Omega Watches Boutique** in Tysons Galleria will impress any fine watch collector (near Tysons Metro, 2001 International Drive, McLean, VA).

Wine and Spirits

Alcohol laws vary in the District of Columbia, Maryland, and Virginia; however, in all three consumers must be age 21 or older to order and buy alcohol. Each state varies in where they sell wine, beer, and spirits. In the two Maryland counties closest to D.C.—Montgomery and Prince George's—you can only buy wines and spirits in the private retail stores or ABC/state-run stores (with a few exceptions such as Rodman's and Balducci's, which sell wine and beer). In Virginia and D.C., wine and beer are available for purchase in grocery stores and convenience stores, while spirits are only available at state-run stores.

You'll find the biggest selection of wine and spirits in a few super-stores located in Washington D.C. Though it's not Metro-accessible, **MacArthur Beverages** (4877 MacArthur Boulevard NW) invests heavily and intelligently in wine futures and offers a strong catalog. **Calvert Woodley Fine Wines and Spirits** (4339 Connecticut Avenue NW, near Woodley Metro station) offers a huge selection of exotic, international wines and spirits, with knowledgeable salespeople eager to guide you. Other good sources for wine, beer, and spirits include **Magruder's** in Chevy Chase (5626 Connecticut Avenue NW), **Schneider's of Capitol Hill** (300 Massachusetts Avenue NE), and **West Dupont Circle Wine and Liquor** (2012 P Street NW).

PART EIGHT

EXERCISE *and* RECREATION

WORKING *a* WORKOUT *into* YOUR VISIT

MOST OF THE FOLKS IN THE *Unofficial Guide* family work out routinely, even when (or perhaps especially when) we're traveling. We walk, run, do yoga—the more "transportable" sports. It's not just a matter of offsetting calories (although those of us who review restaurants need extra help) but of easing stress and jet lag. But picturesque as it is, Washington's summer heat and humidity make outdoor exercise problematic. On bad days, local authorities may declare a "Heat Alert or Code Orange," meaning anyone with respiratory problems should limit exertion and outdoor exposure. Washington is also prone to high levels of allergens, especially in spring and fall. Although snow on sidewalks usually isn't a problem in the major tourist areas because of removal operations, cold air can also be hard on those with respiratory trouble.

The good news is there's less "work" in "workouts" these days and more "create" in "recreation." With trapeze flying, zip lines, climbing walls, rowing and rafting, hiking and horseback riding, the Washington region—whose sweep includes rivers, lakes, mountains, battlefields, and an admirable amount of public parkland—has plenty to entice you.

The BASIC DRILLS

WALKING, RUNNING, AND BICYCLING

THE MOST OBVIOUS METHOD OF EXERCISE—in fact, the almost unavoidable form for tourists—is walking. With its wide-open public spaces, long museum corridors, and picturesque neighborhoods, Washington is a walker's haven (in both senses of the word: security is very good around the Mall at all hours).

Strolling (or running or biking) **the Mall** offers grand views of the **Lincoln, Jefferson,** and **FDR Memorials** and the **Washington Monument,** as well as the **Tidal Basin** and the **Potomac River.** It's almost 2 miles from the Capitol steps to the Lincoln Memorial (and can be longer while the current turf restoration is underway). Crossing the bridge to **Arlington National Cemetery** fills out the 2 miles. You can also walk north along the river past the **Kennedy Center** and the **Thompson Boat Center** to the **Georgetown waterfront.** (This is really nice when the cherry blossoms are in flower; plan to have a drink or dinner at one of the Georgetown waterfront restaurants.) And within Georgetown, the waterfront and portions of the **Chesapeake and Ohio (C&O) Canal Towpath** are very popular; from the canal's beginnings near the Four Seasons Hotel to **Fletcher's Boathouse** is about 3 miles. From the Four Seasons to **Union Station,** going through the Mall and skirting the Capitol grounds, is also 3 miles, so round-trip is 6 miles.

Contained within the city limits is the 32-mile trail system in Rock Creek Park, one of the oldest urban parks in the country. The best place to start your walk is at the park's **Nature Center** (5200 Glover Road NW) near the Cleveland Park Metro. Other stellar walking trails supervised by the National Park Service are at the **National Arboretum** and **Kenilworth Park and Gardens,** both in northeast D.C. The Arboretum has miles of wide paved and mulched trails through various gardens, forests, and meadows. Kenilworth is a photographer's dream, where huge lotus flowers dot the elevated and land-based trails surrounded on all sides by a riot of lily ponds.

Washington offers plenty of options to joggers as well. Most of the better running areas are relatively flat but visually stunning and centrally located, close to major hotels and attractions, making either a morning or late-afternoon run easy to fit into your schedule. Many hotels offer marked-route maps; check with the hotel concierge.

The C&O Canal Towpath offers what is probably the best running surface in town. Runners, cyclists, and hikers love this wide, dirt-pack trail that runs between the scenic Potomac River and the canal. Mileposts along the towpath keep you informed of your distance, but there are also several larger landmarks: **Fletcher's Boathouse** around mile 3 has restrooms and some vending machines. **Glen Echo Park** is about 7 miles out. (You may be able to get a restorative meal and/or drink at the Irish Inn at Glen Echo.) Another 7 miles out, near mile marker 14, is the enormous cataract at **Great Falls.**

In all, the C&O Canal, the entire stretch of which is now a national park (thanks primarily to the efforts of US Supreme Court Justice William O. Douglas), runs 184.5 miles to Cumberland, Maryland, offering hikers, bikers, and joggers another way to enjoy several scenic and historic areas, including **White's Ferry,** where car commuters and recreational visitors still cross the Potomac toward Leesburg; **Harpers**

Ferry, where John Brown made his war-inciting stand; and Sharpsburg, Maryland, also known as **Antietam battlefield.** (This can be done in stages, of course; go to **nps.gov/choh/planyourvisit.**)

There's a second path that follows the C&O Towpath as far as Fletcher's Boathouse but then turns east toward Bethesda and Silver Spring. The **Capital Crescent Trail,** based on the old Baltimore and Ohio (B&O) Railroad right-of-way (and including a bridge over the canal), has both a wide biking trail and in many places a separate running path. It has become so popular (more than a million walkers, runners, and bikers every year) that it is now recognized as the most heavily used rail head in the country. From Georgetown to Bethesda—where the trail emerges at a convenient restaurant neighborhood not far from the Metro—is about 7 miles.

The **Mount Vernon Trail** is a riverside route on the Virginia side of the Potomac that starts near **Theodore Roosevelt Island** off the George Washington Memorial Parkway, goes downriver through Old Town Alexandria, past wildlife refuges and marinas, monument views, jet takeoffs, and so on, and winds up 18.5 miles later at Mount Vernon itself. Roosevelt Island is a sweet little wildlife and woodlands refuge designed by Frederick Olmsted, with a 1.6-mile easy walking loop.

For a more extensive guide to hikes in the area, check out author Paul Elliott's *60 Hikes within 60 Miles: Washington, D.C.,* published by Menasha Ridge Press (**menasharidge.com**).

These trails and routes are great for cycling, too, of course. Adult cruiser bikes (plus helmets, baskets, locks, and so on) are available for rent on a first-come, first-serve basis at **Thompson Boat Center,** at the intersection of Rock Creek Parkway and Virginia Avenue on the Georgetown waterfront (**thompsonboatcenter.com**). Fletcher's Boathouse also rents single-speed cruisers and 21-speed train bikes. **Bike and Roll** rents Trek, tandem, and trailer-hitched bikes from multiple locations, including the National Museum of American History, L'Enfant Plaza, Martin Luther King Jr. Library, and Union Station (☎ 866-736-8224; **bikeandroll.com**).

FITNESS CENTERS AND CORE-STRENGTHENING

MOST MAJOR HOTELS THESE DAYS HAVE A FITNESS ROOM with some cardio and weight-lifting equipment. However, if you are a member of one of the national chains, or are willing to buy a day pass, you have scores of options; many clubs have massage therapists, yoga instructors, and even hair stylists on hand.

Vida Fitness in the Verizon Center is the flagship of a very trendy local chain, now with six branches downtown (**vidafitness.com**) and all with salons on site, so if you want to break a sweat before that breakfast meeting, you're covered. **Sports Club/LA** in the Ritz-Carlton Hotel at 22nd and M Streets NW ($35; **mpsportsclub.com**) is very hip and also boasts a handy deluxe spa for taking the ache out.

Balance Gym has five locations (**balancegym.com**) in the Greater Washington area (Thomas Circle, Foggy Bottom, Glover Park, Georgetown, and Bethesda) and wins top honors in the "The Best of DC" poll for their CrossFit and Dance Trance programs; ask about their "One Day Free Pass" offer.

Intense fitness buffs should try **Solidcore** (**solidcore.co/dc**), with four locations that emphasize a 50-minute, full-body workout designed to work your muscles to "failure" to eventually rebuild them.

There are a dozen **Sport & Health Clubs** (**sportandhealth.com**), some with golf and tennis facilities, spread out over D.C., Maryland, and Virginia. (If you check the companies' websites, you can sometimes find free trial memberships.) **Washington Sports Club,** with 13 area locations, is part of a company that also operates chains in Philadelphia, Boston, and New York City, and gets high marks for high-tech ($30; **mysportsclubs.com**). One of its biggest claims to fame, however, is that one of the employees once asked member (then-presidential candidate) Barack Obama for ID—"and your first name is...?"

YOGA STUDIOS

WASHINGTONIANS LOVE THEIR YOGA, and you won't have to miss a day of practice when visiting, thanks to the **Kimpton Hotels,** which provide a mat in their guest rooms. Several hotels really emphasize healthful travel experiences, and one, **Avenue Suites** in Georgetown, offers complimentary yoga classes on their patio. Dozens of small neighborhood studios offer walk-in classes, so ask the front desk or concierge for recommendations, and inquire about discounts extended to hotel guests. Some popular locations in the District include **Studio DC Yoga Center** (2469 18th Street NW) and **Buddha B** (1115 U Street NW) in Mid City. **Yoga District** (**yogadistrict.com**) with three locations and **Epic Yoga** (1323 Connecticut Avenue NW) offer both hot and barre-style classes. **Flow Yoga Center** (1450 P Street NW) in Logan Circle; **Down Dog Power Yoga** (**downdogyoga.com**), with locations in Arlington, Bethesda, Herndon, and Georgetown; and **Sculpt DC** (950 F Street NW) in Penn Quarter are also good options.

RECREATIONAL SPORTS

TENNIS AND GOLF

WASHINGTON HAS SEVERAL PUBLIC TENNIS FACILITIES, but only two are likely to accommodate visitors. **Rock Creek Tennis Center** (**rockcreektennis.com**), which is home to the Citi-Open tournament every July that draws many of the sport's biggest stars (Sloane Stephens won last year's tournament, but past champions include Andre Agassi, Nadia Petrova, Arthur Ashe, and Andy Roddick), has 25 hard and clay courts,

5 of them heated. **East Potomac Tennis Center** (**eastpotomactennis.com**), on Hains Point near the Tidal Basin, has 24 hard courts, including 5 encased in a year-round white bubble. Make prime-time reservations for both a week in advance, but walk-ups have a pretty good chance of getting a court weekdays.

East Potomac Park also has one of three golf courses operated by the National Park Service and the only one easily accessible by public transportation (and the least expensive, with weekday rates starting at $10 for 9 holes, but realize this is not a championship golf course by any stretch). It offers one 18-hole course, two 9-hole courses, a driving range, and a very picturesque 1930s 18-hole miniature golf course (no cartoon characters here). In addition, East Potomac Park, which is more than 300 acres altogether, has an outdoor pool, a playground, Potomac Grill, and picnic facilities, so it's a good choice for family outings. But check before you go because the facilities are closed sometimes for maintenance. (☎ 202-426-6841; **npca.org/parks**).

The other golf centers are **Langston Golf Course,** along the Anacostia River in Northeast D.C., and **Rock Creek Golf Course.** For more information on all three parks, visit **golfdc.com.**

There are also many courses in Montgomery County (**montgomery countygolf.com**) and Fairfax County (**fairfaxcounty.gov/parks/golf**). However, you'll have to know somebody—and maybe somebody she knows too—to get into Bethesda's famed **Congressional Country Club** (**ccclub.org**), which lists scores of politicos and power brokers among its members. Tiger Woods's Quicken Loans PGA National is played here every other year in late June.

Trumping even Tiger, The Donald recently purchased a 600-acre course in Loudoun County and conducted a radical makeover to transform it into a championship-caliber course. The course has stunning views of the Potomac River, with greens positioned on the water's edge. Trump named it, of course, **Trump National Golf Club** (**trumpnationaldc.com**). The presidential candidate lured the Senior PGA tournament here for 2017, but you have a better chance of winning on *The Apprentice* than scoring a free pass. Ditto the **TPC Potomac** at Avenel Farm in Potomac (**tpc.com/potomac**), which has hosted numerous PGA tours over the years.

SWIMMING

LOCAL WATERS ARE POLLUTED to one degree or another, so unless you have time and money for a trip to the Atlantic beaches, stick to your hotel swimming pool, ask the hotel concierge to direct you to the nearest pool or gym, or check out one of these popular aquatic centers.

One of the nicest is the free Olympic-size pool at East Potomac Park (see above), open June–early October (☎ 202-727-6523; **npca .org/parks**). The year-round pool at **Rumsey Aquatic Center** near the Eastern Market Metro station on Capitol Hill (also called the Capitol Hill Natorium) is also free to D.C. residents, so ask your friends to treat you like family . . . or pay the $7 non-resident fee, $4 for kids over age 6, and $3 for kids under 6 (☎ 202-724-4495). **Woodrow Wilson Aquatic Center** is located near American University and the Tenleytown Metro station (☎ 202-730-0583). The **YMCA National Capital Area** in Dupont Circle (☎ 202-862-9622) has a busy pool and a

unofficial **TIP**
There are only a few hotels that offer pool passes to outsiders, and most of those, of course, are open only between Memorial Day and Labor Day.

popular climbing wall. For those staying in Bethesda or Rockville, the completely accessible and innovative **Kennedy Shriver Aquatic Center,** where some of America's Olympic divers trained, is walking distance from the White Flint Metro station (☎ 240-777-8070). Another option is a day trip to Annapolis to swim at **Sandy Spring State Park** on the Chesapeake Bay; it has a small beach in the shadow of the 3-mile long Bay Bridge that is popular with windsurfers ($4 entrance fee; **dnr2.maryland.gov**).

ROPES AND ROCKS

THERE ARE THREE OF THE ELEVATED-ROPE adventure parks in the Washington area, though none are Metro-accessible: **Go Ape** at Lake Needwood in Rockville, Maryland, a few minutes' drive off I-270 or Route 355; **Terrapin Adventures** in Savage, Maryland; and **The Adventure Park at Sandy Spring Friends School** in Olney, Maryland. **Go Ape (goape .com)** is the first American course from a company that already owns more than two dozen such attractions in the United Kingdom. In a space the size of seven football fields, it scatters zip lines, Tarzan Swings, rope ladders, trapezes, and so on. Each park has restrictions involving minimum age, height, waist size (for harnesses), weight, minimal fitness levels, and so on. (Pregnant women may have to sign a waiver.) For the more challenging routes, you will have preliminary instruction, and most have courses that range from beginner to advanced. Prices start at about $60.

Though farther away, **Terrapin Adventures (terrapinadventures .com)** in historic Savage Mill, Maryland, is even more elaborate, with a 330-foot zip line 30 feet in the air, a giant tandem swing with an 80-foot arc, a multilevel rope course, and a 43-foot climbing tower. It also offers kayaking, tubing, fly fishing, wind surfing, horseback riding, and geocaching.

The Adventure Park at Sandy Spring Friends School (sandyspring adventurepark.org) has 13 separate trails in the Adventure Forest and offers several levels of difficulty. The Monkey Grove has 10 climbing challenges, and the Labyrinth is a wooden structure with multiple bridges, ladders, and ropes. To beat the heat of the day, try going during twilight hours when the park is magically lit with strings of LED lights.

The Trazpeze School is located in the Navy Yard neighborhood, near Nationals Park. The school offers instruction for both adults and kids (ages 6 and older) in all weather—they have indoor and outdoor facilities. Classes range from $40 to $59 for various experiences. To find out whether they offer a class during your visit, check the website at **washingtondc.trapezeschool.com.**

Results Gym (resultsthegym.com) on Capitol Hill has a 38-foot rock wall. But **Earth Treks Rockville,** near the Rockville Metro station (**earthtreksclimbing.com**), is the largest indoor climbing facility in the country, with 38,500 square feet of rock wall; a day pass is $22.

BOATING, PADDLEBOARDING, AND FLOATING

IF YOU'RE ANYWHERE ALONG THE POTOMAC RIVER early in the day or around dusk, you'll see the area's school rowing crews doing drills. The George Washington University Invitational Regatta, which draws teams from all over the country during the Cherry Blossom Festival, is only one of the many contests. And all forms of rowing are increasingly popular in the Washington area; some high-level competitors come here to train.

Canoes, rowboats, and single and double kayaks are available for rent at Thompson Boat Center and Fletcher's Boat House (see page 356). **Key Bridge Boathouse (keybridgeboathouse.com)**, located at the foot of Key Bridge in Georgetown, rents two- and three-person canoes, single and double kayaks, and stand-up paddleboards. **Paddlestroke SUP,** located just north of the city by Angler's Inn in Potomac, Maryland (☎ 301-442-6864), offers rentals and lessons in paddleboarding and river surfing with experienced instructors and in a calm-water environment.

*un*official **TIP**
Inspired by those rowing crews you see on the river? Or maybe you're just a fan of those British-historical romance movies? Thompson Boat Center offers private rowing lessons ($75 an hour) and sculling courses ($150 for a week's course), and even sweep rowing courses, which draw out-of-town Olympic team wannabes ($250 for two weeks).

The Potomac River may look harmless, but please do not ignore warning signs about water conditions, particularly at Great Falls: Both swimmers, jumpers, and world-class kayak competitors have lost their lives here. In fact, rescue crews have nicknamed the gorge section near Great Falls, "the drowning machine" for the frequent loss of life.

For a perfect day trip, take a gentle float down one of the rivers close to Washington, such as **Antietam Creek** near Harper's Ferry. Guides drive you to a drop-off point, and then they float along beside you as the current pulls your inner tube through meandering and fast-moving rapids. This is the perfect family activity because it's safe for people of all ages and levels of fitness (**riverriders.com**).

Prefer something family-friendly and closer to your hotel? Check out the **Tidal Basin Paddle Boats (tidalbasinpaddleboats.com)** on Maine Avenue near the Jefferson Memorial; one-hour rentals are $15 for a two-passenger boat and $24 for a four-passenger boat. The newest boating operation is located at **National Harbor;** the marina rents peddle boats, canoes, paddleboards, and kayaks to tool around on a gentle section of the Potomac River, across from Old Town Alexandria and close to Woodrow Wilson Bridge. Rentals are $15–$30 per hour, with twilight tours available during the summer. For a full listing of pricing, tours, locations, and hours of many Washington-area boating operations, visit **boatingindc.com.**

SEGWAY TOURS

THERE ARE MULTIPLE SEGWAY TOURS available in Washington, and frankly, this is a very efficient way to see a lot of sights and have fun doing it. Segways are two-wheel motorized vehicles that you can steer and propel forward with hand controls. They have an upright post and a platform to stand on. D.C. law dictates that riders must be age 16 or older to operate one in the city.

Tours are offered in the daytime, evening, and by private guide; they involve a 10-minute training session, last about two to three hours, and cost between $65 and $80 per person. Guides usher riders around various monuments and attractions, including the Smithsonian museums, the White House, and the Capitol Building. Tours are usually limited to eight persons, so there are ample opportunities to ask questions and hear the guide's historical facts and interesting stories. Currently, group tours are only offered in English, and there are limits on weight and whether a rider is pregnant (that's a no-go). Reputable Segway companies include **City Segway Tours** (**dc.citysegwaytours.com**), **Segs in the City** (**segsin thecity.com**), and **Capital Segway** (**capitalsegway.com**). They may seem daunting at first, but they're fairly easy to ride and will allow you to cover a lot of ground during your tour. Older teens will love it.

ICE AND SNOW

THERE ARE A FEW YEAR-ROUND ICE RINKS in the Washington area, but the two that would be the most fun for out-of-towners are the one on the Mall and the other within sight of the White House.

Come skating weather—generally mid-November through mid-March—the **Sculpture Garden** of the National Gallery of Art between Seventh and Ninth Streets NW and Constitution and Madison Avenues (**nga.gov/skating**) is transformed into a fantasy ice rink in the middle of the Mall, with the U.S. Capitol and all the Smithsonian museums lit up as a backdrop. It's open until a romantic 11 p.m. on Fridays and Saturdays, and the **Pavilion Café,** a lovely retro-Deco glass-sided eatery alongside the garden, serves until 9 p.m.

Several public rinks are accessible by Metro—and at Metro developments, in fact. The outdoor-café area at the **Shops at Pentagon Row** (part of the Pentagon City complex) and the town square at **Rockville Town Center** are iced during winter. **Canal Park Ice Rink,** near the Navy Yard and Capitol South stations (2nd and M Streets SE) is the newest addition.

For hockey fans, however, the most intriguing facility might be **Kettler Capitals Iceplex,** atop a seven-story office building at Ballston Common Mall (at the Ballston Metro) in Arlington; it's the practice rink for the NHL Washington Capitals (**kettlercapitalsiceplex.com**).

There are several downhill ski complexes within two- to three-hours' drive from Washington: **Whitetail** (**skiwhitetail.com**), **Ski Roundtop** (**ski roundtop.com**), and **Liberty Mountain Resort** (**skiliberty.com**), all located in south-central Pennsylvania. In Virginia, try **Wintergreen** (**winter greenresort.com**), **Bryce Mountain** (**bryceresort.com**), or **Massanutten** (**massresort.com**). In West Virginia, **Canaan Valley** (**skithevalley.com**) and **Snowshoe** (**snowshoemtn.com**) offer the highest vertical drops in the area; all are open to snowboarders and skiers. Maryland has the popular four-seasons **Wisp Ski Resort** (**wispresort.com**) at Deep Creek Lake. All of these resorts offer golf courses, rental cabins, lodges, and restaurants and host regular events and festivals. And all employ snowmaking machines to deal with the unpredictability of the Mid-Atlantic weather.

SPECTATOR SPORTS

BASEBALL

IN 2005, AFTER A 30-YEAR DROUGHT, Washington welcomed a Major League Baseball home team: the **Washington Nationals** of the National League, formerly the Montreal Expos. In 2008, the team moved into an elaborate stadium complex located at the Navy Yard Metro. Tickets can range well into the hundreds, but singles start at $16 on some days, and all sight lines here are good. Nationals Park is more than just baseball; it's a D.C.-area meeting place and social event. The Park has a number of local eateries and hosts the hilarious Racing Presidents: five giant-headed presidential likenesses (George Washington, Abraham Lincoln, Teddy Roosevelt, Thomas Jefferson, and most recently Calvin Coolidge) that compete during the fourth inning by running around the stadium. In season, fans can take an hour-long behind-the-scenes tour on off-days or when the game is at night—or a 75-minute tour on nongame days, including the clubhouse (**washington.nationals.mlb.com**).

In those three decades without a D.C. team, many locals became fans of American League's **Baltimore Orioles,** whose retro-chic Oriole Park at Camden Yards stadium is only about an hour away (**baltimore .orioles.mlb.com**).

For those who see baseball as a stepchild of cricket, Washington's international community supports more than 35 accredited teams, and one of the most popular fields is in West Potomac Park near the Jefferson Memorial, where you can often see white-suited teams bowling away on a weekend. For information go to **wmcl.net.**

BASKETBALL

WASHINGTON'S PROFESSIONAL BASKETBALL TEAMS, the NBA's **Washington Wizards** and its sister team, the WNBA's **Mystics,** play at home at the Verizon Center, located right above the Gallery Place–Chinatown Metro. Wizards games are high-energy entertainment, with lots of community involvement by local youth and military veterans. For visitors staying in Penn Quarter, it's a fun night to schedule a pregame dinner and then attend a Wizards or Mystics game at the Verizon Center. For schedules and tickets, go to **nba.com/wizards** or **wnba.com/mystics.**

Georgetown University (**guhoyas.com**) also plays its home games at Verizon Center. The **George Washington University Colonials** (**gwsports .com**) have many devoted fans (watch for celebs and media faces), and the team's Smith Center home is very near the Foggy Bottom–GWU Metro stop. Two other university teams, with their own Metro stations, are American University's Eagles, who play at Bender Arena, and Howard University's Bison, who play at Burr Gymnasium.

FOOTBALL AND SOCCER

IT'S NOT EASY GETTING TICKETS TO THE **Washington Redskins,** whose fans are famously among the true fanatics in pro sports. Scalpers regularly charge three to four times the regular ticket price—more if the 'Skins are playing Dallas. Driving and parking can be quite hectic, so if you don't mind walking a mile, the Morgan Boulevard Metro station has a dedicated walkway to FedEx Field (**redskins.com**). The **Baltimore Ravens'** stadium, just south of the Orioles' Camden Yards, is accessible via MARC (**baltimoreravens.com**).

The Washington area is also home to the full-contact Independent Women's Football League **D.C. Divas** (**dcdivas.com**), who won the 2015 Championship and play on an outdoor field adjacent to the Redskins' FedEx Field.

Pro soccer is "football" to the rest of the world. The world champion **D.C. United** plays 16 home games each season (March–September) at RFK Stadium (at the Stadium–Armory Metro station). The team hopes to move into a brand-new stadium near Nationals Park (**dcunited.com**) in the next five years.

HOCKEY, ROLLER DERBY, AND TENNIS

WASHINGTON'S PROFESSIONAL HOCKEY TEAM, the **Washington Capitals** (**capitals.nhl.com**), shares ownership with the Wizards and Mystics and also plays at the Verizon Center. Washingtonians are fanatical about their hockey team, and it's nearly impossible to score a ticket to a matchup if they're having a good season. You may notice a sea of red jerseys if you happen to be around the Verizon Center on the night of a Caps game.

Although it's not quite the same sort of "blades," D.C.'s four-team flat-track roller derby league, the **DC Rollergirls** (**dcrollergirls.com**), is just as entertaining. In classic fashion, teams have pun-heavy monikers such as Scarce Force One and the Majority Whips. Teams play a winter-spring season at the DC Armory (Stadium-Armory Metro).

The **US Open tennis circuit** includes a major tournament in August, the Citi Open, at the Fitzgerald Tennis Center in Rock Creek Park; there is shuttle service from the Van Ness Metro station (**citiopen tennis.com**). Washington also has a World Team Tennis franchise, the **Washington Kastles,** coached by Murphy Jensen, which has won five straight WTT Championships in five years. The team, which features such veterans as Martina Hingis, Venus Williams, Sam Querrey, and Leander Paes, plays a three-week season in late July on the Southwest marina near the Waterfront Metro (**washingtonkastles.com**).

HORSE SHOWS AND HORSE RACING

RACING HAS A LONG HISTORY IN THE WASHINGTON AREA, particularly in Maryland, and both thoroughbred and harness racing are available at a number of tracks around Washington, though they're not easy to get to: only **Laurel Park** (**laurelpark.com**) is accessible by (MARC) train. It's a little run down, but Pimlico, outside Baltimore, is home to the Preakness Stakes, the middle contest of thoroughbred racing's Triple Crown, and the third Saturday in May is part of a huge celebration there. Check *The Washington Post* to see which track is in season during your visit.

There are several steeplechase courses in the Washington region, the most famous being the **Gold Cup** lineup every October (**vagold cup.com**). Also in October, the **Washington International Horse Show** kicks off a week of festivities and features more than 600 horses and riders competing in Olympic-level events—dressage, classic equitation, and show jumpers—held at the Verizon Center near the Chinatown–Gallery Place Metro station in Penn Quarter (**wihs.org**). Highlights of the Tuesday through Saturday events are Barn Night, with an evening of competition among younger jockeys, and Kid's Day on Saturday, with kid-friendly activities and free admission.

HORSE RACING

HARNESS:

- **Rosecroft Raceway**—Fort Washington, MD; **rosecroft.com**

THOROUGHBRED:

- **Hollywood Casino at Charles Town Races**—Charles Town, WV; **hollywoodcasinocharlestown.com**

- **Laurel Race Course**—Laurel, MD; **laurelpark.com**

- **Pimlico Race Course**—Baltimore, MD; **pimlico.com**

SUBJECT INDEX

Unofficial Guide Reader Survey

If you would like to express your opinion in writing about Washington, D.C., or this guidebook, complete the following survey and mail it to:

> *Unofficial Guide* Reader Survey
> 2204 First Ave. S., Suite 102
> Birmingham, AL 35233

Inclusive dates of your visit: _____

TRAVELING COMPANIONS

	Person 1	Person 2	Person 3	Person 4	Person 5
Gender:	M F	M F	M F	M F	M F
Age:					

How many times have you been to Washington, D.C.? _____

On your most recent trip, where did you stay? _____

ACCOMMODATIONS On a scale of 100 as best and 0 as worst, how would you rate:

The quality of your room? _____ The value of your room? _____

The quietness of your room? _____ Check-in/check-out efficiency? _____

Shuttle service to the airport? _____ Swimming pool facilities? _____

RENTAL CAR Did you rent a car? _____ From whom? _____

Concerning your rental car, on a scale of 100 as best and 0 as worst, how would you rate:

Pick-up processing efficiency? _____ Return processing efficiency? _____

Condition of the car? _____ Cleanliness of the car? _____

Airport shuttle efficiency? _____

DINING Approximately how much did your party spend on meals per day?

_____

Favorite restaurants in Washington, D. C.: _____

_____

_____

_____

OTHER Did you buy this guide before leaving or while on your trip?

_____

How did you hear about this guide? (check all that apply)

❏ Loaned or recommended by a friend   ❏ Radio or TV

❏ Newspaper or magazine   ❏ Bookstore salesperson

❏ Just picked it out on my own   ❏ Library

❏ Internet

What other guidebooks did you use on this trip? _____

_____

_____

On a scale of 100 as best and 0 as worst, how would you rate them?

_____

_____

Using the

Are *Unoffi*

Have you

Which or

Commen